Women Travel

First–hand accounts from more than 60 countries

There are more than one hundred and fifty Rough Guide titles
covering destinations from Amsterdam to Zimbabwe

Forthcoming titles include
Cuba • Dominican Republic • Las Vegas • Sardinia
Switzerland

Rough Guide Reference Series
Classical Music • Drum 'n' Bass • European football • House
The Internet • Jazz • Music USA • Opera • Reggae
Rock • World Music

Rough Guide Phrasebooks
Czech • Dutch • French • German • Greek • Hindu & Urdu
Hungarian • Indonesian • Italian • Japanese • Mandarin Chinese
Mexican Spanish • Polish • Portuguese • Russian • Spanish • Thai
Turkish • Vietnamese • European Languages

Rough Guides on the Internet
www.roughguides.com

This fourth edition published in October 1999 by Rough Guides Ltd,
62–70 Shorts Gardens, London WC2H 9AB.

Distributed by the Penguin Group:

Penguin Books Ltd, 27 Wrights Lane, London W8 5TZ
Penguin Books USA Inc., 375 Hudson Street, New York 10014, USA
Penguin Books Australia Ltd, 487 Maroondah Highway, PO Box 257,
  Ringwood, Victoria 3134, Australia
Penguin Books Canada Ltd, 10 Alcorn Avenue, Toronto, Ontario, Canada M4V
  1E4
Penguin Books (NZ) Ltd, 182–190 Wairau Road, Auckland 10, New Zealand

Typeset in Bembo and Helvetica to an original design by Henry Iles.
Printed in the UK by Clays Ltd, St Ives PLC.

© Natania Jansz and Miranda Davies, 1999.

688pp

A catalogue record for this book is available from the British Library.
ISBN 1-85828-459-7

Women Travel

First-hand accounts from more than 60 countries

Editors

Natania Jansz, Miranda Davies, Emma Drew
and Lori McDougall

THE ROUGH GUIDES

Acknowledgements

Firstly, thanks to all of our contributors. Like travelling itself there's been a lot of waiting around involved, interspersed with sudden flurries of activity to meet new deadlines and odd requests. Thanks for bearing with us so generously, for submitting great pieces, digging out some wonderful photos at the last minute and being such supportive and inspiring travelling companions. Special thanks to Dea Birkett, Diane Brady, Louise Doughty, Lesley Downer, Miranda France, Kathleen Jamie, Carla King, Kerry McKibbin, Melanie McGrath, Liz Merry, Isabella Tree, Caroline Walton and Sara Wheeler; and to Vivienne Shuster, Cristina Piza and "the Amazonians" for helping with connections.

Thanks also to Bridget Davies, Lucia Reed and Isobel Bruce who patiently opened envelopes and sent out guidelines to all the thousands of respondents to our initial ad.

For crucial book chat thanks to Sarah Anderson of the Travel Bookshop, Katie Hickman, Clare Walsh and Andrew Barley from Waterstones Deansgate, James Daunt of Daunt Books for Travellers; Richard Reynolds at Heffers Bookshop in Cambridge; Michelle Hawkins from Lonely Planet; Dan Hammond from Transworld; Sarah al Hamad from Al Saqi Books, and Wendy Cooper, Maggie Elliot, and Harriet Gaze. Thanks also to Kensington & Chelsea libraries for having such an impressive range of books to lend, and to Eastern Arts Board for agreeing to reduce Emma's hours while she was working on this project.

Thanks to Sandra Heidecker, Barbara Ellingham and Litza Jansz for general back up, to René Véron for help with email glitches and enthusiastic support, Henry Iles for designer flair, Link Hall for stylish typesetting, Ann-Marie Shaw for in-house keeping it all together, Elaine Pollard for attuned proof-reading, Demelza Dallow for tireless scanning, Catherine Marshall for picture design, and, lastly and largely, thanks to Mark Ellingham for all those ideas.

Photo credits

Gail Andrews © Marketa Havlik

Dea Birkett © Jerry Bauer

Margo Daly © Sophie Baker

Dawn Hurley © John Miles

Lieve Joris © Chris van Houts

Laura Pachkowski © Michael Moustafi

Kate Pullinger © Jerry Bauer

Lucy Ridout © Chris Scott

Anita Roddick © Peter Kyle

Isabella Tree © Charlie Burrell

Kate Westbrook © Nick White

Permissions

Margaret Atwood, "Islands of the Mind". Appeared in *Without a Guide*, Katherine Govier (ed). Reprinted here by permission of the author. © 1988 by O.W.Toad Ltd.

Rosalind Cummings-Yeates, "Journey to Yard: A Jamaican Cultural Experience" was first published in *Go Girl! The Black Woman's Book of Travel and Adventure*, Elaine Lee (ed). Reprinted by permission of the author. © 1997 by Rosalind Cummings-Yeates.

Lesley Downer, "Hard Currency". First published in *Amazonian: The Penguin Book of Women's New Travel Writing*, Dea Birkett and Sara Wheeler (ed). Reprinted by permission of the author. © 1998 by Lesley Downer.

Miranda France, "Bad Times in Buenos Aires". Essay first published in *The Spectator*, 15 June 1996. Reprinted by permission of *The Spectator*. © *The Spectator*.

Constance García-Barrio, "A Homegirl Hits Beijing". First published in *Hip Mama* (Winter 1995) and reprinted in *Go Girl! The Black Woman's Book of Travel and Adventure*, Elaine Lee (ed). Reprinted here by permission of the author. © 1995 by Constance García-Barrio.

Katy Gardner, "A Woman's Place". A chapter in *Songs by the River's Edge*, by Katy Gardner. Reprinted by permission of Pluto Press. © 1991 by Katy Gardner.

Joy V. Harris, "Whose Vacation is it Anyway?". First published in *Go Girl! The Black Woman's Book of Travel and Adventure*, Elaine Lee (ed). Reprinted by permission of the author. © 1997 by Joy V. Harris.

Lieve Joris, "The Gates of Damascus". Reprinted by permission of Lonely Planet Publications. © 1996 by Lieve Joris.

Melanie McGrath, "Las Vegas". Reprinted by permission of *The Guardian*. © The Guardian.1998

Isabella Tree, "Islands in the Clouds". Reprinted by permission of Lonely Planet Publications. © 1996 by Isabella Tree.

Isabella Tree, "Living Goddess". First published by *The Sunday Times*. Reprinted by permission of *The Sunday Times* and the author. © 1999 by Isabella Tree.

Sara Wheeler, "Terra Incognita: Wooville 1", from *Terra Incognita: Travels in Antarctica*. Reprinted by permission of Random House, Inc. UK and USA. © 1996 by Sara Wheeler.

About the editors

Natania Jansz was co-author of the first ever *Rough Guide* (to Greece) and helped launch the Rough Guide series. A clinical psychologist, writer and editor, she currently divides her time between co-running a publishing company called Sort Of Books and looking after her three-year-old son. A British Sri Lankan Dutch Burgher (her parents emigrated from Colombo to London in the 1950s) she has travelled frequently to Asia, North Africa and most parts of Europe.

Miranda Davies is a writer, editor and translator with a background in women's studies, development and human rights. She is the author of several anthologies, including *Women and Violence: Realities and Responses Worldwide* (Zed Books, 1994) and two previous volumes of *Women Travel* (Rough Guides, 1990, 1995), co-edited with Natania Jansz. Her travels have taken her to North and Latin America, Morocco and much of Europe. She lives with her daughters, Ella and Lucia, in West London.

Emma Drew grew up in Bracknell, Berkshire. She studied English at the University of Cambridge, and has since held a variety of jobs in the book trade. Currently she is Literature Officer at the Eastern Arts Board, where she works to promote contemporary creative writing and reading to a widening audience in the East of England.

Lori McDougall is a Canadian editor with a strong interest in gender and development issues. Since her first backpacking trip to Asia in 1992, she has worked for the India office of World Literacy of Canada and for the Hong Kong-based business magazine *Asia, Inc*. She holds an MSc in Development Studies from the London School of Economics and is currently based in Delhi, where she is project manager for the BBC World Service Trust.

Contents

Introduction

There's a moment that you wait for in putting together a *Women Travel* anthology: a moment when you find yourself transported by an evocative piece of travel writing and discover, as you add it to the "definite" pile, that a line has been crossed, a critical mass achieved. Like waiting on a bus while yet more passengers squeeze on board, you sense, with a thrill, that the engines will very soon thrum into life and the doors swish shut. A pile of stapled photocopies has become transformed into the first draft of a book. You're on your way.

Welcome to *Women Travel*. This is the fourth anthology that we've put together for the Rough Guides in the last decade and a half, and, as before, we've asked women to send in accounts of their recent travels, sifted through mountains of letters and submissions, leafed through address books, rustled the Rough Guide grapevine, and experienced the same gratified amazement as a book finally began to materialise. Also, as before, we have a clear memory of the batch of articles that swept us across the line. They included Sarah Beattie's description of welding wheelchairs (for landmine victims) in an Afghan workshop under continual threat from the Taliban militia; Rebecca Hardie's comic yet touching account of backpacking around India with her mum in tow (equipped with travel iron and inflatable coat-hangers); Louisa Waugh's drunken revelries and wild gallops across the steppes of Outer Mongolia; Catherine Shorrocks' lucid memories of surviving an earthquake in Indonesia; Dea Birkett's musings on island castaway fantasies in Sweden; Kathleen Jamie's astute portrayal of harassment and friendship in a Pakistan hotel, to name but a few. Without wanting to overstretch an analogy, there were already some inspiring and memorable pieces waiting on board; like Lisa Ball's wonderfully offbeat tales from an Australian rainforest commune (with a naked cyclist crashing through the undergrowth as a wake-up call) or Lesley Reader's trek through the high mountain villages of Bhutan. And others were on their way. Anita Roddick, for instance, wrote to us on her return from Albania where she had been visiting a home for disabled children at the peak of the Kosovar refugee crisis.

While *Women Travel* has undergone quite a few changes in both look and emphasis over the last fifteen years, certain elements have remained the same, and a matter of pride to us. Most importantly we try to cover a broad range of experiences, including as many different voices, perspectives and, of course, destinations as possible. Initially this had a campaigning purpose – travel, well into the mid-1980s, was very rarely presented from the point of view of the woman planning and packing for the journey and we wanted to use our anthology to assert a new female perspective in travel writing. Now, at the turn of the millennium, our task has shifted from pioneering into something more gratifying, and fun: that of showcasing and celebrating women's contemporary travel writing and travel experiences. We've witnessed with great delight over the last five to ten years a minor boom in women's travel writing. Almost every modern travel list contains a good percentage of women writers (rather less than half but with such an astonishing growth rate it seems churlish, or premature, to complain) and we have many other types and forms of travel anthologies that we're proud to share shelf space with. In keeping with this, our anthology now combines extended articles and extracts from our favourite women travel writers and journalists (Sara Wheeler on Antarctica; Isabella Tree on Nepal and Papua New Guinea; Miranda France on Argentina; Lieve Joris on Syria, Melanie McGrath on Las Vegas; Margaret Atwood on the Galapagos islands, to name just some) with over seventy-five entirely new and contemporary travel pieces.

We also, for the first time in print, have put together an extended, annotated, women travel bibliography and essential reading list. In fact, one of our main enjoyments in compiling this edition was running our own private, in-house women's travel book festival, immersing ourselves in hundreds of travel books and articles and selecting the best for review. All the titles we've included in our "read on . . ." lists are recommended, the starred ones especially so and, just to emphasise the choices that now abound, we've plucked from the long list of starred titles our top twenty-five contemporary favourites (ten years ago it would have been a struggle to get as far as double figures).

Finally, added to this heady mix, and impossible to overlook, are the photos at the beginning of each piece. These are a brand-new feature, which we chose to augment the brief introductions prefacing each of the journeys involved. Leafing through the pages we hope you feel, as we did, that you've joined up with one of the wildest, most inclusive women's tours around.

Enjoy the trip and be sure to write.

countries

Afghanistan

Welding wheelchairs under the gaze of the Taliban

Sarah Beattie

Sarah Beattie, a young wheelchair designer with the British-based charity Motivation, was invited to the eastern city of Jalalabad, close to the border with Pakistan, to help set up a workshop producing low-cost wheelchairs for polio and landmine survivors. A month before she arrived, the already war-torn city was seized by the Taliban, an ultra-conservative, Islamic militia, who, among a catalogue of civil rights abuses, achieved notoriety for the severe, yet often arbitrary, restrictions they imposed on women. During her six-month stay, Sarah's position as the only woman in the workshop became increasingly precarious as new laws were introduced banning all women (apart from a few essential healthcare workers) from working outside the home, driving a car, going unveiled in public or mixing with men other than family members.

Before moving to Afghanistan, Sarah and her co-workers spent a few months in Pakistan honing their design and production methods and experimenting with locally available materials. She is currently working with Motivation in Sri Lanka.

I was travelling to Afghanistan with the British charity, Motivation. We had not managed to get the necessary papers to obtain a permit for our project vehicle, so were left having to drive across the Afghanistan border in a rusty old Pakistani taxi. Seven of us – myself, my colleagues, Chris, Nigel and Nick, our driver, a translator and an armed member of the Khyber Rifles, provided by the Pakistani government to take us safely through the "tribal areas" – had to squash onto the four seats. All our possessions were piled to ridiculous heights onto the roof, with Nick's wheelchair teetering at the top.

The trip up the Khyber Pass is its own adventure. The tribal Pathans who inhabit it refuse to recognise Pakistani or Afghan rule, but have their own judicial system. Veiled women spend their lives behind the mud walls of the compounds, in ancient villages lost among the dusty rocky mountains of the Khyber. But it is impossible to do any more than glimpse at their world as you hurry up the pass, through the weapons and drugs bazaars; like all foreigners, we were required not to leave our vehicle, stop or stray from the pass, and to complete our journey in two hours.

The sight of the Taliban guarding the border dispelled any romantic notions I might have harboured about heroic battles fought by rival empires. I had seen enough pictures of these soldiers in the constant Western press coverage of the civil war, but I hadn't anticipated how intimidating they would be in the flesh. Standing, with Kalashnikovs ready, in front of rusty armoured tanks, and staring at us from beneath their imposing turbans, they seemed to be challenging us to question their authority. Suddenly paranoid about the amount of illegal items we had in our luggage – cameras, magazines, music and a stereo – I tried to hide under my veil, struggling to make the two-metre-long cloth stay positioned over my face. We passed through the border, and two hours later were in Jalalabad.

Jalalabad was once a splendid city. The peaks of the surrounding Hindu Kush contrast with a stark rocky desert, making a stunning setting. Traces of faded grandeur lie in the overgrown patterns of the old Mogul gardens and palace ruins. Now, after such a long war, Jalalabad is full of poverty, although relief workers try to alleviate the worst. Children live on the streets, grabbing your clothes to ask for money. Girls as young as ten have grey hairs from the stress they have experienced. I was struck by the absence of women on the streets, and those that I did see were entirely shrouded in a burqua, a garment that covers the whole body, with only an embroidered grill to see out of.

The atmosphere when we arrived was subdued and uncertain. At first the local population seemed to cautiously welcome the new

Taliban regime, grateful for the improved security that came after they confiscated all the civilian-held weapons. They promised an end to corruption and a new moral code. Although it was well known that they would place heavy restrictions on women's freedom and rights, in Jalalabad (a very conservative town) women had traditionally stayed in the house anyway. However it soon became apparent that the restrictions on every part of daily life, and the heavy penalties imposed for breaking the new laws, would nurture a fear of the regime equal, at least, to that of the warlords before.

The new rules were quite arbitrary – from "no kite flying" to "no washing clothes in the street". There were bans on most leisure activities, alcohol, music, photography and TV. Workshop staff told us how their children had had their toys taken away and been told they should study the Koran instead of playing.

Some of the laws seemed to make little sense. For two months women were only supposed to travel in a car if they couldn't be seen; in the back seat, separated from the front seats by a curtain, with the windows also covered. After it was realised that the curtains could be hiding a man sitting next to the women, it suddenly became illegal to have curtains in the back of a car.

One of the most publicised rulings was the ban on women's education and employment. However for the first few months at least, the Taliban made some concessions toward allowing widows and women in important positions (doctors, for instance) to keep their jobs. As a foreigner I was able to work, but I was careful to be very discreet about the fact I was working in an all-male workshop.

In the workshop I didn't really notice the restrictions. Working in an all-male environment can be daunting in any country, and I had certainly been apprehensive about the reception I would get in a wheelchair workshop in Afghanistan. I need not have worried. The men quickly accepted me as part of the team. Although I never felt I had to prove myself, I am sure the fact that I had practical workshop skills, and spent the day covered in rust and grease, welding and using machine tools, helped them to view me as an honorary male.

Soon we had our wheelchairs rolling out of the workshop. Our first test rider was Abib, a fourteen-year-old boy who had lost both his legs aged two, when a rocket destroyed his home in Kabul. We first met him when his uncle pushed him into our workshop in his old wheelchair. It was only six weeks old and had already broken under the strain of wheeling over the four miles of rough track from his house to the nearest road. Our chair, with its three sturdy bicycle wheels, was designed to stand up to being jolted along a dirt track, and allowed Abib to be far more independent and mobile. Soon we were spotting him all over town, speeding down the main road, or wheeling to his friend's house, seeing how fast he could go.

As a foreign woman I was not obliged to wear the stifling burqua that the local women were forced to wear. Instead I had to cover my head and face, except for my eyes, with a large piece of cloth called a *chador*. The chador reached to my feet and took enormous amounts of energy to keep in place whilst walking along. I discovered that the local women learn to "glide" as if they have a stack of books on their head and never move their heads or bend down suddenly. Twice the Taliban religious police came to our house and told my male colleagues to make me cover my face properly.

Inside the workshop I could also dress more comfortably although still modestly. The workshop technicians accepted that it was dangerous for me to wear a chador whilst welding or using power tools, so I was able to keep my head uncovered. Ironically, if they saw me outside work, dressed in *shalwar kameez*, a long, baggy, tunic worn over trousers, with a shawl covering my face so that only my eyes showed, they would often exclaim, "But Miss Sarah, you look so beautiful!"

Clothing restrictions were annoying, but my biggest frustration was my lack of independence. I needed a "male relative" as an escort every time I wanted to go out. Even running out to buy a can of Coke from the little shop on the street corner meant cajoling one of my colleagues to accompany me. I was rarely asked questions directly, but through the man I was with. If I was being accompanied by a local then, all too often, he would ignore my answers and give the ones he considered to be more appropriate, my opinions being insignificant.

Most of the hassles affected us all, male or female. In Afghanistan there is no postal or phone system so every fortnight one of us would make our way back down the Khyber Pass, through the tribal areas to Peshawar in Pakistan, to check email and pick up post: a three-day round trip. We did not have to observe the five prayer times each day, but if we took the wrong road we'd get caught at a prayer block for forty minutes whilst our local staff would be pushed into the mosque to pray. The local currency is so devalued that the exchange rate changes every half-hour and a bag was needed to carry enough cash to buy tools and materials; making the accounts balance took a lot of patience.

Despite the troubles in Afghanistan I found myself leading a surprisingly peaceful existence. No telephones or television and an 8pm curfew meant our lives became very simple. We had electricity for only a couple of hours each day and although we had access to a generator the power was often so low we would have to choose between the radio, hot water or an electric heater. Most evenings we read or played cards, wrapped up in Afghan blankets. Days out consisted of driving into the desert surrounded by the beautiful snow-capped Hindu Kush, where we could put some music on the stereo in the car, I could take off my chador and we'd eat fantastic chocolate cake made from an English packet mix, saved for emergencies.

As the weeks drew on, the stern edicts about women became increasingly restrictive. During Ramadan the Taliban decreed that women did not need to go outside the house. They banned "clothes made from a stimulating cloth" and shoes that made a noise when walking. The local staff preferred not to accompany me into town, as they did not want to be seen with an unrelated woman. One day, when the back of our vehicle was full up with workshop equipment, I unthinkingly sat in the front of the car, and was immediately spotted by the Taliban who took me and the driver to the religious police headquarters, where they beat the driver for allowing me to do so, ignoring my protests that it had been my decision to sit there.

Our housemaid, Nazrin, was a 29-year-old widow with four children and an extended family of seven to support. The Taliban had initially allowed her to work for us in light of her circumstances. Nazrin was the only Afghan woman I was able to form any sort of relationship with, and one of a very few whose face I ever saw not hidden by the grill of the burqua. Despite bringing up her family in Kabul (a city where, according to UNICEF, two-thirds of children have seen someone killed by a rocket and half have seen someone killed by a bomb), and being forced to flee to Jalalabad, she was always cheerful, and endeavoured to make our house feel like a home. She was an intelligent and very resourceful woman, and had previously worked as a tailor. We communicated by drawing pictures and through sign language, sometimes laughing about the absurdity of the Taliban's new laws, but more often despairing over their illogical reasoning.

One day the Taliban decided she should not work any more. My male colleagues spent a hour with the religious police demanding to know how a widow with no income and a large family was expected to survive, but they were only told "Allah will provide". Seeing such a strong woman defeated by such mindless laws was heartbreaking, especially with the knowledge that she is just one of millions of women facing a similar situation.

Nazrin remained a good friend. We bought her a sewing machine, and she made some money by making clothes at home. We often visited and occasionally she would surprise us by sending lunch over to our house in a rickshaw. When an ammunitions dump in the direction of our house blew up with a massive explosion, killing many and injuring hundreds, she immediately turned up to see if we were all okay, even though she knew she'd be in serious trouble if spotted.

Not once in Afghanistan did I meet a person who questioned their faith in Allah. Despite, or maybe due to, living with all the hardships civil war incurs, the Afghan people display an unwavering belief that everything occurring in their daily life is Allah's will. Sometimes this seemed to lead to a worrying indifference to their, and your, mortality. Riding in an Afghan bus was hair-raising, and safety lectures in the workshop proved painfully frustrating, as it was impossible to make the technicians accept that they would be able to prevent accidents from occurring by wearing safety glasses or wiring a plug properly.

However much the Taliban's regime frustrated me, I never felt I had a right to challenge any of the restrictions (although as a Western woman I would have been treated relatively leniently) as I was not there to make a statement but to do development work. But I did take satisfaction in defying the Taliban in small ways. I would sometimes wear jeans under my chador and often hid my personal stereo under it too, knowing they would not dream of looking under a woman's veil (a common way of smuggling men without travel documents across the Afghan border was to dress them in a woman's burqua).

Eventually I began to tire of working within such obstructive rules and regulations. No sooner had we got production running smoothly, than a new law or requirement would necessitate a rethink.

Without warning our visas would become invalid, or we would need different permits for importing workshop materials.

But, despite being relieved to leave these frustrations behind, it was difficult to say goodbye. I had become very fond of the workshop technicians, and they had all helped us to feel welcome in their country. The Afghan character is quite unique, a mixture of fierce honour and warm hospitality. When it was finally time to leave, the technicians held a farewell party in the workshop, presenting us each with a handmade Afghan costume. In the absence of decorations, they had dressed all the machinery and benches with garlands of wild flowers. Afghanistan is a very isolated country, difficult to visit and impossible to contact by phone or post. We knew that once we had left, we would not be able to keep in touch with our friends, making our goodbyes seem distressingly final. Our friends were more fatalistic. When Allah willed it we would meet again.

read on . . .

Dervla Murphy, *Full Tilt: Dunkirk to Delhi by Bicycle* (1965; UK: Flamingo, 1995/US: Overlook Press, 1987). In her first and most famous travelogue on wheels, Murphy chronicles her extraordinary journey from Dunkirk, across a frozen Europe into Iran, through Afghanistan, Pakistan and finally, six months later, arrival in India. With staggering determination she overcomes a series of seemingly insurmountable obstacles – from ferocious weather conditions to ripped tyres, lack of food and three broken ribs, suffered during a fight on an Afghan bus. Murphy's absolute passion for travel, her love of remote, harsh landscapes, her remarkable self-sufficiency and unswerving respect for most of the people (especially the poor) whom she meets along the way single her out as one of this century's most intrepid women travellers. She is also a fine writer.

Sheila Paine, *The Afghan Amulet* (UK: Penguin, 1995/US: o/p). Sheila Paine, an embroidery expert well into her sixties, sets off in search of an ancient embroidery pattern. After travelling in purdah through Iran, she is concealed under a burqua and smuggled into Afghanistan by a group of machine-gun-toting Mujaheddin; she continues her quest in Iraq and Turkish Kurdistan, unexpectedly finding the pattern among a primitive Bulgarian tribe, where women wear red masks. A strange and scholarly quest, undertaken with spirit and an unflappable charm.

Albania

Hosts and refugees

Anita Roddick

Anita Roddick, founder and co-chairperson of The Body Shop, travelled to Albania to visit Children on the Edge, an organisation that works in Eastern Europe to improve conditions for orphans and the disabled. Set up nearly ten years ago by the Body Shop Foundation, Children on the Edge had almost completed its task of refurbishing a home for the disabled in Korce, the regional capital of Southeastern Albania, when the recent crisis erupted in neighbouring Kosovo and thousands of ethnic Albanian Kosovars were forced to flee their homeland under threat of being shot by the Serbian militia. Some walked, some arrived by tractor or bus, some had been herded onto special trains to speed up the process of "ethnic cleansing". Despite their lack of resources – years of Stalinist isolationist policies had left Albania the poorest country in Europe – the Albanian people have done their best to offer open-handed hospitality to the refugees who streamed across their border.

Six hours door to door. It doesn't take much more than that to get from my house in London to Korce, even given that I'm not prepared to risk a direct flight to Tirana, Albania's capital. Instead, I take one plane to Vienna, another to Thessaloníki in Greece, then a three-hour jeep ride to the Albanian border.

Six hours – and a couple of centuries back in time. The border post is little more than a shack with a dirt floor. There is no electricity. The entire area round the border is jammed with trucks laden with bedding, medicine, everything desperately needed by the refugees from Kosovo. The drivers are having to wait up to two days to get through. They've hit the brick wall of Albanian bureaucracy, one legacy of the decades the country spent under the thumb of Stalinist dictator Enver Hoxha. Border officials are dragging their heels because of their anxiety that the influx of aid will stimulate the country's black market. It certainly doesn't help that Albania is one of the major conduits of hard drugs into Europe. Suspicious customs men check everything going in as diligently as the stuff going out. We have to leave the jeep and pick it up on the other side of a no-man's-land.

I'm travelling with Argi, a woman who works with Children on the Edge in Greece, and Liam, my ex-SAS bodyguard. I'm not sure his presence is appropriate but there's a rumour I couldn't be insured for the trip unless he came along. His constant state of alertness is a little unnerving. I guess that means he's good at his job.

The original plan was to visit both Tirana and Korce, but Tirana has been deemed too volatile. So we're driving into the Southeast. What is immediately striking as we head away from the frontier is the extraordinary beauty of the terrain. At first, there are snow-topped mountains, then pointy hills which remind me of China. There is no sense of the present at all – terrible roads, little traffic, no powerlines or billboards. The houses we pass are rough, handmade. It's like a snapshot of medieval Europe – old wooden carts drawn by horses, hayricks, the romance of ruralism. Every so often, a ghastly incongruous concrete structure offers a reminder of Stalin's influence. As we descend to the plain where Korce is situated, the landscape becomes marred by hundreds of concrete mushrooms. Hoxha had these tiny bunkers installed so that Albanians could resist the invasion he was positive was coming. But who would want to invade Albania, the poorest country in Europe?

The country's history is, in fact, one of war, invasion, occupation, ethnic cleansing, and instability which threatened to topple into anarchy at any moment. The anarchy was strictly controlled under Hoxha. With the fall of Communism, it was unleashed. Crime flourished. The Children on the Edge project in Korce had to post armed guards. But the first sign I see of the collapse of order is the garbage everywhere, even in the most beautiful natural setting – bottles, cans, candy wrappers, trashy remnants of the things Albanians were denied under Hoxha. And so many wrecked cars. It gets worse as we near Korce.

We're staying with the family in Korce who always look after the Children on the Edge workers when they're in town. Our host is training to be a doctor. He and his family sleep on the ground floor. We're all bunked upstairs. Rachel, director of Children on the Edge, tells me that every time she comes back, there has been some little improvement made. This time, there's a shower right over the lavatory, a handy time- and space-saving device. They really want to take care of us. I love that – it's the instant concern of the small community. I can imagine the gratitude of the refugees.

Since the troubles of 1997, the streets are deserted by 7pm – where once people would be out promenading on a beautiful spring evening, they are now all in their homes. It gives us a chance to plan our days and find out some more about life in Korce. When Rachel first visited Albania in 1991, she said there was a feeling of hope in the country. Communism had fallen, the standard of living was improving. But the collapse of a national pyramid scheme in 1997 wiped out the savings of maybe eighty percent of the population. The government was blamed, gun law was rife. You could buy a Kalashnikov in Korce for $10. Since then, a sense of hopelessness has overwhelmed Albania.

The economic, aesthetic and spiritual impoverishment runs deep. Although Korce is home to one of the most important mosques in Albania, I see few signs of religious faith, Muslim or Christian, during my visit. Perhaps Hoxha's campaign to make Albania an officially atheist state succeeded after all. Ironic that one of our greatest symbols of faith is Mother Teresa, a native Albanian. Hoxha also crushed the life out of the country in other ways. The food is the most basic proletarian cuisine: meat, cabbage, chips and a soup made with lard. The alcohol of choice is the kind of stuff you drink to forget, a ferocious firewater which reminds me of dry-cleaning fluid.

There is little evidence of local arts and crafts or any sense of street culture – no posters, no graffiti, and the only cinema in Korce closed down to re-open as a bingo hall. Local television seems unspeakable. In our host's house, we can watch BBC 24 and CNN if we constantly jiggle the TV set. His kids watch Italian television stations. They've learned to speak the language. But what else is on offer for young people? Since the 1997 crisis, foreign investment has dried up. There are few jobs. Only the gangsters thrive. They're everywhere in their cheap black leather jackets. Almost all the cars you see – even the taxis – are Mercedes, all stolen elsewhere in Europe. You can guess at the example this sets for the hundreds of unemployed young men who hang around in the town centre all day long. They dream of opportunity in America. The green card lottery is unsurprisingly a national event. We visit a cellar café owned by a nephew of John Belushi, the late American funny man. He is a local hero.

Yet it is these same hard-pressed people who have unquestioningly opened their homes to thousands of strangers. Just how remarkable this gesture is becomes obvious when the reality of Korce's situation is clarified. It's easy to visualise what the city used to look like. Hoxha's destructive attempts at modernisation didn't ruin the exotic Ottoman style of the place. But right now, it's in total chaos. The UN has too much to do elsewhere and small humanitarian groups are trying to cope with an influx of 35,000 refugees with thousands more on the way. This, in a city with a population of 50,000. People are housed anywhere there is room – a chicken factory, a sock factory, a bread factory, as well as any private home with a spare square inch. Impoverished as they are, the local people greeted the refugees with open arms as they streamed into town, welcoming them with fresh water, bread and cheese. But now the city is overflowing.

Thousands of the refugees are housed in Korce's sports stadium. From the highest tier, I look out over an aimless sea of people. Some are trying to sleep on their designated mattress. Kids are playing, teenagers walking arm in arm. The extraordinary physical diversity reflects Albania's own chaotic history. There are stocky, dark Mediterraneans, rugged mountain people, blond, blue-eyed Eastern Europeans. They all speak Albanian, but this ancient Illyrian language is one of the world's oldest tongues and has collected dialects as it evolved and my translator has a little difficulty. Korce can talk to Kosovo, but it takes time. Still, one thing is quickly obvious. These people all have the same kind of story to tell.

They're at home with their families when the door is kicked open by heavily armed men in red berets, carrying automatic weapons and long knives, their faces covered by woollen masks. They're given fifteen minutes to get out of the house. Stay a moment longer and they'll be shot. There's a mad scramble to jam whatever they can into suitcases. The soldiers demand passports and identity papers. These are burned. "Now you'll never be able to prove you're from Kosovo," the men jeer. "Now Clinton will look after you."

Dragging their cases into the street at gunpoint, the families join a silent river of terrified people, herded out of town towards the mountains. They pass fields full of people who have been waiting for hours – doctors, teachers, bakers, plumbers, hairdressers, students, the old, the sick, wailing babies, some of them wrapped in plastic bags to protect them from the rain. In some cases, people talk about being packed into cattle-cars. They are stripped of anything of value. The Serb soldiers joke that the Kosovars are getting free train trips out of the country in exchange for their homes and belongings. Too many of the refugees have stories about killings they've witnessed.

Six hours door to door. This is how the twentieth century is ending in Europe. Will genocide be our century's bequest to the future? But it is another question that obsesses the overwhelmed aid workers: what can we do to help? Because our Children on the Edge workers have been in the area for eight years, they are sought after by other aid agencies for their local expertise. They have been given specific responsibility for providing mobile showers for refugee camps in the Korce area and for providing medical care for refugees staying with families in Korce town. No one from Kosovo has been vaccinated because they were scared Serbs would inject them with poison. Peter, a Children on the Edge worker, says that a mobile health clinic is needed – one that can cross rough terrain so as to reach those refugees that are sheltering in remote villages. Rachel adds that basic sanitation is the issue and this is where mobile shower units would come in – we'd need at least three units. The list of practical needs also includes underwear, disposable nappies, baby food and sanitary towels. Children on the Edge are also looking ahead to setting up a play group for the kids in the summer. A mobile cinema, too.

What is going to happen here? An optimistic projection suggests that the influx of Kosovars, wealthier, more sophisticated and better-educated than the natives, will create a desperately needed infrastructure in Albania. I meet Kosovar nurses who are better-trained than any of the local doctors they're working with. But the disparity is a delicate issue. The Kosovars feel they're stepping back hundreds of years.

They want their children to continue the kind of education they enjoyed in Kosovo, which is already breeding tension in cities like Korce, where there is a high concentration of displaced people. Rachel feels it could be at least three generations before a balance will really be struck. Though no one knows if the refugees are ultimately going to stay or not, it certainly looks as if they will be here for a while. Down the road, the German army is putting up hundreds of tents in a field.

I realise that, as rough guides go, this has to be one of the roughest. I can't recommend Albania unless you feel you have something to contribute. Don't go as a voyeur. One of the most distasteful things I see on my trip is the observers wandering up and down the rows of refugees in Korce's stadium with their video cameras, ignoring the people reaching out to them, the children who want to be held. There is horror in such passive curiosity, and that is one thing the Kosovars need no more of.

read on . . .

Edith Durham, *High Albania* **(1909; UK: Virago, 1985).** Unlike many accounts by Victorian women travellers, Edith Durham's tale of her travels in the mountainous terrain of northern Albania truly stands the test of time. She first set foot in the Balkans in 1900 when she sailed to Montenegro, and became instantly fascinated by the people, culture and politics of the region. Eight years later, during which time she had learned Serbian, studied the history of the Balkans in depth, visited Kosovo (still part of the Ottoman Empire) and spent two arduous months doing relief work in war-torn Macedonia, she set off on a tour of "High Albania". In much the same spirit as Dervla Murphy, she dwells with great sympathy on the local people whom she meets, "reputed fanatical" but often "most friendly" and seems quite unperturbed by bullets whizzing overhead, a frequent lack of food and sleep and the physical strain of walking and riding – albeit with a guide – over rugged inhospitable terrain. Filled with digressions on history, folk tales, religion and politics, this is a passionate, highly individual tale by a woman who became utterly devoted to the Albanian people and their struggle for independence.

Isabel Fonseca, *Bury Me Standing: The Gypsies and Their Journey* **(UK: Chatto & Windus, 1995/US: Vintage, 1996).** Despite their legendary aversion to *gadje* or outsiders, Isabel Fonseca managed to gain acceptance from the Diaspora gypsies of East Central Europe, and, over a four-year period and several journeys, lived and travelled with families from Albania to Poland. Her work of reportage, which includes photos, is a spare and respectful retelling of the lives of the gypsies, matriarchs, activists and prostitutes she befriends on the way. In the Albania chapter, where she spends a summer with the unruly

Dukas family on the outskirts of Tirana, insights into the particularities of gypsy life overlap with more general impressions of a desperately impoverished nation whose people long for nothing more than to leave and "become Europeans". An inspiring and unflinchingly honest portrait of a fast-disappearing world.

Rebecca West, *Black Lamb and Grey Falcon* (reprint; US: Penguin, 1995). A book about Yugoslavia, rather than Albania, but with resonances for the whole of the Balkans. Novelist, historian and critic Rebecca West travelled with her husband through the provinces of Yugoslavia between the two World Wars. She wrote of the ethnic fears and prejudices of the people she met, and their feeling of a "shiftless yet just doom" in terms that now seem startlingly prescient. A book about the ethnic and cultural diversity of the Balkans, that points out the volatility and resentment underlying the tragedy of civil war.

Antarctica

Terra incognita: Wooville 1

Sara Wheeler

POLE

BERT F. SCOTT
ANUARY 17, 1912

The Pole. Yes, but
nder very different
circumstances from
those expected."

In 1991, traveller, journalist and broadcaster Sara Wheeler hitched a lift on a military aircraft from the tip of Chile to King George Island and glimpsed the icefields of Antarctica. "It was as if I was seeing the earth for the very first time. I felt less homeless than I have ever felt anywhere, and I knew immediately that I had to return." Two years later she did, under the combined auspices of the American National Science Foundation (as Antarctic writer in residence) and the British Antarctic Survey, following Scott, Shackleton and a distinguished line of "frozen beards" on their way to the pole. *Terra Incognita: Travels in Antarctica* is her bestselling account of her seven-month stay in "the world's last great wilderness", hopping planes between scientific bases and field camps almost exclusively populated by men.

Sara Wheeler has published two other travel books, about journeys in Greece and Chile (the latter was shortlisted for the Thomas Cook Travel Book of the Year) and coedited *Amazonian*, a collection of women's new travel writing. She currently lives in London with her Canadian boyfriend and their eighteen-month-old son.

In the extract that follows, Sara returns to Ross Island to see out the end of the austral winter. Here she meets Lucia, an American watercolourist, and together they make plans to tow two huts onto the ice and create a makeshift artists' retreat (dubbed Wooville, after the W-00 code prefix used for all members of the American Writers and Artists Programme).

The Woovillian huts were ten feet apart, but we roped them together. "People have been lost in whiteouts in less space than that," Buck had

17

warned. One was a small high-tech affair called a Solarbarn which offered the luxury of a small solar light, and the other was a regular red wooden box hut twenty feet by twelve equipped with a set of built-in bunks. A small dead cockroach lay supine between two panes of plexiglass in one of the Solarbarn windows. Lucia had a sideline in the administration of acupuncture, and when she laid out her needles on the body-sized table bolted to one wall, the red hut quickly became known as the Clinic. We planned to cook in the Solarbarn, so this was named the Dining Wing.

The bathroom facilities consisted of a small metal drum with a lid which lived outside next to the one wall of the Clinic that didn't have a window. It was lined with both plastic and burlap sacks which we removed when full and took back to McMurdo. The contents were frozen, at least. We also established a pee flag by drilling a bamboo pole into the ice fifty yards from the huts. Peeing on the sea ice was allowed, but it was sensible always to do it in the same place, so the ice around our home did not begin to resemble a Jackson Pollock painting.

Now we were alone in our own camp for the first time. Before we set out, Joe in the McMurdo communications hut had dispensed lengthy instruction in radio operation, and we were then obliged to check in with base every day at an appointed time. The call sign of the communications hut was Mac Ops.

"Mac Ops, Mac Ops, this is Whiskey Zero Zero Six, how copy?" I said, loudly and clearly, as instructed. Joe's voice flashed back.

"We're sorry, no one is home at Mac Ops. If you leave your name and number after the beep, we'll get back to you as soon as we can."

Nothing happened. "I didn't hear the beep," I said.

"Beep," said Joe.

* * * *

The weather was good, at first. We had a fine view of the Transantarctics shredding the horizon across the Sound. The landscape was dominated by Mount Erebus, the volcano named by James Clark Ross when he arrived on 28 January 1841 at what was to become Wooville on 2 September 1995. It reached right down to us, as a tongue extending from one of its glaciers extended as far as Wooville.

There, the sea ice had frozen around it. One day, when I was poking around at the base of the tongue, a beam of sunlight on a cluster of ice blocks caught my eye. If it had been at home, the beam would have captured spirals of dust motes, and if it had been in the hills, clouds of midges. The blocks were gleaming in this light like rocks at the edge of the sea made slippery by the rush of a rising tide. In effect, that is what they were.

The temperature leapt capriciously up and down. One day I threw a mug of boiling water into the air, and it froze in midflight. When the mercury hit minus forty, our eyes froze shut if we blinked for too long. After a long session outside we would come in and cling to the Preway like cats. When the wind abated, and we grew hot digging or engaged in other work outside, we licked one corner of discarded items of clothing and pressed them on the iced-up walls of the Clinic, where they instantly froze into position. Despite frequent total cloud cover and limited sunlight, the HF radio continued to run off its solar panel, which we had taped to a window of the Dining Wing.

We made mistakes, but we made them only once. Frozen food brought in a cardboard box was stowed under the front step of the Dining Wing. After the first storm the box had blown right underneath the hut, and we were obliged to lie on our bellies on the ice, prodding with an ice drill to recover our freezer. Forgetting to weigh down the toilet lid with a block of ice resulted in us having to chase it halfway back to McMurdo. The huts were positioned far enough apart to prevent a fire spreading from one to the other – and then we parked the fuel sledge between them. In addition, the sleeping arrangements caused difficulties. On the first night, Lucia slept on the top bunk. I woke up in the early hours to perceive her, through the gloom, climbing down the ladder and dragging her sleeping bag after her.

"What's the matter?" I asked.

"It's like the tropics up there," she said. "I'm sleeping on the floor." The concept of the tropics in our hut was too difficult to contemplate in the middle of the night, so I went back to sleep.

When I woke in the morning, she was already painting.

"I've worked it out," she said. "The temperature differential between outside and inside is so acute that above head height the air in the hut is like the Arizona desert."

"What was it like on the floor?" I asked.

"Glacial," she said. "I moved on to the long table after an hour." Thereafter, I remained on the bottom bunk, where the air remained stable at a pleasant temperature, and Lucia slept on the table.

If there were no jobs to be done at camp, and we needed a break from painting and writing, we would get into the Woomobile – altogether a more successful machine than its infernal predecessor – and drill a few more flags into the ice to mark our route. First, we had to get the small generator going, as the vehicle was always far too cold to start without having a current run through it for an hour. Lifting this object out of the hut and on to the ice was an awkward, two-woman job.

"I bet our arms aren't strong enough to get this started," I said as we prepared to pull the handle.

"We did it on the dry run at McMurdo, didn't we?" Lucia said.

"Yes, but it started first time then. If it doesn't now, and we have to keep pulling, our arm muscles will get tired."

"Wow," she said. "You think we can't do anything."

There was an element of truth in this, and it made me flush with shame. Lucia was quieter than I was, and smaller, and although she lived alone and had travelled extensively, she had not spent months hanging about in the wilderness, as I had. Yet I was the one who approached every practical task with the attitude that we almost certainly weren't going to accomplish it.

When the generator fired up, we both did a little dance on the ice.

The drill, which was three feet in length, resembled an oversized corkscrew, and after many hours of struggle we established our own system for using it effectively. This involved one person standing on the track of the vehicle and leaning down upon the top of the drill, thereby anchoring it in position, while the other grasped the drill handle and turned it furiously, like an egg whisk, spiralling the corkscrew down into the ice. When the pain in the turning arm became intolerable, the driller would change arms, and when that arm ached, we swapped positions. This routine was avoided if anyone was watching.

Drilling to establish the thickness of the ice was more arduous than putting in flags, as it involved going deeper. Even using the new method, it took us more than ten minutes to penetrate three feet of ice, but at least we did it. If ever seawater bubbled up through the drill hole we would get back in the Woomobile, turn round and scuttle off in the opposite direction.

Many cracks radiated from the Erebus Glacier Tongue, and we monitored their progress keenly. A crack is a fissure or fracture in the sea ice produced by the stresses of wind, wave and tidal action. Sea ice cracks generally look like narrow furrows – they were described by a member of the Japanese Kainan-Maru expedition in 1911 as "resembling divisions between rice paddies". Around Wooville cracks did not shoot out like bolts of lightning, or open up like Sesame, so we did not live in fear of an inadvertent midnight swim. None the less, we had received plenty of instruction in the subject. "Profiling" a crack, which meant finding out how deep and wide it was with a drill and whether it was safe to cross, seemed to us a complicated business.

"Now," I said to Lucia one day as we got out of the Woomobile and stood looking down at a rip in the ice. "The effective crack width is determined by the required ice thickness for each vehicle." "Yikes!" she said. "What does that mean?"

"Haven't a clue. It's what Buck said." At this point one of us would usually fetch what was known in camp as "The Book". It was a field manual, written by the staff of the Berg Field Center to assist scientists camping on the ice, and at Wooville it had already acquired biblical status.

Besides ensuring that neither we nor the huts fell through a crack into the sea, we both worked. In addition, Lucia practised acupuncture on herself, and sometimes on me. It didn't seem to matter that neither of us was ill or injured – Lucia said the needles were "a tonic". I would lie on the long table in the Clinic, looking out at the thermals threaded with mist, the moon hanging beyond the tongue, or the miasma of blues and pinks over the Royal Societies. When we absorbed ourselves in our work for too long, we began to exhibit symptoms of madness, with the result that a "Weirdometer" went up on the wall of the Clinic with a swivel-dial for each of us indicating the level of madness to which we had risen or fallen on any given day.

★ ★ ★ ★

In the mornings the sea ice cracked like bullets. If the weather was good, Lucia went out painting in the Woomobile, not to get away, but so she had a different view and could stay what we liked to call warm in the cab. She would position her palettes and her long raffia roll of brushes on the fender, where eventually they froze. Sometimes I went with her, and watched small replicas of our landscape appear on paper like polaroid photographs. The little metal tubes of gaily coloured paste soon gave up the battle for plasticity, and then she would turn to her pastels. If I made notes, everything was defined by the exotic labels on the tubes she held in her long fingers: a cerulean blue sky dropped to French ultramarine in late afternoon, and the Transantarctics at dusk were tinged with burnt umber or flushed with permanent rose.

One of our favourite spots was the configuration of pressure ridges around the southwest end of Big Razorback. The island looked like a croissant from there, with a folded-down triangle at the top. It was a spot much favoured by seals, too, and Lucia always added them last.

"Why have you put three in, when only two are there?" I asked. "Well," she began, "it's to do with composition. Three's better. I mean, it suits the shape of the pressure ridges behind. Or rather, it balances this island here . . . " I could hear myself answering a puzzled question about why I had deleted a particular adjective and replaced it with another. The fact was, half the time neither of us knew why we did what we did. We just knew it had to be done.

Then a weather system suddenly came in, and Antarctica shut down. Big Razorback disappeared into a faint grey smudge and the winds roared across the Sound, battering the walls of the tongue and tossing walls of snow through the air. I had often observed the continent's Janus characteristic, switching abruptly from seduction to destruction, but there, living in the lee of the Erebus Glacier Tongue, I experienced it most intensely. We saw heaven and hell in twenty-four hours, like the human mind as described by Milton. We would be trapped inside for days, the windows mute white sheets, listening to wind which never relented. As Frank Hurley wrote of the ice at such a time, it "lost all its charm and beauty, and became featureless, sullen and sinister". Living there alone without any contact with the outside world except for our brief morning radio schedule with base, we were very sensitive to its vagaries. We came to know what temperature it was even before we looked at the thermometer hanging on the antenna, and we noticed every degree of change. I never could have imagined this happening. Before I had been to Antarctica someone asked me about temperatures, and I replied, not altogether flippantly, that numbers bored me and the only temperatures I recognised were cold and fucking cold. I was amused to read comments in my first Antarctic notebook about "getting used to temperatures of ten below"; that had come to seem tropical. We tried to guess windspeeds, but we were stabbing in the dark.

"I wish we had a windometer," said Lucia one day, "rather than a weirdometer." Windspeeds of up to 200 mph have been recorded in Antarctica, but when the wind got really serious every anemometer invented broke down on the job. The McMurdo weather department had rows of broken anemometer impellers mounted on plaques. An inscription underneath each plaque read, "Damaged by wind", followed by the particulars, such as "95 knots, 25 October 1997'". The last in the long line said, "Dropped by Bill Sutcliffe, 23 March 1990. Winds calm."

When one system came in we were ensconced for five days, with only a three-hour window in the middle when the storm dropped and we ran around on the ice like small children. By the end we were beginning to study the backs of cereal packets and conduct comparisons on the three different recipes for bran muffins printed on our foodstuffs. We ran out of coffee. I grew tired of writing about ice and wind, so for a change I tried my hand at steamy love sonnets (this experiment was not a success). When I turned around to see what Lucia was up to, I saw that she had begun to paint green glaciers.

"I'm fed up with doing blue ones," she said defiantly when she noticed me looking.

The next day she made a batch of muffins over the Coleman stove, undeterred by the fact that all three recipes indisputably called for an oven. They were very good, and very flat. That night the wind was so strong that it kept us both awake. If we dropped off, a particularly violent blast would shake the Clinic and jolt us upright, hearts beating, like a volley of artillery fire. Then it might drop quite suddenly into silence, as if it had been turned off. "At last!" we would murmur, and settle back into the bags. But it was just building up its strength for a fresh attack. If I had heard it at home, I would have expected to see garage roofs flying through the air. It seemed as if the hut would take off over the Sound and that we would wake up looking out on the ventifacts of the Wright Valley.

This did not happen. The door was always frozen shut on those mornings though, and we were obliged to set to with an elongated s-shaped metal tool extracted from one of our tool kits. What its official purpose was, we never knew. We draped a blanket over the door jamb, but the snowdrifts crept past it while we slept. Strange to say, this did not greatly affect the temperature indoors at Wooville – it was always cosy. Sometimes crystals formed on the outside of the window, and when the wind blew really hard, they moved. It was like looking down a kaleidoscope. We watched snow grow up the antenna poles, and as for the Woomobile and the defunct Antispryte, in the moonlight they resembled vehicles abandoned by Fuchs and Hillary on their continental traverse in the 1950s.

When the storm ended, the world seemed new, and the huts shed their extra cladding of ice like the ark dripping water. The snow had been blown from the foothills of Erebus, revealing polished blue ice stuck fast to the rock which, here and there, protruded like an elbow below the treacherously seductive crevasse fields. A thin band of apricot and petrol blue hung over the Transantarctics, and the pallid sun shed a watery light over thousands of miles of ice. The frozen Sound could have been the silent corner of the African savannah where man first stood upright.

The storm seemed to have blanched our interior landscapes too. We sat outside in the evening calm. Often we saw nacreous clouds then, drifting high up in the infinite reaches of the sky – about ten miles up, actually, far higher than the fluffy white clouds at home that send down rain. There might be twenty-five of them, in twenty-five variations of opalescent lemons, rich reds and reedy greens. They were brightest just after sunset, when the glare of the sun had disappeared at ground level but its light still illuminated high clouds. The nacreous ones were small and oval, and they floated along in a line like fat iridescent pearls on an invisible thread. As Gertrude Stein said, "Paradise if you can stand it."

read on . . .

Sara Wheeler, *Terra Incognita: Travels in Antarctica* (UK: Vintage, 1997/US: Random House Modern Library, 1998). Despite the title, Sara Wheeler has produced an astonishingly detailed, scholarly, yet utterly contemporary sketch of this apparently "unknowable" continent. During her seven-month stint as writer in residence as a guest of the American Antarctic Programme (no mean feat for a British author) and the British Antarctic Survey, she trudges out in wildly sub-zero temperatures, scoots around in sprytes and snowmobiles, traipses corridors in science stations and fieldcamps, delves into Antarctica's history and heroic myths, and relays all she discovers in deft and lucid prose. No opportunity gets squandered to illuminate as much territory as possible, be it the disheartening gentlemen's-club atmosphere of the British base camps; the awe-inspiring sweep of nacreous clouds over white mountains; or the secret ingredient for polar minty peas (they use toothpaste). This is travel writing at its most accessible and generous.

Jenny Diski, *Skating to Antarctica* **(UK: Granta, 1997).** Jenny Diski's voyage south in cabin 532 of a Russian-crewed ship becomes the trigger of a far more profound and troubled journey into the darker truths of her childhood and a reappraisal of the damaged and damaging mother she tried hard to disavow. Interspersed with these dread memories is the privileged yet spartan cruise that she takes amongst the ice floes of Antartica, where she battles against reclusive urges to join the other tourists on deck and glimpse life at the edges of this great white continent. Although the travel segments are described with a writerly flair and artistry, they are by no means the focus. For the purpose of this disturbingly personal memoir Antarctica looms largest as a metaphorical landscape.

Argentina

Bad times in Buenos Aires

Miranda France

At the age of 26, Miranda France moved to Buenos Aires to work as a stringer, or resident journalist, for various British and American newspapers. She had read Spanish and Latin American studies at university, had hung out with Peruvian communists in Madrid, and had spent time living in Brazil. Nothing, however, could have prepared her for the proudly melancholic and disturbingly over-psychoanalysed culture of Buenos Aires that she suddenly had to contend with. The bad times lasted two years. Her essay below, distilling this period, won the Shiva Naipaul Memorial Prize. Her highly acclaimed debut book, called *Bad Times in Buenos Aires*, expands on this story.

Argentines have a word for the way they feel: *bronca*. An Italo-Spanish fusion, like most Argentines themselves, the word implies a fury so dangerously contained as to end in ulcers. People feel *bronca* when they wait for an hour to be served at a bank, and then the service is bad because the cashiers have *bronca* too. *Bronca* crackles down the crossed telephone lines and stalks the checkout queues in supermarkets with hopeful names like Hawaii and Disco.

You can easily lose an hour in one of these queues on a Friday evening, among women who look like refugees nudging towards a border, their trolleys piled high with items that might have been grabbed in an evacuation. Coca-Cola and meat, big bleeding hunks of it, are essentials in Buenos Aires. To kill the pre-checkout boredom, people tend to smoke or eat, dotting the shelves with half-finished packets of crisps and biscuits, or even open jars of imported jam, tasted briefly and discarded. "Why is this country such a shithole?" strangers ask one another. "How did we get like this?"

One afternoon last summer, my neighbour Rosa's *bronca* reached explosion point. Several of us were talking in her sitting-room when she burst in like a cartoon housewife, wearing an apron over her nightdress and brandishing a smoking frying pan. The smell of burnt onions drifted dismally in behind her. "I'm 52. Soon I'll die and I won't have done *anything*," she shrieked, before starting to cry. The recrimination wasn't for me but for Pablo, her third ex-husband and her third major disappointment in life: he takes little responsibility for their eight-year-old son, Juan. Rosa's other husbands were worse. The first was blatantly and frequently unfaithful. The second tried to have her "disappeared" during the last military dictatorship. Then, when Rosa's uncle stepped in with a handsome bribe, the police gratefully turned the tables, offering to do away with her recalcitrant husband instead. She declined, and all three ex-husbands are still alive and infuriating.

Rosa lives on the second floor of a slim 19th-century building in the centre of Buenos Aires, and, for a year, I lived on the fifth, in an attic flat that aspired to studio status. The bare rafters spoke against such an ambition: the flat baked in summer and froze in winter. It was impossible to sleep through the tremendous storms which were periodically whipped up in Patagonia, like rioters, and hounded across the pampa to Buenos Aires. When it was heavy, the rain splashed straight through the roof onto my face as I lay in bed, sometimes waking me from jumbled dreams about dictators.

I could stand on a precarious balcony at the front of our building and, seeming to float above six lanes of furious traffic, feel myself almost obliterated by the noise. Another balcony at the back of the flat was much quieter, and perfect for eavesdropping since it overlooked an interior space onto which all the other kitchens had windows. In the evenings I used to sit there drinking *maté* as shouted snatches of the discontented lives below drifted up to me, on clouds of roasting beef.

Eduardo, a retired bank clerk, lived on the first floor, with his 95-year-old mother and a mongrel bitch he had found abandoned outside a tango hall; he called them both "silly old woman" and in all other ways insulted them indiscriminately and noisily. He also shouted complaints – about noise – through the ceiling to Rosa (she shouted back). In the mistaken belief that I was aristocratic, Eduardo once invited me to lunch, to share a sort of shepherd's pie, cooked in my honour. Afterwards, as we talked, I realised how bravely he had faced his life's disappointments. He had never fulfilled an ambition to travel, but was fascinated by Britain. He could quote Wilde and Shakespeare and describe an imaginary walk through central Edinburgh, street by street, monument by monument.

On the third floor lived Jorge, an unacknowledged composer who played the piano beautifully, all day, and late into the night. Away from his piano, though, Jorge was invariably suffused with rage. "Leave this country! Flee!" he used to cry, whenever I came across him waiting for the lift or buying a newspaper from the vendor whose stall was outside our front door. "Get out of this inferno while you can."

The building's only subdued residents lived on the fourth floor. They were the last surviving relations of Arturo Frondizi, still widely held to have been the only honest president this century. Honesty has rarely been the best policy in Argentina. Frondizi, who died last year, was overthrown by a military coup in 1962; some of his family were murdered, the others went into exile. His nephew, my neighbour, returned from Italy after the fall of the military junta in 1982. A strange silence reigned on the fourth floor, such that Jorge's piano crescendos cut straight through the space, apparently unmuffled by the presence of people or furniture. But I did sometimes see Mrs Frondizi, and I even gave her the odd English lesson. She was reading Darwin and spoke wistfully of European art galleries.

The whole building was wracked with disappointment.

★ ★ ★ ★

Porteños, as the inhabitants of Buenos Aires are called, are famously unhappy. All over South America, the joke is about their moodiness, their fixation on Europe and, above all, their arrogance. "An Argentine is an Italian who speaks Spanish and wants to be English", one joke goes and there are many others. "How does an Argentine commit suicide?" a Peruvian asked me once, during a power-cut in the Andes. In the dark, I heard him almost weeping with laughter. "He throws himself off his own ego."

Where did the unhappiness start? When I first arrived in Buenos Aires, I imagined it to be a legacy of the last dictatorship, particularly of the late 1970s, when thousands of people were abducted and executed. One left-wing newspaper still commemorates the anniversary of at least one disappearance every day. The faces smile out of the old black-and-white snapshots with heart-breaking idealism; they all look so very young. Next to the photograph relatives add a few lines of remembrance and, invariably, the slogan: "We won't forgive or forget."

I met the relations of several of these murdered youths, and heard the shameful, tragic stories of others. One teenage protester had been denounced to the police by his own parents, in the hope that his attitude, and his homework, would benefit from a night in prison. But the police killed him. "In effect, the parents murdered their own son," a childhood friend, now an economist, told me. He smiled the sad, wry smile of the Argentines. "How do you get over something like that?"

As I lived in Buenos Aires, breathed the disaffection myself, I grew to feel that the sadness extended much further back, that in fact it was as old as the country itself. The violence that accompanied the birth of the republic had never been resolved. Rather than mix with the natives, as they had to varying degrees in the rest of the continent, the European settlers had slaughtered nearly all of them. At dinner parties, wealthy women with gold stilettos and silicon bosoms still boasted of the "purity" of their blood. Their ancestors a hundred years ago would have collected a cash reward for every dead Indian – a set of severed ears or genitals was required as proof of the patriotic deed.

Argentina had not been settled, as America had, by men and women with convictions and ideals, but by the poor, the homesick, the greedy. The first immigrants had even invented a musical genre to encapsulate their sense of melancholy and frustration. Tango has since been described as the only dance in the world intended to express alienation, rather than joy. It is passionate, but loveless, like sex snatched in a dirty motel. The lyrics dwell on nostalgia, lost love and the lure of suicide. Tango is about the impossibility of human contact at anything other than a violent level. Yet it is regularly dubbed the true expression of the Argentine soul. Is the Argentine soul such a dark and lonely place? Many educated *porteños* told me that it was.

Wherever I walked in Buenos Aires, I felt the pain underfoot. Every street bore the memory of an atrocity or a promise unfulfilled. There was the Plaza de Mayo, where people from all over the republic congregated to catch a glimpse of Perón and Evita on the presidential balcony in the 1940s. Argentina was still a wealthy country then, with prospects to rival those of Australia or Canada. What went wrong? The evidence was everywhere. There were the churches where statues of the Virgin Mary were replaced with ones of Evita. There were the places where Evita's embalmed corpse was hidden by its abductors before they smuggled it to Italy. There were the bars and cafes where military police came looking for subversives in the 1970s. There were the torture centres, with their elegant, European façades.

As the months passed, a creeping claustrophobia took hold of me: I began to despise the country which, through its literature, had fascinated me since my schooldays. I wrote in my diary: "In some places, every idiosyncratic goof is endearing. You feel affection for the noise, the grubby streets, the graffiti, the inefficiency of the bureaucrats. Here you hate them. Everything feels designed to frustrate. It seems that good intentions don't exist."

★ ★ ★ ★

"In Buenos Aires we have two addictions: coffee and psychoanalysis. Times have to be hard – I mean *really* hard – before people give those up," said Alicia, so painfully thin that she risked being engulfed by her sofa, if not by her melancholy. We were sitting in her tiny apartment near the botanical gardens on a mercifully pleasant summer's day. In Buenos Aires, sun is usually accompanied by punishing humidity, and when that is combined with low pressure a half-hour walk can be an effort. On those days, small, squat women from the Red Cross sit on street corners waiting to take people's blood pressure and recommending extra salt in their diet.

Alicia was twice divorced, a history lecturer who worked long hours in a boutique to make ends meet. She had agreed to talk to me about her psychonalaysis. Although there are no official figures, Buenos Aires is thought to be the world capital of psychoanalysis, with proportionately more citizens receiving therapy even than in New York or Los Angeles.

Alicia was typical of her once-monied class: although she cultivated the appearance of wealth, in fact she had very little to spare, and that went on therapy. This was standard amongst her friends. "I know people whose salaries are so meagre they don't know how they're going to get to the end of the month," she said, "but they still have psychoanalysis – it's the only way to survive here."

This same premise was put to me so regularly in Buenos Aires that I became fascinated by it. How could it be that a whole community needed therapy simply to survive? Was there evidence that the treatment was working? How would the nation know when it was cured? Some of my friends spent half their salaries on therapy, with no tangible, positive effect. I hinted at self-indulgence and Alicia's eyes filled with tears. "You don't understand what it's like," she said. "We're stranded here at the end of the world. We don't know who we are or where we belong. We have been forgotten by everyone."

In 1995, Michael Camdessus, head of the International Monetary Fund, publicly chastised Argentines for spending so much money on their psyches and so little on their poor. Rosa was infuriated by this remark. "It's all very well for him to say that, but how are we supposed to get over all these things that have happened to us?" His attitude gave her, she said, *una bronca tremenda*.

However, most visitors to Buenos Aires, even American ones, would agree with Camdessus. My acquaintances, even the newsagent and the cleaning lady, soaked up as much therapy as they could afford. When short of cash, they paid the analyst by doing his typing, teaching him yoga, giving him their paintings, or maybe even their bodies – there were many reports of unethical behaviour.

Newspapers were full of psychology too. When Diego Maradona was suspended from the World Cup on drugs charges, a psychoanalyst writing in one of the dailies suggested that he might unconsciously have sabotaged his chances to punish himself for a deep-buried trauma. Psychoanalysis was huge business, simply because it was the terrain of all those who would claim to be thoughtful. For an intelligent person to dismiss the value of analysis would be like dismissing great literature. "I would be worried", one woman told me, "if my daughter brought home a boyfriend who wasn't in analysis."

Last year, when evading tax became foolhardy for the first time in Argentina, Rosa registered as a French teacher. In fact she is a psychoanalyst. For hours every day and late into the night, she absorbs *bronca*. Even as she watches television propped up in bed, patients ring with mundane worries – one of them keeps her up to date on the state of his bowels. When she goes to the coast on holiday, her patients besiege her hotel with faxes bearing tales of woe about their own holidays. Oedipus is never so much to blame here as bureaucracy, banks, employers, spouses, ex-spouses, the sheer frustration of living in a metropolis where expectations are very much of the First World and the chances of meeting them of the Third. "We were brought up to believe that we could have everything," one of her patients told me. "Wealth, culture, the Malvinas . . . We were conned."

One evening Rosa invited me to try out her new couch, a present from an ex-patient, in lieu of many unpaid sessions. I lay awkwardly on the fashionably zigzagged structure, my feet raised disconcertingly higher than my head, presumably to aid thought, and tried to imagine myself into the mind of an analysed Argentine. I had just been helping Juan to do his English homework and was amazed to find that, in an exercise titled "What does you mother/father do?", psychoanalyst was one of the ten possible answers, along with doctor, lawyer, housewife and so on. Juan had learned how to spell the word in English, but he could not pronounce it in either language. He hoped to get away with "doctor" in the oral exam.

I admitted to Rosa that I was confused by the therapy culture, and her answer surprised me. She suggested that it had something to do with the shock of democracy. "Subconsciously people miss the voice of authority and they're looking for a substitute. Before, they were told, 'you can't do this, you can't go there'. Now they want me, the analyst, to replace the voice of the dictator."

★ ★ ★ ★

Truth, slippery at the best of times, is only ever a matter of opinion in Argentina. Few objective records exist on any point of history. Only fifty years after the death of Eva Perón, one cannot be sure of her date of birth, or her role – pivotal? negligible? – in the revolution that brought General Perón to power. Different government offices cannot agree on the age of the current president, let alone on the past. One friend, while visiting Britain, was intrigued to see how a news story was broadcast, followed up in the press, debated in Parliament, argued on phone-ins – its existence compounded by continuous exposure. In Argentina, serious cases of corruption, murders, even allegations involving the president's family, are news today, gone tomorrow. The result is a feeling of transience which translates into insecurity. What are you if the ground beneath your feet is always shifting, if there is no national stock of knowledge, no set of values, nothing to be held self-evident? If nothing is certain, if nothing exists for sure, then even murders, thousands of them, can officially be denied.

Argentina's new National Library stands as a testament to the belief that truth can be obliterated. A brutalist building, it squats on vast concrete haunches, like a defecating monster, over the spot where the Peróns' presidential palace used to be, until it was ransacked and razed in 1995.

The library took more than 25 years to build and, when I visited, it was an empty universe. Dozens of freshly minted bureaucrats were already in place, waiting with rubber-stamps and cultivating their *bronca* – but nobody knew how many months it might be before the books themselves arrived. The paradox would have delighted Jorge Luis Borges, Argentina's most celebrated writer and a librarian by profession (though briefly demoted by Perón to inspector of poultry). Borges imagined the universe as an "infinite library".

Hovering above the acres of bookless space, on the fourth floor, the director, Enrique Pavón Pereyra, was a crumpled figure with an infinitely sorrowful face which seemed appropriate to his empty surroundings. I had been warned that he would know nothing about the library – his appointment was a political one. But the interview was already arranged and so I took a lift through the space to his office, which was guarded by two cruel-looking young women with red fingernails.

Inside Mr Pavón Pereyra was swinging idly on an office chair behind a vast, empty desk. A flag stood behind the desk and there were various framed photographs of President Menem and of General Perón, an old friend.

My first question about the library went unanswered. Mr Pavón Pereyra's mind was several decades back.

"She died just below where we're sitting, you know." He waved a hand at the newly carpeted floor.

"Evita?"

"Yes, Evita." He looked curiously at me.

"Where are you from, young girl?"

From Britain, I said. I asked another question about the library. The director, far away, ignored it.

Suddenly, shockingly, his eyes filled with tears.

"Why do you no longer love us?" he asked.

"Love you? Who?"

"England. Like a beautiful woman who spurns her lover, England has turned her back on Argentina. How can we forget that love and that desertion?"

Tears rolled down his cheeks. "You must go back to England and tell her to love us again. There must still be some chance – why else would they have written that beautiful musical?"

Had Mr Pavón Pereyra seen *Evita?*

No, he had not, but like most Argentines he knew that it was a wonderful homage. "Don't Cry For Me Argentina" was regularly played in shopping malls and to soothe the checkout queues in Hawaii and Disco.

My questions about the library were redundant, and I was beginning to feel that I might cry too, so I stood up to leave. Mr Pavón Pereyra embraced me. "Come back soon, dear," he said. "Treat this as your home." I walked out, past the cruel-looking girls, and felt the stirrings of a great compassion.

★ ★ ★ ★

Finally, I took Jorge's advice – I fled Buenos Aires. But I ended my Argentine sojourn where it had to end: outside the tomb of Evita, in the Recoleta cemetery.

I once met a woman who worshipped Evita. She had a painting depicting her as a saint, a troubling vision in lipstick and a halo. She had been present, in 1974, when Evita's body first arrived back in Buenos Aires from Italy, where enemies of Perón had it interred as an Italian housewife for twenty years. "Her nose was broken and she was in quite bad shape, apart from her hair, which was beautiful," the woman told me with morbid enthusiasm. "But don't worry, she's been totally recycled now. She'll last for a hundred years."

There are two necropolises in Buenos Aires, both literally mini-cities of the dead, their labyrinthine streets lined with mausoleums, statues and tiny chapels. Death appeals to Argentine snobbery. It is expensive and classy to embalm your loved ones, and display their mahogany coffins in family shrines that have glass doors, a wonderful invitation to voyeurs. Sunny afternoons in Buenos Aires are often spent strolling around the necropolis, peering through the lace-curtained windows at the coffins, and the family photographs which adorn the marble altars. Perón's tomb is in the middle-class Chacarita cemetery. Evita, in a final triumph of social climbing, is in Recoleta, surrounded by the upper classes, who hated her.

Hugo Palavecino, a gravetender, was looking over the cemetery wall the day when they secretly laid Evita to rest. Now he is the only person, apart from her sisters, permitted to enter the shrine. Evita, who had dressmakers, hairdressers, make-up artists, has only Hugo to attend to her now.

"She's quite far down – about five metres under where we're standing now," said Hugo, squinting in the sunshine. "Her coffin's secured behind steel plates, to protect her from assaults."

All that steel and earth to protect Evita from Argentina's *bronca*. And to protect Argentina from hers, too, for there was no rage to rival Evita's. Her writings, her speeches, were all about her fury, a passion so violent it seemed literally to devour her – she died of uterine cancer at the age of thirty-three. On her deathbed, Evita bade her people "burn with the sacred fire of fanaticism". "I don't understand half-measures or balanced arguments," she had written. "I only recognise two words, which I hold like cherished daughters in my heart: hatred and love."

Was the *bronca* connected to Evita? Felix Luna, a historian, had lamented as much to me, saying "she sowed a seed of aggression in Argentina".

I asked Hugo what he thought about when he was five metres below ground, alone with one of history's most famous women. "Perónism was a time of great tyranny," he said. "I try not to think about it at all. It's time for Argentina to put all that hatred and violence in the past."

I asked him if he was contented, and he said that he was. "I think things are beginning to look up for this country, don't you?"

It was a brilliantly sunny afternoon. Hugo was tanned and handsome, with a gentle smile that seemed to have no rueful undertones. He was whistling an old tango, as he walked away. I was almost sorry to be leaving.

read on . . .

Miranda France, *Bad Times in Buenos Aires* (UK: Weidenfeld & Nicolson, 1998/US: Ecco Press, 1999). Miranda France goes to town on a culture that prides itself on its angst, self-absorption and the pursuit of supermodel looks. A bad time is had by all but in this wonderfully adroit and informative portrayal, France manages to emerge with a compelling literary debut. The strangeness of this urban, predominantly middle-class and European-looking society, where acquauintances talk glibly of their rage and trauma on their way to the analyst's couch, is described in telling detail. And there are no cheap shots. At the point where you become most exasperated by the sheer vanity of it all, she reminds you of the scars left by the recent "dirty war", when tens of thousands of the city's young and idealistic were snatched off the streets by the government's death squads. Trauma seems too hollow a term to describe it.

Australia

Welcome to the Rainbow Gathering

Lisa Ball

Lisa Ball arrived in Australia at the end of a long-haul trip that took her across Indonesia, Malaysia, Thailand and the Philippines. To help pay her way she worked in a Thai children's home, drove tractors in the Outback and did dreary office work in Sydney. Finding this last stint incompatible with exploration, she gave in her notice and set off with three male companions for the far north of Queensland, where they lived for a while in an alternative commune. Lisa has now returned to what she refers to as "a temporarily sensible life" in London, where she is a freelance writer and researcher.

Travel, for me, is about surrounding myself with the unfamiliar, but after arriving in Sydney financial need had pressed me into a very grey office job. My dreams of beaches and forests receded as reality struck home. Soon I possessed an alarm clock and a suit. A road, any road, beckoned. I closed my eyes, quit the job and decided to hitch a ride with some guys I knew.

I had met Phil, Duncan and Ezra by chance while travelling, and I have to say that I had my reservations about sharing a small van with three boisterous lads. Could I really cope with their passion for the three "B"s: beer, birds and burgers? I had visions of myself trapped in the back of the van, wedged between empty "stubbie" bottles, rem-

nants of Big Macs and groups of bikini-clad lovelies. I decided to risk it
– the lads had a silly streak and bundles of energy, so I guessed we were
destined to have fun. Also the various types of mind-numbing work we
had all been doing had bonded us. We plotted our escape and attached
plastic silver wings to the wing-mirrors of our beat-up van to ensure a
steady flight. We were on our way.

Meandering through the semi-deserted towns and beaches of the
East Coast, we eventually reached Mount Warning, on the outskirts of
Byron Bay. I could never have guessed that climbing that mountain
would lead me to the heart of some of the more unique elements of
Australian subculture.

The time to climb is shortly before dawn. The mountain is at
the easternmost point of Australia, so to sit at the summit at sunrise
means that you are the first in the entire country to feel the warmth of
the day's sun. Aboriginal people call the site "*Wollumbin*", which
means "Catcher of Weather", and have regarded it as sacred for thousands of years. In the early days of colonial history, Captain Cook
renamed the mountain Mount Warning and used it to navigate his
course around the treacherous coastline. I have reservations about
Captain Cook, so I adopted my own name for it, Mount Morning,
which seemed more appropriate.

We camped at the bottom and set the alarm for 3am when we
planned to start our climb. In the darkness, surrounded by rainforest,
the life of the mountain glowed, watched, sang and scuttled. As we
slowly made our ascent, with only a feeble torch to light the way, the
damp vegetation took on a harsher appearance. Trees became smaller
and more twisted. The air grew colder and soon rain began to pound
against us. The warm van and hot tea seemed a very long way down,
and our romantic notions of night-time mountaineering were beginning to seem ridiculous. I tried to focus my mind on the amazing sunrise, the vast view and the flask of brandy that awaited me. This didn't
really help: I could no longer feel my toes or fingers.

What seemed like hours later, using icy chains attached to the
rocks to assist us, we finally hauled ourselves to the peak. Aching and
sweating but exhilarated we swigged ceremoniously from the flask.
The rain fell in sheets while we waited numbly for the sun to rise and
dispel the morning grey. A realisation was creeping up on me. The
reason for the Aboriginal name was obvious: thick grey clouds clung

to the summit like smog, and I could see no further than the end of my frozen nose. There was to be no sun.

I decided to stretch my aching muscles with some shaky yoga. The boys, preoccupied with emptying the flask, found this hilarious. Bent backwards, grumpy and tired, I shouted in exasperation that they knew where drunks like them could go.

"I'm not a drunk," said a green tarpaulin, which up until that point none of us had noticed. I fell out of my tiger pose with surprise. A large man blinked and yawned, and stepped out of his sleeping bag, apparently oblivious to the hostile weather conditions. Mark, as was his name, made an annual trip to the mountain at the time of the winter solstice, to camp and meditate. I was astonished that anyone would choose to stay on this icy barren summit for more than a couple of hours, let alone days.

Yet there was something undeniably magical about the desolate mountaintop. I had read that Hindus use the word "*darshana*" to explain the mysterious rapture felt in a sacred place. Standing on a mountain pinnacle, my body shivered with delight, and as Mark talked I began to understand the meaning of the word and the reasons for his prolonged visit. Nevertheless, we lesser mortals were at the mercy of hunger and delirium, and we decided to make our descent before legs and spirits gave way. Mark asked where we were going and we gave a collective shrug. "You should go to the Rainbow Gathering," he suggested. "Live out in the rainforest for a while, commune with nature." I had heard of such gatherings before – a by-product of Sixties San Francisco. In Nineties Australia, I didn't know what to expect. Slightly cynical, I raised an eyebrow. He shrugged his shoulders. "What have you got to lose?"

Owning not much more than a few miserable items, it was true that I did have little to lose. Like Dorothy in search of the Wizard, with no real clues as to what we were doing other than vague thoughts of rainforest communes and open skies, the boys and I set off in the van for Daintree Forest above Cairns. Along the way we had fantasised about festive celebrations, music and hippies so as we eventually drew nearer to the camp, we were perplexed by the quietness.

Not for long. "Welcome home!" shouted a chorus of voices through the darkness. Firelight bounced between silver birches, and I sat in the van, confused. I was not home; I was 30,000 miles from home. Something moved outside. A face appeared, grizzly, sun-leathered and contoured by the wind, above a long, raggedy beard. Wild stormy hair poked out of a hat which had once been a selection of animals. The man was bare-chested and had a large knife tucked snugly into his belt. He grinned. My throat tightened.

"Welcome! Welcome! Cam'n join us!" he beamed. Later, as we sat round the fire drinking sweet Indian tea, I was introduced to Cowboy properly. A white Australian, he had lived "bush" for many years. The grizzly appearance concealed a warm heart. While munching on hazelnut damper bread with golden honey, he explained the law of the land. "You are very welcome here. Please respect the environment, as it is the ancestral home of some of the people you will meet. You are welcome to come. You are welcome to go. You are welcome to contribute in any way you wish. We have a communal pool of money and food. There is no electricity, no alcohol, no drugs. Make yourself at home."

Next morning, the night-time buzz of bush creatures was replaced by the sounds of a penny whistle, a guitar and song echoing through the trees. Overnight the van had become a slow-bake oven. Gasping, I stumbled out into the fresh air to be confronted by a naked man cycling through the clearing, bananas and a tambourine slung under one arm. "Morning!" he cried. I blinked twice. "Water," I croaked. "The river's just behind you," came the reply.

I was horrified. A naked freewheeling man might not faze me, but drinking water from so natural a source? No taps, no chlorine! I would contract horrendous diseases! I considered the options: an hour-long mission to find fuel, build a fire and boil water, or fifty kilometres to the nearest town for water purification tablets. I gave in. The river had encountered a stony riverbed and maybe the odd drop of wild animal wee. The water tasted sweet and good, and I reflected that marsupial fluids couldn't be *that* bad for the system and , after all the water I drank in London had probably already passed through at least twelve other people.

The singing I had heard signalled the start of breakfast. Food rituals are fundamental to the set-up of the Gathering. Some people cook, some serve, and others form a circle and sing for their meal. The whole ceremony is performed with the pomp of a Catholic church service. At the first meal we attended, the lads and I shuffled awkwardly as the group sang songs we didn't know. Feeling very silly already, we were then obliged to all hold hands and partake in the hippie version of the "Oki Koki". There is chanting and a collection after each meal. The "Magic Hat" collects anything that you have to give; some offer their money, some simply their love. I was surprised at how well the system seems to work. Like some Biblical story, there was always plenty of food to go around – stacks of it, piping hot, wafted the scent of cardamom across the clearing, like incense.

Breakfast culminated with the "Morning Circle", a meeting of the clan where anyone may speak about anything they wish so long as they are holding the "Talking Stick". For want of a better description, this is basically a twig with bells on that signifies democracy. Discussion ranged from the profound to the ridiculous. One person might offer the service of their mechanical skills or to organise an acupuncture workshop; another might want to discuss the oppression of wild boars by the erection of fences, or whether men may enter the women's circle. I felt like an unpaid extra in a Monty Python film.

Adjustment took time. The meal rituals, the holding hands, singing before eating, primeval chanting, all collected in my head to spell one word: CULT. On the first day I looked for the signs of cultist behaviour that appear in the tabloid newspapers - you know the type of thing: white-robed clones, gurus predicting the end of the world, some sort of bomb factory. These turned out not to exist, although the people and their beliefs were certainly diverse. The atmosphere was relaxed and a sense of freedom and tranquillity pervaded the place. Growing up in London had made me wary of strangers, especially friendly ones. Using the Northern Line underground train every day taught me to keep my distance, avoid eye contact, keep my possessions close by, whereas this was a lesson in trust, learning to welcome people no matter what planet they were on, rather than ignore them. It was far more fruitful - and fun.

We found the best way to meet people was to "muck in". Duncan planted mango orchards, Phil hauled water from the river, Ezra collected firewood. While fiercely chopping mountains of bright yellow starfruits, I gathered tips on how to grow alfalfa shoots in my rucksack and was warned about the dangers of sprouts. Waterfall offered me a place to stay in the Northern Territory; Stream offered to teach me more yoga. Apart from having to suppress a chuckle at the ridiculous names, I began to feel really at home. In remote Australia, the hippie names of the Seventies do seem to have stuck: I even met a man called Lentil. For a while I contemplated changing my own name to Mung Bean, as I was quite taken with them, but as Mung Bean Ball sounds like some kind of vegan take-out food I stuck with "Lisa".

One of my favourite people was Loma, whom I literally bumped into in a paddock full of Asian cows. I don't quite know how I missed her; wearing a fuschia-pink dressing gown, a baseball cap and a shock of blonde hair, she stood out dramatically from the cows. A fat hand-rolled cigarette hung from her lips and bright red markings like tribal scars flushed across her cheeks. She explained that the herd had been lent to her as a form of organic lawnmower. As we walked home for some tea, I realised that little in Loma's life engages with the conventional.

In one corner of the field stood a wall-less Bedouin style tent. For such a simple dwelling, Loma's home had an opulent and elegant air. From within it reminded me of the impossible and precarious architecture of the Dr. Seuss children's books. A raised bed dominated the room, towering, flimsy and fantastical. A neat pathway led to an outdoor kitchen, where the oven was made from a selection of termite nests. Like a microcosmic city, the oven bustled with industry. The creatures continued to inhabit the warm walls, sensibly avoiding the direct heat in the centre. I wondered how friends at home would view such human-insect co-operation.

"Try this," Loma said, handing me a large green-black fruit, "it's a chocolate pudding fruit." I was sold on the name alone, and the taste was almost indescribable. Delicious, chocolate-avocado-fig. Heaven from a tree!

The land resembled Eden that day. Fat jackfruit lazed on the boughs of trees and the ground exploded with vividly coloured vegetables. Coconuts clung to the palms. The river roared by. For the first time in my life I imagined actually living like this. Life seemed infinitely richer and somehow more real. My Lycra-supported, air-cushioned existence, viewed from here, now looked farcical. Back home I strove so hard but to get where? To achieve what? To have the luxury of buying my beans in a can, or a bottle of wine to relieve the stress, or my two weeks in the sunshine.

I did realise that as an outsider I was guilty of romanticising the lifestyle. Life in the Gathering was anything but simple. Money was always a problem. No electricity meant a lot of extra work and often not enough hands. There was still need for contact with the outside world and tools and medicine are not cheap. The land was abundant, but often cruel. Crops fail, droughts occur, pests develop and people lose interest.

Some weeks later the Gathering left en masse for Cairns. The Australian government wanted to mine uranium from Aboriginal sacred ground. In protest, about a hundred of us painted our bodies with ochre mud from the forest and paraded through the streets, wielding banners to the sound of didgeridoos and drums – all very silly and great fun. I overheard Stream suggest to a policeman that he should chew parsley while on traffic duty, to protect himself from harmful pollution. The policeman looked bemused. I guessed he was more used to having insults thrown at him than homeopathic advice. The day was deemed a success; the press turned up and the issues got some decent coverage.

On my last morning at the Gathering, I awoke sharply when an overripe starfruit landed forcibly on my head. Nature's alarm clock works in strange ways. Once I would have sworn at being rudely awoken at six in the morning, but I just brushed the jam from my face and the ants from my ears, hung up my bedroll and made my way down to the river. I felt both excited and sad about hitting the road again. The Gathering had inspired all of us: Duncan was going to Indonesia, I was going to learn Thai massage, Phil was going to create an artistic masterpiece. We were bubbling over with energy and ideas. It was time to move on. I had come to miss friends, caffeine and the telephone, but I worried that when surrounded by all the temptations of city life I would succumb to fast-food binges, copious quantities of wine and Tube rage, and would forget all I had learnt at home in the forest.

Scattered around the world now, some of the inspirational ideas conjured up by the lads and myself are prospering. For me back in London, chewing parsley furiously on the Northern Line and thanking the trees in Hyde Park just make me feel silly, though practising a smile rather than a scowl still feels pretty good, as does roaring loudly in large open spaces.

In your own backyard

Margo Daly

Margo Daly was living in London when she was offered the job of researching the *Rough Guide to Australia*. She returned to explore her country with a notebook and the requisite eye of an outsider. Her initial research took her to South Australia and Victoria, where she travelled in the middle of a rainy winter, mainly by bike. She recently edited, with Jill Dawson, the fiction anthology *Wild Ways: New Stories About Women On the Road* (Sceptre 1998) and has written the *Rough Guide to Sydney* and is completing a novel.

After two years living in England it was odd that I chose to write and research a guidebook to Australia. For as long as I can remember I had dreamt of escaping my home country, fuelled by all the books I'd ever read. I was the first of my siblings to go abroad, having schemed to leave since I was sixteen when my best friend and I had gone as far as a guided tour of a cruise ship berthed at Sydney's Circular Quay. Our Year 12 leaving magazine judged us most likely to embark on a Women's Weekly World Discovery Tour. Instead, two weeks after my high school exams, I flew alone to England, my father's birthplace, for a very unglamourous year as an au pair and a bar attendant, with a few forays into France. At the same time my older brother had taken a year off from university to travel around Australia, writing to me in London as the Australian Pioneer Explorer – or APE for short. In his letters he chided me for going overseas without seeing Australia first, and it sunk in that he might be right.

The problem was that I had had a rather appalling glimpse of the "real" Australia as a child, which had made me dread the country's interior. I was eleven when Dad dragged us from the leafy, hilly northern suburbs of Sydney to northwest New South Wales. Wee Waa was suffocatingly inland, 500km from the sea, and the terrain around the small town was monotonously flat. The hotel where our father took

45

us to live was one of only a few double-storey buildings in town; while he was its publican, we lived upstairs. On the Namoi River, Wee Waa is at the centre of Australia's highest yielding cotton-growing district. Sharing the climate and crop of the USA's Deep South, in the mid-1970s it also echoed some of the same racial attitudes.

I saw life here for the first time and it was brutal. The locals called my father's pub the "black hotel": the town's Aboriginal population drank in its public bar. There was an unspoken apartheid system in operation, which even extended to my best friend, an Aboriginal girl, who was not allowed to sleep over, despite my tears. At the height of the cotton-chipping season, at the hottest point of the summer, when most men were working and had money to throw about, the bar and the beer garden seethed. On hot Saturday nights, Country and Western music floated up to my bedroom and I'd fall asleep listening to the plaintive tones of *Satin Sheets to Lie on, Satin Sheets to Cry on*, to be woken up by the shouts and broken glass of a brawl. The "bull wagons" routinely pulled up outside the hotel on these nights and the police would literally pile the black population into the back. Or so it seemed to me, hanging out on the balcony, allowed a privileged view of Main Street.

Nature too, entered into my view of the "real" Australia. Wee Waa got its levy bank eventually, not long after we'd left, but in between the Namoi swelled its banks twice. My mother cooked knee-deep in brown water in the kitchen, while customers still sat at the bar on high stools, the salvageable contents of the cellar piled high before them. The Aborigines from Tulladunna, the Aboriginal reserve on the fringes of town, were put up at the two-storey Central School, and townies made cruel jokes afterwards about it needing to be disinfected. Afterwards, fine silt covered everything, and a smell like damp clothes left to rot pervaded.

When we left four years later I hated rural Australia, seeing no romance in the outback: boring stretches of backward nothing. Give me the sea and the city, I thought; give me culture, an outlook. And yet I remember as a young child in Sydney being amazed when I learnt that people came to the city for holidays, and being driven across Sydney Harbour Bridge and the glittering harbour thinking, sullenly: why would anyone want to come here, it's so boring. I had still to learn that in order to really know and love a place, you need comparisons. Returning to Australia to begin work on the guide, I realised it was more complicated: that a place changes, becomes something else, each time you go away and come back to it. Now I was returning to Australia, not Sydney. I was thinking of my home as a continent, not a city or a state.

Just as my preconceptions about my country began to collapse on being tested, so did my ideas about myself. I had chosen to cycle on my first trip out to Australia, alone, and the decision for me was a big one. I was allowing myself to believe in my abilities, to say, "I can do that". I had always hated sport at school because it was competitive; I was a clumsy child, always tripping over my own feet. But being clumsy (and pale) doesn't prevent an enjoyment of physical activity and I loved swimming and walking. What I saw as a very Australian mania for sports and sun-worship had always been a mystery to me and sometimes made me feel like an outsider in my own country.

I had learnt to cycle quite late, at eleven, when my experience was restricted to the flat roads of Wee Waa. My first adult taste of cycling was a few months before leaving England for South Australia. Renting a mountain bike, I spent a weekend pedalling along the Ridgeway between Oxford and Marlborough. Covered in mud, rain pouring down, I sometimes wept as I tackled another hill, my friends furiously speeding off in the distance. But I had learnt that the sense of achievement at the end far outweighed the tears which, after all, were only temporary.

It was not that I had planned to cycle in Australia – the thought never crossed my mind until I was confronted by the realities of South Australia's negligible transport system. I'd taken the bus to the Barossa Valley, one of Australia's most famous wine-producing regions, but once there, how was I to get around? South Australia is a car state, made easy by lax registration laws so everybody, it seems, can charge around in a battered old bomb. Consequently, the transport system is abominable, with buses to the main centres but no public service to any spots off the main route. I couldn't afford a car and petrol, let alone the nightmare, cost and responsibility of a breakdown, but clearly needed my own transport to properly research the book. After renting a bike to cycle around the Barossa, I knew I had the answer: a pleasurable and inexpensive means of transport – idiot-proof too – that allows you to be part of the landscape, rather than viewing it at full speed through a glass screen.

In Adelaide, a city surrounded by vineyards, I based myself with some kind friends of friends who became my mates too. To them, with their full-time jobs, it must have seemed as if I was forever flitting off for mini-wine tours. Away I'd cycle to the Franklin Street bus station, load my bicycle, and arrive back a few days later with some more choice bottles for us to enjoy. My first expedition was to Victor Harbour, a seaside town on the Fleurieu Peninsula just south of Adelaide. With little to discover there, I cycled east along the coast to Goolwa, a river town on the Murray Mouth, and ventured into a surf life-saving club en route. Surfers, those almost mythical Australian characters, still intimidated me – a teenage hangover of a suburbanite attempting to brave the wilds of beach culture. I faced my fear, using the cover of the travel guide to speak to one for the first time, extracting all sorts of information about local surfing and finding this "waxhead" was in fact a human too.

Cycling demands carbohydrates and after the forty-kilometre return ride I craved a huge bowl of pasta. Italian restaurants are few and far between outside Adelaide, and in Victor Harbour I happily found one, its walls encouragingly lined with photographs of Italian cyclists. I stuffed myself with spaghetti, perfect fuel for the next morning's cycling. It was a liberation to be eating as much as I wanted, like I had as a teenager, with an enormous and unselfconscious appetite. Instead of living in my mind, I discovered that I had a body. My body was a machine, use of which was exhilarating. Like a car it needed water and fuel; when it was cold and started suddenly it would crank up, causing a painful left knee.

The Fleurieu Peninsula, besides its impressive coastlines on both its Gulf St Vincent and Southern Ocean coasts, has the undulating vineyards of the Southern Vales inland. With about forty wineries in a small concentration, mostly in bush settings, the area around its centre, McLaren Vale is perfect for cycling. Perfect any time but winter, perhaps; Adelaide and its surrounding areas have a Mediterranean climate, just right for grape cultivation, of dry summers and rainy winters. I didn't know this until I'd done my research; ill-prepared with no waterproof gear whatsoever.

My second expedition (this time with a fetching, bargain-basement, clear plastic, wet weather suit) was to the Clare Valley, another wine region which has more in common with a down-to-earth farming community than the boutiquey feel of McLaren Vale and the Barossa. It is as much sheep as wine country, and my first night was spent at Bungaree, a grand old sheep station. Waiting for a night-time lift to the property, I sat drinking tea in a milk bar. The women behind the counter were curious about this night-time manifestation with a bicycle and amazed that I was brave enough to cycle around by myself. They insisted I must be scared, by which I knew they meant rape and deserted country roads: cars and men. But except for once or twice, I was never frightened and I knew why. It was as if I was on a mission. I had such a sense of purpose, and I was so busy getting on with it that there wasn't room for fear. I was determined not to fail, and besides, I never felt alone. My bike was company.

I found these wine areas refreshingly sophisticated yet with friendly, rural attitudes. But the Riverland – the long, irrigated strip on either side of the Murray River from Blanchetown to the Victorian border – came as a shock, resembling that atmosphere I'd experienced as a child in northwest NSW. The towns here all have the same raw edge, with little charm or sophistication, and an undercurrent of violence most apparent on drunken Friday nights. I found the area menacing, and several things happened there to make me hate it.

I'd planned to stay at the backpackers' hostel in Berri. Figuring that in the middle of winter there wouldn't be much competition for rooms, I left it until late afternoon to call, just to check if it was open. I didn't bet on the number of people fruit-picking at that time of year – the man who answered the phone said they were full up. I begged him to squeeze me in somewhere, as I had to come and look at the place for the travel guide anyway. Also, it was now early evening and there was nowhere else in Berri where I could afford to stay. Seemingly unimpressed, he insisted that there was no room. When I returned the next day to look at the hostel, after telling him of my panicked 24-kilometre cycle in the dark along a busy highway to the next town and a cheap place to stay, he sheepishly confessed that they weren't quite full, but he had turned me away on account of my Australian accent. Hostels are for travellers, and if you're travelling within your own country, you have to make the distinction between traveller and itinerant worker (read untrustworthy drifter) clear. Unfortunately it is often Australians who misbehave at hostels.

As travel goes, what seem like the worst of days can provide some of the best moments. I'd made an appointment to interview Ian

Abdullah, an Aboriginal painter who lives in Barmera, a Riverland town known for its annual Country and Western music festival. I had first seen his paintings in Sydney at the Museum of Contemporary Art. Bright and childlike, the painting of the floodlit rodeo at night struck at childhood memories. It was already getting late as I hurried to make the 14km from Berri to Barmera for the night. Riding along the highway towards a turning with a few cars waiting to pull out, I was disconcerted by the crude comments shouted at me from one vehicle; although it's a disturbing fact of life that men in cars in Australia heap verbal abuse at female pedestrians, I'd never experienced it on my bike. But at least he didn't knock me off, like the bloke who then turned left, without looking. Picking myself up, all I could think about was my bike, my new bike. I shook my fist at the man and screamed that it was my right of way, in too much of a hurry to check if I was hurt or to take down his licence number. My bike was OK, so I headed on, feeling angry but strangely pleased that I hadn't burst into tears.

As in all of Australia, the Riverland's pubs double up as hotels, an often misleading term stemming from a legal requirement that drinking places provide at least a few rooms where customers can sleep off the night's excesses. Struggling on to Barmera, I arrived to a scene of typical Friday night drunkenness, men spilling out onto the streets from the very heavy hotel where I'd planned to stay. As I pushed my way into the public bar, I got the usual quota of stares and sexist comments. In public life, Australia has one of the best records for sexual equality in the world. However, an equivalent change in attitudes has not necessarily followed. Around the time that women achieved equal pay, public bars of hotels – which until then had traditionally refused to serve women – were stormed by women's groups. Now, you can get a drink anywhere, but the way in which these places are set up with two bars continues to reflect the old bias: you'll still see signs for the "Ladies Lounge", and it's nearly always a long way from the public bar to the women's toilets. My shabby, unheated room seemed as spitefully far from the ladies as was possible. Sitting on the worn orange towelling bedspread under a dim dangling light bulb, I examined my left leg and the painful yellow, purple and green bruise spreading across my shin, and did finally burst into tears.

The drinkers were still going strong when I wearily got on my bike to make my appointment. Beyond the hotel were fields and pitch darkness and I cycled as fast as I could in sheer terror through the unlit streets. I knew Ian Abdullah's house by the red, black and yellow Aboriginal flag outside. In 1970s' Wee Waa such a thing would have been unheard of, especially in – what I later learnt – was a mainly all-white street. Things in Australia were beginning to change; white Australians were fascinated by Abdullah's paintings with their rural black perspective. Mostly evocations of his childhood and early adulthood, they show South Australia's Noongahs growing up along the banks of the Murray. For many they provide a realisation that tribal existence was only one aspect of traditional Aboriginal life; just as my best friend in Wee Waa would look confused when I asked her about carved emu eggs and didgeridoos, Ian Abdullah began by trying to paint tribal images which didn't feel right and belonged not to him but to the Aboriginal people of the Northern Territory. The Murray River, teeming with water-life, supported a large Aboriginal population, and the area along the Murray still has a large black community. Abdullah is not tribal, but he had never moved far from his roots, working on the land, in the tradition of the unsung Aboriginal rural worker.

After the Riverland, I was glad to get out of South Australia and head for Victoria. I caught the interstate bus to Melbourne and my old friend Jackie, who lived in a turn-of-the-century run-down terrace house right near the Victoria Markets, just to the north of the city centre. The Market, operating every day except Mondays and Wednesdays, is a lively showcase for all the varied cultures that thrive in Melbourne. Every vegetable and fruit imaginable is sold by all varieties of people hawking them in loud, raucous voices; and the food halls burst with delicacies, among them hybrid creations like brie wrapped in eucalyptus leaves.

When I cycled to Jackie's doorstep it was 6am but she'd already got up and lit a fire in her room to welcome me. It was a notoriously cold house and the all-women household used to take long hot baths to warm themselves in the midst of Melbourne's bitter winter. It was also the house where Helen Garner, one of Australia's most famous writers, had once lived, immortalized in her classic novel *Monkey Grip*, a tale of obsessive love and heroin addiction, played out in the shared communal households of the 1970s. Still gloriously ramshackle in best Melbourne inner-city grunge style, the house of women continued to be unconventional: artists, a dancer, a women's refuge worker. They all cycled, too, and were envious when I'd get out my gear and go off on a jaunt, away from the bars and the bands and the late nights of the city. Everybody, it seems, cycles in Melbourne, a mostly flat city with a transport system predominately of trams providing a quieter, less polluted and more predictable cycling environment. Cycling within the state is made easier with a bicycle-friendly and extensive train system. The high population density in Victoria, the second smallest state, means the system has stayed intact so it's very easy to get to out of the way places.

My grandfather had come from Victoria, and there was some mixed-up story about him being orphaned in a fire. He and his brother got shipped off to an orphanage while his four sisters were sent to a convent and became nuns, to torment my mother during her childhood. Mum said I still had some second cousins in Victoria, but could never quite remember whether they were in Ararat, Ballarat or Bendigo, all within the gold-rush area, north of Melbourne. I kept a lookout but it was not until Shepparton, in the fruit-growing centre of the Goulburn Valley northeast of Melbourne, that I spied a Doyle's bus. With about an hour to kill, I looked them up in the phone book, expecting mild disinterest. Instead, a very excited Ken Doyle insisted I come straight round to the bus depot, where I found a short, very friendly man who looked just like my mother. He took me back to meet his mother, who sorted out the complexities of the blood ties for us: our grandfathers had to be brothers. A big dinner was arranged for me out on his sister's farm where I met Ken's wife Joyce, of Aboriginal descent, who taught Aboriginal studies at the local technical college, and their three blonde, brown-eyed children. I was touched by the kindness of distant relatives, so far removed yet familiar. I saw a photograph of my grandfather's brother, dressed in his World War II uniform. We'd lost our only photograph of Grandad, who'd died when I was five, and this seemed the closest I'd ever get to his dimly remembered image.

Throughout my journey, strangers became friends and friendships were strengthened. On my last night in Melbourne, I cycled with Jackie at midnight across the city to seaside St Kilda to see the last set of a local band, and drink some long, cool beers. It was exhilarating, the impulsiveness of our ride and having the tramless, near–deserted streets to ourselves. For once I took my friend's lead, launching myself across traffic lights and abandoning all rules of the road. Although I was leaving the next day, I felt as if I'd finally come home.

The Flying Postman

Bronwyn Denny

Over thirty years ago Bronwyn Denny left her home in Sydney to travel independently along overland routes to England where she has lived ever since. In 1986 she picked up an illness while in the Far East, which left her with a long-term neurological condition. Her health has since improved, but she now travels in a more calculated way, using organized group itineraries, transport and accommodation. At the age of sixty she revisited Australia and

managed to fulfil an ambition to join the "world's longest mail run", a two-day, 3000-kilometre flight from South Australia to Queensland with 27 landings and takeoffs from airstrips made up of a few hundred metres of gravel or sand. The flights, which only accept bookings for the cooler months, normally take on just two tourists. Bronwyn took an early morning flight from Adelaide airport to Augusta to meet the plane.

There were two other passengers on the transfer to Port Augusta: a pair of hairy legs in shorts and an uptight young woman who announced that we could go now that she had arrived (half an hour late and having already missed two flights). I duly followed their example and collected my in-flight meal from a box: fruit cake wrapped in cling-film and a carton of juice. Before long I was in the tender care of Tray-cee. As part of the remarkable package, I spent the rest of the day in a four-wheel drive being taken wherever I wanted to go in the local area by a woman of about my own age. We chatted about our families and the terrible things we did when we were young – she swimming in tidal mangroves and me taking to the ocean alone in a canvas canoe – as we visited the recently established Arid Lands National Park. We went into the bushland of the Flinders Ranges, made a brief stop at the Flying Doctor Base and spent my lunch voucher on a generous meal at a museum tracing the history and environment of Outback Australia. By early evening I was delivered to the *Standpipe Motel* for dinner and an overnight stay. Next morning at half past six, after breakfast in my room, a taxi transferred me back to the airfield.

Our plane, a Rockwell Shrike Commander carrying the pilot, Bill (a 28-year-old surfer), and up to three passengers, was delivering and collecting mail and supplies from Port Augusta in South Australia, over the north Flinders Ranges, the Strezleki Desert to Birdsville (where the airstrip is quite rightly outside the pub), then on to Boulia in Central West Queensland. Then it zigzags down the Birdsville Track, over the open coalmine at Leigh Creek and back to Augusta.

On the way "up" we took a woman into Queensland for a bar-bie under the coolibah tree in the town where she was heading. It was a surprise birthday party for her friend so the pilot came in the long way round in order that the 65 inhabitants wouldn't know that a plane had landed. Over a hundred people managed to get to the event! It appeared immaterial that every place at which we stopped beforehand knew that there was a party planned in Bedourie, and even that "there should be a good fight if the ringers come on from Sandringham". No one came to meet her and help her with the booze and the toaster she was carrying as a present so, having made use of the toilet marked "Sheilas", she set off along the wheel tracks to the settlement, a few kilometres into the desert. We picked her up again early the next morning as she had to get back in time for work the following day.

The only other passenger was an Aboriginal stockman with his name embroidered on his uniform shirt, who was en route to some-where near Mount Isa, well beyond the plane's final destination.

The whole of north-central Australia had been seriously flooded for several months, to such an extent that in some places it was only otherwise heard of in Aboriginal tales. Now the waters had receded from vast tracts of land, leaving only a few of the homesteads still isolated and cut off even from our plane. Flying at between 2000 and 4000 feet, I sat next to Bill; if I leant forward it felt as though I would fall out. The slowly changing landscape was incredible. With all the unreal vegetation that had sprung up as the waters withdrew, between parallel flowing ridges of dunes, flying was like swimming along the bottom of the sea. The partial cloud cover lent an eerie green light and deep reflective purple-blue above. I was almost afraid to breathe for fear of drowning but partly from the sheer sense of exhilaration. We flew over the Channel Country where the waters had drawn back to reveal great expanses of the desert's natural drainage network. These capillary-like channels fan out as though from some never-ending delta and were stained red while the surrounding area had been left as yellow clay. Thus we were suspended over what looked like a giant human brain for perhaps an hour, its patterns continually changing and pulsating.

Stops at homesteads were between ten minutes and a couple of hours apart. The first of many refuellings was at an airstrip three kilometres from the nearest dwelling. An old truck rattled out to us with a blue oil-drum in the back. A hose was connected at one end to the drum and at the other to the rear of the plane, and the fuel was pumped through by hand. At another property, a seven-year-old girl drove the truck out alone, barefooted. Sometimes no one came out, so we collected their mailsack and left anything for them in an old oil drum on a post or, in one case, in an old-fashioned refrigerator.

Birdsville pub is one of those notches that a traveller's life has to acquire. Being a woman and, worse still, a Pommie by the locals' reckoning, I did not get off to the best start. Both of these attributes, by tradition, are simply bait to the chauvinistic attitudes that are part of life out here. God forbid what it would have been like if I'd been a shapely young 'un. A sign in the bar states: "This is Australia. If you enter wearing your cap back-to-front you will be thrown out." And another reads: "MENU. Zap pie, zap pizza, seven-course meal (six-pack and pie)." Fortunately my fellow passenger at this stage, a down-to-earth Aussie with a job in the city, had often worked here during the annual Birdsville Races when the population swells for a few days to several thousand people, so we were given special service. I sheepishly handed over my touristic meal voucher in exchange for "zapped" lasagne.

By evening, we reached Boulia, our destination, which appeared to have the expectation of becoming a boom town. "Now they've sealed the road through from Longreach everyone will want to come here." I tried to visualise the empty, hugely wide dirt road through the town crawling with developers who wanted to build more veran-dahed, galvanised steel and wood houses. Or tourists clamouring for the shade of one of the gum trees. Even the Colonial pub and store might be stretched.

I was collected at the airstrip by a man with a gangrenous foot who used a lump of wood to control the pedals of his small, sometime white, open-backed truck (the kind known in dehydrated Aussie-speak as an *ute*). The stockman climbed into the passenger seat next to the driver and I threw my sack into the red dust and hairy bits at the back. As a woman, and appropriately in line with local custom, I began to haul myself in after my luggage. It was Harry, the driver, who insisted I should sit in the front cab too. It was a mixed blessing, as anyone who has ridden in a cab astride an old-fashioned gearstick will know. I was reminded of hitchhiking in my youth, when we used to take it in turns to squeeze in beside the driver.

The inimitable Tray-cee had forgotten to notify the pub that the plane was bringing a passenger who would need an overnight stay. As the normal accommodation was full, it was decided to move some shearers out of a room above the bar and put me in there. The con-sensus of opinion, however, was that I wouldn't "get any rest" (I didn't ask for more detail about this), so finally I was given Bill the pilot's motel room. Bill quietly and graciously insisted that this was the best option and tiredness got the better of my maternal-type guilt feelings – until the next morning at breakfast when I noticed that he was still doing his paperwork. I had an interesting little room, en suite with direct drainage through the floor into the dirt below. Sleep had seemed to move in rhythm to the all-night drumming coming from shacks at the back of the motel, and someone called Rosie was in great demand until the early hours. I reassured myself by repositioning the safety pin that fastened the thin curtains together.

Next morning it was back to the airstrip, where supplies were being loaded onto the plane, and the return trip south. We were unable to stop at some of the homesteads as the ground was still too soft to land after the floods, but we did land at Bedourie to pick up our party visitor, this time accompanied by her friend who had come along to say goodbye.

"Were there any fights?" I asked innocently.

"Well, sort of half a one. You know, Joe set up Bob, and then the ringers were in from Glengyle, but were called back by three a.m. But they went as far as the pub and it got a bit heavy and Sue spat the dummy and called the police, so they jumped in the truck."

By this time the mail and supplies had arrived by *ute*, the driver on this occasion a woman all of ninety years old, who also happened to be the postmistress, nurse, midwife and storekeeper. As the loaded plane circled the settlement the space under the coolibah was already filling up again as the party entered its second day.

The Birdsville Track had been impassable for months, so it was necessary to restock the roadhouse at Mungeranie. This was one of many such places, often spaced several days' travel apart along the outback roads, and which provided accommodation, supplies and a welcome. To rest while I was waiting and to avoid some of the glare from the stones, red and mirror-polished by the wind, which form the desert's surface in this part of Australia, I decided to lie down on the smooth panned earth of the road. But I couldn't sleep. The vast areas of water nearby had attracted hundreds of huge pelicans, which seemed always on the move, lumbering along and catching the light on their plumage. Bill said, "Make sure your seatbelt's on when we fly. We might have to dodge a few of these." And we did, too.

In the evening we passed by the purples and reds of the Flinders Ranges, dry-ice clouds spilling from the ridges, over the opencast mine at Leigh Creek and on back to Port Augusta for the night. My box of juice was still in the refrigerator where I had left it, and the taxi was waiting the next morning to take me to the airstrip. After a big hug from Bill I was whisked away with a planeload of twelve commuters back to Adelaide.

read on . . .

Julia Blackburn, *Daisy Bates in the Desert* **(1994; UK/US: Vintage, 1997).** In 1913, when she was 54 years old, Daisy Bates, an Irishwoman, went to live in the deserts of south Australia where she became one of the first travellers to take up the

Aboriginal cause. Although Mrs Bates left behind a detailed record of her life, little of it was discovered to be true. Julia Blackburn relies on her own vivid and original imagination to fill in the gaps, interweaving in this meticulously researched biography moments of fiction that are seamlessly and beautifully crafted. Scenes such as living in a tent among sand dunes, digging out rabbits and lizards for food, beating the ground in Aboriginal rituals and hunting for souls under the milky light of the moon are effortlessly evoked.

⭐ **Annie Caulfield,** *The Winners' Enclosure* **(UK: Simon & Shuster, 1999).** Already a successful comedy scriptwriter, Annie Caulfield has penned a travelogue with all the panache and pace of a great comedy act. She flies to Australia in order to unearth the history of her Irish great-uncle, an irascible misfit who was shipped out of harm's way to Queensland, where he successfully earned a living as a jockey. In researching the truth behind the family myths she hopes to establish her own links with this faraway continent. Not all that she discovers, however, is good for a laugh. Her tales of racism and misogyny make salutary, even harrowing reading, such as when she visits the scene of an almost-forgotten nineteenth-century massacre, accompanied by Bill, an Aboriginal stockman. Yet, in this deceptively informative, many-layered portrayal of two generations of Caulfields' experiences in Australia, it's the irrepressible humour that lingers.

⭐ **Robyn Davidson,** *Tracks* **(1980; UK: Picador, 1998/US: Vintage Books, 1995).** In her late twenties, Robyn Davidson broke the mould of the gung-ho adventure yarn with this unusually honest and self-revealing account of riding a camel alone across the Western Australian desert. Davidson arrives at the frontier town of Alice Springs with her dog, a few dollars and a, "lunatic plan" to acquire and tame four wild camels to lead across 1700 miles of wilderness. With the help of a sympathetic Afghan herder, an Aboriginal elder and some loyal friends, she ultimately succeeds and her journey becomes a travel classic. Interestingly, it's in the moments when failure lurches closest, when her motives and even her sanity are thrown into question that the epic scope of this sensitive, often moving, travelogue is most clearly revealed.

Monica Furlong, *Flight of the Kingfisher: A Journey among the Kukatja Aborigines* **(UK: Flamingo, 1996).** The biographer and novelist Monica Furlong travels to the sacred lands of the Great Sandy Desert of Western Australia to live among the Kutkatja community of Wirrumanu (translated as "the flight of the kingfisher"). In exploring her hosts' remarkable closeness to the natural world, she finds that her own attitudes and priorities are subtly transformed. Her deft handling of spritual anthropology, travel memoir and historical research make this an engrossing tribute to Aboriginal values.

Susan Hawthorne and Renate Klein (ed), *Australia For Women: Travel & Culture* **(US: The Feminist Press at the City University of New York, 1994).** A wonderfully hotch-potch collection of essays, poetry, and fiction by 57 women, including Elizabeth Jolley, Dale Spender and Ruby Langford, plus helpful listings of music and arts festivals, cafés, galleries and "circus seasonal events". Don't be deterred by the rough production, this is a book brimful of surprises about women's history and culture in Australia.

⭐ **Jan Morris,** *Sydney* **(UK: Penguin, 1993/US: o/p).** In 1962 Jan Morris recklessly dismissed Sydney as "no more than a harbour surrounded by suburbs". Three decades later she returns to pay the city its full due, in this well-observed, stylishly evoked portrayal. "What a fine and interesting city", she finally exclaims.

Bangladesh

A woman's place

Katy Gardner

Katy Gardner lived in Bangladesh for sixteen months while undertaking field research for her PhD in Social Anthropology in London. An acquaintance at a local development project suggested that she settle in his family's village in Bangladesh's northern-eastern Sylhet district. This is an excerpt taken from her book about that experience, *Songs at the River's Edge: Stories from a Bangladeshi Village*.

On arriving at the village of Talukpur, Katy is welcomed into the compound of her host family and is introduced to the customs and rituals that mark Bangladeshi rural life. Under the patient care of Amma, her daughters Bebi and Najma, and various relations, she gradually learns how to behave with the modesty required of a village girl, including how to wear a sari, how to bathe in public, and how to eat gracefully with her fingers.

On the evening of Hushnia's wedding, I went to visit Sufia in the small thatch and bamboo house she shared with Kudi Bibi. She was squatting in the kitchen, rolling out *pitas* (rice cakes) into small triangles when I arrived, and I happily joined her. It was one of the easier culinary tasks, and I had almost mastered it. From time to time Sufia would hold a pita up and declare, "This is a woman, and this one, a man!" and then collapse helplessly with laughter. The bari was virtually empty, since everyone was still at Hushnia's homestead, and Kudi Bibi would not be back for many hours. It was a good time to ask her about marriage. With just the two of us there, she could tell me many things and would not be ashamed.

"Of course I cried at my wedding," she said, casting a critical eye over my handiwork, taking one of the pitas I had just completed and rerolling it with a skilled hand. "Every woman cries at her wedding. If she didn't, people would say that she was bad. They'd start whispering, and say 'That girl has no shame'. Did Hushnia cry a lot? Didn't you like the wedding?"

I replied that she had, that I hadn't liked it, and that in my country we were happy to get married. Shocking as it might be, we usually loved our husbands before we married them.

"Ah well, your country is different. You Londoni people have one way, and we have another."

"But don't you feel sorry for Hushnia?"

"Katy, you don't understand."

She was right. I didn't understand how she could be sitting there so complacently, telling me that arranged marriages were fine, crying was great, and weddings were lovely, especially as she'd been through it herself.

"Listen. Hushnia is only crying because she must leave her parents' home, where she has been all her life. She's not crying about her husband. She knows that all women must marry, and that is what Allah willed. What would happen to her life if she had no marriage? She trusts her parents that they'll find someone good for her. Don't they love her? They have found her a fine husband. Perhaps in your country people don't cry because they are always separate from their parents – that's true, isn't it? Slowly Hushnia and our new brother-in-law will start to love each other. You'll see."

She paused, and then added softly, "I remember the words of my husband every moment that I am awake."

Later that week we walked across the fields to one of the lineage baris to see a new bride. She had been brought back from her father's village the evening before in a ramshackle minibus decorated with tinsel which had raised great clouds of dust as it bounced along the country track. She was to be the new wife of yet another of my family's cousins.

The bari was crammed full of people. All the rooms were over-flowing with guests sitting on the beds and chairs, while inside great piles of food were endlessly served.

"Have you seen our bride?" Rahela, the groom's youngest sister, asked after touching our noses with hers, in greeting. "She's not beautiful. Black!" And then she laughed and hurried past. Later on, I was to realise that to insult one's new babi is the order of the day, marking the beginning of an informal and jokey relationship.

The bridal chamber was even fuller than the other rooms. Toddlers screamed and pushed, and old women in starched white saris sat with their hands on their laps, looking at the scene with approval. In the middle of a mass of teenage girls and overexcited children, sitting on the bed with her face covered and her head down, was the new bride. They were fingering her hair and her bangles, tugging the veil from her head as she vainly tried to pull it back, and examining her hands. From time to time she dabbed at her eyes with her handkerchief.

"Come and see her!" they cried when they saw me. They seized her face and pushed the veil roughly back, then forced her eyelids open with their fingers. She was lovely.

"Hello," I said lamely, "my name's Katy. What's yours?"

But of course she didn't reply, just looked away in horror.

"Do you think she's beautiful?" a little girl decorated for the festivities with great patches of red rouge on her cheeks and lips, and plastic flowers in her hair, asked me. She thrust a sticky hand into mine. "The new babi's so black!"

"No, don't be rude. She's very pretty. Wait till you have to be married and then you'll be less of a horrible little girl."

The remark had its desired effect, for the hand was instantly withdrawn and the child screamed in terrified embarrassment at my risqué mention of her future. Little girls learn their roles young, and know they must be ashamed at the prospect that one day they too might be married. The other children squealed in delight and continued to press around the bride, pulling at her orna and heavy gold earrings while she shook with sobs.

★ ★ ★ ★

The young woman's ordeal was to last for three days, as it does for all new brides in a conventional marriage. After this, as is the local tradition, she was taken back to her father's bari for a visit, to cushion the jolt of marriage and exile. Like Hushnia, from the moment her own family women bathed and spread holud over her at home, she could do nothing for herself. At her husband's home, her new female in-laws helped her with everything: they led her to the latrine, changed her clothes, and no doubt even blew her nose for her if necessary. When senior kinsmen came to visit, the women helped her to her feet and pushed her gently to the ground, so that she should touch their feet respectfully. She never spoke, and covered her face with her sari as much as possible.

I was to see many brides before I began to realise that this display, though partly a genuine expression of the fear and grief that I had seen in their faces, was also an age-old way for a girl to demonstrate that she had been well brought up, and would do her duty as a wife. Her averted eyes and covered face assure her new family that she will be obedient and knows her place – behind the veil of Islam, and at her husband's feet. She is the personification of *sharom* (shame).

Sharom is what, if you are a Muslim woman in a village in Bangladesh, you feel when a strange man catches sight of you; it is what you feel if your marriage is mentioned; it is the reason for covering your head, and not letting your sari rise up above your heels; it is why you hide behind your mosquito net if male guests arrive, and almost die of mortification if anyone sees the stains of menstrual blood on your sari. Shame, I soon learnt, was part of the natural state of being a woman.

Hand in hand with this in-built shame is the state of purdah, the veil. For the women whose families can afford for them not to go out in search of work, purdah means a shielding from strange men, a life spent rushing for cover whenever a man who isn't a relative or close neighbour appears. It was normal for the family women suddenly to fix their eyes upon the distant horizon and exclaim: "Who's that?" as we sat chatting out in the yard or at the pond. Far off, across the fields, a male figure would be making its way along the path to the bari.

"It's Alim Ullah."

"No, it's a stranger. Come in."

And they'd cover their heads and hurry back inside, or to the back of the homestead, which was always the women's territory. After a few months, I was behaving in exactly the same way.

Purdah means that the lives of the village women are very closed. The richer ones have been to Sylhet, and a couple to Dhaka, but no woman would ever travel alone. Even if she is just going to the next village, she always takes at least a child with her. Some have never been further than the distance between their husband's and father's villages. For months on end, they stay on their bari; their world is the house, the yard, and the pond. They might visit female friends and kin in the village, but the young wives of village men often come from outside, and therefore have none. Twice a year, they are taken home to their father's bari for a visit. A question that I was always asked whenever I was on a journey outside the village was: "Are you alone?" After about six months of this I began to dread the question, and hate telling my travelling companions that yes, I was, and seeing the shock in their eyes.

All the women who could afford it in Talukpur had a burqua. Many of the younger ones had theirs in pretty shades of pink or cream, with frills at the cuffs or down the buttons at the front. "Isn't it lovely?" I was often asked, as this garment was produced for my admiration. I could only ever smile weakly and say, "But don't you feel hot in it?" Even in the winter, a walk at midday is a sweaty affair. In the summer, when by 7am the sweat is pouring off most people, to go out with a burqua over the top of a sari must be torture. After seeing the perspiration dripping from exhausted women visitors who had walked to our bari in their burquas, and the speed with which they tore them off once safely in the confines of the building, I decided that this was one garment I would not try.

★ ★ ★ ★

It was quite useless for me to question the state of purdah, just as it was useless to query the natural superiority of men, which everyone assured me of, for these beliefs were the very bindings of village culture.

"You say that women aren't as good as men, isn't that right? In my home, we say that we're equal. We believe that women and men are the same. We don't cover ourselves. We can go out if we want . . .

63

we're free," I used to declare to any woman who would listen, hoping, in my first months of naivety, that they would eagerly accept my notions of liberation, and confide their hatred of their subservience with glee. Not so.

"Yah Allah, Beti, you have much to learn," the more patient ones replied. "Isn't it so that Allah made us this way? Of course men are more powerful than women. That is the way our God created it. If you don't cover your head and go around like a man, then you will be punished."

"But look at me! I'm not a man, but I've come here, and I can study at college, and I think that's good . . ."

"Your ways are different. So. But *we* say that there are two paths in life, that we must choose. One is white and pure, the other is covered with thorns that make your feet bleed. The first way is our Islam. We cover our heads and hide ourselves from men, and Allah is pleased. The other way – the women go in skirts, and show themselves like in your country, and those who take that path burn in hell."

"So I'll burn in hell?"

"In your country it's different. Your women are just the same as men. But here, you follow our ways."

Everyone was always too polite to admit that since I continually resisted their pleas to convert to Islam, hell was undoubtedly where I would end up.

On other occasions, I tried to ask why it was that women should follow such rules: "But why did Allah make it like that?"

"Because it's good. It's our custom."

"But don't you want more freedom?"

"Listen – we have men to care for us. We have brothers, and fathers and our husbands. That is their duty – so why should we want freedom?"

Any thought of sisterly consciousness-raising was rapidly revealing itself as a patronising and hopeless proposition. Anyway, I was slowly beginning to understand that what the women said they believed was not always the same as how they really saw themselves. I was being presented with an ideal, which the women did not wish to question openly but knew was often far from the truth. After all, if it was all so perfect, why were there abandoned and destitute women who begged from village to village? Everyone knew, too, that women often held the baris together, and were by no means less intelligent than men.

"More powerful than us, but no more intelligent," older women would sometimes declare, with shy smiles.

The young brides might have appeared shrinking violets to my uninitiated eyes, but the older women were clearly of a different ilk.

"He does nothing, just pray!" Amma snapped one day, when I asked why it was she, not Abba, who was negotiating the sale of some of the family land. "I'm just a woman, but haven't you seen how people respect me?"

read on . . .

Katy Gardner, *Songs at the River's Edge: Stories from a Bangladeshi Village* **(UK: Pluto Press, 1997).** Katy Gardner's tales of village life in Sylhet, Bangladesh, are told with both empathy and honesty. As a doctoral student in social anthropology, Gardner spent sixteen months in Bangladesh, steeping herself in the traditions and concerns of her subjects. However, this is no distantly observed case study: instead, Gardner has opened the doors to her mud-floor bari (house), allowing us to share in all. We see her own discomfiture in shedding her urban identity and in adjusting to expectations of female modesty, as well as her pleasure in her deepening bonds with local women. Gardner traces the themes important to these women – from absconding husbands to shrewish mothers-in-law to constant trust in Allah, all is told through all-too-rare first-person dialogue, giving us an insight into the humour, tolerance, and resilience that the writer so clearly admires. Grim tales of poverty and gender bias can be heard all over South Asia, but Gardner's lively narrative delivers more human understanding than hard statistics and theoretical analysis can achieve alone.

Sara Wheeler, "Requiem", in *Amazonian: The Penguin Book of Women's New Travel Writing* **(ed Dea Birkett and Sara Wheeler) (UK/US: Penguin, 1998).** Sara Wheeler buys a flight to the most densely populated country on earth in an effort to shake off her yearning to return to the expansive emptiness of Antarctica. Her ruse appears to fail. Other ties, a boyfriend and a pregnancy, cloud her leaving, and her confidence in her own adaptability and taste for the jostling Bangladeshi street life is seriously undermined. Yet, from this uncharacteristically fragile and self-doubting approach, Wheeler produces one of her finest set pieces. "Requiem" is a profound evocation of the claustrophobia of travel. Vignettes of her journey – the street scenes of Dhaka, the train to Chittagong, the watery Sundarbans – coalesce in a surprisingly informative portrayal. Finally, in the mangrove swamps, she realises that her Bangladesh trip marks an ending. Her old life has at last begun to peel away, leaving space for a fresh look ahead.

Bhutan

Big Mother beckons

Lesley Reader

Lesley Reader, an educational psychologist, traveller and writer from England, first flew to Bhutan in the 1980s to take up a post as a volunteer teacher in a remote mountain village. She remained there, the first Westerner to make her home amongst the villagers, for two and a half years and, through her attempts to master the obscure dialect of Bumthangkha, achieved fame as "the foreign teacher who can speak our language". Shortly after her first trip she took a voluntary job working in a refugee camp in Thailand, but the pull of the clear mountain air and the memory of Bhutanese friends proved irresistible. She returned as a school inspector, spending her time trekking between some of the country's more inaccessible villages to provide support to local teachers. Since then she has re-established her base in London, and, as a contributor to the *Rough Guide to China*, and co-author of the Rough Guides to *Indonesia; Bali and Lombok* and *First Time Asia*, she has roved around most parts of the Far East. She still returns to Bhutan from time to time, mostly working as a tour leader for the exclusive package trips encouraged by the government.

I may have thought I'd finished with Bhutan, but Bhutan had certainly not finished with me. One night, while I was living in Thailand, my Big Mother came to visit me. Big Mother, "Ama Jigpallah", is the title for your oldest maternal aunt in Kengha, the language I had struggled with in Buli. My Ama Jigpallah is the aunt of my best friend in the village. In that strange state between sleep and wakefulness, more vivid than reality, more substantial than dreaming, she appeared and spoke: "Kuzuzangpo, Lopen" – Hello, Teacher. She smiled and vanished. I feared she had died, and sent letters to her village, enquiring. She appeared again and again, always at the same time; she always said the same words. And then, out of the blue, came news of another job in Bhutan, a job I knew was for me. Once I'd made up my mind I didn't see Ama Jigpallah again until I saw her in the flesh in Buli. Neither she nor anybody else in the village was surprised to hear of my visitations in Thailand. I know that Westerners will see Ama Jigpallah as proof that I'd gone bush, been taking strange substances or finally cracked up. It can't be helped.

I returned to Bhutan two years after leaving. There was no overwhelming excitement, no tears, no drama. I stood in the clear mountain air and breathed deeply, gazed into the brilliant blue high altitude sky, and I was home.

The new job and life were very different from the old. Instead of living in one village and teaching in the local school, I was committed to visiting the eighteen schools in Shemgang District, or the Keng district as it is called.

The area is one of the most remote in Bhutan. Roads are very few, the villages are widely spaced and the countryside is wild and difficult. Rivers thunder through steep-sided gorges several thousand feet deep, with sides covered in thick inhospitable forest. People have settled wherever a water supply and enough flattish land are available for cultivation. Most of the villages are many days' walk from the road and Government services are widely dispersed. Schools, health units, malaria eradication officers, agricultural workers and animal husbandry officers cover wide areas and ease of access to these facilities varies greatly; some children live within half an hour of school (although this may involve a difficult river crossing on the way), others may walk for well over an hour in each direction while others again board at school from the age of six as the only way to receive education.

Within these villages electricity is a dream (a dream that is coming true as Save the Children provide small solar panels to run school lighting schemes), water supplies are sometimes clean, sometimes worrying, knowledge of latrines is rudimentary, there are no shops and life varies from hard through very hard to almost impossibly hard, depending on your village and the time of year. Everything that a family needs they must produce themselves, or they must have the cash, time and energy to trek to the road (two, three or four days' walk away) to buy it and carry it home. Every box of matches, every bar of soap, every bottle of kerosene for lighting has to be carried on the back of a man or woman or horse over countryside that is sheer up or sheer down. I never learned the word for flat in Kengkha: it's never used. To make that journey you must also carry your food for the trip, your pots to cook your food on the way and enough clothes to keep you warm while you sleep in the forest at night.

As well as family needs every pencil, book, piece of paper and blackboard for the school, every aspirin and needle for the health unit, every improved seed or grain of chemical fertiliser, all of these necessities of development must be carried along these well-trodden but often very difficult paths. One day I met a group of men carrying new "improved" blackboards to the schools, donated by an aid agency that had better remain nameless. Produced after much thought and consultation, the blackboards were three feet wide. Many of the footpaths in the area are much less than this. These men had to walk sideways like crabs for hours and hours on end, their loads strapped to their backs as they struggled up hill and down dale.

My job was to visit the eighteen schools scattered around this area as often as possible and support, help and advise the teachers and heads. I was based in Shemgang, the district headquarters, but most of my time was spent trekking from village to village.

I would pack my rucksack, get a lift down to the place where the footpath left the road, hire a porter from the first village for the trek to the next, and off I would set. At each village I would stop and change porters. Sometimes I would stay overnight in a village if the schools were too widely spaced; sometimes I would reach the next school within the day. Sometimes the day's walking was long, ten and a half hours of solid slog; sometimes the day was short, six hours of solid slog.

At each school I would stay for two or three or four days, do my work and move on. There were various routes around the district and I always varied my route to explore new paths, visit new villages, meet new people. Six or seven weeks after leaving the road I would arrive back, hitch a ride to Shemgang, settle down for a week or two to recover, write my report, read my mail and do the washing before setting off again.

I became a nomad and learned that I could sleep equally well on the floors of classrooms, kitchens, forests, huts or supposedly haunted temples. I discovered that I could cope with leeches on any (and I mean any) part of my anatomy without having the screaming abdabs, was not much distressed by fleas, bedbugs or scabies and could sleep equally well with the headmaster's children or village grandmothers snoring beside me. I have the cast iron stomach of the truly lucky, but still cringe to recall the maggots I found in one plate of meat. I wish I had discovered them before digesting more than half of it.

I learned from my porters which water sources to trust and which not, which ferns to pick for curry and which plants never to touch, the almost dried leaves of which tree I could roll up and smoke if I so wished. For the porters, sometimes men, sometimes women, sometimes young, sometimes old, were my companions for hour after hour. Unfailingly cheerful, they chatted if I had breath to do so, sang and chewed betel nut while carting my rucksack up sheer slopes, knew how to cross raging rivers in the monsoon, cut new paths through the forest if a landslide had taken the original one away and were a fine source of gossip and fun.

In a region where Westerners are very rare, I was initially regarded with some concern: would I be able to climb the hills, drink the local booze, sleep next to Grandma? One endless source of delight was the look on people's faces when they realised I could speak Kengkha.

There was often initial uncertainty as to what I was. Dressed in trousers, T-shirt and walking boots, I reached one village. The old couple ploughing in the field stopped, looked at me, frowned and quizzed the porter: "Is it a man or a woman?" When I replied and pointed out that I did have boobs, at first I thought they were going to die from the shock and then thought their uncontrollable laughter might finish them off.

As well as bringing news and gossip from Shemgang and the villages along the way, I spent endless hours describing my own country and family and I usually managed to pack a different set of photos on each trip for people to look at. For people were as keen to know about me as I was to learn about them. In one house there was a belief that Western women did not drink alcohol. I soon put them straight on that.

Depending on where the school was in relation to the village and where I was sleeping, so my social life in each school was determined. If I was staying with a headmaster who maintained a distance between himself and the local people, then I tended to mingle with the school staff and their families; but if I slept in the classrooms or the head was of a different disposition then things were very different.

In one village I think I was probably visited by every woman who lived there in the course of my stay. There was a constant stream of visitors from dawn to dusk; they often woke me in the mornings and left after I had crawled into my sleeping bag and nodded off at night. If they missed me in my off duty hours they would often arrive at the classroom windows for a chat.

One old lady, unaware of the conventions of schools, wandered into the class as I was teaching, a bottle of the local distilled alcohol in one hand and a mug in the other. "Have a drink," she demanded.

I said I would drink later.

She thought I was making excuses and wanted to know what was wrong with her drink.

I tried to explain I was teaching.

"So?"

I said I couldn't drink while I was teaching.

"Why not? Here's the bottle, here's the mug."

My Kengkha was not up to the task. I gave in. The mug was very big. I taught the rest of the morning sitting down.

My novelty value was considerable. Washing in the local stream often attracted a crowd, particularly on my early visits. At first I thought that little old ladies standing beside me were waiting to get to the water, but they soon put me right: "Oh no, we've just come to watch you." As I struggled to wash all parts while keeping most covered the comments were uninhibited: "Isn't she fat?" "Her flesh is white." "She has hairs on her legs." One day I got up at four in the morning to wash in solitude.

Although in some ways my life was difficult, I was lucky in that every village I visited gave me something to look forward to; the prospect of someone or something that got me up the final five hundred feet, helped me forget my aching legs, my rumbling stomach and the discomforts I would find. In some villages it was a special family, friends; in others it was a wonderful stream for washing, a glorious view, a peach tree in season, a headmaster who always had fresh vegetables, a group of teachers to laugh with.

Yet whatever my hardships, they were nothing compared with those of the people I came to know and admire more and more as I learned about their lives.

I learned that Buli is a fortunate place: the people have paddy fields and enough rice, vegetables and forest food to keep them going for the year. Such is not the case throughout Keng. I visited villages where soil, rainfall and terrain make rice a luxury, where maize or millet are the staple crop. These are lower grade grains than rice, harder to digest, providing less goodness. In one village slash-and-burn agriculture is the method of production, difficult back-breaking work. Forest experts may condemn this, but with no land flat enough for a permanent field it is difficult to see what else people could do.

I learned that sickness is a constant danger. I stayed in a tiny village in the middle of nowhere. One of the women in the house started taking her clothes off. "Please check my baby." She was pregnant, five or six months. I protested my ignorance. Her shoulders slumped; her last child had been stillborn and she was worried about this one. I suggested she go to the nearest hospital. It was the middle of the monsoon, the paths were diabolical, the rain, mud and leeches almost intolerable. It had just taken two of the worst days' walking I had ever done to reach the village. She pointed up at the mountains over which I had come, the almost sheer paths across them and shook her head. "It's too late. I can't walk." No health workers ever visited; she and her baby were in the hands of fate. I heard later that both were fine.

This time.

I learned about festivals and pilgrimages, about a Lama reported to be able to bring water forth from dry stones and about poisoners, black magic and superstition. On my first trip back to Buli I explained my job and the route I would take around the district. Ama Jigpallah began to cry. She shook her head. "You must not go to Picor." This is a particular part of the district. "The people there will poison you, they are poisoners."

"I have to go. It's my work."

Ama Jigpallah looked stricken. "You have just come back, and now we will never see you again. You will die."

Her younger sister scurried into a back room and staggered out, pulling a sack of rice. "Do not eat in their houses. Take this rice: you must cook it and eat it yourself."

I gestured to the sack and my already bulging rucksack. Even they could see the point. I suggested I was going to eat in school: the Head was not from those parts. The sack was divided, divided and divided again. They packed and repacked my rucksack, squeezed in as much rice as they could and finally I promised to be careful where I ate, under no circumstances to touch a boiled egg (especially dangerous) and to send a message by some means, any means, to let them know when I was safely out of Picor. After several safe returns from the dreaded Picor and my admission that I ate anything I was given by anybody they decided that, as a Westerner, I was obviously immune in some way. Gradually I learned more about these poisoners and their awful characteristic – although they do not choose to hurt people, they sometimes harm people years after they have eaten in their house, and very often the trait runs in families. They appear to be looked on with a certain amount of fear, but without blame.

In contrast, black magicians, reputed to be rife in certain other villages, are generally feared and detested for using their learned arts to cause illness and death. The local prison held those convicted of black magic, while other prisoners had taken the law into their own hands and attempted to murder an old lady believed to practise such evil arts.

It seemed that every day I learned more, and gradually my perceptions of what I was seeing altered. On my first trip around the district the scenery filled my mind. During the monsoon I became aware of which bridges were likely to be washed away and which paths were prone to rock falls; I learned where I was likely to encounter a snake, where most leeches lurked and simply have to close my eyes to see again the tiger footprints in one part of the forest. I learned which paths had the cruellest inclines or no drinking water, and where and when my favourite wild fruits would be ripe. And while I enjoyed the friendship and good nature of the people, so too I saw the unrelenting hardship and the darker, sadder side of their lives. This was a privilege.

For some months now I've been back in England. To explain my comings and goings both to myself and to my Bhutanese friends, to explain why I feel no sense of culture shock in moving from one place to the other, I suggest that my soul is half Western and half Bhutanese and needs both places to thrive.

This time when I left I promised to return. I'll make sure Ama Jigpallah doesn't have to come and get me.

read on . . .

Katie Hickman, *Dreams of the Peaceful Dragon: A Journey into Bhutan* (UK: Coronet, 1989). Still in her twenties, Hickman travelled on horseback with Tom Owens, her photographer partner, and Karma, their guide, into the kingdom of Bhutan. Her account of their arduous but exhilarating trek from village to village evokes the sparsely populated Himalayan landscapes and rural culture as vividly as any series of snapshots.

Bolivia

The importance of seeing Ernesto

Fiona Adams

Fiona Adams spent a year teaching English and history to children in a South African homeland before returning to London University to study for a Masters degree in Latin American Studies. She graduated in 1995 and went backpacking in South America where, having spotted an ad for a journalist quite by chance, she got a job on Bolivia's local English language newspaper, *The Bolivian Times*. She has since reverted to the freewheeling life of a freelance and lives in a "wonderfully dilapidated old house" in La Paz where she continues to write for the same paper, in addition to contributing articles to *The Guardian*, *The Sunday Times* and Australian *Marie Claire*. The following account tells of an early trip into the Bolivian mountains where she was determined to track down the ghost of Che Guevara.

My arrival in Bolivia was dramatic. Aeroplanes don't just land in La Paz, they narrowly avoid crashing. At 4000 metres above sea level, the land rushes up to meet the plane. The pilot, in turn, accelerates because at this altitude we could stall in the thin air. Passengers are hurled forward in their seats as flashes of white mountain tops flick past the windows like an old movie reel. As the plane bounced down on the tarmac we all erupted into applause, I wasn't too sure if it was because we were happy to be in Bolivia or just glad to be alive.

When not in the throes of revolution, military coups and cocaine scandals, Bolivia spends much of its time in wonderful contradiction. The country is landlocked, yet there is a Bolivian Navy. Officially, it has no earthquakes but in just one week of my stay the newspapers reported 84 tremors. And despite the fact that Bolivia has lost every single war it has fought, in 1967 its army managed to defeat one of Latin America's most charismatic communist revolutionaries, Ernesto Che Guevara. I'd harboured a secret crush on Che since my otherwise rather unradical university days. I was now visiting the country that had last seen him alive. And in a morbid sort of way, it was exhilarating.

Bolivia had seemed like the perfect starting point for Che's plans of extending the war against imperialism across Latin America and even beyond. Bang in the heart of the continent, it borders Peru, Brazil, Chile and his own homeland of Argentina. It also has a militant history. But ultimately Che's choice was ill-fated. If you're not struggling for breath in the high mountains, you'll be sweltering in impenetrable Amazon forest. Horizons are infinite in Bolivia, a country twice the size of Spain with fewer than eight million inhabitants. This may be an ideal landscape for llamas, pan pipes and the adventurous tourist, but its vast uninhabited spaces and appalling communications system made it a dismal place for Che's brand of guerrilla warfare. Che and his bedraggled column were eventually cornered in a remote hamlet just outside the eastern town of Vallegrande and shot on the spot.

I must admit that it wasn't just Che the communist crusader that grabbed me. Like thousands of other students. I was seduced by his popular image. He simply oozed sex appeal. I fell in love with even the most outmoded posters of him: the beret at a rakish angle, the combat trousers years before they came in vogue. I devoured the recently published adventures of his motorbike trip across South America, just as he had qualified as a doctor at the age of 23.

It wasn't long, however, before I was cursing my schoolgirl crush. There are only two directions to travel in a country like Bolivia: up or down. I had plummeted through every weather known to man heading east to Guevara's old haunts. Leaving La Paz by bus, it turned out, was no less hazardous than the flight in. Once we had contested the Andes (magnificent with a layer of freshly fallen snow) we descended thousands of ear-popping feet into the semi-tropics. Bolivians counteract the dangers of travelling on some of the world's most frightening roads by garnishing their dashboards with rosaries and plastic Madonnas and blaring out salsa from ancient stereos. By the time we pulled into the town of Vallegrande, after half a dozen near-death experiences, I was practically on the verge of converting to Catholicism myself.

It was in Vallegrande that Che's bullet-riddled body last saw daylight, and where for thirty years his bones had lain in an anonymous mass grave under the town's disused airstrip. A Cuban-Argentine team of forensic pathologists and archeologists had dug him up just a few months before my arrival and whisked his remains off to Havana. Now, a wooden cross in a dusty hole is the only sign that Vallegrande once hosted the world's most wanted revolutionary. With the exception of this historical hiccup, Vallegrande is much like the rest of Bolivia. There's a dusty plaza in front of a church and dozens of hole-in-the-wall bars serving *chicha* beer and homemade apricot wine at plastic tables. The biggest excitement these days in town is Sunday mass and the occasional cockfight.

Before his unceremonious burial at the airport in 1967, Che's corpse had been laid out in the laundry room of the local hospital, a whitewashed, balustraded building on the town's outskirts which is still up and running today. Rumour has it that nuns from the neighbouring convent, so impressed by Guevara's resemblance to Christ, had sneaked into the laundry room to cut off locks of his hair for keepsakes.

No such undercover antics are needed for today's laundry room pilgrim. The doctor on call took one look at me – dishevelled in my Che T-shirt – and pointed towards the rose garden. "You'll find it back there," he said before turning to deal with a bleeding taxi driver.

I'd certainly been pipped to the post. The pink laundry room was brimming with graffiti and freshly cut flowers. Some green twigs had been squeezed into a little vase and placed on the double concrete sink where Che's body had lain. I could only find enough wall space to etch on my initials and the date. All the rambling poetry I had composed for this moment had to be ditched for lack of room. Probably for the best, my words would have been shamefully shallow in comparison to all the calls to join the revolution and death to the capitalists scrawled across the walls.

I decided to venture further afield into the scrubby mountains where Che had fought out the last few days of his life before his execution in the tiny hamlet of La Higuera, a morning's truck ride from Vallegrande.

Clearly, this was the only transport heading south that week and everyone, myself included, was making full use of it. No one batted an eyelid as more and more *campesinos* and farm animals boarded the already overflowing truck as it left town. By way of compensation, the late comers handed round sugar-coated wheat puffs. A slavering black mongrel took up position on my lap and tried its best to look winsome every time the sweets were passed my way. We idled away the hours discussing the various merits of living in Bolivia as opposed to England. Everyone wanted to know how much a chicken cost in London. I regaled a now captive audience with fantastic stories of British house prices and the Queen.

The conversation on board was going swimmingly until they asked me how old I was. "Good God, girl," my neighbour squealed, "we thought you were about fourteen." I wish I had been. My single status was now looked upon with pity. One kindly gentleman with a droopy moustache said he had half a dozen sons to whom he could introduce me. Another woman pulled out a plump breast and started nursing her baby, maybe in the hope that it would bring forth any maternal feelings in the unmarried childless gringa sitting opposite.

Outside, the terrain became more rugged and mountainous as our strange party bounded uphill into guerrilla country. The road appeared to peter out into a gathering of small cottages that seemed to have been deserted for at least twenty years. I was prodded and told that this was my stop.

La Higuera, which means "place of the figs", epitomises the Bolivian one-horse town. Its inhabitants eke out what appears to be a miserable existence. The soil is parched, the trees thorny, and the rivers just tentative trickles. Long gone were any signs of figs. I wasn't surprised that Che, camped out in the woods below, had been forced to slaughter and eat his beloved mule to avoid starvation. I'd had similar macabre thoughts myself in Bolivia, a country not known for its culinary delights. Only the day before I had walked past a *confitería* with an enticing cream cake propped up in the window. My mouth watering at the prospect, I walked in and ordered a slice only to be told that it was made of papier-mâché, put there to attract custom. They had freeze-dried potato soup, if I was still interested.

I was met by a stocky man with a machete called Pablo, who assured me he knew everyone in La Higuera and everything that went on here. Not difficult considering the town's population must have been around forty at a stretch. His wife sweetly offered me a glass of homemade lemonade before quizzing me on my intentions. On the wall behind her, a yellowed newspaper cutting carrying a photo of Che had been lovingly glued up between a bikini-clad girl advertising beer and a poster of a young woman who, on closer inspection, appeared to be none other than Shirley Temple.

Everyone in La Higuera had something to say about Guevara and the bearded revolutionaries that descended upon their village thirty years ago. All remember Che fondly, sometimes with tears in their eyes. I had to keep reminding myself that these were the children and grandchildren of those who ratted on him in the first place. Pablo's neighbour, Irma, told me that when she had seen the guerrillas come into the village she and her sisters had been so terrified that they had hidden inside the house and hadn't emerged for two days.

But a lot can change in thirty years. In the west, Guevara has risen the ranks from persona non grata to those of a sex symbol. These days his face sells everything from Swatch watches to skis. Rock bands tour with his image on stage and no university campus is complete without his poster. In La Higuera, Irma (like Pablo's wife) now has pictures of Che decorating her sitting-room walls. Here, she told me in a whisper, Ernesto Che Guevara is no less than a saint.

For a moment I thought I'd landed in Cuba. Fidel Castro's favourite motto *Patria o Muerte* (Fatherland or Death) is scrawled across La Higuera's walls under stencils of Guevara's face and red paint proclaiming that Che Lives! The village's one street is called "8th of October", the date of Guevara's death. On the same date each year the town hosts a boisterous fiesta, the highlight of which is a candlelit vigil up to the old building where Guevara was executed. At the end of 8th of October street there is a hideous stone statue of Che looking far more gorilla than guerrilla, which someone once had the bad taste to colour in with black and red powder paints.

Maybe my arrival had been a little premature. In ten years' time no doubt La Higuera may have its own *Holiday Inn*. The hamlet has recently been placed on the map by the Bolivian tourist board eager to cash in on Che's currently chic status. But I'd thrown the village into turmoil with my request to stay the night. Irma told me that most tourists just passed through. No one really stayed more than an hour or so. And despite my volunteering to leave they wouldn't hear of it. There was a free bed at the doctor's surgery, Pablo informed me, I was to sleep there.

I couldn't believe my luck. It was the doctor's surgery, then the village school house, where Guevara had been imprisoned and killed thirty years earlier. Yeah! I was to sleep in the exact spot where Che was shot. I was delirious with excitement.

Don Giovanni, the village doctor, had been educated in Cuba. He assured me he wasn't a communist but shared my passion for Guevara and that was what had brought him to La Higuera two years ago. But my infatuation with Che paled into insignificance against this man's. There was more Che paraphernalia than medicines inside his surgery. He kept a book in which dedicated Guevarists, like myself, were permitted to enter their names and addresses. A bronze placard had been placed on the wall describing the events of October the 8th, relegating a government cholera information poster to a dimly lit corner.

Giovanni's favourite pastime was scooting about on a motorbike into the mountains where Che had fought. He insisted on taking me for a hair-raising spin get a better view of the guerrilla fields. I fully admit, that during one particularly frightening wheelie, the thought did cross my mind, that if me and the doctor crashed in such a remote spot, who was going to stitch us up?

But Giovanni's driving was worth the view. Looking down into the desolate valley below, I could see the Rio Grande spiralling its uncertain course through the forest. I could imagine Che, half-starved and plagued by mosquitoes, planning his next move against the Bolivian army. If I'd looked closely enough, I think I may even have been able to see his ghost camouflaged in the woods below. You fool, I thought, why did you choose Bolivia? It's not exactly the sort of place where things go according to plan.

Unscathed, I dreamt that night, not of the enigmatic Ernesto Che Guevara (on whose very execution spot I was lying), but shamefully of motorbikes, Madonnas and chocolate cake.

read on . . .

Ernesto Che Guevara and Mart-Alice Waters, *The Bolivian Diary of Ernesto Che Guevara* (reprint; US: Pathfinders Press, 1994). A compelling historical document of the idealism, mundane realities and hardships of Guevara's Latin American campaign.

Lucy McCauley, "Soroche", in *Travelers' Tales: A Woman's World, ed, Marybeth Bond* (US: Travelers' Tales Inc., 1995). A short but atmospheric essay about a woman fending off an awkward attempt at seduction in La Paz, while disorientated by Soroche, or altitude sickness.

Botswana

Stranded in the Kalahari

Chrissie Mann

Adventure turned to adversity when Chrissie Mann and friends Ellen and Maggie miscalculated their food and water supplies on a hitchhiking trip across the Kalahari Desert, setting off woefully unprepared for a trip from Maun, Botswana to Windhoek, Namibia. The trip was to prove that the kindness of strangers is alive and well. Chrissie is currently reading for a degree in American Studies at the University of Sussex in Brighton, England.

Ellen, Maggie and I awoke in our tents, hungover and gasping for a drink. The evening before, at a bar in Maun, Botswana, we had toasted our decision to venture forward together on the next leg of our journey, to Namibia's capital of Windhoek. According to our map, only two routes lay open. One of these routes looked substantially shorter, as it involved a direct trek across the Kalahari Desert. This suited Maggie, as she was anxious to reach Cape Town quickly and catch her flight back to the US to start school. It also suited our budgets: since this route offered no regular public transport, it forced us to rely on hitching rides for 500 miles. The idea didn't bother us much, as we'd become used to hitching in other parts of Africa with little trouble.

We hauled our heavy packs the half-mile from the campsite to the main road, grumbling all the way. Settling down by the side of the empty road, it was soon apparent that not many cars were on the road. We'd forgotten it was Sunday; all days seem to merge into one when you travel. Yet this didn't dampen our resolve; we simply prepared to wait, and were joined by local residents, who stayed with us by the roadside, helping us watch out for passing trucks.

Eventually, a truck came and we grabbed our belongings in frenzied excitement, convinced it would drive off before we were safely on board. The villagers looked on as we struggled to climb up – not an easy task laden with rucksacks and bags. Landing in a heap, we tried to gain some degree of poise before the truck jumped into gear and trundled off down the road. Happy to be on the road again, we waved to all the people we passed, and they waved back. Travelling in the back of a truck is not the most comfortable experience, but I loved the unrestricted freedom of it. The trees and vegetation around us thinned out, and the land lost the look of human occupancy. We sat back and took in every aspect as we watched the route we had covered fade away behind us.

The Kalahari Desert of central Botswana is not an archetypal desert with sandy dunes. It is scrub land, with a scattering of trees and fauna. Spontaneous bush fires are very common, as we found out when the smell of burning earth and leaves hit our nostrils. Looking ahead, we saw a raging fire spitting up smoke and sparks on either side of the road. Our driver didn't seem worried, safely tucked up in his air-conditioned cab as we bounced around in the back. We sighed with relief as the truck rumbled on, into clean air.

Our ride soon came to an end, and we said thanks as we jumped down. We sat in a sliver of shade thrown by an old gnarled tree, feeling more and more lethargic as the temperature rose. We took turns to wave down the few cars that came along, but none were going our way. Ellen listened to her Walkman, singing aloud in doleful tones. Maggie studied her guidebook, tracking our route. I wrote some letters, signing off "Lost somewhere in the Kalahari Desert".

As the hours passed, it became clear there was no way we were going to reach Namibia that night, and it was pretty unlikely we would find accommodation further along the road. Somehow, we hadn't expected the trip to the Namibian border to take more than a full day. How could we have been so naive to have underestimated the risks of setting out across the desert with a limited supply of drinking water and food?

We broke our only loaf of bread with great solemnity, sandwiching hunks together with crisps and peanut butter. Two young boys entertained us briefly as they bobbed past us on the rumps of their donkeys, waving sticks around and grinning cheekily. To our relief, a truck finally pulled up and we clambered aboard. It was the first female truck driver we had encountered, but apart from indicating her direction, she had little to say. In the dying sun, we travelled for several miles before being dropped off a couple of miles from Ghanzi, a small settlement some 200 miles on from Maun.

We thanked our driver, and unloaded our bags. But instead of driving off, she demanded money. In our haste to accept the lift, we hadn't asked if there would be a charge for petrol. This was a huge oversight on our part. The situation became very tense as she got out of the vehicle, rolled her sleeves up, and steadied herself for the first punch. All we could do was quickly offer her our remaining currency from Botswana and an American dollar bill, which seemed to do the trick.

By now, we needed water desperately. Maggie was voted chief investigator, and she and Ellen set off down the road to see what they could find. I remained by the side of the road to set up camp for the night, trying hard not to focus on the bliss of drinking a frosty glass of Coca-Cola. I cleared the prickles carpeting the ground, and pitched the tents, racing against the setting sun. Praise be: Maggie and Ellen arrived with fresh water, courtesy of a kind villager. We settled down to a torch-lit supper of sausage meat, raisins and the remaining bread, washed down with water flavoured with purification tablets. Wild dogs began to congregate around the camp. Maggie, Ellen and I swapped travelling tales in the darkness, giddy that we'd managed to cope.

Our stories rolled on as the moon rose. We gazed up at the darkening sky, enjoying the shooting stars and the sounds of the desert around us. Suddenly, the dogs began barking, signalling that someone was approaching the camp. Unable to see anything in the darkness, we waited to see who would emerge out of the blackness. It turned out that we scared the living daylights out of the stranger too, who suddenly turned tail and ran after hearing our foreign voices. Realising it was a woman, we cried "Hello" and the stranger returned. Zinniah was a sturdily built woman, whose warm eyes shone in the torch-light. Laughing, she explained that she thought we were thieves and was about to send for the police. We offered her some of our meal, but she declined. She was amused by our situation, and assured us that if we got up early enough, we would definitely catch a lift into Namibia.

The night was a disturbed one, as the dogs circled our tent, snapping at each other. I woke very early, and refused to let my mind wander onto the subject of food. We ate little for breakfast, wanting to preserve our remaining provisions, then packed up quickly and took up our positions by the side of the road. Suddenly Zinniah appeared, balancing a silver tray that shone brightly in the morning light. She bade us good morning and poured tea for us from a tin pot. She'll never know how much that sweet gesture meant.

Despite such a promising start to the day, not a single car had passed by mid-morning. The journey ahead seemed more ominous as the hours ticked by. I sat motionless and watched a green-blue lizard sunning himself. At last a lift arrived, and I grabbed the front passenger seat. Safely inside the air-conditioned cab, the driver turned up the radio and we sang along with abandon. Our lift ended at another deserted crossroads, with not a tree in sight under which to shelter. The heat had intensified and the whole area looked desolate. Maggie was stressed; the thought of sleeping out for another night by the road was too much. If we could only cross the border to Namibia, the distance to Windhoek would seem so much shorter. To bolster our flagging spirits, I cracked open our last tin of peaches.

To our relief, a truck soon came in sight and Maggie squeezed into the cab along with four others and a crying baby. Ellen and I joined ten adults and a small child in the back. I stood precariously against the railings, as there was no space to sit. I held on tightly as the truck bounced over the rubble; the dust made my eyes smart, the air dried my throat, the side rails cut into my thighs, and the wind fixed my hair into an abstract design. I just wanted it to be over. Ellen had fared better, fitting her backside snugly into the centre of a spare tyre.

With much satisfaction, we reached the border. One of the passengers sent round a bottle of local whiskey, and I took a celebratory nip – only to quickly feel dizzy and sick as exhaust fumes smothered us. Our lift took us toward the town of Buitepos. Flying high on the fumes of the truck, I thought I was hallucinating as we approached the town. The commercial buildings sparkled and shone; the petrol station had Mars Bars and a public loo. Heaven!

We covered the final 150 miles in a comfortable minibus. Arriving in prosperous Windhoek, I felt mild culture shock. Our two-day journey across the desert had felt like a lifetime; the three of us were exhausted but elated. Tonight, we would enjoy the rare luxury of a proper bed. Our resting place, a guesthouse called *The Cardboard Box*, pampered us with the most blissfully warm showers. All the scrubbing in the world couldn't shift the dirt, but it still felt wonderful. We changed for dinner, and ordered the largest pizza we could possibly eat.

That night, Ellen, Maggie and I reflected on the trip. What had looked like a simple journey on the map had been both a personal and physical challenge. Certainly, I'd never experienced anything like it before. Our lack of organisation was undoubtedly dangerous, and we would advise others to be much better prepared than we were and to never hitch alone. However, what I'll remember most is the feeling of exhilaration. We had survived, and we formed ties of friendship that seem strong enough to last a lifetime.

read on . . .

Bessie Head, *Serowe: Village of the Rain Wind* **(UK: Heinemann African Writers Series, 1981).** The story of Serowe over the last hundred years, largely collections of testaments by residents.

Bessie Head, *When Rain Clouds Gather* **(UK: Heinemann African Writers Series, 1989).** Set in the heart of rural Botswana, this outstanding writer's first novel deals with a South African exile who becomes involved in an agricultural project. The book deals with love, friendship, drought and the fierce forces of tradition. Among Head's other books (all published in the UK by Heinemann in its African Writers Series), *Maru* (1987) is on one level about racial prejudice and loneliness, but is also a beautifully told love story that is firmly in the mystical realm, while *A Question of Power* (1986) goes much further into subjective states and suffering, sliding in and out of sanity. By comparison, the short stories in *The Collector of Treasures* (1977) are mostly light and amusing, and alongside her first novel are the best introduction to her work and village life.

Marjorie Shostak, *Nisa: The Life and Words of a Kung Woman* **(1990; UK: Earthscan, 1996).** Compelling, if harrowing, story of the life of a woman from the Kung San tribe, living in the Kalahari Desert. In her own words, recorded in interviews with anthropologist Marjorie Shostak, Nisa describes her early childhood and fury at being weaned, her first sexual adventures, how she bore four children (all of whom died) and the practicalities of survival in one of the world's harshest environments. Told with resilience, even humour, her testimony stands out as a dignified tribute to a vanishing culture.

Brazil

The luckiest woman in Rio

Cherry Austin

In the early 1990s, Cherry Austin took a break in her career as an advertising executive to spend some months travelling in the northeast of Brazil. She funded her trip by working as a hotel receptionist and tour guide. Since then she has returned at least once a year to compile and update the Brazil chapter for the *South American Handbook* and raise funds for the Passage House, a Recife-based project which helps homeless girls.

Back in Rio, I was smiling. The corners of my stiff upper lip started curving when I stepped off the walkway into the airport, with its tropical mouldy-concrete smell. The taxi driver's nonstop conversation and three-lane Grand Prix performance made me laugh, as did the Coca-Cola balloon floating next to Christ, up above a gleaming bay. The sunshine did the rest. By the time I'd settled myself down with a cold beer, the smile was downright smug. One of the world's most stunning beaches in front of me, one of its most exciting cities all around; it was February; I was hot; I was happy.

The first time I went to Rio I hated it. I stayed three weeks, determined not to let any damn city get the better of me, and for three weeks I was miserable. Then I caught a bus to explore the rest of South America. I never left Brazil: just under a year later I was sashaying down Copacabana beach, making every second count before I had to force myself to board a plane for London. Brazil had got the better of me. It taught me a lot, changed some of my ideas, most of all, it changed my attitude to myself.

People tend to ask the same two questions about Brazil: "Weren't you worried about the violence?" and "Did you get a lot of trouble from the men?". When I first arrived, my mind was ringing with warnings. I was scared, mistrustful, and everything bewildered me.

Copacabana is erotic. Brazilian flesh comes in an infinity of shades of brown, and it's paraded – toned, tanned and glistening – not only on the sand, but around the streets, on the buses, in the shops. Surrounded by all this sexiness I felt threatened. I certainly couldn't compete, but worse than that, I didn't understand. My bikini was bigger than some of those girls' street clothes, and they were wiggling muscles I didn't even know existed – but they were so beautiful, they surely didn't need to be quite as obvious as that. There could only be one explanation. I remembered the voice of a friend who'd been here: "They're all prostitutes." "All of them?" "Yes, all. Some of the men, too." Her tour guide had confirmed it. Clinging on to my bag for fear of thieves, I tried not to stare. But people were staring at me. I felt like the unwelcome guest at someone else's party.

It didn't get any better. The streets sprouted market stalls on every spare inch; I fumbled about in a maze of lurid colour, confused by sounds, smells and sights that were totally unfamiliar to me. I stepped over whole families living in doorways and old women with leprosy. Permanently on the defensive, I marched through a forest of bronze bodies, and everywhere I went people stared. Back in my room each evening, I laboriously calculated the day's dollar rate against the cruzeiros I'd spent to see how much I'd been ripped off. Then I battled with my Portuguese handbook for an hour or so, trying to make sense of the day's abortive conversations. Not much wiser, I would put on some makeup and go out for dinner, steeling myself against the dangers of Rio at night, against beggars, robbers, and the approaches of incomprehensible men.

The calculations were a waste of time. Give or take a dollar, my sums always tallied. No one cheated me. I found it hard to believe: clumsy and uncomprehending, I was such an obvious target. I had to face the shameful fact that I was expecting to be short-changed, because in their position I thought I might have tried it. The traders on the streets of Rio were not only poorer than me; they were more honest.

Someone did try to rob me, one hot Sunday afternoon. He was scruffy, shoeless, dishevelled and dirty, and carrying a big stick. He was too slow – I saw him coming. It was easy to hop on the bus with my bag under my arm, as I have done so many times at home in London, and then I wondered why I'd been letting fear restrict my movements. Years of roaming freely around my own risky city had already given me a fine street sense – and a philosophical attitude towards the occasional minor loss. There was no reason to assume Brazilian handbag thieves were any cleverer than our own sharp operators: ours don't even do you the favour of warning you by their alarmingly poverty-stricken appearance. Better still, nobody was planting bombs in the Rio metro. On balance, Rio was probably safer than London. Having rediscovered my common sense, I relaxed.

My Portuguese was improving, too. With my new-found confidence I started to stroll the length of Rio's black-and-white mosaic pavements at a slower pace, absorbing the sunshine, the music and the view. I took time out to enjoy the permanent party atmosphere around me. The realisation dawned that maybe I wasn't the centre of attention after all. Everybody stared, certainly, but then everybody was staring at everyone. It was just what people did. Meanwhile, I still had to work out how to handle the constant onslaught of people wanting my money.

The critically poor were everywhere, most of them trying very hard to make or beg an honest living. Like other visitors to developing countries, I found it difficult to strike a balance between giving and ignoring, buying and rejecting. Whatever I did, I felt inadequate. And the kids broke my heart. Energetic gangs of good-looking youngsters hung out on the streets day and night, harassing passers-by with cynical humour. All the guidebooks told me to avoid them – but when you're eating a meal big enough for three, how can you refuse a homeless urchin asking for food?

The first time I offered, the child said something I couldn't understand. He looked at the plate, then at me, with open contempt, and moved on. Watching what the Brazilians did, I learned to use a toothpick to transfer the food, without touching it, into clean paper napkins, which the child can wrap up and take away. It's also quite normal to ask for the remainder of your meal to be packed in a foil container that you can give to someone hungry. However famished that boy may have been, he was not prepared to trough in my plate.

It was becoming obvious that, by Brazilian standards, my manners were appalling. With enough Portuguese by now to manage everyday transactions, I observed and copied all the small conventions that keep any society running smoothly. As soon as I learned to take time over greetings and thanks, life became simpler. People smiled and waved, "Come back soon!" The incessant cat-calls that had been bothering me now translated themselves into such comments as "Hey, Blondie!" – not very creative, but neither very threatening.

I had one big problem left to solve: a painless way to get rid of unwanted admirers. The action around me gave no clues. It seemed unlikely that the entire city was populated by hookers, but I could certainly understand why my friend had thought it was. The local girls were consistently seductive, polite, and charming to all comers, but trying to imitate them proved a big mistake for me. I couldn't work out what to do: merely showing lack of interest was not enough – the would-be suitor simply doubled his efforts. Guidebook advice about pretending to be married, or with someone, was useless. The average Brazilian man is convinced that he's the greatest lover in the universe, and will carry on giving you the opportunity to try him out for as long as you let him talk. I have never been seriously harassed in Brazil, and know of no other woman who has been (groping, Italian-style, is almost unheard of), but I was getting into some very complicated situations, simply because I couldn't find any tactful means of persuading someone so persistent to go away. One day, I tried a quote from the previous evening's soap opera: "I need to be alone!", delivered as dramatically as possible. "Ah!", came the response, verbatim, "Sometimes it's good to be alone." Pushing my luck, I repeated the next line, which went something like: "Yes, there are many things I must consider. In solitude." I could hardly believe it when my new friend told me where to find him if I got tired of thinking, and left.

By the miraculous intervention of television drama, I'd hit on one of the few reasons allowable, in a sociable Latin society, for rejecting company. It wasn't ideal: it meant finishing conversations as soon as they'd started, when I wanted the practice. But it saved me from having to get up and leave places before I was ready, from shouting matches in the middle of the night, and from the near-fatal insult of telling a macho male you don't actually fancy him. I must have gained one hell of a reputation as a deep thinker around Rio de Janeiro.

The girls in the tiny shorts obviously weren't all claiming to be in permanent need of solitude, and I was no closer to understanding what it was they were doing. Women in Rio had no interest in me, other than commercial, and there was little more to be learned from stilted conversations with hotel staff, so to try and find out more about this intriguing culture I headed up to the northeast in search of the perfect beach and a small, friendly town with few foreigners.

I found it, and that's where I stayed. Maceió, the shambolic capital of Alagoas (an impoverished state the size of Wales), is one of hundreds of towns, villages and cities along that coastline, a seemingly endless chain of glorious beaches. My journey took me from crowded Salvador to São Luís, on the marshy fringes of the Amazon: two old slaving ports, each retaining its colonial architecture and an intense mystical culture carried over from West Africa. I tried peculiar fish and strange Amazonian fruits in Belem; drove through toffee-scented sugar plantations; drank cocktails by a lush river in the dozy town of Mossoró, visited dusty hamlets in the colourless Sertão, a desert covered with thorn bushes.

My new-found skills in Portuguese were largely useless when faced with varying regional accents, but people were generous with their time and patience. My answer to "Why are you travelling alone?" was simply that no one had been able to come with me. The idea that I had been so eager to visit their country that I'd actually left my family and friends behind appealed to most people. I rarely was alone.

Everyday life in Brazil is set to music. It seems most people can play an instrument, and know the lyrics to hundreds of songs. Children learn to dance as soon as they can stand; ordinary couples will get up and perform a dazzling lambada between the tables at a café; teenagers samba-reggae outside the record shops. In the northeast especially, everything seems to happen to a syncopated beat; Brazilians even walk with a swing. The smallest gathering around a roadside bar could turn into a party, with old ladies teaching me to samba ("Imagine you've got a piece of chalk in your bum – now try and draw a figure of eight with it"), and the kids who sell oranges to the bus passengers practising their English – usually one obscene word, picked up from television – to universal hilarity. I was invited to impromptu parties on starlit beaches, where guitars and drums would magically appear as if they had been somehow hidden in the palm trees, to dinner with extended families of twenty or more, and to birthday celebrations at two-room houses in *favelas*, where the one chicken that was cooked meant the entire household would do without meat for the rest of the week.

I was never allowed to contribute more than the other guests did: maybe a couple of rounds of beer; often nothing at all. When I took some chocolates to a dinner party, as I might at home, the hostess was embarrassed. Such kindness to a virtual stranger astonished me: the humiliating reply to "Well, wouldn't you do the same if we were alone in your country?" was so painfully clear that nobody forced me to answer. Unable to return all this hospitality, I tried to be good company: at the least, my stiff-backed attempts to dance were a guaranteed source of amusement.

Many of the people I met lacked the money for basics such as dental care or changes of clothes (brothers and cousins shared their wardrobes, with one spare outfit between them). Competition was fierce for jobs that would barely pay the rent, and sometimes children had to work to supplement the family income. Their education was in any case limited by the inadequacies of the state school system, so families could easily become trapped in a cycle of deprivation.

The thing that brought the reality of hardship home to me was not the overcrowding in the poorest houses, nor the malfunctioning drains flooding dirt roads where children played, nor the treatable illnesses suffered by people who could not afford to buy medicine. Perhaps all this was too far from my own experience. It was a comment by my colleague at the Maceió hotel where I found a job, that helped put this poverty into perspective. An educated girl of immaculate appearance, she was describing the life of a cousin who had managed to "escape" to Germany, where she worked in a factory. It sounded pretty grim to me. "She always has food in the fridge," enthused Lídia, "and she's got dresses she hardly ever wears!" Lídia had plenty going for her, including a decent job. She had five changes of clothes. If she was ill, she had to ask our boss to pay the doctor – and the boss decided whether treatment was necessary.

I could see why Lídia and thousands like her would marry almost any man, no matter how unpleasant, or would be willing to work in any demeaning capacity to break out of Brazil's oppressive economy. What I couldn't hope to explain to her was the sheer drudgery I imagined her cousin enduring, the greyness of a winter in Hamburg, or the apathy we Europeans call civilised behaviour. The vitality and determination Lídia took for granted in her surroundings were an inspiration to me: people often had to do two full-time jobs to make ends meet, plus an adult education course to improve their prospects, yet never seemed too tired for laughter, gossip, or their deeply complicated emotional lives. Every day was lived with relish.

The estimated proportion of adult women to men is eight – some say as many as thirteen – to one. Despite equal opportunity laws, the culture generally gives economic preference to men. Parents try to buy their daughters a home as early as possible to help defend against financial risks, but this doesn't alter the figures: some form of sharing is inevitable. Rather a lot of Brazilian men have a tendency to fall passionately in love several times during their lives, resulting in several families. Some of the women they set up house with might also have children from a previous lover.

The scenario is further complicated because households often cannot afford to move – so all the families end up living in the same neighbourhood. As a result, many of the young people on one block may be closely related, with fathers, half-brothers and sisters, mothers and stepfathers all living in different households. It doesn't take much imagination to see how intricate sagas of love, jealousy, friendship and treachery develop in such a setting. I began to understand why Brazilian TV soaps are so famously outrageous: nothing the scriptwriters invented could hope to rival the extravagant passions dominating their viewers' own lives.

These people respect their emotions, and talk about them: listen to a group of men, drinking beer at a café, and they'll be discussing football, politics – and relationships. To someone from a culture where it's better to admit to a case of measles than to being unhappy, it was a revelation. Portuguese has words for feelings that don't even exist in English. Experimenting with this new vocabulary, I did become more aware of changes in my own state of mind – and more sensitive to others' feelings. It was incredibly liberating; and, unexpectedly, I found my difficulties with over-persistent admirers dissolving. I started to make friends.

There were, of course, still plenty of men whose conviction that I'd come to Brazil purely for sex was unshakeable. These studs, ready to oblige, could be very hard to get rid of: one leaped into a taxi with me, and had to be removed by two incredulous drivers; one invited me to dinner with his wife, forgetting to tell either of us he was planning a little orgy after the pudding; one, having been refused entry to my hotel room, sat outside on the kerb all night "in case I felt like it later". Then there was the guy who asked the man I was with if he could borrow me for a while, asserting with total authority that "gringas" are liberated – and therefore sleep with anyone who asks them! The mystery of my sudden irresistibility was solved, especially when I took a closer look at the pornographic magazines displayed on every news stand – most of the images are imported from the USA, and represent, to some fevered Brazilian imaginations, all "first world" women. It's a rough equivalent of the way some British men think about Swedish girls.

I got talking to two girls at a beachfront bar one evening. They had been laughing at the amount of attention I'd attracted during the day, so I asked them about it: it did seem ludicrous, asking two golden women whether I was cramping their style, and so it turned out to be. "Look", said one of them, "You're foreign; you're different from us, you're from the first world. You're . . . "

"Exotic", filled in her friend, trying not to laugh too much: "But in the end, our men have got nothing in common with you. You seem like a nice person, but you're a diversion; you're just passing through . . . "

I met one of Brazil's lamentably few female bank managers. She was always glad to see me on the beach because, she said, people thought it was peculiar when she sunbathed alone. We weren't by any means the only two unaccompanied females on that stretch: getting a suntan is something of an imperative, so if your friends can't be there, you go on your own. What made this woman different was that she was married. While she was bronzing her skin, her husband was with his long-term mistress. At four-thirty, the bank manager's lover – a friend of mine – finished work, and joined her for a few hours before going home to his wife. The bank manager knew everything about her husband's extramarital activities; but if he had known about hers, he would have killed her – perhaps literally. Male pride is a serious matter in this land of epic emotions. My friend had many other lovers, but adored his wife to the degree where he would – and did – drop everything if he thought she was in trouble. It would have destroyed him to know that she, too, had a gentle friend who kept her company while her husband was out.

At first, all this confounded me: I couldn't quite believe that so many people's lives were so complicated, but, in context, I found it all a good deal more acceptable than I might have done at home. Spending my evenings drinking beer under palm trees with people who gave their phone number to anyone they were interested in, I started to wonder which was the better way. Letters were arriving from friends in England: a woman who was secretly frightened her man was being unfaithful; a man in distress because he thought he loved two women; a girlfriend depressed because she never seemed to meet any available men. Perhaps the oh-so-controlled British were not really very different from my Brazilian friends: just significantly less honest. At least the people around me respected – and enjoyed – their own and each other's sexuality.

There's a phrase, heavily used in Brazilian cosmetics advertisements, which, translated as "it's your duty to be beautiful", I found offensive. My samba teacher put me right. The phrase is a Brazilian proverb: "Whatever is beautiful should be shown off!". While teaching me to dance with my body "opened out", she also had to teach me what every Brazilian learns from birth: that my body is beautiful. I was about 40lb too heavy when I flew to Rio. Within two months, I'd lost all the excess weight without trying. Brazilian food is delicious, and I ate plenty of it. I believe it happened because I'd started to lose the negative feelings I had about my appearance. This wasn't because of any special event, it was in the air. Taking a closer look at those gorgeous people with the slinky walk, those sequinned dancers in the carnival, I could see that very few of them had perfect bodies. What they had was confidence. You don't have to be skinny to be beautiful in Brazil. All you have to do is be proud of what you've got, and show it off with style.

By the time I got back to Copacabana I had the tan, the shorts and the walk. I could get into deep conversation with strange men, exchange phone numbers, and saunter away with a smile. I could see newly arrived visitors staring at me with the same bemused distaste that they showed toward the other half-clad women on the avenue. By now, I knew the answer to the question that was puzzling them. Some of the girls are hookers, some aren't. Some do it part-time. For going on a date with a holidaymaker, spending the night and sharing his breakfast, they can make the equivalent of a whole month's pay. Me, I had a brand-new positive outlook, a fresh attitude towards people, passion and politics, a better body, a sense of rhythm; a ticket to London and a passport to a country with a stable economy. I felt like the luckiest woman in Rio.

Speaking in tongues

Lucy Needham Vianna

For the past nine years Lucy Needham Vianna has lived on the outskirts of Rio with her Brazilian husband Herbert (leader of the successful Brazilian band, Paralamas do Sucesso). In 1996 she recorded a series of radio programmes about Brazilian traditional music for BBC Radio 3, which she devised and worked on with an English friend, Jo Shinner, a world music specialist. Lucy was nearly seven months' pregnant when the two friends travelled together by plane and small rental car, seeking out the authentic rhythms of Bahia and Minas Gerais in the northeast of the country. She has since worked with various Brazilian and British production companies and last year published her first book in Portuguese, *Viajandao com as Criancas* (Travelling with Children). A third baby is on the way.

I was thrilled when my university mate Jo called from London to say that the BBC had commissioned our project to make six radio programmes about Brazilian traditional music. I had been exposed to much of this music through its influences on my husband Herbert's compositions, and always felt that it would be interesting to show how much more there is to it than Carnival Samba and the Bossa Nova hit, *The Girl from Ipanema*. Moreover I had itchy feet and wanted to travel. Marriage, a first child and work commitments had slowed me down – now I had the chance to hit the road with a purpose and investigate some of the nooks and crannies of Brazil's geography and culture.

I had journeyed by bus all over the northeast of Brazil with another close girlfriend nearly ten years before. We had experienced very few real scrapes that I could remember, so the fact that I was six-and-a-half months pregnant was not going to stop me now. In fact I knew it would be a positive advantage. Men would be much more respectful of someone who they presumed had a husband somewhere along the line, even if they could not quite believe that a fellow coun-tryman would let his "gringa" wife charge round the country in such a delicate state. Women related to me as a mother rather than some foreign hack and on meeting me would immediately start to rub my bump affectionately.

Meanwhile I also had a protector in the form of Neguinho do Samba, conductor of the phenomenal Olodum Drummers and a good friend of my husband. As part of our project we interviewed him about his latest cultural venture, the all-female percussion group Didá, after which we were lucky enough to see him conduct the Sunday night rehearsal of the Olodum Drummers in Salvador's Pelourinho Square. There were thousands of Bahians crammed into the square, waiting for Neguinho to take up his position, but he was much more worried about safely steering "minha irma" ("my sister"), as he had taken to calling me, and my bump, through the swarming crowds. I was eventually delivered onto the steps of the Jorge Amado Museum, from where I had the best vantage spot for watching the solid mass of dancers, vibrating to the syncopated samba-reggae rhythms of Olodum, devised by Neguinho and now the core beat of all Bahian music. (The drummers also made guest appearances on Paul Simon's album *Rhythm of the Saints*, and on Michael Jackson's hit *They Don't Care About Us*, for which Spike Lee shot the video in this very place.)

The next day, despite Neguinho's protests at my driving, Jo and I headed off in our ultra-basic Fiat Uno towards Cachoeira to track down some "Samba de Roda" groups and record their music, with its links to the Afro-Brazilian religion, Candomble.

The Portuguese colonists would not let their African slaves practise their original faiths, and forced them to convert to Catholicism. To this day every Catholic saint has his or her equivalent deity in the Candomble, as the original slaves adapted the saints to represent their own gods. Some ethnomusicologists believe that Samba de Roda is the purest translation of the original African rhythms that exists outside of Africa. It also has a very important connection with Candomble: being party music and made for dancing, it was permitted by the plantation owners – in fact, its repetitive, almost mesmerising form was usually a precursor to the trances that are said to bring forth African deities and to the subsequent more secret practices of Candomble which used to start up once the slaves' masters were safely tucked up in bed.

In Cachoeira we were looking for a woman called Dalva, the leader of a Samba de Roda group who had named themselves "Samba de Roda Suerdick" after the German tobacco factory where they had all once worked. Cachoeira is pretty small and after stopping for directions just three times we found ourselves outside her door. Dalva was a typical portly but very beautiful black Bahian of around sixty, living with her extended family in the ground floor of a simple old colonial house. We had spoken briefly by phone a few days before, but the whole concept of some foreigners wanting to record her group had seemed beyond her. This time, after an informal chat and more explanation, we arranged that we would come back to record the group on the following Sunday (the musicians and dancers all had day jobs during the week). Then she very casually mentioned that today was the birthday of Cachoeira's important Candomble priestess, or "Mae de Santo", and that since she was a daughter of Lemanja (goddess of water) there was to be a big procession to lay gifts for her in the river.

Dalva's pre-adolescent granddaughter, dressed in the customary bottom-hugging Lycra mini-shorts and cropped top, led us down to a much poorer corner of Cachoeira and into a small whitewashed courtyard which was obviously a *terreiro*, the temple where the Candomble rituals take place. Next door there were numerous elderly Bahianas dressing themselves up in beautifully intricate white lace shirts and full skirts. I was aware of intruding on something very sacred and private, but unlike at many *terreiros* in larger cities, we strangers were made to feel very welcome. We caused immense curiosity and were encouraged to take photographs. After a couple of hours of hanging around, the women assembled with the *atabaque* (a tom-tom-like African drum) drummers, and the procession, pulling a small wooden boat full of gaudy offerings, began to make its progress. We wound our way through a flattish *favela*, then through the grounds of an abattoir scattered with skulls, and up onto the rail line that would lead us to the river. The drummers beat a relentless rhythm and within ten minutes a white-robed woman collapsed to the ground, "received" her deity and began speaking in tongues. I had had considerable exposure in Rio to Afro-Brazilian customs and religion, but nothing so raw and primeval, or in such a bizarre setting. Half an hour later there were at least six deities "present" and we had arrived at the water's edge. The "Mae de Santo" had by now also received her deity, Lemanja, and was being carried into a small canoe, along with the offerings and one of the drummers to maintain the trancebeat. The small mirrors, sweets and jewellery carried in the boat were laid in the river as a gift to Lemanja, who is traditionally seen as vain and sweet-toothed. The entire procession then proceeded to stagger back along the disused railway line to the *terreiro*, where things got even more intense as women, completely possessed by their spirits, danced for hours to the beat of the hypnotic drums. When we left to head back to Salvador at ten o'clock that night, I felt that the celebrations were only just starting to warm up, but my bump had swollen so much from being on my feet so long that it was about to burst out of my dress, and we had to be ready for a full schedule of work the next day.

There were moments during the trip when I wondered why I was putting myself and my unborn child through all this. The lowest point was when I began to throw up so badly on a plane from Salvador to Belo Horizonte that extra sick bags had to be drafted in from surrounding passengers. I ended up spending a day in bed staring at a dingy ceiling in a budget hotel, punctuated by trips to the toilet and reassuring phone calls to my doctor. Meanwhile Jo struggled to pull things together for a story on Minas Gerais, with next to no Portuguese.

The following day I was on my feet and back in action. We were looking for a replacement story for Minas as we had a gut feeling that the original idea, of recording the Afro-Mineiro rhythms with the percussionist Djalma Correa, was just not going to work. He seemed rarely sober and when we did try to get something down on tape he was so smashed within half an hour on *cachaça* (lethally potent Brazilian sugar-cane rum) that the music sounded appalling. Then someone mentioned the Familia Alcântara, a 38-member choral group encompassing four generations of the same family, who could trace their roots back to their slave great-grandparents. They sang in an original Yoruban dialect. Minas is not usually considered an important centre for Afro-Brazilian history but there had been as many slaves here mining gold and precious stones as there were toiling on the plantations of Bahia.

One member of the family worked as a nanny in Belo Horizonte, and we arranged to meet her on the Saturday and drive to their hometown together. We were back in a trusty Fiat Uno rental car with Nini the nanny as our guide. Our destination was Joao Monlevade, not a big hit on the tourist map as it is the centre of the Minas steel industry, in which most of Nini's family were employed. It took us about three hours to drive there, one hour of which was spent winding our way through Belo Horizonte itself as Nini only knew the bus route through the city, hardly the most direct. We arrived to find assorted members of the family gathered in the back yard of the matri-arch's house. The choir ranged from a ninety-year-old granny to young children. Dressed in African attire, they sang a range of African spirituals and Brazilian *congadas* in a strange mixture of Yoruba and Portuguese. Congada is an important rhythm stemming from the slave culture and features to this day in one of the big Afro-Brazilian reli-gious festivals in Minas. We had another programme in the can.

By the time we had recorded the six programmes, my unborn child had been blessed by African and Brazilian deities, sung to in indigenous languages, sexed by a Country and Western virtuoso gui-tarist and former prostitute, and had inspired numerous verses of *repente*, rap-style improvised poetry accompanied by accoustic guitar which remains an important means of passing political and cultural information around the backlands of northern Brazil. The baby had been jigged around to so many different drumbeats that I was sure that it would come out dancing samba!

As I had anticipated, we never felt threatened travelling as two women, although every man we encountered appeared to fall in love with Jo on sight. Even when I left her in Salvador for a few days at the end of the trip, she was able to fend off admirers without too much trouble. Brazilian men are intrinsically *machista* and cannot resist trying it on with a European woman, but they were not aggressive when turned down. Pregnant, I was regarded as sacred, like the Virgin Mary.

read on . . .

Alma Guillermoprieto, *Samba* **(US: Vintage, 1991).** For one year, Mexican-born, US-raised ex-dancer and journalist Guillermoprieto lived in Manguiera, a poverty-stricken village on the outskirts of Rio de Janeiro. Her aim was to learn about the rapturous rythms and lifestyle of samba, the immensely popular sensuous song and dance, and to take part in the run-up to Carnival. Whilst serious samba aficionados carp at her musicology, no one can deny the courage and verve with which she approaches her theme.

Alma Guillermoprieto, *The Heart That Bleeds: Latin America Now* **(US: Vintage, 1995).** In this varied and evocative colllection of essays (or "dispatches" as she prefers to call them) Guillermoprieto anatomises the Latin America of the early 1990s. Originally published in *The New Yorker*, her writings on Brazil range from a description of evangelicals in Rio, through an account of the off-screen dramas of TV's telenovelas (soap operas), to a discussion of the corruption scandal involving President Collor, a man she once described as "sleek as a Borzoi".

Annette Haddad and Scott Doggett (ed), *Travelers' Tales: Brazil* **(US: Travelers' Tales Inc., 1997).** An outstanding collection of excerpts and articles from travel writers, journalists, anthropologists, historians and other travellers, including Diane Ackerman, Augusta Dwyer and Alma Guillermoprieto. As with the rest of Travelers' Tales' country-based titles this covers a surprising spectrum of outsider views.

Burkina Faso

Welcome to the land of whole people

Melanie McGrath

Melanie McGrath is the author of *Motel Nirvana*, a much-acclaimed book about the New Age cult heartlands of America, and *Hard, Soft and Wet*, a commentary on the digital generation. Besides her transatlantic jaunts she has done a fair amount of globetrotting, including the trip, described below to Burkina Faso where she spent a month in Ougadougou with documentary film-maker Carlyn Saltman. See also her pieces on Mali (p.378) and the USA (p.596).

About two months after my father died, in early 1991, a friend called. "I think you should go away for a few months. Is there anywhere you just can't picture yourself?" "Africa," I replied. There was a pause down the line. "Good. I know just the person you should meet."

For four weeks in February and March Carlyn and I rented a big stucco house under bougainvillea vines in the northern outskirts of Ouaga. Carlyn was away much of the day, so to pass the time I would sit out on the porch with the radio on tuned to the World Service. At lunchtimes I was often joined by Moise, who was studying for his *baccalaureat* under a mango tree at the edge of the compound. "*Paris, c'est tous, tous riche, quoi?*", Moise used to say, which was his unqualified thumbs up for France and everything French. He didn't know about the black ghettoes strung out along the railway tracks north of the Paris *périphérique*, or about the rows of Senegalese traders flogging trinkets on the Place Vendôme. Nor did he invite discussion of such things. To him, France was free and rich, Burkina impoverished and politically second-rate. It was as simple as that. One day he would work in France and send money back to his homeland, he said. He didn't know how, only that it was inevitable.

Moise did not feel it safe to discuss politics. About a week after we met, he brought with him a leaflet headed "Le Patrie ou la mort, nous vaincrons," Burkina's national slogan. Inside was printed a crude history of the country's political struggles and a puff for the ruling party. He asked me to keep it as a memento of a particular point in time, which, although not significant in itself, made up part of the greater narrative. He said that if the government fell, the leaflets would be burned and new ones printed; mine would always remain as evidence. Evidence of what? He did not say, but I understood that he felt the struggle to live made a tawdry puppet show of politics and patriotism. At the back of Moise's leaflet was a little note: "*Bienvenue au terre des hommes integres*, Burkina Faso." Welcome to the land of whole people. I noticed it when I was back home, unpacking. There was a smear of sand stuck over the word *terre*, which drew my eye.

During the dry season in Burkina, the White, Red and Black Volta Rivers dwindle to little more than salt scars cutting the savannah. The mosquitoes are worse in the rains but even when the water was sunk low in the nearby reservoir, or barrage, thick curranty clusters of the creatures pestered women washing their clothes. When the water level fell, it left behind it deceiving mud banks whose depths were as pliant and dismal as quick sand. A tyre up-ended in the mud vanished the following day. Plastic water bottles filled with silt and sank like stones. The water itself, on the other hand, always seemed inviting enough; steel blue and shiny under a matte Harmattan sky.

In the heat haze, it was easy to mistake the fishermen and their craft for fat-bellied water birds. Moise had told us it was forbidden to fish, but then, people have to eat. All the talk around

Ouagadougou at that time was of drought and food shortages, because the January rains were not good, and there would be no more until July or later. There was no mention of hunger, you understand, because it is too commonplace to be of much interest. Outside the cities hunger is a way of life. The predictions they were making on the street were for famine.

People begin to suffer long before the pot-bellies and fly-blown eyes of television images; long before the hatching of what will later become "a story". The suffering starts as a series of delicate acts of neediness. A child picks up some mango peelings and stuffs them into his mouth without brushing off the dirt; a woman takes a peanut from the road, closes her hand over it and walks on. The famine flashpoint is not a point at all but the accretion of many such tiny degradations, each of which helps edge the country nearer to starvation. West Africans treasure what little they have that can be relied upon; the weight of tradition, sincerity, an understanding for the value of acceptance. Beneath the brilliant currents of colour and theatricality which bring tourists to West Africa there persists a grave and subtle stoicism as unchanging as a well-used pathway. On the far bank of the barrage, beyond the scarlet pirogue, there were always vultures blustering about, picking at things not visible.

Just south of the big house, past the barrage and into the Bois de Boulogne is a compact copse of whitewashed acacia trees leading in to the centre of Ouagadougou. This was our route into town in the mornings to pick up baguettes from the bakery near the *Hôtel Indépendance*. If the sky were not blush and hot with Sahara dust from sunrise to dark you might momentarily imagine yourself bumping along some unloved road in southern France. Early each morning, a woman would set up her trestle table at this corner, a youngish woman in a blue *pagne* printed with portraits of the Pope. We bought our carrots from her, always three brilliant orange carrots tied up with plastic twine. Each day the same wide seductive smile, no teeth, baby on her back balanced inside a *pagne* of purple striped calico, another in the shade under the trestle. "*Française?*" asked the woman once. "Yes." In Burkina, all points between or at either side of Africa and France are secret *départements* of the French motherland or remote geographical irrelevances. Why didn't I wear earrings, the woman wanted to know, why didn't I plait my hair, why was it so short, do I have fleas? She said that I looked "*comme un homme, quoi*" and wiped tears from her eyes with the back of her hand. Then she threw in a mango with the carrots to thank us for our custom and waved us away, same wide smile. If I were to stop by on the way back she'd plait my hair, she said, laughter big enough to split her spleen.

One morning, about three weeks after we arrived, Carlyn had the idea of visiting an aquaintance of hers in the bush. He was old and illiterate, and she was unsure whether or not he was still alive; there had been no news of him. We drove our mopeds into town in search of kola nuts good enough to present as gifts. There were few sellers, since it was out of season and the nuts, in any case, have to be brought up from – where? – the coast, I think. In Burkina a gift is a sign of the measure of respect accorded by the visitor to the visited. An ill-considered or mediocre gift is regarded as an affront to the dignity of the recipient. Better to bring nothing but company. Towards late afternoon we found what we wanted and turned our mopeds north, back towards the big house.

Moise and his friend Jean were sitting in the shade of the porch, waiting, although the door was open. Solemn African patience. To what purpose did we so wholeheartedly lose ours? Perhaps, after all, we never had it. Jean had come with a message from his mother to ask if we would like her to bring over some of her cassava. We shuffled about and made eyes, locked in inner diplomacy; cassava to us tastes like mashed potato and raw egg yolk left in the sun to putrefy. No sauce, no accompaniment can resurrect it. It lies beyond the culinary pale. Finally, Moise said; "So what did you both do today?" Burkinabe are, as a rule, informal but effortlessly courteous people. Even the aggressive style of market haggling has its own implicit protocol. Overstep the mark, and you will find yourself outside the system altogether, with no possibility of re-entering it, as though the market had folded in on itself and become a dream-world, excluding all spectators. It's one of the strangest paradoxes of Burkina, and of West Africa in general, that a culture so embalmed in its customs, so riddled with social rules, can be at the same time so much more relaxed and sensitive than our own.

Next day two 50cc mopeds headed out on the Kaya road early, rumbling the silence and kicking up ochre dust, Jean and Moise driving, we two content to be passengers clinging on behind; pragmatism before feminism – one of the first great rules of female travel. A few miles north of Ouaga the burnt red soil gives out to a sickly chalk white laterite, which is where the savannah truly begins. Grey brown baobab trees stretch to the horizon, and along the route here and there are thatched mud *zakse* strung about with granaries and knotted into compounds. Yellow *termetières* make a coral reef of the plain. For the most part the road is unpaved piste, rutted into escalier, but every few miles there is a metalled section still surviving from the last grand government infrastructure construction scheme. Wherever there is a proximal village women will have set up impromptu arrets on the tarmac with stalls selling oranges, ginger beer and peppery brochettes. A string of women passed us on the road, headed towards Saaba for the market, their heads hatted with eliptical paniers full of calabash-es, dry dates and bread cakes; the country's nervous system, these women. Now and then we scattered dwarf goats grazing in the drainage ditches either side of the road. A taxi brousse passed, leav-ing a dust devil whirling behind it. Grit built up in our eyes and noses, clinging to the skin like red barnacles, and matting the hair into hempish ropes. Heat pinched the air into strange smoky flues. By ten we had turned to the east, towards Nakambe – the White Volta – across a track razed from the bush.

The old man was sitting under a carob tree about twenty yards from his compound. Two years on and his left eye was cataracted over. On his head he wore an embroidered skull cap fixed with a hairgrip. Carlyn knew him at a distance from his *boubou*, the same tear in the shoulder revealing a ladder of sinews. Hearing the put-puts, the old man looked up, stared without look-ing as one does when retrieving some detail from the memory, then smiled a big moon smile. Under the shade of an awning he inspected our kola nuts, pulling off a lobe and pushing it carefully around his mouth as if it were a piece of hardened wind-dried meat. When his wife returned with a calabash of *dolo* we gave her a piece of scented soap.

The old man produced a faded Polaroid of his family, set in rows. He asked Jean to tell us that his sons and nephews were absent, working the fruit plantations down in Abidjan. He shook his head. "Burkina is become a nation of women and old men", he said, "just women and old men". When we left, he said "You have made me happy so I will leave your footprints in my compound until the wind takes them away," He squeezed his wife's arm. "She won't need to sweep today, so she's happy too."

To save ourselves from the worst of the sun, we stopped off at Saaba. A light hot breeze carried with it the smell of ammonia and tannin, and the stench of goat. A woman with heavy tribal cicatrices beckoned Jean and Moise with her right hand palm down, hissing. Who were we? Not development workers? The general feeling about development agencies in Burkina is that they should give more and get out.

Saaba's menfolk were settled under a carob tree, eating brochettes made from giant snails and playing cards. A couple of girls pounded millet together in desultory fashion, but it was too hot that afternoon to do anything much but doze and idle. The noise of a generator rose up on the heat haze. Inside a nearby hut a local entrepreneur had set up his video to show kung fu movies to the village youth. Jean and Moise headed over to the hut leaving Carlyn and I to begin negotiations for a handful of mangoes. The stall-keeper was a fat woman with lean eyes, the kind you wouldn't trust if you made contact with them on a city street. "Where are your children?" "We haven't got any." She stared out from those silted eyes with a mixture of amazement and scepticism, then reached for my earlobe and pulled. "How old are you?" She peered at the earlobes, trying to guage whether or not they were pierced; was I a woman as I had claimed, or merely some strange sexless thing? "Twenty-seven." "*Ah, trop agée, quoi?*" She shook her head. A man with cicatrices came up behind her and exchanged greetings. She said something to him in More, the language of the Mossi people, which made him laugh. "She wants to know where are your children?" he said in broken French. "We don't have any." He said: "What have you done with them?" The woman pressed his arm and leaned in towards his face. "She doesn't think you are telling the truth. You are not telling the truth. That is very bad. We like openness here." The woman reached behind her and produced a calabash of *dolo*. "That'll loosen your tongues. *Nous sommes en Afrique, quoi*," said the man with a smile on his face.

Cambodia

A surface serenity

Sheila Keegan

Sheila Keegan and her eight-year-old daughter, Carolyn, were seasoned travellers by the time they arrived in Cambodia, having started their journey in India (see p.262). Yet little prepared them for what they were about to experience in a land riven by civil war, where the ancient glories of the Angkor temples stand in regal contrast to today's cowboy towns, populated by gun-toting bandits and bored taxi girls.

Cambodia was an impromptu stop for me and Carolyn, my eight-year-old daughter. I was booking our flight from Bangkok to Saigon when the travel agent suggested we stop over in Cambodia. Why not?, I thought.

It was a country linked hazily in my mind with civil war, rebel groups and *The Killing Fields*. My guidebook described the turbulent recent history of the country: Nixon's secret 1969 bombing of suspected Viet Cong base camps that killed thousands of civilians; Pol Pot's terrible Maoist experiment that led to the deaths of at least one million citizens between 1975 and 1979. After booking the flight, I studied *The Bangkok Post*, which carried news of rising tensions between the government and the Khmer Rouge guerrillas. I felt uneasy. Was this really the place to be bringing a child on holiday? But by then, it was too late. We were on our way.

Given this backdrop, Phnom Penh was a surprise. It has wide, tree-lined boulevards and decaying colonial buildings, the legacy of French rule. Unlike most Asian cities, there seemed to be little traffic. Cycles and motorbikes outnumbered cars. Phnom Penh has the feel of a country market town rather than a capital city. It exuded a sense of calm and order. In Cambodia, however, few things are as they seem.

We flew north to Siem Reap, to visit the Angkor temple complex. The temples were built between seven and eleven centuries ago, at the height of the Khmer civilisation. There are about 100 temples still standing, spread over several square kilometres, though these constitute only a small number of the original buildings. They truly are one of the great wonders of the world. To be so close and not visit seemed sacrilegious.

We stayed at guesthouse No. 279 in Siem Reap, a newly built wooden house, on stilts, with a wide veranda and frilly blue curtains at the windows. It is owned by Pen Buntha, a bowed middle-aged man who displayed what seemed a characteristically Cambodian mixture of faultless politesse and rigid determination. He guided us to Mr Phally, who was to spend two days chauffeuring us around the temples in his air-conditioned car. This was a wicked indulgence, but I decided that Carolyn, who has no interest whatsoever in ruins, could not reasonably be expected to spend two days walking around the temples in the fierce heat. It turned out to be money well-spent.

We were advised to stick to the main paths while touring Angkor, as many areas are still rife with landmines left over from the civil war. "It is full of Khmer Rouge," proclaimed Mr Phally, waving vaguely in the direction of the surrounding jungle. "You mean they're behind the bushes? Are we going to get killed? Do they ever attack the town?" asked Carolyn, more in excitement than terror. "In May 1993 they attacked," Mr Phally told us solemnly.

As we drove toward the main entrance, on a paved road through the jungle, Mr Phally announced that we were taking a sudden turn to the left. "Why are we going down here?" I asked in alarm. The entrance to the temples was clearly visible ahead. My imagination was given full rein in Cambodia. Was Mr Phally spiriting us off to a Khmer Rouge camp? Were we to be the next foreign hostages? We passed a couple of burnt-out tanks. My anxiety increased.

"It is better." "Better? What do you mean, better?" "If we go main entrance, you pay $41, get ticket. Here is better. Side entrance.

Give guard money and lets you through. No ticket." Ah, it was simple, comprehensible corruption. I relaxed. We pulled up at the checkpoint. A simple wooden pole blocked the dirt track. There were two guards: one manning a small booth, the other asleep in a hammock. I walked up to the booth, a little apprehensive. How were you supposed to handle corruption in Cambodia? I looked back at Carolyn. She grinned conspiratorially from the car window. "Please can I have a ticket?" "$41." "My friend paid $28. Please can I have a $28 ticket?" I smiled. He looked at Carolyn's grinning face and nodded. I sauntered back to the car. "Piece of cake." The guard waved us through. "They must be very rich," I commented to Mr Phally. "No rich. They drink, drink, drink, spend money on girlfriends, go to nightclubs. No rich." I decided that there must be more to Siem Reap than first appeared.

Over the next two days, we visited the main sites. Carolyn drank Cokes in air-conditioned splendour while I sweated over the ancient ruins. Angkor Thom, a fortified city, extends over ten square kilometres. At its exact centre is the Bayon, a huge twelfth-century monument with more than 11,000 carvings covering nearly every inch of its stone surface. Smiling carved faces look down menacingly at every turn. The city was deserted and the air hot and still. The chatter of cicadas rose from the encroaching jungle. I looked about me nervously. I felt an eerie solitude. Was it the spirit of the ancient Khmer people that fed my unease, or the present-day threat of stealthy Khmer Rouge guerrillas? This was a strange, alien world. In some of the temples, the trunks of huge trees had insinuated themselves into the fabric of the buildings, their muscular roots heaving up the stones: a mosaic of the living and the dead.

Walking back to our guesthouse, we heard shouts and looked up to see a group of women gesticulating from the balcony above, urging us to join them. We climbed the steps to a frenzy of giggles as more women materialized from nearby rooms, clustering around us, urging us to sit. The women were in their twenties, with vibrant make-up and bright gold earrings. The exceptions were a stout, raucous woman of fifty or so, with a gutsy laugh, and a thin, solitary man, who seemed to distance himself from the group. I didn't know what to make of them. Most Cambodian women are watchful and reserved. We laughed and chatted, with not a common word between us. They pushed each other aside, competing to have their photo taken with Carolyn. One woman playfully grabbed Carolyn and dragged her into a bedroom, closing the door. The others could not control their mirth.

Suddenly, it dawned on me. We were in a brothel. We were a useful diversion in the long afternoon, before the evening's business began. Later I mentioned the women to Pen Buntha at the guesthouse. I was curious to see if my assumption was right. "We visited some women who live over there – a group of them." "What! No. You must not go there. The child must have a shower," he exclaimed. "But they are my friends," protested Carolyn. "No," he continued, agitated now. Drawing me to one side, he continued, "They are taxi girls." "Taxi girls?" "Taxi girls! Taxi girls! They are not good girls. You must not go." I spent the next half-hour trying to explain to Carolyn what a prostitute is, in terms that were neither condemnatory nor too explicit. "But that has nothing to do with us," she retorted. "They were nice to us. They're our friends."

I was left confused about where I stood on the issue. I agreed with Carolyn, but ended up with the lame excuse that, if we visited them again, Pen Buntha would be upset. Somehow I felt that, by ignoring Pen Buntha's well-meant advice, we would be abusing his hospitality and causing him anxiety. Later, Pen Buntha brought his young grandson to meet us. "How old is he?" I asked. "He is four. His father is a doctor," he added with pride. "You just have the one grandson?" "Yes, my daughter's child. I have one daughter. My other three children, they die. In 1975. I was teacher. I was moved by the Khmer Rouge to the Thai border. It was very bad. No food. My children die because there no food. The one, nine, she live. The others, seven, five, one. They die." He laughed, a nervous laugh. I was too overwhelmed to pursue the subject. I looked at my sturdy, happy child and tried hard not to cry. Later, he asked me, "How many children you?" "Just the one." "Only one? Two, three, four is better. If one child . . . is ill, what do you do?" Just for a moment, I had a glimpse of how awful life under the Khmer Rouge regime must have been.

Back in our hotel in Phnom Penh, we prepared to fly out to Vietnam the following day. The atmosphere was tense. *The Bangkok Post* was reporting that 400 Khmer Rouge soldiers were only 25km to the north and marching on Phnom Penh. I felt uneasy. I was looking forward to reaching the calm of Vietnam. I had taken Carolyn with me to the Killing Fields memorial, just outside of Phnom Penh, and she asked endless questions. How did they kill the people? Why? Who dug up the bodies? What happened to the children? I had serious misgivings about my decision to bring her to Cambodia. I put her to bed. "I'm scared, Mummy. What if they come here? What if the soldiers come?" "They won't come here. They're only in the country areas. The big towns are quite safe."

But it was later that night that I felt real fear for the only time in Cambodia. I heard a commotion in the street below our room. I looked out to see more than a dozen armed men, some with rifles, others with machine guns. On the back of a pick-up truck stood a bare-chested man, wearing a red bandanna and cradling a machine gun. I crouched behind the balcony of our second-floor room, watching. I was shaking. The men surrounded our hotel and a group of them charged inside, their guns raised. Had Phnom Penh been overthrown? Were these Khmer Rouge? I suppressed my panic by making plans. I would hide Carolyn in the wardrobe with her passport and directions to get to the *Foreign Correspondent's Club*, where I thought she would be safe. We had discovered the club earlier that day; a delightful colonial throwback, on the top floor of a building overlooking the Tonle Sap river. I sat in a comfortable teak armchair, drank Gordon's gin with Schweppes tonic and read the Sunday newspapers while Simon and Garfunkel songs drifted at a discreet volume over the heads of the assembled Westerners playing pool.

Where was that sanctuary now? Could I possibly be in the same country? Minutes later, the gunmen emerged from the hotel with a prisoner, a revolver to his head. They beat him over the head with the gun. Blood spurted. He ran off. There were loud shouts and all rifles were pointed at him. Please, don't let them shoot him, I prayed. But they were distracted and he escaped. The gunmen stayed. For two hours, all was confusion and noise. At one point a gunman charged into the hotel with a rocket-launcher. Mercifully, Carolyn slept throughout and I crept downstairs to find out what was happening. On the first floor of the hotel, I discovered a nightclub. Outside, a polite row of painted women in short, tight dresses waited to be propositioned. We stared at each other in mutual amazement. Another brothel.

Reality was becoming strained. I could see the headlines: "Irresponsible mother and eight-year-old daughter killed by Khmer

Rouge in Cambodian brothel." The hotel receptionist reinforced the surrealism. "It's nothing. No problem. A traffic accident." Later, without warning, the men leapt into their trucks and roared off. I never discovered what it was all about and I was on edge until we arrived safely in Saigon.

Cambodia is a fabulous country. The people are gentle and welcoming, the countryside is verdant, the history and architecture are fascinating. But it is a country of extremes, racked with contradictions and tensions. There is a palpable sense of fear in the air, as if everywhere hang the ghosts of the recent past, as if the surface serenity is a mirage.

read on . . .

Lucretia Stewart, *Tiger Balm: Travels in Laos, Vietnam and Cambodia* (1992: UK: Chatto & Windus, 1998). In 1990 Lucretia Stewart overcame her fear of travel to investigate the mysteries of Indochina, a region shortly to embrace tourism following fifteen years of isolation in the wake of the Vietnam War. After a frustrating stay in sleepy Laos, she has more success as an independent traveller in Vietnam and, finally, Cambodia which takes up the last third of this highly readable book. Stewart is a fluent, compassionate writer with a great sense of humour (quite often at her own expense) and an excellent eye for detail, especially where people are concerned. It is her encounters with people, like the elegant widow Somaly, with whom she develops a lasting friendship, and the various officials and guides who illuminate her trip, that bring the book alive. Interleaved with this contemporary scene are harrowing accounts of the country's traumatic past as well as vivid depictions of its many spectacular monuments, in particular Angkor Wat.

Carol Livingston, *Gecko Tails: A Journey through Cambodia* (UK: Phoenix, 1997). This vivid portrait of a country struggling towards democracy combines wacky humour with serious insight into Cambodia's recent history and the day-to-day impact of the UN presence.

Canada

A sneaking civic pride

Carolyn Steele

Carolyn Steele has been a psychologist, an ambulance person, a maker of wedding cakes and an occasional stand-up comedian. She was running her own small business in London, offering training courses in first aid, when she spotted a newspaper ad for someone to spend two years in Canada looking after an elderly lady with Alzheimer's. She decided to go for it and within weeks had landed in Toronto with her son Ben, then aged nine. Carolyn has since kept an ongoing record of their impressions and experiences. The following extract, written nine months on, deals with some of the aspects of Canadian life that make it so different from England.

I have a confession to make. I only began to read books by travel writers when I knew I was about to travel, and then it was reading with cribbing in mind. Where do you find all those culturally curious little anecdotes that tell the world what it's like better than you ever could? The answer appeared to be to sit in a bar until fascinating situations happened round you.

I tried it. But I've never been much of a one for solitary drinking, even at home where pubs provide the lone female with a dingy corner to hide in. Canadian bars are empty and well lit. They also sport waitress service, even the ones called *The Fox and Pheasant* to make them sound English – all guaranteed to make one feel conspicuous, so although a fascinating situation did happen round me once I didn't turn into Bill Bryson overnight.

I can recommend sitting in a bar with pen and paper when you're poor and thirsty though. Sooner or later someone can't restrain their curiosity and you get bought a beer. I met two amazing women this way who I initially took for mother and daughter. It turned out that the older woman was the girlfriend of the ex-husband of the younger (Got that? It took me a while). After a merry evening they rang said ex-husband/boyfriend to come and drive them both to their respective homes. They made him buy me a drink first of course. The poor man was in his pyjamas when they called.

Our education proper began in the restaurants, as we adjusted to being allowed to enjoy our food. Brits just don't revel in their comestibles. It's not polite. Ben and I learned to cope with the "all you can eat". yardstick for portion sizes fairly quickly, although it took a while to stop apologising for having things exactly how we liked them. Then we started to discover ever newer and more dizzying ways to adore the stuff on your plate.

There's *Harvey's* for example, the fast-food hamburger joint where each meal is lovingly garnished by hand as you watch. First you choose from a complicated selection of toppings. Then you gaze with appreciation as your server creates a delicate montage atop your bun with the sort of dedication I haven't seen since my mother prepared me meals with faces on.

Harvey's kept us happy for ages, give or take the odd argument as to the correct pronunciation of "tomato". Sadly Ben has gone native over this issue, the better to be understood garnish-wise. He calls his trousers "pants" as well and always uses the "washroom", all in an accent as impeccably English as the day we landed. He's under orders to hang on to it, too. He's always been relatively cute; over here the accent contributes to a kind of cuteness squared. Quite a social asset.

I digress. Back to food. Then we found *East Side Mario's*. After the standard mountain of pasta (all you can eat, naturally), another new experience. Each server's uniform includes, clipped to the belt, a little viewer like the ones you can buy at any seaside town. You know the sort of thing, binoculars with a circular set of slides fitted in, so you can hold them up to the light and squint at a selection of sea views. Only these aren't sea views. These are the desserts.

Yes, once you have read the mouthwatering details of your towering triple chocolate thingamijig with extra whatnots, you can inspect a photograph to ensure that it actually does tower enough. OK, I know Brits put their puds on a trolley. It serves the same purpose, but we still get away with the idea that we don't really want to eat it. We point and say, "Oh all right, I'll have some of that then."

Here, by the time you've read the description, borrowed the viewer, scanned through to find and inspect your chosen confection and ordered it by name, there's no way to pretend you're just eating it to be polite. I honestly didn't realise we felt so guilty about our food until I lived with people who don't.

A friend of ours tells a story about England. Her daughter went into a pub for lunch and ordered a ham and cheese sandwich. But she couldn't have a ham and cheese sandwich. She could have a ham sandwich or a cheese sandwich. That's what it said on the menu. Obviously she ordered one of each, deconstructed them at the table and ended up with exactly what she wanted. I still wouldn't do that.

We've lived here for a while now – nine months to be exact – and I can confidently state that the best way to figure out what makes Canada different is to sit back and wait for surprises rather than go looking for cross-cultural charm. Canada Day was a surprise. Not the fireworks, nor the fact that they were free, along with the rest of a day-long festival sponsored by the local university. It was the traffic jam.

I've never encountered much traffic here before. There's generally too much room, but 55,000 people attended this particular Canada Day extravaganza. The sensible ones walked there. The rest of us sat for one and a half hours waiting to get out of the car park. And I mean waiting. No one swore or shouted, no one hooted a horn, no one got out of their car to "remonstrate" with the chap at the front who actually couldn't go anywhere anyway. We waited. Had this been Harringay (where we lived in North London), blood would have spilled in the first ten minutes. Flabbergasted, I mentioned this to a friend the following day. She told us the standard Canadian joke. "How do you get 25 Canadians out of a swimming pool? You ask them nicely to please get out now."

And nicely is how everything is done. I'm not using the word in its pejorative sense here, although as a snotty self-styled sophisticated Londoner I probably would have done a few months ago. Take the

Waterloo Busker Carnival, for example, or the Summer Medieval Festival. I'm not used to local extravaganzas – unless you count the Notting Hill Carnival, which isn't quite the same as I won't attend that for less than ten pounds an hour on emergency standby – so it took a while to get into the spirit of things.

My first impression of the Busker Carnival, "an annual international celebration of street theatre", was that you could see better in Covent Garden any weekend of the year. As I wandered about though, and clocked the performers carefully making a fuss of as many kids as they could, I began to understand how all-consumingly nice these events are. The main street was out of action for almost a week for the construction of stages. No one moaned. All the shops and businesses sponsored something. The final family concert ended with dancing in the street. One or two of the acts weren't bad but hey, who needs talent as long as everyone gets involved?

The Medieval effort was similarly low level, but we all turned out and put our hands in our pockets anyway. And the kids had a wonderful, wonderful time. Soon the free winter entertainment will begin: ice skating outside City Hall, Christmas lights and carols in the park, that sort of thing. The kids invariably have a ball.

As they did at Halloween. Let me state here and now that I have a big problem with Halloween. I disapprove utterly. Probably because in our part of London it isn't so much a cute kiddies' tradition as an excuse for the local yobbos to demand money with menaces from old ladies. It's different here of course; the cute kiddies' tradition is alive and well. In the weeks leading up to the big night, houses began to sprout pumpkins all over their front doorsteps and scary costumes invaded the shops. Eventually the houses festooned with early pumpkins were populated by plastic "pumpkin people" (stuffed with leaves and amusingly arranged in reclining garden chairs on the front porch), alight with spooky lanterns, and full of bags of sweets for scary tots to make themselves sick on.

The trick-or-treating code goes: "If a house has its outside light on, you'll receive a warm welcome. If not, don't call." In spite of myself I started to thaw. That's actually quite a good idea.

I now know that pumpkins go soft if kept indoors, which is why they have to live outside, with faces on. You can even get Halloween garbage bags – pumpkin orange, with whimsical grins – to liven up your property still further. OK, I admit it, we bought some. And, yes, I relented: for the first time ever Ben was allowed to go trick-or-treating. For a child who still can't quite believe his freedom (he still pinches himself when I wave him off on his bike saying "come back when you're hungry"), this was the ultimate transatlantic experience. It certainly knocked Niagara Falls into a cocked hat.

Not that he isn't as bowled over as I am by spectacular places. He's quite a geologist now, and a nifty map reader. It's just that we were expecting lakes and waterfalls and trees and stuff. The little things you don't anticipate seem to leave a bigger impression. Like having to be home by dark, instead of not going because Mum can't take you. And filling a bag with leaves just because it'll look like a madly grinning pumpkin.

As soon as the pumpkins disappeared from people's porches they were replaced by big red bows on all the gateposts. At the beginning of November I was a little bemused by the idea that these might be Christmas decorations, but sure enough they were followed with alarming speed by coloured lights in trees, little wooden sleighs on chimneys and plastic snowmen lurking in the undergrowth. It's as though houses must be "trimmed" for something the year round. As soon as one festival ends, the decorations for the next appear. The words "vulgar" and "kitsch" come to mind so often that I'm starting to dislike my attitude even more than I dislike the lights, and the cutesy little wooden shepherdesses hibernating in garages waiting for summer to come round again.

I had a ponder along the lines of "Why don't we do this at home, then?" and concluded that most of the decorations would be stolen or vandalised if we did. I still think it's all very nasty but have become a tad less superior on the subject. Ben doesn't want ours to be the only house in the street without "stuff". Oh dear.

The biggest surprise of all was the leaf hoover. It all started with the delivery of a leaflet from the City of Kitchener Public Works Department regarding their municipal leaf collection scheme. I'm not sure why I'm surprised. It stands to reason that if you live somewhere with a lot of trees, you end up with enough leaves to be a municipal issue. It's just another of those tiny but unexpected aspects of living somewhere different that no one tells you about because they're so obvious.

So, you rake your leaves into the gutter and a nice man comes and hoovers them up, then they get made into mulch for all the parks and gardens. Fascinating. No, really. First along the route is a lorry with a huge hose on the front, spurting water at the leaf piles. Presumably they fly around less if damped down. Then the hoover lorry lurches by with a huge hose on the back, slurping up little mountain ranges of leaves and churning them into goo.

I'm not noted for my enjoyment of outdoor pursuits. I've never quite seen the point of getting sweaty and tired in the garden when you can have a nice sit-down in front of the Test Match, but I felt such a glow of civic pride as I contributed to the municipal mulch that I think I may go and rake some more. Canada sort of does that to you.

Hitching through the Yukon

Kate Pullinger

Kate Pullinger, a Canadian novelist, has lived in London since 1982. Her latest novel *Weird Sister* is due to be published in 1999. Other recent fiction includes the highly praised *The Last Time I Saw Jane* and a collection of short stories, *My Life as a Girl in a Men's Prison*. She travels less now than she used to but still longs to get away. Here, in one of her much earlier jaunts, she hitch-hikes through the Yukon Territory, a massive area north of British Columbia.

The Yukon is basically the "Great Outdoors", and not much else. Exceptionally underpopulated, with less than 25,000 people in an area almost as large as France, it is a mountain-lake-forest-river-lover's dream come true. I think the best way to see it, at least in summer, is to hitch-hike. I have always found hitching in the Yukon relatively fast, easy and safe, mainly because towns are far apart and nobody is going to leave anyone standing on the side of the road in the middle of nowhere at -20°C, or, in summer, in all that dust.

Last summer I stood on the side of the road outside the Yukon's capital, Whitehorse. My thumb stuck out, I was heading for Dawson City, 556km away. The first vehicle to stop was an old Ford truck, bed on back with two extremely large sled dogs hanging out over its sides. They barked at me ferociously. A woman jumped out and asked how far I was going. I told her, and she said she was only going 85km, but that was a good start. So I jumped in.

She was young, had long plaited hair, and was wearing men's shorts and a felt hat. Next to her sat a small, dark baby, who looked at me curiously. The woman didn't say anything so neither did I. After a few miles she reached above the windscreen and pulled a cigar from behind the sunshade. She smoked it as she drove, clenching it between her teeth when she changed gear. I looked out of the window over the hills and vast, peopleless landscape. After 85km she pulled off the road on to the dirt track that led to her house and I thanked her and jumped out. I slammed the truck door so it shut properly and she and the baby sped off. The sled dogs barked at me until I was far out of their sight.

I stood again at the side of the road. A small Toyota two-door stopped. I put my pack in the back seat and climbed in front. This driver was also a woman, she wore a skirt and her hair was wet. We began to chat and I learned that she was just driving home from a swimming lesson in Whitehorse – a trip of 340km, which she made every Friday. There aren't very many swimming pools in the Yukon. The conversation led to a familiar story: she came up to the Yukon ten years ago to visit a friend and stayed. She said she wouldn't leave for anything, and now her brother lives up here too. I began to think there must be something special about this place.

Where she dropped me it was very quiet. There were trees everywhere I looked. In fact, all I could see was trees. I had to wait here around twenty minutes before I heard what sounded like a truck. I saw the dust before I could see it, great clouds of dirt billowing up into the sky. Then I saw the truck and stood on my tiptoes and tried to make my thumb bigger. The driver saw me and started to slow down. It took him a long time to do so and he went past me. I could no longer see, there was so much dust, and I held my scarf over my mouth. When it settled I walked to the truck – a long way up – and negotiated the lift, another 85km.

After hoisting my pack up I climbed in. The driver started the engine and headed down the road. I smiled to myself, thinking I was in front of the dust now. The truck driver seemed to change gears a hundred times before we were up to the right speed. Steaming along, past the endless lakes and hills, he told me about his children going to school, having babies and working in Edmonton. I listened and then asked how long he'd been here. He said he came for a year thirty years ago. There is something about this place.

Dropped at another turn-off I ran into the bushes for protection from all that dust. When he and his cloud were out of sight, I climbed back to the road. A few more cars went by and then a van stopped. It was a newish van, brown, with a sunset painted on the exterior. I knew about this kind of van: lush interior, shag carpets on the walls, a stereo. They call them sin-bins, glam-vans, or more straightforwardly, fuck-trucks. Thinking of my vulnerability, I took a look at the driver. He was male, of course, and looked about forty-five. He was wearing a nylon shirt with bucking broncos on it. He had a skinny black moustache and shiny hair. He asked where I was going and said he was too, he didn't know these parts and would like some company. The voice inside me said he was okay. I got into the van.

The driver was called Dan and came from Fort St John. He talked away about his family and I began to relax. He said he was a professional gambler which made me sit up: gambling is illegal in most of Canada. Dan told me all about the gambling circuit in British Columbia, the late-night games in Trail, Kelowna, Hope, the nights when he'd walked away with $4000 in his pocket. He told me about the cards, the passwords and the bribes to the Mounties. I was astounded; this was a whole new side to "Beautiful But Boring British Columbia". I asked him what he was doing up here. Then I remembered: Dawson City is the only place in Canada where gambling is legal. And Dawson City was where I was headed.

It was evening by the time we arrived and Dan dropped me off at the crossing to the campsite. Satiated with gambling stories, I sat down beside the river and waited for the little ferry to take me across. It was full of other hitch-hikers: Germans, Americans, Québecois. It was 8pm and the sky was as bright as mid-morning. I ate and then took the ferry back across to the town, strolling along the Wild West wooden sidewalks, past the false-front saloons, hotels and shops and ending up in front of *Diamond Tooth Gerties*, the casino. I went in, thinking I wouldn't play, just have a look around. The place was full and everyone was drinking, smoking and gambling. There were dancing girls, and a vaudeville show and card-dealers with waistcoats and bow ties and armbands. I had a drink and wondered if this was what it had looked like in 1905. Standing beside the blackjack table I figured out how to play, and watched as people won and lost. I wasn't going to play, just watch.

Many bottles of Molson Canadian and five hours later, I came out, $10 up. It was 2am, broad daylight; if the sun ever went down, I missed it. Running to catch the ferry back to the campsite, I talked and laughed with all the other gamblers I had met. Feeling rather rich and drunk, I crawled into my tent. Someone had built a campfire and people were milling about doing campfire sorts of things but it didn't seem right, campfire and campsongs in broad daylight. I closed my eyes and thought that perhaps after a few nights of lucrative gambling I would hitch that brief 250km up into the Arctic Circle. There is definitely something about this place.

read on . . .

★ **Kate Pullinger,** "The Good Ferry", in *Amazonian: The Penguin Book of Women's New Travel Writing,* **Dea Birkett and Sara Wheeler (ed) (UK: Penguin, 1998).** Beginning with the ferry ride to Vancouver Island where her parents live in a retirement community, Kate Pullinger casts a retrospective glance over her thirty-something years, using the journeys she has made between and within Canada and England, as markers. Written with the calm intelligence and sympathetic insight that she brings to her fiction, this beautifully composed narrative extends the boundaries of travel writing to offer, entirely unpretentiously, a meditation on travel and autobiography.

Margaret Atwood, *The Journals of Susanna Moodie* **(UK/US: OUP, 1970/ 1973).** As if to underscore Moodie's place in the canon of Canadian literature, Margaret Atwood, one of the country's best-loved novelists and poets, has recycled odd bits of her text to create this epic poem exploring themes of nature and alienation.

★ **Eva Hoffman,** *Lost in Translation: Life in a New Language* **(UK/US: Penguin, 1989).** To the teenage emigrant Eva Hoffman, watching her beloved Poland slip away from the deck of a passenger ship "the word 'Canada' has ominous echoes of the 'Sahara'". The loss of identity that she subsequently experiences at the hands of the anodyne and cruelly uninterested society of late-Fifties Vancouver – where her name is casually changed in a school registration – is described with palpable hurt and loss. In the end Hoffman rescues herself through her mastery of her new language and love of its literature, achieving via a New York persona, academic eminence and a newly comprehensible world. A deeply humane and utterly memorable book that covers every nuance of exile.

Susanna Moodie, *Roughing it in the Bush: or Forest Life in Canada* **(reprint; US: Carleton University Press, 1990/Canada: McClelland & Stewart, 1996).** Susanna Moodie, an Englishwoman of genteel background, had already achieved some critical success as an essayist, poet and writer of children's stories, before she sailed with her family to Canada to begin a pioneer life in Ontario in 1832. The enterprise was a failure, with Moodie and her husband struggling against adversity and slow, but inevitable, ruin. This finely drawn account, a classic of pioneer literature, was published twenty years after she arrived. She died three years later .

China

A homegirl hits Beijing

Constance García-Barrio

Constance García-Barrio had already studied Mandarin for three years when she decided to improve her language skills still further and take a month's intensive course in Beijing. She also needed a break from home. She is a native of Philadelphia, where she teaches Spanish at nearby West Chester University, and has just finished a novel based on the city's black history in the 1830s. The following account was reprinted in the anthology *Go Girl! The Black Women's Book of Travel and Adventure* (see p.652)

"Take a solo trip like that," my girlfriend said, "and you'll never come back."

"Drug dealers work the corner a block from my house," I said. "I could catch a bullet from a deal gone sour and never come back from the grocery store."

"You're crazy."

"Insanity and seventeen-hundred dollars will get me to Beijing."

I cooked austerity meals to save the seventeen-hundred dollars. The insanity came ready-made. In 1991 my son, then sixteen, had me on an adrenaline seesaw. His grades rollercoastered. Our fights, when he stayed out late, topped ten on the Richter scale. Beijing was as far as I could get from him without leaving the planet. My husband, calmer about our son's antics, agreed that I needed a break.

Truth to tell, there was more to it than that. I teach Spanish at West Chester University, twenty miles from my Philadelphia home. Eager to learn a non-Western language, I studied Mandarin at West Chester – three years' worth. The time had come to take the plunge. The Beijing Languages Institute (BLI) offered a month-long intensive course during the month of June. I graded my students' finals and hopped the plane.

After twenty-six hours in transit, I reached Beijing. I'd written to BLI, asking to be picked up at the airport. Other passengers from my Air China flight jostled me as I craned my neck, looking for someone holding a sign with my name on it. After much searching, I gave up. It was nearly midnight. I had no Chinese money. Everything was in characters, and I understood every fourth or fifth one. I didn't know a soul in the place. I was dead-tired and a little scared. Would people understand me when I spoke? Had my teacher urged me to make this trip too soon?

I found one currency exchange booth still open. When I told the woman there that I wanted to change a hundred dollars, she understood me with no trouble. Emboldened by this success, I asked what a fair price was for a cab ride from the airport to BLI. She told me twenty dollars, and a pack of American cigarettes as a tip, if the service was good. I'd been advised to take a couple of cartons of Marlboros and some jars of instant coffee, so I was ready.

The ride from the airport took me headlong into one of China's greatest political dilemmas. "Why are the police stopping cars?" I asked the cab driver as he slowed down at a checkpoint.

"Today is June first," he said. "The anniversary of Tiananmen Square is coming up. The government doesn't want trouble."

"It was awful those students were killed."

"Yes. A very sad thing."

After fifty minutes and one more checkpoint, we reached BLI. Despite the strange bed, I slept like a rock. I awoke the next morning to the voice of a *tai qi* teacher outside my window. From my dorm room, I saw about sixty Chinese people of all ages doing the slow, graceful movements of this exercise. I dressed and went downstairs to watch.

The Chinese fascinated me from the start, and so did BLI's four-hundred-plus students. They came from all over the world. One of my class-mates, an Italian girl, was learning Mandarin for a career in diplomacy. A Nigerian man wanted enough Mandarin to study traditional Chinese medicine at Beijing University.

I lived in Building Ten, a four-floor concrete box. Everyone got clean sheets and a roll of toilet paper every ten days. We had hot water four evenings a week. For eighty-nine dollars a month, I couldn't kick. Classes ran from eight in the morning until noon. Teacher Ma, a plump, lively man, had us sing Mandarin tones each morning. "Bring a thermos of green tea," he said, "to soothe your throat." He spoke nothing but Mandarin, wrote nothing but characters. For me, memorizing characters exacts flesh and blood. Between classes, homework, and private tutoring (two dollars for ninety minutes), I studied nine hours daily.

The cafeteria served Chinese and Western food, but I hadn't come to China for cheeseburgers. Most mornings I paid ten cents for a *youbingr*, a large, flat, circular bread with a light texture and doughnutlike taste. Two more cents got me a tablespoon of hawthorn preserves. A glass of green tea cost one cent. Sometimes I went to the Muslim dining room upstairs. It served no pork. There I got a quiet meal and an inside view of Middle Eastern politics.

The infirmary, too, offered both Eastern and Western options. I'd sprained my ankle before leaving home. When I reached BLI my ankle was slightly swollen. The second day it had ballooned. The third day, I saw blood under the skin. Dr. Tang took an X-ray. "It's the muscle," he said. "You don't need medication."

"Then what?"

"Massages."

"For how much?"

Dr. Tang charged fifteen *kuai*, about three dollars, for thirty-minute deep-muscle massages. After a week of them my ankle was fine.

★ ★ ★ ★

Located on Beijing's outskirts, BLI is a suburban island complete with stores, tennis courts, a track, a bank, a post office, and a pool. All you could need. But I felt marooned there, distanced from China's people. I decided to hit the road.

A hard-seat train ticket in China gets you a wooden seat, a cheap fare, and pore-to-pore contact with the Chinese. On a 220-mile ride from Beijing to Cheng De, I saw farm wives open huge bundles of food. People took out tin cups for the green tea served free in hardseat coaches. Vendors hawked snacks. People threw garbage on the floor. A voice on the loudspeaker asked people not to let their children urinate on the floor.

Halfway to Cheng De, I became the car's main attraction when a twenty-year-old medical student sat beside me.

"How old are you?" she asked.

"Forty-four."

"Not bad for forty-four," said the woman across the aisle.

The medical student felt my Afro and giggled. People stood up and peeked at me.

"You have long legs," she said.

"It runs in my family. My father was six foot, six inches."

A collective gasp came from overhead. Other passengers had gathered for a narrated close-up of a rare sight: a black American woman riding hard-seat. The Far East was meeting West Philly. After that ride, Cheng De's exquisite temples seemed anticlimactic.

★ ★ ★ ★

I met my Waterloo the next weekend. I'd taken a train to Tian Jin, an hour south of Beijing. I'd heard of the city's famous Culture Street and Food Street. I browsed in the Culture Street's bookstores and handicraft shops then, hungry, went to the Food Street. It had restaurants both swank and shabby. I went in a decent-looking one. When they saw me, the two hundred people who'd been lunching put down their chopsticks and stared at me. They seemed neither hostile nor condescending but, rather, eager to inspect the novelty that had wandered into their midst. Still, as the object of such intense interest, I wanted to evaporate. Finally, a young couple invited me to sit with them and their eight-month-old baby.

"Are you from Africa?" the man asked me.

"The US."

"What are you doing in China?"

"Studying at BLI," I said, giving him the short version of the answer. I didn't have the vocabulary, or the inclination, to explain that

I was getting a breather from home, and opening another window on the world for myself by learning a language spoken by a billion people. I could have added that I wanted to see if, in middle age, I could come to the edge of the cliff and leap.

★ ★ ★ ★

Toward the end of June, I cut class and took a six-day solo trip south-east to Shanghai, Suzhou and Hangzhou. Shanghai, with its traffic and pickpockets, could have been Mexico City or Manhattan. Suzhou held surprises. After an argument with the manager at a nice, new hotel, I wound up in a six-dollar-a-night room whose amenities included a spittoon, a small black-and-white TV, and three large squares of toilet paper. Like other guests, I didn't have a room key. Whenever I returned from shopping or sightseeing, I asked the staff person on my floor to let me in. Still, give the devil his due. I was the only foreigner in the hotel, and the staff bent over backward for me.

En route to a famous temple the next day, I saw the many canals for which Suzhou is called the Venice of China. Barges hauled every-thing from coal to produce. Wandering one temple's gardens, I saw barefoot Chinese tourists stepping up and down on pebbles embedded in the ground.

"Why are they doing that?" I asked the group leader.

"It's like getting a massage," he said, massaging my left shoulder a moment to be sure I understood.

"I see."

The trim, twenty-something tour guide looked around, saw no foreigners near me, and asked, "Are you alone?"

"Yes."

"Would you like to join us?" When the tour ended, I had tea in a private garden with the others.

. ★ ★ ★ ★

I doubt I would have had such invitations if I hadn't been alone. I liked the flexibility and surprises that travelling alone brought me, though I had to stay vigilant. I never changed money on the street despite the attractive rates. (I could end up with counterfeit money,

BLI students had warned me.) I'm sure I paid more than the Chinese would have for clothes and fruit in the marketplaces, but that was a small price to pay for my independence.

On the other hand, I never feared for my safety in China. I felt as if I had an angel with me. Still, I paid great attention not only to what people said, but also to their gestures. I scrutinized body language because I didn't understand every word of the spoken language; sometimes the hours of alertness wore me out. In my travels, I found that foreigners, black and white, greeted me warmly – we were all outsiders for the Chinese. You rated with BLI students and faculty if you had enough Chinese to travel on your own. I loved that taste of equality.

On the last day of class, we received certificates. I was pleased, but I valued the trip's intangibles more. I'd jumped in, talked with people, had bizarre, exhilarating excursions. When I returned to Philadelphia, my son looked at me with new respect. Not a bad solo trip a for someone my age, he said. He'd enjoyed telling people, "Could you call back? My mom's in China." He's matured since my trip. I've mellowed, too. The last time I talked about China over dinner, I surprised myself by asking him, "How about us doing China together?"

Flying beneath the radar

Carla King

Carla King is a San Francisco-based travel and technology writer and author of the *American Borders* dispatches, the Internet's first realtime literary travelogue. Raised in the North Carolina countryside, she learned about motors by tinkering with the machinery around the farm. When she was sixteen, her family moved to Silicon Valley, where she learned about computers and became a technical writer. Carla didn't begin to travel until she was 28, when she took a solo motorcycle camping trip around France. She hasn't stopped travelling since. A contributor to many magazines and travel anthologies, Carla celebrated her fortieth birthday by riding a motorbike from Beijing to the Tibetan border. Below is the overview she wrote for *Women Travel* of the experiences recounted in "The China Road Dispatches," a twenty-chapter odyssey in words and digital photos found on the Internet at *www.verbum.com/jaunt*.

The villagers were felling birch trees right into the road as I passed slowly, avoiding the tangle of soft green branches. For a moment I was invisible. They were far too preoccupied with their harvest to notice the motorcycle, its Beijing plates and its foreign rider. The air smelt of green sawdust and spring leaves. In the dappled clearings between the houses, women sat stripping the fragile branches from the trunks and placing them carefully in neat piles sorted by size, their black hair gleaming in the pools of sunlight.

It was my fifth week alone in China, my fifth week of riding straight through any number of beautiful villages that dotted the mountains, deserts and river valleys between Beijing and the border with Tibet, on a crazy journey that was really someone else's idea. But the promise of a wild new adventure, and one that came with the loan of a classic Chang Jiang motorcycle . . . seemed just too good to pass up.

The idea for this trip began nearly a year ago when I checked my email one morning over coffee. "Come to China," a message read. A flurry of exchanges began. "Forget the handover in Hong Kong, the real story is what's going on in the countryside . . . there's a bike waiting for you in Beijing." The communiqués were from Rick Dunagan, an American expat who had adopted me after reading my online dispatches from a trip that I made around America on a Ural sidecar in 1995.

He liked my choice of bike. The Ural, a reverse-engineered 1938 BMW that the Russians have been making since 1945, is almost identical to the Chang Jiang, or "CJ", manufactured from the original BMW mouldings on the banks of the Chang Jiang River; the Yangtze as we know it. Rick and his friends are all CJ fanatics. They spend their weekends riding to the Great Wall and the Ming Tombs and other sights, and back in their offices they surf the Net. My dispatches from the American jaunt had intrigued them. They each had dreams of making similar trips around China, but as they hadn't the kind of lifestyle that allowed them to spend two months on the road, their energy went into making it happen vicariously.

Half a year later, I made my first trip over the International Date Line to Beijing. The expats welcomed me with a group ride and camping trip in the countryside. It was autumn, and the peasants sold piles of persimmons, apples and walnuts by the road. We pitched our tents on a remote watchtower on the Great Wall of China and watched a full autumn moon rise over Mongolia. I was hooked before we set up the barbecue and roasted hot dogs on an open fire. I shared round a bottle of Tennessee whisky I'd bought for the occasion and heard myself say, "Yes, I'd love to come back in spring," and we talked about what a trip it would be, an Internet saga to be created on the road, in realtime, with my laptop computer and my digital camera.

The following April I returned to Beijing. The CJ they'd prepared for me was registered with the numerical equivalent of the Yin-Yang symbol; the number 69. A good sign, I thought. Balance. Harmony. Wholeness. Beijing had just begun experimenting with letting foreigners drive around the city with an international licence, but it didn't seem as if they were going to let me go running around the entire country alone. Yes, they were open to the idea of independent tourism now, but it would take months to get permissions from each of the provinces I planned to visit and if any of them said "no", then I'd be forced to cancel the trip. But what if they weren't actually asked . . . ?

"Just go!" the expats urged. "They'll only make you spend a night in jail while they figure out how to send you back." So I rode nervously out of Beijing, alone, and I found wilderness split by rough country roads stretching for miles through pyramidal mountains. When I came to Heibi province even poorer conditions revealed themselves. Here was the Chinese equivalent of a hillbilly backwater: a population rife with malnutrition, iodine deficiency and inbreeding, not to mention the absence of education, social and health services. Darkness fell, the few people I met stared rudely and couldn't tell me the way to the nearest large town, Liajang, and no roads were signposted.

It is altogether likely, I thought, as I rode through another tiny village lit by cooking fires, that these peasants have never been more than ten miles from their homes. It is altogether likely that these people have never imagined that they would see a foreigner, in the flesh, in their entire lives. It is altogether likely that my first day on the road I will run out of gas in the middle of nowhere, far from Liajang, and end up sleeping in a ditch.

The air became colder and the road became narrower and ever more potholed until it deteriorated completely into dirt and gravel. I dodged piles of asphalt, and some stray bricks fallen from a cart. The dark shapes of trees loomed above me on either side so thickly that I might have thought I was standing still had my headlights not caught them running by. Kublai Khan had ordered the trees planted, centuries ago, to give solace to travellers. The trees did not give me solace.

What gave me solace was the sudden appearance of a building strung with white lights that might be a hotel and, a little further on, two gas pumps under a brightly lit shelter. I pulled up to the pumps and a woman sauntered out the doorway. She wore opaque knee-highs that left dents halfway up her short calves, pink rubber pool sandals, and a lime green dress sprinkled with large white polka dots. She tried to hide her astonishment at my appearance as she pumped gas through a filter in my tank, and confirmed that the lit building was indeed a hotel. It cost twenty *yuan* per night. Armed with a full tank of gas and this happy information I rode the short distance back and in through a cement archway and open wooden gates. The three-sided single-storey cement compound was lined with red, motel-style doors. I switched off the engine and unfastened my helmet with cold, stiff fingers. My back ached and my left ankle throbbed from the effort of shifting the big bike. I tossed my helmet, gloves and scarf into the sidecar and scratched my itchy scalp, then I looked up to face my hosts. A dozen girls in orange polyester pyjamas looked back, their eyes lined heavily in black, their mouths shining with bright colours of lipstick.

It seemed that I would be spending my first night on the road in a brothel.

I don't know how I managed to say hello, but it came out. "Nee how?" I said, and smiled to reassure them. They burst into giggles, covering their mouths with their hands and looking at each other in astonishment. Finally, a very thin young man in an ill-fitting pinstripe suit and a flat-top haircut strolled casually toward me. One lock of hair had been left long to hang rakishly over one eye. We exchanged greetings, and after a moment's hesitation he took the twenty *yuan* I handed him and began ordering the girls around importantly. I was accompanied by a swirl of bobbing orange pyjamas to my room, which was a basic cement box with a bed, a desk and a television turned on at full volume. Later the manager and I sat at the cheap wooden desk and struggled with the hotel registration form. He, unable to read my passport, and I, unable to read the form, filled in the blanks together with a mixture of Pinyin and Chinese characters that told my story: USA. Female. 39. Beijing. San Francisco. It was a scene to be repeated nightly for many weeks to come.

I locked the bike and stuck a hotel alarm in the doorjamb then watched, amused, as the truckers roared in and, waving empty liquor bottles aloft, literally fell from their cabs into the arms of the waiting girls. I put my earplugs in and slept soundly.

Waking early, I rushed outside to find myself in a lovely river valley enclosed by jagged mountain peaks. The brothel was quiet as I topped off the oil, tightened the wheelspokes, and gave the motorcycle the necessary daily check for loose screws and oil leaks. At about 6am I rolled the bike outside the gates of the brothel so as not to wake the tired girls with the sound of the motor, and took off through a landscape that left me breathless. The air was clear and clean, the mountains steep and green, and the peasants were already hard at work hoeing or dragging ploughs by their shoulders through the earth, or carrying straw basketfuls of produce on their backs. I passed a man, miles from anywhere, struggling on a steep downhill grade with two twenty-foot tree trunks balanced precariously atop a barrow.

An hour later I stopped at a busy village marketplace spilling with fruits and vegetables, boxes of newly hatched chicks and cages filled with tiny pink piglets. It was the first time the crowd grew so thick around me I felt I would choke, and it was the first time that I was rescued by the elders. Someone barked an order and everyone stepped back, immediately, to let pass an ancient couple dressed in Mao blue. Their faces were all smiles and creases as they beckoned me to their fruit stand where they pulled out a toddler-sized stool so I could sit and finish my snacks in peace. Relative peace, that is.

The elders stared, touched my leather jacket, played with the Swiss army knife and phrasebook, and wouldn't let anyone else near. From then on I would look for elders before I stopped so that I could park my bike next to them and ask for their shelter from the masses.

On my trip this lack of privacy would eventually depress me, as would the effort of trying to meet my most basic of needs. Between the Yungang Caves and the Genghis Khan Museum, the Gobi Desert and the Labrang Monastery, the problem of shelter would plague me most. I would never, during the entire trip, be able to identify a hotel building. There are several types of hotels, the most basic being a small dormitory-style inn called a *luguan*, and the most elaborate old-style tourist hotels with their misleadingly gilded lobbies – the rooms basic and the blankets threadbare. The Chinese characters for these places are impossibly long and complex and there is no one style of building that might help in the identification process.

Every evening I was burdened with the task of asking a series of surprised locals where I might stay. Now that the old two-price system (one price for Chinese, one price for foreigners) was no longer in place, all accommodation was open to me, and I did not even have to register with the PRC before bedding down, as had travellers before me. I could stay anywhere, even in homes. One would think that with such an abundance of possibilities would come greater ease of accommodation, but this fact confused the locals more than me, and in a large town the process of finding a place to sleep could take as long as an hour. Many times a volunteer would ride on the back of the motorcycle to direct me. Grateful, I'd insist upon taking them to their destination, but they always refused.

Gas was no problem, however, and food was abundant. I ate well from roadside stands. Noodles were standard breakfast fare, but for lunch and dinner I'd find fresh fruit and breads and small hot packets of pasta called *jowza* stuffed with an endless variety of ingredients: *bok choy*, garlic, onions, ground pork, chopped vermicelli, spinach, garlic, red peppers. I learned to look for the stacked brown baskets when I smelled the pungent scent of soy and garlic.

My biggest worry was the motorcycle. Just before I reached Hohhot, the capital city of Inner Mongolia, blue smoke began to blow from a tailpipe, signalling a problem with a piston ring in one side of the engine. I was led to the local CJ mechanic where he and his family lived tucked away in a narrow, tree-lined alleyway crowded with one-room shops that also doubled as homes. One neighbour sold produce, another plastic buckets. In front of his shop a dozen motorcycle cadavers were lined up neatly, waiting for repair or organ donations, one couldn't tell. A shallow plastic dishtub held a tangled pile of grimy tools. The ground was littered with cigarette butts, spark plug boxes, nuts, bolts, shattered plastic and wire. One large tree provided shade to work in.

The mechanic, all machismo, started the CJ and revved it up, inspecting the blue smoke that came from the tailpipe. Before I could protest he mounted and took off down the road. The crowd turned its attention to me, but the mechanic's bent old mother grinned tooth-lessly from the doorway and beckoned me inside. Ducking beneath the lintel I entered a two-room building with a floor of pounded dirt. Motorcycle parts cluttered all the corners and were stuffed underneath the two low single beds shoved up against the wall and covered in greasy white sheets. Loops of clutch and brake cables hung on a wall over one of the beds. The kitchen consisted of a small iron pot-bellied stove that sat next to the door, and was surrounded by filthy bowls that would be used, unwashed, for the next meal. The place smelled of dirt and motor oil, soy and ginger. It was a scene I'd become accustomed to, this unclean hospitality. It was an honest hospitality, though, and it was in the company of mechanics that I experienced the small mira-cles, the artful creativity, scrupulous billing practices, and the placing of incense beside a crude altar. This last was the only overt sign of spirituality I'd see outside of a monastery.

She fed me leaves of green tea in boiling water, and left me alone. When I went back outside the CJ was parked and the mechanic was working on a red Yamaha. He looked up at me to announce brightly "A-okay!", giving me the thumbs up.

No amount of argument would convince him to replace the ring. "It's not broken," he insisted. "Not yet," I protested (speaking from my guidebook), "but I go Tibet!", hoping that the idea of the length of my trip would make him understand that I needed preventive maintenance. But this concept was as foreign as I was.

"No, no. . ." he laughed. "It is A-okay! Only needs more oil . . . lots of oil!"

Thus dismissed, I bought all the parts I'd need for my imminent breakdown, took a quick visit to the Hohhot museum, and prepared for my departure the next morning. It was not to be. A few blocks from my hotel the battery died. Typically, the mechanic I knew didn't sell batteries, and it took hours to find a replacement.

I was to spend yet another day in Hohhot, so I decided to visit a Tibetan monk named G—, who I'd met the day before at the local monastery. He'd been exiled for having attempted a border crossing into India to see the Dalai Lama and was unhappily assigned to the small Buddhist monastery here, surrounded by what he felt was scandalous behaviour by the other monks.

"China monk, he take wife," declared G unhappily, "and Mongol monk drink alcohol."

He wasn't so righteous about smoking cigarettes, and used the change from my beer and grocery money to stock up a good supply.

The monks invited me to stay in the monastery and I happily accepted. When the doors were closed to the public I brought the motorcycle in to work on it and wrote in my journal while they prepared a simple meal of noodles (made from scratch with flour, salt and water) mixed with broth and fresh vegetables prepared over a pot-bellied stove. Joining us for dinner was the ninth incarnation of an important lama, a fat Chinese man who padded around the compound in Nike's and a royal blue leisure suit. During dinner the television blasted a static-ridden soap opera about a high-class Chinese family, this episode centering on the wife of a politician getting caught with a hickey on her neck. The programme was intensely studied by the four monks present, none of whom displayed the least embarrassment at the sex, deception and excess materialism. After helping G practise his English we retired, all of us on a large *kang* padded with thick Persian rugs. I was given several heavy blankets of cotton batting and a beanbag pillow. We all made up our beds and climbed in fully clothed. Sleep came immediately.

In the morning G and I took off on the bike to a mountain monastery nearby. He'd never ridden on a motorcycle, and it was clearly a thrilling experience for him. His innocence was joyful to experience. It was indeed an adventure – an American who couldn't speak Chinese accompanied by a Tibetan monk with no sense of direction attempting to find a remote mountain monastery in a Mongolian province. The day was sunny and warm, and the uphill pull combined with G's added weight caused the CJ to overheat.

We waited on a rocky hillside. G lit a cigarette and I looked at the sky. How often does one get the chance to do such a thing, I was thinking as I settled back on the grass. A goat stumbled, sending rocks down the hillside. I slid a little further away from G's constant smoking. This good-natured young man, all smiles, his 24-year-old face aged with weather, had made eight pilgrimages across Tibet to be blessed by the Dalai Lama in India. The eighth time he was caught when he slipped and broke his foot and was unable to escape the Chinese border guards. They had exiled him here, to this pitiful little monastery. What more could I do for him, other than bringing him here to worship at this special little monastery, other than buying food and cigarettes, I was thinking, when something hit me on the side of the head.

A rock? No . . . G had knocked into me somehow. No . . . he was kissing me, he had actually tackled me, his lips landing on my cheek so forcefully that the connection was like a blow. I easily removed him and held him at arm's length. His eyes darted over my face, and he said one word: "Kiss!"

It was a proclamation. It was an expression of desire and frustration and boredom and a statement of an opportunity not to be lost. I looked around. The CJ was pinging a few yards away. Other than that, we were completely alone.

"No kiss." I responded simply and firmly.

"Kiss!" His face was all confused child.

"No kiss." Jeez, I thought. And all that talk about wives and alcohol distracting monks from their holy purpose. I could have laughed.

He hesitated, perhaps reading my thoughts. "Okay. No kiss." He looked at the ground; abashed, picked up the cigarette he'd left burning, and puffed away.

"Listen," I said. "Really. No kiss . . . okay?"

"Okay." Another puff. "No kiss."

The monastery was only a few miles away. It was an ancient place, remote and wild and beautiful. G made his rounds amongst all the Buddhas and Bodhisattvas, lighting incense, offering money and bowing incessantly. I took photographs of the outside walls painted in intricate, mysterious scenes.

Another evening passed like the last, only slightly tainted by a nagging sense that my familiar manner had been at least partially responsible for G's lapse in protocol. I suspect that in Lhasa it is not unheard of for young American women seeking spiritual solace to find more inspiration amongst the maroon robes of some handsome Tibetan monk. At any rate, I had found comfort and acceptance in the monastery and was sorry to have to go.

G couldn't understand my hurry, other than that he had greatly insulted me. Despite the troubles I slept peacefully again in the *kang*, waking in the morning to the noise of tin pots banging together. Jumping out of the *kang* I found all three young monks outside harassing a young Chinese girl who had been sleeping against the monastery walls. She was shocked and bedraggled, and probably cold with only two thin blankets between her and the cement. "Leave her alone," I pleaded, but the monks laughed and continued shouting and banging the pots.

"Many girl father lock out house for go to clubs with boy late," G explained.

I stood helpless as the monks exhibited a total lack of compassion, shouting at her to get up and leave. She shouted back. The monks laughed. The girl said something ugly and spat at the ground. The monks pulled her up by her clothes and began pushing at her. She looked to be a teenager, dressed in a plaid miniskirt and her hair cut stylishly short. I must have looked as bedraggled as she, for she started at the sight of me, turned and left in a huff, her blankets trailing behind.

Thus awakened, I was fed tea and noodles. G was morose, but brightened as I presented him with a small red mag light, a pair of thick wool socks and some money to take the bus to Tibet when he could go. All for seeing the Dalai Lama again, I told him, and also gave him one of my extra English/Chinese phrasebooks for writing me the letter he promised. G promised prayer, too, writing my name and address carefully in his notebook.

I took my leave ungraciously as always, feeling so pressed to stay. Every host seemed to take my parting as a personal affront, proof of their failure to keep me entertained and it would take a few miles at least to overcome the awkwardness of my offence. Then, as the bike settled into a steady cruise the familiar tingling dread of unknown adventures once more gained a hold.

Friendships confused

Kerry McKibbin

Kerry McKibbin, originally from the Isle of Man, lives in London where she works as a TV producer/director. After graduating from university in the early 1990s, she taught for a while in Japan. When she tried to cut short her two-year teaching contract, her boss (a man with dubious underworld connections) adamantly refused to allow her to go and even threatened to have her intercepted at Tokyo airport. She decided to make her exit by less conventional means and took a boat to China.

On board the China Shipping Line ferry from Japan, I had no need of my guidebook's hints on "How to Meet the Chinese". My fellow passenger, Ken Ki Cho, had volunteered herself as my guide and together we spent three surreal days speaking pidgin Japanese in the ship's sauna. Curiously darting glances across at each other's naked bodies, this unusually intimate situation provoked deep discussion of our recent histories, our relationships and future plans. Like the majority of passengers, Cho had just completed three years of privileged study in Japan. Her professors had shown her countless newspaper and magazine articles written by Japanese businessmen worried and amazed at the rapid expansion occurring in China. What did her family think of that, I asked. She wasn't sure. Her only contact with China had been an occasional letter from her mother and sisters. But they worked on the land and would know nothing of the changes occurring in Beijing or Shanghai. Now in the luxurious heat of the sauna she dreamed of a high-flying, well-paid career in electronic engineering.

On the third day there was sudden commotion. Mah Jong boards were abandoned and card games gathered up as passengers piled on layers of thermal underwear. I stood shivering on the deck with wet hair. The afternoon was overcast. It was sleeting heavily. This was my first solo backpacking journey outside the security of Japan and for the first time, it struck me that everyone else was going home: Cho was meeting her student friends in Beijing, other passengers were giddily returning with gifts for their relatives. I was nothing more than a lone speck on some exotic map. As I stared down at the armed guards marching along the Tianjin harbour wall a knot twisted in my stomach.

In the chaos outside the ferry terminal a hoard of khaki-coated men pressed in on Cho and myself and bundled us onto the nearest bus where I sat squashed up against a frozen window while the driver – a Castro look-alike in an ex-army greatcoat complete with shoulder stripes – revved the engine to screaming point before lurching forward onto the main highway, a string of plastic grapes swinging wildly across his windscreen. Unwilling to halt at signals, he blasted his way through traffic lights, passengers haring after us, prostrating themselves across the doors and clambering in while we were still in motion. Oil constantly leaked from the gear box and mixed with spit and tea leaves on the floor. On he raced, Beijing Opera music flooding out of the front speakers. A mother sitting next to me leant over, slid my window open slightly and stood her little boy on my knee so that he could pee through the crack.

As we neared Beijing, a fight broke out between the tight-faced woman ticket-collector and a male passenger. Cho anxiously revealed that the initial fare had inexplicably gone up and that those who refused to pay would be thrown off. After several frenzied attempts at extracting the supplement from us, the woman dragged us from our seats, out of the doors and dumped our bags down into the slush. And so it was that I first entered China, bouncing along the black, shiny streets in a smart sidecar, grinning up at my new friend Cho who was strapped behind the solid woman driver. "My business!" shouted back our driver proudly. "International taxi service!"

Was it a year spent walking clinical Japanese streets that made the outskirts of Beijing so shocking? The road ahead was pitch black, cars and lorries flashing their headlights to warn us of their presence. Fruit sellers displayed their wares by candlelight; I was surprised when we overtook a horse-drawn cart. This was more an Elizabethan landscape than a capital city. In the lights of the headlamp I picked out four chickens dangling upside down each side of a bicycle's handlebars. The owner had tied them on by the feet and cycled along, legs held at right angles, out of pecking range. Street lights began to appear and I could make out low, crumbling houses with felt roofs held down with bricks. Outside, cabbages were slung over coal cellars. We raced past one narrow *huton* (alley) after another. Each was incredibly narrow and muddy. I wondered down which *huton* Cho would sleep that night.

At the hotel Cho found me, the owner claimed she only had double rooms. The building felt suspiciously empty. I was surprised to find a caretaker on each landing. The first was reclined, feet up on her desk; the second was knitting with a bright yellow ball of wool; the caretaker on my floor was almost asleep. Scowling, she led me to my room and dumped a flask of boiled water on the table. Two cups sat still filled with the dregs of jasmine tea and the bed was unmade. A locked door in the en-suite bathroom adjoined the next room where a woman and man were arguing. I lifted the toilet gingerly – all was mercifully clean. The woman's voice grew more high pitched and frantic; from the car park came the sound of a windscreen shattering. Shouts, a scuffle, the sound of running footsteps. Beijing felt out of control.

I did not want to leave that hotel the next morning. Dire though it was, I dreaded setting forth into the street; but I had to find my bearings. Men loitered on the street corner but said nothing as I walked by. Outside a noodle shop, children played a game with fistfuls of straw. Garbage cans with their lids up lined the street, overflowing with rotting vegetables. At the end of the street, a mountain of cabbages stood twelve feet high. I turned down a narrow alley where a group of workmen were squatting by the gutter, slurping noodles from metal basins. A woman took my arm and led me away, indicating that it would be dangerous to continue. Suddenly we were on a wide boulevard with high-rise buildings, cars, trees in tubs. It could have been anywhere in Europe.

These were the streets Cho insisted we stick to when I met her later. I noticed that the white leather shoes she had carefully cleaned before we stepped off the boat were now scuffed and muddy. "Look at that posh hotel!" she would exclaim. "That wasn't there three years ago . . . Over there on the right – that's an American clothes shop, isn't it?" We ate at Kentucky Fried Chicken, drank coffee on the top floors of glass-fronted hotels and shopped at the Friendship Store. Cho was ecstatic to be back in Beijing.

She insisted we arrive at Tiananmen Square by taxi. The square was very large and very empty. I looked in vain for evidence of the atrocities I had read so much about but it was as though nothing had ever happened. A few families bought ice cream from stalls and hawkers tried to sell wind-up paper birds which flew for a few seconds before clattering down on the paving slabs. In the subway beneath the square, a football match might have just finished. Hundreds of locals were packed together, some squeezed behind stalls. A man at the plimsoll stall held a bewildered old woman by the throat, shouting into her face. Cho dragged me to the train station where the same frantic atmosphere awaited me. I had been warned about queues at stations but had never imagined that each would be six bodies deep. As the customers pushed against each other, one would suddenly pop out of line and fight to regain their place. At the front, a man flung himself at the grille which protected the ticket booth. Two uniformed women stood on a ledge level with the counter, beating him back.

I was determined to travel to Guiyang in the south of the country and bought a ticket from a black marketeer. Guiyang had its problems (six million beneath the Chinese poverty line), but according to my guidebook it was typical of the current economic development in China. I wanted to see what this great and unexpected twentieth-century miracle looked like there. Cho couldn't understand why I should trade Beijing's luxury for Guiyang, but she waved me off from my hotel as I took a rickshaw to the station the next day.

Like every transaction in China, negotiating the bicycle rickshaw for the short journey to the station involved lengthy negotiation. The driver had started with complicated Chinese hand signals to signify numbers, but we soon reverted to bargaining on paper. As fifty yen became twenty-five, shoemakers, cooks, a butcher and an ironmonger stood watching from the sidelines. Each gave his opinion on whether the price was fair or not. Eventually the driver strapped my rucksack between the bicycle and his two-wheeled cart and moved off into the sea of traffic.

A cook pedalled hard next to us, a steaming canister sloshing about behind him; a bus screamed across our path. I shut the canvas side flaps of the roof canopy, praying for a safe arrival. The driver snorted, coughed and spat onto the street, first to the left, then to the right. I remembered the signs in English I had pointed out to Cho: "Do not spit!" According to her, the Chinese translation was slightly different: "Aim your spit carefully!" The driver snorted again, this time using his hand to blow his nose with great precision, spraying mucus first over my left foot and then over my right. On the way he'd met a collaborator. They had cycled level with each other, plotting. On reaching the station, the collaborator thrust his head through the canvas side flap. "Fifty yen" he hissed, flicking a knife blade in front of my face.

Guiyang city centre assaulted my senses the moment I stepped out of the hotel. Red brick dust blew in my face. I had to walk the main street with half-closed eyes, my scarf pulled right up to protect my mouth. Every building was gutted; every road surface mercilessly torn up. A man picked his way across a crumbling wall, silhouetted against two gleaming, new towerblocks. My ears nearly exploded with the constant pounding and drilling. I passed a team of men who were breaking bricks by hand. Others were tottering in plimsolls over heaps of jagged rubble, shoulders breaking under heavy yokes.

Rain had begun, transforming the brick dust into a light brown, swimming mud. A line of hard-faced women stood freezing at a makeshift bus stop, hands in their trouser pockets, stiletto heels perching them high above the slime. Buses and jeeps spliced their way around exposed, metal sewer covers, leaving the women angry in their spattered patent. Everywhere, crazed development was out of all proportion and control. A butcher sold sheep's innards from his bicycle; the bright red stomach hung over the crossbar like a deflated rubber ball, passing shoppers fingering it despondently. Disorientated inhabitants emerged from breeze-block shacks with hungry eyes; they neither knew nor cared that Cartier had hit Shanghai. They stared as I photographed the plastic tables with their gaudy, fringed umbrellas which stood next to the noodle stands – a touch of the Bahamas on the edges of Hell.

Back at the dank and freezing hotel lobby in Guiyang, the receptionist was chatty as usual. We were the same age which, in China (as I would later discover to my disadvantage), spelt instant camaraderie. She was preparing for a wedding reception that afternoon but found time to devour my British postcards. "Who sent you to China?" she constantly asked me. It was beyond her comprehension that I could have earned enough money alone. "No matter how hard I work, my money is worth nothing outside this country" she sighed. "China's face is changing but it's still the same people who travel and fill the beds in this hotel." I recalled the moment at the airport where I had surprised a group of Mao-suited, communist die-hards swilling copious amounts of imported whisky in the splendour of the first-class waiting room. "And I don't even want to emigrate," she continued "only go outside – only to look." Her words stuck with me. I was sure this natural desire to get away and put one's life in perspective was inherent in the collective frustration, the fighting and the tension I had witnessed on the Beijing streets. There the people aren't just accepting flimsy promises of material change. They want to experience the results now.

The wedding party trooped past singing at the tops of their voices. Heartened, the receptionist translated the song as a wish for the birth of a baby boy. Their song still echoed in my ears days later as I tramped along the backs of the fields below a certain Yunnan mountain. Women were bent over their vegetable patches and hadn't noticed this Western traveller closing in on them from behind. Looking down, I had been balancing along the grass strips which separated some disused patches when suddenly – shockingly – I had spied a baby's skull sticking up out of the soil. Another lay close by, barely covered by a thin layer of earth; a few more holes were dotted around. I watched the women intently, but if any really had murdered their baby daughters, they didn't flinch – just carried on, heads bent, tilling the soil.

Buying breakfast on my first day in this isolated Yunnan village I had met the local entrepreneur, James, as he called himself. Emerging from behind a screen, he had drifted over to take my order. He was wearing a smart jacket with a fur-lined collar, which gave him a luxurious air I had seen in few Chinese people. Discovering we were both born in 1969, we chatted as Chinese equals and he invited me to join him and his friends on a hike.

Our party consisted of James (sporting a bright red cravat and trilby), his friend from the rubber factory (where a power failure had resulted in an impromptu holiday) and an old man who insisted on buying bread and bananas before our ascent.

The vegetation was semi-tropical. Big palms and ferns lined our path. No one wanted to carry the bag of bananas so we stopped regularly to eat, admiring the village lake below us. Half way up the mountain, I went to pee behind a line of fir trees, finding when I came out that our chaperones had disappeared. The climb up to the top would be too much for the old man, James explained. As we continued climbing right up into the snow James began to annoy me; he insisted on taking my hand to help me over icy patches on the slopes. Completely alone on the mountain side, we eventually stopped. "Karee", he began. "Perhaps we can become special friends." Warning bells were clanging. And what exactly did he mean by that? "We can write to each other" he explained. "Then one day, we can get married like my friend. He met a Dutch girl here. Now he has his own car and apartment in Amsterdam and", he added, "his wife is still a modern career woman."

He was offended at my amused refusal. "Don't you like me?" he asked incredulously. I mumbled a guilt-ridden criticism of oppressive regimes restricting free travel. "Agh! But you misunderstand my heart!" he retorted, angrily. "Can't you see? The gods have sent you! We were both born in the same week of the same month of the same year – the year of the Rooster. You are my chicken and I your cock!"

Yet another free enterprise venture was operating outside Yangshou village. Having spurned the tourist pilgrimage to Moon Hill, I had rented a bike which soon revealed itself to have a flat back tyre. Not to be put off, I ground heavily onwards out of the town, marvelling at the mysteriously formed hills rising sporadically like salt pillars from the surrounding flat plain, determined to seek out the real Yangshou. A mile later it came to me. A wiry, upright woman with bright eyes and an open smile neatly propped her bicycle against the hedge and proceeded to pump up my back tyre with great vigour. "Do not worry!" she called over her shoulder. "I only want to practise my English." After giving the tyre a last professional squeeze, she whisked a pocketbook out of her bicycle basket and handed it to me for examination.

It was crammed with foreigners' accounts of this woman, who introduced herself as Lee, a local farmer. The accounts praised her desire to improve her English, thanked her for her generosity in inviting strangers into her own home. Would I care to come to supper too? All she asked was that I buy a few traditional print postcards of the surrounding area. It was the least I could do. I congratulated myself on my good luck as I whizzed behind her back along the main road, the white-painted tree trunks which lined the ditches blurring as we passed.

Swiftly hoisting the bikes over the threshold, Lee slammed the huge barn door behind us, leaving only a square of light to come in through an open back door. She steered me towards a reclining, wicker chair piled high with knitting and offered me a cup of jasmine tea. Somewhere, a pendulum clock ticked. Did I like pork? she inquired. Was it too dark in here? Suddenly a naked bulb dangling from the ceiling was snapped on, illuminating a side of bacon hanging from the same wire. She took a cleaver, hacked off a slice and exited through the back door, leaving the bacon swinging. Huge, yellow, bulbous vegetables dangled from the exposed rafters. A large black-and-white photograph of a stern old woman dominated the white-washed back wall. Every few seconds a fizz and a hiss emitted from a collection of sealed pots beneath a table. Lee lifted one of the lids to reveal slowly pickling vegetables.

Two young girls snuffled their way in from school, unsurprised to see a foreigner shelling peanuts in their living room. Lee shrieked instructions from the outside kitchen and the reluctant pair took over the shelling. Directly outside was a red, iron pump with a sandstone drainage area. A line of brightly coloured hand towels hung drying on a bamboo pole tacked to the wall. Next to this was a cotton holder with pockets containing four upright toothbrushes. Lee was merrily chopping vegetables on top of a smooth, stone slab. Behind her, a tarpaulin roof protected three squat brick ovens on top of which woks sat comfortably sizzling. My camera burned in my pocket.

At the low table, Lee urged more pork on me and taught me to push the rice quickly into my mouth by putting the bowl rim inside my bottom lip. As I brought the dish up, a bracelet bought in Yunnan glinted in the light. Would I buy one from her? At last an opportunity to show my gratitude (though I was embarrassed that her hospitality should be reduced to money). She pocketed another ten yen and produced the pocketbook which I dutifully filled with praise: "By opening up her home, this woman is doing more for international understanding than the whole government put together. Keep up the good work." Immediately I had finished, she snapped it shut. Silence. The children perching on their upturned stools stared intently. The clock ticked. "One person; one meal – twenty yen", Lee stated in a business-like voice.

The children giggled mockingly as I set off on my heavy bicycle. Silly, gullible foreigner jolting over pot holes in the pitch black, blinded by truck headlights, only the white-painted trees preventing me from falling into the steep ditches along the side of the road. How dare she mock my gratitude with her fake hospitality! I was angry at her and yet, as I pressed on, I realised I was most sickened at myself. In her wisdom, Lee had managed to expose the holes in my dubious Western, political correctness. I had thought of myself as a traveller, not a tourist, determined to seek out the real, contemporary China, to be a living part of history in the making. But she knew that at the bottom line, I had wanted to see inside a real, Chinese, peasant farmer's house, to gawp at how she survived with no running water, to store details of her uneven, earthen floor. If what I had wanted had been given freely within the framework of simple, unassuming peasant hospitality, I could have ignored my guilty motives. How did her neighbours regard her? I wondered. Did they admire her for making more money in one afternoon than they could imagine in a week?

The moon loomed behind the mysterious hills with all the beauty of Lee's picture postcards, but I didn't stop to savour the scene. Could no one see past my white, Western features in this country? I recounted those I had met on my travels. Almost every person I had been in contact with had been obsessed with the get-rich-quick syndrome and when they had spoken to me, it was to ask advice on how this might best be done. Had Cho, too, only been using me as a rice ticket, showing me glitzy Beijing hotels so that, with me, she could gain entry; showing me around the city just so she could exchange her

People's Money for my foreigners' currency? I had hoped that our lengthy discussions meant more than that. I pedalled harder, breathing heavily to extract the doubt which stuck in the back of my throat.

One year later, I dropped into The Chinese Shopping Emporium off London's Kilburn High Road. The owner, Mrs Woo, obligingly agreed to translate a letter I had received that day from Ken Ki Cho. Fetching her glasses, she leant over the counter. "She says you were the first British person she'd ever met," she began. "That you shared many thoughts together and that always you are in her mind. What's this?" she squinted. "Something about a sister?" Then she looked across at me, smiling admiringly. "As a Chinese, she pays you the greatest compliment of all. She says 'I want to call you sister'."

read on . . .

Jung Chang, *Wild Swans* (UK: Flamingo,1993/US: Anchor World Views, 1992). This gripping, often harrowing, story of three generations of Chinese women whose lives spanned the political maelstrom of the twentieth century achieved enormous popularity in the West. Jung Chang's grandmother, born into a feudal society, was a warlord's concubine; her mother struggled with the hardships of Mao's revolution and rose to become a Communist official before being denounced during the Cultural Revolution, while Jung Chang herself lived, breathed and spouted Mao until the discrediting and crushing of her parents and her own "re-education" in the countryside, indelibly tarnished her convictions. The story ends when she's sent abroad to study in England and stays on. Unsurprisingly, this extraordinary autobiography, written in a spare, documentary style, was banned in China.

Martha Gellhorn, "Mr Ma's Tigers", in *Travels with Myself and Another* (1978; UK: Eland Books, 1983/US; o/p). In 1941, reacting to news that Japan had joined the Axis, war correspondent Martha Gellhorn persuades the editor of Collier's to let her report on the Chinese army in action. "I felt a driving sense of haste. I was determined to see the Orient before I died or the world ended or whatever came next." Her account, written with her usual incisive honesty and adrenaline, includes spiralling night flights out of a semi-blockaded Hong Kong, a chilling description of the just-bombed city of Kunming and the sordid realities of rampant cholera and tuberculosis.

Anchee Min, *Red Azalea* (UK: Gollancz, 1996/US: Mass Market Paperback, 1995). Having distinguished herself as a zealous "Little Red Guard" by denouncing a beloved teacher, Anchee Min is sent to join a peasant collective on the China Sea coast. There, under a regime of relentless toil, and conditions of near starvation, she embarks on a passionate affair with her female squad leader, before escaping the farm by competing successfully for the starring role in Madam Mao's latest opera, called *Red Azalea*. Production is halted by Mao's death and after years of menial film work, and a slow recovery from TB,

Min manages to emigrate to America. Her haunting and salutary memoir, written with the occasional obliqueness of a second language, was an instant bestseller. No other book illustrates quite so clearly the political suggestibility of youth, nor its resilience and hope.

Harriet Sergeant, *Shanghai* **(US/UK: John Murray, 1998).** Using first-hand accounts, skilful research, and imaginative reconstruction, Harriet Sergeant charts the rise and fall of the city known throughout the 1920s and 1930s as "The Whore of the Orient".

★ **Alice Walker,** "A Thousand Words: A Writer's Picture of China", in *Living by the Word: Selected Writings 1973–1987* **(US: Harcourt Brace, 1989).** Pulitzer Prize winner Alice Walker documents a trip she took to China in the early 1980s with a group of eleven women writers, including her close friend and travel companion Susan Kirschner, Paule Marshall and Tillie Olsen. Her account, divided and styled around fifteen imaginary or mental "snaps", touches on a wealth of personal impressions and observations: from a critique of the renowned Chinese author Lu Xun to a disheartened musing on the Great Wall, a surprised enjoyment of Beijing, and concern about the treatment of less eminent Afro-American guests.

Marina Warner, *The Dragon Empress: Life and Times of Tz'U-His, 1835–1908, Empress Dowager of China* **(UK: Vintage, 1993).** Despite having never studied Chinese, Warner has managed to piece together a portrait of the mandarin's daughter who held supreme power in China for just over four decades until 1908, which tallies, apparently, with vernacular sources. The empress is shown to be an unsavoury mix of corruption, megalomania, xenophobia, ruthlessness, vanity and malice – Warner could, and does, go on. She also outlines the combination of forces, including endemic poverty, civil war, foreign exploitation and invasion, that brought the Ch'ing dynasty to its knees.

★ **Jan Wong,** *Red China Blues: My Long March from Mao to Now* **(UK: Bantam/US: Anchor Doubleday, 1996/1997).** Part political history, part travel memoir, *Red China Blues* is a fascinating account of daily life in Cultural Revolution China. A Maoist wannabe from Montréal, Jan Wong arrived in Beijing in 1972 and spent the next six years struggling to uphold her faith in the world's biggest social experiment. Though she married a fellow idealist – the only American draft dodger to seek shelter in China – disillusion gradually set in, and she decamped for the West, returning in the 1980s as a journalist for *The New York Times* and *The Globe and Mail*. Her front-row coverage of the Tiananmen Square massacre lingers in the mind long after the final page of this often-painful, highly personal book.

Colombia

At home with the street children

Judy Seall

Judy Seall works as a drama teacher in the rural south of England. A few years ago she took a break and flew to Bogotá, on the invitation of a Colombian friend from college who had just moved back there. She arrived fully intending to stay just a few weeks before launching herself on a tour of neighbouring South America but, after a chance meeting with an organiser of one of the local street children charities, she radically changed her plans. Instead she spent the next twelve months becoming increasingly immersed in working, and playing, with the street children of Bogotá, including running drama sessions at a new home established just outside the city. She is currently making plans to return.

Arriving late at night in the dimly lit El Dorado airport felt very daunting, especially as Lucia, my one friend in Latin America, was nowhere to be seen. Almost immediately I was surrounded by enthusiastic men, women and children wanting to carry my ruck-sack, offering me lifts and trying to persuade me to stay at their par-ticular *hospedaje*. Strangely, I felt most threatened by the small chil-dren with their unwashed faces and scuffed knees. Tiny hands clutched my arms, and when I pulled away their persistent wolf-whistles followed me. Retreating to a quieter corner I waited hope-fully. The airport felt uncared for - flies had been squashed on the once white walls, and little mounds of rubbish were beginning to collect in the corners. A portly man with bad teeth and a nervous smile watched me with interest. I smiled nervously back but felt uneasy. Within minutes I was rescued by Lucia – apparently there had been no record of my flight having landed.

Lucia is an old college friend who had returned to live in Bogotá after years of studying and working in Europe. We jumped into a taxi and headed for her apartment in Chapinero, a relatively safe area in the north of the city. Taxi drivers are a curious breed in Colombia. A fare can be agreed quickly, only to be doubled a mile down the road. Fortunately Lucia had already taken care of this. We passed clusters of wooden huts placed precariously on the roadside lit up by candles and paraffin lamps. Several of these huts were shops and bars. Faces were hidden in the shadows and unmoving. As we travelled over the unfinished roads, our taxi driver dodged the piles of rubble and tiny children collecting cardboard. I learnt much later that the more rubbish there is the better for the families living on the edge. Metal, plastic and cardboard are sorted and sold for recycling. The roads widened and the huts were replaced by apartments and the odd tired-looking tree. Lucia had only just moved into a brand-new apartment which she shared with Nino, her slightly nervous Italian partner. There was no furniture, no telephone and only intermittent electricity. It was January and cold.

The next morning Lucia and Nino set about advising me how to handle their city. A woman travelling alone in a male-dominated society obviously needs to be a little cautious. The latest scam in Bogotá, apparently, was taxi drivers offering sweets which had been drugged. Tourists were gratefully accepting innocuous-looking boiled sweets while stuck in the inevitable *trancon* (traffic jam), and the next thing they knew was that they were lying in an alley having been stripped of all their possessions. I made a mental note never to accept sweets from taxi drivers. Lucia then outlined which areas of the city I shouldn't walk alone in at night, and Nino emphasised I should be wary of the underpaid and overworked police officers.

In my first week I discovered a city of contradictions. I was woken early by a lone cockerel and battled to get to sleep with angry car horns. Small children with the clothes falling off their backs made mischief outside the famous gold museum. The heat was oppressive by day, and yet the temperature dropped so much at night that whole families huddled for warmth under blankets of newspapers. In the beautiful Candelaria district, thieves plotted in shadows while the wealthy struggled to feel safe behind elaborate security railings.

My initial plan had been to spend a month travelling in Colombia and then move on through Ecuador, Bolivia, Peru and Chile. It all seemed highly appealing. Then I met Rosanna, a Colombian, and had my whole approach to spending time in her country turned on its head.

Rosanna was waiting for her weekly English lesson at the British Council while I was raiding the library. We fell into conversation. She was working with a local charity supporting the city's street children, and I quickly became fascinated. These children live on the edge of society and are frequently treated by the authorities as an irritant, like a splinter that needs to be removed. When an important person arrives in town the streets are "cleaned" by death squads and the bodies dumped in forgotten scrubland. It is difficult to assess exactly how many street children there are – some only work on the street and return home at night, many drift between unhappy homes and the uncertain life on the streets, and a smaller group has nowhere else to go. But Rosanna told me that the local projects were starting to have an impact in alleviating the very worst of the conditions that the children have to face. Not so long ago the streets had been so dangerous that the children had crawled into the sewers, and become known as the sewer rats. Now at least they were able to resume life in the open. Trying to get my head round such terrifying realities was impossible. I had been working with mainly middle-class children in rural Berkshire and had never come across such stories.

Just before her English lesson began Rosanna invited me to visit the children's home, to meet her colleagues, and of course, the children.

A few days later I was picked up outside a baker's by Francisco, Nancy and Arturo, the driver, in a rusty jeep. As we travelled through choking traffic, the gear stick unscrewed itself and the windscreen wipers shuddered to a stop. Francisco a young, energetic man, was the director of the charity's latest home. He greeted me warmly and made me feel immediately welcomed. By contrast Nancy, a teacher at the home, seemed slightly distant, as if waiting to discover what my motives might be. She had seen too many young students from the

States and England come to visit the home, involve themselves briefly in the work and then disappear. My interest could have been no more than a passing flirtation with the rough edges of Colombian city life. Despite the low pay and long hours Nancy had carried on with the project, and was clearly depended on by the children as their reliable friend. I didn't blame her for her initial wariness.

An hour later we reached the home, built on a hill in Subachoque, overlooking small farms. It was cold and the place was shrouded in mist. I found myself clutching my purse and immediately felt ashamed. Two small boys in worn out sweaters and patched jeans many sizes too large, raced up and hugged me tightly. Very tightly. Their names were Cristofer and Carlos Angulo and they couldn't have been more than eight years old. The other boys inspected me from a distance. The home was a tough place and these were tough boys, who were suspicious, inconsistent and unpredictable.

After hugs with the adults the boys resumed their "games": throwing stones at each other by way of greeting, butting heads and kicking balls hard at the windows. For my self-appointed hosts, Carlos Angulo and Cristofer, I was the new toy to be yanked around their home, introduced to the temperamental alsation and occasionally fought over. It was exhausting. The most extraordinary part of the day, however, was listening to the stories the children told me. Jesus told me how his stepfather had abused his mother and his younger brothers and sisters over many years. Jesus would come home from working on the streets and find his mother sitting hunched as if holding her body together and his sisters with blackened eyes crying in the comer. Meanwhile his stepfather would be teaching his brothers a lesson on the other side of town. When I asked Jesus if he was ever beaten up he shook his head and showed me his muscles proudly. He wouldn't dare, he claimed. One night it was so bad Jesus sought out his stepfather and stabbed him to death. I swallowed hard and stared at this wiry young teenager. He smiled and this alarmed me even more.

Travelling back later that day I questioned Francisco about Jesus. He was one of their most challenging children. He'd been brought up by his grandmother as his mother had died when he was a baby. His grandmother had become very old and couldn't look after him so he'd drifted onto the streets. I wanted to interrupt, surely we were talking about a different boy. But no, Jesus had re-invented himself for my attention – he'd learnt to make up stories as a means of making adults listen and care. Months later I realised that it wasn't entirely made up. It certainly wasn't Jesus' story, but the sad truth was that it belonged to many other street children in Colombia.

Arturo dropped me off at the bakery, and Francisco asked me if I wanted to return the following day. I did. And I kept on returning, though never quite committing myself in those initial stages to more than one day at a time. My friend, Lucia, encouraged me and, I liked the challenge. I pushed any feelings of guilt that I could only be there a short time away. I stayed. I was curious. I became more and more involved.

Rosanna asked me to run drama workshops for the children, and much to my surprise I agreed to give it a go. I spent six weeks with the children, getting to know them, and deciding what kind of drama sessions I could do. We played games together and they taught me dirty street words. Fights were a regular occurrence among the boys, and I soon realised that the only way to stop them, or, at least to limit the damage they could inflict on each other, was to step into the middle and separate them physically. Initially I was quite frightened. They were always very careful with me, however, no matter how out of control they seemed to be, and were terribly upset when I ended up with a black eye in the more serious fights. But there were also good times and my favourite were when we shared stories and jokes.

Most of the children living in the home had drifted onto the streets very young, had never been to school, and treated all adults with suspicion. Adults could have them picked up, locked up, beaten up – even killed. Consequently many of the children had low self-esteem and struggled with feelings of worthlessness. Daniel's mother had been tortured and murdered in front of him, Delia was repeatedly raped by her stepfather, and Ruth's face had been badly burnt after her home had been set alight by the death squads. These children had known more loss than I would ever understand.

Unlike the special homes the Colombian government had set up, which the street children described as being like prisons, Subachoque tried to involve them in making choices about their lives. This necessarily included the choice of whether to stay at the home or return to the street. No activity was compulsory, but generally they all wanted to do everything. By the time we arrived the children had been up several hours and were working. This could include planting potatoes, sorting out the laundry or removing bricks. Physical labour was considered an important part of their rehabilitation.

The boys were looked after by a variety of staff overnight – "Ojitos" (Big Eyes), an ex-street child himself, Sofia, a fragile young student, in hiding from the police after witnessing two police officers killing a street child, and Patricia, a tough, no-nonsense mother of three cheeky boys. Once the day team arrived the boys attended lessons which took place in a large shell-like building resembling an aeroplane hanger. There were 21 boys when I first started working there but the numbers went up and down like a yo-yo over the next few months. The boys were divided into two classes which were run by Francisco and Nancy. There was no syllabus as such but most of the lessons focused on basic numeracy and literacy. In the afternoon various workshops took place, such as mop-making, brush-making, plastic bag-making and, more recently, baking. The home sold as many of the resultant products as possible, and Francisco's dream was for the centre to become completely self-sufficient, with each child having a trade to fall back on. When the children finally leave the home they are all offered support, but it is always on the understanding that they in turn will help another street child. The opportunity for them to write a different life story was there but it wasn't always easy. Right from the beginning small children were expected to help themselves – in order to come to Subachoque they had to leave their bottles of glue and knives on the street.

In the drama workshops we explored traditional stories like *Hansel and Gretel*, stories full of wicked step-parents, neglect and very little money. These were common enough experiences yet what the children seized upon in these stories was the change of fortune. Hansel and Gretel escape from the gingerbread house, find the treasure and are reunited with their father who really loved them all along. Happy endings, conventional marriages and traditional family life were the most popular outcomes. Such a romantic view of family life was common and strongly desired despite all they had lived through. The father of Luz Mari's third child turned up at the home every so often, proud of his virility, demanding to see his child. Yet he was only about thirteen himself. And Luz Mari? Behind her round moon face and her tired grey eyes she had dreams like any other fifteen-year-old. Despite all the sexual abuse she had received from so many men, her dream was to get married and live happily ever after.

Wiry Richard, who used to perform circus acts on the street was one of the most regular attenders. If there was no football Carlos Angulo would turn up, climb the walls, punch other members of the group and shout a lot. Luz Mari listened intently in a corner of the room. I became known as the "Gringa from Gringolandia" who spun a good story but had strange eating habits preferring to bring a sandwich rather than eat a "delicious" soup of boiled chicken heads and claws. Delia taught me to salsa, Cristofer – representing the whole of Colombia – beat me at football each week, and Jairo drew diagrams explaining the sewer network in Bogotá.

Several evenings a week I went out with the night patrol to visit various *parches* or street gangs in Bogotá. Our role was to try and keep in touch with these fragile communities, give advice to any children who were in trouble with the authorities, take them to hospital and pay for any treatment, even play hide-and-seek with the smaller ones. The first time I went with the patrol the brute reality of these children's situation hit me like a punch. It was about 11 o'clock at night and drizzling intermittently. We parked in a shopping precinct car park and Adonias, the psychologist, called out some names. The dark streets seemed particularly menacing that night and I felt painfully vulnerable. There was no sign of anyone. We approached a small children's playground and a few scrawny-looking bushes. Still no sound. Then the giveaway - smoke from a cigarette and several pairs of eyes blinking. There were five children smoking dope and staring at me hard. Nothing could prepare me for their stares.

During night patrols I spent most of the time listening to their stories – of how they had been spat at, stamped on and shaken by members of vigilante groups. Too many of these children were sex toys from a very young age so they had a confused understanding of forming relationships. Children as young as eight or nine would attempt to stroke my breasts and kiss me passionately. Being very firm from day one was essential, explaining that we didn't have that kind of relationship. They offered me a sniff of their plastic bags filled with cheap but extremely potent glue, and explained how the drug *bazuko* was very effective at numbing the effects of the cold nights. Many of them were shrunken in weight and had severe breathing problems. It was not uncommon to come across children from the home who might have had a disagreement with a member of staff or were concerned about their friends still on the street. One night we ran into Jesus with a bag of glue hidden up the sleeve of his jumper – he was as high as a kite and didn't recognise us. He had been found with a knife on him earlier that day and refused to hand it over, so he'd left before he'd been thrown out. There were times when I felt utterly depressed about the hard facts of their lives and couldn't face joining the night patrol. But I also grew to recognise their amazing optimism about life and their important sense of loyalty to each other.

At weekends and during holidays I took time out and travelled by bus, seeing as much of Colombia as possible. Perhaps these breaks were a rehearsal for when I would leave the children to return to my own life. I knew after a very short time that I could not stay for more than a year. I wasn't strong enough.

Colombia is a beautiful and diverse country with scenery ranging from the impressive Andes mountains where the temperature regularly drops below freezing, to the humid Amazon River where it becomes impossible to count your mosquito bites. I trekked through dense tropical rainforest in search of "*La Ciudad Perdida* " (Colombia's Lost City), observed an Easter parade in the sparkling white town of Popayan and discovered strange archeological remains in San Agustin. I met some wonderfully exotic and interesting people, and was offered opportunities of a lifetime including an invitation to appear in the popular soap opera *Fiebre* (Fever), and work alongside a group of indigenous people in the Amazon. But the street children haunted me in my dreams, and I always returned.

I finally left Colombia just before Christmas almost a year later. Cristofer and Carlos Angulo came to see me off at the airport. Their grasp of geography was limited, and despite my protestations insisted that England was just another state of America, inhabited by Mickey Mouse and Sylvester Stallone. As we waited for the plane, and the boys tucked into burgers and chips, Cristofer told me that he would be the next Valderama playing for Colombia. Carlos Angulo insisted that he wouldn't. Both Cristofer and Carlos Angulo were used to adults leaving them and accepted it with a stoicism well beyond their years. They both promised to write. I knew they wouldn't and I wondered if I would ever see them again.

My decision to stay in Colombia and work with these children had been the right one. I felt honoured to have been accepted into their lives for that short period. As Avianca Flight 018 left the runway I thought about individuals. Luz Mari had decided to have her third child adopted and was training to be a hairdresser. Richard was impatient and had made up his mind to leave the home and go back to performing his circus acts. And Jesus was still on the street. I'd been told that he was wanted by the police in connection with a stabbing.

Now back in Reading, I'd like to be optimistic about the future of these children but it's hard. I send Christmas cards every year but hear nothing. I want to return but am afraid of what I might find. I only hope that these children aren't dreaming their dreams in vain.

read on . . .

Joan Didion, *The White Album* **(1979; UK: Flamingo, 1993/US: Noonday Press, 1990).** This second collection of essays from one of America's pre-eminent writers includes her impressions of Bogotá in the early 1970s. From the plush excesses of the city's Hilton and Hacienda district to the shacks of its shanty-towns, Didion presents a telling and prismatic view. As with all her writing, flashes of brilliance are threaded with sober insights.

Cuba

Falling among friends

Jane Mathieson

Jane Mathieson trained as a doctor in France then worked for Medecins du Monde in South Africa and Tibet and for Oxfam in Rwanda. After her son, Oliver, was born, she took a break from aid work, and became a full-time single parent. He was two years old when they embarked on their first travel adventure together, on a trip to Cuba. They currently live in the English Lake District.

Years ago, when I was living in Johannesburg, two Cuban doctors came to stay. Their country was reeling under the effect of the demise of the Soviet bloc. Politely but compulsively, they went around the house turning electric switches off. As we flew into Havana, lights broke the uniform black I had been staring at through the plane window, not in confluent bright patches as over Western cities, but paler, flickering intermittently: Third World lights. Cuba still has no power to waste.

Once firmly on Cuban soil, the unpredictable electric supply lost the exciting, romantic appeal it had exerted on me from the air. A power cut shut down the computer of the immigration officer we had been waiting to see for nearly two hours, at which point we had to change "queues" - or rather join another group of tired, irritated, travellers waiting amorphously in front of a faceless booth. Luckily, Havana airport is modern and clean. My maternal eye scanned it for hazards: as the waiting time increased, so did the number of lighted cigarettes held at the height of Oliver's face. Depressingly, there also seemed to be more, rather than fewer, people crowding in front of us, more legs through which he might disappear. When I tightened my grip on him, he cried pathetically, "I want go home". Our home in Cumbria seemed immeasurably far away.

In daylight, Oliver was again prepared to share my enthusiasm. We'd slept fitfully through night traffic sounds and cockcrows in the first of the six double beds we were to share over the next three weeks. The freshly laundered sheets cloaked the smell of city drains. Our only booking from home was for this room in a *casa particulare,* Cuba's equivalent of a "bed and breakfast", in Havana Vieja: high-ceilinged, shuttered, opening onto a starlit terrace. None of our fellow guests complained about our late arrival and early rising. My choice of accommodation seemed to clump me with tolerant people who could have been my friends: elderly communists, students, a photographer, a film maker. They welcomed me to the fold with a few tips over coffee, while Oliver charged through the house, discovering caged song birds and wicker rocking chairs.

We set off at pushchair speed with a vague mission to locate my Cuban medical friends, whose address I'd lost. We headed up Neptuno towards Avenida 23, where the Ministry of Health is located. Oliver focused on the cars, motorbikes and potholes ("tarmac broken", he observed), while I looked into shop windows (mostly boarded or empty) and open doorways. We paused to glimpse – through a mass of shoulders and legs – the National Dance Company gyrating to salsa. The smell of sweat and sensual, heated bodies just reached us, sweet and intoxicating. Further along, we were invited into a similar hall to sit on wooden benches while a big band practised. Oliver was mesmerised by the decibels, I by the drummer who raised his eyes to mine in friendly seduction.

Finally we reached the Ministry; the receptionist was sceptical but sent me towards a narrow concrete stairway at the back of the building, leading to a windowless, dim-lit corridor. A figure emerged from a doorway, wearing the immaculate white pleated shirt and neat moustache I associated with Cuban doctors. "Ah, Fernando, he is in Cienfuegos, do you want to call him there?" My guide led me through the rabbit warren of offices to the phone. I wondered silently how they can do their job with so few computers.

I talked to Fernando, and we made a loose arrangement to meet. But my elation and relief were immense: I was no longer "alone" in Cuba, I had friends.

A cloud crossed our path as we walked back towards Havana Vieja along the Malecon. This seafront avenue is separated from the rocky shore by a low wall, a metre wide, irresistible to an adventurous child. Oliver ran along it, ignoring my outstretched hand and pleas for caution. Once in a while spray would splash him, to his delight. His co-ordination is good, and I was only a little concerned. Then I saw him throwing pebbles over the wall. An irrational malaise touched me as I looked closer and realised that he was taking them from what must have been a *Santeria* shrine. *Santeria*, the Cuban equivalent of Haitian voodoo, is a marriage of animist practices brought to Cuba by African slaves, and Catholicism. The rough, naive drawing of a church-like building had been chalked onto the horizontal surface of the wall, its spire pointing seawards; a cockroach had been crushed in the centre of the edifice. The pebbles Oliver was busy removing had been placed, like miniature foundation stones, along the chalked outlines. Banishing superstitious thoughts, I put Oliver back in the pushchair and proceeded, full speed ahead.

The bad luck caught up with us a few hours later, in a play ground full of equipment that looked like the rest of Havana: as if the ravages of the blitz, or an earthquake – or, more accurately, several hurricanes and decades of neglect – had been swept aside, but not repaired. I was suspicious of the lopsided swings and the jagged seesaw, but unwary of the slide which Oliver joined several children on. The parents' bench was intact. I relaxed, he fell, maybe two metres, with a thud and screams. He looked a terrible mess, blood was pouring from a cut on his forehead, and from his mouth and nose, and his cheeks were grazed and plastered in sandy grime. More worryingly, he was crying plaintively, and was bleary-eyed and drowsy.

As I picked him up, a man ran to me, saying that he'd take me to a health centre around the block. We were seen immediately by the female duty doctor. She gave me a comforting embrace after calling an ambulance, which arrived within minutes to take us first to a paediatrician in a neighbouring health centre, then on to hospital. Oliver was momentarily distracted by the frenetic drive through Havana. The ambulance was sponsored, according to a large sticker on the rear window, by Medicos del Mondo, the aid agency I was employed by for several years. Oliver stared at the plastic seats, muttering "broken". Such kindness, such competence, and broken seats. By the time we arrived at hospital Oliver had perked up and after an hour's observation, we were allowed home. No stitches, no fee, just a large dressing on the forehead. As we waited for a taxi under the hospital porch, a lady selling sweets offered Oliver a lolly. I had no *pesos* to pay her. No, she wanted to give it to him. I gave her a dollar, she smiled, shook her head, and emptied half her box into my bag.

The next morning, Oliver still looked like a war victim, but was vastly improved by a wash and a neater dressing from my first aid pack. I had already been asked several times: *"hijo o hija?"* ("son or daughter?"), so decided it was time to give Oliver's baby curls the chop. Our meanderings through the streets of Havana took us to an arcade, where a man was leaning, chatting, by a doorway in an off-white top, scissors in hand. He ushered us into the dark, mirror-lined interior, and sat Oliver in an old fashioned chair higher than the others, which must have been specially designed for children. Children: consistently catered for, never a problem. Oliver sat spellbound, enchanted, as the barber snipped away. Motherhood brings unforeseen moments of emotion; and this little rite of passage from babyhood to boyhood had me pushing back tears of pride. A professional job, just as I wanted without having to say a word, short on the sides and a few curls on top. The price listed on the wall was 0.80 *centavos*, less than a twentieth of a US dollar. When asked for three dollars, I pointed to the list. We settled on one. It was a fair compromise, I felt, considering the average Cuban monthly salary is about ten dollars.

I had planned to head from Havana to the beach. Oliver loves trains, and I was intrigued by conflicting stories about the Cuban rail network. So the following evening, I booked seats on the Santiago train. Verdict: Cubarail beats Branson on punctuality, but not on comfort. I blessed disposable nappies after failing to induce Oliver to wee into the stinking bottomless toilet bowl. We travelled through vast sugar plantations, which had been set alight, to ease the labour of harvesting and improve the produce. Once, tongues of flame lapped hot towards the open windows, where the railway sidings had caught fire. "Daishenaws" (dinosaurs), commented Oliver, retreating hastily from the window. He hadn't yet learnt the word for dragons.

Most of the night, there was no light; occasionally a bright neon would flicker above our heads. Across the alley, a woman with an enviably well-behaved child warned me not to leave my luggage overhead, where helpful hands had already stored it. I half followed her advice and made sure my valuables were wedged safely, though somewhat uncomfortably, against my body on the seat. In the middle of the night, I was woken by the only raised voices I heard during our stay in Cuba: a fellow passenger had been robbed, his bag had disappeared. A glance in the direction of my rucksack, and I was already being assisted in lifting it down.

I hardly recall asking for help in Cuba: it was always there, spontaneous and gracious. If Cubans could export good manners, civility, generosity, care, or the many technical and professional skills which their excellent education system has endowed them with, they would be the richest people on this planet. As we approached Santiago, I struck up a conversation with the man whose bag had been stolen. He offered to try to get us on the bus to Guantanamo, from where we could catch another to Baracoa. It was not our lucky day. The bus was full, and by the time our new friend had called the airport and discovered there was an eight o'clock flight to Baracoa, it was already seven-thirty and all the taxis registered to carry foreigners had left the station. However, he eventually persuaded a *pesos* taxi to take us.

Ten minutes later, the driver dropped us at a roundabout, pointed towards a traffic-free, roller-coaster-like dual carriageway, saying he could take us no further because of police controls, and the airport was only two hundred metres away. I struggled to the brow of the first rise, to find there was no sign of the airport: only another rise a few hundred metres ahead. A car passed at speed, probably also late for the plane we were trying to catch. Eventually, scarlet-faced and shaking from exertion, I flagged down a bulldozer. Two men jumped off and grabbed our bags. But where could they put them, let alone us? The arrival of a bus on the scene deprived us of a more original ride. Room was made for us although the bus was full. We reached the arrivals lounge at five to eight, to find the plane was delayed . . . or maybe it wasn't going to fly at all . . . "Come back and ask at ten". By eleven, there was still no news, Oliver was protesting vehemently at being confined to the pushchair, my bladder was bursting and there were neither ground floor toilets nor lifts to go upstairs. I trusted child and luggage to the care of an airport attendant and dashed off. Oliver was in such a foul temper by then that I was pretty sure no one would want to kidnap him; and I would almost have been grateful to be relieved of my bags.

At twelve-thirty we took off in a plane the likes of which I have seen only on vintage movies: a dozen seats arranged length-wise, piles of newspapers, which slipped every time we hit an airhole, and a general Cuban "few screws missing" look. Thankfully, the noise, the spectacular views of the Sierra Maestra mountains, and the threat of being vomited on by an overweight Afro-Cuban granny sitting opposite, diverted my attention from other, more life-threatening, hazards.

Oriente. The eastern region, where Baracoa is located, is lush, sub-tropical, fertile and remote. Formerly home to the exterminated *Tainos* indigenous population, it claims to be Christopher Columbus' first landing point in the Americas. Turquoise ocean, emerald mountains, yet Baracoa, for all its charm, cannot help exuding an air of poverty and neglect. We stayed at the hotel *La Rusa*, the cheapest in town. Previous guests included Fidel and Che, who were supported in their guerrilla activities by the Russian proprietress. As I unpacked, it was my turn to "want go home". Checking my cash, I discovered that exactly $300 were missing. I'll never know whether, in a moment of stress, I mishandled the cash, or whether it was stolen. It's the first time I've lost money while travelling.

Oliver tried to comfort me. "Mummy worried." Then he started "helping" me in my desperate search through our belongings for a fictive purse I might have put the money into. Shoes, toys, keys, padlocks, were sent flying under the bed and across the floor. I led him to the bathroom, checked there were no electric fittings or breakables in reach, shut the door on him, and returned to tidy the room. A couple of minutes later, I relented and went to open the door. Impossible. Somehow, he had locked it from the inside. He stopped crying when I explained what had happened; but he was incapable of unlocking the door. I ran down to reception, and within minutes, the doorman came to the rescue with the biggest screwdriver I have ever seen. Oliver emerged, more curious about this latest adventure and the man in our room than perturbed by his captivity. The next day, Oliver fell asleep just before check-out time, then woke as I carried him downstairs. He was crying miserably at reception while I paid the bill. The manager asked why, then insisted I should take him back to our room to finish his sleep – one of the many small kindnesses that make Cuba such an unique country.

From the hotel, we walked along Baracoa's *malecón* to the home of Francisco, an eleven-year-old boy with whom Oliver had struck up a friendship the day before, playing in the street. I had asked him where we could buy a pizza, one of the few items tourists can buy with *pesos* from street vendors: nutritious, tasty, and at three *pesos,* a bargain. He bought us a pizza, refusing to let me pay. Then he took us home to meet his parents: a breeze-block interior, which I would have whitewashed before parking a car in and sparsely furnished. The only embellishments were a few plastic flowers, dolphins and nymphs, and two television sets, neither of which worked. The boy's mother made us delicious, sweet coffee on a bunsen stove, while we talked about the beach and where we might stay – I had just discovered that the cheap hotel I had selected from my guidebook was now charging $45, which was way beyond my budget. Francisco's older brother, Victor seemed to have some ideas, but was reluctant to commit himself, fearing that the authorities might mistake his help for hustling, which is illegal.

I decided to lighten my bags by giving a few surplus items to our new friends: some clothes, a dictionary, crayons and exercise books, and a bottle of ketchup. In exchange, our friend's brother, a cobbler, did a much needed repair to the pushchair, while I found a taxi that could take us to a much cheaper, beachfront *casa particulare* – both unregistered for foreigners. On arriving, we were told to wait at the side of the street while scouts were sent off to check there were no police around. Within minutes, a woman came running towards us, saying we must move on fast, because a meeting of all the police in the vicinity was taking place in the village that day. I grabbed Oliver and a bag, my guide took another, and we ran through a palm grove, past grazing oxen, across a stream, and finally along a white sandy cove.

The house where we were to stay for the next two weeks stood alone on the beach, among palms and almond trees. A piglet was attached by rope to a stone by the doorstep. By the time I had been introduced to my hostess, Oliver had disappeared. I ran to the sea; had he already drowned? I called, no answer. Then a member of the hastily assembled search party laughed and pointed under the partially elevated house, where Oliver was busy watching some chickens. We had landed in paradise – at least, that's how Oliver saw it. He didn't mind the absence of running water: he had his potty – and he was taken on the ox cart to a nearby stream to fill the water barrels, a treat to which I was never entitled. Sun-browned, he looked more Cuban by the day, and was learning a few words: *muchacho, mira, adios, gracias*. Once I had ascertained that he had a healthy respect for the sea, I relaxed and let him entertain himself all day outdoors, half naked, chasing the domestic animals, or playing the fool with the many compliant and appreciative adults of the extended household.

It was like landing in a García Márquez novel, the characters of which I had all day to observe, making charcoal, coffee and coconut oil, scaling fish, slaughtering the piglet, and most of all, preening and playing. Manicures for the women, dominoes for the men, television for all in the evenings. I slept early. For my hosts, I surmised, the nights were shorter: they were incredibly beautiful, their bodies shone, sexual. There were rarely any other tourists on the beach, although sometimes local children came to gather driftwood, and would join us building sandcastles or collecting seashells. Nothing else ever "happened", apart from routine police alerts, when we would be sent off to hide in a nearby cove with a backwater perfect for paddling and many overhanging almond trees whose nuts we extracted by smashing the shells between rocks. If the police lingered in the village, an emissary would arrive with guavas, coconuts, and a child to play with Oliver.

The permit for official *casa particulares* costs $100 to $150 per month per room, the fine for illegal tourist activities is $400. The concept of taxation is unpopular, the attitude defiant rather than fearful. I was told there is a plan to expropriate my hosts and to build a hotel on the beach. Although unwelcome, this prospect did not seem to arouse passionate opposition. It would attract more tourists (tourism is now apparently Cuba's leading industry) and tourists bring dollars. As we were leaving Cuba, measures to combat prostitution and hustling, as well as other unregistered tourist activities, were being reinforced. It is unlikely that the many people we met during our stay would still feel free to respond so openly and spontaneously to us. Cuba is changing.

We headed back from the Oriente towards Cienfuegos to see Fernando, via Santa Clara. Our train arrived on time again, at 2.30am and it took another two hours in a taxi to reach Fernando's sleepy suburb. Although I would have gladly settled Oliver to sleep through the remains of the balmy night in his pushchair, the taxi driver insisted we must wake our friend. "We Cubans don't mind being woken – and what about the baby?" A few minutes later, Fernando emerged. "Please remind me of your family name," he said, rubbing his eyes and putting on his glasses – then confessed to having mistaken me on the phone for another South African contact. Seemingly pleased to discover my true identity, he embraced me, admired Oliver and, uncomplaining, led us two blocks down the road to a comfortable *casa particulare*.

Over the next few days, he took time off work to show us around town, and we slipped back into the easy friendship which aid workers in foreign countries often share. We recalled how he'd earned his nickname, "The Handkerchief Man", comforting me over a failed relationship. He updated me on the project we helped set up together, arranging for Cuban doctors to work in disadvantaged South African communities.

Our last evening in Cuba, we were invited to share a delicious meal with Fernando's family. A week's wages had been spent shopping for us. Fernando explained that state salaries did not cover the basic food basket requirements of the average Cuban family. He himself is in the privileged position of having earned hard currency working outisde Cuba, but will only be able to maintain his comparatively comfortable lifestyle by securing other overseas contracts. "Fifty percent of Cubans now have access to dollars. You see, Jane, Cuba is a fabulous place to live if you have dollars." What about the other fifty percent? I was left hankering after the poor, yet caring, quasi-egalitarian, society which I had experienced. I still need to be convinced that dollars are the answer to Cuba's problems.

read on . . .

Susan Eva Eckstein, *Cuba under Castro* (US: Princeton University Press, 1995). A thoughtful reappraisal of Cuban Communism that looks behind the Marxist-Leninist rhetoric and cult of Castro to show a far more tolerant and flexible system of government than is usually portrayed. Illuminating background to some socio-political musings.

Wendy Gimbel, *Havana Dreams : A Story of Cuba* (UK: Virago, 1999/US: Knopf, 1998). Driven by rosy memories of childhood holidays in pre-Revolutionary Cuba, Gimbel returns in 1991 to investigate the regime she has come to despise. She focuses her attention on three generations of privileged women, all closely linked to Castro; Dona Natica, a half-English former socialite; her daughter, Naty, who once had a brief affair with Castro; and Alina, the Miami-glam daughter from the union who has yet to be fully acknowledged by her father. A highly readable portrayal, but one occassionally dragged down by the author's own prejudices and bitterness about a childhood idyll overturned by history.

⭐ **Alan Ryan and Christa Malone (ed),** *The Reader's Companion to Cuba* (US: Harcourt Brace, 1997). An extraordinary distillation of a century's worth of travel-writing about Cuba, from Anais Nin, on the "fairyland" of Havana in the 1920s, to Frank Mankiewicz on a 1970s excursion around town with Fidel at the wheel, to Martha Gellhorn's return to Cuba in 1985 and Pico Iyer's 1990s update, with hosts of others hitting the tarmac in between. A great anthology, that could only be lifted by including a few more women writers.

Mirta Yanez (ed) and Dick Cluster and Cindy Schuster (trans), *Cubana: Contemporary Fiction by Cuban Women* (US: Ballantine Books, 1998). Havana editor and novelist, Mirta Yanez, has assembled an impressive cast of women writers in this atmospheric and illuminating collection of contemporary fiction. Cubana offers a tantalising sample of the literature that's flourishing in her country, for all its apparent economic stagnation.

Ecuador

Islands of the mind

Margaret Atwood

Margaret Atwood, the renowned novelist and poet, was born in Canada where she continues to live. Just over a decade ago she took her parents on a cruise around the Galápagos Islands, which are designated Ecuadorian national parks, and closely protected from the damaging impact of tourism. It was the last trip they were to take together before her father, a zoologist, suffered a series of strokes. "Despite the physical discomforts," she wrote, "I'm very glad that we managed to do this with him, as it was always one of his dreams to see Darwin's favourite stomping grounds. The trip was worth every itch, scratch, heat rash, and cockroach." Her most recent novel. *Alias Grace*, was shortlisted for the Booker Prize.

I am not the world's most intrepid traveller. I don't like planes or airports. The sun fries me. If there are insects to be had, they bite me. Bacteria invade me. I get seasick and am susceptible to bad smells. I live in terror of the day when someone, somewhere, will dish me out an eyeball, and in the cause of international relations I will feel compelled to choke it down. Insatiable curiosity propels me around the globe, but I travel with a mini-drugstore of ointments, bandages, sun creams, disinfectants, and pain-killers.

The point is that if I can make it to the Galápagos and back, almost anyone else not actually in a wheelchair probably can too. But for the usual delights of a tropical vacation – working on your

tan, poolside romance, pina coladas under the palms – go elsewhere. One of my acquaintances asked me in all innocence if there
were any tennis courts. There aren't.

This is how it all came about. I hang out, some of the time,
with birders. (Some people refer to them as bird-watchers, but to a
birder that is like what being called a lady painter is to a female
artist.) Birders take birds seriously, and among them the Galápagos
Islands rate high. One of our chief birding connections, Marylee
(*Canada's National Parks: A Visitor's Guide*) Stephenson, had been
there the year before and had been longing to get back ever since;
but birders are often short of cash, since they spend it all on scopes
and binoculars. Marylee decided to charter a boat, fill it, and go
along as a sort of summer camp counsellor.

When my father heard we were on our way to cruise among
the islands where Darwin had cruised, gawk where Darwin had
gawked, and throw up where Darwin had thrown up (the great
man never got over his seasickness, which makes him, for me, even
greater), he did not say, "Why do you want to go *there?*" as he had
when informed about previous expeditions of ours. Instead, his
eyes began to glitter, and he went to the bookshelf and began
pulling out book after book, a sure sign of interest and even
approval. My father is a zoologist. Darwin and the Galápagos rank
for him as the Mohammed and Mecca, respectively, of any true
biological believer.

It struck Graeme and me that possibly he might like to come
with us. After a remarkably short period of deliberation, he accepted. "It's about time a reputable zoologist got down there and discovered the theory of evolution," he said. The one hitch was the
fact that my mother gets motion sickness in just about anything
other than streetcars, and we all knew he'd never go without her.
But she gamely opted for medication, and Marylee filled in two
more blanks on her list.

We had signed in blood by January; the trip was to start in
mid-May. In the interim, we studied up.

The Galápagos are a group of islands in the Pacific Ocean
west of Ecuador. There are sixteen main islands; all are volcanic in
origin, and all are geologically recent. All things living on them
have come trom the mainland, and, isolated from other influences,

they have evolved, often into something distinct from parent stock. Thus Darwin's interest: for him the islands were a living laboratory where birds and animals could be caught in the very act of adapting themselves through natural selection to conditions new to them. This is what makes the islands unique, and this is their attraction for naturalists.

The Galápagos, we learned, could be expected to yield numerous bird species found elsewhere: there are three kinds of boobies and many sea and shore birds such as petrels, oyster catchers, pelicans, shearwaters, frigate birds and tropic birds; there are flamingos and yellow warblers, great blue herons and ospreys. But what gives the Galápagos five stars among birders are the species unlikely to be found anywhere else: the flightless cormorant, with its vestigial wings; the exquisite Galápagos penguin; the lava gull, with its amazing red-lined beak; and the thirteen varieties of Darwin's finch, most prized of which is the woodpecker finch, which uses cactus spines as tools.

As a birder, I'm a good botanist; I prefer things that stay still long enough for me to actually see them. Secretly, I was focussing my hopes on the volcanic formations, the cacti as big as trees, the sluggish marine and land iguanas, and the sea lions and fur seals that were supposed to be fearless enough to allow you to play out any fantasies you might have retained from reading *The Jungle Book* as a child. (This fearlessness, not to be confused with tameness, results from the fact that there were no large predators on the Galápagos for most of the islands' history. In this respect the Galápagos fauna are unique. Mockingbirds sit on your hat; sea lions swim with you and nuzzle your legs. Frigate birds stay on their nests and let you photograph them. You have to take care not to trip over the land iguanas. I was also yearning for some porpoises, up close, and a hammerhead shark, at a discreet distance.

As the date approached, we began receiving sheets of printed material from Marylee, who, never having organised such a trip before, was determined to leave nothing to chance. We were ordered to get polarizing filters for our cameras, to buy our film in Canada before leaving (Marylee had an in-bulk deal), to supply ourselves with waterproof camera bags and with a plastic bag for carrying our film unharmed past the X-ray machines in airports.

On the appointed day we assembled at the Toronto airport, twelve of us, the oldest of whom was seventy-seven and the youngest seven. We flew to Guayaquil in Ecuador, via Miami.

We spent the day in Guayaquil to recover from our jet lag, catch up on our culture shock. And to hold Marylee's hand because our tickets to the Galápagos proper had not yet arrived at our hotel as promised. But many phone calls were made, and next day we were headed for the islands, 600 miles off the coast in the middle of the Pacific Ocean.

I had expected the plane to be a bit like a flying boxcar, but it was an ordinary, full-size plane. Stuffed with tourists, half of them Ecuadorian, half of them perspiring foreigners, it flew in the normal way to Baltra, where there is a World War II landing strip, a tiny airport, and a lot of cacti. A bus, which *was* like a boxcar, took us a short distance to the dock; and there we were met by our ship, the *Cachalote.*

You can visit the Galápagos Islands only by ship. You cannot camp on the islands, which are highly protected Ecuadorian national parks: you must eat on the ship, sleep on the ship and confine your garbage to the ship. All ships are licensed by the government parks administration. They come in three sizes, which correspond to three price ranges: small, medium, and large. The small ones are converted fishing boats, usually without sails. They take eight or so, roll around in heavy swells, and are good for the young, the poor, and the adventurous. The large ones, such as the *Santa Cruz,* take eighty or ninety and have waiters and fans for the rooms. You are woken by loudspeaker, taken ashore in groups of twelve to twenty, and treated to slide shows and lectures in the evenings. The big ships go out for only four days, don't make it to the outlying islands as a rule, and are not allowed ashore at certain places, where the trampling of so many feet might damage the wildlife.

The *Cachalote* is in the middle group. It carried twelve of us, though nine would have been optimum, and four crew. It had sails, so it was not at the mercy of its motor – a cheering thought. Because we had chartered it, scheduling was flexible: we could go where we liked, when we liked. Life aboard was informal, to say the least, but not punitive.

However, none of these advantages flashed through our minds as we were ferried out to it in two nervous bunches, in the *panga,* a small motorized boat we would come to know well. What struck us was that the *Cachalote* was, somehow smaller than it had looked in the diagram. I began to wonder what we had let ourselves in for.

Our first meeting with the crew made us even jumpier. There were lots of dos and don'ts, many of which had to do with the correct way of working the toilet valves. (This lesson was not properly learned by everyone in our group; several times there were disasters.) The main feature was that if you didn't screw the head down properly, the sea would come in and the ship would sink. The other big items were sand on the feet (frowned on) and getting up the ladder from the panga without stepping on the head of the person behind you or getting a leg crushed. I noticed that the ship was equipped with a net that extended from scuppers to railing and went all the way around. It was like a giant floating playpen. Pepé, our guide, was probably just as nervous as we were, since he had to make it through two weeks without losing any of us overboard or allowing us to fricassee or mangle ourselves. To him, we must have looked like a challenge.

The rest of the crew – a captain and a cook, both named Hugo, and a blond, curly-headed American motor expert called Matt – were in charge of the running of the ship, but Pepé Salcedo was in charge of us. He was Ecuadorian, twenty-four and looked like a genial buccaneer. Some of the naturalist guides in the Galápagos do their job only for money, but it was evident at once that Pepé does his for love. He first came to the Galápagos on a school trip, and fell in love with the islands. He opted out of the professional future expected by his social class to become a guide, which involves being able to speak a language other than English and Spanish and completing an intensive three-month course. Pepé also studied at the University of British Columbia for a year, taking courses in geography, geology, ornithology, theory of evolution, and entomology. Every evening he went over the next day with us, telling us what we were going to see and why it was the way it was. There wasn't much he didn't know, and when we would encounter other groups ashore, they'd creep around to listen to Pepé as he held forth on why flamingos are pink (it's the brine shrimp; deprive them and they bleach), why the flightless cormorants stretch out their wing stubs (vestigial behaviour, from when they had real wings and dried them that way), or why the large flying thing somebody saw was not a hummingbird (there aren't any; it was a hawk moth). He could make noises like sea lions and many other things as well, and never wore shoes, as the soles of his feet were like bedroom slippers. He was astoundingly good-natured. Jess, our daughter, fell in love with him at once; everyone else took a little longer. My father, having heard him expound on grasshoppers, concluded that he was "a good man," by which he meant scientifically acceptable, a phrase he does not bestow lightly.

My father approved of Pepé for many reasons. Like my father, and indeed like Darwin himself, he had defied convention and expectations in order to go adventuring in search of natural truths and wonders. Like my father (and Darwin) as well, he was initially self-taught and irrepressibly curious. Again like the two of them, he had a healthy respect for bees and beetles.

And then there were what one might call his literary abilities. At one point, Pepé told us he wasn't too fond of what he called "life listers", birders who are interested only in adding to their collection of names, to the exclusion of the birds themselves, their environment, and their welfare. One such man was going too far, in Pepé's opinion: seeing things that weren't there and whining to Pepé on days when he hadn't logged any new species.

"But I got him back," said Pepé. "One day I said, 'Look! A flightless cormorant!'

I pointed up into the sky. 'Where?' the guy said, swinging up his binoculars."

Since this was exactly the kind of deadpan prank my father himself was quite capable of playing, he referred to Pepé after that as "quite a boy".

The first afternoon on board, Pepé wisely steered us to a mangrove swamp within easy sail. We racked up ten species of birds, including the lava gull and the large-billed flycatcher, and began to feel a little more confident. After dinner, we crammed ourselves into our respective hunks in an optimistic mood, only to entounter what was to remain a major problem on board: sleeping.

There were, altogether, ten bunks, and eleven of us, plus our daughter, who could not in fact sleep on the floor as we had thought. The six people below deck sometimes found it hot and stuffy (since the ports had to be closed when the ship was moving), and noisy because of the motor. Twice someone forgot to close a port, and waves came in on sleepers, drenching them and their bedding. The four above also found it hot when the engine was on. The best place to sleep was outside, on top of the cabin, or (second choice) on the deck itself; but some nights it rained. In any case, there wasn't room on deck for all. Graeme staked out the chart table, and there was sometimes a territorial scramble for the saloon table. Bad nights resembled a giant slumber party, with people in nightgowns bumping into each other in the dark. On good nights, however, the *Cachalote* rocked gently at anchor, the ports were open, and you were lulled to sleep by the sound of sea lions hunting fish, blowing and wheezing two feet from your head.

This is the place to mention that all boats in tropical latitudes have cockroaches. They are large, live under the floors, are impossible to exterminate, and come out in the darkness, when they sometimes walk on you. Apart from an experimental nibble or two to see whether you're a moldy crumb, they don't bite. You can't expect zero cockroaches. All you can hope for is an acceptable passenger-cockroach ratio, and this the *Cachalote* had. The acceptable ratio may vary with the passenger, however. My father was likely to greet any new cockroach discovery with "Ha!" The reaction of some of the others was less gleeful.

The routine during the days varied, depending on where we were and what the weather was like. Mostly we staggered up early, ate breakfast, which often included papaya and eggs (served separately, not together; there was some growling over the first platterful of eggs until people realised there would be more), were briefed by Pepé, slathered ourselves with sun block, and were taken ashore early to avoid the heat of noon. After being stunned by natural wonders (this is not meant ironically), we were brought back for lunch.

The food on the *Cachalote* was excellent by local standards, and the cook knocked himself out for us, whipping up two impromptu birthday cakes and serving up tasty hors d'oeuvres of rock lobster the crew had caught. The fish was fresh caught too:

we'd often trail a line behind the boat and pull in something: wahoo, mahimahi, tuna. But there were several occasions when we didn't feel much like eating it.

For it must be admitted that although none of the sailing was bad by *Cachalote* standards, some of it *was*, by those of nonsailors. Also, the distances between the islands were a lot greater than they looked on the map. During the worst weather we held singsongs to distract people, and things got more like summer camp than ever. Even in moderate winds we found that the best thing to do was climb to the cabin roof and stay as close to the exact centre of the boat as possible, since it moved the least.

I had, I confess, times of doubt: during the roughish sail back from Hood Island, for instance, when I stood on the deck gobbling down the Gravol and trying to focus on the horizon, while the rain poured down the neck of my jacket and my mother turned a delicate Lifesaver green on the bench inside the cabin. (My father, having come from a long line of privateers and other forms of salt, did not get sea-sick, exactly; he merely went to sleep. But even excessive sleep can be anxiety-producing in the guilty.) Had I shown total wisdom in suggesting this trip? Would my parents get damaged? In the event, they did not: the sprains, falls off the cabin roof, infected feet, and peeling sunburns were all suffered by other, younger people.

("The thing is," Marylee said to me, when we had returned from a jungle stroll on mainland Ecuador that included an unexpected, and for me, hair-straightening tiptoe along the slippery edge of a washed-out dam, with a rocky precipice on one side and a mountain stream on the other, "most people, when they're in danger of losing their balance, slow down. Your mother speeds up.")

In fourteen days we covered the major islands, from Tower in the north, where the frigate birds were mating, to Hood in the south, almost the spot where the waved albatrosses breed, launching themselves from the cliff there because they don't take off from flat ground. A list of what we saw would read like a list; or if better written, like Tui De Roy Moore's *Galápagos: Islands Lost in Time*, which I recommend. My favourite things were the eight-mile lava flow on James Island, which was moonlike and, when explained in detail by Pepé, totally engrossing; the land iguanas of Plaza Sur, eating yellow portulaca flowers in an idyllic prehuman torpor; swimming in a grotto with the fur seals; swimming anywhere with the sea lions; and watching the Sally Lightfoot crabs, which are bright red and spectacular against the black rocks.

The highlight for Jess was our snorkelling expedition to the Devil's Crown, an extinct volcano in the sea that has eroded to a jagged rocky rim surrounding a placid centre, home of many bright tropical fish. At first she was dismayed by the name and the ominous look of rocks and the lack of beach to climb out on; she held onto the panga and wouldn't let either of her parents float off with her. But Pepé, indispensable as ever, swam to the rescue and took her with him. He dove down to the bottom of and broke open a sea urchin, so that all the fish within smelling distance came to eat out of his hands.

"This is my cathedral," Pepé said to Graeme. This was what he wished to convey to his flock; that the Galápagos should be viewed not as a vacation but as a privilege.

For my father, the Galápagos were disappointing in only one respect: there were not enough insects. Wingless grasshoppers, true, and fire ants, and an indigenous bee, and a hawk moth; but not an entomological proliferation. However, this relative scarcity did explain one troublesome fact. Darwin, as is well known, began his scientific career as an amateur beetle collector, which was, in my father's opinion, right and proper. But the actual theory of evolution was deduced from finches and other lesser species, not from beetles. Why had Darwin strayed from the path? Now all was clear.

The deficiency was made up for during the four-day excursion into the cloud forest of Ecuador that we made on our way back. Here there were more insects than birds, and many never before scrutinised by my father's eye: giant crème de menthe-coloured katydids, enormous blue morphos and exquisite clear-winged butterflies, a parade of leaf cutter ants, a red-spotted beetle that remains a mystery to this day, and many kinds of moths, which fell nightly into the soup. Happiness may he a warm blanket for some, but for others it is a large arboreal termite nest. Luckily, we were able to locate one. "Hmm," said my father, inserting a stick into it so that the termites would come out to be viewed. This is the sound all male Atwoods make when profoundly interested.

Midway through our time in the Galápagos, we anchored at Puerto Ayora on Santa Cruz to restock. We visited the Charles Darwin Research Station, where the various species of giant Galápagos tortoises are raised to a good age and then put back where they belong. Several species are already extinct; they were heavily used by early sailors, who would stockpile them upside down in the holds of ships, where they would stay alive for months.

Pepé arranged a meeting for me with one of the young scientists. We talked about conservation – the difficulties involved in trying to keep the Galápagos the way they are, or, in the case of some islands, in trying to restore them to what they were. The big problems are caused by species introduced by man, against which the indigenous birds and animals and even plants often have no natural defences. Pirates and fishermen deliberately introduced goats and pigs so they would be able to kill them for meat; rats, burros, dogs, and cats were accidental. The cats eat the marine iguanas and their eggs and are threatening the Galápagos doves; rats, dogs, and pigs have decimated several species of giant tortoise; goats have been devastating to plant life. Because of the climate, animals such as goats breed much faster than they do further north: a few left on Pinta by local fishermen in the 1960s rapidly became a population of 30,000, now reduced by feral-animal control programs to a few hundred.

Controlling these animals, which are pests in their context, costs about $72,000 per species per year. The money goes for transport – all supplies, including water, have to be taken by boat to the islands – and for equipment: tents, guns, and provisioning for the crew of twenty hunters. The Darwin station, which employs a federal-mammal specialist, a botanist, a herpetologist, a marine biologist, an entomologist, and a human ecologist, costs $600,000 a year. Some comes from foreign zoological associations, the rest from donations (you can contribute through the World Wildlife Fund, earmarking the money).

Later I talked with Pepé about the same problem. I had the usual anxieties about being a tourist: was I, by mere presence, helping to further threaten a natural balance that was already under

Lucy Ridout in Mauritania

Lisa Ball at the Rainbow Gathering in Australia

Sara Wheeler in Antarctica

Frances King in Japan

Nicki McCormick and "Betty" in Pakistan

Isabella Tree with Dani warrior in Irian Jaya, New Guinea

Jean McNeil in Mexico

Sheela Keegan's daughter, Carolyn, in the Thar Desert, India

siege? But according to Pepé, the Galápagos are one example of tourism actually encouraging conservation. Since the development tourism as a major industry - which has exploded only since the mid-Seventies – the local people have realised that if they wipe out the indigenous animals and plants, nobody will want to come any more. Most of the fishermen have become tour operators, and local inhabitants are themselves helping to stamp out feral pigs and goats. Many mainland Ecuadorians are now visiting their own national treasure; in Pepé's view, this is how they may first encounter the idea that nature is fragile and will not support infinite exploitation.

Pepé had yet another example of human-animal harmony in his bag of tricks. He took us to visit the Iguana Man, a kindly painter who has been living in the Galápagos since the Thirties, having had a difference of opinion with Hitler. His house was visible from the *Cachalote's* mooring, identifiable by the marine iguanas that covered its tin roof. They went up there to sun, said the Iguana Man, who also told us that, since the iguanas had had the site first, he'd made a deal with them. In return for their land, he would trade them roof basking and food. This seemed fair enough.

Their names were all Annie, he said, after the first one with whom it had been his pleasure to become acquainted. Toward sunset he brought out a large metal dish full of what looked like oatmeal porridge, and banged against it with a spoon, calling, "Annie, Annie, Annie!" Quick as cats, the iguanas slithered and plopped down from the roof and into the dish of oatmeal, where they swiftly became covered with porridge and proceeded to lick each other clean. Their benefactor looked on proudly, noting correctly that this was something we'd be unlikely to see anywhere else. "Who says they are stupid?" he beamed.

"Quite a boy," was my father's comment. You can be quite a boy without being a good man, and vice versa. Possibly he was thinking that, deprived of the chickadees that festoon his hat at certain locations farther north, he might not be entirely averse to iguanas.

Pepé saved the most idyllic location for last: the haunting and indeed haunted island of Floreana. He spent the evening before our landing on it getting us into the right mood with some history and legend. In suitably hushed tones, he told us about the German dentist who, equipped with steel teeth and his wife, had arrived more than half a century before in search of a noble-savage Eden; of the gun-toting baroness who had disembarked with her two lovers and a large supply of bubble bath soon afterward; of the rivalry between the two factions; of mysterious disappearances, possible murders, unexplained deaths . . .

On some of the islands, black with lava flows, smelly with sea lion dung, or white with guano, it would not have been possible to imagine this romantic saga. But on Floreana, with its gentle hills covered with palo santo trees, its tender inland lagoon, and the most beautiful white-sand beach we'd been on yet, the search for paradise, however doomed, was plausible.

On the last night, we slept on deck, where, in the morning, we found ourselves covered with small black smuts disgorged from the motor when it was started up. It was the *Cachalote's* way of telling us our time was up. Somewhat melancholy, we cruised toward Baltra; as port was sighted, I looked down into the clear bow wave and there, hanging suspended for a moment almost beneath the bow, was a hammerhead shark.

We disembarked at the dock and, dragging our by now pullu-lating luggage behind us made our anticlimactic way up to the little airport. Pepé, dressed in a set of spotless whites he'd dredged up from somewhere, saw us off. At the same rime he was locating the incoming group, sizing them up for potentially hazardous quirks. We spotted them too: washed, whey-faced, immaculate. We knew they would not remain that way for long, but we envied them any-way. They were about to experience something unique on the planet, and every lurch and dry heave would, we knew, be worth it. We wished we were going too.

read on . . .

★ **Annie Dillard,** *Teaching a Stone to Talk: Expeditions and Encounters* (1982; US: Harperperennial, 1992). Four stories in this collection relate to journeys that Pulitzer prize-winning author Dillard made to the Ecuadorian jungle and the Galápagos

Islands. *The Deer at Providencia*, her best-known and most frequently anthologised short travel piece, set on the banks of the Napo river, is as good an example as any of the tough-minded lyricism of her writing. Dillard has an almost uncanny ability to tilt a composition and reveal its most prosaic and awesome aspect. The Galápagos-inspired narratives, *Life on the Rocks* and *Teaching a Stone to Talk*, are written with similar virtuosity.

England

A Celt abroad in London

Lesley Riddoch

Lesley Riddoch is an award-winning Scottish journalist. Her many achievements include being voted *Cosmopolitan* magazine's Woman of the Year for Communication in 1993 and editing the *Scotswoman*, a special edition of the *Scotsman*, written and produced for International Women's Day. She is also founder and director of the feminist magazine, *Harpies and Queens*. Lesley has worked extensively in London, where she learned to survive with the help of a bicycle and her indomitable Celtic spirit. However, she has now decided to "come home" to experience the novelty of working and living in the same place.

Back in Glasgow she has set up Worldwoman, a project that aims to publish on the Internet a newspaper written by women from every country in the world on International Women's Day in 2000. She is contributing editor to Scotland's new national newspaper, *The Sunday Herald*, and, as co-founder of a community-based political party, the Highlands and Islands Alliance, she is also very active in her country's national politics.

Living in London is a love-hate experience for many Celts. Part of you is annoyed that all the bright lights, connections, best opportunities and biggest names seem to have been bagged by this unlovely town. Part of you wants to join them. The mere fact that I was making a living in London in the 1980s as a tediously outspoken Scot meant that against my will I had to admit Scotland wasn't enough. So from the start I wasn't even inclined to try and appreciate London, and its roads, trains, tubes and buses certainly helped me along. I was determined to endure London through gritted teeth.

Archway Road and I were just made for each other: a piece of tarmac so familiar to every truck travelling north that I never once managed to cross it in daylight. When I started work as a BBC trainee in the early 1980s I was elated at finding anywhere to live, then realised I would never sleep properly again. Despite double-glazed windows the traffic noise outside the house of little bedsits was incessant. And it was not just a noise. It was a warning – from the man-made river outside the door that poured unnatural forces from scary container park seas right past our sleeping heads – a message sent over and over again from the thundering great Amazon of the M1 motorway heading north to the coiled anaconda of the M25 that encircled the city. Everyone has their price. Keep working. We know what they all want. We will deliver. Crossing the Archway at traffic lights was like parting the Red Sea. Its power was almost biblical.

I found the dirt and the endless anonymous movement of steel, tin and expressionless drivers terrifying. A river fertilises its banks; these terrible torrents of freight did just the opposite. Every house was dirty, every garden strewn with litter, every person head down walking fast with absolutely no sauntering, no dallying, no hanging around. Even the climate on the banks of the Archway seemed harsher; if it drizzled the spray soaked the thin pavement the whole way from the Underground stop to my door. There was always a wind – and dust and smog.

Traffic flow. It was not a flow – that would be sinuous, organic, natural. It was a threat, London's traffic threat, not of being struck or knocked down or even polluted, but of life being reduced to a series of mindless mechanical moves. No beauty, no surprises – just getting the trucks on the road every day, doing what massive cities do best.

My best friend Sarah lived nearer to the centre of the city at Finsbury Park. Holloway Road had even scarier qualities than Archway. At places it is three times as wide, bordered by a shambles of shanty shops and ropy estate agents, dodgy-looking Indian restaurants and even a strange unmodern Marks and Spencers department store complete with sullen, uncommunicative staff. One day, waiting for a bus, I was seized by the thought that the whole system could be completely overwhelmed if just one extra person got on a bus that was already full, because for most people travel was absolutely routine, regular and infinitely repeated. Coming home from overnight shifts I would often be the only white person on the tube. Time is the most sophisticated colour bar. BBC shifts seem to have been constructed to avoid rush hours, so it took months to realise that the groups of office staff hanging round in pubs drinking Perrier water at six o'clock were just trying to avoid the crush on the tube. My heart was telling me to get out, my head was putting up no opposition, so I moved away.

I went back to live and work in Scotland without regrets and with enough cash to visit the pals I hardly saw when I was living in London. But I knew I'd be back. Strangely, being there a second time around cured me. By the middle of 1998 I neither hated London nor felt I had anything left to "prove" by working there.

There were two possible tactics: cycling or living slap-bang in the middle of the city. Both cut out the most depressing and alienating aspects of London life, Amazonian roads and toilet-like tubes. Cycling from North London to White City, where I was working in the BBC TV newsroom, took about 45 minutes, which was quicker than the tube and – thanks to an alternative cyclists' guide to London – took me away from most junctions and busy main roads and through such absolute delights as the back streets of Notting Hill, which I still remember as if they were another country. This was not just because almost everyone was black, still unusual back home in any part of Edinburgh or Glasgow, but because they were communicating with each other – chucking out rubbish, chatting on street corners, having a cigarette before starting the day. Life like it trickles on in all the towns I've known, measured not frantic, purposeful not completely random. Such behaviour is built to last, as if people knew they'd be seeing their customers, neighbours, or even me on the bike, again and again. City life is about rhythms and patterns so why can't they be celebrated, intimate, shared?

Sharing cabs late at night after twelve-hour shifts in the TV newsroom was an extra cycling challenge. Forty-five minutes cycling mainly downhill during the day at the height of your energy is one thing. Cycling home at midnight was another. As the names on the taxi list were intoned by yet another tired soul on autopilot, I'd wait to see if my fellow traveller was a humble worker, in which case I might try and persuade them to help prop the bike up against the cab divide with our feet, or a late-working executive type, in which case I went for it without hesitation or, as it turned out, any refusals.

My tube memories bring back nothing positive at all. My bike memories are full of shortcuts through lanes with the billowing hedges and endlessly blossoming shrubs of a suburban spring, past great old houses covered with the kind of flamboyant, enveloping ivy, creepers and clematis that most god-fearing Scots disdain, and then the bold dash towards Marble Arch. Before traffic lights were installed this was Britain's biggest free for all: six entry points, two, three or four lanes wide, right at the heart of London, and used by pompous, pressurised people installed behind their expensive steering wheels, and me on my bike. The key to survival was speed – and luck – in finding the precise gap through which to burst into the lanes of traffic, and then weaving the bike through the aisles of glass and metal in order to come out intact at the other side.

I suppose I could have taken the bus, or opted sooner for tactic two – living in Soho (or as near as damn it). It wasn't quite living because I was really just working there two to three very long days a week before racing home to Scotland like a woman who couldn't quite hold her breath any longer and needed desperately to exhale. The hotel in which I stayed was run by East Europeans. They were working there illegally, as I discovered one Tuesday night on returning from presenting a BBC2 *Midnight Hour* debate on the Tories' immigration laws: the staff had all been seized in a Home Office raid. Luckily Stefan, the young Slovakian snowboard-champion-cum-barman, had been spared. His sister, employed at another hotel in the same group, had tipped him off when her workplace was raided that afternoon. He told me this as we stood halfway down the stairs to the wine cellar at two in the morning, the only time the lack of customers could justify his absence from the security camera record, and the only place a smoke detector could not pick up our cigarettes. His wages were so low that he was forced to live outside London and face a ten-hour shift and a ninety-minute tube journey to and from his bedsit, and people wonder why few Londoners want to do these service jobs.

He stayed, however, and sneaked me the single hotel fan during that overheated, non-air-conditioned summer, and lent me the only hotel bar-heater in the freezing winter. He egged me on to go running up to Regent's Park every morning. As a fitness fanatic he somehow did the same when he arrived every morning at 5.30. On his very last day, when he decided no longer to live in fear of the next raid, he poured us both massive Taliskers, my favourite malt whisky, and stood before the security camera saluting the health of Slovenia, Scotland, the other hotel staff – except the manager – and Ken Livingstone, the former socialist leader of the Greater London Council. Then I never saw him again. At least we had been able to connect. Somehow that happened more often in the very eye of the hurricane than at its perimeter, perhaps because Soho and Piccadilly are so congested.

I came to relish my weekly walk from Broadcasting House to Millbank by the river Thames: past the little synagogue with the same man washing the steps every week; along Poland Street and its Asian wholesale jewellery shops, which were quite prepared to sell me the most outrageous diamanté clip-on earrings on the basis that they'd be seen on the small screen five hours later; through narrow streets clogged with rails of dresses being whisked into back shop entrances; off pavements onto half-cobbled bits of street to avoid couriers arriving and signing delivery slips, or lovers, friends, business associates, offbeat tourists, adventurous mums and daughters, everywhere human exchange in the air; then down past the flaming torches that define the grandiose, neo-classical Institute of Directors, down the broad sloping steps to Pall Mall, St James' Park, and then the rear view of Whitehall and the centre of government; through the busy dusk scamper-past of civil servants who might have liberated a country or sealed a fate or concealed or promoted or just sat with their feet up all day; towards Westminster Abbey and the vast, white, fluted, impregnable fortress of Parliament, whose absolute power I've always worked to remove – that of Whitehall, not the impotent House of Commons of course. Poor old London, home to the biggest façade in Europe, allowed to fester without proper administration for decades thanks to the whim of a London-hating, suburb-loving series of governments that Londoners foolishly helped to elect. London: relegated to a couple of soap operas and local evening news bulletins; driven through, endured, tolerated, and left behind by a powerful class of people who will never ever slow down long enough to connect.

I was groomed to join them. And the Celtic chip on my shoulder made me both hate London and crave its approval. Thankfully I walked (or cycled) my way out of that one.

read on . . .

★ **Dea Birkett,** "Folkestone: A Love Affair", **Kate Pullinger,** "The Good Ferry" and **Imogen Stubbs,** "The Undiscovered Road", in *Amazonian: The Penguin Book of Women's New Travel Writing,* **Dea Birkett and Sara Wheeler (ed) (UK: Penguin, 1998).** Three out of eleven narratives from this excellent collection relate to modern England. British travel writer and broadcaster Dea Birkett relishes an escape from metropolitan life only to become dispirited by small town conservatism at the seaside; Canadian-born novelist Kate Pullinger travels along her curriculum vitae, from writer in residence at a men's prison in middle England to becoming a visiting fellow at a Cambridge college; and Northumberland-born actress Imogen Stubbs returns with an unimpressed five-year-old daughter to her grandmother's lakeside home. An evocative spree around parochial England.

★ **Clare Boylan,** "A Journey with my Mother", in *Without a Guide, Katherine Govier (ed)* **(UK: Riversoran Press, 1997/US: Hungry Mind, 1996).** Dublin-born novelist and essayist finally manages to persuade her ageing, self-effacing mother to accompany her to London for a short holiday. The ensuing clash between the two women's fantasies of the capital, and of each other, is described with subtlety, insight and wit. A profoundly moving pre-midlife quest to create some small space for honesty amid the forced illusions of motherhood. London, somehow, does the trick.

★ **Angela Carter,** *Nothing Sacred* **(UK: Virago, 1982) and *Shaking a Leg: Collected Journalism and Writings* (UK: Vintage, 1998/US: Penguin, 1998).** Angela Carter, one of Britain's most celebrated and original contemporary writers and social commentators, died of cancer at the height of her literary powers in 1992, aged 52. These two overlapping collections of essays, articles and reviews, many of them autobiographical, go some way towards demonstrating the passionate engagement, honesty and intellectual acumen of her writing. Snapshots of her early childhood among the coalfields of South Yorkshire are included, with astute reflections on the concept of Englishness as manifested in cities as different as Bradford and Bath, plus a witty look at the Lake District where "the ghosts of poets don't walk – they hike".

★ **Granta,** *London: The Lives of the City* **(UK: Granta 65, Spring 1999).** Granta's usual superlative mix of fiction, memoir and reportage focuses this time on London. Lucretia Stewart describes the harrowing banality of becoming a street crime statistic, Helen Simpson imagines planes dropping from a jam-packed sky, and Doris Lessing and Penelope Lively provide sharp prose images of selected slices of London life.

Helene Hanff, *84 Charing Cross Road* **(UK: Warner, 1982/US: Penguin, 1990).** In the austere late 1940s, an extrovert American author writes to an antiquarian bookshop in London's Charing Cross Road on the trail of some obscure titles. She receives a typically repressed reply from a bookseller who signs himself FPD and a surprisingly touching and enduring correspondence is launched. Sadly, both author and bookshop have passed away.

Irma Kurtz, *Dear London: Notes from the Big City* **(UK: Fourth Estate, 1997).** American journalist Irma Kurtz arrived in London from Paris in 1963, shortly before the explosion of the "swinging Sixties", and never left. In this witty, thoroughly readable memoir she chronicles her relationship with the city she has grown to love, taking us to the areas she has worked and lived in, peopled by the chaotic cast of characters who dotted her life as she gradually found her niche as writer and, most famously, agony aunt, in the fashionable world of glossy women's magazines. Intimately engaged with her subject yet with the unjaundiced eye of the outsider, Kurtz offers many astute and entertaining insights into her chosen home.

Doris Lessing, *Walking in the Shade, 1949–62* **(UK: Fontana, 1998/US: HarperCollins, 1997).** The second volume of Lessing's autobiography spans the London years between her arrival as a single mother from Rhodesia in 1949 and the publication of her most famous novel, *The Golden Notebook*, in 1962. Her love affairs, psychotherapy and increasing disenchantment with the Communist Party are all disclosed with the deft prose, candour and remarkable insight for which she is acclaimed. A seminal piece of writing on London in the 1950s.

Miranda Sawyer, *Park and Ride* **(UK: Little, Brown & Co., 1999).** Feature journalist and Wilmslow girl Miranda Sawyer whoops it up among the multiplexes, heritage centres, B&Q stores, and prestigious hotel nightclubs of suburban England. A surprisingly affectionate portrayal of life in the motorway slipstreams.

Estonia

In the shadow of the bear

Sue Gyford

Sue Gyford became interested in Estonia after making friends with an Estonian student during a high school exchange in the USA. She has since visited the country on two occasions, first for three months as a student of social anthropology and later for almost a year to learn Estonian. Each time she found herself captivated by Estonian hospitality and the fascination of watching a nation and its people unfold and blossom after decades of suppression under Soviet rule. During Sue's second visit she and three American friends spent a weekend as paying guests on a farm on the island of Saaremaa, where they were accompanied almost everywhere by their delighted host.

The world tends to view the Estonian people only in the shadow cast by the big bear looming ominously behind them. In recent years, however, while Russia has whirled from one crisis to another in the hands of an elderly and somewhat drunken leadership, Estonia has been cutting its own path. The new leaders of *this* country are thirty-something businessmen, ruling by the ubiquitous mobile phone rather than the vodka bottle, and far happier dealing with Brussels than with Moscow.

The difference is not just a post-Soviet novelty. Estonians have been ploughing their own furrow for centuries, and shouting – or rather, singing – about it since at least the late 1800s. The establishment of vast song festivals, sometimes with as much as half the population in attendance, was an instrumental feature in the "National Awakening" that first suggested to Estonians that they might achieve independence. Although the Estonian Republic was established for only twenty years before the bloody imposition of Soviet rule, the national ideal persisted. After decades of suppression, it bloomed once more in the singing revolution of the early 1990s. Perseverance and passion, along with the pacifist tactics of holding hands and singing in the face of a crumbling Mother Russia, finally won Estonia's independence once again.

I had first heard accounts of life during the singing revolution thousands of miles away, while a high school exchange student in Utah, USA. Chatting before an aerobics class with another student, Kadi, whom I had taken to be German, I discovered that she was from Estonia. Thus, in the rather random way in which life tends to conduct itself, seeds of curiosity and enthusiasm were sown and bore fruit three years later when I stepped off the tiny Finnair flight from Helsinki to Tallinn. As a student of social anthropology, I had come to conduct three months of anthropological fieldwork (to hang out, take the air, sing a lot, as it transpired), and, in due course, to work out for myself what the Estonians and their visitors figured was so damned special about the place.

Most people's mental checklist of Estonia begins very much like my own, with strained reminiscences of the news stories covering the independence movements in the Baltics in the early 1990s. Partly due to the co-operation of the Baltic states at this time, those who can identify Estonia as distinct from Russia tend to know of it only as one of the Baltic trinity of Estonia, Latvia and Lithuania. At a conference on Human Rights in Kaunas, Lithuania, I debated, drank and danced with students from each of the Baltic nations. The jokes flying around about "warm Estonian men" (from Lithuanian women with irony heavy enough to sink your boots) and "crazy Lithuanians" were enough to put paid to any ideas of Baltic homogeneity.

If you happen not to have chewed the fat with a group of mixed Balts, a quick anecdote will give you the general impression. As the Baltic nations established their independence at the beginning of the decade, one of the most symbolic tasks was to remove the towering statues of Lenin from their city centres. The Estonians hired a modern

Finnish crane, and lifted Vladimir Ilych cleanly, quietly and efficiently from his podium. The Latvians formed a committee. And the Lithuanians massed around the base of the monolith in their thousands, cheering and frantically beating at it with hundreds of hammers, before blasting it into fragments with dynamite.

By the time I first arrived in Tallinn, a lot of water had passed under the bridge since those early heady days of symbolic gesture and hopeful new horizons. The reality of independence had bitten hard and the struggle had begun in earnest to build something lasting out of the initial euphoria. Kadi found me a room in a flat with a local woman, Ella, and her seventeen-year-old daughter, Krista. Ella's husband had been an opera singer who had died young, and now Ella sewed furs in a factory in town, working hard to keep body and soul together. Unlike many Estonians at the time, she had only one job – many people needed several to make ends meet. More typically, every weekend after the snow thawed, she would head off to her mother's house in the countryside and spend the daylight hours working on her land, to return home exhausted on a Sunday night with bags of rhubarb, bottles of milk and bunches of dill, that staple of Estonian cuisine.

The hospitality afforded me by Ella and Krista matched that I found as I knocked, time after time, on strangers' doors throughout the university and the town to ask if they could help me in my newfound occupation of being professionally nosy. Both they and fate guided me into membership of two different choirs and a whole host of friendships. A year and a half later, when I returned to study Estonian at the University of Tartu, I found that I was not the only one to have been so beguiled by the place; other foreigners, like me, had been away and returned; others had never got around to leaving. There was little need to discuss what brought us back as it didn't seem to need explaining – friendship, the countryside, the city of Tallinn, the people, the places, the summer, the winter, whatever. Perhaps the strongest pull of all was being witness to Estonia and its people unfolding and blossoming after so long in the dark.

Being in a state of very rapid transition, the country is full of bemusing contradictions. Sharp-suited businessmen in Mercedes cars whizz blindly past elderly women selling handfuls of cornflowers at the side of the road. Wooden houses with no toilets or running water languish at the feet of multi-storey glass business centres. Maria, one of the friends I made in a choir during my first stay, had, by the time I returned, had a son and moved to a house in the country. She could only be reached by turning down an unmarked track through the trees and, on reaching a clearing, wading through waist-high grass until her home hove into view. She padded barefoot around her new domain with young Jasper on her shoulders and her long hair swinging around her hips, looking every inch the earth mother. I was shown the vegetable patch, from which most of their food would come, the latrine at the end of the garden, the well (which was the only source of water) – and on returning to the house for tea, the gleaming PC in a back room awaiting an imminent Internet connection.

Nowhere are the extremes of this painful game of "catch-up" more visible than in the growing rift between town and country. The fairytale old town of Tartu has been progressively undergoing a well-deserved wash-and-brush-up: buildings painted, roofs repaired, and customer service smiles defrosted. This urban concentration of tourism and trade could not be more different from the beleaguered outlook of the Estonian village. Estonians say that they are close enough to their neighbours if they can see smoke from the chimney. Villages are, therefore, spaced out in a sprawl, and thinly populated. These days they are often presided over by the silently ruminant hulks of abandoned *kolkhoz* (collective farms), the inheritance of the last era of agriculture. The ultra-free market economics of the new state swiftly harvested off agricultural subsidies for its own coffers, all but domestic smallholdings perishing as a result. Young people from the villages no longer want to stay in them, no one wants to move *to* them, and they are emptying steadily and surely.

I spent one afternoon walking around the lakes near Tabivere with Kadi, passing the occasional house from which morose faces would sometimes peer out. On spying the unblinking observers of our passing, Kadi remarked that it was probably the event of their week. Her suspicions were confirmed when an elderly gentleman sporting a battered hat and driving a blindingly yellow old banger chugged up the road and drew to a halt at our side. "So who are you then?" he enquired. "Have you just moved into the area – or are you researchers?" Such, it seems, is the fate of the Estonian village, abandoned by all except the sociologists.

If the countryside of the mainland is a time-stalling kind of place, the islands of Saaremaa and Hiiumaa are where even the country folk go to chill out. For fifty years Saaremaa was one of the most westerly points of the Soviet Union. This signified two things: it was a long way from Russia (relatively speaking) and it housed a missile early warning system. The latter meant that even mainlanders needed special permission to visit; islanders needed permission to swim (lest they try to cross the Baltic to Sweden).

One spring weekend, finding our brains full to bursting with Estonian grammar, I and three fellow students packed our bags and hit the long winding road to Saaremaa. My American companions, Cori, Julie and Judy, were part of a random batch of the "foreigners" who turn up in Tartu every year, often returning to the land their grandparents fled during the war, either to perfect or to take their first steps in the language of their forebears. We rented rooms on a homestead just outside the island's capital, Kuuresaare. Reaching the farm necessitated a bumpy taxi-ride through a flat, boulder-strewn landscape of such vivid green that one's eyes almost vibrated in their sockets. It transpired that the taxi driver was an old mate of our host, Toivu, who waved us up to our rooms on the first floor while he caught up on the latest gossip from town.

We enquired about the possibility of a sauna and some beer to go with it. As in Finland, saunas are a staple of Estonian life. The former was definitely on, and the latter off, the agenda. We resigned ourselves to a sober night and followed Toivu for a quick tour of his domain. Trailing unprepared to the back of the house, we stood aside as he creaked a door open and stepped after him into the steamy, sweet-smelling gloom. On the right was a horse, and behind it a pig. Chickens flounced about indiscriminately and cows munched along the left-hand wall. And, in the furthest dimmest corner sat Toivu's wife, silently carding wool in the dark. Slightly embarrassed, we stepped forward as bidden to see a day-old calf in the stall next to her, tottering shakily before its uninvited audience. After much polite nodding (at both Toivu's wife and the calf), we bundled out again, blinking in the sun as Toivu pushed the door shut, leaving his wife carding away by herself in the blackness of the communal barn.

While the sauna heated up during the afternoon, we wandered about through dandelion-carpeted fields, returning in the early evening. Dinner was served in our guest loft, Toivu's wife making her second appearance of the day to deck the table with bowls of home-grown vegetables and small slivers of meat, before disappearing meekly downstairs. Toivu himself sat with us, ate with us, whipped out the vodka and started talking. He showed us album after album of family photographs and told us of his loneliness: "All this land and no one to speak to." Sadly enough, none of us had the front (or the Estonian) to mention his wife eating alone downstairs and no doubt awaiting our dirty plates.

His hospitality knew no bounds. It transpired that he had sent his friend the taxi driver to bring us a few bottles of beer from Kuuresaare. Furthermore, he had been down to a distant shed to siphon off some of his own home-brew into a foot-wide wooden tankard, where it now swilled about milkily in the anteroom to the sauna, awaiting our pleasure. The Saaremaa Brewery's beer is renowned throughout Estonia for its quality and potency. Toivu's own version looked rather like Horlicks but was rather less conducive to a peaceful night. He had also taken the liberty of inviting his three sons over for the evening to share in the beer, the sauna and the good times. As on so many occasions, our linguistic ineptitude, combined with Estonian reserve, combined to save us. The evening passed more demurely than should be humanly possible when several adults are dressed in steaming towels and absolutely lashed about the gills.

The rest of our stay passed with the same bemusing mix of generous hospitality and downright optimism on the part of our host. Toivu appeared at nine the next morning, sauntering across the lawn with the tankard, terrifyingly refilled. He volunteered to drive us around the island, showing off to the locals by taking us all to dinner in a minuscule local café that served only anonymous lumps of reformed meat and potatoes. Finally, as we packed to leave, he refused to take us back to Kuuresaare, demanding instead that we stay another night, free of charge. How could we refuse?

France

Whose vacation is this anyway?

Joy V. Harris

When Joy V. Harris treated her two nieces to ten days in Paris, the trip proved not quite the "holiday of a lifetime" they had hoped for. Fortunately it hasn't put her off making further travel plans. She still hopes to visit every continent and all fifty states of her native USA. Joy currently resides in Berkeley, California, where she is working on her first novel, supported by jobs as a consultant in financial systems and as a real estate developer. This Paris account was first published in *Go Girl! The Black Women's Book of Travel and Adventure* (see p.652).

June of 95 marked a proud moment in the life of my niece, Ronya. She had accomplished one of the most revered achievements in African American life: graduation from high school and acceptance into college. What better gift to share with an African American princess than a guided tour of my most beloved city, Paris. For expanding her view of the world, Paris seemed to be the perfect place to start.

Paris in June. The very phrase brought up an image of cosy cafés and street musicians, quaint shops on narrow streets, centuries-old cathedrals, museums, and gardens in full bloom. And I haven't mentioned fashion and food. The last category alone would be worth the journey.

195

I had extended the invitation for this ten-day excursion the previous Thanksgiving, giving me more than six months to plan the details. Her mother agreed that this was an opportunity of a lifetime and would pay the airfare as a graduation present. I would cover other transportation, hotel costs, entrance fees, and dinner every night. When my other niece, twenty-one-year-old Helesha, got wind of the plans, she refused to be left out. The three of us would take Paris by storm.

I wasted no time, spending hours at local bookstores reading travel books. I spoke to everyone I knew who had been to Paris in recent years and even learned how to get on the Internet to find the best sights and locations. We would stay in an area I knew on the Left Bank in the sixth *arrondissement,* not far from the Sorbonne and the Luxembourg Gardens. We would have easy access to everything via Boulevards St Michel and St Germain, with the Louvre and Notre Dame a mile away.

After a flawless red-eye flight from Boston, we arrived in Paris shortly after noon; by 3.30, the girls were asleep in our Art Deco hotel. I napped for about half an hour, but even in my sleep my skin tingled, knowing that Paris was just outside the window, waiting beyond the balcony. I let the girls continue to snooze as I slipped into the street, literally dancing the four blocks to Rue de Seine. I bought a scrumptious chocolate fudge and bit into it. The Paris of my dreams came back to me; it felt just as I remembered it from my last visit. After pressing my nose against some antiques shop windows, I ducked into a *brasserie* and bought some bread and cheese for the girls' late lunch.

They were still asleep. Jet lag, I supposed. I sat on the balcony and ate, gazing at geraniums filling the apartment windows across the way. At ten o'clock, when the sun was beginning to fade away, Ronya turned over and smiled and asked about something to eat. By eleven, the three of us were cruising the streets of Paris on foot looking for a McDonald's. I let the choice of dinner pass this time, especially when I realized that the golden arches were just three blocks from Notre Dame. So, at midnight on our first day, we were walking along the Seine watching couples in the glow of the lights shining on the cathedral's buttresses. Paris had them hooked, or so I thought.

The next morning I woke up late and bathed quietly so as not to wake the sleeping beauties. The Luxembourg Gardens were just two blocks away; I decided to have a croissant and hot chocolate by the fountain and people-watch from a warm, comfortable vantage point. How could I be so selfish, I thought, sitting there so close to heaven and let my nieces miss this lovely scene. I forced myself back to the hotel a little past noon.

"So, what should we do today, Eiffel Tower or the Louvre?" I asked, spreading maps on the bedcovers while my nieces stirred beneath them.

"I'm a little hungry," Helesha answered, "but this is vacation. We really don't have to do anything."

"What's at the Louvre?" Ronya yawned. The stunned look on my face must have signalled that she'd better follow that up with something more. "I've seen it in a book somewhere, but I don't know what it is, or what's in it."

I started to explain to the two high school graduates that some of the world's finest art could be found there and that the building itself was once a palace. The only thing that got a hint of interest was the *Mona Lisa*. *Winged Victory* was pretty easy, right up the main stairway. Then, along with hundreds of other tourists, we crowded around *Venus de Milo*. The girls were smiling now, the Louvre had them hooked, or so I thought, until I found out they were laughing at the gum they had left at the base of another statue. I gave them that girl-I'll-kill-you look that has been passed down in my family for generations, and they retrieved it. After a few more notable paintings and sculptures got only a cool response, I decided to get the *Mona Lisa* over with.

"It's so much smaller than I thought. Why is this so famous?" Ronya asked, perplexed.

We had a brief art history discussion over bottled water and a croissant. They shrugged off my comments about the confident gaze, the use of colour, and the approach to portraiture. It was still early, so I suggested a stroll up the Champs Elysées, or at least to the Tuileries gardens, which were right next door.

"If we have to walk, never mind. We walked here, we've walked around the Louvre, and we have to walk back. Let's just go back to the hotel."

For dinner that evening the only thing we could agree upon was pizza. We found a pizza café on St Germain where the food was decent and cheap and a Heineken cost the same as a Coke. This place would become our second home.

"What do we do tomorrow?"

"We could go to Versailles Palace or Monet's garden at Giverny, maybe get out of the city," I offered.

"Shopping. It's time to shop," they said in unison.

By Thursday I had devised a strategy to satisfy my Paris sightseeing addiction. I would rise in silence and sneak into the bathroom to write in my journal, then take off for breakfast in the Luxemburg Gardens and some close-by sites. I'd then double back to the hotel at around one, wake up the girls and wait for them get dressed until three, then we would head out. Today it would be shopping near Boulevard Raspail.

The lesson on prices turned into more than just calculating exchange rates. I had to agree with the girls that this stuff was expensive, even in the less chic shops. Shoes were seventy to ninety dollars and a simple T-shirt was close to forty.

"Where is the mall?" Ronya asked.

"Galeries Lafayette is not too far, and there is a bargain department store along the way."

We arrived at the department store, Tati, just about the time office workers get out of work. Bedlam. People were packed in the narrow isles speaking very brisk French or Algerian or Chinese with a French accent and with a more aggressive approach to shopping than I had experienced even in New York. We were badly battered as we considered purchases. At one point I looked over my shoulder and caught pitifully bewildered looks on my nieces' faces and suggested they go outside while I paid for our purchases. I went to rescue them with a couple of extra gifts, cheap umbrellas. It had begun to rain. We gave up on shopping and returned to the hotel in silence.

After a late dinner that consisted of nine-dollar sundaes at the Haagen Daz café, they finally let me have it full force.

"We came here for a vacation," Ronya started. "When I go on vacation, we sleep late, then go to the beach. And everybody speaks English and everything is real cheap. It's not like that here."

I began to explain that we were not in a resort or back home. We were in Paris. This a place where you see historical things you've read about and learn a little about another culture by watching, listening, and being curious. Then it was Helesha's turn.

"These are just old buildings to us. The people here are mean and try to run you over in those little cars. We came here to shop and we can't do that without more money; we don't know where to go and we can't ask anyone because they don't know what we're talking about."

And then the final blow.

"We were thinking we should leave, maybe go to London or just go home." Ronya nodded in agreement as Helesha spoke.

Go home? Leave Paris? After three thousand dollars and three thousand miles? I closed my eyes and began breathing deeply to push away the vision of tossing two young black bodies over the balcony. I checked my tone of voice and began what I thought was a reasonable defence.

"How could you leave Paris after only three days? You haven't even seen half of it. We are staying right where James Baldwin and Langston Hughes met friends in cafés. Josephine Baker sang not far from here. Friends of mine who are artists had studios and jazz clubs in the next block. You haven't even given it a chance."

"Those people are all dead. We have given it a chance," Ronya pouted. "We'd rather just chill." End of discussion.

I awoke on Friday depressed. In Paris! Unthinkable. After going through my normal routine, including some scorched expletives about these two young sisters in my journal, I returned from my garden breakfast and walk to find them still sleeping. I threw some francs on the table and wrote a note that I'd be back at three.

The closest travel agents were in the area near the Opera House and I walked toward them with a vengeance, talking out loud to myself. How could anyone not love Paris? Couldn't they see that there was life outside of Roxbury? You can take the child out of the ghetto, but . . .

The third agent spoke better English than the others and I began to explain my problem. As I asked about making reservations to return to the States early or taking a ferry to London the next day, tears began to roll down my cheeks. She looked at me sympathetically or maybe she thought I was as crazy as I was beginning to feel. We came up with two plans of escape, but I would have to make a decision and confirm arrangements by the end of the day. I had an hour. I jogged past the Louvre, across the Pont Carrosel, up Rue des Sts Peres to Rue de Seine. I walked the rest of the way to the hotel and arrived breathless to find the room empty. I sat on the balcony and just as I began to feel a twinge of panic the two of them burst into the room, laughing, with arms full of shopping bags. For the first time in days, I was thrilled to see them.

"We found some good places to shop, up around the University," Ronya gushed, showing me the outfits and gifts she had bought.

"Yeah," Helesha said, unpacking her wares. "We walked in the store and they started talking in French. We stared at them and they laughed and started trying to talk in English. I can understand almost anybody if I'm trying to shop." They pulled out skirts, jackets, scarves, and barrettes purchased at some of the very places I had passed on my solo adventures.

Relieved that they were alive, and jealous that they were having a better time without me, I explained where I had been and the choices we had. We decided to compromise with a trip to London but to give me two more days in Paris.

"We think we can stand it two more days," Helesha smiled, "and anyway, I've got to bring back a picture of the Eiffel Tower."

For the next two days my routine changed. I got up and out early and went to see Giverny one day and the Rodin Museum and the flea market at St Sulpice the next. I'm not sure what the girls did, but we met for a decent dinner each evening and finally found something that impressed them: the Eiffel Tower at night. I even got Ronya to try something other than hamburgers and pizza. I figured a ham and cheese crepe was at least a step in the right culinary direction.

London turned out to be delightful. Some brothers hit on the girls in English our first night, and we found blocks upon blocks of shopping on Praed Avenue. Somehow we squeezed in Buckingham Palace, Westminster Abbey, and the Houses of Parliament to appease me. Ronya and Helesha liked the city so much that they began planning to return the next summer.

On the flight home I pondered it all. True, they had acted a bit spoiled. On the other hand, maybe I had been heavy-handed in wanting to expose them to the things that touched my soul. But how would I have viewed Paris if I had taken Spanish and African American studies instead of French and World History? How would I have done if my first visit had been with a guide who had her own view of what was important instead of letting me discover Paris for myself?

I ended up seeing that it hadn't been such a bad vacation after all, just two different ones – theirs and mine.

Cycling on the French Riviera

Carla King

Carla King, a San Francisco-based travel and technology writer, was 28 when she first embarked on a solo motorcycle trip around France. She hasn't stopped travelling since. In 1993 she moved to Nice and wrote a guidebook to mountain biking the French Riviera's Alpes-Maritimes, followed by a cycling adventure through West Africa. Since then she has undertaken two major motorbike journeys, across America and China (see our China chapter) and is currently planning an epic journey around India. Her travel experiences are also recounted in words and digital photos on the Internet at *www.verbum.com/jaunt*.

I stood on the edge of the cliff and surveyed the terrain I'd covered that April morning. The Mediterranean sparkled blue only 15km away as the crow flies, but I'd cycled 40km along smooth, curving, black-paved, lonely roads to get from sea-level to my 1000-metre-high perch. Behind me, in the distance, were the snow-capped Alps. The guys who passed me on their racing bikes had told me they often go there on weekends, after the snow has melted. Unlike these kilometre-counting, colour-clad fanatics, I was happy to stop in the field of grass and wild flowers atop this protruding, round-faced cliff the Niçoises call a *baou*, and call it a day.

I was loving this time I was spending in Nice and the towns and countryside around it, much more than I had on my previous trips to France. Soon I realised that being on a bicycle was the key to my current experience. Besides my own sense of personal accomplishment and well-being, the French, being cycling fanatics, almost always treated me with respect and kindness – despite my less-than-perfect grasp of the language.

I was biking in the *arrière pays*, or "back-country", which is situated behind the Riviera, in front of the Alps, and southeast of Provence-proper. In the tiny villages perched in the hills, though, it was Provence. After the first climb of the morning I'd stop at a little café to rest, eat something, and contemplate the Alps to the north, the Mediterranean to the south. It was just me and my mountain bike, the trusty five-year-old Rock.Hopper I'd modified with suspension and touring racks for previous, more ambitious tours. The children ran their hands over it, pointing out my California license sticker, and asked me questions about America while I sat under the perpetual sunshine of the Côte d'Azur. The waitress worried over me. "You should eat more than that, *chèrie!*" she said, slipping me an extra portion. "Think of the energy you will use." I could almost hear the Italian mamma in the accents of many of these village women, insisting, "*Mangez! Mangez!*"

It had taken all morning to get to my perch on the cliff and from now on it was downhill. I felt pretty proud of myself. After my last tour, a three-week stint in Switzerland three years before, I hadn't done much bike touring. In California I had been considered a mountain-biking dilettante by my more athletic friends. But now I was doing three or four day-trips a week from Nice, of forty to a hundred kilometres each, navigating by contour maps to find the forgotten roads and tracks, preferably leading to a castle ruin or an old fort.

"Aren't you scared riding around by yourself in the woods?" a French woman asked me. It could be lonely on the trails and the fire roads, but I was never frightened. Occasionally, teenage boys on motorcycles would race past, barely glancing at me, and the few others I met were usually busy collecting mushrooms or herbs. They would give me chanterelles and puffballs and fill my packs with leaves and berries to make a tisane, good for strength.

It was the solitude I liked about biking. I listened to my body work, I had time to think, time to enjoy the abundant natural beauty, and time to contemplate the history of this area. Each mountain has its tiny village *perché* with fountain, church and a cobblestoned square. Here time seems to have stopped; women in black scarves tread slowly along in groups, carrying bags of produce from the marketplace; old men play *pétanque*, a form of boules, on a flat dirt court. Others sit at the nearby café and drink beer or pastis, the perpetual column of smoke from their Gitanes curling up past their hat brims.

To reach some of the more remote villages I had to take a train into the hills. The controllers were bored and never minded that my French was bad or that sometimes the train wasn't authorized to carry a bike. A lot of them were cyclists themselves and were anxious to give advice on the best roads, the best areas, the best bakeries and crêperies (cyclists eat a lot). After two or three hours of pedalling through the mountains I'd descend to the platform, the only passenger at some deserted station, and start my journey back to Nice.

The hills were a relief from the city, which I loved but sometimes found tedious. At Nice train station men would freely offer their opinion on my physical appearance: "I don't like women with muscles", one might say, looking me up and down disapprovingly. Another would point out my legs to someone else and grin: "Look at those legs . . . *très musclées.*" The men in Nice are not shy.

Interestingly enough, I was hassled less when I wore skintight biking gear – ten times sexier than the baggy shorts and T-shirts I wore riding around town. I attribute this difference in attitude to image. When I was dressed in professional biking gear, men saw me as an athlete first, a woman second.

In Nice I had a room in a villa converted into apartments, rented out to students and long-term tourists by Madame and Monsieur Dupuy. This couple immediately became like family; Madame Dupuy helped to correct my French and Monsieur Dupuy, always the clown, taught me all the words that weren't in the dictionary. After telling them about my day I'd run down to the beach to take a quick swim before going out in the evening.

Nice has many good clubs and bars, including, for foreigners, three Irish pubs, a Dutch pub, and a big American-style place called *Chez Wayne's* in the old section that attracts a young rowdy crowd. A cosier place is *Jonathan's*, a basement club where Jonathan, an expatriate

American hippie, sings and plays his guitar – mostly American and British folk songs – and lets French bands try their hand at Bruce Springsteen and The Beatles. The club feels like a corner-bar, which made me comfortable there alone.

The old section also has markets and a good selection of cafés and small shops selling quiches, snacks and sandwiches. *Bar René-Socca*, popular with everyone from students to business people, is cheapest for lunch when everyone relaxes for a while with their *socca* or pizza, washed down with a beer or glass of the local rosé, always served ice-cold. But here, like everywhere else, I found it too easy to meet French men, and too difficult to meet French women. For one thing, women seem to prefer jogging or aerobics classes to cycling. And their culture is still traditional enough to keep them occupied with most of the housework even though many work outside the home. They just don't have time to sit around in cafés unless they schedule it into their day. I had one French friend I'd worked with in Lyon several years before; another brief friendship with a woman I'd met who worked at a tourist office; and I met two women, a mother and daughter, by trading English-for-French lessons. But we were always working our meeting times around their husbands' or boyfriends' schedules.

During a slow month my landlord, Monsieur Dupuy, and I often went to the railway station in the mornings to meet the trains from Paris and Rome to recruit tenants for his other apartments, but many people were too suspicious to take us up on it. Monsieur Dupuy would lean on the open door of his Renault, smoking, squinting under his cap, while I tried to convince people that we weren't working a scam to rob them, but truly had a nice, reasonably priced apartment to offer as the tourist season was slow.

My bedroom with shared bathroom cost 2400F per month, and though I thought this was a bit steep, the other foreigners I met were envious of my deal. The Dupuys' place was behind locked gates in a quiet residential neighbourhood on a hillside only a five-minute walk from the beach. The back garden was shaded by orange and peach trees, and we ate at the tables by the flower beds. I made friends with a couple from Vancouver who stayed there for a few weeks, and it was always fun to play *pétanque* with everyone in the evenings before dinner.

Though I lived in one of the safer areas of town, someone mangled the cable lock on my bike, and if they'd had bigger snippers they'd have owned it. In town, even small towns in the hills, I locked my bike with two locks. A friend at school locked his with three. Petty theft is an everyday occurrence and violent crime is not uncommon.

Theft, harassment and violence is most apparent around Nice's primary tourist attraction, the Promenade des Anglais – a wide sidewalk built next to the three-metre-high sea-wall that stretches the several kilometres between the airport and Nice's shipping port. The promenade, overlooking the town's stony beaches, is where everyone walks, jogs, exercises their poodles, or just hangs out. I wanted to rest on one of the promenade's blue chairs that the city has so thoughtfully provided, or on its benches, or on the wide edge of the cement sea wall. I wanted to stare out to sea, to write, to read . . . but the men who hang out there are relentless. My first day in Nice, I had only taken a few steps on the promenade when I was approached by a man. "Are you Swedish?" he asked in English. I shook my head and kept walking. "Danish?" he continued. "English, American, German, Italian, Spanish?" he persisted. "Why won't you talk to me?" he pouted. Finally I replied in French, "I want to be alone." He stopped with a scowl and I continued on my way. One minute later: "Hello. You are American, I can tell." Another persistent fellow.

Every foreign woman I met had the same experience, no matter what nationality or mode of dress. French women seem to have the best defence system against excessive harassment. I was advised by a local: "When they look at you, don't ignore them. Before they speak to you, look back at them like they're the lowest life-form on the planet." It's cold but it works. Being polite has no effect.

I would not walk on the promenade late at night, though it is well-lit. At that time the guys who hang out there are often high or drunk. During my stay I saw three knife fights, one of which was over a girl who'd walked by – they were fighting over who got to say hello to her first.

This seemed to be more of a problem in Nice than in the other towns in the Côte d'Azur. I visited all the coastal cities between Cannes and Menton, and occasionally crossed the Italian border to bike in the hills behind Ventimiglia – an entirely different world.

All in all, my bicycle seemed the perfect method of transportation. I could throw it on a train going to Antibes, and ride to the

Picasso Museum. Or to Menton to see the Cocteau Museum. Everywhere I went people were nice to me because of it. "*Courage!*" they would shout as I puffed up a hill. I never lacked a subject of conversation. I learned all the French words for bicycle parts and tools. I passed cars sitting in city traffic jams. I could take long trips or short trips or just give up and take the next train home.

In the end I was sorry to leave. Even after six months I had not seen all the perched villages, I hadn't seen all the museums and forts, nor had I begun to look at the caves and important archeological sites. I hadn't gone to Corsica as I had intended. (An eight-hour ferry ride away, it's reputed to be a hiker's and mountain-biker's paradise.) Next time I will stay with the Dupuys again. I'll go to the Alliance Française and study for a language certificate. I'll ride my bike to all the caves. I'll see the perfumeries I missed in Grasse and go to the culinary arts museum in Biot. Maybe I'll take sailing lessons or rent a kayak, go horseback riding, learn to hang-glide or para-sail. Or I'll start a women's bicycling club. Back at home now, I find myself flipping through the brochures and guidebooks as eagerly as if I'd never seen the place.

read on . . .

Émilie Carles, *Wild Herb Soup* **(UK: Indigo, 1996).** An inspiring and moving autobiography of a girl born and raised in the remote Alpine valley of the Névache near Briançon in the early years of the twentieth century. As well as giving an interesting account of peasant life, it records the development of social conscience and an extraordinary moral toughness as Émilie becomes aware of the brutality and harshness of peasant life, sees her brother die in World War I, experiences Resistance in World War II and finally finds herself, as an old lady, leading the campaign to stop the desecration of her beautiful natal valley by the construction of an autoroute.

Dorothy Carrington, *Granite Island* **(UK: Penguin 1984/US: o/p).** A fascinating and immensely comprehensive book, combining the writer's personal experiences with an evocative prtrayal of historical figures and events. By far the best study of Corsica written in English.

Karen Connelly, *One Room in a Castle: Letters from Spain, France and Greece* **(1995; UK: Black Swan, 1997).** "It's possible that I will write only postcards from this place, because the image on the card will show you that at least the exterior is beautiful", writes Canadian author Connelly of her temporary home beside medieval ramparts in a ghetto neighbourhood of Avignon. What follows are brief, beautifully composed and deceptively telling vignettes of an outsider's life in this famous medieval city. Her disconsolate loneliness, her chance affair with an Algerian man, her brushes with racism and her pleasure in the company of a gypsy woman neighbour are penned as short but beautifully composed prose pieces.

Janet Flanner, Natalie Danesi-Murray (ed), *Darlinghissima: Letters to a Friend* (UK: Rivers Oram Press, 1988/US: Harcourt Brace, 1986). From 1925 to 1975, the American correspondent, Janet Flanner wrote her letter from Paris for *The New Yorker* magazine. Resolutely European in outlook, Flanner's authoritative observations on the cultural, social and political life of Europe made her one of the most respected journalists of her day.

Gisele Halimi, *Milk for the Orange Tree* (UK/US: Quartet Books, 1991). Born in Tunisia, the daughter of an Orthodox Jewish family, Halimi ran away to Paris to study law, emerging as defender and advocate of women's rights, Algerian FLN fighters, and a host of other unpopular causes. A gutsy autobiography.

Gertrude Stein, *The Autobiography of Alice B Toklas* (UK: Penguin, 1989/US: Vintage, 1990). The goings-on at Stein's famous salon in Paris. The most accessible of her works, written from the point of view of Stein's long-time lover, gives an amusing account of the Parisian art and literary scene of the 1910s and 1920s.

Gillian Tindall, *Célestine: Voices from a French Village* (reprint; UK: Minerva, 1996/US: Henry Holt, 1997). Intrigued by some nineteenth-century love letters left behind in the house she has bought in Chassignolles, Berry, Tindall researches the history of the village back to the 1840s. She produces a meticulous, thoughtful and moving protrait of rural French life and its slow but dramatic transformation. A well-written, warm-hearted and unique serving of social history.

Freda White, *Three Rivers of France* (UK: Pavilion Books, 1992/US: Faber & Faber, 1984). Freda White spent a great deal of time in France in the 1950s before tourism came along to the backwater communities that were her interest. An evocative book, slipping in the history and culture painlessly, if not always accurately.

Gambia

Love through open eyes

Carina Marong

Carina Marong was working as an office manager in Scotland when she first went to The Gambia on a package holiday. There, she met Lie, a charming hotel receptionist, with whom she fell in love. This is the story of Carina's first trip to Lie's family home in rural Gambia, days before their marriage. Carina and Lie now live in Brighton, England, and have recently had their first child.

Lie started a conversation, but I kept my eyes fixed on the sea. Having already run the gamut of hopeful Gambian men since arriving on the beach, I was in no mood to indulge yet another handsome flirt. Then he made me laugh and I turned to look at him and saw a supremely confident man, whose eyes were intelligent and full of life. There was none of the "you're white and have money and I'm poor and black" attitude that so many men exude. Instinct prompted me to trust him but it would take many months, and many tests, before I could allow myself to do so.

There are women tourists who think that offering a steady stream of beer and cigarettes is a fair exchange for a holiday fling with a beautiful young man. At least they have some notion that a deal is being struck. However, those who are looking for a serious relationship should beware. Plenty of men view holiday romances as the quickest means of getting a foreign visa, and their motives soon become transparent. I'd always thought that the women who insisted on bringing their young lovers back home with them were rather sad. I saw one TV documentary that featured a woman in her forties who had married a nineteen-year-old Gambian who spoke no English, had no exportable skills, but was clearly out for whatever he could get. It was love, she insisted – no man had made her feel this good. Yet my enduring impression was of a thin and wretched-looking boy, sitting shivering under a woolly jumper while he watched his lover tell the camera that things had not really worked out and that he seemed somehow "different" to the boy she had met in Africa. You just knew his return flight had already been booked. The same, I vowed, would never happen to me.

I returned to Scotland. Lie promised to write first, but I feared he would meet someone off the next flight and forget. Then the letters started arriving. Instead of requests for expensive electrical items, he sent thoughtful words and gifts, along with pressed flowers still holding the scent of Africa. We wrote and phoned constantly, and before long I was flying back. It was on that second visit that he insisted we declare our faithfulness to each other in a traditional engagement ceremony. The few doubts that remained were beginning to slip away.

Three trips followed, each one undertaken with a list of mental questions about our relationship and the extent to which we could adapt to the other's culture. Lie took the issue as seriously as I did. It mattered that our answers were convincing.

A year later we agreed to be married in a simple civil ceremony in Banjul. While my friends knew of my decision and were supportive, I didn't dare tell my family in advance of the ceremony. They knew me to be impetuous and often foolish in love, and I didn't want to risk getting married with their active opposition. The shock I caused them was inexcusable, but I'll always be grateful for the way they rallied around, giving Lie and I much support and love.

A wedding trip

I had been on Gambian soil for 48 hours, barely long enough to wet my toes in the Atlantic, yet there I was at Banjul Ferry Terminal, bound for a village in the interior and an introduction to my future in-laws. Once on board the ferry, we bought violently coloured drinks and a bag of cakes from one of the omnipresent sellers. An elder in grubby white robes boomed Koranic prayers through a megaphone and drinks sellers wobbled along the ferry deck, keeping a grip on their trays of goods as we swung heavily round into Barra harbour, narrowly avoiding the naked children dive-bombing off the end of the pier.

At Barra, it seemed there were hundreds of bush taxis honking their horns to attract passengers heading into the provinces. We scouted for a car heading due east, into the rice fields, where Lie's village lies. The taxis sagged visibly beneath the weight of bulky packages tied to the roof with blue twine. We found a rusty jeep going our way and peered in the back seat, meeting the mildly curious gazes of what seemed like hundreds of faces.

"Get in," Lie said cheerfully.

"But where?", I muttered as I trod clumsily over chickens, a bundle of dead fish and bumpy toes. Everyone smiled graciously at me and I perched on the spare tyre. Lie followed, squeezing his six-foot frame into a corner, and with an alarming grinding of gears and a sudden lurch, we were off, hurtling out of Barra in a cloud of red dust.

As the dust worsened, everyone vanished under scarves. There was not a spare inch of space, but we adopted a philosophical attitude to our discomfort – I because I am a spoilt European to whom this was an adventure; the Gambians because there is no option, and they're not easily fazed.

By midday, dust had penetrated every cavity and we had our first diversion. A man flung his frail frame at the taxi, desperately begging us to carry his sick wife to hospital. It seemed there was no space for a small bag of rice, let alone an elderly woman in great pain. I was sure that a journey in our bone-rattling taxi could only make her condition worse, but the taxi represented her only hope of survival.

We all squeezed together a bit tighter, and the taxi rattled on until Lie spotted his village from the crest of the hill. We unfolded ourselves from the taxi and were met with chirrups of welcome from all sides. Lie's family homestead was enormous, indicative of the wealth his father once commanded as a successful groundnut farmer. Dwellings encircled an open clearing and Lie's parents welcomed us in the main house. Tall and charming, they smiled broadly and the family resemblance was clear.

Lie's mum is his father's third wife. She bore eight of the fifteen children in the family, of which Lie was their first together. As we were talking, somebody pushed through the crowd at the doorway and planted a chicken in my lap. Lie leaned over and whispered that it was to be slaughtered for a feast that night in my honour. I felt mean posing for photos with the unsuspecting bird, which trembled slightly as it was lifted by its ankles and dragged away to the pot.

Though I know only a few words of Mandinka, the warm words of welcome needed no translation. Lie's mother constantly pressed my hand between her own, happy to have lived long enough to see her first son married. I smiled and nodded at everyone, grateful for their kindness. Still, I knew that Lie's family had silent questions of their own – about whether I was good enough for their son; whether I had an honourable character; whether I would be a loving and honest wife. Lie's brother, in particular, watched my actions closely, and although it didn't make me nervous, I was glad they seemed to approve of the match.

We were taken to our room for a much-needed shower before a tour of the compound. Lie's father's three wives share a house, and I often wondered how they felt about each other: were they offended when a new wife came along, did they plan their babies at different times and was there much rivalry? Lie assured me that there was usually much debate within the extended family before an established wife could be reconciled to a new one. Often, the prospect of bickering and fierce resentment at home led men to stick to monogamy.

I had gone to the Gambia pitifully ignorant of Islam and innately mistrustful of organised religion, but found that far from being oppressive and restrictive, Islam is a very personal religion. With no priest to mediate, the interaction between God and believer is direct. I also found that Islam, as it is practised there, affords women the highest respect. It expressly forbids abuse of any kind towards women, and I sensed neither fear nor subservience in the females I encountered. Indeed, the easy banter exchanged between men and women indicated a surprising degree of gender equality. I remember how I used to remind Lie constantly that I was a Western woman, with freedoms and rights I would never relinquish. Gradually, we rid one another of our preconceptions – he now accepts that alcohol per se is not evil, and I have conquered the prejudices I held about him as a black man and a Muslim.

In Lie's household, meals were arranged by rota, with the first wife responsible for the breakfast, the second for lunch and Lie's mum for dinner. She showed me how it was coming along, and I saw my chicken bubbling away in a stew of spices and onions. After dinner, we sipped green tea with the family before going to bed, lying down on a mattress stuffed with straw. Though I was tired after the long trip, sleep escaped me utterly. Some species of rodent life was performing gymnastics in the roof thatch and a high-spirited crowd milled past our hut on the way to the village wrestling ground. Their roars of approval set off the wild dogs, and all this incredible noise filled me with a sense that I was in a very alien place. I wondered how anyone ever slept here; Africa is never, ever truly silent. How, I wondered, would Lie adapt to life in a Scottish village, where for hours at a time, it is so quiet I wonder if I have gone deaf?

In the morning, all the village elders came to see us off, shaking hands and offering marital advice. The rounded-belly gestures needed no translation and we duly promised to be as fruitful as we could. Most of the family accompanied us through the village, dropping away until only a handful were left with us beneath the baobab tree, waiting for the bush taxi to arrive. Near Banjul, we rounded a bend and saw mudflats dotted with tiny fishing boats and the most exquisite birds I had ever seen: cormorants, pelicans, egrets and storks shimmering in the twilight. The scene radiated serenity and I knew, with the certainty one can only sense deep in the gut, that I would go to my wedding in three days' time with no doubts whatsoever.

Now three years on, I think that our long-distance courtship was important to building a strong marriage. Such things bring you closer, testing your determination, trust and commitment. Neither one of us has changed who we are, and any initial hiccups were due more to my reluctance to cede a solitary life than to cultural differences.

Lie is the same man he was in Africa, and has adapted to British life with an ease that astounded me. He found work at the airport as a catering supervisor, and he keeps in touch with his family by phone or fax every few weeks. As unlikely as it might have once seemed to our family and friends, our marriage works well, and is kept strong by scrupulous honesty and constant communication.

Lie and Africa have enriched me, and we hope to spend our old age under the mango trees, with our children ensuring that the links to both cultures stay strong.

read on . . .

Rosemary Long, *Together Under the Baobab Tree: A New Life in Africa* (UK: Verulam, 1994). Rosemary Long enjoyed a comfortable existence as a Glasgow journalist, divorced with three grown-up children, when she fell in love with Ray, twenty years her junior, while on holiday in the Gambia. Here the cliché more or less ends. Based on her "Into Africa" columns in the *Glasgow Herald*, Long has written a refreshingly straightforward, touching and often funny account of her subsequent marriage to Ray, her ready acceptance into his family and the life they have built together in the African bush.

Ghana

Hard currency

Lesley Downer

Lesley Downer was a Japan specialist until, under the guidance of a Ghanaian boyfriend, she discovered Africa. In this extract of a piece first published in *Amazonian* (see p.230) she describes her six-month stay in Ghana, travelling in the shadow of K, an aspiring politician, who returns determined to influence the destiny of his country. Their relationship begins to fray under the strain of their diverging perspectives and eventually Downer returns alone to England. They have remained friends, however, and still visit each other, although, as Downer writes, "Every time I meet him, he is more African and the gulf between us grows deeper and deeper. " About Ghana, she continues, "But to this day, when I step out of the plane and my foot touches the red earth of Africa, I feel the old surge of exhilaration and joy."

Lesley Downer is the author of several books about Japan, including *On the Narrow Road to the Deep North*, which was shortlisted for the Thomas Cook Travel Book Award. She has written and presented a series on Japanese cooking for the BBC and now works as a journalist, dividing her time between New York and London.

"Hey, everyone, this is ma woman! Meet ma woman!" It was that lethargic moment when daytime turns to evening. On the terrace of *Kin's Hotel* on the edge of Accra, a group of men sat arguing and laughing over beers. The light had faded but the heat was still intense, heavy with the smells and sounds of the tropics. Vines swarmed across the trellises; leaves and blossoms made a ceiling. In a corner a light bulb flickered. Mosquitoes circled, while ants scurried across the table. Hi-life – the feverish, rhythmic, body-swaying music of Ghana – pounded from a ghetto blaster. On a dusty patch of ground opposite, some lads were kicking a football around, yelling exuberantly.

I knew two of the men already – Charles, bearded and mellow, and the irrepressible George, crackling with ideas and wit. The others turned expectantly to greet us.

The newcomer grabbed a chair and pushed me forward. "Meet ma woman!" he cried, his smile huge in the darkness. I was glad to be his "woman", not his "wife" or his "girlfriend". Calvin Klein T-shirt notwithstanding, he was no soft city dude but a brother, a homeboy, back among his people, rough, tough and manly – or so the word seemed to imply.

I shall call him K, because most men's names in Ghana begin with K: Kofi, which in the Twi language means "a male born on a Friday"; Kwesi, "born on a Sunday"; Kwame, "born on a Saturday"; and Kojo, "born on a Monday". Not that the story I have to tell is in Western terms especially shocking. But Ghana is a claustrophobic society and, like the inhabitants of many small countries, Ghanaians are extremely sensitive, particularly when it comes to their country's image. I would not like to endanger his position there in any way.

Fresh off the plane, K was still spangled with the allure of London, where he had lived for a decade and a half. Now he was home and Ghana was soon going to know all about it; he had every intention of making his presence felt. Charming and charismatic, he was bubbling over with plans, ideas and idealism. The others might have had their dreams battered out of them by years of poverty and hardship, but his were still intact. He ordered me a Coke, then threw himself into the discussion. It was February 1992 and there was plenty to argue about. The country was still dominated by the military. Police and soldiers armed with ancient rifles were highly visible. We had already had a run-in with the police and had been in the country barely twenty-four hours. After twenty years of military rule, Ghana was to go to the polls at the end of the year. Its masters had decided it was time for at least the appearance of democracy.

★ ★ ★ ★

We had arrived at night, the plane sweeping low across the swaying silhouettes of palm trees. As I stepped out, the sweet febrile air of Ghana, as fierce as a sauna, swept me up in its embrace. It was my first moment in Africa. I felt its intoxication – the passion, the pulse, the red earth beneath my feet. Hoisting his bag on to his shoulder, K walked into the airport. Already soaked with sweat, I followed behind him. Customs officials swarmed around us, "porters" hustled to carry our bags and arms grabbed at us. K brushed them all off like insects and strode out to where Charles and George, his half-brothers, were waiting.

By the time we had loaded Charles's ancient green Peugeot, it was sinking on its axles. The boot was flapping open with suitcases piled high. K had spent his last weeks in London shopping with the desperation of a man who might never have the chance to cross the portals of Paul Smith or Harvey Nichols again. As for me, I had kept my baggage to a minimum in order to carry his, plus his new state-of-the-art ghetto blaster, which I took as hand luggage.

We had not gone far when a leathery-faced policeman flagged us down. Charles, the quiet, reasonable one, got out to see what the problem was. The excitable George was next. The voices grew louder and louder. "Stay here!" barked K, flinging open his door. I sat, hardly daring to breathe, while he joined in what was by now an enormous row. Then a younger policeman strutted up, making much play of his rifle. Fresh from the placid streets of London, I was petrified.

Finally, the voices lowered. The three men got back into the car and we drove off, arguing vociferously. What had been the problem? I ventured. The policeman, apparently, had accused Charles of running a taxi service, for which he had, of course, no licence. He was therefore committing an offence. Some "dash" – a monetary gift to the policeman – would have ensured that it was overlooked, but K, fresh from England and full of Western notions, refused to countenance such shameful Third World practices. Hence the row and the rifles. I never discovered how the argument had been settled.

Down a dark bumpy road lined with tiny stalls, we stopped to buy food. On each stall an oil-soaked wick flickered with a yellow flame. A roly-poly woman wearing a bandanna sold us kenkei, fermented cornmeal wrapped in banana leaves, with a chilli-hot sauce to dip it in and some grilled herrings. The whole lot was rolled up in newspaper, a hot greasy bundle which I held well away from my lap as we headed for Charles's, where we were to spend the night.

★ ★ ★ ★

I had never planned to come to Africa. It was the last place I had ever expected to find myself. My roots were in Asia, my work in Asia. I had spent a large part of my life between two complex, complicated, rather cold and passionate small islands – Britain and Japan. My father, a China specialist, had always said there was one country in the world which one fell in love with. In his case it was China; in mine, Japan.

But then I met K at a party. At the time, he was going out with an acquaintance of mine. Years later, when they separated, K called me. On our first date he took me to the gym. On our second he showed me a photograph of a formidable African matriarch, stern and frowning, with a bouffant head of hair. "This is my mother," he said. Then he opened an atlas at the map of Africa and pointed out a small oblong country on the hip of the continent, bordering the Atlantic, a little above the equator. "This is Ghana. This is where I come from." He always explained matters to do with Africa in simple language, as if talking to a child. It was only after we had been seeing each other for some time that he deemed I was ready to learn his surname.

I had never before met anyone who knew with such clarity what he wanted. K had a life plan: to study at the London School of Economics, get experience in local government in London, then go back to Ghana to set his country in order. Unfortunately, when we met he had already completed the first two stages. He was due to move to Ghana in less than six months, which I assumed would mean the end of our relationship. But there was another part of his plan too, and that involved me. He had decided that I was to go with him, as his woman.

My preparations for visiting Ghana were patchy. From time to time K sketched out fragments of the complicated political situation, the good guys and the bad guys. His hero, Kwame Nkrumah, had won independence for Ghana in 1957, making it the first country in Africa to free itself from colonial rule. In 1996 Nkrumah was overthrown in a military coup. Colonel Acheampong, a pudgy potato-faced character, the Mobutu of his day, salted away millions of dollars in Swiss bank accounts while the country's economy lurched into a hopeless downward spiral. I heard about the terrible hardships that followed when, even if people had money in their pockets, there was nothing in the shops to buy.

Finally, a dashing young flight-lieutenant, Jerry John Rawlings, led yet another military coup, taking a stand against corruption. Larger, fatter, less dashing but immensely popular, he was still in power thirteen years later. He had set the economy on its feet again and was now planning to legitimise his rule with elections.

K also explained that Ghana was a matriarchy; perhaps, I thought, that was why he had shown me the picture of his mother. I didn't know the half of it. Later, when I met her, I began to understand better. She was an extraordinarily powerful woman who, even in old age and illness, dominated the lives of her sons.

And he told me about his grandmother, who had brought him up. Following Ashanti tradition, she had carefully moulded his head, pressing it every night with her hands and giving him a rounded pillow to sleep on. You could tell Africans who had grown up in Britain, he said, because their heads were square, flattened at the back from sleeping on a flat surface. As for him, his shaven head was a smooth and aesthetically perfect egg shape.

But there were many things about Africa which he didn't or couldn't tell me, and which I could not even begin to understand until my feet had touched its red soil and I had breathed the moist scented air.

★ ★ ★ ★

On my first morning in Ghana I was woken by children's voices. Safo and Selassie, Charles's children, unable to control their curiosity any longer, had pushed open the door a crack, anxious to see their uncle and new auntie. Outside a cock was crowing lustily. I dropped into the kitchen to greet their mother, a tiny, warm and high-cheekboned woman named Julie. Charles had introduced me to her the previous night, pronouncing her name in the African way as "Jilly".

While Selassie, who was two, clung to my hand, five-year-old Safo ran ahead to show me his domain. Charles was a farm manager. His house stood all alone at the top of an escarpment. Together, the children and I surveyed the grasslands which spread as far as the hills on the distant horizon. The land was not tamed like the English countryside. There were no fields, no hedgerows; there was no sign of the hand of man. It was simply bush, wild, uncultivated, undeveloped. In the distance herds of skinny cattle roamed, nuzzling under rocks and around thorn bushes for blades of grass. Behind the house was a large shed where chickens lived.

While K had had the good fortune to be out of the country during the bad times, Charles had lived through them. He spoke of hiding under the table while mortars exploded and of how, five years before, his car had been impounded by the military at gunpoint. He told the story almost as a joke. "Things have improved since then," he said, smiling.

K was hypercritical of his newly rediscovered country, burning to change things. But Charles was content to watch and comment and joke. He had seen enough of life and death and had an almost preternatural calmness. I thought he seemed one of the wisest people I had ever met.

The latest news was that the leader of the opposition had been imprisoned. His "crime" was that he had not stood up quickly enough for the national anthem on some major state occasion. The brothers discussed this with a combination of outrage and incredulous humour. I listened in silence, trying to get to grips with what kind of country this was.

Charles turned to me. "Do you know what the national anthem sounds like?" he asked, teasing me.

"No," I confessed.

"You'd better find out," he said with mock sternness. "And make sure you stand up quick when you hear it."

Driving into town there were plenty of reminders that this was a country under military control. From time to time we would come to a police barrier set up across the road and a soldier with a rifle (always ancient and usually rusty) would peer into the back seat and order us to open the boot to ensure that there were no hidden arms caches. My presence as a white female, however, rendered it less than likely that we were on our way to perpetrate a military coup so quite often they would just wave us through.

Accra was the greenest, poorest, most laid-back city I had ever seen. I kept expecting to reach the bustling commercial hub of the place or at least to pass the odd skyscraper or an enticing shop or two; every city I had ever been to, even ones as poor as Manila or Canton, had enticing shops. But there were none. With Charles's ancient car sputtering along, spewing out smoke, we drove through street after dusty street of low flat-roofed houses with mud walls painted pink and blue, surrounded by palms and banana, plantain and papaya trees. It was like a city sprouting in a jungle which threatened to swallow it up at any minute. The only shops we saw were strictly functional, selling fabric, watches or electric fans, or cavernous buildings like warehouses with fridges and cookers piled outside.

We passed the military camp and the firing range where the potato-faced Acheampong and two of his predecessors had stood a few years back, lonely and blindfolded, to face their nemesis. Perhaps, then, they regretted the ruin they had caused. The eight numbered boards stood side by side in a row on a bleak escarpment beside the road where the Atlantic waves lashed the shore, a grim reminder to anyone passing by. I wondered what had become of the millions of dollars they had stashed away in Swiss bank accounts.

While I looked around with the magpie eye of a journalist, snatching up shiny nuggets of information, K's experience of the country was very different. For him it was a homecoming, in some ways a tortured one. But this was his country. He needed to rediscover himself there. The quirks, the inefficiencies, the ramshackle banana-republic nature of the place which I found endearing, to him was infuriating. How could his country, for which he had given up his Notting Hill flat, his VW Golf and his managerial position in the civil service, be such a mess?

For me all the allure of this seductive new country, this breath-taking new continent, focused on him. I would run my fingers across his velvety skin, admire his neat bottom, his expressive hands, his huge liquid eyes set wide apart. In the morning, if I woke up before him, I would lie in bed just looking at him, incredulous that such beauty could be mine. But already I knew that I was losing him. He was moving into a different world. I could see him changing.

* * * *

A couple of weeks later we were on a bus, rattling and bumping our way upcountry along a broken red road, pitted with ruts and potholes. In Nkrumah's time, it had been a splendid highway. Then for twenty years, while the country's economy crumbled, so did the road. Under

Rawlings's rule, parts of it had now been resurfaced. In others, the bus slowed to a crawl, cautiously manoeuvring around yawning furrows as deep as ditches.

We passed villages of mud houses with straw roofs, out of which the occasional TV aerial poked, and a small town of decaying plaster houses with balconies and shutters, zigzagging up a hillside. Mainly we were in rain forest, "semi-deciduous", as K insisted. It seemed to go on for ever, mammoth trees caressed by sinewy vines, familiar plants – Swiss cheese plants, rubber plants – sprouting to monstrous proportions in the clammy greenhouse air. Little villages huddled in clearings, but there was almost no cultivation. It was pure virgin forest.

The bus driver put on a tape of gospel music. Ghana, I was discovering, was passionately Christian. Taxis and trucks were emblazoned with ornate stickers proclaiming "Trust in God" or, rather alarmingly, "I am covered by the blood of Christ." It was just as well that God was their insurance; they had no other.

The tape came to an end and a voice crackled from the recorder, urging us to repent, to go to the Lord, before we suffered eternal damnation. For a while we endured it, then the passengers became restive. "We want more songs," bellowed a deep female voice from the back. The other passengers took up the complaint. "More songs," they chanted, "more songs. Stop the preaching!" But the driver had control of the tape recorder and the preaching continued.

Our first stop was Kumasi. In the nineteenth century, before the British took over, Kumasi was a splendid city, the capital of the Ashanti people and the home of the Asantehene, the Ashanti king, who was wealthy and powerful enough to employ Europeans as military trainers and economic advisers. In the colonial wars it was razed to the ground, but it had risen from the ashes. It was a charming place, far more of a city than Accra, a jigsaw of shuttered buildings three or four storeys tall, painted in creams, pinks and beiges, which spread up the hill around the central market. It even had appealing little shops stacked with rolls of colourful fabric, clothes and shoes. There was a prosperous feel to the place. For a moment, as we pushed through the throngs of people beneath the rusty corrugated-iron roofs of the market stalls, I lost sight of K's shaven pate among the myriad black heads and wondered how I would ever find him again. In London he had been the exotic one. Here it was me who stood out from the crowd.

We climbed a hill, past a football ground, to the Asantehene's palace. It was hidden behind a high wall and we could see no more of it than a forest of coconut palms swaying behind. A peacock stalked past the gate, spreading its tail feathers. An elderly woman, very dignified, in a colourful cloth draped like a toga, was standing on the road outside, bidding farewell to some guests. She waved in our direction. "It's the queen mother," hissed K. "Go and speak to her." But I was too bashful.

Later he told me the tale of the greatest queen mother of all, Nana Yaa Asantewaa, who in 1900, at the age of sixty-one, led the Ashanti troops in their last desperate attempt to drive the invaders out. The British were holed up in Kumasi Fort, a rather ugly redbrick building which is now a military museum. The battle raged for days, but in the end the Ashanti lost and the lands which now make up Ghana became the British colony of the Gold Coast. Outside the palace some lads were kicking a football about in a swirl of red dust. Inside, I suspected, life continued with as much splendour as ever before.

On our way down the hill we visited one of K's friends, who had lived in London and played in a band. Now he was home, in a mud-walled house with a central courtyard open to the sky. While the two reminisced about clubs, concerts and friends, a woman was pounding fufu, dropping a pestle the size of a small tree trunk into a barrel of cassava dough.The rhythmic thud punctuated their words.

The next day we were up at six. At the bus station we boarded a minibus and waited for it to fill up. "Full" meant at least four, if not five, people squeezed along a seat made for three, petrol cans hanging off the back and sacks of rice and a trussed, squawking chicken under the seats. Barefooted hawkers gathered around the bus, balancing tin basins on their heads piled with Chinese toothpaste, shoe polish, batteries, tooth-cleaning sticks and nail clippers. One skinny lad in a ragged jersey peered through the window as I sat scribbling notes. "Your handwriting is very good," he observed. I stopped, thinking the bus was about to move off. "It's OK," he said urgently, as if his life depended on watching me write. "You can write. Write it! Write it!" He did not care what I wrote, it was the act of writing that fascinated him. Perhaps he was illiterate; yet he could speak English, even if not perfectly.

Half a day later, sweaty, sticky, dirty and battered, we straightened our cramped limbs and stepped into the stillness of the noon heat. The huge trees with their thick foliage and the hummocky red track which led away from the road were bleached of colour in the fiery sunshine like an overexposed photograph. We were in Abofo, where K had spent the first fifteen years of his life. As we picked our way along the earthen track, goats and chickens zigzagged back and forth in front of us. I had never felt the gulf between us so strongly. For all his designer T-shirts, expensive trainers and Armani body lotion, for K this village with no electricity, no running water and no sewerage system was home. As he strode purposefully in front of me, I tried to imagine the schoolboy growing up in the bush. How had it been, arriving for the first time in the crowded metropolis of Accra? Even more unimaginable, how had it felt to travel to the grey streets of London at the age of sixteen or seventeen? But K had without a doubt been at least as cocksure and confident then as he was now. He had probably just strutted into these new worlds, certain he was the coolest guy on the block and that whatever he got was the very least he deserved.

Queen for a day

Naomi Roberts

Naomi Roberts first went to Ghana in the late 1980s to live and work in a village compound in the forested coastal strip of the country, approximately 120 miles from the capital. When she returned to Bristol to resume her work as a clinical psychologist, she kept in contact with her Ghanaian village friends through letters, occasionally sending money to help with village projects. Eight years later she returned for a brief visit.

My friend Susie and I left the carpeted wastes of Heathrow on a cold November evening and arrived at daybreak in the dusty echoing concrete hall of Accra's Kotoka airport. Our plan was to spend a few days in the capital together before splitting up and visiting the villages where we had each worked as volunteers almost eight years before. Our flights and hotel in Accra had been arranged through a tour operator that advertised in the Sunday papers. No longer were we the brave and high-minded development workers, leaving our homes, family and comforts to work in the field. This time we were tourists on holiday.

We sat on a low wall outside the airport and waited for our agent to turn up. Cars and taxis came and went as the tropical heat settled around us. We shed our English layers and pushed up our sleeves. An hour passed and there was still no sign of a car, but the waiting had a familiar Ghanaian feel to it and the heat had a slowing down and calming effect. It was just as I remembered; a lot of waiting and a lot of heat, but this time there was no anxiety about trying to get anything done. We waited and surprised ourselves by not getting rattled as we certainly would have done back at home.

Eventually the car turned up and we were driven round the edge of the city to a hotel which turned out to be in a suburb with wide dusty roads and new pink- and blue-painted houses with ornate wrought-iron fences. Between the new houses, though, were the same rows of low concrete sheds which were each neighbourhood's local shops; each unit open in front displaying stacks of bottled drinks, bread and soap powder, and alongside the shops the little wooden stalls selling peeled oranges and street food. It was the same juxtaposition of new development and hand-to-mouth, day-to-day trading although the expensive sports club seemed new, with its high walls and flags flying, and a glimpse of a blue swimming pool with expats jumping from the boards.

Our hotel was one of the new buildings, not big, surrounded by high pink walls and with a steel gate and a guard in raggedy brown shorts. In front was a small, beautifully tended garden full of glossy-leafed palms and the scent of flowering shrubs, and our room had comfortable beds, a television on which we could watch the BBC World Service, a shining tiled bathroom, air conditioning and a fridge stocked with bottles of Ghanaian beer. This shining cleanliness, this relaxed, modern efficiency was something I had never come across in all my time as a volunteer. In those days, we took pride in being dedicated and poor and eschewing the luxuries that were taken for granted by the expat community.

We spent a few days in Accra; sometimes passing the hottest part of the day lying on our beds with the air conditioning on, other times sitting out on the balcony of our room, watching the people walking up and down the unpaved orange mud road outside the hotel. Some were smart, returning home from work with briefcases, and others poor and shabby carrying loads on their heads, but they all shared the slow, calm, easy walk. You don't rush here. Sometimes we would go out, too, to wander slowly down the dust road to the local row of shops and catch a taxi into town; still the rusty, low-slung, suspension-free taxis that we remembered.

I had written to my friends in the village, had told them what plane I'd be on and the name of our hotel. I half-expected that one of them would turn up but nobody came and there was no way of making contact before I took off on a bus for the village. Over the intervening years I had kept in touch by letter with the family of one of the subchiefs of the village. I had lived in his compound in one small room and my particular friends had been his sister-in-law, Beatrice, and her son, Kofi, who was then just ten years old. Through my subchief's cousin, who was a teacher, I had sent some money to the village and this had gone towards buying bricks and corrugated roofing sheets for a little three-room nursery school which, when it was finished, had been called after me – the Naomi Roberts Kindergarten.

Taking the bus to the village was only a little bit more luxurious than before. You still had to make your way through the bus station, a vast, open, muddy space with a thousand or so buses, minibuses, taxis and lorries going, it would seem, in every direction, and find amongst hundreds of other low wooden ticket huts the right one to buy the tickets for your particular destination. Then, after sitting in the bus in the heat until every seat, including the makeshift seats that are let down into the gangway, are filled, you take off, lurching and hooting, through the log jam of vehicles. Once out of the town, though, there was an enormous change in evidence. Where the road before had had so many deep potholes that the 125-mile journey took six or seven hours, now a sleek, smooth ribbon, built, I later found out, by the

Japanese, curved gracefully through the forest, past villages and small towns, streaking through oil palm plantations. The journey time to the village was cut by half although there was still no clean water and the electricity stopped six miles down the road.

I was dropped off on the main road in the middle of the village from where it was a short walk up to the compound where I had lived. In just a few seconds I was surrounded by shouts of "Auntie Naomi, Auntie Naomi, how are you? Welcome." My bags were pulled from my hands and carried for me to the subchief's compound. But when I first stepped into his family home there was no one there that I recognised. I was beginning to wonder if I had made a mistake and might have to go and find somewhere else to stay. I waited in the shade and after a while Beatrice appeared and ran towards me with her arms outstretched. We had a long hug.

She described how her family had grown since I last saw her. She had three more little boys. In fact I already knew about two of them, and Kofi had once written asking me to tell his mother to stop having more babies. Beatrice and her husband were now living in their own house, round the back of the compound, and Kofi had moved to the other end of the village. Kofi, she explained, had gone to Accra to meet me, but we had missed each other and it would take many more days before we finally managed to coincide.

I was given a room that I never knew existed before, the sub-chief's guest room. It had a big and extremely comfortable bed in it with very clean white sheets and curtains over the window and the door. It had been prepared for my coming. I set out my things and lay down to rest on the bed and a great wave of relief and happiness washed over me. I was already finding staying as a guest much more comfortable than being an aid worker. Over the next few days, I was content to sit around all day in the compound and do nothing except watch life and chat to people. I think to live successfully in a rural setting in Africa you do have to slow down; something I hadn't understood in my earlier attempts to be a useful aid worker.

The next morning I went over to visit the nursery where about fifty tiny children were housed in two rooms. Some were running about and playing while others were squeezed onto little benches in rows facing the big blackboard. There were no tables and not quite enough room on the benches either so that little children were constantly falling off the ends to be replaced by others. There were no toys and no books.

The rest of that first day I spent sitting on a little wooden stool outside Beatrice's house watching her cook and look after her baby. My first grandson, who was slightly younger, was doing very similar things at home, smiling, sitting on the ground playing with a plastic lid, although he was very much larger in size with a much louder scream. Beatrice wanted to know about babies' medicines in England and I discovered that she was much less confident that "nature is best" than my daughter and her friends. Beatrice had gripe water, vitamins, special herbal nose drops and cod liver oil. She said the baby was often "hot in the head" and for this she ground up herbs which she dripped into the baby's nose off an old rag.

On the second day, rumours begin to reach me that the main chief of the village, whom I had only ever met once before, had returned and that I was expected at the palace. (All villages have palaces, just rather larger and grander compound houses than my sub-chief's house.) Beatrice and I walked down to the palace and found that a crowd had already assembled outside and the village elders were sitting round the edge of the great courtyard. As is the custom, I walked around the courtyard shaking each of them by the hand before sitting down. The elders then took it in turn to come and shake *me* by the hand. Slowly it dawned on me that the formality was leading somewhere. I was going to be made a queen mother (an honorary female village elder). But the main chief wasn't there yet and obviously we couldn't go home again until he arrived, so everyone sat down and waited. We waited for about an hour and we chatted and more and more people crowded into the palace courtyard. It was very strange to feel that all this gathering together and milling about was because of me.

Eventually the chief arrived, wrapped in an elaborately woven cloth, and sat amongst the elders on the raised platform to one side of the courtyard. The linguist of the village stood up and, holding a golden carved staff, made several speeches the point of which was to ask me to accept the "stool". I realised that whatever my own thoughts on the matter might be it was not going to be possible to decline this offer. I then made several short speeches (I am always aware of my plummy, schoolmistressy voice on these occasions) about my pleasure and surprise, and mimed my English friends' reaction to my becoming a queen mother in Africa, which got a big laugh. I was then told to be ready at six the next morning when women would come to my room and help me dress for the ceremony.

Just after eight o'clock the next morning three ladies arrived and went with me to my room. They were late because they had had to borrow the right clothes and jewellery for me to wear. First one *kente* cloth (an elaborately and beautifully woven cloth of coloured stripes) was tied tightly round me like a tube, then another. Then two heavy bead necklaces, dotted with gold nuggets, were lowered over my head and, to complete the effect, a gold ring, gold and black traditional sandals and a gold and black crown. My hair was a great problem, whether to wear it in or out. It was decided that it should be tucked in, exposing my great pale forehead. I took a brief and horror-struck look at myself in a little mirror – so wrinkly and gaunt, glasses and all.

Hundreds of people arrived, many of the women were waving cloth (old rags, curtains and so on) in unison to create a very necessary cooling breeze. At last I was taken outside and seated upon a palanquin, with four bearers. At first it felt safe and then rather alarmingly, the whole thing lurched to one side as the bearers beneath it swapped places. I was told to wave and move my top half around in a wriggling, dancing motion, which I did but, oh! – it would have been impossible if anyone I knew back home had seen me. I kept thinking, what shall I tell people? To be the object of adulation, cheered and screamed at just because I was rich enough to give some money. For really it did seem that hundreds and hundreds of people (the schoolchildren were out to line the route) just couldn't get enough of me, especially when I tried to dance and wave and twirl my hands. I don't believe in all this royalty thing and there it was happening to me. Yet I couldn't have said no – not really.

The tallest boy even held a big umbrella over me and when we got near the palace someone came rushing out with the official parasol, pink plush with a fringe, and knocked my crown off with it. Then I was carried up the palace steps and the bearers danced and jiggled before putting me down.

The actual ceremony involved lots of walking back and forth across the courtyard, a great deal of hand-shaking, bottles of schnapps being presented and lots poured on the ground, while the linguist delivered more speeches. For the most part I had to sit and look dignified. At one point I was taken to a side room and rewrapped in the cloths so I could part my knees better and sit in a more regal fashion. Lots of photos were taken. And all along I was told what to do: get up, greet these people, sit down, look at the linguist while he speaks. I was sitting next to another queen mother most of the time and at one point I thought she said to me "Long life", so I said it back. It turned out she was saying "Don't laugh", so from then on I sat with as solemn an expression as possible, knees spread, feet parallel, hands on knees.

But at the end there was some dancing at which I acquitted myself pretty well – losing my inhibitions and wiggling along with the best – and that got the most cheers and excitement of all. Everyone in the village was by now milling about. Some were drunkenly pushing forward, shouting at me and waving, and being pushed aside by others, but on the whole nobody minded and the atmosphere was relaxed. It was nothing like the strict humourless formality of ceremonial occasions in England when nobody moves a finger out of place. There was such a mixture of "pomp", a real attempt to turn a new person into someone to look up to and then get help from, and also so much informality. For me it was embarrassing, I felt ridiculous, but the villagers were thanking me with total sincerity.

This was the high point of my last visit to Ghana and I came away really gratified to have been made a queen mother but also alarmed. What was expected from me? I will go back again, sooner this time, and before I go I will have to think clearly about my role in the village, what I can and cannot do; it is so easy to get it wrong. It is no longer just a place I can visit from time to time for a holiday and to see old friends. That easy relationship is lost to me now. Instead I have responsibilities. I am seen as a benefactor now, a provider, and that I find much harder to get right.

The day after the "enstoolment" I again sat with Beatrice, watching her cooking and looking after the little boys. I felt much the same person as before, in T-shirt and shorts again, but excited and proud too and looking forward to meeting up with Susie in Accra and telling her all about my my new queenly status. We met as arranged in the hotel and I also eventually met up with Kofi. The years had transformed him into a tall man with a deep voice but he was still very shy and clearly out of his element in the city. We sat together in the posh hotel lounge where I bought him Cokes. You could tell that the hotel staff were curious about this country boy who'd been waiting for the foreigner from England, although they treated him kindly.

My last evening in Ghana was spent with Kofi, Susie and an ex-colleague of hers, driving through Accra in the tropical darkness with a soft warm wind blowing through the open windows of the car. We stopped to eat. Kofi had never been to a restaurant before and found the knife and fork awkward to manage. He was given a bag in which to take away the food that he didn't finish.

Two days later I was back at my desk and wondering how best to explain to my colleagues the surprising fact that I was now a queen mother.

read on . . .

Lesley Downer, "Hard Currency" in *Amazonian: The Penguin Book of Women's New Travel Writing,* **Dea Birkett and Sara Wheeler (ed) (UK: Penguin, 1998).** Contains the original, longer version of the story above which shows more of the cracks appearing as Downer and K cope in their disparate ways with police corruption.

Ama Ata Aidoo, *The Dilemma of a Ghost* and *Anowa* **(UK: Longman, 1995).** Aidoo, one of Africa's relatively few female authors, deals in *Dilemma* with the unusual theme of a black American girl married into a Ghanaian family and in *Anowa* with a Ghanaian legend about a girl who refuses her parents' chosen suitors. *No Sweetness Here* (UK: Longman, 1995/ US: NOK Pubs, 1979) is a collection of short stories, most of which handle the theme of conflict between traditional and urban life in Ghana. *Our Sister Killjoy* (UK: Longman, 1988/US: Feminist Press, 1995), Aidoo's first novel, explores, in an experimental fashion, the thoughts and experiences of a Ghanaian girl on a voyage of self-discovery in Germany. *Changes* (US: The Women's Press, 1992) is a love story, used to portray urban African women – and the social forces that combine to make them both powerful and vulnerable.

Maya Angelou, *All God's Children Need Travelling Shoes* **(UK: Virago 1986/US: Random House, 1991).** In this fifth volume of her often riveting autobiography, black American writer, poet, editor, dancer, actress and political activist Maya Angelou emigrates to Ghana with her seventeen-year-old son. After the initial joy and excitement of being for the first time black in a black country, she gradually dismantles the myth of "Mother Africa" and reaches a new understanding of herself, her people's history and the meaning of motherhood. Written, as always, straight from the heart.

Wendy Belcher, *Honey from the Lion: An African Journey* **(US: Dutton, 1988).** Belcher returns to the Ghana of her childhood to take up a job with a Christian organisation. Her lyrical account is packed with cross-cultural insights, a strong cast of characters and a spectrum of West African landscapes.

Gracia Clark, *Onions Are My Husband: Survival and Accumulation by West African Market Women* **(US: University of Chicago Press, 1994).** Although strictly in the realms of economic anthropology, this portrayal of Kumasi market women contains some fascinating insights and details.

Mary Gaunt, *Alone in West Africa* **(1912; UK: o/p).** Widowed, middle-aged and strapped for cash, the Australian writer Mary Gaunt set sail for the Gold Coast. Her fearless travels, which sent her, swaying in her hammock with her sixteen African bearers, deep into the Asante heartland, enthralled her Edwardian public. Sadly, this book has not been reprinted, but Dea Birkett's *Spinsters Abroad: Victorian Lady Explorers* (UK: Gollancz, 1991/US: Blackwell, 1989) provides some illuminating anecdotes of her trip and helps place her amongst her contemporaries.

Greece

A hairy tale

Armelle Ellison

Before setting off for university, Armelle Ellison took this rite-of-passage trip to the Greek island of Rhodes with her schoolfriend Jenny. Despite their many misadventures they have remained close friends. Armelle is currently completing a postgraduate course in information studies at Glasgow University. Jenny, who has recently had a baby, continues to live in their home town on the outskirts of Nottingham.

I remember that Jenny was muttering something about how great our summer holiday had been and what a shame it was that we were going to have to head home to England. I was nodding in agreement. "So let's not go," she announced. "Let's stay here instead!"

Her plan was simplicity itself. To finance our extended stay on the island of Rhodes we would take up hair-wrapping – plenty of girls were doing it on the main tourist streets of Rhodes Town but there were none in Faliráki, just a few kilometres south. This small town seemed peculiarly lacking in devil-may-care entrepreneurs, but we could fill that niche. Hair-wrapping didn't seem a particularly taxing project and hey, we looked the part already in our tie-dye gear and tassels.

The high point of Jenny's plan was that it enabled us to stay on in Greece, instead of returning to Nottingham to struggle by on the dole. Sitting on sandy beaches watching swirly clouds float across an azure sky was a far more appealing prospect, though admittedly, to the more seasoned traveller Faliráki might not have seemed so paradisiacal. Most shreds of the "real" Greece had long since departed the town, eaten up by the wall-to-wall pubs, clubs and "caffs" serving full English breakfast. We, however, remained undeterred – Faliráki's brash commercialism was the ideal backdrop for two teens bent on having a wild time.

All that remained was to ring our mothers and tell them not to expect us back. Characteristically, Jenny's mum reacted with easy-going acceptance while my own mother blew a fuse. Though I'd turned eighteen a month previously, she hadn't yet come to terms with the fact that I was an adult and accordingly, she insisted I came home. Safe in the knowledge that there wasn't a thing she could do, I told her my mind was made up. If I could support myself I'd be staying.

It was pretty daunting that first evening, sitting down beside the busy main street for our debut, setting up our amateurishly hand-chalked sign. It was make or break time. To draw the customers Jen set about wrapping a strand of my hair and incredibly, this attracted a lot of interest – we were in business. Our trade seemed to catch the eye of a wide spectrum of people. The vast majority were female – from tiny girls to young women – but a gang of tipsy guys who strolled past thought it would be amusing to have long hair-wraps sprouting from their short-back-and-sides cuts. Though we assured them it was virtually impossible they persisted, assuring us that if it fell out the next day they wouldn't care, and offering to pay double the going rate. Unable to resist this bribery, we gracefully obliged.

The story we'd fabricated (about our previous experience hair-wrapping our way around the islands) went down well, and we had a wonderful, profitable night, happily exchanging trivial banter with the holidaymakers while we worked.

Afterwards, to celebrate, we went out and bought the biggest bottle of syrupy ouzo we'd ever seen. High on success, we shimmied back to our apartment and, with the lads from next door (attracted by our drunken, siren-like singing) we proceeded to whoop it up. The guys were Geordies, slightly older than us (in their twenties), and a good laugh. One was gangly and awkward, with a mop of curls, one was dark with very pointy features and the other had longish blonde hair, wanton blue eyes and fancied himself loads.

In the morning I was rudely awoken by the hotel-owner strolling unannounced into the bedroom. At the sight of his stormy countenance the guys, who had passed out in our room, hastily scuttled off. His wrath was fierce – entertaining men overnight was forbidden, therefore we'd have to pay for the extra two people. This was despite the fact that the room was minute, only had two single beds and that they had their own room anyway. Bleary-eyed, we declined and he shuffled off, muttering to himself. The previous night was actually a bit of a haze to me, but two images were etched in my memory. The first was of Jenny, keeled over in a suitcase with just a pair of disembodied, mosquito-raddled legs poking out. The second was of the boys, inexplicably dressed in our clothes. I swore to myself that I wouldn't touch ouzo again.

The next night saw Jenny and I back at our spot beside the main street, peddling our wares once again. We were more confident now, our expert status affirmed by the miniature rainbow of coloured thread we had bought with the previous night's takings. Between us sat skeins tinted crimson, mulberry, cyan, terracotta, indigo and sappy green, and heaps of shiny, candy-coloured beads. The only flaw to the evening was when one of the previous night's customers reappeared.

From what I could make of her she seemed nice, a bit of an airhead maybe, but harmless enough. She'd decided that the hair-wrap spoiled the line of her sleek, centre-parted bob and wanted it removed, then replaced underneath her hair where it wouldn't be so conspicuous. Dutifully I obliged with a new wrap in the position indicated, but, for the life of me, I couldn't unravel the original one. Practised as I was by now at putting wraps in, I'd never tried taking one out and it was nigh-on impossible. As I wrestled ineffectually with the tight knots more customers were queuing up waiting to be served, so finally, at my wits' end, I resorted to the scissors.

To my heartfelt dismay great chunks of hair came away at the same time as the yarn, and began to waft away on the breeze. My victim, still chattering away, was happily ignorant of my blunder so I grabbed the decapitated locks, stuffing them down my trousers, out of sight. Then, the offending hair-wrap removed, I sent her on her way. When she'd gone, I explained what had happened to Jenny, producing the hair from my trousers with a flourish. Giggling helplessly, we watched the blonde tresses float off down the street. The next few nights I lived in fear of her coming back to seek retribution, but saw neither hide nor hair of her again.

For a week or so our days were full and perfect. In the mornings we'd saunter onto the beach and pass the time dozing, drinking strawberry-slush confections brought to us by waiters called Spiros, and swimming in the ocean. Sprawled on a towel which was by now none too clean, and buttered with coconutty unguents, I willed the sun to brown me like a giant piece of toast. Days spent relentlessly seeking the "sun-kissed look" had so far only resulted in the "onion effect", skin peeling away from my body in translucent layers. I consoled myself with the thought that I had the whole summer to catch up with Jenny, who had turned a warm brown. At night we went downtown to do our wraps.

Faliráki at night was a sensory overload. Our view from the side of the busy road was of a flowing torrent of flesh, of a fantastic, boisterously colourful creature with hundreds of legs. Riots of smells assaulted our nostrils, each vying to drown out the rest – perfume, smoke, the sea, fried food, alcohol and sweat. The people who interested us the most were those who, like us, were young and capricious. There were droves of them to watch, from the smug local lotharios, sporting a different girl on their arm each week, to milky-faced damsels, fresh off the plane, who would change colour with their background like chameleons and become brandy-cheeked temptresses, flushed with wine and weather.

On one particular evening the air was balmy, trade was steady, and as my hands worked, my mind drifted. The easy, rhythmic motion of fingers on threads lulled me into an absent-minded reverie and the minutes winged by in unseen flocks. Soon it was twilight and we were thinking about packing up when a middle-aged Greek chap came up to enquire how much it was for a hair-wrap, professedly for his girlfriend. Unsuspecting, I told him prices started from 500dr (about £1.50/$2). That was it. Brusquely remarking that we must be making plenty of money, he told us he was a policeman and he was arresting us for working without a licence.

We were in a state of shock and utter incomprehension as we were whisked down to the station in Rhodes Town. I tried explaining that as Greece was a member of the EU we hadn't thought we needed a licence, but my sputterings fell on deaf ears. With no idea what was going to happen to us, we huddled together in the back of the car and awaited our fate.

On arrival at the police station we were deposited in a cell which was already jammed with bodies. Our fellow jailbirds were mainly young British people, staff from numerous local bars, and there was a tangible sense of community in the small room, a sense of being in the same leaky boat. There's nothing like a common calamity to promote intimacy and everyone chatted as if they were old friends in the local bar not strangers in a jail cell. This sentiment of camaraderie dulled the blow of being arrested to a certain extent. It was reassuring to be surrounded by others, who didn't seem to regard the predicament we were in as a big deal. Left on our own, Jenny and I would doubtless have worked ourselves into a state of hysterical terror. As it was, we managed to hang onto a few shreds of sanity.

Intermittently we were shepherded out in batches to be finger-printed, then herded back to the cell. Further additions were constantly being made to our number, as more villains were caught in the act of pulling pints and in course we were joined by a guy called Jim who'd been through it all before. Having a captive audience (in every sense of the word), he proceeded to tell us what we could expect. Apparently, every summer the police would perform a random swoop, round up all the unlicensed Brits working in the various bars and restaurants and bang them up for the night. The next day the cases would go to court, where the owners of the bars and restaurants would also be tried. Inevitably everyone would be found guilty, but the proprietors would be the ones to foot the hefty fines. This, Jim told us conspiratorially, was the object of the mission – to line the cops' pockets.

We all heaved a collective sigh of relief: no one was going to be deported, or left to rot in prison. Then suddenly a thought occurred to me – Jenny and I were effectively self-employed. There wasn't anyone to come and bail us out, and though we were doing okay (considering), we weren't in the same financial league as the fat-cat bar-owners. It was conceivable that we would be jailed. The rest of the night I spent picking my cuticles raw, nervously waiting for dawn.

Sleep was pretty much out of the question due to the cramped conditions (although the few die-hards who had turned in were snoring up a storm). Visits to the loo were under escort, and the cubicle didn't have a lock. Still, it wasn't as unpleasant as it could have been – at one point a kind policeman went and bought us cans of pop, pizza and even cigarettes. I couldn't eat the pizza (worry had taken away my appetite, and the cheese had gone all congealed and waxy-looking) but it was nice to see a friendly, compassionate face amongst all the slate-eyed men of steel.

Scared as I was, I still knew we didn't have it all that bad. The boys in the neighbouring cell were a couple of Greek kids, in for dope offences. These guys looked no more than sixteen and green as hell, one in for possession, the other for dealing. Just a couple of skinny urchins – it was hard to believe that they'd be behind bars for the foreseeable future. Their eyes seemed unnaturally jewel-bright but there was no aggression in their faces, just a mix of bewilderment and incomprehension. Strangely, we avoided looking at them much. I decided later that it was because their predicament so entirely dwarfed ours. We needed our resources of pity to feel sorry for ourselves, so we pretended they didn't exist.

When the morning eventually came round we were marched in a bedraggled, shame-faced procession to the courthouse. Just before our case came up one of the court officials took Jenny and I aside to examine our passports, telling me that a month earlier I'd have been too young to be prosecuted. I smiled ruefully as we were called up to face the music.

The hearing only took a few minutes. A policeman with hair grey as a louse's back gave evidence against us. This was in Greek, and therefore totally unintelligible. We were then asked if we had anything to say. The confident, reasonable argument that I'd hoped to make came out a tremulous, unconvincing garble and, judging by the impassive faces of the magistrates, the cursory interpretation of my halting words hadn't gained much in translation. We were sentenced, again in Greek, and told to step down.

As the next batch of workers were sent to the stand, I asked a nearby official what the verdict was. Unsmiling, he told me we'd been found guilty and sentenced to ten days in prison. My overwrought brain fought to assimilate this information and I lost all composure, my face crumpling as I held off imminent tears. The thought of spending any more time locked up was anathema. Luckily the official soon put me out of my misery, announcing that the alternative was to pay a fine. We were fined just over seventy pounds each, the same as the bar-workers, and counted ourselves lucky. The owners of the bars were stung for a grand each.

After that we didn't do any more hair-wrapping, the occupational hazards were too formidable, and soon we were flat broke. The last of our meagre funds went on two one-way tickets home. My feelings about leaving Faliráki were pretty contradictory, swinging from deflation and disappointment, to excitement at the thought of seeing family and friends again. Mum seemed pleased when I rang her to tell her we were on our way back. I didn't say anything about our brush with the law, though. There are some bits of news, like pregnancy scares, nights spent sleeping rough or getting arrested, that are best told later.

A Lesbian holiday

Deb Herman

Deb Herman, a "struggling but garretless writer" from Leeds, flew with her girlfriend to the island of Lesbos in the north Aegean. They were on a package holiday to Skala Erossos, a small coastal village reputed to be the birthplace of Sappho and the only lesbian resort in the Mediterranean. This was Deb's second visit. Her girlfriend is apparently now firmly converted to beach bunnyhood.

The trouble with homophobia is that when you go on holiday it tends to go with you, but in the little beach village of Skala Erossos it takes a back seat. For this resort is on the island of Lesbos, birthplace of Sappho and the only (lowercase) lesbian holiday destination. It may be a cliché, but what a wonderful cliché. All the ingredients of a classic

Greek vacation are there, history, scenery, beaches and food; added to which are the joy and relief of being unremarkable. Since the 1970s, queer women have been travelling to Skala Erossos in ever-increasing numbers and have turned the village into a place of pilgrimage. I first learned of the present-day scene on Lesbos some years ago, when I read Armistead Maupin's novel, *Sure Of You*, part of which is set on the island. Since then I've been there twice, most recently in September 1998 when my partner and I stayed one all-too-short week. In the time between my visits, the scene has passed from tents and campfire cooking to studio apartments and beachfront tavernas. This, unsurprisingly, has led to a warmer welcome from the locals; modern Greece is not noted for sexual tolerance, but money has a most persuasive voice.

We flew directly to the island's capital, Mytilene, a bustling town of strange houses resembling Wedgwood china and score upon score of mopeds and motorbikes. Everyone rides them, from teenagers, girls and boys, to elderly ladies some of whom prefer side-saddle pillion. We had been dyke-spotting with little success on the plane, but were rewarded at the airport where we saw a dozen. Unfortunately, all but two of them were flying out, not in, but we were cheered nonetheless. In order to escape reality as quickly as possible, we had booked a taxi to get us to Skala Erossos which is on the west side of the island, about two hours' drive away (there are funky Fifties coaches to get you there if you've the time and the inclination). The driver was from Erossos and friendly enough to make us feel safe and welcome. We began to relax into being an everyday couple on holiday. As we quickly left the town behind our city-battered senses revived in the unpolluted atmosphere. The journey was mostly through rough, beautiful hills and the ubiquitous ancient olive groves, with occasional glimpses, when the roads bent the right way, of heartbreakingly blue sea. We tried not to notice the many roadside shrines to victims of the alarming hairpin bends. Every so often we swept through villages that belonged to the twentieth century only by virtue of the plastic chairs and Coke machines outside the cafés. Our smiles broadened with every mile we travelled.

The travel agent had booked us into a studio at the *Hotel Antiope* which is owned by locals but run by two women (one Greek and one German) who met on the island. *Antiope* is women-only and very popular. Even quite late in the season it was fairly full, mainly with German and British couples. We dumped our bags, sat on the sun-terrace, ordered our first beer and gazed contentedly at the nearby sea. A little later we slapped on the sun-cream and took a slow walk to the beach – four minutes instead of two. The village is tiny, a few residential streets lie behind a quarter-mile stretch of bars, souvenir shops and beachfront tavernas either side of a main square. To the east of these is a dinky fishing harbour and to the west another quarter-mile of perfect sandy beach. Hills enclose the village and the beach giving a pleasing sense of being cradled and protected. At the far end of the beach is "Sappho's Mountain" the edge of which is said to resemble her profile, but probably only by the deluded or blind.

Along the row of cafés and bars there is something of a divide between progressive and traditional. Most are run by locals who vary in their acceptance of their queer clientele from slightly hostile to positively welcoming. Straight package-tourists do go, but in fairly small numbers, so the yearly dyke invasion has a beneficial economic effect. Foreign women, in love with Lesbos, have started to buy or run some of the businesses and become accepted as residents; no mean feat on any Greek island. One British woman, after having spent her summers on Lesbos for years, was celebrating her purchase of the village launderette. At the height of the season, she told us, the beach is crowded, the parties can last all night and everyone runs out of clean clothes!

Like most beach towns, Erossos is quiet in the winter. *Hotel Antiope* want to open at Christmas, but there is little work for the resident women and most of them winter elsewhere, returning in early spring for the lazy start to the season. What struck me most about the women who stay and work in Erossos was the continuing freshness of their love for the place. There is as much enthusiasm in the praises of ten-year veterans as there is in those of new tourists.

There's not much to do in Skala Erossos. One goes from breakfast to beach to lunch to beach to dinner in a satisfied haze. The toughest decisions we had to make all week were what to choose from the menu or even which tentacle to have from the octopus hanging from the roof. One tentacle or two? We did venture out of the village one day on a rented motorbike that was the stuff of fantasy and once more braved the scary shrines to arrive, a little numb of derriere in Kalloni, Lesbos' second largest town. Had we not been so high from the bike ride, we might have been more put out by the sudden return to blanket heterosexuality. Outside Skala Erossos, Lesbos is like any other part of Greece and our behaviour automatically became more circumspect. On the way back we stopped at the beautiful monastery of Limonos. We were banned from the chapel by a little sign that read "Woman not allowed". However, we were permitted to view the museum's large collection of bizarre Greek Orthodox icons. We found a portrait of St George, his arm sweetly and campily draped around gorgeous pouting St Demetrious, while their equally camp horses kiss. We rode back to Erossos pondering on the nature of a church that produces and displays such an image while keeping all women who are not virgin mothers from its ritual and burning Sappho's poetry. Oh well, the Church of England might be slightly more tolerant of women, but is much less so when it comes to displays of affection between same-sex saints.

Back at the beach a thunderstorm was brewing. The normally calm sea was almost surfable. I wussed out and sat on the shore as my partner and a few other women braved the breakers. They bobbed up and down, gasping and screaming in at least four languages, grown women rediscovering the pleasures of childhood, unabashed and unafraid. It was moving and wonderful. The first (and only) rain of the week happened that evening. Hollywood rain, great claps of thunder, precise strokes of lightning. Women crowded into *Sappho's* bar and settled in to watch the show. Unsurprisingly the barriers came down and what had been an atmosphere of friendly politeness became camaraderie. I put it down to the large number of British women. All Brits, dykes included, are united by a bit of bad weather. In the evenings of the sunny days, people drifted onto chairs over-looking the beach and watched the ridiculously perfect sunset sizzle into the sea. Service was on hold in *Sappho's* while the waitresses stopped to watch. It seems to be impossible to become blasé about the beauty of a Mediterranean sunset. Afterwards it was back to the tavernas for another round of squid, sardines or shrimps depending on what had been caught that day. The menus didn't vary much from place to place, so we ate in the same one most of the week. The friendly, slightly harassed owner brought us free halva one night, pre-sented for lovers with two spoons. We kissed on the beach in the moonlight without once having to check over our shoulders for trouble. If you understand what a big deal that is, then you want to take your lover to Lesbos.

Over the last twenty years or so, gay men have colonised a few resorts, mostly on the Mediterranean, where they can meet, party and be safe. In these homo-havens, however, you might have to buy a magazine to see another woman. On Lesbos women are starting to experience the heady power of profit over prejudice. Women go to Skala from all over Europe and North America. We go in groups, in couples and alone. Lesbian-feminists made an icon of Sappho in the early 1970s and went to worship. In these less political times most women go simply to relax, to be in love unchallenged by threatened straights, to meet other dykes, to have a good time. We spend more money now than we used to, which, of course, makes the uppercase Lesbians welcoming. Even the ever-present stray dogs and cats are feeling the benefit. Well, you know what they say about lesbians and pussies! (I say, thank God for quarantine.)

Visiting Skala Erossos gave me an experience I've only ever had before on Gay Pride Day, that of being in the majority, being the norm. It is a heady feeling, one that is taken for granted by most straight people and should not be underestimated. It gives one power or at least the illusion of it. Women can find themselves making impossible dreams possible. You don't have to meet a man on a Greek island to stay there. The only wonder is that any of us leave at all.

read on . . .

★ **Fionnuala Brennan,** *On a Greek Island: A Personal Experience* (UK: Poolbeg Press, 1998). In the late 1970s, Brennan, her poet husband and their two children settled on the island of Paros. Her vividly evoked landscapes, clear thumbnail sketches of the local people and sensitive account of their gradual assimilation, including the children's involvement in the local school, are underscored by an obvious and enduring affection for the island.

★ **Katherine Kizilios,** *The Olive Grove* (Aus/UK/US: Lonely Planet Journeys, 1998). At seventeen, exactly the age her father had been when he emigrated to Australia from his native Greece, Kizilios boarded a flight to Athens. Several trips and well over a decade later she returned to spend a few months floating round the Dodecanese, journeying into Thrace and Turkey and re-appraising the modern experience of Greek life from a village vantage point. Sections of carefully researched war history and her sympathetic treatment of the thousands of displaced people are clouded a little by lacklustre prose and a tendency to sneer at fellow-tourists. However Kizilios comes into her own on her travels to Istanbul and musings on the key themes of Greekness – lost glory and relations with Turkey.

★ **Patricia Storace,** *Dinner with Persephone* (UK: Granta, 1997/US: Random House, 1996). American poet, and fluent philhellene, Storace spent a year in Athens in the mid-1990s. Using the deceptively naive stance of the lone American abroad, she deploys a mass of friendships, chance encounters, cultural events and television soaps to tune into the nuances of Athenian Greek. Her dry self-awareness, lucid yet exuberant prose, and flair for research (of both the scholarly and open-eyed type) combine to make this a richly informative and enjoyable read. Not least, she manages the complex task of rendering the "Macedonia Question" just a little more comprehensible to an outsider. If you want to know why Greek humour is streaked with bitterness, or understand the tensions between east and west or the peculiar sense of continuity that places classical Athens at the centre of modern Athenian consciousness, then this is the book for you.

★ **Sara Wheeler,** *An Island Apart: Travels in Evia* (UK: Abacus, 1993). An entertaining chronicle of a five-month ramble across Evia, one of Greece's largest, but least-visited, islands. Wheeler's sure touch with Greek history and culture, and a frank and open approach to the people she meets – Orthodox nuns, goatherds, Albanian-speaking villagers, intellectuals – brings this island buzzing to life.

Guatemala

Faces at a roadblock

Louise Doughty

Louise Doughty, a novelist, critic and broadcaster, travelled with her younger sister from Mexico to Guatemala City using local buses. During a routine military roadblock on the road to the capital she discovers that the terror of 36 years of civil war and state repression is by no means forgotten. A short story based on material from this trip appears in the anthology *Wild Ways* (see p.651)

Louise Doughty's first book was *Crazy Paving* (1995), which was shortlisted for four awards and followed by the critically acclaimed *Dance With Me* (1996). Her latest is *Honey-Dew*, which she is adapting for film. She has also won awards for short stories and radio plays. Besides the Americas, she has travelled in Africa and Australia and is in the process of visiting various Eastern European countries as research for her next novel. She currently lives in London.

We crossed the border at dawn. A small stone bridge took my sister and I into Guatemala. Ahead, the road plunged on and upwards through dense, lush greenery. Here and there, palm trees sprung through like jack-in-the-boxes. The air was cool and clear, the sky white but becoming tinged with gold. The early morning mist was rising from a distant volcano.

We had been travelling for two weeks, stopping off on our journey from Mexico City to enjoy the colonial prettiness of Oaxaca and the beaches of Puerto Angel. From the Mexican coast, we traversed wide scrubland plains punctuated by the occasional maguey plant. At an oil refinery town called Salina Cruz, we had hit a bus strike, and crawled towards Guatemala on local buses through the night, finally reaching Tapuchula at the border twenty-four hours after we had left our cosy wooden *posada* in Puerto Angel. In a deserted bus hall, we had been accosted by a cleaner who sold us some *quetzales* (the local currency) at rip-off rates. We had run out of water and all we had for breakfast was a packet of sticky boiled sweets.

By contrast, our first impressions of Guatemala were of a tropical idyll, hazy blue skies, grey volcanoes and a thousand different types of greenery. The hill beyond the bridge rose sharply to a small, yellow-painted hut fronted by a porch and hatch. Even the military jeep parked next to it seemed somehow picturesque.

A young soldier sat in the hatch. We offered him our passports and he scanned our visas carefully, then extracted a piece of paper from his desk and fed it into a small, old-fashioned portable type-writer. When he had typed up our details, he charged us one *quetzal* each and waved us on.

As we made our way up the hill, a plump man in a straw hat came charging towards us, shouting and waving frantically. He grabbed both our bags, one in each hand – ignoring our protests – and ran back up the hill. We gave pursuit. Only when we mounted the rise to a lay-by did we realise he was a bus driver who had just seen his first two customers of the day. We sat on a nearby stone and chatted to him while he swabbed down his vehicle – the wheels of all buses had to be clean by law, he explained, to prevent the spread of crop and livestock diseases. When my sister enquired tentatively when the bus might be leaving, he glanced heavenward and shrugged. When it was full, he said eventually.

It filled up – eventually – with local people. It was still too early for other travellers. Rachel and I remarked upon how friendly everybody was, in notable contrast to Mexico, where as two women travelling alone we had met with a fair degree of hostility. Nearly everyone climbing on the bus paused to exclaim and smile when they saw us. We had been on our guard for over a fortnight and felt slightly dislocated by this welcome.

Our sense of dislocation increased when, after passing through a few hamlets and villages to pick up more passengers, the bus hit the main route for Guatemala City, a clean tarmac road through gentle hills. The landscape reminded me of Leicestershire, where we grew up. The road was uncannily like the one from Oakham to Melton Mowbray, which our parents used to take when we all drove over to visit Gran and Grandad. Then, suddenly, we would pass over a wooden bridge with sentinel crops of palm trees on either side or a volcano would rise before us.

We played a game, shutting our eyes, then opening them and describing where we thought we were at that particular second. (This sense of unreality has followed me wherever I have travelled, which makes me realise what a homebody I am. New or unusual landscapes always make me feel as though I am watching a film of myself travelling through them. If I listen to a Walkman, then I can do it complete with soundtrack.)

We were probably about two-thirds of the way through our journey when the bus rounded a bend and we were reminded sharply of exactly where we were. A long stretch of road lay straight ahead. Vehicles were pulled over onto the verges, as far as we could see. Stretched across the road itself was a row of military trucks. Ranged in front were soldiers with sub-machine-guns.

The chatter on our bus ceased immediately. Rachel and I craned our necks, more excited than frightened. The bus slowed its pace and crawled past the parked vehicles, towards the roadblock. On either side of us we could see cars, vans, trucks, buses. Everything had been stopped. There must have been several hundred soldiers questioning the occupants of each car, examining papers. As we neared the front, I saw on the left that the driver of a battered Ford had been spreadeagled over its bonnet. He was face down with his arms splayed. Three soldiers were gathered round. One of them was shouting.

The bus pulled up in front of the roadblock and the driver dismounted to talk to the soldiers. He seemed at ease with them, chatting as he handed over his papers. Meanwhile, an unsmiling soldier climbed onto the bus and then stood at the top of the aisle, his gun held across his chest, scanning each passenger in turn. We were sitting at the front of the bus and I could have reached out and touched him, yet he seemed as odd and remote as a statue, his combat hat pulled low over his forehead. I was reminded, absurdly, of the cadet corps at school, where I had been – briefly and ineffectually – Corporal Doughty. The only thing I had been any good at was the shooting, earning a marksman badge with a .22 rifle.

It was only when I glanced behind me at the other passengers that I began to realise how out-of-kilter, how ignorant, my observations were. Their faces were impassive, blanked by the desire not to be noticed. I turned back to the front and watched the young soldier as his gaze worked its way slowly down one side of the bus to the back, then back up over the passengers seated on the other side. At one point, his look hovered, then flicked back to a seat midway down the aisle. I became aware that I was holding my breath. After a brief stare, his gaze moved forward again. I was united with the other passengers in a slow, silent exhalation.

Somebody banged on the side of the bus and the soldier turned and seated himself at the wheel. The keys were still in the ignition and he began flicking switches on the dashboard. Another soldier who was standing by the door was looking towards the back of the bus and shouting.

Eventually, the soldier dismounted and the driver was allowed back on. He started the engine and there was much calling and waving between him and the soldiers. The bus inched forward, and we then sat in front of the roadblock with the engine bubbling beneath us while we waited for the soldiers to move one of the trucks and allow us through.

On the other side of the roadblock, other vehicles had been stopped but fewer. Within a few minutes we were clear and bowling down the wide empty road. It was only then that we felt able to lean forward and ask the driver what the roadblock had been about. I waited while Rachel translated for me. Drugs, I wondered? Insurgents? I was lamentably ignorant about the detail of the political situation in Guatemala but I knew about the rebellions and the army massacres of indigenous people.

Rachel leaned back in her seat with an ironic smile.

"What did he say?" I asked.

"It was a road safety check," she replied. "They were checking the lights."

It made our encounter seem laughable, fun, a story to tell the folks back home.

It was only when I returned to Britain six weeks later that I decided to correct my ignorance and got hold of an Amnesty International report on Guatemala. It made sobering reading. In 36 years of civil conflict, thousands had been killed, tortured or "disappeared". The indigenous peoples had been at the heart of this conflict. The situation was particularly bad in the early 1980s and full details of that terrible time are only just coming to light. In the Rio Negro massacre of 1982, for instance, 177 women and children were killed by the armed forces and their auxiliaries. (There were no men to kill because they had all been massacred one month earlier.) A grave containing 143 victims was not exhumed until 1994 – other mass graves in the area remain undisturbed.

Our encounter with the roadblock was essentially anecdotal. It was far more serious for the other occupants of our bus. Our driver had seemed relaxed about it – it clearly happened often enough to him – but even he had said casually to my sister, "Everyone on this bus is glad you are here." As foreign travellers, our presence had been a form of protection for them. Even the Guatemalan military knows the value of tourist dollars.

The human rights situation of any country presents the traveller with a dilemma. There is a terrible tendency – terrible but understandable – for a traveller to be thrilled by a brush with danger, to bring it home like a souvenir and hand it out to friends. I have been guilty of that – my sister less so. She has a degree in Spanish and Latin American Studies and now works for Amnesty International.

One alternative is to boycott such countries altogether – but ignorance is oxygen to oppressive regimes who are perfectly happy for the rest of the world to pass their activities by. Burma keeps its borders closed for a good reason.

My solution to this dilemma has been to go to such places but to bring home responsible awareness as well as souvenirs. On my return from Guatemala I tried, unsuccessfully, to sell a feature about the human rights situation to various national newspapers. (I was told that Guatemala wasn't hot news.) I used the roadblock incident in a novel I was writing at the time. The novel wasn't published either, although I have since written and published three others, but an entirely invented encounter between a Mayan boy and the Guatemalan military surfaced in a story which was recently published in an anthology. Such gestures are hardly going to shake the Guatemalan government but I do believe that the spreading of knowledge is an intrinsically good thing. The alternative is the darkness of ignorance, and soldiers who massacre prefer to do it by night. And, yes, I joined Amnesty International.

A positive taste of hardship

Sue Balcomb

 After several years travelling and intermittently working as a tour guide and development worker in Mexico, Central and South America, Sue Balcomb eventually returned to England, seven months pregnant. She had planned to settle here after the birth of her daughter, Katalina, but soon felt the pull of Latin America. Also Katalina's father is Mexican and Sue wanted her to have some first-hand experience of her culture and roots. She improved her Spanish to degree level and eventually found a voluntary placement in rural Guatemala which would accept her as a single mother with a three-year-old daughter in tow.

I knew some of Guatemala's history and politics from my involvement in Central American solidarity groups and from the talks that I had given as a tour guide in the early 1990s. Since then, the "civil" war of 36 years had been declared over and the Peace Accords signed. Nevertheless, political repression had not been eradicated and I wasn't sure how safe we would be.

Feeling both frightened and excited, I booked us tickets for a year. What would it be like? Would it be dangerous? Would I be lonely? Would we get ill? How would Katalina manage long, uncomfortable bus journeys and basic living conditions? I scribbled a list of potential hazards and possibilities, and once down on paper the negatives diminished and became manageable. We could always come home.

249

In January 1997, we flew to Guatemala City where we spent a few days recovering from food poisoning we had contracted in Heathrow Airport. So much for the health dangers of "abroad"! We stayed with the director of Casa Guatemala, a non-governmental organisation (NGO) set up to help abandoned, malnourished and orphaned children. The project has centres and a clinic in the city for children under two, and a home, school and farm for those aged between two and eighteen in Eastern Guatemala. Based on the Rio Dulce river in steamy jungle, the branch of Casa Guatemala we were to call home was accessible only by boat.

We arrived in the late afternoon, the sticky heat pricking at our skins. The project leaders told us the centre housed some eighty children, cared for by a team of international volunteers, local teachers and care workers. That first night, as we lay in our narrow bed under the eaves, I was confused by the sound of loud cheering. Someone, somewhere must be watching an exciting football match yet I knew that the generator had been turned off – there was no electricity and anyway I hadn't seen any sign of a television. I tiptoed down the creaky wooden stairs and outside in the direction of the crowd, to discover that the swamp surrounding our building was swarming with mating frogs, calling to each other in the watery blackness.

We lived in a huge building, the *"ranchon"*, along with forty other children and eight adults. Katalina and I had our own room, windowless and desperately hot in the dry season, which came with a collection of unwelcome night-time visitors. Our "pets" included fighting rats, vampire bats that bit the children's noses (leaving two neat puncture marks as evidence), small ant-eating bears, scorpions and cockroaches with such long legs that Katalina thought they were spiders.

My work was to set up and manage a hydroponics greenhouse (meaning cultivation without soil), establish a large chicken hut and attempt to find a crop which could be cultivated on poor, cleared jungle soil. My days were physically hard with long hours. While I was on the farm, Katalina attended the kindergarten and learned to fight her way among the emotionally and physically scarred young children. Like all new children to the project, she was bullied and had to find her place within the group, but her basic grasp of Spanish helped and she soon made friends with some of the *chiquitos* (small children) and younger girls.

The basic diet and hygiene conditions affected our health. Katalina suffered from sores that were difficult to heal, and within a couple of months had contracted amoebic dysentery. We tried numerous cures: belladonna from a homeopathic travellers' kit brought from home, a local concoction of crushed burnt tortillas mixed with cooking oil, hefty stomach massages given by the local women, and drinking bottled water brought in from the mainland. Finally we consulted a doctor on the river, who suggested yet another medicine. Katalina had been taking this latest potion for several days, when I looked it up in the excellent healthcare book, *Where There is No Doctor*. I was shocked to read "Dangerous – do not use. This drug can cause blindness, paralysis and even death"! She stopped taking it immediately while I watched her closely over the next few days for any side-effects. Katalina survived unscathed and thankfully the amoebas didn't; we were healthy for the rest of our stay. Apart from outposts like this one in the jungle, access to medical care was easy, quick and, for a Western budget, cheap.

Although I had difficulty with the constraints of institutional living and sometimes felt very drained and lonely, there were many positives or we wouldn't have stayed so long. I loved swimming in the wide river with Katalina in her rubber ring, out of our depth, gazing at the verdant jungle around us and marvelling at our isolation. The chickens' growth from being one day old to producing eggs was a joy to me as well as the children, and our diet was greatly improved by the regular addition of eggs to the main staple of beans and tortilla. I was stimulated by conversations with other volunteers and overwhelmed by the beauty of occasional starlit rides along the inky river to drink beer in the nearest tiny town.

The project was constantly thwarted by shortage of funds and by the lack of a coherent developmental approach. Rules were made and changed with little or no consultation and children were transferred to other homes without any preparation. There was a high turnover of staff due to low morale and lack of involvement in the decision-making process; projects were started and then abandoned as people came and went. In terms of providing the children with better care than on the streets, where many would have died, the project was a success. However, in terms of development work or empowerment of the young people and staff, it was sorely lacking. After nearly six months, once the baby chicks had grown enough to produce eggs and the programme had been set up to pass on skills to the teenagers, I felt I had achieved enough to move on.

Through a contact in Antigua, I eventually found work with SHARE Guatemala, a large NGO which had recently set up a programme of participatory rural development in 24 regions in the country. It seemed as if I was to use my community work skills at last.

With SHARE I was placed with a smaller co-operating agency based in the department of San Marcos, in the western mountainous region of Guatemala. Within weeks we were settled into a new routine. I was found lodgings with a local single mother and her family. We had our own small room and access to a beautiful rose-filled courtyard, shared with a verbose parrot. My brief was to join a team of local rural development workers, working on a programme designed to promote, support and facilitate teaching-learning processes and the exchange of resources in three main areas: family health and nutrition, better management of family resources and community organisation with a focus on sustainability. Our first task was to carry out village diagnoses (a kind of needs survey) and help find ways of solving the priority problems.

I worked in two villages, one a bus ride of an hour and a half from my base, the other a further ninety minutes' mountainous walk uphill from the bus stop. When the weather was fine the views were spectacular; for miles and miles, the hills rolled and dipped, the steep, deep-green slopes dotted with small villages and fields. Across the clear blue sky, the Santa Maria volcano smoked in the distance. I could hardly believe that I had the chance to work somewhere so stunningly beautiful and pure.

Travelling with a child opened up social opportunities for me. My motherhood helped bridge a cultural gap and exchanges were open and positive. We were rarely hassled and generally I felt much safer than when I had travelled solo; everyone talked with us. I have vivid memories of Katalina skating up and down the darkened aisles of rickety buses to sit next to gnarled old *campesino* men. They chatted to her about their lives and families, and laughed with her in a way that we have never encountered in Britain.

At work we held meetings to discuss and analyse aspects of village life. We established family vegetable plots and trained women to set up their own credit unions. I spent many hours sitting on damp mountainsides with groups of women, the swirling mists alternately revealing and hiding their faces, the beauty of their woven traditional dress a poignant contrast with the poverty of their living conditions.

Katalina attended school near our home until the long summer holidays. From October until January, she came with me to work. The one daily bus would bump and shake us along the unmade, rutted road, high up into the clouds, to live a remote village life. For a few days each week, we slept in the same room – and sometimes the same bed – as the rest of our host family. Lithe and wiry Jose and the small, rounded midwife Liandra provided us with a home, along with their numerous children and extended family. While I was busy working with groups of people in the community, improving my Spanish and learning a smattering of the local indigenous language, Katalina ran round with the children in the maize plantations. She was cherished and cared for by adults and children alike. In a world unspoilt by consumerism, we taught the children English games like the Okey Cokey and Pass the Parcel and Katalina learned to be resilient and imaginative. For my part, walking through the swaying twelve-foot-high maize to the latrine in the dead of night, with my stick against the *chuchos bravos* (fierce dogs), grasping a dripping beeswax candle in a carved stone, I felt I had time-travelled to some core of my being.

These months were so full of good experiences that it is hard to pick the most influential moments. Being a single mother, I had an instant bond with the many women whose husbands were away as illegal workers in North America or who had died through illness. On frosty mornings we huddled together around the stone stoves and patted tortillas while sharing stories of love and ambition. Some nights, Katalina and I stayed with the local mayor, and he and I would share a single beer on a walk through the moon-washed mountains to the lookout, way above the nearest town.

Among the real highs was finishing the diagnostic process in the villages and presenting a slide show, which had the audience in stitches; many people had never seen images of themselves and they wanted to see them again and again. It was great to see villagers, especially the women, stand up in front of a large group and speak about their communal problems and future. I hoped that the women, with their new-found confidence, would be participating more in their community's development. Sitting in a dirt-floored kitchen, shrouded in smoke from the wood-burning stoves, while the Improvements Committee told me that no one before had ever worked and lived with them with true respect, was truly inspiring.

There were lows too, during which I was forever being reminded of the desperate state of the world. While capitalism, consumerism and planet destruction continue to hurtle on, poorer nations and peoples (for there are also some very rich people in Guatemala) are left to struggle harder and harder for wood, water and food. I spent evenings with men in sombreros who told me how they had been ripped off by an unscrupulous water architect, who took their money and left without the study they needed to provide water for the village. They shared with me their lives. "How many children do you have?", I asked the 43-year-old treasurer of the group. He looked at me for a long while before softly answering, "I have five children alive, and seven who have died."

Sometimes, when I felt lonely and unconnected, I struggled to deal with the same old questions – "Where do you come from? Where is Katalina's father?" – and the lack of privacy. It was hard to enjoy the rain and mud, and diet of days and days of tamales, a flavourless mixture of dried maize, soaked, ground and wrapped in leaves before steaming. It was frustrating to have lengthy arguments with the professional men in the office base, when I would win because my point was justified but ultimately lose since they could not bear to be "beaten" by a woman. I loathed the way the evangelical church would blare out their lambastic sermons through loud speakers attached to the outside of buildings. In one village, church leaders had spread rumours that the free school breakfasts were "contaminated" as they believed the aid had come through the "enemy" Catholic church. Despite my attempts to dispel these myths, many children didn't eat the food and nothing was ever resolved.

At the same time, the community spirit did win through. We trained volunteers to begin to co-ordinate and run the projects and develop problem-solving strategies. Subsidised food for under-threes encouraged women to have their children weighed and attend health education sessions; the diagnostic process was completed and documented; the vegetables were planted and reforestation planned. The Improvements Committees began the long task of campaigning for drinking water (in a neighbouring village this had taken thirteen years!) and for a paved road. As our date for departure loomed closer, I felt desperately sad to leave.

Looking back, I realised that the fears on my list had scarcely materialised. Katalina had been ill, but she recovered and developed a good immune system. Her Spanish improved immensely and we both delighted in the contact with the "real" world. Long journeys were always helped by cheerful conversation and the sharing of laughter and food. Living conditions were basic, but we soon became used to them and grew to appreciate the comforts of life in Britain. People had responded positively to my status as a volunteer, incredulous that I was willing to work just for food and a place to stay – a luxury simply not open to them. Some went out of their way to thank me for what I was doing, despite all my assurances that I was receiving way beyond what I gave. When it finally came to leaving I knew that we would keep in touch and that I would one day return.

read on . . .

Louise Doughty, "Lady Chatterley's Chicken", in *Wild Ways: New Stories about Women on the Road,* Margo Daly and Jill Dawson (ed) (UK: Sceptre, 1998).** A backpacker attempts to shrug off a fellow traveller after a one-night stand in Puerta Angel, only to find herself stalked by him along the bus routes of rural Guatemala. Her attempt at escape brings catastrophe to a young Guatemalan truckdriver. In this wonderful, lucid fictional account, Doughty starkly evokes the Guatemala experienced on the backpacker's route and one woman's travel malaise.

Lucy McCauley, "What I Came For" in *Travelers' Tales: A Woman's World,* Marybeth Bond (ed) (US: Travelers' Tales Inc., 1995).** McCauley returns to Guatemala with her mother to seek out her grandmother's mountain grave. Having married an American adventurer, her grandmother left her North Carolina home to begin a new life in the jungle. McCauley delves sensitively through her mother's childhood memories and eye-witness accounts to shed light on her family's settler lifestyle.

Mary Morris, *Nothing to Declare: Memoirs of a Woman Travelling Alone* (1988; UK: Picador, 1999/US: St Martin's Press, 1999).** Weary of life in New York, novelist Mary Morris packs up her bags and goes to live in the small dusty town of San Miguel de Allende, north of Mexico City. Her subsequent travels take her down through southern Mexico and into the lush mountains and jungles of Guatemala. As with her second travel book, *Wall to Wall*, Morris manages effortlessly to weave her own personal story with fine description and astute observations of the places and people she encounters.

Jean-Marie Simon, *Eternal Spring – Eternal Tyranny* **(US: Norton, 1987).** Of all the books on human rights in Guatemala, this is the one that speaks with blinding authority and the utmost clarity. Combining the highest standards in photography with crisp text, Simon's book allows the facts to speak for themselves, which they do with amazing strength. If you want to know what happened in Guatemala over the last twenty years or so there is no better book, though Simon does, however, clearly take sides, aligning herself with the revolutionary left – there's no mention of abuses committed by the guerrillas.

India

Innocence and experience

Rebecca Hardie

Kerala's palm-fringed coast and languid backwater canals have long attracted travellers seeking a retreat from India's dusty northern plains. London-based Rebecca Hardie discovered Kerala's charms on her first trip to India. She was planning a return trip when her mum – a novice backpacker — suddenly decided to come along. Rebecca is also the author of "Monkey Brain", about getting to grips with meditation in Thailand, starting on p.560.

"Mum!" I yelp again, gritting my teeth slightly. A rickshaw skims past, perilously close. I had tried to imagine what this trip would be like, but had given up – the variables had simply been too overwhelming. In India, with Mum. I had struggled to make sense of it. Two mutually exclusive concepts, but here they were, forced together in the face of furious oncoming traffic.

The conversation had gone something like this:

"What are your holiday plans this year, darling?" A perfectly innocent question.

"I think I'm going to try and go to India in October." A perfectly reasonable answer.

"Who with?" A mother's usual concern.

"Mum!" She knows how I like to do things. "On my own."

"Oh, don't worry sweetheart, I'll come with you."

★ ★ ★ ★

And so it had come to pass that after a long and sleepless flight from London, via Sri Lanka and several Middle Eastern duty-free shopping opportunities, we were aiming for Quilon, a provincial town in the south Indian state of Kerala, where we were to embark on a backwater boat trip.

I had been determined to launch Mum in at the deep-end, and didn't want to stop until we'd reached our destination. Landing in Kerala's capital city of Trivandrum, we begin to navigate our way through the tiny airport, through the scrum of rickshaw and taxi drivers wrestling for our business. And I begin to suspect that I might not really have considered her in this at all. Easy for me to find my way around, to glance about and adjust in the blink of an eye, but I had done all this before. Mum had spent 55 years doing nothing of the sort, but desperately wanting to.

Luggage in hand, I pull her onto a screeching local bus, full of sweaty strangers staring openly. I am too tired to think about anything but the ninety-minute journey to Quilon, and certainly too tired to reach out to the mother beside me, who is keeping her eyes firmly closed, against the jolts both of the bus and of what might lie ahead.

Quilon is a sweet sight after our fifteen-hour journey. I insist that we walk to the hotel, wherever it may be, and stride off as Mum lugs obediently behind. Eventually, the *Shah International* towers above the street, its magnificent name emblazoned for all to see. We are effusively meeted and greeted, and led to our room. It is tiny, dark and frayed. The air-cooling unit, when we try it, sprays a storm of insects straight out over the beds: temperature control by means of the whirring of a thousand tiny wings.

Mum, now I am actually bothering to pay any attention to her, is displaying no signs of either disappointment or surprise. She checks the bathroom, and comes out puzzled. "Darling?"

"Mmmm."

"Why do you think there are mothballs in the sink?"

I smile to myself. I'd forgotten this particular sub-continental conundrum. Why in the world *are* there always mothballs in the drains, in the sinks, in the showers? For the subtle, fresh scent of Napthalene? And with that smile, I feel myself easing back into India;

my exhaustion relaxing into a sense of arrival. I am beginning to remember the India – and the Kerala – I had visited five years before, full of the quizzical situations that had undermined my Western pre-conceptions, full of the foibles and contradictions that had demanded laughter in place of crying.

I sit back and begin to watch Mum settling in. She pads around, unpacking, seeing to this and that. I mention that we will have to get her a small purse to put her change in. This will mean she can avoid having to tangle with her array of money belts (one round the waist, one round the neck). It will also, perhaps, mean we can avoid looking quite so ripe for the pocket-picking.

The garrison of accoutrements she has brought disarms me. I find it hard to react to inflatable coat hangers. So hard, indeed, that in a trice I find myself blowing one up so Mum can hang the dress she is ironing. A travel iron, a hair-dryer, immaculately labelled pharmaceuticals, an umbrella, a fold-away rain hat that ties under your chin, a washing line with suction pads for attaching to the wall . . . a precaution for all eventualities. She looks just as she does at home. Her daily routines, transported. Arming herself against the unfamiliar, just in case.

After a quick nap – it's only 4pm locally – we decide to go out for a wander, to stave off real sleep. I had thought that Kerala, in all its lush fertility, would make a perfect starting point. We could embark on a languid backwater trip, through the lagoons, lakes and rivers that stretch along the coast, blurring the land into the Arabian Sea. But Quilon itself is an unremarkable town – for tourists, it is little more than a door to those waterways. However, sometimes it is just this sort of town that can turn out to be the most extraordinary. To reveal the essence of everyday life lived in the country with the second-largest population on earth, in the world's largest democracy. And for my mother, in her exhausted and tender state, it is Quilon that will be her first real taste of Indian chaos.

Refreshed by our rest, my eyes are now fully open. She, however, appears to have dispensed with the need to blink. She is, quite literally, agog. She simply cannot believe her eyes. Basic movement seems too complicated, and she's hardly spoken since we left the hotel. We stand, stock-still and silent, as she tries to process what is before her. The jumble of shops and buildings, piled one on top of the other, defying gravity and Western standards of form. They knock into their neighbours, brilliantly painted signs clashing noisily, fronts wide-open to the world. Shop after shop selling the very same things: brightly coloured buckets and mugs sitting dusty in the sun, stainless-steel cooking vessels reflecting a million street scenes just like this one, suitings and shirtings, brilliant saris heavy with embroidery and jewels, towering pyramids of gorgeous sweets flecked with silver and gold, stalls teeming proudly with Y-fronts, rubber sandals and suitcases.

The people weave by in a hot haze of activity. In and out of the shops, through and past the stalls, up and down and across the screaming roads. Loudspeakers wailing Bollywood film music compete for air-time. This is how "Honk your horn for Jesus" translates in this land of a million Hindu deities. And there are offerings everywhere — tiny collections of bright flowers and leaves, jasmine opening up as the evening approaches, mango leaves to welcome you inside. The whole of life is here, lived on the pavement, in the rising stink of auto-rickshaw fumes and evening cooking. "It's just like it is on the telly. But it's real," is my mother's breathless best that very first day.

★ ★ ★ ★

Things move very slowly for a while after that. And very much led by me. The expected parent-child role reversal seems to be happening early, as I do all the talking, all the handing over of money, make all the decisions and plans. I choose the food, advise and inform and explain. My mother's tongue is tied for the first time in her life. She resembles nothing so much as a startled, but highly enthusiastic, deer.

"Fifteen rupees, Madam." After a period of intense, frowning concentration, she brings out a selection of coins, and a thinly disguised smile of blank incomprehension.

"Fifteen, Mum."

She squints at the coins, one by one, then consigns the money to me, aware that she isn't participating as she might. She is at the mercy of my interpretations, of my familiarity with the place. And I am at the mercy of the dependence she has allowed herself to assume. I can feel the responsibility draining me. Worse than that, I can feel it irritating me, and my eyes begin to close once again to her perception of all of this, to the demands that are being made on her by this frenetically new environment.

"Oh God," I wince exaggeratedly. Four days in, and we are embarking on our journey through the backwaters. "We're even going to have to go on a special tourist boat now," as if to let her know how very different things would be if I were on my own. I leave her with our packs while I go and get tickets, complain bitterly about the price and rush off to the nearby market to buy some provisions for the journey. I make a show of being busy. By now I'm fed up, and doing little to demystify the way to get things done. She sits calmly, looking around her. Placid as a baby blowing bubbles.

We cut through great swathes of water hyacinths, their roots reaching way down, choking all in their path. Their flowers coating the surface in rippling colour, their strong waxy leaves deadening the sound of the boat's mechanical progress. Impossible not to be lulled by this, and by the view stretching out before us. As if we are sailing out into the middle of nowhere. We are on a watery highway to the horizon, flanked by lazy palm trees, the merest frisson of a warm breeze flicking their leaves in a shimmer of green.

Every now and again the scene changes from wilderness to domestic. Mud-and-straw huts appear. Whole communities live in this flooded place, on tiny reclaimed slivers of land that they cultivate as if they were ordinary fields.

We stop for lunch at a village en route. Mum gives me a look, suspicious that I might be keen to try what's on offer. But I get stuck into a thali – an assortment of curries served with rice on a tin plate – and she agrees it's delicious. With time to kill as the other tourists look around cautiously for a toilet, peel their bananas and wonder whether the potato chips might be safe, we walk further into the village.

A group of village women and children are gathered around slicks of silver fish. The chatter sounds brittle, until it is cut by unfurling peals of laughter. I approach, pointing encouragingly towards my camera. They nod, slap thighs, laugh some more. There must be five generations here, going about their daily business. Grouped by geography, by having all grown up under the same patch of sky.

I laugh and joke along, squat amongst the fish and faces. I'm having fun – mingling nicely, thank you. Until I hear a great crash of hilarity, and turn to look. There is my mother, sitting in the dirt, her sunglasses on upside down and she's pulling faces for England. Exaggerated mimes and japes to communicate. Those around her, young and old, are clapping their hands with glee. And it is mutual. She catches my gaze, pleasure transforming her face. And I return it, smiling straight out to her, basking in the warmth of her sudden comprehension.

Carolyn came too

Sheila Keegan

Sheila Keegan first followed the hippie trail to India in the early 1970s. Twenty-five years later, she packed up her market-research company in London and set out to revisit her old haunts with her eight-year-old daughter, Carolyn. Their seven-month trip spanned India, Thailand, Cambodia, Vietnam, Laos, Indonesia and Australia. See also their adventures in Cambodia (p.108).

I knocked on the head-teacher's door. I felt like a child, not a grown woman. "How would you feel about me taking Carolyn out of school for two terms?" I blurted out.

"Why do you want to do that?"

Nervousness made me blunt. "I want to travel with her".

"Where will you go?"

"I don't know. We'll play it by ear. Through Asia. To Australia eventually, I think".

She paused for a moment. "I think that's a brilliant idea. She'll learn such a lot. Some children wouldn't cope, but Carolyn will be fine."

"I'll take school books with us. I'll make sure she does some work every day," I gushed, full of gratitude. She smiled. "Yes, well, you could do that. But it would be a shame if it spoiled the experience for her. Enjoy it, both of you."

I felt more nervous about the trip than I let on. My business partner, Rosie, and I had been running our market-research company for ten years. Closing the business had been a big decision, and one that we had been thinking about for several years. We had set up the company when she was pregnant with her first child, Beckie. We had built the business around our four children – three of hers, one of mine. We were juggling home, family and work, rushing from business meeting to ballet class, as is the way of working mothers. The company had survived the recession. We were doing well, but we felt stale and in desperate need of a break. My life as a single parent had become so regimented, so pressured, that there was never time to ask whether there was a better way of living. I needed a break.

There seemed so much to do before we left: sorting out the business and the house; getting our injections and malaria pills; loading up with mosquito nets and an emergency blood-transfusion kit with sterilised needles, and then cramming it all into two small hold-alls. It wouldn't fit. The clothes had to go. They could be picked up en route.

We set off from London at the end of January. I should have felt euphoric. Instead I felt scared. I had no idea how we would fare. I prided myself on being a seasoned traveller, but that had been twenty years before – many comfortable beds, bottles of Chardonnay and beach holidays ago.

Carolyn is an adventurous and outgoing child, but is still a typical eight-year-old: obsessed with television, sticker books and disdainful of any food that does not emanate from McDonald's. I had gone back to work when Carolyn was just two months old, so we were used to being apart much of the time. How would we survive being together for seven months, 24 hours a day?

Arriving in India, we headed straight for Goa, which we had visited several times before. It was supposed to be a holiday, before we began the "proper" travelling. It was difficult. We fought non-stop as the realisation of our interdependence dawned. Was it going to be like this for seven months?

Next, we headed south by train, to the "real" India. Suddenly we were thrust into the chaos and poverty and excitement of a country that is like no other. I had spent time in India as a wandering hippie in the early Seventies and I was keen to revisit old haunts.

Certainly it is easier now; third-class train travel has disappeared and poverty is less acute, but India still shocks the senses.

Carolyn was stoical as she watched the limbless beggars tugging at her clothes, and acquiesced to the constant stares. She was less stoical about the "hole in the ground" toilets. She was afraid she would fall in. On an early attempt to use·one, a giant cockroach emerged and she ran out the door, knickers around her ankles, to the amusement of the local women. Squatting over an Indian toilet is an acquired skill. With practice, she soon mastered it.

Almost everywhere we went in India, we were greeted with friendly curiosity. Where was my husband? Why was I travelling on my own with a child? I invented a husband working at home, to cut conversations short. Carolyn was a spectacle in her own right: her pale skin and red hair were irresistible, as women often leaned over to touch her hair and marvel at her freckles. She took all this in her stride.

I allowed her much more freedom than I would do at home because India felt so safe, so child-friendly. I would send her out to buy bananas with a few rupees – she always managed to bargain a better price than me. She would come back with a mango or some nuts, which she had been given as a present.

In many ways, Carolyn coped better than I did. On one occasion, we got lost in the Western Ghats, along the far southwestern coast, and had to take six local Indian buses to reach the city of Cochin. It took us several days, and in the process we turned up in small towns were Western children were undoubtedly a rare sight. As we waited at a bus station, we were surrounded by thirty or forty men who just stood impassively, staring at us. I became enraged and shouted at them to go away. They remained impassive, staring. "Calm down mum. Just read your book," said Carolyn as she reached into her rucksack, pulled out her *Famous Five* book and settled down to read.

One of the magical times in India was a four-day camel trek in the Thar Desert in western Rajasthan. We set off from Jaisalmer, an exquisite twelfth-century town of golden buildings, with filigree sandstone carvings so delicate they could have been cut from butter. Each of us had a camel – Carolyn had insisted on her own, Peacock; an incongruous name for the hefty, balding beast. With a typical eight-year-old's preoccupation, she looked on in horror as Peacock leaned forward to catch the droppings of the camel ahead in his mouth.

"Ugh. That's disgusting. Mum! Look! That's disgusting," she yelled, as she stared, fascinated.

Once we had become accustomed to the lurching of the camels, we settled into the timeless serenity of the desert. Our days assumed a routine. Up early, breakfast cooked by our guides, Baru and Garth, on a campfire built with twigs and camel dung, saddle up and trudge through the desert until the heat mounted like a furnace, and then stop to sleep till the day cooled. Afternoons were the best, as we ambled into the sunset, stopped for supper around the campfire and then settled down for an early night under the open sky.

We became accustomed to the groans and farts of the camels tethered nearby and to the strange, haunting songs of Baru, which seemed to be born of the solitude and other-worldliness of our desert surroundings. The props of the twentieth century had gone. We were suspended in time.

On the final night of the trip, Carolyn and I lay side by side, wrapped in our blankets, chatting. "It's time for sleep," I said. "Lie back now and just look at the stars."

"But where are the stars? There are no stars tonight."

Suddenly, lightning flashed across the far western sky, silhouetting our camels. It flashed again. We watched, fascinated. A wind started up. "Quick. Cover your things. A big sandstorm is coming," shouted Baru. We packed everything away, put the camera in a plastic bag, tied up our hats, and Baru build a barricade around us, piling up everything from the supply sacks to the camel saddles.

Carolyn was sobbing: "I don't like this, Mummy. I don't like this."

"It'll be alright. I'll tell you a story."

We buried ourselves under the blanket. The wind roared around us and we could hear the constant thunder. It started to rain and the blankets grew sodden and cold. Baru fixed a large plastic sheet over the top of us, burying the edges in the sand. "For the baby," he said. "The rains are coming more."

The sand covered the blankets and plastic sheet. It was heavy and we could not move. I remembered hearing stories about sheep lost under snowfall and were only discovered days later. Who would ever find us buried together out in the middle of the desert? Feeling claustrophobic, I tunnelled out with my hand to reach fresh air, but the sand blew in and got in our mouths and eyes.

It was four hours until the sandstorm passed. We were both exhausted, but we could not sleep. We lay there waiting for the faint light of dawn. When we got up, Baru had already lit the fire. He was cheerful. "Day is day. Night is night. This desert life," he said.

Heading back on our camels toward town, I could see Jaisalmer Fort, dramatic against the flat skyline. We reached the road, and jeeps roared past, belching exhaust fumes. It was noisy. It was crowded. And despite our sandstorm scare, both Carolyn and I were reluctant to let go of the desert. "I want Peacock. I don't want to leave him," sobbed Carolyn back at the hotel. She was inconsolable. We headed out to the shops, where we bought a tiny silver camel that we named Peacock. Back in England, months later, we wrapped him up and deposited him in Carolyn's "safe" drawer, which houses the mementoes of her life to date: the wrist tag from the hospital where she was born, the curl from her first haircut, the stitches from her broken arm.

Travelling with a child is very different to travelling on your own. I am, by nature, an adventurous traveller. At times I felt very frustrated that I had to curtail my plans because they would be unfair to Carolyn: the going would be too tough, it was not safe, she would be bored. However, equally, when I chose to do something I knew she would enjoy, I often reaped unexpected rewards.

For instance, much of our two-and-a-half-month journey through India was plotted according to the availability of animals to be fed, stroked or ridden. We chose to visit Bandipur National Park near the southern city of Mysore because of the promise of elephant rides and tigers. As a result, we experienced a most entertaining and novel safari trip. The tour started in the late afternoon, when the animals in the sanctuary were supposedly stirring after the heat of the day and contemplating supper. About twenty of us – travellers with cameras, Indians with babies – clambered into a rickety minibus designed to seat eight. The windows had two flimsy aluminium bars across them, low down, with a space above that could easily accommodate a marauding tiger. Obviously none was expected and we shortly understood why.

Grating and clanking, the minibus set off, spewing noxious exhaust fumes as the driver pounded his foot on the accelerator and skidded down the dusty path through the scrubby bush. Large notices inside the bus demanded "Silence", presumably so we could catch the stirring animals unawares. They fell on deaf ears. The babies cried in relay and then in chorus. The adults chattered and shrieked, and no amount of admonishment on the part of the driver made any difference. They had come along for the fun of the ride, not the animal spotting. They urged the driver towards a more neck-breaking speed. The travellers strained out the windows, cameras at the ready, waiting to snap any passing specimen. But the combination of the rattling, belching minibus and the deafening occupants ensured that no self-respecting animal would come within miles. We were a ghetto-blaster on wheels.

We did spot an elephant in the distance, but as there was a man riding him, we did not consider this to be a valid form of wildlife. Then, to our joy, we noticed a stag who, presumably, was deaf. He stood, head held proud, a brilliant white neck and chest thrust forward, like a Victorian gentleman posing at a photo sitting. I positioned my camera awaiting the decisive moment. I missed it. We whistled passed him at such a speed that all I got was a cloud of brown dust and a glimpse of what looked like a subtle leer on his chops. I never did get a photo of an animal in Bandipur, but I got some nice pictures of tigers at Mysore Zoo.

Food was another area of compromise when travelling with Carolyn. It would be gratifying to think I had reared a child who would tuck into curries with gusto and sample local delicacies with genuine interest. But no, I had a normal London-reared eight-year-old. Weaning her on garlic and seaweed had had no noticeable effect. At age five, she rebelled and refused to eat anything but burgers, pizza, chips and ice cream. By age eight, nothing had changed. For two-and-a-half months in India, she lived largely on rice, chapati and vitamin pills. I watched in alarm as her weight dropped until she was skin and bone, and I went to extraordinary lengths to find food she would eat.

We once travelled on a train for 28 hours in order to find a Wimpy restaurant. Delhi turned out to be a culinary haven for Carolyn. As she tucked into chicken nuggets and a strawberry milkshake at Wimpy, she announced: "After this, I'm going to have a double burger." She did, and then vowed we would be back for supper.

"But Delhi has some of the best restaurants in the world, " I protested.

"Yes, and this is one of them," she retorted.

But there were compensations. The social life in Delhi's Wimpy was a revelation. It was full of young adults who had obviously dressed up for the occasion. The men wore jeans and leather jackets, in spite of the heat. They preened and swaggered in front of the women who sat, poised, made-up and bejewelled. This appeared to be young Delhi's prime pick-up joint. I spent many a contented hour observing courtship rituals while Carolyn stocked up on lamb burgers and thick shakes.

Many people were horrified when I announced I was taking my eight-year-old child through India. She would be ill. She would hate it. She would never catch up at school. She was ill – once – and it was scary, but she recovered. She did hate some of it, as did I, but this was more than balanced by the good times. Carolyn and I had to learn to work together as partners. It was not always easy, but we did it. She would wriggle through crowds to secure seats on overcrowded buses, while I struggled behind with the luggage. She would haggle in the markets and negotiate rates in hotels. She became adept at sign language and at establishing an easy rapport with all sorts of people.

She was disappointed to receive few letters from home, so she wrote to the Queen and the Prime Minister, asking them to write back to her, care of poste restante. She was delighted when she received replies from both.

The trip made her streetwise. It gave her a confidence that has stayed with her. It also gave us a closeness that I hope will see us through the teenage years. Back in London, Carolyn settled more easily than I did. She was glad to be home and "back to normal". She learned not to discuss the trip too much with her friends; they were not interested. Her school-work did not seem to have suffered. On our trip, she had discovered reading and devoured books. Her maths had been honed by hours of haggling; by eking out her £1 a week pocket money and by changing it from one currency to another as we travelled across Asia.

I was less keen to be back. I would have happily stayed away another year. Rosie and I re-started our company and we are back at work, but we have organised it so that we are not as tied. We take more time off. We are involved in other things. I would like to travel more with Carolyn. I am nostalgic for that space. But Carolyn's fantasy holiday is to travel first-class to the States to visit Universal Studios, whereas mine is to spend six months living in a jungle in Borneo.

Stopping to learn

Eleanor Simmons

Eleanor Simmons, a London-based researcher and writer, set off on a six-month solo trip around India. She had planned to stick to the usual backpacking circuit, travelling from north to south on trains and local buses. In order to visit a family friend, however, she makes a detour to Orissa, one of India's least-visited states, where a large tribal minority faces extreme rural poverty. Here, she finds herself drawn into the world of development work.

I had chugged past hundreds of train stations like Berhampur during my months in India: dusty, sun-baked and crowded with encampments of people, luggage and the odd cow. All seemed like whistlestops en route to the usual tourist destinations: Agra, Goa, Madras. There never seemed any reason to stop until now.

Govind fished me out at the station, greeting me like a long-lost daughter. It all seemed a long way from the damp English November, when Govind, a visiting family friend, had first heard about my plans to travel in India, and insisted I come and see his development organisation in Orissa.

Relaxing was not high on his agenda. He ushered me into a jeep, and within seconds I was reminded of his extraordinary zeal for his work. His conversation opener was, "What is your opinion of the poverty in India?" I'd found the all-pervasiveness of poverty in India deeply shocking. Leprous beggars and malnourished children were just the most visible end of the spectrum. Skinny rickshaw drivers and small children working in restaurants seemed like success stories in comparison. Aware of the helpless banality of my answer, I replied: "It's appalling."

Govind grinned. "And now you will find out what is to be done," he said.

Stunned, I listened as Govind outlined his plans for my stay. What I had thought would be a social visit of a few days was transforming itself into a month-long crash course in development studies: I was to accompany his colleagues on their rounds, he told me, in order to see how his organisation operated. I could ask the villagers whatever questions I wished.

How could I do this? I wanted to protest that I was not an expert aid-worker, a VIP or even a journalist – just a Western traveller who had momentarily strayed off the tourist route. Yet as Govind spoke, my curiosity began to win over my nervousness. My best experiences in India had all been when I had just gone with the flow. "You will enjoy it, too," said Govind decisively.

Orissa is one of India's poorest states, with some of the lowest literacy rates and largest tribal populations in the country. Its sweeping golden beaches and palm trees seem an unlikely setting for the impoverished fishing villages where Govind's many small-scale projects take root: loans to fishermen to buy new boats; water filters for local schools; health education in malaria-infested villages.

My own education began the very next day. Govind's colleague, Bikram, arrived to take me to a scheduled-caste village where the women had formed a *sangam* (committee) and built a community centre. Off we drove, Hindi film music blaring. Now I was really in wilder territory than I had yet experienced. I'd even found the tourist trail in India challenging – on the rare occasions when I had ventured off the circuit for a day-trip, I had needed all my courage not to jump on the next train back.

We stopped eventually at a building of rough bricks with a corrugated-iron roof. A straggling line of thatched huts comprised the village. Bikram ushered me into the dark hut, and a mat was found for me to sit on. I could see nothing except for the glint of nose rings. A young woman handed me a green coconut and disappeared back into the shadows before I could thank her. Bikram, also privileged with a mat, whispered: "Two years ago, these women would have been far too frightened even to greet a stranger." I knew how they felt.

I wished desperately I possessed more panache; that I had the type of personality that could break barriers instantly. Eventually, after an awkward pause, I waveringly made the prayer-like gesture that signals general goodwill all around India. Instantly, the stares were accompanied by cautious smiles, and the gesture was returned. Communication had begun.

The villagers told Bikram of their achievements and setbacks, requesting help for this and suggesting ways of improving that. A young woman in a pink sari holding a baby grinned at me suddenly, then looked down. Bikram asked me, "You have questions?".

I smiled at the woman holding the baby. "How old is her child?"

The question was translated, and the woman shyly mumbled a response. Approving mutters from my audience suggested I had asked the right question. Encouraged, I started to have the first real conversation I had ever had with village women in India. I learned that the women were all agricultural labourers with no land of their own. They earned fifteen to twenty rupees a day during the six months of the year that work was available. They had set up their *sangam* to come up with ways of finding an income for the remaining six months and to establish a communal bank account into which they deposited the few rupees they managed to save. To open this, they had needed to learn to sign their names. They had built the community centre themselves in the evenings, after the working day was done. I looked round at the building in awe.

Impressed though I was, I was frustrated by the superficiality of my questions. I wanted to know what made these women tick; how it felt to be an Indian village woman; what thoughts went through their heads; what their opinions and emotions were. Yet all that I seemed to manage were simple, fact-based questions.

Then Bikram said: "They would like to ask you some questions too." So, shyly at first, the village women asked me about myself and about England.

"What food do you eat in England?"

"Do you have mangoes/ coconuts/ bananas?"

Both were surprisingly tricky questions. They could not understand that we ate lots of bananas but could not grow them. Here, people grew their own food or bought it locally grown from the market.

And then, of course, there were the personal questions: husband, parents, sisters, brothers? I told them of my family, yet was aware that the big question was left unasked: what was I doing here, so far away from home? Still, our differences didn't matter at all as they painted intricate henna patterns gleefully on my feet and put flowers in my hair. As we left, they tried to give us more food. Bikram refused, and an elderly woman began jabbering angrily at him. Bikram translated: "They are angry because now you will go back and tell the English that they didn't give you food."

It struck me that our meeting was as near as these women would ever get to travelling themselves. Even the middle-class people in Govind's organisation asked me wistfully what Bombay or the Taj Mahal were like. As we returned to town, we were travelling further than most of the village women would ever go. They could not even envisage England, let alone go there, but they had now spoken with an English person. They had travelled without leaving their village.

Back at Govind's home, I was able finally to relax and assess. At dinner, Govind's daughters served me, and it occurred to me that this deference that made me so uncomfortable was a standard part of Indian hospitality. Playing the part of the memsahib was alien to me, but accepting genuine kindness was not, and I had to adapt to the Indian way.

And so it was that I enjoyed the next month tremendously. Each day, shortly after sunrise, I was taken to a different village demonstrating a particular type of project. I was shown everything, from newly planted papaya trees to health-education projects. I was treated to special performances of songs with educational messages ("Put on shoes before using the latrine" being a particularly catchy number). Fishermen punted me out on the beautiful Lake Chilka – setting for many a Bollywood movie – while telling me of their struggle to get the market rate for their catch.

Day by day, my awkwardness dissolved. Although I was witnessing what it was like to live with poverty, I still found it hard to understand. I realised, to my shame, that it was only now that I was truly regarding villagers as people and not just exotic curiosities.

Govind, himself the proud father of four daughters, constantly lauded me as a strong woman. Everywhere we went, he told villagers that I had had the courage to fly to a far-off country and to travel round that country alone for several months. Yet I was uncomfortably aware that these women who were expected to admire me combined a long day's work – such as breaking stones for road-building – with child-rearing and household chores. And they still managed to build the huts we sat in. They were stronger than anyone I've ever met, yet they did not have many of the freedoms I take for granted: to argue with men, to travel outside wherever they want, to spend money as they pleased. If they were to break free, they needed to lose their sense of inferiority, and that was where getting to know me was – in Govind's view – an education.

After leaving Orissa, I travelled in India for two more months with much-sharpened perceptions. I had an inkling of what a figure of mystery I must be to so many Indians, and how much more there was to learn about Indian society. But for all that, my month in Orissa revealed more similarities than differences between us. People who got to know me would often ask to call me "sister": a wayward sister, it was true, but one proud to be claimed as part of a global family.

read on . . .

Elisabeth Bumiller, *May You Be the Mother of a Hundred Sons: A Journey Among the Women of India* (US: Fawcett, 1991). Bumiller's urge to make sense of India's contradictions, and those of her own expat life, led her to choose women as her window. Using profiles of both village women and leading figures in Indian public life, she explores such issues as arranged marriages, dowry and domestic violence, female infanticide, feminist movements and population control. Bumiller makes the most of her privileged access to such personalities as filmmaker Aparna Sen, pioneering trade unionist Ela Bhatt, Bollywood legend Rekha, Jaipur princess Gayatri Devi, and police chief Kiran Bedi. Her interviews are now ten years old, and one longs for a follow-up volume featuring newer feminist voices. Even so, Bumiller's excellent introduction to India's gender issues stands the test of time.

Robyn Davidson, *Desert Places* (UK/US: Penguin, 1997). Nearly two decades after her lonesome camel trek across Australia in *Tracks*, Davidson once again trudges the desert, this time attaching herself to the nomadic Rabari tribe of Rajasthan. Pelted with stones by village children, frequently exhausted and undernourished, made ill by worm-infested water and enraged by the suspicion and scrutiny she's relentlessly subjected to, Davidson writes from the brink of endurance. She survives the ordeal (a feat of both physical and moral courage), but her romantic illusions about the vanishing nomadic lifestyle are left in tatters. Her writing, which switches from travel to anthropology as the tribe fails to roam, is remarkably raw. She ends up cursing as much as she venerates, yet she leaves you in no doubt about the ravages inflicted by poverty and her fury that this should be so.

Leila Hadley, *A Journey with Elsa Cloud: A Mother and Daughter Odyssey Through India* (UK: Thorsons,1999/US: Books & Co., 1997). Lengthy memoir brimming with detail of a mother's reunion with her wayward daughter, now a student of Buddhism, and their travels in style from New Delhi to a final meeting with the Dalai Lama in Dharamsala. Although Hadley veritably overflows with knowledgeable observations about India's culture, architecture, landscapes and religions, the country is very much a backdrop to her story rather than a central theme. It is the interwoven reflections on her unhappy, privileged childhood, her failed marriage, the disconnectedness of her relationship with her daughter, even the admonitions of her analyst in New York, that form the essence of this honest, occasionally irritating yet compelling book.

★ **Justine Hardy,** *Scoop-Wallah: Life on Delhi Daily* (UK: John Murray, 1999). *Thwarted Ambition* might have been a better title for Justine Hardy's entertaining memoir of a year living and working as a freelance journalist in Delhi. Tired of approaching India from the outside, Hardy opted to string for a local paper, *The Indian Express*, where, instead of rattling off stories on civil unrest or penning trenchant political columns, she found herself consigned to earnest investigations of Delhi's public-toilet crisis and first-person articles on yoga, complete with self-portrait in suitably tortured pose. Hardy, however, is at her best not with grand themes, but with wry character sketches of her friends and associates. Foremost among them are her landlord, Raj Kumar Yashwant Singh, a gay Rajasthani prince; Alka Singh, the wistful wife of a tea-plantation manager in terrorist-plagued Assam; and Johnny Whitright, a hippie chef on a divine mission to "cook with love" at a Tibetan Buddhist festival.

Zia Jaffrey, *The Invisibles: A Tale of the Eunuchs of India* (UK: Weidenfeld, 1997/US: Vintage, 1998). Jaffrey, an American daughter of Indian parents, makes use of her outsider status to draw closer to, and understand, the life of India's *hijras*, or eunuchs. This is a personal, rather than academic, study written in a light, even colloquial, style, yet her fascination for and obvious sympathy with her subjects carries her through.

Imogen Lycett Green, *Grandmother's Footsteps: A Journey in Search of Penelope Betjeman* (UK/US: Pan Books, 1995). Penelope Betjeman, writer, avid traveller and wife of the former Poet Laureate, died on a Himalayan mountain in 1986, only a year after leading her eighteen-year-old granddaughter, then "floundering on the far side of sulky adolescence", on one of her legendary trips across India. In an attempt to recapture the remarkable grandmother she felt she had only just discovered, Lycett Green retraces their steps six years later. Her skill as a writer, and the rich treasure trove of experience provided by the subject she adores make this an immensely readable, affectionate book in which travelogue and memoir are seamlessly combined.

Sarah Lloyd, *An Indian Attachment* (1984; UK: Eland Books, 1992). Caught up in a love affair with a placid, beautiful, opium-addicted Sikh, Lloyd spent two years living in rural India, first in a mud-built Punjabi village then later in a cramped brick hut within the community of a dubious holy man. The relationship, predictably, floundered. "In parting from Jungli", she wrote after boarding her plane to London, "I had lost my place in a community, and a belonging more tangible than any I had known in the country of my birth." If her lover's main role was to provide her with a bridge to village India, then she used it for the best of purposes, to provide an honest and enlightened account of the rural Indian way of life.

★ **Gita Mehta,** *Karma Cola* **(1979; UK: Minerva, 1990/US: Fawcett Books, 1991).** A satirical look at the psychedelic 1970s freak scene in India, with some hilarious anecdotes, and many a wry observation on the wackier excesses of spiritual tourism. The book was an instant bestseller along the backpacker routes. Author-filmmaker Mehta has followed this up with a charming and magically Indian set of short stories delving into the human heart, *A River Sutra* (UK: Minerva, 1994/US: Vintage, 1994), and, most recently, a collection of critical essays and social commentary, **Snakes and Ladders: Glimpses of Modern India** (UK: Minerva, 1998/US: Doubleday, 1998), which offers an unflinching assessment of India today. Evocative reports range from India's political corruption scandals, to its presentation of ancient cultures and the latest trends from Bollywood.

★ **Dervla Murphy,** *On a Shoestring to Coorg: An Experience of Southern India* **(1976; UK: Flamingo, 1995).** Accompanied by Rachel, her five-year-old daughter, Murphy, renowned for her cycle ride from Ireland to India, chooses to take the bus this time. They start in Goa, and after a series of lengthy rides enter the beautiful yet little-visited tropical mountain province of Coorg, where they spend a couple of months alternately roughing it and enjoying the hospitality of some of the region's wealthy landowners. Murphy writes with her usual disarming honesty, echoed in some of her daughter's remarks, as when she is told she cannot attend a funeral: "I wanted", she wails, "to find out if burning humans smelt like cooking meat." Less adventure-packed than some of Murphy's books, but a strong sense of place and keen observation of people, plus the novelty of having Rachel in tow, make this a compelling read. A classic India travelogue that for many years was the closest anyone came to producing a manifesto for the budget traveller.

Heather Wood, *Third-Class Ticket* **(UK: Penguin, 1984/US: o/p).** A party of elderly Bengalis leave their home village for the first time to tour the subcontinent by train. Absorbing and poignant, though the ersatz fictional style grates after a while.

Indonesia

The Kuta cowboys

Denise Dowling

Denise Dowling first encountered the "Kuta cowboys" during a college semester abroad, studying Indonesian language and culture at an American school in Bali. She returned six years later to write about the cowboys and their customers for the Australian edition of *Marie Claire* magazine. A teacher and freelance journalist in San Francisco, Dowling has written successfully on similar "tawdry" topics such as pimps, perfect couple competitions and septuagenarian strippers for the Australian and UK editions of *Marie Claire*.

Part I: Women who ride the Kuta cowboys

Kuta sweats sex. The combination of heat and anonymity is a powerful aphrodisiac in this resort town in Bali. Sex whispers in the tree leaves at night; it vibrates in the bass of techno that drugs the discos. But it's not really sex, more of a humid hedonism, the electricity of heat lightning. Then there's the fumbling drunk guarantee of a good time in clubs where Australian surfers and surfie chicks go, because Kuta is their Fort Lauderdale. But that's fast-food sex from a drive-thru. That's Kuta, but not Bali. Bali is the brown navel of a Brazilian girl swaying, hips straddling midnight and sunrise. A solipsist who believes that she's the only one who exists, but knows the figments of her imagination are watching her in the mirror.

I travelled to Indonesia on assignment with a women's magazine to write about sex, which isn't hard to find, but it's hard to find people who will talk about it. The article is about older Australian women with "Kuta cowboys", young Indonesian gigolos. Shhh . . . the guys don't like it when you use that word. They're boyfriends, the young men insist, they're not just paid for sex. The story might have a happier ending if sex was the only thing the women wanted. Well, you know women: some of us think sex should be wrapped in love. That's the package these women buy, and the Kuta cowboys have learnt to sell it that way. But you know how you can purchase something in a store, blinded by the dressing room light, then you get home and it looks completely different? But you've already taken the tags off so you can't return it? That's what happens sometimes with these relationships. Indonesia is a poor Third World country with poor electricity, so it's hard to see what you're wearing. Bali is seductively dim; even when the power's on, it's the flattering flicker of candlelight.

The cowboys hunt at Kuta beach when it's early enough to "make a promise" to meet a woman later that night. The women have just started to apply sunscreen when a cowboy trots over. April is a low season for tourists and competition is fierce; many of the boys are with minnows, but they hope to fry fatter fish.

"I like the older women because they have more money," says a twenty-one-year-old gigolo who calls himself Montana. "We say, 'No money, no honey.' The young ones just want to party. The old ones are nice; they take care of me and give me massages. I not care if her body's old. We say, 'A face like Italy, a body like Toyota.' I tell the woman she's the only one, because otherwise it sounds cheap," Montana adds, pulling out a wallet thick with snapshots of the only one from Sweden, the only one from Australia, and the only one from France.

Kuta cowboys say falling in love is a hazard of the profession, but through on-the-job training, they've learned to avoid that trap. "I don't give love any more because I was hurt by one girl who said she was coming back but she never did," explains twenty-four-year-old Made. "If the woman says, 'I love you,' I say 'Me too.' I lie because I care."

Made is courting four women scattered around Europe in hopes that he'll win a trip there. After they return home, many women wire money that the cowboys use for rent and clothes, and some pay for a flight so that he can visit. If a boy is really good, Santa gives him a marriage licence, a one-way ticket off the island. That's what the boys really want – our paradise is their purgatory. Newspapers in Bali are cluttered with ads from university graduates seeking jobs and former economics majors can be found hawking necklaces on the street. Many Indonesians won't consider a local girlfriend. The cowboys claim they aren't attracted to Balinese women, "because they're too naive and just want a rich boyfriend. Besides, I like the blonde hair, the blue eyes," Made adds, before chasing a Japanese woman in a tiger-print bikini.

The cowboys are blind to every colour but green and any tourist resembles an ATM machine. Not every woman goes to Bali to shop for a souvenir boyfriend, but one usually winds up in her suitcase. When you drape your blanket on Kuta beach, you don't intend to get those beaded braids that only look good on Bo Derek. You already have plenty of sarongs, thank you. And you don't want a pedicure, because the sand just scratches it off. But so many peddlers are pushing stuff that you leave with poodled hair, pastel toes, and a sarong slung around your waist.

Sally is a thirty-six-year-old nurse from Queensland who brought her teenage daughter to Bali as a graduation present. She and the daughter were at a local disco one night when the singer-slash-guitarist came over and sat with them after a set. She thought the twenty-six-year-old musician was after her daughter until he invited her to his room that night.

"When I met Matt, it was the best sex I'd ever had," Sally says. "That part of my marriage had just died and I thought, 'Maybe this is all I need – an overdose of sex!' My husband and I'd had problems and I guess at the time I didn't feel very good about myself. I wanted to feel better by doing something for somebody else. And I guess there was the thrill of being with a younger guy," she continues. "If someone offers you a new car or a second-hand one, which would you choose? Especially if the second-hand one is falling apart?"

She really wants to know what I think, so I ask what kind of mileage the used one gets. I don't tell her this, but I'd probably take the second-hand car because I'm not into that shiny, prancing kind of new vehicle. Which is exactly what her new boyfriend is, and it only takes one flick of his mane to see. Besides, as a freelance journalist, I doubt I could swing the down payments on a new one.

When Sally returned to Australia after meeting Matt, she assumed it was a resort romance with an expiry date attached. But when she'd call Matt from overseas, she was "charmed by his smooth talk". She sent him money for an airfare to visit, not sure if the funds would be used for a ticket. As he stepped off the plane, Matt didn't recognise Sally because he was so strung out on heroin. She had no idea that Matt was a junkie, and suddenly realised what he'd done with the money she'd wired for a boom box. So Sally did what any nurse in the world would; she straightened her Florence Nightingale cap and weaned him off the drug.

She estimates that she's spent nearly $7000 on the relationship since meeting Matt six months ago. She paid for the ticket to Australia, paid for them to fly back to Bali and go to Java to visit his family. Now she's flat broke and returning to Australia in a week. But Matt *really, really* needs a motorbike and does Sally think she can put it on her credit card before she goes? Pretty please?

"When Sally leaves, it will be hard not to see other women because I am a man," Matt says. "I want to marry Sally. I think this is forever, because I get everything I want now."

"Right now I'm thinking, 'What have I done?'" Sally says, lighting a Marlboro. "I've lost my marriage, my kids, and my house because of Matt. My oldest daughter says, 'I don't know what you see in him, he's just a parasite.'" I try to talk to Matt about it, but he doesn't want to listen, he doesn't understand. There's something definitely there," she's quick to add. "I mean, I'm in love. It's been exciting and adventurous. But my life in Australia is so different and spending all this money is totally out of character for me. It would have been more economical to have met an Australian guy!"

Sally sighs and drags on her cigarette when asked what she gets from the relationship. "Well, I hold the purse strings, and maybe I'm a person who likes control. Sometimes I feel like I'm his mother. Matt says to me, 'You're my guardian angel, you saved me.' That makes me feel good. You know, in retrospect, I would have been quite happy to be by myself," she adds. "But then I met Matt, and it just sort of happened . . ." She trails off, like she wishes it wasn't too late to return Matt and get her money back.

Jean is a forty-nine-year-old ex-farmer's wife from Western Australia who's been living with her twenty-five-year-old boyfriend,

Heri, for four months. She and Heri are like teenagers, giggling and arm-wrestling with each other. While we talk, she flips through photos of her and Heri partying with other cross-cultural couples and shots of Heri grinning impishly after Jean dressed him as a girl. Heri proposed three weeks in to the relationship, but Jean said no.

"I want to marry Jean and live in Australia because I can work there," Heri explains in stilted English. "If I stay here and marry an Indonesian girl, I think I have less of a future." Jean doesn't want to rush into anything, nor does she want Heri to feel that he has to make a commitment, because she can't give him children.

"From Heri, I get a lot of happiness, love and affection," Jean says. "I was married very young, at seventeen, and my ex-husband wasn't a demonstrative person. He was very busy with work and I felt like something was missing. With Heri, I'm finding I can express myself more freely. For the first time in my life, I'm independent. Heri has taught me to like myself for who I am and not what I look like. Sometimes I feel a bit insecure, like, 'Why should a young, handsome man be interested in me when there are so many nice looking young girls around?' Heri says it's because he loves me. He knows I haven't got a lot of money," she adds. "I know about the Kuta cowboys, but Heri has proven that he's not like that. But can you ever really know how they feel? They think that because they say they love you, that's enough. Heri is so quiet, and his English is limited.

"Heri said, 'I've got nothing to give you.' I told him that I may buy his cigarettes and food and put a roof over his head, but he doesn't realise how much he's given me. Before, I felt unattractive, I felt fat," she says, pinching the skin sagging from her arms. "With Heri, I feel young. He makes me feel alive."

Part II: If you go

No matter what your intention for vacationing in Bali, paradise can be hell if you're a woman alone, especially in the resort area of Kuta. With that in mind, here are some tips to pack for your trip.

Take The Back Seat In A Taxi.

The drivers often mistake your thigh for the stick shift.

Always Wear A Bra, Even If It Means Unsightly Straps.

My first night in Kuta, I check out the *Sari Club*, popular with
Australian surfers who can afford to gorge on alcohol. While the rest of
us squander our resources on shirts, surfers opt for a strictly below-the-
belt wardrobe, leaving them more money to spend on drinks served in
goldfish bowls. A dread-headed surfer next to me is watching the
women, summoning his courage, grasping for the right opening line.

"Sooo. . . " he turns and anchors his hand on my back pocket.
"You here to party?" After one drink, it is time to leave the *Sari (I Went)
Club*. Balinese moths hover outside while I try to unlock my bike.

"I have a big dick," says one. "Do you want to see?"

"No thanks," I tell him. "I've seen enough pricks for one night."

"Cheap price," he adds. I don't say anything, so he starts haggling. "Okay, for you . . . tonight . . . free."

I laugh and fumble with damn key, which is writhing in a rusted
lock and bent by haste. I've got to escape before the boy hits puberty.
He is very concerned with my plight and supervises over my shoulder
while I'm hunched over the lock. I straighten up to curse and notice
the boy has swallowed a canary.

"Come on," he purrs. "Let me see them again."

The Police Will Be Happy To Help If Something Bad Happens. Just Be Sure To Bring Rupiah, Because They Don't Take American Express.

Therese is a cherub-faced Swede who was eating with her fingers and
drinking warm tap water when we met at a food stall. I see her a few
nights later in a boat-shaped club called the *Bounty* where Balinese
waiters are dressed like the Good Ship Lollipop. Surely being chained
to a sewing machine in a sweatshop for fifteen hours and a dollar a day
is less degrading than this line of work.

I go to ask Therese her opinion on this human rights abuse and
notice a purplish blush on her right cheek. She explains what happened
while she pats the bruise, that she'd been talking to an Indonesian man
at a club and walked outside with him. When the man realised that
Therese was headed home without him, he punched her.

"I don't know what to do," she says. "People tell me to report
him, but what would the police do? Besides, I don't want to start
trouble."

Even The Australian Guys Speak Another Language.

I am not interested in Max, an Australian friend. "Blah, blah . . . space. . . work," I explain, hoping he will read between the lines. He apparently needs *Cliff's Notes*.

"Is it because we're not here for very long and you're afraid of falling in love with me?" His surf-blue eyes are sad with hope. I lower puppy-eyes, chew a chapped lip and chip at a sienna sunrise nail.

"Yeah," I say. "That must be it."

The Expats Only Look Sophisticated.

Goa 2001 is a nightclub popular with expatriates. We go there to moan about how broke we are – even though we shop before our afternoon massages. Three British expats introduce themselves at the bar. Maurice, the chap to my left, has swallowed one goldfish too many. His friends are discussing "Dutch Wives", these pillows that are on the beds in Bali. Maurice turns to me, "And what do you sleep with?"

"A baseball bat," I say sweetly.

After Maurice has offered to "maybe" introduce me to a connection for the article I'm working on, he alludes to later that night, when he'll be "sucking on my nipples until they're five times larger".

"We'd be a good match," I coo, "if sucking on your IQ had the same effect." I turn to exit as his French girlfriend walks in. She gives me a look that could stale a baguette, but reserves her wrath for Maurice. I never would have passed high-school French if I didn't make every vocabulary test "open book". Yet I can still translate her ranting *tu* and *merde*.

If You Get Mugged, It's Your Fault For Carrying Money.

Jost is a German tourist who believes that Western women are to blame for how Indonesian men treat us. He thinks we're like matadors, waving sunburnt shoulders and scabby knees in front of the bull while local women shroud themselves in pants and short-sleeved shirts.

I tell him that when I was studying in Bali, we dressed like the Indonesian women, showing a minimum of skin. According to Jost's theory, the Indonesian men would think that women in tank tops were loose, but would respect us for respecting their culture. So certain incidents should not have happened – like the father who wanted to spend quality time with my classmate who lived with his family, so he took her to a deserted bungalow. Or the X-ray technician who felt a breast exam was necessary when another woman lost two teeth in a bike accident. And when my foot was stung by fire coral while scuba diving, the divemaster shouldn't have tried to check if the sting had spread to my genitals. But I guess I asked for it with that bathing suit. Remember to wear pants and a long-sleeved shirt when you dive.

With Some Men, The Timing Just Isn't Right.

As I'm walking to my hotel one afternoon, there's a crowd of people standing over what looks like a beached shark. When I get closer, I see it's a sheet draping bony calves and pruned toes. A man bends down and unrolls the cloth. It's a Balinese boy, maybe ten years old, his red swim trunks streaked pink with salt. His left profile is perfect but the brown jaw is splotched white.

"Not good . . . looking," an Indonesian hisses. He could mean it's not nice to look or that the boy is not good-looking. Everyone is walking to the other side and I follow, thinking that not knowing would be worse than what I'll see. Sand and rocks have scraped his face raw, leaving a skull with just enough flesh to evoke humanity. The eye is a socket of white and his mouth is exaggerated gums and teeth. There is blood where lips should have been.

A man squats down to take pictures. The shutter clickclickclicks, drowning the surf. An Indonesian in official blue pants and starched white shirt lights a clove cigarette and hands it to his friend. No one moves to load the body onto the patrol truck. We simply stand, as if our presence might breathe life into the boy.

I sleepwalk to the path that leads to the hotel. It's where I live, but not home. "Wait!" A man calls from the crowd, following me. "Where are you from? Do you have a boyfriend?"

There's No Charge For Room Service.

I need to bury the boy with teeth so wide he could have been laughing. His face is etched in my dreams when a knock stumbles into my nightmare. Made, who works the late shift at the hotel, is muttering in Indonesian. I speak the language, but I don't always understand. I open the front door, thinking it must be a phone call at the front desk. Made staggers like a boxer, fishing with his hands, his whiskey-stale voice whispering of thirst. I try to shut the door and Made steps back like he's rehearsed this part, slurring words of apology.

283

I close the door and lock it. I sit down. I walk to the door. It's definitely locked. The boy is still there, grinning.

You Could Always Stay Home.

When I phone my mother, I tell her about the boy who was one of the two hundred locals and tourists who will drown this year in Kuta. "So, you don't swim in the ocean any more, right?" She knows my Piscean roots, that I'm a mermaid in cowboy boots. But she'd rather I didn't test the water. She'd prefer I hadn't returned to the other side of the world.

"I still go in the sea. I know it's dangerous, but I'm careful." I don't mention Made or the words that echo from the street men. I don't say anything about the man who waited on a jungle path, his fingers busy with a bloated zipper. I tell the truth but I omit the facts.

"I'm not going to let it stop me from swimming."

Caught in an earthquake

Catherine Shorrocks

Catherine Shorrocks is a 33-year-old British journalist who took a year off to travel. After working and travelling in Australia, she and her partner set off for Indonesia. They planned to travel through the archipelago by land and sea but, shortly after arriving on the island of Flores, disaster struck. Since returning home, Shorrocks has resumed her career in journalism and now lives in Manchester with her partner and their two children.

The village had resumed an air of normality. Dogs and chickens scratched in the dust, a woman swept the ground in front of her hut with a bunch of twigs, and barefoot children ran about, inventing games with sticks and stones. I stared up at the mountains and marvelled at the savage beauty of the Flores landscape. Centuries of volcanic activity had tortured the island, carving knife-edge ridges, thrusting up craggy peaks, scoring deep valleys and creating the fertile soil that allowed lush tropical vegetation to flourish. It was a week since the earthquake and the waiting seemed interminable.

We had arrived in Indonesia on the short-hop flight from Darwin, Australia, to Timor, and had been intending to travel through the archipelago by land and sea. Flores, our second port of call, was known throughout Indonesia for the Keli Mutu crater lakes – three coloured pools in the caldera of an extinct volcano at the island's centre. At dawn, the mists rose to reveal deep, still waters that according to legend were inhabited by the souls of the dead. We, like many other travellers, had made a long journey just to see this strange, otherworldly landscape.

After a night in the port of Ende, we had set out on a tortuous minibus ride along the mountain road that snaked beside a ravine up to Moni – the village used by tourists as a base for travel to the crater lakes. I asked the owner of the *losmen* – the guesthouse where we were staying – whether the journey was a dangerous one. "Yes," he replied cooly, "it is very dangerous." But our driver was unworried by the narrowness of the road, negotiated its twists and turns with skill, and waited patiently while gangs of workmen removed the boulders that had crashed down from the mountainside the night before.

Our arrival in Moni was marked by the switching-off of the engine, the blaring music and the two metal fans that had gone some way to cooling passengers in the oppressive heat and humidity. But as we got our wallets out to pay for the trip, it seemed as though the engine had been turned back on and had developed a violent knock and rattle. Or was some unseen crowd angrily rocking the vehicle from side to side? It was to be many hours before we knew that what we had experienced was a 6.9 earthquake with an epicentre just nineteen miles off the northern coast of Flores. In the next few minutes, 2200 people lost their lives as the quake rocked the whole island, pounding the port of Maumere, less than fifty miles away, with 80ft tidal waves and sweeping away the entire population of a small sand island off the coast.

The driver shouted to everyone to get out of the bus. Beneath our feet, the road buckled and heaved as great waves of energy shook the earth. In our confusion and panic, it seemed as though the world was pulling itself apart. The spasms subsided three, maybe four times, just for a few seconds before the ground bounced and juddered again, and the trees resumed their frenzied dance. We tried to brace our legs against the shaking and put our hands to our ears to block out the deafening roar. The scene was truly apocalyptic. Villagers came screaming from their crumbling homes and gathered in little sobbing huddles, raising their arms to the sky and looking towards the volcano. "Keli Mutu! Keli Mutu!", they wailed. Someone brought out an enormous crucifix, others had grabbed religious pictures as they fled their homes and held them aloft, crying for mercy. I began to wonder what horror would end this torture – a boiling flow of lava? A shower of boulders? A deluge of mud? One way or another, I was sure we were bound to die. Then the ground settled, there was a sickening smell of sulphur, and the air was dusty and hot.

The tourists quickly sought each other out. There were those who were already staying in the village and those of us who had just arrived on the bus from Ende. Altogether, we numbered fifteen or twenty: Australians, Americans, British, a Danish woman, a Canadian. The flow of information between us was swift. There were only two roads out and God knew what sort of a state they were in now. The lakes were very close and did you see how flimsy the sides of the crater were near the top? The behaviour of the villagers began to worry us. They ran across the football pitch to stare up at the mountain. More than once, they came screaming back toward the village warning that the crater lakes had burst and that we were about to be engulfed in a sea of mud and debris. These were false alarms, but they sent us fleeing in terror towards higher ground all the same.

To our Western minds it seemed inconceivable that there was no source of information about what had happened. We knew that Flores was frequently hit by earth tremors but this was clearly a major disaster. Desperate for information that could help us decide what to do next, we switched on the BBC World Service to listen to the news. It would be a few hours before news of the earthquake filtered through to London from this remote corner of the world and hearing the newsreader tell us calmly about the Maastricht Treaty and the possibility of a Beatles reunion concert seemed to add to the surreal nature of our situation.

One of the villagers, Joseph, pulled some wooden chairs out of the rubble of his house and brought us glasses of hot, sweet tea. It was still less than an hour since the earthquake had smashed up his home, and we felt humbled by the kindness of this stranger. Over the next seven days we were to experience the most extraordinary acts of humanity as the locals, who had lost so much of the little they had, persisted in treating us as their guests, showing us remarkable hospitality in the face of their own terrible misfortune.

We decided to take Joseph's advice and walk back up the road to higher ground, where we would have a better chance if the lakes did burst from the crater and wash down into the valley. So, with our rucksacks on our backs, we joined the little procession of refugees struggling up the hill. In places, heavy banks of soil and roots overhung the road and we hurried along, taking shortcuts across fields and vegetable patches, arriving in a tiny village of just a few corrugated-iron- and grass-roofed huts as the sun was going down.

It seemed the Moni villagers had decided they had gone far enough and would camp out for the night. We all sat down on the warm dirt road. The villagers put down their bundles of salvaged possessions and stared at our ghostly white faces, tutting and muttering about our plight as much as their own. Someone came down from Nuamuri, the little village beside the road, and said one of the families was offering us a hut for the night. Many of the buildings had collapsed, one of them burying a five-year-old girl who had died from her injuries, and most of the Nuamuri villagers were now huddling together on the ground outside the village chief's house. We weren't sure whether we should take up the offer as there must surely be others who needed shelter more, but the family, who had moved into the back part of the hut, was insistent and once again we accepted the unexpected hospitality with gratitude.

Later that night, another villager arrived with bowls of steaming meat and vegetable stew, but with the food came bad news. There had been a report on the radio that another earthquake was predicted and was expected to affect the Moni area much more severely than the first. It would happen in the next few hours. We felt as though there was a death sentence hanging over us but somewhere at the back of my mind lingered a doubt. Surely that was the whole point – earthquakes could not be predicted and that was why steps were never taken to evacuate areas before they happened. I clung to that belief during a terrible night spent lying in the open with the villagers (no one wanted to stay indoors now) as tremors rumbled on and died away. As we lay awake, staring up into the black sky above, we saw shooting stars.

Dawn broke over a misty landscape and the villagers began to stir and pull their blankets and sarongs tighter round their shoulders. We had survived the night and although aftershocks were coming with worrying regularity, we felt the danger of another earthquake was probably over.

During the morning a sturdy shelter of green bamboo was swiftly erected for us on a piece of open ground. This, and a second, bigger shelter built using corrugated sheets for the roof and walls, was to become our home for the week. We slept there, squashed in side by side, glad of our sleeping bags during the cold, damp nights. Our sleep was fitful and we were often jolted awake by earth tremors and would crouch, alert and watchful in the dark.

At first the onlookers who crowded around our shelters scrutinised us with an unsettling air of detachment, as though we were actors on a stage. We had the feeling they knew us all by name and were beginning to assess our personalities and discuss our actions, while we still found it difficult to identify individuals in the sea of curious faces that watched our every move. But after a few days and with the help of signing, pointing and a few words of Indonesian, we began to make better contact with our hosts and eventually came to know many of them by name. There was Katerina, who brought traditional medicine to help our fevers and offered massages to ease our tension; Agnes, a little girl who invited us all to her hut; Nimos, a cheeky boy who played tricks on us; Ketut, the twenty-year-old sent from his beloved Bali to serve as local policeman; and a bald little child with a swollen belly whom we called Buddha.

The village chief, wearing a traditional hand-woven sarong and a khaki camouflage T-shirt, brought us bowls of steaming cobs of corn and chunks of *ubi*, a thick white root. We bought pineapples and bananas and munched through our supply of biscuits. The villagers, small and wiry, seemed to survive on very little but worried that we needed much more to sustain our larger frames. One night, a procession of women arrived in the village with huge bowls of hot food. The ingredients for this feast had been dug out of the rubble of a local restaurant, along with china plates and metal spoons and forks. Our hosts dished up a thin soup of noodles and tiny quails' eggs, mounds of steaming rice, fried meat and vegetables. It seemed to me the most delicious food I had ever tasted.

As we sat crosslegged in a circle, the women crouched close by, watching us eat and grinning in pleasure at our obvious appreciation of their efforts. In the centre of the circle, giant insects hurled themselves at a hissing hurricane lamp. The thick black night wrapped around our little group and for a few brief moments the food and warmth, the smiles of the villagers and the ring of bright faces gave me a false sense of security. I felt cocooned, as though the savage forces of nature could no longer harm us in the sanctuary of Nuamuri.

But as the week dragged by, we became more and more concerned that no one knew we were trapped and began to worry that we might never be rescued. The group was split over the best course of action, and gradually our numbers dwindled as people left to embark on the long and dangerous walk to Ende. By the sixth day, those of us who remained were clinging to the hope that the Australians in the group had managed to get a message through to their embassy and that a helicopter rescue would eventually be launched. Our families – and we hated to think of the torture they must have been going through – must surely have reported us missing and would have made their own attempts at alerting the authorities. We began to despair and, with the threat of illness and weakness from lack of food weighing heavily on our minds, we decided to walk out the following day.

We never found out who sent the Indonesian army helicopter that swooped down the next day to take us away. Crowds of villagers ran shouting and waving into the road as it landed. They clutched our arms, rejoicing, and hurried us out through the dust. It was a strange parting with no time for proper goodbyes. We began giving away clothing and possessions in a last-minute attempt to express our deep gratitude, and watching the villagers eagerly accepting these cast-offs, I realised how much restraint they had shown over the past week and how to them we must have seemed rich beyond compare.

The landscape of Flores looked even more stunning from the air: the green-furred volcano ridges plunging steeply down into the sea. But even as we soared across the island toward Ende, I was thinking about the people of Nuamuri, who faced the long task of rebuilding their homes from the rubble. I had been constantly taken aback by the decency, apparent lack of envy and great resilience of the villagers. The shared trauma of a terrible natural disaster had flung us together with these people, whose lives were so far removed from our own, but instead of resenting our presence at such a difficult time, they had shown nothing but kindness and genuine concern for our safety. For a few days, our money and possessions, even our education, meant nothing and I think it was the villagers who saw more clearly than we did how much – not how little – we all had in common.

read on . . .

Tracy Johnston, *Shooting the Boh: A Woman's Voyage Down the Wildest River in Borneo* (US: Vintage, 1998). Thrilling account of rafting down the treacherous Boh river through the Borneo jungle as sponsored writer in a mixed party of adventure-seekers, including two American fashion models, a wealthy Italian and a Chicago lawyer. The adrenalin-fuelled moments of being smashed against boulders, or dragged underwater with lungs full of watery froth, are tempered by slower-paced trials involving leeches, ants and an entire forest floor animated by ravenous crawly things. Against this context Johnston, the only member of the group over forty, attempts to come to terms with the sure signs of menopause – an incongruous juxtaposition, that's rendered profoundly moving by her crisp, yet passionate, prose. Interestingly from such a, literally, breathless escapade she finds herself re-valuing the much quieter, more sedentary love of the partner who stayed behind.

Louise G Koke, *Our Hotel in Bali* (New Zealand: January Books, o/p). The engaging story of two young Americans who arrived in Bali in the mid-1930s, when the island was still relatively untouched by tourism, and almost immediately set about building a hotel on Kuta beach. An affectionate account of the locals, expats and visitors caught up in their grand enterprise, this book includes some wonderfully atmospheric black-and-white photos.

Anna Mathews, *Night of Purnama* (UK/US: o/p). Evocative and moving description of village life and folk in the early 1960s. Focusing on events in and around Iseh in the aftermath of the eruption of Gunung Agung. Written with a keen sympathy and recognition of the gap between West and East.

K'tut Tantri, *Revolt in Paradise* (UK: Griffin, 1990). A fascinating, if somewhat embellished account of the expat life of Muriel Pearson, British artist and adventurer, who lived in Bali and Java from 1932 to 1947. Known as K'tut Tantri in Bali and Surabaya Sue in Java, she relates astonishing tales of hob-nobbing with the raja of Bangli, and building an early hotel on Kuta beach. Later she joins the Indonesian Independence movement, smuggling arms and supplies between the islands and operating an underground radio before being caught by the Japanese invaders and suffering torture and two years' imprisonment. A remarkable account by a truly remarkable woman.

Louise Williams, *Wives, Mistresses & Matriarchs* **(UK: Phoenix House, 1999).**
Williams, an Australian journalist and specialist on Asian affairs, interviewed factory labourers, business magnates, mistresses, prostitutes, a princess and a prime minister for this book of insights into the lives of women in Asia. These are fairly superficial snapshots but revealing nonetheless, as in the conversation with a judge of the Islamic Court in Indonesia. A female pioneer in her field, strongly in favour of women's right to education, Ibu Mahdiah believes in stoning women for adultery and upholds polygamy as a safeguard against men having extramarital affairs. Three further chapters on Indonesia illustrate the aspirations, achievements and contradictions faced by women in this rapidly changing society.

Iran

Learning to love my chador

Kay Hill

Kay Hill's travels began when she left England with husband Ed to drive to Kathmandu in Nepal in an ancient Land Rover. She was excited at the prospect of visiting Eastern Europe, Turkey, India and Nepal, but Iran seemed remote and forbidding. Up-to-date information was hard to find and she knew no one who had visited that country before, so her curiosity was tinged with foreboding as she headed overland further and further away from home. Her tale starts in Turkey where she was introduced to an equivalent of the voluminous black chador that she would be expected to wear in Iran.

"Oh, you must have the one with the pleats, it's so much prettier," giggled Fatima excitedly as she eyed me in the tiny changing room's dim mirror. Her mum and two sisters nodded in agreement as they twirled me around, prodding and adjusting the layers of black polyester in which I was now enveloped. Mum, her eyes bright and laughing from under her veil, gave me her seal of approval. "She says you are Muslim woman now," translated Fatima with a grin.

It's a disconcerting feeling to look into the mirror and see a stranger staring back. With my figure and hair vanished from sight and my face looking unflatteringly plump and white thanks to my jet-black nun's wimple headgear, I hardly recognised myself.

My shopping trip, in the eastern Turkish town of Erzerum,

would have been far more testing had it not been for the timely intervention of fifteen-year-old Fatima and her family. As I was heading into the Islamic Republic of Iran I needed suitable clothing, so I'd gone in search of the *char sarf*, the Turkish equivalent of the black Iranian *chador*. Unfortunately, *char sarf* also means "bedsheet" in Turkish, so I was being shown plenty of linen by bewildered storekeepers but no clothes. Fatima, seeing me gazing disconsolately into yet another shop window, seized a chance to practise her English. "Can I help you?" she murmured shyly, and hence we ended up crammed into the top-floor changing room of a draper's shop, trying on endless versions of black robes, all of which looked identical to me.

At first, Fatima had just done the translation, convincing the proprietor of my earnest need for Islamic clothing. But it soon transpired that I needed even greater assistance, when, once in the changing room with my bundle of black cloth, I realised I hadn't a clue how to put it on!

It was Fatima's mother's turn to help. "She used to wear *char sarf*," said Fatima, "but now she is modern." Dressed in a floor-length raincoat with a bright silk scarf wound tightly over her hair and face, mum bustled confidently in, dressing me like an infant as I raised my pasty limbs to order. The waist of the complex gown needed to be elasticated, so Fatima raced down the street to the haberdasher's for a yard of knicker elastic which was then deftly installed and knotted to fit. My hair was tied back, and the headdress bound tightly across my forehead and buttoned under my chin, while the rest of the fabric was draped to form a cowl top. Finally, despite my protestations that I wouldn't need it, a yashmak was elasticated around the back of my head and tucked tightly in so that only my eyes were visible. Mum eyed me approvingly, then, tutting a little at my bare hands, dashed out of the changing room to return with a pair of black nylon gloves, "the finishing touch" according to Fatima. Fortunately for me they were far too small, so I was at least left with one tiny bit of bare skin for ventilation!

Back in the hotel afterwards I wasn't sure whether to laugh or cry. True, I felt I could safely jettison the yashmak, but I did have a month of travelling in Iran ahead of me when I would have to stick to the rules which allow only face, hands and feet to be shown. I looked like a demented nun and the enforced conformity reminded me unpleasantly of my hated school uniform.

Driving towards the Iranian border and further away from tourist Turkey, the first signs of the sexual segregation that was to be a fact of life for months to come also began to emerge – I was ushered into the curtained "family areas" in restaurants and the women's section of tea shops. At first I was resentful, but I was soon to learn to appreciate these havens from the ever-present attentions of men.

Camping in Dogubayazit, the Turkish border town in the extreme east, I met Maike, a Dutch woman, and we shared our nerves about the following day's border crossing. Her Islamic outfit was a little more user-friendly than mine as it came in two pieces – a long skirt and a combined headdress and shirt – but the end result was much the same. The crossing was, for us at least, uneventful. Both of us were travelling with our husbands so we had little to do but watch as we were processed in the same way as our men's bags. I noticed that most of the Iranian women passing through immigration did not have their own passports but appeared to be black-clad accessories to their husbands, who sometimes had two or more identically dressed wives in tow. If ever a pop star or head of state really wanted to escape public attention, they could do worse than don a chador, since it seems to render the wearer instantly both anonymous and invisible.

With our heads full of dire warnings about crackpot fundamentalists and hate-filled revolutionaries, Iran couldn't have come as a more pleasant surprise. On our first evening we strolled around the park in Tabriz, chatting with the locals and eating ice cream under the watchful eyes of a giant poster of Ayatollah Khomeini. People were warm and friendly but not pushy, and I found many Iranians spoke some English or German, making communication fairly easy. Even in the heartlands of religious Iran, the holy town of Ghom and the massive shrine to the Ayatollah outside Tehran, we were always made welcome – I was taken right up to the revolutionary leader's grave by a party of young Iranian women, then persuaded to sit down and share a picnic with a family outside the shrine.

Tehran itself is a busy, crowded, modern city with all the accompanying traffic problems. When we were there petrol cost only a penny a litre, so almost every family had a car or motorbike, often driven at alarming speed. Crossing the road was a major undertaking and the air a stifling haze of blue exhaust fumes. At times I felt just as I would in any Western city – the hotels were clean and well equipped, the tap water drinkable, the roads well maintained – then I'd walk into a hotel lobby and see giant posters reminding female foreigners of the dress code and of the sinful wantonness of letting hair stray from under your scarf.

A sudden storm while I was walking around the monolithic Freedom Monument in Tehran reduced me to near hysteria: as well as the usual problem of dust blowing into my contact lenses, I was suddenly trying to cope with an outfit that threatened either to send me skywards like Mary Poppins or straight into the nearest jail cell for being a Western hussy. My skirt blew up, the cowl puffed out like that of some giant Michelin woman and my hair started escaping in all directions. In the end, clutching fistfuls of black, head down against the wind, I hurled myself back into the Land Rover in a flurry of forbidden limbs.

After the gentle pace of eastern Turkey, Tehran was frenetic and overcrowded. People always seemed to be hurrying and prices for food and accommodation were high, so it was a relief after a couple of days to push the Land Rover through the gridlocked traffic towards the open country beyond. Outside Tehran, the scenery was harsh and lunar. Much of Iran seems to be inhospitable desert, though towns are linked by excellent roads punctuated with gigantic bus-stop restaurants and the occasional roadside mosque. Except for the occasional bus we saw no one for hours on end; with internal air fares costing as little as ten pounds, only the poorest people travel between cities by road. Bumping along at our maximum speed of 55mph, with a choice of suffocating from the heat with the windows closed or choking on the dust with them open, it took us a whole day to drive to the next major city, Esfahan, the nearest thing Iran has to a tourist destination. A few coach parties of rich Britons, French and Japanese come here to see stunning Islamic architecture and medieval bridges, while a steady stream of backpackers and overlanders pass through the town's one cheap and friendly hostel on their way to and from India. It was a relaxing place, somewhere to talk travel and trade tips, to enjoy burgers and pizza (the murals may read "Death to America" but the Iranians appear to have welcomed American junk food with open arms), and to see the sights.

The great mosque in Imam Square is an awe-inspiring building coated in radiant blue tiles. As I wandered around I found myself mobbed by a coach party of schoolgirls, resembling a flock of chattering starlings in their black chadors. There was lots of giggling, self-conscious practising of English and photos all round. When I finally escaped I found Ed in earnest conversation with a pot-bellied pirate of a man called Ali. His opening gambit had been: "Do you know where Salman Rushdie lives?" He insisted on taking us for tea. We walked across the giant square, and tea came to us in the form of Hussein from the Nomad Carpet Shop. Kilims were spread on the grass and the four of us, soon joined by another passing backpacker, settled down to sip golden tea and put the world to rights. Bearded Ali, impressed by my chador-clad modesty, was a huge fan of the Islamic revolution. Everything was better now, he affirmed, and if only he could get rid of Rushdie it would be almost perfect. His proudest moment, it appeared, was being kicked out of America because they thought he was a spy.

Hussein, defiantly clean-shaven and snazzily dressed, told me I looked ridiculous, along with all the other Iranian women. He had lived for ten years in Turkey to avoid the Iran/Iraq war and fancied himself as rather cosmopolitan. For Hussein all these wretched rules put off the tourists and meant that he sold fewer carpets.

Back at the hotel that evening there was a tap on the door. "My dad wants to meet you," announced twelve-year-old Mahmud in perfect English. The youngster was so keen to practise his talent for languages that he had a standing arrangement with the hotel. They let him know when any English people arrived and his family could take them out for the day to help with his conversation. Accordingly, the next day we found ourselves sightseeing in the company of Mahmud, his parents, Morteza and Parwani, his sullen older brother, Nazer, and his cute younger one, Sahid. The men and children went off to climb a nearby hill where one could visit an old fire temple, while Parwani (her name means "butterfly" in Persian) and I chatted in the cool shade. With me she was relaxed and talkative, but when Ed was around she kept her chador right across her face, gripping it in her teeth while she poured his tea so that he didn't get an inappropriate glimpse of her.

The status of women in Iran struck me as a strange mixture of freedom and restriction. In contrast to places I'd visited in eastern Turkey and, later, Pakistan, where few women seemed to work outside the home, in Iran we came across female police officers, insurance clerks, bank staff and newsreaders. Even the Deputy Prime Minister was a woman. Yet a small breach of the dress code might still lead to arrest, and married women appeared to me largely governed by their husbands. Ed and I spent a delightful evening having dinner with an Iranian businessman who was charming, well educated and friendly. After I left, he asked Ed how often he had to beat me to keep me so well behaved.

After Esfahan we moved on to Bam, the desert oasis which produces most of Iran's dates. At the edge of the town are the remains of an amazing medieval city, built out of sun-baked mud and deserted centuries ago. The lush oasis scenery and the incredibly ancient buildings were beautiful, and fascinating to explore, but I found myself stumbling, sweating and cursing as I struggled to enjoy the visit while being slowly suffocated by polyester. I longed just to wear leggings and a T-shirt and feel the wind in my sweat-sodden hair. However, it's amazing how quickly Islamic modesty seeps into the psyche. When the hotel clerk in Ghom knocked on my door to get a form signed I forgot myself and opened it straight away, wearing a long-sleeved shirt and ankle-length skirt, but with my freshly washed hair still damp and loose. The shock in his eyes was electric, as if I'd walked out into the hallway stark naked, and I found myself slamming the door as I blushed scarlet and fumbled for my scarf. Within a week I had the same habitual tick as the women around me, always running a finger along my hairline to check for escapees, always adjusting, covering, checking for decency.

Later, at the Pakistani border, a friendly customs officer pointed at my dusty chador: "You take off now, Pakistan is free." I observed if anything, though, that the women in rural Pakistan were even more covered up than in Iran, peering through tiny eye slits or viewing the world through mesh panels in their *burquas*.

I had set out thinking of Iran as simply a place "on the way" to the more important destinations of India and Nepal, but in the end that country, together with Pakistan, proved to be the high-spot of the entire trip. I discovered people who were open-hearted and more than willing to give their time, friendship and hospitality to visitors who make the effort to show respect for local traditions and culture, and if that meant dressing a bit differently for a couple of months it was a small price to pay. Besides, although it was hot and awkward, I did, in a small way, learn to love my chador. At least for a time anyway I never had to worry about what I was going to wear or having a bad hair day.

read on . . .

Christina Dodwell, *Traveller on Horseback in Eastern Turkey and Iran* (US: Walker & Co., 1979). Seasoned traveller and prolific writer Dodwell journeys by bus through Iran to Pakistan and back to Turkey where she completes her loop of the mountainous borderlands on horseback. Her usual brand of intrepid adventures, sharp observation and historical research are spiced by some splendid colour photos.

Shusha Guppy, *The Blindfold Horse: Memories of a Persian Childhood* (UK: Penguin, 1989/US: Beacon Press, 1993). Poetic and romantic memoir of life in pre-revolutionary Iran, by a Persian-born, French-educated, London-based writer and songwriter. Guppy describes, with more than a touch of yearning, the gently civilised world of her large parental home, with its big walled gardens, overflowing with family, friends and devoted servants. The smells, stray sounds, characters and customs of Tehran are caught and beautifully conveyed, just before the city lurches through cataclysmic changes.

Dervla Murphy, *Full Tilt: Dunkirk to Delhi by Bicycle* (1965; UK: Flamingo, 1995/US: Overlook Press, 1987). Murphy's account of her extraordinary bicycle journey to India includes just two chapters on Iran where, thanks to a deliberately short haircut acquired in Teheran, she is largely taken for a man. Despite its "physical dirt and moral corruption" she finds much to like in the country, especially the people she meets. Such obstacles as a disintegrating bicycle, physical exhaustion and a badly sunburnt arm barely seem to dent her incredible spirit.

Israel

A kibbutz with a view

Joanna Nathan

Joanna Nathan, a journalist from New Zealand, had long been curious about kibbutz life. In 1997, with thoughts of the English winter ahead, she exchanged her flight to London for one to Israel. Her spur-of-the-moment plan was to spend a couple of months working as a kibbutz volunteer before touring the Middle East. She ended up spending half a year working in the kitchens and fields of a kibbutz in the Jordan Valley, 30km from the Sea of Galilee, before finally moving on through neighbouring Arab states. She currently lives and works in London.

I couldn't believe it when the bus driver stopped at some factory gates and told me that this was the kibbutz. When I checked again I received a curt nod so I disembarked, still disbelieving. Factories? Iron gates? Asphalt car park? I'd imagined cottages, orange groves, traditional folk costumes – folk dancing, dammit! Passing through the barbed wire fence however I found not a county idyll of yesteryear but a relaxed low-rise 1990s community. It looked, I decided, like the rolling campus of a university dotted with the units of a retirement village. Crop tops and hipsters abounded rather than any sort of peasant garb, and loud Hebrew rock music blared from many a stereo. The elderly whirred past on motorised scooters, children were pushed about in what I later found out to be laundry carts, and everyone else was on bicycles. Traffic was confined to a perimeter road, and bustle and rushing to another world.

Despite having long wanted to go to a kibbutz, I had only a vague notion of what one was, that is to say a sort of commune of happy peasants sharing all they had. During a summer job apple-picking at home, I was foolish enough to share these thoughts with my boss, a fierce capitalist. "Ha!" he roared, "I'll give you a toothbrush and you can come up to my place for meals. Then we can call this a kibbutz." Persuading the security staff of El Al, Israel's national airline, of my nebulous intentions proved difficult. After an hour-long interview by two teams of interrogators, they looked sceptically at my plans. No, I didn't know anyone in Israel, or any Arab terrorists. No, I didn't know which kibbutz I would be going to. No, I didn't know how I was going to find a kibbutz. And, um, Jerusalem, Nazareth and Bethlehem – to me Biblical, fairy-tale names – were the only places that came to mind when I was asked to identify where I was heading. However, after my questioners had rifled through my photos and address book, questioned me on friends and finances, and heard a day-by-day, blow-by-blow account of the previous six months of my life, I was allowed to board. From that point it all worked out very easily.

I quickly found a hostel in Tel Aviv and, upon seeing the nine smelly boys with whom I was to share it (the sort that seemed to fill many Israeli hostels, working illegally in construction after having drunk and smoked their air fare home), even more quickly found a kibbutz agency. My only criterion was safety, as I had heard tales at the hostel of volunteers being sent unawares to kibbutzim right on the Lebanese border with daily background rocket fire. Kibbutz Maoz Chaim lay one kilometre from the now-peaceful Jordan, and the bomb shelters there were these days used for table tennis.

As a volunteer I worked six days a week for my keep: meals, an allowance for the kibbutz stores and pub, the occasional group trip, free tampons and stamps, and all the clothes you could wear from the stockpile of kibbutznik cast-offs. Everything a small village needed was at hand, like the small grocery and clothing stores, laundry, library, garage, swimming pool, health centre, basketball and tennis courts, post office, beautician and hairdresser – although my one trip to the last left me looking like a psychopath. I could not understand how the kibbutz women all managed to look so glamorous. Judy, an enthusiastic volunteer leader, found me wandering about looking bewildered and quickly got me kitted out in (really ugly) acid-wash jeans, circa 1985, and an army jacket. She soon became a familiar figure out and about on her senior citizen's tricycle. I was grateful for the extra clothes, as it had never occurred to me that the Middle East could be so cold. The Jordan Valley is reputedly the lowest place on earth and consequently can feel freezing. So much for skipping winter!

This was not the hotbed of communism that my former boss had scorned. Today's kibbutzniks tout mobile phones. They have a personal allowance so they can choose whether to eat in the dining room or buy and prepare ingredients themselves. Many of the children go to university, whilst low-paid workers from as far away as Thailand come to work in the plastics factories and fields that pay for it all. From the look of the designer labels and consumer durables it seemed that people were doing quite nicely. What I saw barely related to my socialist ideals – this was the reality of the kibbutz project, which people had been living for sixty-odd years.

The other volunteers were mainly under twenty and many were away from home for the first time, which some found hard (there was seemingly a competition to see how disgusting the bathroom could be made). All kinds of nationalities passed through. I felt both fortunate and ashamed to speak only English, as French, Danish, South African, South Korean, Swiss, German, Mexican and Italian volunteers, together with the kibbutzniks, chatted away in my mother tongue. It was more of a challenge when a Colombian arrived, as his only English was from American love songs and a phrasebook containing such useful expressions as "I want money not food stamps". He was a quick learner, though, and soon came up with: "Latin men are hot in the bed."

The South Koreans, when there were more than one, tended to stick together, and I became accustomed to the grilling each new arrival from Korea faced. It appeared that one 23-year-old was desperate to find someone younger in order to hand over the cultural obligation of looking after one's elders. From time to time amongst the volunteers there were misunderstandings. One man with little English and no Hebrew was asked to leave over allegations of "kissing children". He appeared bewildered and protested that he was only being friendly, and no one really knew what had happened, but this was the kibbutzniks' home and there were no second chances.

Something that amazes, and sometimes upsets, newcomers is how little attention the kibbutzniks pay the volunteers (unless one particularly wants to sleep with you), but of course they have seen many come and go; the record while I was there was fourteen hours. I found people dignified and often ashamed of their usually very good spoken English. "I must sound like the Russians speaking Hebrew," apologised one woman, the Russians being the newest immigrants to the kibbutz. We were very much left, therefore, to entertain ourselves. There was a school camp atmosphere – two to a cabin, barbecues in the evenings, afternoons of catching up on years of neglected reading and writing, swimming and cycling. Occasionally we would take a trip across the Galilee to the beach. On Fridays the pub would open, which was *the* big event for the volunteers. No night was complete without the huge stereo system blasting out *One Night in Bangkok*, and vodka on ice at three dollars a bottle. I even became accustomed to Hebrew rock. Such evenings probably contribute to the volunteers' generally bad reputation, as the young residents struck me as a relatively sober lot, though they can move into shared apartments at fifteen.

I did not find the kibbutz at all exotic, unless you count the turtle in the bathroom. *The Simpsons* were regularly on TV, chicken nuggets seemed to be the snack of choice, and sprinklers kept the grass green all year round. It was brought home to me that this was the Middle East when a young volunteer was out late at night and was confronted by a kibbutznik wielding an M16. Previously I had only ever seen a gun twice but here grandfathers would cycle by on their way to monthly target practice clutching automatic weapons. At the weekends, when teenagers on military service returned home, M16s were considered too awkward to manoeuvre through the aisles, so there would be a stack of them at the counter. It turned out that one of the men with whom I was working had trained as a sniper during his national service, and a woman, now working in the dining hall, had been a bomb disposal expert. Despite this, or perhaps because of it, I can honestly say that I never felt more safe. The kibbutz was 8km from the nearest town and children roamed unsupervised within its boundary fences. One night we heard gunfire and my room-mate and I lazily argued as to who was to lock the door, normally left unbolted, but both of us fell asleep.

The volunteers were set to work pruning date palms using ten-metre-high hydraulic ladders, laying irrigation pipes in the fields, picking mangoes, milking cows, or loading chickens into the dreaded battery. At first I was assigned to the kitchen, which ran like an incredibly smooth and well-ordered household, albeit on a huge scale. The dishwasher was a triangular conveyor belt in relentless motion throughout the day, the toaster was cleaned with an air hose, and salads were mixed in bowls the size of baby baths. The food seemed designed for maximum weight gain: bowls of chocolate sauce and sour cream for breakfast, and deep-fried peppers and cauliflower on offer at lunch. The kosher chicken, served up in different guises on most days, was for some reason horribly furry. The kibbutz, though, was not particularly Orthodox; meat and milk mingled freely, and all was dished out by an Arab chef who pulled up to work in a Mercedes.

After a month I was glad to escape the monotony of large-scale food preparation to go to work in the garden, although finding enormous discarded snake skins in the bushes was a bit off-putting. The day started early. In April the temperature shot from 15 to 40°C so I began at five in the morning to beat the heat. The garden supervisor, Moshaun, was a chivalrous (at least to girls who didn't speak Hebrew) pot-bellied man, well past most countries' retirement age but still putting in enthusiastic thirteen-hour days. He spoke little English so we soon developed a personal mixed and mimed language of gardening terms. As a woman I always got the front seat in the garden "golf cart", and raked, clipped dead roses and pruned olive trees. Big tractors were for the boys. On my one day in the fields I was sent to make breakfast for ten men; gender division on the kibbutzim seems alive and well. Often men who are toned and tanned from work in the fields were married to women plump and white after a life in the children's houses and dining room.

Breakfast, with a few hours of work already accomplished, was at eight. Morning tea, with all the watermelon that you could eat, was at ten. By one o'clock, the working day for volunteers was over. It took me a while to relax into a lifestyle where the biggest source of stress was a bra not returning from the laundry, but within weeks I could spend hours on the porch watching the world go by. I painted a mural and started my own garden. As the months passed the people who originally I had found gruff and taciturn began to thaw and stopped to talk. When I went on holiday trips, kibbutzniks that I had never seen before would ask how they went, and I started to get invitations for coffee, aerobics classes and Sabbat drives. Someone offered to re-bind a book of mine that had been savaged by dogs when I left it outside. Someone that I had worked with in silence for months suddenly bought me an ice cream. I listened to many stories of things that people have had to do or live through that I will never experience: there remain photographs of the years when the kibbutz was under daily bombardment and surrounded by a slavering ring of guard dogs. Most people I found well-informed and liberal, an important counterbalance to those in the country of a hard-line religious persuasion. Everyone I asked saw a Palestinian state as inevitable, although interestingly it seemed to be the young who had the most doubts about this.

I was continually surprised by how little the kibbutzniks appeared to do jointly as a community, coming together mainly for big Jewish festivals, and even then people tended to pack up as soon as the formal programme concluded, returning home to continue the party there. One man I talked to pointed an accusing finger at private televisions, which had only been allowed ten years before. Things have changed a great deal since Golda Meir, Israel's first and only female prime minister, described kibbutz living in the 1920s: children raised en masse, shared clothing and partitioned cubicles in which to sleep, and people unable to make a cup of tea without making a cup for everyone. Today many families have three or four generations living on the kibbutz and have very established ways. One morning an elderly woman asked me to work on the small flowerbed adjacent to her porch – but only as far as the exact boundary to her neighbour's flat. "If she likes it messy then that's her business," she almost snarled.

It felt amazing to cycle about knowing everybody and seeing different generations regularly sit down to lunch together. Getting married and starting a family in one's mid-twenties seemed to be the norm. Up to five children in one family was not unusual and divorce was rare. Dads, with short working hours and no commuting, could often be seen picking up their kids from the children's houses.

I found the kibbutz life easy to slip into, punctuated as it was only by the annual cycle of festivals: dressing up and drinking at *Purim*; two weeks of dry crackers rather than bread at Passover; barbecues for Independence Day, and the solemnity of Holocaust Remembrance Day. I found myself putting off leaving, and putting it off again. Two months turned to six, and when I finally did go I promised to come back "home", as Judy put it. I wonder how long Maoz Chaim will survive, as a kibbutz at least. In many ways it was already a small capitalist village. A few kibbutzim have even challenged one of the fundamental tenets of their foundation, and have recognised through variable allowances the hugely disparate hours and tasks that people do. Change is inevitable. Young people do not display the same pioneer zeal of the older generations and many want more challenging jobs and the bright lights of the city: like many elsewhere, they want what they see on TV.

read on . . .

Orly Castel-Bloom, *Dolly City* (UK: Loki Books, 1997). Irreverent, Kafkaesque surrealist novel by a young Tel Avivian author who has won many prestigious writing awards within Israel.

Risa Domb (ed), *New Women's Writing from Israel* (US: Vallentine Mitchell, 1996). An anthology of short stories by Israeli women writers including well-known names like Shulamith Hareven and Orly Castel-Bloom.

Nur Elmessiri and Abdelwahab M Elmessiri (ed), *A Land of Stone and Thyme* (US: Interlink Publishing Group, 1998). A collection of short stories by a new generation of Palestinian writers from within the Palestinian territories and beyond. Censorship and repression of writers within the camps has meant that some of the stories focus surprisingly on inner struggles, employing a symbolic and allusive prose style, while Diaspora writers can be more overtly political.

Michael Gluzman and Naomi Seidman (ed), *Israel: A Traveler's Literary Companion* (US: Whereabouts Press, 1996). A modern, varied and very refreshing collection of Israeli short stories for the traveller, exploring different destinations, different styles and different attitudes.

Sahar Khalifeh, Elizabeth Fernea and Trevor LeGassick (trans), *Wild Thorns* (1976; UK: Al Saqi Books, 1985/US: Interlink Publishing Group, 1998). With its unsentimental portrayal of ordinary Palestinian men and women going about their everyday lives in the Israeli-occupied West Bank and Gaza strip, ***Wild Thorns*** captures and chronicles the experience of occupation. A sincere and uncompromising look at the effects of oppression.

Bettina Selby, *Riding to Jerusalem: A Journey through Turkey and the Middle East* (UK/US: Little Brown, 1995). Spurred on by the notion of pilgrimage (the leitmotif of her epic bike rides) and hopeful about the effects of the Jordan/Israel peace treaty of 1994, the intrepid and highly popular travel writer Bettina Selby cycled from Cyprus to the Holy Land. Here she draws on her significant knowledge of Christian history and a typically idiosyncratic Christian-feminist viewpoint to explore her religious heritage and also the religions of the Jews and Muslims she meets along the way. An intriguing, gutsy and learned historical exposition on wheels.

Margarita Skinner, *Between Despair and Hope: Windows on My Middle East Journey 1967–1992* **(UK: Radcliffe Press, 1998).** Health and welfare worker Margarita Skinner spent twenty years working with refugees in Jordan, Gaza, the West Bank, Lebanon, Syria and Iraq. This graphic and compassionate account of her life and work provides a disturbing portrait of how ordinary families in the Middle East are being caught up in the spiralling brutality of sanctions, displacement and war.

Helen Winternitz, *Season of Stones* **(1991; o/p).** American journalist Winternitz witnessed the gathering momentum of the Intifada when she spent two years living in a small Palestinian village of shepherds and peasant farmers near Bethlehem on the West Bank. She survived the growing atmosphere of suspicion, antipathy and eruptions of violence towards American strangers, which included having her car stoned, by learning to speak Arabic. She writes about this period, the characters and everyday concerns of village life with enormous honesty and clarity.

Italy

A student in the city of chic

Helena Smith

Helena Smith spent a month in the university city of Perugia in Umbria on an intensive Italian language course. Back in London she works as a full-time editor for the Rough Guides and has helped update the Rough Guides to Scotland and Europe. She is a winner of the *Vogue* and *Independent on Sunday* writing competitions.

I arrived in Perugia dazed after a long train journey, took a frantic taxi ride to arrive two minutes before the accommodation office closed, and was given the address of my flat which I struggled to find; it was on a curved street of high shuttered buildings. On the top floor I found my silent apartment, with a cupboard-sized kitchen and tiny bathroom, whose small square window framed the hulking silhouette of the cathedral. Eventually the landlord, a rotund and smiling dentist, lumbered up the stairs, apologised elaborately for the state of his teeth and his breath and explained that he had just come "from the restaurant". He amiably insisted on taking a large deposit for the room and left me alone. I hung up my clothes, which looked lost in the depths of the wardrobe, and huddled under the thin quilt; I had been unable to get the ancient gas heater to work. I was woken starkly at 3am by loud voices. Three witches were walking up the street below, talking animatedly. It was All Saints' Eve: Halloween.

I was in Perugia to study Italian at the Università per Stranieri (Foreigners' University), a non-profit-making institution founded by

307

Mussolini to improve the image of Italy abroad, the only trace of these suspect origins being a 1930s marble concert hall embedded in the ornate eighteenth-century university building. Higher-level students were taught in this *palazzo*; as a total beginner I was sent to a more recent building on the leafy outskirts of the city, which was apparently a mental hospital until Umbria's "care in the community" policy decreed that the residents should be released. This appeared to account for the high proportion of eccentrics on the streets of Perugia, who did add a certain surreal medieval colour to the city. One wore a striped football strip and shouted up at the same window for hours on end, while another thin and aesthetic man stood guard in the main square dressed as a medieval knight, holding a tall pike and with a greyhound by his side.

My first few days in the city, before the lessons got going, felt both liberating and lonely. I walked energetically, mapping the ancient streets, looking in at the glowing shops, and absorbing the sudden panoramas, when a thin street of tall houses would open out onto tumbling rooftops, great churches which clanged the hour, and infinitely diminishing mountains. I was cocooned by my lack of language, almost mute, until the life in my apartment began to open up. It was home to three German girls, two Finns who spoke beautifully exact English, and me. We visited each other's rooms, and spent hours in unguarded adolescent conversation, sitting cross-legged and wrapped in our quilts, drinking tea.

Then the classes started, and my month in the city really began. The ex-asylum/classroom was actually lovely, but the first lesson was utterly daunting as it was, of course, conducted in Italian, and therefore incomprehensible. There was no other common language to bind the group; the other students were from Colombia, Belgium, Austria, Serbia, Greece and Australia. Some were learning Italian for fun, some for work, and some were escaping trouble in their own countries and hoping to make Italy their home. Our two teachers were instantly adorable: one was small and voluble, laughing with exasperation at our mistakes, the other sophisticated and expressive, eventually coaxing us into conversing about Italian culture. We were forced into language, bullied and cajoled into stretching a handful of nouns and verbs into a phrase, a sentence, then the beginnings of a conversation. Some students reacted against this process, refusing to employ necessarily childish language, or finding it humiliating to do so. The rest of us regressed happily to infant school, and competed to impress the teachers with our eagerness. And our own relationships with each other developed with our language. There was an earnest anti-war film festival in Perugia, and we went together to see Bergman and Tarkovsky movies, which were dubbed into Italian to add to our muddle. After a couple of hours spent in a nineteenth-century Perugian café discussing *Ivan's Childhood* with a gregarious Serb, an elegant Belgian and a rather haughty Austrian, I began to feel actively, if confusedly, European.

Umbria as a region isn't renowned for its nightlife, but the presence of so many foreigners in Perugia seemed to have contributed to a healthy drinking culture. The British-style pubs, the best of which had a good dash of Continental chic in their design, were genuinely vibrant magnets for Italian students and foreigners, little pockets of hubbub, life and light; every night I went out with people from the apartment or the class. And the whole city seemed to attend the rather bad production of *Romeo and Juliet* we went to in the beautiful eighteenth-century Teatro Morlacchi. The theatre itself was the real star, frescoed and chandeliered, with tiers of little *Dangerous Liaisons*-style boxes giving wonderful views of the stage, and, perhaps more importantly, the audience. Touchingly, and typically of this idiosyncratic place, the medieval knight (who came to all the anti-war films wearing camouflage) appeared at the play in a startling white frock coat, top hat and gold-tipped cane.

It is a cliché to compare a city to a stage, but Perugia's magnificent main street, from the *duomo* to the Piazza Italia which looks out to Monte Amiata and Assisi, is the perfect setting for the twice-daily social pageant of the *passeggiata*. In the evenings particularly, whole families turned out onto Corso Vanucci, to window-shop in the gorgeous boutiques, chat, and generally pose. Only the most Euro-chic students, however, could achieve the sartorial standard required, and most of us felt excluded, perpetual spectators of an event where the scruffy were utterly ignored, rendered almost invisible. A sort of Sloaney, horsy look was all the rage, the men pristine in Barbour jackets, and the women immaculately jodhpured and booted, an odd antithesis of urban fashion in this otherwise cosmopolitan place.

This somewhat fetishistic preoccupation with style extends to the city's perception of itself. Unsurprisingly, there is a strong sense of civic pride in Perugia, with its Etruscan walls, gateways and well, wonderful medieval civic buildings and houses, and the dramatic centrepiece of the grand thirteenth-century fountain. A slender stone bridge which once served as an aqueduct bringing water to the fountain runs through the lower part of the city, decorated with sculptures depicting the months of the year and Old Testament scenes. While I was there this focus of municipal pride was being restored, and the city had fountain fever. The shop windows all had obsessively fountain-related displays: bookshops showed it in antique engravings, a delicatessen embedded a picture of it in a loaf of bread and a cake shop sculpted it in miniature from swirls of sugar icing.

But there was a less sophisticated side to the city, manifested in the crowds of insistent lads (*ragazzi*) who lounged outside the university building and bars, waiting to pounce on stray foreign females. Every few nights, minibuses ferried students out to colossal nightclubs, palaces of out-of-town tackiness with trashy disco decor, Day-Glo cocktails and Eighties tunes, with a few numbers by chubby Italian crooner Eros Ramazotti. Eros provided a chance for the *ragazzi* to make their move, and there was much smooching and swaying under the mirror balls. Having got into a reluctant conversation with a couple of leather-jacketed ageing Romeos, my friend and I were disturbed to find them waiting outside our flat one morning; they had followed us home the night before and shadowed us for several hours, but were eventually seen off by a combination of my friend's Finnish frostiness and my own blank inability to communicate anything more complex than a request for a ticket or an ice cream – I was still new in town.

Otherwise my contact with Italians, apart from the two teachers, who provided us with a great farewell Christmas feast of *panetone* and cola, was limited. I had an Australian friend who stayed with a lovely signora in a pretty room, perched above the Etruscan arch. My friend had quickly abandoned learning Italian in favour of having a good time, but she and her landlady went to Mass together. I went with them once, but their solemn choreography of genuflection and communion-taking was unfamiliar, and I felt excluded, slightly envious of their easy rapport.

On my last morning, my friend and I went to the university for breakfast (a powerful cappuccino and a *bombolone*, a big sticky doughnut), and then we spent hours wandering round Perugia. A strange thick mist had fallen on the surrounding area, but the city stood above in clear sunlight, like a fortified island looking down to the sea. The whole view was obscured except for the faint snowy Monti Sibillini in the distance. It was the last day of November, and the streets were being hung with long strips of blue-and-white stars for Christmas.

I went back to the flat and packed, and the dentist/landlord arrived post-haste "from the restaurant". I was wary, thinking he planned to keep my deposit; he grinned, grabbed my hand and placed it on his tubby chest so I could feel how his heart was pounding and gauge how eagerly he had rushed to bring the deposit. He handed over the cash and was unexpectedly sweet, suggesting that we keep in touch in order to further European unity. I said goodbye to my high, beamed room and to my friends, who took me to the bus-stop across from the great Etruscan arch. I watched both it and them disappear, and the bus plunged out of the medieval heart of the city into the urban sprawl towards the railway station, where I took a train for the colder climes of Milan.

read on . . .

Anne Calcagno (ed), *Travelers' Tales: Italy* **(US: Travelers' Tales Inc., 1998).** The latest offering of this excellent series of travel anthologies combines newly commissioned writing with an inspired selection of extracts, interweaving male and female perspectives. Frances Mayes, Lisa St Aubin de Teran, Patricia Hampl and Mary Taylor Simeti are joined by the likes of Tim Parks and, for evocative period detail, H.V. Morton. Jan Morris introduces the literary tour.

Barbara Grizzuti Harrison, *Italian Days* **(US: Atlantic Monthly Press, 1988).** Born in Brooklyn of Italian-American parents, Grizzuti Harrison had long wanted to tour Italy, lingering in palazzo hotels, wandering through arched alleys and, most of all, relishing the seductiveness of Rome. Her stylish prose, peppered with personal visions, emotions, and well-turned nuggets of history, art and politics make this a multi-layered and evocative read.

Clare Longrigg, *Mafia Women* **(US: Vintage, 1998).** Fascinating look at the new, active role of women within organised crime in the 1990s, mainly in Naples and Sicily. Intimidation and fear are shown to be the oil that turns the Mafia wheels, the supreme place of the family appearing to justify almost any outrage or amount of complicity.

★ **Mary McCarthy,** *The Stones of Florence/Venice Observed* **(UK: Penguin, 1985/US: Harcourt Brace, 1985).** A mixture of high-class reporting on the contemporary cities and anecdotal detail on their histories; one of the few accounts of these two cities that doesn't read as if it's been written in a library.

Frances Mayes, *Under the Tuscan Sun* (UK: Bantam, 1998/US: Chronicle, 1996) and *Bella Tuscany: The Sweet Life in Italy* (UK: Bantam, 1999/US: Broadway Books, 1999). Bestselling accounts of the author's "love affair" with Italy as she and her husband, Ed, first set about transforming an old abandoned villa into an idyllic home, then settle down to further appreciate the sensuous joys of Tuscan living and explore more of their chosen country. An American poet and professor of creative writing, Mayes writes in an often lyrical if slightly breathless style, overflowing with enthusiasm for every detail, from the twining vines which "open their pure pink faces to the morning sun" to the wonders of her "tiny bathroom equipped with mimosa bath salts and the thickest American towels". It's hard not to feel a twinge of envy. She is also a passionate cook and food writer, and both books are scattered with recipes including, in *Bella Tuscany*, a truly delicious-sounding lemon pie with roasted almonds.

Fiona Pitt-Kethley, *Journeys to the Underworld* (UK: Chatto & Windus, 1990). English poet searches Italy for the Sibylline sites, spending a good third of her time in Sicily – a healthy appetite for sexual adventure provides her with plenty of distractions.

★ **Lisa St Aubin de Terán,** *A Valley in Italy: Confessions of a House Addict* (UK: Penguin, 1995/US: HarperCollins, 1996). St Aubin de Terán moves with her family into a huge, dilapidated palazzo deep in the Umbrian hills. A year later she throws it open to celebrate her daughter's wedding. That dull, tired theme of "foreigner moves to Italy to discover the joys of rusticity and self-catering" has been wonderfully reworked in lucid, bright prose. St Aubin de Terán might have become a refurbishing addict but she has yet to become a cliché.

Jamaica

Journey to yard: a Jamaican cultural experience

Rosalind Cummings-Yeates

Rosalind Cummings-Yeates is a freelance writer and arts critic living in Chicago. This account of her trip to Jamaica, where she went to holiday and write an article on the island beyond the tourist resorts, was first published in *Go Girl! The Black Women's Book of Travel and Adventure* (see p.652). She is currently in the process of getting her short story collection, *Dancing like a North-Sider*, published, along with a play entitled *Ginseng and Jerk Chicken*.

> *Mi born in foreign but mi love yard still.*
> – "Warning Sign", Born Jamericans

There's a lot to be said for a black person visiting a black country. There's something that touches the spirit and reconnects what has been lost, stolen, and forgotten. It outlasts photos and souvenirs, burrowing deep within. Jamaica possesses this power; it can weave an unbreakable spell on the most cynical tourist, but its true essence can only be absorbed by touching the culture – the people, the dialect, the food, the lifestyle.

Soon after my feet first touched Jamaican earth, I was angry. Rolling down the winding road in a bus from the airport to my hotel, I was surrounded by loud, rum-swigging tourists. Their "irie mon" comments and subtly arrogant attitude toward Jamaicans irritated me. As the only black face on the bus, apart from the Jamaican guides, I felt resentful that I had to endure the same narrow attitudes toward people of colour that I had just left in the US. I had come to relax and work – I was writing a travel article on the Jamaica beyond the beaches and resorts – and I didn't need that kind of aggravation. I journeyed far from the tourist arenas and this was my only encounter with such attitudes.

After I checked in, I rushed to the hotel restaurant for jerk chicken but learned quickly that I wasn't going to get anything authentic as long as I was in a hotel. The chicken was slathered in barbecue sauce and lukewarm, not unlike poultry in your local American chicken shack. The waiter grinned at me and told me about the stall that served the best jerk. "Gal, yuh got to go outside a here," he said. And that's exactly what I did.

Negril has intangible attributes that are just as striking as the turquoise water and white sand beaches. There is a thick, enveloping aura that permeates the town. It feels moist and seamy and it hangs around you, lurking just above the dirt roads. Part of this feeling comes from the fast-paced atmosphere that accompanies tourism: clubs, fast money, and drugs, mixed with the conservative, strongly Christian yet frankly sexual Jamaican sensibility.

Another part of this feeling can be attributed to the aggressively intense manner of many of the men I encountered. I found that despite the stereotype of the well-hung, smooth-talking, Jamaican playboy there are many brutally direct, woman-loving, beautiful men. Nevertheless, one must still deal with the smooth-talkers, and I quickly developed my own method. I had been warned by friends who make annual pilgrimages to Negril that there is a "rent-a-dread" market, where single women pay the way for male companions who may incidentally sport dreadlocks. In part, that explains why strolling through Negril alone I drew unwanted comments and offers; it was assumed that I must be looking for a man. To avoid such advances, I dressed in "roots" fashion: long dresses, flowing African garb, and headwraps. This is a style I favour anyway, but I detected a certain level of respect for my attire. Tourists in skimpy shorts and ultra-revealing swimwear usually trigger disdain and catcalls among the townspeople. Jamaican women observed my clothes and I saw them nod in approval. The men smiled but weren't so quick to approach me. It's much easier to get around in conservative Jamaican society dressed conservatively.

It's also easier if you shun behaviour based on stereotypes, such as saying "hey mon" and expecting every Jamaican you meet to have a "no problem" attitude, falling over themselves to meet your needs. I found that being respectful and not too familiar with the people I met helped ease cultural barriers and smoothed the way to glimpsing Jamaican life.

For an up-close look at Jamaican life, I looked up Don, a friend of a friend, who knew the streets and people of Negril. We started the day by hopping on one of the mini-vans that serve as public transportation. Since most people commute from surrounding towns, it was crammed with folks on their way to work. It was a whirlwind ride, the van lurching down narrow roads, barely stopping to let passengers out. Nobody seemed to mind, though, and it was interesting to see the landscape of coconut trees, cows, marketplaces, merchants, and uniformed schoolchildren as we whizzed by. We paid our fare at the end of the ride and climbed out in front of Negril Craft Market. Noted for unbelievably persistent vendors, the marketplace can be a web of hard-sell frenzy. Both tacky and exquisite jewellery, sculpture, clothing, and paintings fill stalls lined up side by side.

"Come, I give you a spe'shell deal!"

"Just take one look, no pressure! No pressure!"

Proposals and pleas rang out from every crevice, making for an overwhelming experience, although the presence of a native Jamaican did help. Don cautioned vendors to let me decide if I wanted to buy and they backed down. I was able to concentrate on the beautiful craft work and select what I wanted in peace. When I was on my own it was much easier to buy souvenirs from roadside displays or vendors along the beach. Local gift shops usually stock less creative, higher-priced items.

I wanted to sample Jamaican food prepared for Jamaicans, not the watered-down dishes aimed at tourists, so Don steered me to a small eatery that was a local favourite. Furnished with bright curtains and tablecloths, it didn't look like a restaurant, but rather, a kitchen. I had slightly spicy, curried chicken with plantains, which are sweeter cousins of the banana family, and Don had "manish water," or fishhead soup. I drank sour sop juice from the sweet creamy tropical fruit, and Don had Irish moss, a thick beverage made from seaweed. The service was quick and no-nonsense and the atmosphere was relaxed and unpretentious. Since Jamaica is not really an "eating out" society, it's a treat to go to a place that caters to local tastes. The prices are low and the food will usually be well prepared.

On the road back to my hotel, I sampled sugar cane from a roadside vendor. They cut the long stalks and I sucked the sugar cane juice from the pieces. It's very hard and chewy but the pure sugar rush is unlike any you get from mere candy. I also bought a small sampling of local fruits – "pawpaw" (papaya), june plums, sweet sop (even sweeter than sour sop), and mango. Needless to say, they were all bigger and sweeter than anything imported to American supermarkets. The only problem was figuring out exactly how to eat the more exotic fruits. I had to get instructions from the "higglers" (market women) on what to cut with a knife and what to bite.

After a short nap made necessary by the relentless afternoon sun, I met Don at my hotel for a tour of popular nightclubs. My first clash with Negril mores came when I discovered him waiting behind the wooden blockade manned by a hotel employee. "Visitors are not allowed, Miss," I was informed in crisp, British-inflected words. Translated, hotels make it a policy to bar local people from entering, lest the hotel guests be "bothered" by beggars or vendors. When I protested, Don just shrugged it off. "It's a way tings are," he said calmly.

Another thing about the way "tings are" in Negril is that foreigners are recognised on sight and usually treated with condescending wariness until they prove that they deserve otherwise. The looks I caught when I entered the first club were mocking and slightly challenging. I couldn't understand how they knew I wasn't Jamaican just by looking at me, before I opened my mouth. "It's your skin," Don explained. Although I'm the same walnut-brown as Don, my skin didn't have the burnished look that his had from being in the sun.

I heard murmurs of "rent a" across the room. Since I was the only non-Jamaican in the club, they assumed I was paying for Don's escort services. Tourists rarely venture into local clubs for any other reason, he told me. But after they observed that I didn't pay for any of Don's drinks and that I was familiar with the latest Buju Banton records, the attitudes vanished.

The clubs and dance halls of Jamaica have a culture all their own, unseen at hotel bars or beach concerts. They tend to be dark, all the better for the couples "wining" in corners along the walls. (Wining is the Caribbean way of suggestively gyrating your hips to the music's rhythms. It can be done solo or by rubbing up against a partner.) Dancehall tunes with heavy bass lines are usually favoured, along with flashy, sexy clothes. Sometimes the music slows down for a show by partially covered strippers, who tend to be plump, in accordance with the taste for "mampy" (extremely voluptuous) women, but they don't do much more than the wining the patrons do themselves. Both men and women performed, and I didn't feel any of the lasciviousness that I would have expected. The spectacle was treated the way most Jamaicans treat sex – as something natural.

I saw more deeply into Jamaica when I travelled down the southern coast. I passed through Savanna-La-Mar, or "Sav-La-Mar," as the locals call it, where a crumbling fort serves as a swimming hole for children. Here you can see agile little bodies bobbing and diving all along the edge of the waterfront, which also boasts a bustling market-place. You can buy everything from goats to pencils from the efficient vendors, but I preferred just to soak up the sights and sounds of every-day life.

Effortlessly negotiating prices and carrying bushels of produce, the women looked self-possessed and strong, comfortable with who they were. The men were easygoing and masterful. I saw a clear rela-tion to the African sense of community that so many black people around the world struggle to hold on to. These people didn't look like they had many material comforts, but their bearing pointed to emo-tional and spiritual strength that warmed me with pride.

As I travelled along the coast I marvelled at the beauty of the waving sugar cane fields, the lush greenery, and colourful scenes of rural life – a part of Jamaica not seen on T-shirts or tourism ads. Though most of Jamaican tourism emphasises Bob Marley memorials, a lesser-known memorial lies in the town of Belmont, on the south-east coast. This tiny fishing village claims to be the resting place of Peter Tosh who was a noted member of the Wailers and a popular solo artist.

Further along the southern coast is the Maroon town of Accompong. The Maroons were escaped slaves who established settlements in the hills, out of reach of the plantation owners. They have retained African culture and some language, due to centuries of isolated self-government. Accompong was established in 1739 and was part of a treaty agreement with the British. Today, it is an autonomous state.

The road to the village is treacherous and narrow, but there has been talk of expanding it for the visitors who come for the January 6 celebration of the Maroon victory over the British. Accompong carries an aura of battles and hard-won survival, and I saw this in the strong Ashanti faces of its people. Visitors must first obtain permission from the colonel, who is the elected leader. I visited the monument to Cudjoe, the Ghanaian-born leader of the Maroon War of 1729, which lasted ten years and won the Maroons the freedom to govern themselves. I also saw the Peace Cave, where the 1738 treaty for Accompong was signed, and the three-hundred-year-old *abeng,* or horn, used to warn Cudjoe's warriors of approaching British attacks. I found visiting Accompong to be a deeply moving experience. Witnessing the unbroken legacy of the strong African spirit of resistance should be an essential part of any visit to Jamaica.

Ruff spots and rent-a-dreads

Katy Noakes

Katy Noakes works in a black arts resource centre in Bristol. She went to Jamaica with a friend, Fiona Parker, in the mid-1990s. It was their first trip to the island, and, like the previous writer, they were determined to avoid the usual tourist circuit.

Going to Jamaica was accidental. We'd planned to go to Cuba, but lacking the stamina to face the travel agent's queues, we grabbed the first bookable flight heading anywhere south of America. And so we came to be at Montego Bay's Donald Sangster airport, armed only with a five-year-old guidebook listing hotels which were way over our budget even then, and surrounded by a planeload of Bud-swigging red-faced American college boys. A group of women in national costume danced and sang in the sweltering heat, adverts for lord knows how many different types of rum plastered the airport walls; everybody everywhere seemed to have something to sell and were intent on selling it. The realisation that we were in at the deep end slowly dawned, but like well-briefed independent travellers we set about looking confident, acting as if we knew what we were doing and trying to give off a "no messing or ripping us off" vibe. We should have known better.

Jamaica relies on tourism for nearly fifty percent of its income; the island attracts over a million visitors a year, its population is only 2.2 million and more people of Jamaican origin live outside the island than on it. It doesn't take a mathematician to work out that the islanders have an international outlook and a streetwise front isn't really going to fool anyone – most people have seen it all before.

Opting for the taxi driver with the most trustworthy face, four wheels and at least two doors, we set off from the airport on our quest for those stretches of calm, idyllic palm-lined beaches. Women don't need to worry especially about using public transport; if a journey is dangerous it probably won't have anything to do with gender. More people die in road accidents than by other means, but once you see how many people can fit into a car you realise that the number of deaths isn't necessarily related to the number of actual accidents. Jamaican taxis are known as the eighth wonder of the world. This could either be because at least eight drivers will be vying for your custom or because eight is the average number of passengers. You might not see any need to lose weight before exposing all in a bikini, but if you haven't the money to rent a car to yourself, a diet merits serious consideration.

Having found a cheap hotel we decided to take a walk and get our bearings. Unwanted attention comes in many well-rehearsed, usually good-humoured forms and it doesn't take long to work out that in Jamaica you have to deal direct. Apologetically, we tried telling the women who wanted to braid our hair "Not now", which means later on. We tried just walking by and nodding a smile, which means you want to talk, preferably business, and we tried laughing and saying our hair was too short. If you're not interested in what someone has to sell, just say no and say it firmly. It is actually possible to braid short hair. The unfortunate consequence of an over-polite attitude can be seen on cropped and braided tourists on beaches island-wide.

Depressed by the recommended tourist option of private beaches, we headed for a secluded cove on the way into town, planning to relax and catch up with some sleep. A group of dreadlocked men and small boys waded in the sea with a large fishing net. The late afternoon sun still beat hot on the otherwise deserted beach and just as we were enjoying our guidebook moment a boy appeared from nowhere brandishing an aloe vera leaf and pouncing enthusiastically on my leg. "Yuh wan some aloe?" he piped.

"Um, well not really, no", I replied.

I was too late. The pace in Jamaica is generally slow except when it comes to cash transactions. "Got some dollars for me?" he asked, pronouncing the magic word which summoned five of his friends who all kindly offered to relieve us of our Western burdens such as cigarettes and money. George, the oldest of them at nineteen, warned us that the town was seething with thieves and "nuff bad bwoys". We needed a guide, he told us in a tone which managed to convey both menace and concern. Noting our scepticism, he pointed to the scar around his neck and chatted merrily about his recent stint in prison by way of proving how dangerous the town is. It wasn't so bad inside, he said, because most of his spars had all been in there at some point too and anyway, he shrugged, it was just part of life. Suitably impressed by his scar, we decided that our first day maybe wasn't the best time to accept George's offer to see more of his life, and headed back to the hotel.

The next morning we accepted the offer of a lift to Negril from a hotel resident. With its seven miles of white beach, the reddest sunsets and a renowned laid-back attitude left by the 1960s' hippies who favoured the town, we were convinced that tranquility was finally within our grasp. When Leon, our driver, dismissed our destination as a "ruff spot" we shrugged it off as another display of over-zealous tourist control.

The hour-long ride took in a technicolour landscape of cane fields, colonial relics, ramshackle huts and random, roadside traders who appeared for work from no apparent nearby town. The combination of heat, blue skies and lush, vividly coloured fauna was overwhelming. Corrugated iron houses sprung up here and there and a young girl walking through a fishing village had handwritten "Gun girl dunnomess" on her T-shirt. Jamaica's contrasts were certainly striking.

Negril's parish of Westmoreland is a lively farming region with more than its fair share of pot-holed roads and booming sound systems. Leon dropped us off to catch the bus to one of the cheap, rented huts which line the beach. "Your destination blow-job city", wisecracked the bus conductor. Another undue warning, we thought, and laughed.

Most of our time in Negril was spent laughing; it was the best strategy for dealing with what would otherwise be infuriating. A human free-for-all (except everything has its price), Negril is home to one of Jamaica's most popular tourist souvenirs. This is where the walking, talking and frequently dancing male dolls, commonly known as "rent-a-dreads" or "rastitutes" make their living by patrolling the beach and "entertaining" unattached visiting females. From sixteen to sixty, female tourists are bombarded with lyrical sweet talk. This was something we were unprepared for and it took me several looks in the mirror to check that I hadn't turned into a Kim Basinger clone before I realised what was going on.

Being in Negril must be something like experiencing a twenty-four-hour Chippendale extravaganza. Madonna may have coined the phrase vogueing, but these boys have claimed it as their national dance, breaking into a move every time a fresh female opportunity presents itself. "I have children in France, one Italian an' I have one in Germany. I an' I a good father, seen", belched Desmond, Rasta of thirty-something years and one of Jamaica's leading export agents. Perched by the bar, keeping a keen eye out for future female investments, Desmond took a swig of his cocktail and explained his theory of paternal responsibility. "Dis Jah a say, I an' I have control over my life an' de youth they 'ave theirs." Exactly how a six-year-old is responsible for their own life somehow got lost in the mesh of Rasta soundbites and rum. "Dis place like Sodom anyhow", he belched, another cocktail and a good few rejections later.

Male prostitution differs from female prostitution in that the men remain in control. "We run t'ings seen," said one disgruntled man who wasn't going to take a rejection standing up. The number of female tourists who are happy to play the game can make it difficult when you're trying to persuade someone that you didn't just come to Jamaica to sample the "big bamboo" they are offering – a situation which is exacerbated by the high profile of resorts like Hedonism, where American students spend their holidays dressed in strategically placed tassles and fuelled on intravenous rum.

Respect has to be earned and while women will be implored to "go natural" by countless sweet-talking men who are all pitching a "positive t'ing", women who concede will be branded for "running around". When I said how good it was to see a German woman out partying with her daughter one night, one of the men who hung around our rooms shrieked with laughter, "Rassclat! That woman went with three different men last night. She act like a one woman Oxfam show!"

Despite everyone's warnings we were still determined to reach Kingston and decided to head back to Mo' Bay for the weekly train through the Blue Mountains. Peace and tranquility still eluded us, but something had obviously woven its magic because we didn't bother to check the timetable. The train wasn't running. There's a saying about travel in Jamaica that getting from A to B is no problem; it's what happens in between that can throw you off track.

Our diversion took us via a funeral party at St Ann's on the north coast, in completely the opposite direction to Kingston. Leon, who had originally driven us to Negril, assured us that we would be welcome and that there would be lifts to Kingston from the party. Keen to see more of the island and its people, we accepted without reservations. Leon was at least sixty years old and his friends were all respectable, middle-aged businessmen with whom, we reasoned, we must be safe.

Set in a million-dollar mansion on the top of a hill, surrounded by acre after acre of verdant land, the party was hosted by ex-ministers, businessmen and general cronies of the Jamaica Labour Party leader, "don" Edward Seaga. Most of the people there lived in North America, coming back to their Jamaican playground at weekends. The women were mostly light-skinned or Syrian and the men's main concern was money, with which they could buy and use anything – us included.

The house came complete with a dark-skinned family who had a yard in the gardens and their own bit of patio to dance on, marked out by a white line. It was apartheid in our faces and taking the first lift out, we fled. When we came across an overturned truck in the village at the bottom of the hill, our accountant driver beeped his horn impatiently and the female passenger shouted out for a "nigga ghul" to come tell her what had happened. The thought that these village people had inconvenienced them by having an accident outraged them. The thought that someone might need help just didn't occur.

The party prepared us for Kingston, which spread out like another bad traffic accident at the base of the Blue Mountains. Our bus route had taken us through the heartland of Jamaica, past small towns and huts where images of poverty were countered with land for subsistence and breathtaking scenery. The ramshackle huts crammed together along the freeways under the city smog had not even this appeal. I couldn't help wondering what had happened to make it go so wrong.

The disparity between rich and poor which we had glimpsed in St Ann's was magnified in Kingston, where a sharp divide separates the uptown gentry from the downtown ghettos. Denham Town and Jones Town were like embers around the blitzed debris of Trench Town. Market women piled up their fruit on the cracked slabs of paving stone and the people trying to scratch out a living far outnumbered those who had come to buy. Meanwhile, the middle classes in new Kingston spoke with American accents, ate in American diners, watched satellite TV and kept their eyes firmly averted from life at the bottom of the hill.

Without any contacts and feeling too voyeuristic to walk around town alone, we cut our stay in Kingston short. Heading out of town on a bus, we made the mistake of asking fellow passengers what all the graffiti about Jim Brown meant. The bus went suddenly silent and the faces froze aghast. We'd involuntarily raised the issue of politics and no one was prepared to risk a comment.

Our return to Westmoreland was a relief. The rent-a-dreads knew by now to leave us alone and once that barrier had been overcome we were free to enjoy their friendship and accept their invitations to homes in nearby villages. We spent surreal afternoons watching Scarface and Kung-fu videos in a yard full of Rastas and rudeboys, went on overnight drives over mountains and past lakes under skies of the clearest, brightest stars, sang along to calypso and Madonna at the top of our voices and spent endless heated hours discussing the position of women in Jamaica. "I like you ragga English", said a self-styled bandalero after one such verbal wrangle, "You take the bait every time, but you think I dunna know the score, huh?" Slapping me round the backside with the fish he was preparing for tea, he ran off giggling.

Our journey back to the airport was a day later than planned – we'd totally forgotten the date. A friend agreed to drive us and in true Jamaican fashion we set off with a car crammed full of people who came along for the ride. Running into a police roadblock, we were asked to get out and spread ourselves over the car to be searched. The police found a fingernail-sized amount of ganja at the bottom of my bag and vindictively fined Tony, the driver, five hundred Jamaican dollars for "failing to stop". It was obvious that we weren't travelling with a family of official guides and the authorities apparently felt that such unsanctioned mixing should be punished.

Leaving Jamaica was the first time I have cried at an airport. Our time had been frustrating, hilarious and eye-opening. Even with the most blood-boiling kind of hassle, the humour at least, was hard to resist. "Hey strong English", shouted one man as we took our bags out of the car, "Yuh wan come use your leg muscles an' chop off my balls?"

read on . . .

Ziggi Alexander and Audrey Dewjee (ed), *The Wonderful Adventures of Mrs Seacole in Many Lands* (1957; UK: OUP, 1990). Mary Seacole, a Jamaican nurse and heroine of the Crimean War, writes about her life and travels.

Cedella Booker, *Bob Marley: An Intimate Portrait by his Mother* (UK Penguin, 1997). Marley's mother goes on record with her own version of her son's life, including his embracing of Rastafari, his attitude to sex and ganja, his approach to the cancer that eventually killed him and the financial wrangling that followed his death. An utterly excusable addition to the myth-making that has eclipsed the history of this reggae star, which includes some telling scenes of rural and urban Jamaica with occasional stylistic excursions into Jamaican patois.

Carolyn Cooper, *Noises in the Blood* (UK: Caribbean Publishing, 1993/US: Duke University Press, 1995). Provocative study of Jamaican popular culture, particularly the use of language, that looks at Marley's lyrics, the "slackness" of the sexually explicit DJs and the Jamaican oral narrative tradition.

Lorna Goodison, *Baby Mother and the King of Swords* (UK: Longman, 1990). Rather dark collection of contemporary short stories set in Jamaica.

Sistren with Honor Ford-Smith (ed), *Lionheart Gal – Life Stories of Jamaican Women* (1986; UK: The Women's Press, 1994). Edited by Sistren theatre collective's long-standing artistic director, Honor Ford-Smith, this book is based on testimonies collected in the course of the group's work with ordinary Jamaican women. A powerful anthology, bursting with the spirit of resistance.

Andrea Taylor, *Baby Mother* (Jamaica: X-Press, 1995). Popular fictional account of one woman's journey through single motherhood, Jamaican style.

Japan

Boxing with shadow puppets

Frances King

Frances King, a British puppet designer, was invited by a rural Japanese puppet troupe, Yuyake, to help make shadow puppets for a street parade and to tour the show to schools around the countryside. Living in the attic of the puppet workshop – a former train station in Shizuoka prefecture – Frances set about learning a new set of performance skills, including how to sing Japanese and play percussion.

I woke with a start. What was that noise? Outside it was still dark except for a few shimmering stars, but my room was aglow with luminous neon. Bleary-eyed, I looked out of the window. In the narrow lane below, four huge vending machines disgorged cans of beer and cigarettes. I lay sweating on the futon, unable to sleep, as insects buzzed in a distant corner of my attic room. In just one day, I had been catapulted from my home in Yorkshire to this village in Okuyama, where I was to spend the summer working on designs for a puppet theatre. No wonder I felt adrift.

My tiny *tatami*-matted room was part of the puppet workshop, located in a traditional wooden building that had once been the village train station. Downstairs, sliding paper screens concealed trunks of puppets, theatre lighting and higgledy-piggledy chests overflowing with materials. The bathroom was a corrugated iron lean-to with an aluminium bath. No high-tech Japanese gadgetry there.

A few days after my arrival, my new employer, Mac-san – a transplanted New Zealander who had lived in Japan for 25 years – had to go abroad. She left me with all the main tools for survival: keys to a Toyota van, a roughly drawn map directing me to the nearest grocery store, and instructions on how to deal with earthquakes, tidal waves and poisonous snakes. Strangely enough, the prospect of natural disaster was far less terrifying than negotiating my everyday needs. I was completely alone: an urban British artist living in a Japanese farming community. Spoken Japanese was just a blur of indistinguishable sounds; I was an illiterate mute who felt entirely invisible. How would I cope? Could I find food? Would I be able to drive to the supermarket? Or the hardware shop? I might get lost. Who would help me? What if the van broke down? My mind was besieged by panic.

The antidote was to concentrate on the essentials and shop for food. At first, I was overwhelmed by the unidentifiable vegetables and packets of coloured squashy things. Then, I came to relish the sensual aspects of this search for edible ingredients. What to do with the many available varieties of fresh fish, fish paste or soy bean products? I had no inkling, but by smelling, prodding and taking cues from the colourful packaging, I was soon able to cobble together a simple meal, moving on from miniature cucumbers and pickled ginger to steamed rice and miso soup.

This temporary inability to communicate reawakened other senses, making everyday experiences intensely vivid. The surrounding landscape was a patchwork of pine forests, tea plantations, bamboo and orange groves. Mist-shrouded hills evoked a brush-stroke painting, and green paddy fields spoke of the miracle of life. It was for me that the bullfrog chorus sang at dusk. I alone saw the blue flash of a kingfisher on the riverbank, noticed the evening smells of eels cooking and the fragrant incense from the roadside shrine. I kept the company of spindly-legged wasps who built a beautiful nest under the eaves and centipedes who visited the humid bathroom. The only external acknowledgement of my existence seemed to come from the sailor-suited children who cycled past me daily through the village to school, nodding as they passed.

Each day was a feast of the senses. Whether it was swimming with water turtles in a nearby river or sitting in my aluminium bath listening to the rain, I began to feel alive. Solitude and cultural alienation enhanced my relationship with this otherwise strange world in which I lived.

My initial contact with villagers was limited to polite greetings as we passed each other on the way to our respective workplaces. But I was very touched to come home one day and find a young woman and her two children waiting for me. Handing me a bag of freshly picked chestnuts, she said, "We want to be your friend." I discovered she was part of the extended family that owned the beer shop across the road.

That evening, I cautiously ventured into my nearest drinking establishment. I armed myself with my phrase book, poised to deliver the Japanese equivalent of "Good evening. One beer and a packet of crisps, please". A group of farmers sat on stools, chatting to the Mama-san. They smiled politely and said hello, their conversation trailing off into silence. I looked at all the bottles, wondering whether my choice of beer should be informed by the graphics on the label, the logo, the shape of the bottle or the odd slogan in English. When it came to snacks, I was spoilt for choice – the choice being packets of dried fish, dried octopus (with eyes), dried squid, whole or in strips. At last I found a kind of fried dried beans. These turned out to be deliciously salty, and later became a favourite.

Two of the men began talking enthusiastically, their shyness doused by alcohol. Asking me where I was from and whether I liked Japan, they became visibly excited when they discovered I was English. One man pointed at the other saying, "He – English – learn." As if to demonstrate, he continued, "This is a book, this is a pen", repeating the sentences over and over like a mantra. I appreciated their friendliness, and said goodnight before returning home to another quiet evening in my creaking train-station attic.

Soon, I began to meet more villagers. One morning, I heard a truck outside emitting a loud sucking sound. I slid open the front door to see a man with his arms down a drain hole frantically waggling a long stick. Seeing me, he began chatting away, but all I could grasp was his request for water. Grinning, he stuck out his bum and patted it repeatedly. From his eccentric performance, I guessed that he wanted to use my toilet. We smiled helplessly at each other for a few moments before it dawned on me that he was the sewage collector making his rounds – a necessity in a community like ours, with many older homes having pit toilets.

At work, I began to feel more at home when I was joined by two colleagues, Hirasawa and Fukagawa. Hira-san was a woman in her early forties who defied the Japanese stereotype of femininity. She was assertive, confident and lively, and expressed her opinion in a manner that sometimes seemed brusque. She managed to combine working as a travelling puppeteer and musician with running a household for her husband and two children. This was no mean feat in a country where women are expected to prioritise child care. She had boundless energy and enthusiasm. I loved the way she would simply laugh at her mistakes. She related well to children and was an excellent storyteller, speaking the voices of various characters in the show, and singing beautifully.

Hira spoke more English than I did Japanese and her style was emphatic and full of Americanisms. In fact, she learned much of her English from listening to the Beatles and the Carpenters over and over. I soon got used to her puttering away in the workshop, singing Karen Carpenter songs in a clear soprano voice. Even so, I was still amused by her creative use of English. One day we were eating miso soup with some unidentifiable vegetable floating in it. I began to ask her what it might be, but before I had finished my question she burst in with "Bamboo, baby!" It took me a minute to realise she was telling me we were eating fresh bamboo shoots.

Fukagawa-san was a carpenter who made the bamboo base structures for the figures I was working on. His name meant "deep river", and it described his introspective personality and flowing energy exactly. In his fifties, with greying curly hair and small beard, he would sit shoeless and cross-legged, working patiently with fresh green bamboo that he had cut himself. Sometimes, he presented us gifts of spinning tops, bamboo whistles and instant chopsticks. He once made me a *mimikaki*, a Japanese ear-cleaner in the shape of a bird; its beak is meant to scratch about the ear canal. He gave me a demonstration of this, wincing and saying "Iteh, iteh" – Ouch, ouch – to warn me from poking in the beak too deeply.

Fukagawa was partial to flea markets, especially retro ones where he found gems like antique spectacles and lacquered–wood boxes. After visiting his beautiful house, which he had built in the classical Japanese style, I realised he was a true craftsman who appreciated these fast-disappearing traditions of Japan. I noticed the details of his personal effects; his handmade wooden tools, his well-worn leather bag and his traditional wooden *geta* (slippers). This appreciation seemed to run in his family: he also owned a large collection of price-less kimonos that his parents had once rented out as part of their cos-tume-hire business for kabuki theatre.

When the clock struck noon – announced by a jolly electric keyboard version of Beethoven's *Ode to Joy* over the village loudspeak-ers – Fukagawa, Hira and I would sit down with our respective lunch boxes and say "Itadaki-mas", a secular thank-you, before tucking in. Fukagawa always carried a beautiful lacquered-wood box from which he ate his daily meal of cold rice and pink pickled plums. My lunch, meanwhile, was a miserable sweet potato thrown haphazardly into whatever container I could find. This changed when Hira showed me how to cook noodles Japanese-style. After that, we'd often cook *soba* – fresh, thick white noodles eaten cold in a hot fish stock and sprinkled with sesame seeds, finely chopped spring onions and shrimp croutons. Very refreshing as the July heat intensified.

We worked through the summer humidity, our concentration interrupted only by intermittent exasperation at the rivers of sweat that ran from our skin. From time to time, we mopped our faces, or worked in front of a whirring electric fan for light relief. We looked forward to our breaks where the three of us would cool down by drinking ice-cold flasks of *mugi-cha* – barley tea – and eating chilled watermelon from the freezer. Fukagawa once presented Hira and me with gifts of antique folding paper fans that had once belonged to his family. With these we fanned our way through every tea-break until the arrival of the rainy season.

I felt honoured to have such a personal introduction to Japanese culture. It helped alleviate the initial sense of isolation that I experi-enced on arrival in Okuyama. After a month in the village, I ran away to Kyoto for the weekend, to stay with an English friend who had lived in the city for many years. It was a joy to share my experience of everything that was foreign about Japan with an old friend. Living alone in the village, I'd really missed meaningful conversation.

Things got better in the autumn, however, when we started an extensive tour, performing some fifty shows to schools in Northern Honshu and Hokkaido. Performing was a challenge, as I had to oper-ate puppets and lights, sing in Japanese, play percussion, and play my button accordion before and after the show. The most difficult thing to come to terms with, however, was that I received no feedback on my work – either during the rehearsal period or the tour. Influenced by the traditional relationship of master and apprentice that governs the learning of any Japanese craft tradition, you are expected to learn by your mistakes. Yet sometimes, this lack of praise or criticism made me feel even more isolated.

Although shadow puppetry is not a traditional Japanese art form, it rose to prominence in Japan in the 1970s, inspiring hundreds of small companies that now tour in nursery and primary schools around the country. Our performance told the story of "The Big Turnip", a Russian folk tale well-known to Japanese children, about how a farmer enlists the help of his entire family to harvest a giant vegetable. The set consisted of traditional-style woodcut images printed onto a roll of paper, with silhouette puppets made from card.

Our young audiences of three- to seven-year-olds were always enchanted by the show. As we unloaded trunks of puppets from the small Toyota van, children would rush to greet us with excitement and curiosity. Afterwards they ran amok, playing instruments and inspecting both the puppets and me. With my shortish hair, very young children frequently asked me whether I was a man or a woman. Often they called out "America! America!" and I became aware of how culturally insignificant the UK is to the rest of the world compared with the US. The entire crowd including teachers would usually wave us off, asking us to return soon and calling out "O genki da ne" (Stay healthy forever).

For three months, we were constantly on the move, staying with local people or in *minshuku* – Japanese-style inns. I felt privileged to be driving through the Japanese countryside in autumn, when trees are red and gold, visiting mountain hot-springs and camping in the woods. Most of all, I felt privileged to enter into the warm, but fleeting, relationships with strangers that are common to the travelling performer. Our hosts were always welcoming and generous, our audience responsive.

Being part of the puppet company enabled me to see Japan as I never could have done alone. In a society that appears so inaccessible to foreigners, it was a wonderful way to meet people, and unlike many travel encounters it felt like a mutually enriching experience.

Mama-san's babies

Sarah Dale

Driven by the need to escape for a while from the cloisters of law, Sarah Dale left her job as a solicitor in the south of England, gathered her savings and flew to Thailand for an extended holiday. Two months later, having almost run out of money but reluctant to fly home, she heard about "hostessing" in Japan. The last of her savings went on a flight to Tokyo and a bright red silk dress.

The hostess, I learned, was the modern equivalent of the geisha, a centuries-old and highly venerated profession that attracts Japanese girls like a vocation. Geishas are the embodiment of that enduring Japanese icon: feminine perfection. They exist to serve men and preserve the traditional arts such as singing, dancing and playing classical instruments like the *samisen*.

Her modern counterpart, the bar hostess, has exchanged silk kimonos for cocktail dresses, and the *samisen* for a karaoke box. She is considerably less expensive than her predecessor yet she shares the same values: to be the feminine ideal, to entertain, to listen, to be serious, to dazzle with her wit and charm. It is not considered a demeaning job. Certainly no sexual favours are expected – just mild flirtation, perhaps a glimmering eroticism. Many Japanese girls claim to be proud to serve men in this way and be recognised for their "skills". The pursuit of this feminine ideal is revered in Japan like an art form.

Hostess bars, I learned, abound in their thousands in Japan. Each bar has a manageress, always called "Mama-san", who will set the particular, and distinctive character of her establishment. Western girls, particularly of the blonde-haired, blue-eyed variety, are considered a special treat and a myriad bars boast them like a range of exotic fruit. I was enchanted. This would be much more fun than writs and wills and I set out for Tokyo in search of a dissolute life.

As soon as I arrived I found myself a room in a cheap hostel known as a "*Gaijin* House". These are always full of foreigners working as hostesses or English teachers who usually have good job-hunting tips to offer. "Just walk into bars on spec and ask for work," they told me. So that same night I staggered out in a haze of jet lag, to the hostess Mecca: "the Ginza". It was impossible to decipher what was and was not a bar, so I took pot luck. My enthusiastic smile and carefully articulated "hostess" was met each time with a horrified hiss of "gaijin", arms arranged into a cross in front of the face and a closed door. Clearly crossbones meant "no" and "gaijin", I realised, was Japanese for foreigner. Literally, it means "outside person". It was the first Japanese word I learned.

Perhaps I kept walking into private parties that night or perhaps I was just damned ugly. I didn't understand and I didn't find work. I crawled away from the Ginza and headed back to the "outside person's" house.

By Monday morning I was freshly resolved. I scoured the expats' newspaper, *The Japan Times*, and found several bars advertising for Western girls to work as hostesses. I made some calls, had an interview and got a job at a bar called *San Michel* in Akasakamitsuke. Not quite the Ginza but nevertheless a thriving business district.

All dolled up in a silk dress I'd had run up cheaply in Bangkok, I tottered off on high heels to my new life. On entering the bar I was immediately faced with a full-length portrait of Mama-san reclining in a cocktail dress that she had thrown on. Mama was a middle-aged lady, petite, shrew-like and a bit tawdry. She had been born in Japan but was third-generation Korean and so still considered *gaijin*. Starting life herself as a bar hostess she had saved enough money by whatever means and started her own enterprise. She spoke no English and used "Boy" as her interpreter. Boy was a girl – or at least that was the consensus of opinion – and her job was to greet customers, bring drinks to the table, and fire hostesses.

Mama called me her baby, plucked a hair out of my chin and barked at me to sit. A posse of women gathered round, all sporting that ubiquitous silk dress. There was Danielle, a skinny American with flaming red hair. She had just graduated and was hostessing to repay college loans. Anna and Femka, two marvellously tall Dutch girls saving for another season of going gaga in Goa. Sophia, a sexy Swede, with an unrealised dream to be a model and legs that undulated from beneath her skirts, and Domarra, an Italian linguist perfecting her Japanese. Completing the group was a loud fat woman from

Manchester, whom I got the distinct impression I had been chosen to replace. All these gorgeous girls and then us two.

Our guests arrived. A group of Japanese salarymen, that is businessmen, on a corporate razzle. Prohibitively expensive for the individual, hostess bars are mostly frequented by salarymen on the obligatory evening out with the boss. The company foots the bill and all the salaryman has to do is drink himself into oblivion and remain there until his boss says he can leave.

We jumped to attention and in concert squealed: "*Irrashaimasse*", meaning welcome. High heels scurrying, we fetched whisky and water, glasses and ice, bowls of sweets and hot wet flannels . . .

The flannels, "*oshibori*", were for the guests to wipe their hands with, a Japanese ritual unfailingly observed before eating or drinking. Mama pointed to where each of us should sit and the party began.

Assiduously we catered to their every need; we topped up drinks and clinked ice cubes in glasses, we lit their cigarettes, and, intermittently, unwrapped a sweet to delicately pop into a guest's mouth.

The usual questions and small talk commenced. You know, the subjects that always surface when people don't know each others' language very well. Then gradually as the whisky unlocked our guests' tongues and inhibitions took flight the conversation became increasingly bawdy. Each hostess's innuendo was met with admiring guffaws from the guests while more serious comment was politely listened to and ignored.

We were perfect young ladies. Never so inelegant as to cross our legs, lean back in our seats, bite our nails or play with our hair. Never so rude as to divert our attention for a second, our admiring gaze for an instant from these latter-day Samurai who, weary from another day fighting for Japan's economic miracle, would look to us adoring *gaijin* girlies to ease away their tensions. Departures from this strictly observed code of etiquette were met with a public shriek from Mama and a whispered interpretation from Boy.

Domarra felt that hostessing was the perfect opportunity to practise the Japanese language and exchange cultures. I found there was a limit to how much you could discuss with a middle-aged Japanese man who has worked for Mitsubishi all his life, cannot speak a word of English and is four sheets to the wind. The salarymen I met were more interested in exchanging saliva. Like little boys they would giggle and tell me their hobby was "girl-hunting". Tentatively they would try to touch our legs but the gentlest of reproaches, such as a clucking no, a surprised giggle and a firm push or a wiggle of the hips and a motherly slap, was enough to bring an immediate retraction and a resumption of that blank expression, as if nothing had ever happened. Femka believed in preventative measures and employed the beguiling tactic of "lovingly" clinging onto her guest's hands so that she knew exactly where they were. Mama was approving. This was a "decent" bar. We were all her babies. The only thing we were to massage was ego.

The art of hostessing we learned was mere coquetry. Never yes, never no, but a tantalising maybe. To our guests it was the stuff of dreams. It kept them coming for months.

For me the evening's climax was certainly before the guests' arrival. We would sit around swapping travellers' tales and talking about our lives back home and what we planned to do next. There was a strong sense of togetherness and we rallied each other along. I don't think any of us could quite capture the reality of the job we were doing. Our bizarre placement seemed more and more hysterical.

Our guests frequently asked us to sing karaoke. These requests were met each time with some moments of feigned modesty, as was required by Mama-san, and then a rather undignified scramble for the microphone as we each sought a three-minute retreat from wandering palms and inane conversation. Microphone firmly in hand I yelled out *Sonny* and everyone danced. The guests were at their wooden best and the girls were not much better. No one had their heart in it, no one had the beat and a domino of glances passed through us. I remember it like a framed picture.

San Michel closed at a quarter to midnight. Depending on the caprice of their boss, the salarymen would either stagger hiccuping to another bar or to their homes for a few hours' sleep before doing it all again the next day. After bowing to our guests the other girls and I would leave the bar. Once around the corner we threw off our heels, and like a fleet of Cinderellas ran in stockinged feet through the streets of Tokyo for our last trains home.

I suppose what really got to me about hostessing was that I had put a price on my freedom. Ordinarily, when faced with a slobbering old man with a red face and a preoccupation with asking "How big is your boyfriend's dick?" one might shout some abuse, turn away, and leave. In this situation, however, I had relinquished such rights; I had sold them to Mama-san. It was mental prostitution.

So I decided to "empower" myself. Throwing away such girlish things as make-up, high heels and Bic razors I claimed back my sanity and decided to be myself. Openly flouting the rules of decorum, I recklessly crossed my legs, deliberately leaned back in my seat; heedless, I unwrapped those sweets and popped them, horror of horrors, into my own mouth. Most offensive of all I offered opinions, disagreed, argued, behaved just like the owner of a pair of Doc Marten boots should. I played the raconteur and clowned around, but in my own way and not in the freeze-dried, vacuum-packed fashion they expected. Curiously they responded with laughter and fascination. Perhaps they were bemused to see this in a woman.

Something would just not let me quit. I suppose I was curious to see how long I could last being me: two weeks basically, and Boy was sent to fire me. She gave me a big hug and my wages up to date; £50 for each night I turned up and an inexplicable £15 deduction for the use of toilet paper!

A lot more money than this can be earned! The sleazier the bar, the more Japanese you speak, the longer you've been around and, of course, the longer your legs, the higher the rates. You can double, triple this basic with tips earned for anything from being wined, dined or complimented to singing a soulful ballad or performing an exotic belly dance. The job can be as risqué as you want it to be and consequently you can earn as much money as you like. A woman able to handle the masquerade and approach the whole affair as some peculiar brand of performance art can make a killing. I got my fifty quid for just turning up!

With the hostessing mystique shattered, I found myself a job as an English teacher, which is an option open to anybody with a degree and English as their native language. Within weeks I was wearing a suit again, even carrying a briefcase. I had been sucked back into respectability despite myself.

I later met up with Anna, one of the Dutch girls and she told me that she had been fired a few days after me. It seemed Mama thought she smelt. Anna didn't care. She shrugged and told me, "Nobody care zat I smell in India. Oh well, tonight I go for job as bunny girl." Mama-sans do hire and fire indiscriminately, but there is always another hostess job just around the corner. Femka, meanwhile, was doing famously holding court to a string of admirers. Somehow she was able to slip on the mask more comfortably than I, the deodorant more successfully than Anna. Danielle, like me, took a teaching job and no doubt Domarra is there to this day, exchanging cultures.

The loud fat one from Manchester left a few days after I arrived. Hostess with the Mostest, she had been at *San Michel* the longest. Six months of hostessing had made her enough money to do an overland trip to Israel. On her last night she gave a sonorous rendition of *My Way* on the karaoke and then gave me all her old clothes in exchange for a packet of condoms.

About ten months later, when I was living in a different part of Japan, I was waiting for a train and spotted Sophia pasted up on a billboard – all legs, she was modelling shoes. She had realised her dream.

The women I met who hostessed throughout their stay developed a jaundiced view of the country. I could see how this could happen; working at night and sleeping in the day meant that it was easy to miss some of the fragments that make up Japan. As a teacher and through living with a Japanese family I saw women treated in a different way. Marriages, which are often arranged, are an economic necessity. The family is like a small business, producing the next generation of mothers and salarymen. In the most sinister privatisation of all, the chemistry in human relationships seems to have been disentangled, set apart and sold as a service. Instead of relaxing at home with their families, Japanese salarymen go out in droves to relax with strangers. When I was teaching, my students bowed and called me "*sensei*" in hushed tones. This was refreshing after the hostess bar, but eventually the rigid formality seemed almost ridiculous – it had a sterility about it. Accustomed to living in a melting pot of emotions and responses it was difficult to find my role.

I'm glad I had a short stint at hostessing. It gave me first-hand experience of an aspect of Japan that is often missed by travellers. I was surprised to see how deeply rooted and unshakeable were my principles. My need to be appreciated for everything I am as a woman, rather than just one feminine façade, was more intense than I had ever really known. Hostessing helped me to work out what I don't want with my life.

read on . . .

Isabella Bird, *Unbeaten Tracks in Japan* (1880; UK: Virago, 1984: US: C.E. Tuttle, 1971). After a brief stop in Meiji-era Tokyo, intrepid Victorian adventurer Bird is determined to take to the wilder routes of Japan that are untrampled by tourists. The journey she chooses is the northern route to Hokkaido, which she describes in vivid prose.

Angela Carter, *Nothing Sacred, Selected Writing* (1982; UK: Virago, 1993). Some of the most brilliant writing in this collection of journalism and autobiographical essays is devoted to the two years Carter spent in Japan in the early 1970s. Her fascination for the country radiates from the pages, be it a description of the tranquil ennui and cosiness of the gentrified district where she lived ("you could eat your dinner off the children") to a smart retrospective of the ancient art of tattooing, or a clear-sighted enquiry into the ubiquitous comic-strip rape fantasies "read at idle moments by the people whose daily life is one of perfect gentleness, reticence, and kindliness". See also **Shaking a Leg** (UK: Vintage, 1998/US: Penguin, 1998), a further eclectic mix of writing, including a travel section entitled "Home and Away" that ranges from the 1960s until her death in 1992.

Cathy Davidson, *36 Views of Mount Fuji: On Finding Myself in Japan* (US: Plume, 1994). Davidson and her husband moved to Osaka in the early 1980s to teach spoken English at a major women's university. Over four journeys, spanning nearly a decade, she settles her dilemma of whether or not to live permanently in Japan deciding against the constant, if mild, humiliation that *gaijin* (foreigners) routinely face. Her stylish and stylised prose (she relies on literary devices to exemplify the emotions so carefully hidden from view), the breadth of her experience and her transparent love of the country make this a memorable and important narrative.

Josie Dew, *A Ride in the Neon Sun: A Gaijin in Japan* (UK: Little, Brown & Co., 1999). This latest travelogue by one of the youngest of Britain's pedalling scribes begins with her rather confused arrival at Tokyo Airport (a week earlier she'd been heading for New Zealand), after which she spends two weeks cheerfully lost in the city before finally hitting the road. The rest of the book follows her progress across the country, still "in various degrees of disorientation", on a journey punctuated with odd, usually very brief, encounters with people like the "jaunty workmen" who buy her a beer and give her a lift on their fork-lift truck, the policeman on his annual cycling holiday and Meredith, the former Coca-Cola roller-skater girl, now working as a gas pump attendant for her Japanese father-in-law. More entertaining than illuminating, this is a book filled with snapshots of a country few foreigners can easily decipher.

Lesley Downer, *The Brothers: The Hidden World of Japan's Richest Family* (UK: Chatto and Windus, 1994/US: o/p). The Tsutsumi family are the Kennedys of Japan and their saga of wealth, illegitimacy and the fabled hatred of the two half-brothers is turned into a gripping read by Downer. Also look out for **On the Narrow Road to the Deep North** (o/p), her book following in the footsteps of the poet Basho.

Norma Field, *From My Grandmother's Bedside: Sketches of Postwar Tokyo* (US: University of California Press, 1997). The daughter of an American GI and a Japanese mother, Field returns to Tokyo to minister to her bedridden grandmother who has suffered a second stroke. In the midst of this emotive and arduous family duty, childhood memories of Japan come bubbling to the surface: taking loyalty oaths in the US embassy, sharing a warm futon with her aunts and grandmother, the public shame caused by the break-up of her parents' marriage, and, throughout, the minutiae of everyday life. Her reflections memorably include an indictment of the bomb and America's refusal to acknowledge the holocaust that followed. This is a collection of quiet reminiscences and observations that add up to a powerful, allusive evocation of Japanese post-war culture. Field's earlier book, *In the Realm of a Dying Emperor: Japan at Century's End* (US: Vintage, 1993) offers an insightful look at the cracks in the imperial image that began to show after Emperor Hirohito's death in 1989.

Leila Philip, *The Road Through Miyama* **(US: Random House, 1989).** As an extension of her East Asian studies programme at Princeton University, Leila Philip lived for two years in a small Japanese town where she set about learning the potter's craft. Her astute and poetic memoir of this period charts the progress of her general apprenticeship into all aspects of village life – scything rice stalks, harvesting bamboo, ceremonial tea-pouring – as well as the complex, delicate and time-consuming process of moulding and firing pots. An alluring read, packed with fascinating detail of the culture and customs she was privileged to witness.

Kazakstan

New tenants on Mametova Street

Liz Williams

Liz Williams works for a British educational consultancy with contacts in several of the former Soviet republics, including Kazakstan, Uzbekistan (see p.624) and Kyrgystan. During the summer of 1996 she lived with her partner, Charles, in the Kazakstan capital, Almaty, where she began work on a book of interviews with women from the region. Despite maddening bureaucracy, pollution, days without gas or electricity and a regular lack of sleep, she soon grew fond of the city and plans to return.

I first arrived in Kazakstan one summer night, flying in from Heathrow via Vienna. From the air, in the early hours of the morning, the heart of Asia was invisible. Its principal city, Almaty, was indicated only by a few lights scattered across a vast plain of darkness. At the time, this seemed symbolic of this mysterious, unknown land. Later, I learned that Almaty simply cannot afford street lighting. So much for romance.

On landing we abandoned any semblance of British politeness and shoved our way to the front of the plane in order to be first on the bus to the terminal and therefore first in the visa queue. There we contended with a dormant *apparatchik* on a 24-hour shift and having secured our visas, headed for the exit where a driver was waiting. During the wait for our visas, my partner Charles asked someone if smoking was allowed. The man looked at him as if he were deranged and said flatly, "Nobody cares." This bald pronouncement echoed throughout our stay, from the state of the roads, to the buildings, to the possibility of another devastating earthquake. The Soviet tide has ebbed and left Kazakstan high and dry. Now nobody seems to care.

The next day we awoke to find ourselves in an ordinary Soviet-style city; the air was redolent of dust and unburned fuel, smoky with exhaust emissions and fumes from numerous *shashlik* kebab stands. To the south arched the foothills of what eventually become the Tien Shan, the Celestial Mountains, which stretch to the Chinese border in a long snowlit switchback. Almaty lies sandwiched between steppe and mountain, and comprises row after row of grimy apartment blocks. Removed from its stupendous setting, it would not be dissimilar to some parts of London. Yet despite the dust, the functional architecture and the hot *samal* wind which blows down from the mountains and sets everyone's nerves on edge, the city in summer is very green – one more happy legacy of the 1910 earthquake, after which Almaty was rebuilt and every citizen encouraged to plant a tree. Its name means "Father of Apples"; oak and sycamore line its quiet, wide streets. Beyond the city lies a hinterland of *dachas*: from mansions to garden sheds, surrounded by allotments crammed with cherry, plum, apple and blackcurrant.

We were to live in a private apartment, rented by the school for which Charles was working. Our landlady, Marina, lived downstairs and her family supplied us with such essentials as light bulbs and plums. Periodically, according to the last British tenant, her father would appear on the landing in a string vest, taking refuge from the prayer meetings held regularly by Marina and her mother, which, happily for him, coincided with *Baywatch* on our TV. Marina was an easy-going landlady; the sole rule she imposed upon us was that if anyone came to the door, we were to lie and tell people we were American pastors. We whiled away a considerable amount of time speculating on the reasons for this (the secret police? religious convictions?), but it turned out to be Marina's entirely justified fear of the taxman. Our rent was more than the average monthly salary, and undeclared. Upstairs lived a very old woman, who used to leap out onto the landing at random moments and shout at people, and who complained every time our phone rang since her own was connected to it by some Byzantine party-line network.

Mametova Street possessed several amenities. There was Vasily's eponymous café and *shashlik* (mutton kebab) stand, dominated by an immense hollow tower which was a cooling vent for the mythical, unfinished Almaty Metro. There was also a *faux* Turkish restaurant (for though the Kazaks are proud of their Turkic heritage, their enthusiasm is impeded by the fact that relatively few people have been to Turkey), and a breathtakingly expensive Korean nightclub, complete with its coterie of teenage prostitutes in hot pants. At the end of the street was one of the biggest mosques I have ever seen, apparently constructed out of oil drums and scaffolding; religious zeal had not lasted long in this case, for the previous *imam* had run off with the money before the congregation could get round to the plastering.

During the first few weeks, our principal difficulty was getting any sleep. Vasily's idea of a good time was Russian rock and Tajik pop, played at ear-splitting volume all night, every night. If we closed the windows, the apartment was a furnace. If we opened them, we were deafened. Towards dawn, the music would die down and there'd be a brief window of peace before the *muezzin* from the half-finished but still defiant mosque began. After that, came the milkman, sweetly intoning "Malako! Malako!" as he did his circuit with a tank full of unpasteurised dairy products.

Despite these attendant disadvantages, however, it did not take long to become fond of Almaty. It was not an exotic city, but one soon began to notice its more surreal aspects. There was a huge pile of rubble carefully placed in the middle of Abai Street so that cars would not inadvertently drive into the enormous crater which lay behind it. There was the bouncy castle positioned in front of the improbable pink wedding-cake structure of Zenkov Cathedral, and a museum built like a giant *yurt*. The women selling roses and onions outside the market all had doctorates in physics; out of work, they took what jobs they could get. Almaty was full of odd things that you'd glimpse from the corner of your eye and fail to believe.

Apart from the cathedral and the mosque, the city was filled with the usual imposing architecture of totalitarianism: huge facades designed to impress, set against the floating backdrop of the mountains. Perhaps they were impressive once, but now . . . nobody cares. The roads were pitted with potholes and buildings were falling down, undermined by frost and earthquake damage. Sometimes there was no gas or electricity for days when the government couldn't pay its bills from neighbouring Uzbekistan. In retaliation, the Kazakstanis would cut off international phone lines, ensuring that the Uzbeks could not speak to anyone outside of their own borders, and eventually a sullen compromise would be achieved. In the meantime, we would retreat to *Vasily's*, which had the basic but prudent facilities of a kettle and an open fire.

Post-perestroika economics impressed no one. Many people hadn't been paid for months, but still turned up regularly for work. One of these stoic individuals remarked with a laugh and a shrug, "We pretend to work and they pretend to pay us . . ."

Perhaps unsurprisingly, there seemed to be a general nostalgia for the Soviet Union; I met twenty-something entrepreneurs who still carried a cherished Party Card in their breast pockets. Yet I found only one statue remaining from the old days, a bronze bust of Lenin that sat on a plinth in the park. When I went back a week later to take a photo, Lenin had gone. His place was being taken by Kazak heroes; the dignified figure of the poet Abai now sits in a pool of flowing robes where the founders of Communism once stood.

It took me a little while to adapt to the role of post-Soviet housewife. There was one main department store, Tsum on Abai Khan, which was a cavernous, stuffy emporium where you could buy anything from socks to three-piece suites. Tsum reminded me of an aquarium. I preferred the Green Market on Makataeva. In need of a syringe, or a mosquito coil, or Korean salad? You could find everything and anything in the market, including a magnificent range of vegetables. Rumour had it that the meat section was rigorously checked, but having turned round one day to encounter a flayed horse's head, we became primarily vegetarian. Post-Soviet housewives take the kids and a bucket when they go shopping: there is no such measure as "under a kilo". I became stronger, but perpetually tired.

It was easy to find somewhere to eat in Almaty. *Vasily's* was our local haunt and great so long as you weren't trying to sleep. Highlights of the unchanging menu include *shashlik* (mutton kebab), *plov* (mutton pilau) and *mantis* (mutton dumplings). You may notice a theme developing here: Kazakstani cuisine is monotonous in the extreme. At *Vasily's* the food was good, however, and there was always something going on. The patron's accessories included Kalashnikovs and once, memorably, a boa constrictor. Frequently people danced, often led by a young lady of Tajik extraction whom I christened Tess of the D'Urbovitches, due to her position as the local *femme fatale*.

On Saturdays we would escape the pall of pollution overhanging Almaty and head for *Media*, a hotel and spa with an ice-rink on the edge of the foothills. From here, you could walk up into the quiet butterfly-filled woods, or climb the leg-tremblingly long flight of steps which led over the avalanche dam, on which wedding parties self-consciously posed. Ahead rose the mountains, remote and glacier-crowned; behind lay the empty, heat-shimmering steppe. Almaty, lost beneath the smog, could do its vanishing act again.

Once, Vasily and his wife, Maria, took us to Lake Kapchugai. The shore was dusty and somnolent below the striped rocks of the steppe cliffs, but there was, excitingly, a boat for hire. It was a wallowing ex-military craft captained by a former fisherman from Vladivostock. He let us drive, with erratic results, and sang the *Internationale* with great verve. It was very quiet, and the song echoed out across the sparkling waters of the lake towards the blue curl of the mountains.

Vasily and Maria were typical of their fellow Kazakstanis – a friendly, hospitable couple who would insist on taking you to their home, stuffing you full of food and pouring vodka down your throat. One of my hazier memories is of sitting in a Chekhovian cherry orchard and drinking dubious toasts to Josef Stalin in the company of Vasily's grandfather, who wore a coat stiff with medals despite the summer heat, and who was impervious to alcohol.

When we left Kazakstan autumn was drawing closer, and the snow line was beginning to creep down the mountain slopes in preparation for Almaty's transformation into a winter city. I was glad to be going home, away from the dust and heat and reek of fuel, but I find that I miss Almaty. I get cravings for *shashlik*, sometimes, and cherry trees, and unlit streets. I'm planning on going back.

Laos

A sisterly venture

Emma Dowson

A trip to Laos beckoned to Emma Dowson and her sister, Lucinda, as a novel Christmas break. That impression was confirmed as they sampled the pleasures of an herbal spa run by nuns and travelled around what they found to be a serene country poised between a communist past and a capitalist future. Emma is a book publicist who lives in London; Lucinda co-ordinates women's health projects in Asia. Both have travelled extensively in the region, sometimes alone and sometimes together.

My sister, Lucinda, and I wanted to escape Christmas in London. Our mother was marrying again and selling the family home. For the ten years since my father had died, we'd always made a point of being together, just the three of us, for Christmas. Now all of our lives were moving on and it seemed appropriate to do things a little differently this year.

We chose Laos mainly because it had recently opened up to independent travellers and partly because we liked the idea of a country whose currency was named the "*kip*" . Our first impressions of the capital, Vientiane, were of a torpid backwater. Ochre-coloured houses sat among coconut palms that stretched languidly along the banks of the Mekong River. Golden temple spires dominated the skyline. Traffic was comprised of slow-moving bicycles and the occasional VW

Beetle. Jasmine trees poked their roots through dusty paving stones and dragonflies hung like clothes pegs from telegraph wires. It was Asia on Valium.

We obviously looked exhausted and scruffy when we checked into our guesthouse in Vientiane, because the elegant-looking receptionist suggested we head to the local herbal sauna for a tranquillity top-up. Good advice. We hired a *tuk-tuk* to take us to the peaceful grounds of an ancient Buddhist temple, Wat Paa, where we were to find an alfresco beauty parlour. A dozen women lay on wooden benches amongst tropical flowers, being pummelled by nuns in white robes. The sauna itself was a wooden chamber raised on stilts above a torpedo-shaped boiler heated by an enormous fire. An elderly nun plucked clumps of herbs from the garden and threw them into the bubbling cauldron balanced above the fire.

Lucinda and I wrapped sarongs around ourselves and squeezed onto a rickety wooden bench inside the sauna. A woman beside me was rubbing thick white paste all over her body, as if preparing to swim the English Channel. Dusty shafts of sunlight streamed though cracks in the ceiling to illuminate steam billowing through a pipe in the floor. I could distinguish lemongrass, mint, coriander, sandalwood and eucalyptus, but not the other 27 herbs that apparently make up this intoxicating potion.

Emerging into the cool air twenty minutes later, we both felt slightly woozy. We hauled up water from a well to cool ourselves with, although to allow the herbs to soak deeply into your pores, you are not supposed to wash for three hours after the sauna. I had opted for the full restorative overhaul, and soon one of the nuns was oiling me with warm coconut oil and kneading my joints to ease my travel aches.

With their shaved heads and flowing white robes, the nuns looked intimidating at first glance. Yet they were not quiet or distant as I had imagined, but joked and gossiped with the local women. One of the nuns tip-toed up to me with a bowl of water and pretended to toss it over my head. Everyone howled with laughter at the impromptu joke.

The local women were friendly and curious. One, who told us that she was the manager of a textile factory, spoke good English and acted as question mistress. Why was my hair red and my sister's blonde? How did we get it that way? Why did we have hair on our arms? She asked if we had husbands or children, and everyone looked sympathetically at us when we shook our heads. We were in our late twenties and most Lao women of our age would have already married and had several children. We should work on our skin, suggested another woman – that way, we might still have a chance to catch a man.

We were curious about their lives, too. Amongst our group were shopkeepers, housewives, a couple of bank clerks and secretaries, and an extremely youthful-looking woman who claimed to have 21 grandchildren. All were taking a much-needed break from work and domestic duties. Our novelty value soon wore off, but our question mistress kept up a running commentary, pointing out which woman's husband drank too much *lao lao* (the local moonshine), which one's daughter was to be married to a rich man the following week, and so on.

By the end of the treatment, Lucinda and I were firm believers in the Laotian adage of healthy body, healthy spirit. Feeling refreshed, we decided to check out Vientiane's nightlife. It was Saturday night, and groups of beer-swilling teenagers squeezed into fairy-lit wooden bars lining the Mekong River. The atmosphere was more that of a seaside town than a capital city, and it was hard to believe that during French rule, Vientiane was renowned for its decadence. Unlike many other Asian countries, women had few qualms about drinking alcohol in public, which made matters much more comfortable for us. In general, Laos was one of the easiest places I've ever travelled in because the people were not only friendly and easy-going, but also seemed to respect space and privacy. We rarely received unwelcome attention from local men. Even *tuk-tuk* drivers – often aggressive in Thailand – court Vientiane passengers with barely a raised eyebrow.

Yet change is slowly arriving in Laos. At one bar, we met Malee, a woman who was visiting her homeland for the first time in more than twenty years. "My father was a doctor, and like thousands of other fairly well-off families, we left Laos just before the communists took over in 1975. We fled to Australia as refugees," she told us. "Vientiane looks much the same as when I left, but there are little signs of change everywhere." She pointed to a derelict Art Deco-style cinema, where, as a child, she had watched movies dubbed into Lao.

Now crowds gathered around generator-powered TVs, enthralled by soap operas beamed from Taipei and Tokyo.

Another obvious symbol of change is the recently completed Friendship Bridge, which spans the Mekong, linking Laos to neighbouring Thailand. Malee said she had noticed that the older generation fears that contact with the outside world will destroy the equilibrium of their fragile country, while younger people consider it the height of sophistication to listen to Western pop music or slip the odd phrase or two of Thai into a conversation.

A couple of days later, Lucinda and I caught a bus to Vang Vieng, a small riverine town 160km north of Vientiane. The river, Vang Vieng's most valuable resource, was filled with pencil-thin wooden fishing boats and every inch of its silty banks had been turned into vegetable plots. The whole town congregated here. Schoolchildren wearing pristine uniforms filled buckets at the water's edge, while an old man cleaned a silver teapot with meticulous care. Women washed themselves furtively beneath their sarongs; one wedged a baby between two rocks for safekeeping while she bathed another child.

Women, renowned in Laos for having better business skills than men, dominate the market and by 5am each morning, every woman in Vang Vieng was up buying and selling. Stalls sagged under a dazzling array of exotic fruit, pyramids of baguettes or enormous slabs of tofu floating like jellyfish in plastic bowls. Roasted rats complete with singed tails were served on sticks like grotesque lollipops. Hawkers pressed wedges of succulent mango into our hands – no obligation to buy. The abundance was seductive. No one here looked starving or homeless, and the only beggar we saw was a muttering, ragged man holding a pin-thin dog by a string. He was obviously an anomaly as children pointed and giggled at him with naive curiosity, as they sometimes also marked out tourists. It was often hard to remember that Laos is one of the world's poorest countries.

Travelling around Laos can be difficult, as roads are poor and buses are occasionally hijacked by bandits. The journey back to Vientiane from Vang Vieng – considered to be a safe stretch of road – was uneventful until the bus ran over a calf. The driver stopped, slung the dead animal on the roof, and continued on, nonchalantly ignoring the blood dripping down the back window.

On Christmas Eve, we steeled ourselves for Lao Aviation's forty-minute flight to Luang Prabang. Windows rattled as the antiquated eighteen-seater Chinese plane skimmed jagged mountains at 12,000ft, swooping toward the ancient city, where rhino-horn-shaped temple spires below threatened to impale us. Christmas morning dawned in Luang Prabang with clinking bicycle bells, hammering silversmiths and bellowing hawkers – and a squeaky rendition of *Jingle Bells* emanating magically from a string of fairy lights beneath our window. "To make you feel more at home," beamed the guesthouse owner.

Still, nowhere could feel less like home. Luang Prabang's narrow streets were lined with scarlet and golden temples, buildings with apricot walls, peppermint shutters and powder-blue doors, all thronging with saffron-clad monks and Hmong tribespeople wearing indigo tunics fastened with bright pink sashes – their legends say they floated here from South China on magic carpets. The city's plumage seems to belong to another age, its colours enduring to make the modern world look monochrome by comparison.

We followed an aromatic trail of incense from the medieval-looking Wat Vixoun, filled with 400-year-old Buddha statues, past a succession of low sweeping roofs and gleaming gables, and up 332 steps to the peak of sacred Phou Si Hill. The mighty Mekong below was reduced to a tea stain. We sat beneath a huge frangipani, its branches weighed down with petals like tiny pieces of origami, and simply breathed in the magic of the place.

Laos is on the brink of enormous change, yet many people seem happy to linger behind the times. Buddhist-inspired Lao culture dictates harmony, and the phrase "*baw pen nyang* " (why worry?) hangs in the warm air like an incantation. Laos is an extremely laid-back country, yet one where women work incredibly hard. Tam, the tiny, middle-aged woman who had turned her home into the guesthouse where we stayed, was quite an entrepreneur. She also ran a small weaving business from home, specialising in intricately patterned wall hangings. You could often hear her chattering away to guests in French or English as she pedalled an ancient-looking loom in the garden. Tam was constantly busy, yet went about her tasks in a cheerful, unhurried way. Lucinda and I vowed to try and imitate her instead of rushing through our London days.

On Christmas Day, Tam invited us to eat with her family. We feasted on sticky rice, watercress seasoned with chilli, and *laap* – a salad of minced buffalo, tossed with lime juice and garlic. After the meal, Tam poured *lao lao* into tiny glasses. "Good luck to you," she said, downing a measure. I had heard these words stitched to the ends of conversation all over Laos – by market vendors, nuns, bus drivers and schoolchildren. These well-meant words stayed with us all the way back home to Britain.

read on . . .

Lucretia Stewart, *Tiger Balm: Travels in Laos, Vietnam and Cambodia* (1992; UK: Chatto & Windus, 1998). In 1990 Lucretia Stewart overcame her fear of travel to investigate the mysteries of Indochina, a region shortly to embrace tourism following fifteen years of isolation in the wake of the Vietnam War. Her trip begins in Laos where she spends a frustrating month in Vientiane, waiting for a permit to leave the sleepy capital and explore the country independently. She whiles away the time in the company of various male "guides" – one of whom pursues her obsessively – and miscellaneous foreigners until, denied the necessary *"laisser passer"*, she moves on to Vietnam and Cambodia.

Louise Williams, *Wives, Mistresses & Matriarchs* (UK: Phoenix, 1999). Williams' exploration of the lives of women in contemporary Asia is based on interviews with a wide range of subjects, from factory labourers to business magnates, mistresses and a judge of the Islamic Court. However, the chapter on Laos contains more of her own reflections about a country she has visited several times over the years. Intrigued by official claims of it being the one nation in the world to have eradicated prostitution, she tries to find out more from the Women's Union but her hosts' "inexhaustible politeness" forces her to give up. Observing the cars and glitzy shopping malls currently invading the capital, Vientiane, she concludes that the days of moral re-education are definitely numbered.

Lebanon

Start of the holiday season

Nicki McCormick

Two years after crossing Asia by motorbike (see Pakistan, p.464), London-based writer Nicki McCormick was restless to return to the Middle East. Looking for a short holiday that was a bit exotic, a tad adventurous, with maybe even a hint of danger to write home about, she bought a ticket to Beirut.

Lebanon, at first sight, was a disappointment. I'd arrived with voyeuristic expectations of bombed-out buildings, battered infrastructure – a phoenix rising from the ashes. I was also looking forward to the chaotic clamour of the Middle East. What I found was a surprisingly chic country of Mercedes, mobile phones and designer clothes – a sort of Cote d'Azur with extra cranes. Construction was continuing apace: the entire coast north from Beirut to Byblos is an unbroken jumble of high-rise concrete squeezed in below the mountains. The airport was sparkling-new, the road system excellent and there wasn't a bomb-crater to be seen. Apart from the odd pock-marked building and the proliferation of army checkpoints, there was no sign of a war. It seemed the phoenix had already risen.

I'd been planning to buy a motorbike and had optimistically packed my helmet. However, it appeared that due to galloping infla-tion, this was going to be out of the question. I consigned my helmet to the care of a campsite and set out to explore the country by any other means of transport I could find.

Lebanon is a small country. About the size of Wales, it contains enough history and geography for an entire continent – as if God had made a scale model of Creation before embarking on the real thing. Within one hour, you can descend from soaring, snow-capped mountains to sandy beaches, from lush mountain valleys to semi-desert. Sprinkled among such geographical diversity are ruins from a myriad of civilisations. The Lebanese may be frantically eliminating all traces of their modern ruins, but their ancient ones have been painstakingly preserved. Nearly every town boasts a site of outstanding archeological merit, and the tourists are starting to trickle back.

All major routes and a good few minor ones are served by shared taxi or buses. Anywhere else, hitch-hiking was easy and rewarding – wherever I was, I'd stick out my thumb and within minutes would have a lift. I'd been mentally prepared to spend my stay fending off advances from lecherous men, but was surprised and delighted to find that, on the whole, the hassles I'd experienced in other Middle Eastern countries did not exist in Lebanon. Men and women seemed open and friendly, and genuinely pleased to see foreigners (of the unarmed, non-invading type) returning to their country. I felt very safe.

While hitching around the country, I was picked up by mechanics, farmers, housewives, school groups, priests and, most memorably, by Simon and Hannan, a just-married couple on honeymoon. I'd decided to visit the Jeita grottoes, a vast cave system near Beirut that was used for most of the war as an ammunition dump. The taxi dropped me off near the turn-off to the caves and I started walking, hoping for a passing vehicle. Simon's BMW, still adorned with straw wedding bows tied to the door-handles, pulled over as I was starting to despair. He and his bride were going to the caves too – their first visit.

"We couldn't visit our country for so long," explained Hannan, immaculate in a peach-coloured linen suit, despite the heat that was turning me into a sweaty mess. "It's exciting now to be tourists just like you." They were childhood sweethearts, and had been engaged for ten years; the past five years had been spent waiting to marry, as Simon's military service prevented him from doing so. The five long years had expired three days previously; Simon was now an officer and the couple had married on his thirtieth birthday.

After we all explored the caves together, Simon and Hannan insisted I visit them the next day at their home in a small village near Baalbek, in the Bekka valley. And so I arrived to find their house full of Hannan's extended family, cooking, organising and giving advice, while Simon looked slightly bemused by this influx of females into his home. We sat under grapevines and drank small cups of repellantly strong coffee before Hannan insisted we go for a drive. Just beyond the village church where the pair had married was a building-sized Hezbollah mural. This area was the guerrilla army's stronghold. The Hezbollah is now the only militia army still fighting the Israelis – all the others have been absorbed into the Lebanese army. They are now gaining support due to their social welfare programme among Lebanon's Muslim community.

I wondered what Simon and Hannan's opinion of them was, as they are Christians in a Muslim stronghold. The reply was unequivocal. "Originally, this village was almost all Christian," said Hannan. "But then when I was young, many Muslims came and tried to make us move. I remember one year when I was a child and the Christians refused to leave, each family stored barrels of fuel in the house and the men and boys vowed that they would fight to defend their homes. If people tried to hurt the women and take our houses, our fathers were ready to burn the whole family in the home rather than surrender. The house we have now was empty for a while, then a Muslim family took it over and refused to pay rent. They broke everything, they were dirty, they are bad people".

Though Christians and Muslims live side by side all over the country, and women covered in modest black robes mix in the shops with girls in mini-skirts and lipstick, I got the impression it was often an uneasy relationship. I have never met such pure religious hatred coming from educated people as I did from Simon and Hannan and several others. Growing up in a war zone can explain a lot, but when, on our way back to my hotel, we passed a café named *Lady Dianna*, Hannan came out with a comment that made me bite my lip: "They love her round here," she nearly spat. "Everybody loved her – I did too. But then she accepted a Muslim. If she was going to marry him and reject her faith, I think she deserved to die!"

Having spent many enjoyable years living and travelling in Muslim countries, I found this hard to swallow, and the contrast with Hannan's otherwise warm and bubbly personality was frightening.

However, I met a couple of people who denied there was tension. "I'm Muslim, but many of my friends are Christian; it makes no difference," insisted one young woman with whom I hitch-hiked. It was refreshing to hear such a comment.

In the course of my explorations of the country, I'd soon realised that my first impressions of Lebanon had been a little hasty. The country bears many scars, both physical and mental, from nearly two decades of unrest. The concrete coastline I'd seen, for example, used to be a pristine beach. Development had sprawled, unchecked by government, and pollution is a growing problem.

Johnny, a tour guide and historian, gave his opinion: "The youth, especially, had no authority when they were children – a whole generation has grown up with a selfish, short-term mentality. There was no point in looking after things if they might get destroyed anyway." Most people I spoke to did not share his disillusionment; I got the feeling I was in a nation hell-bent on putting the (recent) past behind it as quickly as possible and getting on with the important task of rebuilding.

Johnny invited me to stay with his family in Bcharré, a steep, red-roofed village perched on the edge of the Qadisha gorge, and offered to take me through the famous valley to some rarely visited, difficult-to-reach churches. I accepted with trepidation, but he sensed my reservations and made it clear from the outset that he had no designs on me. The only difficulty I had during an energetic ten hours of scrambling up and down impossibly steep cliff paths (the Maronite monks, who once occupied the Qadisha Valley, spent centuries being persecuted, and dedicated themselves to making their retreats as inaccessible as possible) was keeping up with a non-stop commentary – in French – on Lebanese history. Johnny had been a guide in the region for many years, and was eager to show me the best of his country.

From a goat-track winding along the valley side, we clambered up hundreds of metres of loose scree toward an uninspired-looking cave mouth. Halfway up, Johnny took a slight detour and pointed out a pool of water in a rock crevice – a natural spring. We drank our fill and carried on. I was starting to wonder whether it was worth it (my lungs were bursting and some of the panted French explanation was going over my head), when we ducked under an outcrop and I found myself in a cool, vine-draped courtyard. What looked like a cave from below was a simple but surprisingly spacious monastery on two levels, now deserted but once home to about a hundred monks. This being a religious area, the cave chapel was still cared for – fresh stubs of candles flanked a portrait of one of the area's many saints.

We ate our lunch, gazing in silence over the hazy depths of the Qadisha, nearly a kilometre deep in places. Then, Johnny suddenly tugged at my sleeve. "Come, I've got a surprise for you," he insisted. We climbed a ladder at the side of the chapel, and, taking out a torch, he beckoned me to follow as he squeezed into a narrow crack in the rock wall of the upper chamber. Nervously I complied, hoping the surprise wasn't going to be an unpleasant one. We wriggled deeper into the rock. Johnny grabbed my hand to steady me on the uneven floor – I began to feel scared. Then, shining his torch above our heads, he showed me his surprise. We were in a grotto of glittering marble-veined walls and delicate, cake-icing rock formations. "This passage goes on for miles," he explained, his voice echoing, as it bounced off surfaces at unseen heights. "I found it when I was a child. I think there might be tunnels running from here down to the valley floor – the monks used to use them as escape routes when they were in hiding here." I was entranced, and regretted doubting him.

The next day was my last in the country. I descended from the mountains to the bustle of the capital and spent the evening at a jazz festival in a newly restored street in downtown Beirut. The smart young things of a new Beirut sat out at tables gossiping, networking and drinking beer, surrounded by still empty buildings. It felt slightly surreal, but to the Beirut residents I was with, this was normality.

I left Lebanon feeling confused and ignorant. None of my ill-informed preconceptions of the country remained, but no coherent image had replaced them. It is a fascinating, beautiful land, but there is so much under the surface that it is difficult for a first-time visitor to absorb in a few weeks. As I waited for my plane, a security guard asked me what I thought of his country. "Nice," was all I feebly managed to reply. "I had a very nice holiday."

read on . . .

 Mai Ghoussoub, *Leaving Beirut: Women and the Wars Within* (UK: Al Saqi Books, 1998). In this moving and important autobiography, London-based writer and sculptor Ghoussoub trawls her memories of Beirut and considers what might have happened had she stayed. Her reminiscences, darkened by everyday acts of revenge and retaliation where grandmothers might harbour thoughts of murder or a gentle grocery boy might double as a torturer, are threaded with more scholarly research and ethical enquiry into the years of civil war. She leads us to the sobering insight, reinforced by recent scenes in Kosovo, that her Beirut, the tragic city she loved and left, is everywhere.

Bettina Selby, *Like Water in a Dry Land* **(UK: Fount, 1998).** Observant, erudite, no-nonsense cycling scribe Bettina Selby reprises her 1985 journey across Lebanon, Jordan and Syria and on to Jerusalem at a time of intense political initiatives for change.

Libya

Trailed in Tripoli

Sarah Johnstone

Sarah Johnstone is a freelance journalist based in London. She knew that her two-week visit to Libya would carry travel restrictions but hadn't quite bargained for the persistent presence of her requisite official guide, Omar. Whether the recent lifting of sanctions will bring about a relaxation of the visa requirements that governed her stay remains to be seen. Johnstone has written for *The Independent on Sunday*, *The Times* and *The Face*. (See p.510 for an account of her trip to Soweto.)

By the time we travelled back up the long road to neighbouring Tunisia, I wasn't so much grateful to have survived as dying to do simple things, like buying a newspaper, for myself again. I'd gone to Libya looking for adventure, the undiscovered and perhaps even a little danger. Instead, during thirteen days and across 4000km of this pariah state, I found myself on the receiving end of, variously, unbelievable friendliness and generosity, straight-out leering, and mostly a desire to do things for me rather than let me do anything myself. After that, I was nearly able to convince myself that ordering a meal in French without the interference of my Arabic-speaking guide was like striking a major blow for feminism – right up there with winning the vote and burning my bra.

At least at this late stage I could have set my bra on fire without going broke. Since the US air-strikes which killed leader Moamar al

Gaddafi's young daughter in 1986, Libya hasn't been the best place to brandish American Express travellers' cheques. Given the UN embargo since 1992 over the Lockerbie bombing, it's no surprise that credit cards have been useless there, too. For those reasons, I'd been packing some serious money in my lingerie for the past two weeks. A few extra nights in Tripoli's exorbitantly priced hotels and some meagre souvenirs meant it was, oops, D cup to A cup. Thank god – or *Hamdu lillah*, as the Libyans constantly say – for the Wonderbra.

Actually, I'm exaggerating a little there. Taking what was supposedly the easiest route to Tripoli under the air embargo – flying to the Tunisian resort of Djerba and then making the 300-kilometre journey overland – I'd already managed to dump the bulk of my fake cleavage with my guide, Omar, when I paid him as we met in Djerba.

"None of this road existed before direct flights were banned," Omar said, as we sped down the new highway through small hamlets and later past hawkers selling petrol and Libyan dinars. "There was nothing here."

"Mmm," I nodded, intrigued, but exhausted by an impromptu overnight stay in Tunis airport and a trifle distracted by finding myself flat-chested again. I fell asleep and only really woke up when we reached the border.

The Libyan government might recently have been inviting more tourists to come and spend hard currency seeing its fabulous Roman ruins and traversing its stunning deserts, but nobody seems to have told the guys on border patrol this. They go slow while long queues build up, they leave you waiting during hour-long shift changes, they analyse every detail of your visa as you sit there sweating, and they may even take possessions of yours they fancy. Even after we smoothed our way through immigration and customs with small gifts, Omar and I were stopped in quick succession for two or three passport checks.

Such Orwellian bureaucratic control would only add to my feelings of impotence during my stay. The way Omar told it, I *had* to have a guide, even if I hadn't chosen it as the safest option. He said local travel companies no longer helped independent travellers get visas, after tourist photos of roadside checkpoints ended up in an Italian newspaper. Today, not only the tour company sponsoring your visa would stay by your side, but if there were five or more of you, a "tourist policeman" would accompany you to watch where you aimed your cameras. At least that system doubled up as protection for most visitors against kidnap by bandits or terrorists. Me, I didn't have a tourist policeman to watch over me. And as Omar pocketed my passport at the border, I began to feel strangely like his captive.

Since Gaddafi came to power in 1969, and according to the Green Book in which the Colonel later formulated his "third way" between capitalism and communism (he's recently accused British Prime Minister Tony Blair of nicking the term), women in Libya enjoy a certain equality under law. And it is true that more of them than ever before go to university, hold responsible jobs and even undertake armed service. However, as with so many things, official theory and cultural practice are more than a trifle misaligned. Just how circumscribed women's movements are in public was impressed upon me as soon as we arrived in Tripoli.

I stepped out of the hotel grounds alone for a bit of an initial reconnoitre and cars screeched to a halt and crawled slowly along after me. Some men hissed, and yelled "*Bonjour*", "*Buongiorno*", "Hey you, come here". Others stood in my way, forcing me to pace back and forth like a trapped animal. My friends will attest to this: I'm not a woman who's easily intimidated. But ten minutes along the palm-lined Al-Fateh Street on the Mediterranean waterfront was all I could bear before I scuttled back to my hotel womb. Undoubtedly a lot of this attention was due to my being a Westerner – still not a common sight in Libya – but even when I returned outside with a scarf on top of my shapeless neck-to-toe ensemble, the hassle didn't entirely subside.

Tripoli, or Tarabulus as it's known in Arabic, still intrigued me, though. From my window, I could see the green shutters and doors of its Italian colonial buildings starkly contrasting against white facades. I could see the grandiose monolith of the Al-Fateh tower rising above the horizon and the upside-down bottle shapes of the neighbouring Dat El Amad complex. I wanted to see more of this and of the Senussi kings' palaces. I wanted to get closer to the ubiquitous billboards of Gaddafi, which amused me in their singularity. So the next day I arranged for A—, the friend of a Libyan friend of mine in London, to show me around the city after she finished work at four.

A is 27 and a civil engineer. She's one of the many younger women who shun the headscarf, dress like they were wandering down

Oxford Street in London, and initially she comes across like a thoroughly modern miss. Yet like virtually all unmarried Libyan women, A still lives at home with her parents and must ask their permission any time she leaves the house. Later, when Omar and I were to ask her to come for an afternoon's sightseeing in the nearby Roman ruins of Sabratha, she would have to decline on her father's wishes. Even that evening, we had to ask her father before we could go 100m down the road to the post office. Not that we had planned to visit the post office that day: we were supposed to be looking around the city, after all. However, although A had told her father she needed the car, he'd casually let her brother take off in it instead, and for hours, we were stranded. We couldn't catch a taxi into town, because unless a male relative is with them Libyan women don't like being in the same car as strange men. So, we had no alternative but to spend our time indoors, looking at photos, chatting and eating.

Don't get me wrong. A and her family, like many of their compatriots, were among the sweetest people I'd ever met. It just would have been nice to see the city as we talked.

Finally, we heard the rattle of the clapped-out Peugeot, and ran downstairs to meet her errant brother, U—. Before I went to Libya, I told myself how different it would be being a woman there, and promised myself to behave meekly. This was the first time I was to find that, when it came to it, I often just wouldn't be able to help myself. A was upset with her brother, but didn't look like she was going to say anything about it. I thought I'd try to make the point jokingly.

"Where ya bin? We've been stuck," I mocked U, hands on hips. Then, in my best Keystone Cops manner, I gently slapped the air in front of his face.

However slapstick the intention, the gesture didn't go down well.

"Gee, tough girl," U recoiled. "I didn't know we had tough girls such as these in this house."

"Oh, she's been living in Britain," said A airily, as if that explained it all. Then she drove me back to the hotel.

★ ★ ★ ★

"We were supposed to. We were supposed to. That's a phrase that you'll learn to use a lot in Libya," laughed Kahlil, when I bumped into him at breakfast and told him how my previous day's plans had been thwarted. Kahlil was a regular visitor to Tripoli from Beirut, and his gallows humour had kept us all in stitches on the long flight from London. He was selling books to the Ministry of Education.

"I used to turn up to meetings at eight, when I was supposed to," he said. "But there'd be nobody there, and they'd shrug their shoulders and say 'Such and such didn't come in today'. Now I go in at ten."

★ ★ ★ ★

Two days later, Omar and I left the capital and set out for Benghazi, Libya's second city and 1000km to the east. On the way, we were supposed to stop at some Roman ruins, overnight in Muisrata and drive straight on for the next 800km. But, oh no, Kahlil was right. Omar had alarmed me by confiding in me that this trip felt "like a honeymoon", had bought the plastic cups to match – decorated with a wedding couple being showered in confetti – and seemed to be on a mission to seriously impress.

The sheer size of the former Roman city of Leptis Magna, one of the best archaeological sites in the world, wasn't enough to overawe me on the long journey, apparently. We had to spend about an hour finding a tiny Islamic museum, full of nothing but ceramic chips. We had to stop to photograph the fallen statues of the Phaleni brothers, heroes of the former Roman empire; we made a detour to see one of Omar's favourite beaches along the unspoilt miles of coastline. Only my objections about how late we were running meant we got to defer a visit to the Great Man-Made River Project – a dam like any other dam I've seen – until we were on the way back.

"Just for you, Sarah. I do it just for you," Omar enthused as we continued stopping at more and more places where I couldn't understand why were stopping.

By the time we arrived late in Benghazi, even the car seemed to be protesting at all these additional pitstops: its brakes were starting to fail. While Omar raced to buy new brake pads from another shop, I stayed behind at the garage with a dozen mechanics. I don't know what they made of this strange female creature who started investigating the inner working of the BMWs and Mercedes in for repair, but, they were certainly less threatening than the men in Tripoli.

"Would the girl like a drink?" one of them asked. "How sweet," I thought, dug my head into an engine in embarrassment and came up covered in grease.

The countryside beyond Benghazi was beautiful. The green mountains, housing caves where the Libyan resistance fighter Omar al-Mukhtar waged a twenty-year war against the Italian forces which invaded the country in 1911, rose to the mish-mash of Greek, Byzantine and Roman ruins at Cyrene, and fell away in a grand sweep towards the sea.

As we made our way through the mountains the next day, another battle ensued, with another Omar – a battle of wills. *My* Omar wouldn't have a snack unless I shared half of it. He wouldn't have a drink of water unless I did, too. He started calling me "dear" and "darling" and insisted on tying my shoelace when it came undone. There'd be a fight if Omar thought I should take photo of something and I didn't want to. If I wanted to chase down the architectural wonder of a hotel where Mussolini lived, Omar would show me a valley where his favourite waterfall used to flow.

There's no denying that Omar was a helpful person, a kind person. He seemed to know his way round the country and out of nearly every bureaucratic cul de sac. Given that English was once banned in Libyan schools, and not many people speak it, his mediation was often necessary. But then he began not just insisting that I eat all the food on my plate, but ordering it, too. This, I felt, slightly exceeded his job description.

"Er, just a salad for me," I'd protest, before the waiter emerged with a starter of soup, salad and spaghetti, followed up by a huge main course.

"I just want you to be happy," was Omar's reply.

Such events strengthened my growing conviction that Omar harboured a fantasy of marrying a foreigner and being able to travel freely around the world, as he often mentioned his best friend had done – a dream, according to my friend Fatma, of many middle-class Libyans living under the embargo.

Back in Muisrata, on the return journey to Tripoli, he picked me up for dinner, took me to his house instead and tried unsuccessfully to seduce me, I think. As he was showing me around his home, I just couldn't shake the weird feeling that he was trying to display his wealth, as a way of inviting me to share it. In the living room, he slipped on some romantic music, and got on his knees to give me a series of presents. "This is for you," he said, handing across one multicoloured bauble, "and this," he added of another, "this is for A, from us."

"Us?" I spluttered. "Omar, there is no us."

He wasn't listening.

"So, this is my home. It can be your home too if you want. Do you want to stay?"

"No, Omar," I almost whimpered, hoping the ground would open up and swallow me. "I want to go back to my hotel room RIGHT NOW."

★ ★ ★ ★

Nearly everywhere I went there was someone who told me how crazy or brave I was for coming to Libya alone. The Italian travel agent I met in Ghadames did too. Unlike me, Sigmundo was ready to write off the rest of the country, apart from this 2000-year-old, covered desert town. The diet was monotonous. There were no elephants or zebras or lions. The desert was vast and flat. However, "with Ghadames, they certainly seem to have something very special".

As for me, I found Ghadames fascinating, but despaired at how it underlined the division between the genders which permeated this entire land. Up until the 1980s, when most of the population moved into new housing, Ghadamesi men had had the run of the main floor of the family home, the women spent most of their existence on the floor above. Because they were only supposed to come downstairs with their husband's permission, or in his absence, the town's women-folk often moved around the town by going from rooftop to rooftop.

At one stage, Sophia Loren had run across the tops of these houses during the making of one of her early films. Today, Omar, our local guide Mustafa and I climbed up there to look at the town. Having Mustafa with us put me at ease: it made it harder for Omar to act in such a proprietorial manner towards me.

After this desert sojourn, there was one last chance to try to see Tripoli properly and to take a few photos of it. The first time I attempted this, I found myself ending up waylaid by A, and sitting in a coffeeshop with her. (We had to hide behind a pillar, because she thought it incredibly risqué for a woman to sit where she could be seen from the street.) The second time, when I got out on the streets with my camera, I nearly got arrested twice. Every card in Libya seemed stacked against me in this quest. Then, on the last day of my stay, I did manage to get a real glimpse of Tripoli by giving Omar the slip. That wasn't easy. Thirty seconds or so after I sat down for breakfast, he had appeared at my side and wanted to come with me. Later when I returned to the hotel, I turned around to find him coming in the door, and wondered if he'd been following me, anyway. By this point, the nicer Omar tried to be to me, the nastier I couldn't help myself from becoming. At the time, I thought this probably just reflected our different cultural concepts of what it means to always be doing someone a favour. I figured that, as a lone woman, it might have seemed to a Libyan man as if I were looking for somebody to look after me. But later A would confess that she'd found Omar a bit over the top, too.

Out on the streets, I was so frustrated by not having been able to do my own thing for so long, that I hardly noticed the catcalls that followed me nearly wherever I went. Gaddafi himself was in town that day, his cavalcade racing back and forth along the streets. Maybe that was the reason, maybe it was because I had a better idea of where I was going, but people didn't seem to pay as much attention to me as I wandered happily past the shops and mosques.

The next morning we set out in the cold and rain for the long drive back to the airport. Only on the plane from Djerba was I truly alone again. After a fortnight of spending fourteen hours or more with a hitherto total stranger, I could look forward to running my own life once more. I lay back in my seat and contemplated how wonderful it would be go out and have a proper drink with friends. I lingered over the thought of how I would go to the cinema or see a band, and of all the myriad possibilities open to me once I returned to London.

The strangest thing was that for a week after I did, I didn't know what to do with myself and felt lonely and miserable instead.

Malawi

A sista and a mzungu

Tatum Anderson

Tatum Anderson, a London-based IT journalist, spent nine months in southern Africa, beginning with a stint as a physics teacher at a private school in Harare (see p.642) before travelling in South Africa, Namibia, Botswana and Mozambique. This is the story of her trip from Malawi to Tanzania.

I was completely unprepared when I started to travel in southern Africa. I think I was probably the only traveller with Coco Chanel perfume and a little black dress in my backpack.

My excuse was that I'd come to teach, not to backpack. I had taken a break from working in London to take up a job teaching science at a secondary school in Zimbabwe for the winter term. When the contract finished, I wanted to see more of Africa. I stopped wearing Chanel in Namibia. The dress was left somewhere in Botswana. I sold the travel iron, bought a tent, and set off on a two-month trip to Tanzania, via Malawi.

In Zimbabwe I could move around incognito. My background is a mixture of Indian and Jamaican and I was hardly ever targeted as a tourist but in Malawi it was different. This was because I was travelling with a *mzungu*, or white person, a Danish student called Marcus who I had met in a backpackers' hostel in Harare. Later, when Rachel, a white Australian, joined us, locals began asking if the other two were my parents, even though – apart from the obvious – one of the *mzungus* was younger than me. I was attributed a number of possible origins, from Chewa to Swahili. When I opened my mouth, I was a black woman who spoke like a *mzungu*. I was drawn into conversations about black people in England and Jamaica, how many children I had, or why I wasn't married or staying at home and looking after my parents instead of wandering around.

But wandering around is the best thing to do in Malawi. The country snakes along one side of Lake Malawi, the third-largest lake in Africa, and many travellers follow it north toward Tanzania. Some head for Cape McClear, for the cheap diving courses, others to climb Mount Mulanjie Massif, or to check out the authentic 1970s gear in nearby Zomba market. Hastings Banda, Malawi's head of state for 37 years until his death in 1997, banned travellers with hippie clothes, long hair and mini-skirts from entering the country. Many travellers, throughout the late 1960s and 1970s, sold their clothes at the border.

We headed north, staying at various resthouses and backpackers' lodges by the lake. It was cheaper to stay in tents on the beach most of the time. When I ran out of cash, I traded Manchester United postcards for a bed for the night.

At Nkhata Bay, a busy port about halfway up the lake, I was woken by singing at five each morning. I watched the red sunrise over the lake and the silhouettes of fishermen hauling narrow boats onto the shore, yards from my tent. Nkhata Bay was a good point to wait for the weekly Mtendere ferry taking passengers south, toward Monkey Bay.

After an early morning swim in the lake, we would sit in cafés and watch locals buy ground maize, music and plastic containers in the market, or play a board-game called Bao with any willing contenders who passed. I gained brownie points by playing (badly) the male version of Bao, which has easier rules for females.

I spent most of my time gossiping with the kitchen staff at the backpackers' lodge, or the fishermen on the beach, or wood carvers fashioning tables, or the women sitting at the hairdresser's. The proprietor of *Sue's Hairdressers*, Mrs Mlaglia, was always happy to chat while she sat barefoot with a client's head between her legs, pulling their hair in one direction and their heads in another.

I slowly got the hang of backpacking. I could find anything in my backpack in under a minute and put up a tent. I coped with open-air showers and could make a fire to cook the day's catch with rice. But I couldn't get used to the polite segregation between many travellers and locals.

By the time Marcus and I reached Kande beach, I had met just too many travellers who saw Africa primarily through the lens of a camera, and were more interested in wildlife and the beach than any meaningful contact with Malawians. Too often, the only contact they had was limited to ordering beers and food.

I had been incredibly intimidated, at first, by the hard-core travellers who seemed to know about most places, and were self-sufficient and confident. But I soon began to tire of the endless "been there, done that" conversations that were their stock in trade. When I heard a woman say in a bored voice, "I've been everywhere in the world", and reel off, like some advanced memory exercise, all the places she'd been to, I knew it was time to leave.

Marcus and I were offered dinner one day by a Malawian boy on the beach. His name was John and he said his mother would cook us a meal for a small amount of money. Just before sunset he came to collect us with a couple of his friends. We took a convoluted route through a maze of bushes to his village, which was a collection of huts set back from the beach.

About twenty children greeted us. A chair was put out in a space between the huts, but this was for Marcus, not me. I was ushered away from the men, and a baby was plonked in my arms as I was taken to meet the grandmother and lots of aunts.

I walked into a small round hut that was the kitchen. John's older sister was stirring a huge pot of *nsima* – maize flour cooked with water to the consistency of dough – over a fire made from fine twigs. We sat talking, wiping eyes streaming from the smoke. She was my age and grew up in Bulawayo in Zimbabwe, which is why she had perfect English. She told me she was about to go to university when her father had died. He had originally come from Malawi, and the family had been forced to move back to Kande to live with her father's relatives because there was no breadwinner. She cooked three meals a day for at least twelve people.

Outside, kids were marvelling at a chocolate bar and deciding how to divide it. John's brother showed me the Walkman he had swapped with a traveller. He was listening to Bob Marley.

We ate a fine meal of tiny *kapenta* fish, sugar beans with tomato and onions, and the Malawian staple of *nsima*. Before John and his friends led us back in the pitch dark along the beach to Kande, I had to run into the lodge to get my address for his sister who wanted to write, and a Fanta for John because he was not allowed in. The lodge seemed to be the sole accommodation option for travellers in the area and only paying guests were allowed in.

Mzuzu, up the coast, was the nearest place to buy supplies. We stopped off on our way to Tanzania and soon fell in with Rachel, the Australian. She had seen us trying to hitch on the wrong road for the border and came over to give us advice. In the end we decided against hitching and caught a chicken bus instead, to Karonga, near the Tanzanian border. These are local buses that transport both chickens and people. The men stood up in unison every time we went over a bump, so to preserve their manhoods.

We arrived in Karonga to find a water shortage. Rachel and I walked for 45 minutes in the dark to the lake for a wash. We knew we were at the lake only when we felt the water on our toes and heard the gently lapping waves. After a sweaty journey on the bus it was quite possibly the best bath I'd ever had. We hitched a lift back in a jeep blasting out hip-hop, with two Malawians who were talking in their best American accents.

The nearest resthouse to the bus depot doubled as a lively brothel, judging from the revolving-door clientele. The three of us checked into a single room. The window had no glass, but the room was still stifling because of the corrugated iron roof, hot from the day's sun. There was as much wildlife inside the room as out, so Marcus put up his tent next to the bed to keep out mosquitoes, lizards, and whatever else managed to squeeze in between the window grille. We had padlocks to fasten the doors with, because Rachel had already spent a sleepless night crouched behind the door in another Malawian brothel, crying as drunken men tried to get in.

Karonga may not be pretty, but it does have a sense of humour. The banks are social meeting points. Security men, with crash helmets and money-stuffed briefcases chained to their wrists, stop for a chat while waiting in the queue. Tumbledown shacks with names like the *Ultramodern Guesthouse* lean at the roadside, and you can get a drink at the *Hangover Clinic* – one of Karonga's many bars.

The next morning, we paid for a ride to the border in a pick-up truck. I was interrogated by a border guard, who didn't believe I could hold a British passport. I gave him a short black British history lesson, and he asked me to send him some reggae tapes when I got home.

And so we walked into Tanzania, winding our watches forward an hour, listening to Swahili conversations, and noting that the cigarette brands had changed. The touts offered me a different exchange rate to the other travellers. Because I was "a sista", they said.

Malaysia

A natural high

Madeleine Cary

Until 1990 Madeleine Cary juggled her life as a single parent with a career as a media producer. That year her son Ky, aged sixteen, was killed in a tragic accident. After some time trying to recuperate and heal with family and friends she decided it was time to seek life-affirming experiences again. With a backpack, a few savings and no clear itinerary in mind, she flew to Bangkok, marking the beginning of a ten-month low-budget trip through Southeast Asia. She currently lives in Brighton, on the south coast of England, where she writes short fiction, for radio and various magazines, including *Metropolitan*, *The New Writer*, *Acclaim* and *Interzone*. She also has a story in the anthology *The Ex Files* (Quartet Books) and is working on a second novel while the first, *Twisted Braid*, is being agented.

The river journey to the jungle's base camp echoed every dramatic image I had of jungle adventures, from Vietnam movies to *The African Queen*. The muddy brown river widened and the jungle on either side became denser, trees and shrubs stretching higher. Suddenly it looked as if the scale of nature had shifted. Every living thing seemed larger. The scents from the myriad shrub and plant life wafted past and changed constantly, from sweet jasmine-like fragrances to pungent, almost menthol scents. Occasionally tribal inhabitants of the jungle, the Orang Asli ("Original People"), would appear from behind bushes to watch us. Scaly creatures would bob to the surface of the water. The birds darted by in flashes of vibrant colour.

I was experiencing a child-like excitement about this adventure. After four months of travel in Southeast Asia, I had failed to undertake a jungle trek. For every guided tour on offer there would be a story concerning inexperienced guides, rapes, thefts, obnoxious travelling companions and the inevitable Western insensitivity to the local environment. There were tales of stoned tourists staggering down jungle trails, chanting Bob Marley songs at high volume and frightening off every bit of wildlife in the area. It had not held much appeal. I was also embarrassingly aware of my fear of the demands of a trek. Then I met a traveller whose frequent treks had left him something of a self-styled aficianado of jungle lore. His enthusiasm about jungle living was infectious. When he asked if I would like to accompany him on his foray into Malaysia's Taman Negara jungle, I saw it as a welcome chance to finally experience the adventure of trekking. With that intuition that develops after months of lone travel, I had decided that he was a good sort and had already reached an uncomplicated level of friendship with him. It was really down to whether his claims to knowledge and experience of jungle life were genuine.

The Taman Negara jungle in central Malaysia is one of the richest in Southeast Asia. Being home to such a variety of animal and plant life, including the tualang, the tallest tropical tree in the world, it is considered a magnificent example of unspoilt tropical rainforest. As the wooden longboat sputtered down the murky river, I revelled in my good luck at being able to spend a week in this renowned jungle with an experienced trekker. But we had not yet escaped civilisation. Suddenly, a huge holiday complex loomed out of the tropical mist as we turned a corner into the base camp. Here, luxury chalets were available for the rich and cautious who could take walks on small, safe paths in the jungle area around the site. We had to register, pay a nominal fee and I also needed to rent a tent from the supplies office. My friend was content to simply sling a hammock in a tree, but I was not so hardy as to shun insect and waterproof shelter. His fluent Malay and hard bargaining got me an old tent for a pittance. Its poles, string and pegs were missing, but he was confident that we could improvise with twigs and vine.

My only trepidation about the trek concerned the nine-mile hike we would have to undertake to our campsite. My companion had already planned the route and warned me that after six or seven miles of fairly easy trekking, there would be a steep uphill climb for the last two miles that would be backbreaking. I am not afraid of a bit of hard work when necessary, but I knew that I would be carrying a week's supply of food and a tent and was beginning to question whether I would stay the course.

When we finally left the base camp with rucksacks efficiently packed and strapped to our backs, with every available bit of skin covered to fend off the leeches and full water bottles hanging round our necks, I was too excited to feel the weight of my pack or to notice the cloying, damp heat of the jungle we were taking a trail into. In his khaki clothes and jungle boots, bandana tightened round his forehead and machete at the ready in his belt, my partner looked like he had been brought in from central casting. I had to hide my amusement when I first saw him as his usually buoyant mood had given way to a serious, almost nervous state. I decided it must be the remnants of some primordial male pre-hunt ritual.

As expected, I started to feel exhaustion after the first two hours and we were still nowhere near the dreaded steep climb. My companion, used to the demands of a trek, was blazing a trail at full steam. By comparison I seemed to be moving like a snail. However, I found myself ahead of the game when we came to a small river with a fallen log across it. I have a good sense of balance and managed to walk the log effortlessly whereas my companion confessed his fear of walking logs and had to remove his footwear and wade thigh deep through the unpleasantly opaque water. As the sky slowly darkened with an impending rain cloud, we had to decide on a course of action now that we were falling behind schedule. We agreed that he should charge on ahead in order to set up camp before evening rains and darkness. Feeling enervated and intrepid, and not wishing to be accused later of holding us up, I insisted I would be all right alone so long as my energy held out. Here was not a man to treat a woman like a "lady". He gave me clear instructions about which trail to stay on, promised he would come back and look for me if I had not arrived at the camp by nightfall and with that dashed off into the distance like a gladiator.

That is how I ended up breaking the number one rule in the trekker's safety code: never travel alone. I did not see that we had any choice but to operate in this way. And, strangely, I felt no fear as I continued alone on the trail in this magical environment. There were supposed to be tigers and elephants in the area, but local people had stressed that they usually keep clear of human visitors. Naturally, there would be snakes and other reptilian creatures, not to mention the millions of different insects. Yet, as I did not know what to look for, I plodded on regardless. I could hear the monkeys high up in the gigantic trees and the hornbills with their "hoo-hoo, ha-ha" laughter. My only real cause for panic was whether I had sufficient stamina to complete the journey. Energy levels were running dangerously low. Every minute I would stop to give my back and shoulders a rest from the overwhelming weight of my backpack. And this was still relatively flat territory.

When the uphill climb started, I had reached zero energy and was staggering around like a drunkard. I stopped to eat provisions, drink water and rest until I felt refreshed. Later, I could only manage half a minute of the upward haul before I had to stop again. The hill turned out to be an almost vertical climb with tree roots for steps and stalks and trailers to hang onto for support. At every point where I arrived at what I thought was the summit, I looked up to see yet another stretch of several hundred metres reaching skywards. Counting, swearing out loud and concentrating on anger helped spur me on. I thought of *Pilgrim's Progress* and wondered how I must look bent over like a harridan, crawling on hands and knees, spluttering out expletives and panting as if close to death.

I think it was a near-death experience, looking back. Now, whenever I have to try to achieve something which I think I cannot do, I always remember that nightmarish trip up that steep jungle hill where sheer willpower got me to my goal against all odds. When I finally reached the summit and saw camp-fire smoke curling up through the trees in the valley, I felt ecstatic, switched gear and ran downhill, leaping over fallen trees and sliding on carpets of dead leaves. The reward for this arduous expedition was the sight of our arboreal home, an idyllic clearing by the river. In an adjoining stream a smooth rockpool with a light waterfall above formed the perfect bathing area. The first thing I did when I arrived was fling off all my sweat-soaked, muddy clothes and plunge my aching body into the pool. I lay exhausted in the cool, crystal water but on the most incredible natural high I have ever experienced.

My friend already had his hammock set up in a tree with a small shelter made of tarpaulin. My tent was soon erected by improvising with twigs and vines. Then, before I could think of having a rest, the trees started to sway in ominous winds, announcing the imminent arrival of our first major jungle downpour. By hanging tarpaulin over the fire we kept sufficient flame going to boil water for tea and rice. After such an exhausting day, even lumpy rice with cold tinned goat curry tasted sublime. As the rains subsided we fell into a state of almost comatose relaxation and sat back to enjoy the evening chorus. It was the cicadas who started the symphony, providing the base maraccas rhythm. Another cicada joined in with a sustained, almost electronic-sounding, haunting trumpet pitch which rose through one slightly mournful key and died out on a rapid staccato. As one trumpet sound faded away, another would start up, sometimes nearer, sometimes further away. Then the counterpoint of monkey chatter and birdsong would bring the performance to its crescendo. In the mornings, the same creatures would provide a wake-up call that was remarkably different in tone and key. If the evening symphony was slightly ominous, the dawn chorus was full of life and promise.

Our week in the jungle soon fell into a routine based around the frequent and predictable rainstorms and the survival needs of cooking, cleaning the utensils, washing clothes and gathering wood. The reward at the end of each day would be an hour or two of the weird concert provided by our unseen companions. We divided the chores of cooking and washing, but nearly came to blows over the most effective way of starting a fire when all available tinder was sodden with rain. I was probably asking for trouble trying to tell this overgrown boyscout how to play the survival game, but I have never been able to keep quiet when I think I have a solution to a problem. It took a couple of days before he realised that I was not impressed with his constant display of survival techniques and I realised that this was not the most suitable place to make an issue over my right to prove my competence. Every day we would have to start the fire around three o'clock as the rains would come by six, which gave us enough time to get a good flame going for boiling water and cooking rice. Even though it was a daily occurrence, it was still alarming as the light dimmed and the gigantic trees swayed threateningly in heavy gales which always preceded rainstorms. One of the most dangerous aspects of jungle life concerns the frequency with which large trees topple over in the gales or under the weight of the rain. Sometimes we could hear them crashing around us and were never sure, when we heard a nearby crack, if a huge tree was about to collapse onto the camp.

I felt a strange combination of peace and serenity with an underlying sense of danger in the jungle. It was a stunningly beautiful environment in which to contemplate and reappraise life and, once really settled in, to leave the past behind and live life on an immediate level. The dense cathedral of trees and shrubs that surrounded us formed a spectrum of green, gold and brown shades with patterns of light filtering in as the sun moved across the sky. The fragrances changed throughout the day as the various shrubs and plants opened out in the baking sun and then the steaming damp. All day, fascinating insects and butterflies hovered, particularly attracted to any gaily coloured items we had lying about. I did not think it was possible for living creatures to have such vivid colours and patterns: Day-Glo orange, turquoise, lime green, stripes, dots and even some eccentricities like dangling pom-poms or long tail-spikes to aid camouflage. Some butterflies liked to sit on my hands and taste the salt, allowing me a close view of their beauty. Spotting stick insects as they played at a variety of disguises became another favourite pastime.

The only real hazard came from the minuscule leeches which would somersault at high speed across the leaves to attach themselves to your skin or clothing. The tiny, thread-like creatures could worm their way through fabric unnoticed, so body checks became necessary rituals throughout the day. One morning we were invaded by wasps and another by a troop of large stinging ants. On both occasions my friend was impelled by testosterone to take action rather than stay sensibly and patiently in the zipped-up tent. The result was that he managed to get stung and bitten and did not even succeed in getting rid of the pests. Once insects decide to investigate in large numbers, you just have to wait in shelter until they have scouted and then moved on. There was evidence of larger creatures in the area, too: the occasional wafts of animal urine scent on the air, the mounds of recent elephant dung and the large cat prints we saw in the mud by the river bank one day. One night we heard what sounded like a feline growl in the distance. We must have spent many hours around the evening campfire discussing how we would respond if a hungry tiger wandered through or a herd of elephants came on the rampage.

On one of our daily explorations away from the camp, we found an abandoned Orang Asli settlement with its bamboo shelters, the remains of old fires and herbs dried out in the trees. Bunches of flowers, which tribal girls wear in their hair, were hanging from the shelters. I was hoping we might meet some of these people, but we only managed to hear the laughter of their children one day echoing through the jungle.

I was just getting used to being so blissfully cut off from civilisation when, one day, a telephone engineer from Ipswich wandered into camp. His legs, covered with leeches, were bleeding profusely. We welcomed him and got a pot of tea going. He was a real loner and seemed disappointed to be in the company of other humans. He pitched his tent and stayed the night but had disappeared by dawn, giving rise to a few sick jokes about hungry tigers.

After a week our food supplies had run out and we reluctantly packed up and began our return journey to the base camp. The trek back was much less tiring; our load was a lot lighter without the food and we were both refreshed and fit from our week of getting back to nature. For most of the journey we were pelted by torrential rain. When we got to the river which we had crossed easily the previous week, it was flowing rapidly and was clearly several metres deeper because of the rainfall. This time, as we discussed all the options, I noticed my companion was not so keen to play leader. Either he had run out of steam or had realised that I was worth listening to when it came to bright ideas. Or perhaps he had never tackled a dangerous river before. I wandered along the bank until I saw a part of the river which looked shallower where the water was bumping over stones and forming patterns. I reported back and we decided to give it a try. When he insisted he go in first to test the depth, I did not argue; he was taller and stronger than me. The water at the deepest part came up to his knees which meant that it would reach my thighs. We formed a cortege of legs and walking sticks to ford the waters. I battled against the flow and more than once was nearly knocked over. As with the pilgrimage a week before, I felt I was tapping into some unknown strength and determination as I stumbled slowly through the crashing water. When we finally reached the safety of the bank on the other side, we both collapsed, exhausted and dripping wet. Like a couple of kids, we fell into hilarity and self-congratulation about our boldness. Then we looked back across the river to the dense jungle territory we had left behind and a sad silence fell. Leaving this temple of nature to return to society was a hard wrench. The first sight of civilisation we saw was the rear end of a panicking tourist, naked from the waist down, desperately trying to pick leeches out of his bleeding groin. As we began to pass the well-heeled tourists from the base camp, the artificial scents of cosmetics and toiletries hit our noses with a nauseating impact. They, in turn, stepped aside with expressions of disgust as we passed. No doubt we smelt as wild as we looked by now.

One more week in the jungle and I might have wanted to adopt it as a permanent lifestyle. The experience had left me spiritually high, emotionally calm and in superb physical shape. I had learned not just practical survival techniques, but also how two people must stave off bad humour and competitiveness in order to co-operate for the mutual good. Most importantly, I had shown myself that I could achieve something which I previously thought was beyond me. I now had a new perspective on my own capacity for bravery and determination, not to mention living on wits and intuition. I was looking forward to continuing my lone travels into other parts of Malaysia, but I had great difficulty refraining from inviting myself along when my friend started to plan his next trek. As we waited for the boat which would take me out of the jungle, he chatted in Malay to an Orang Asli tribesman. They spoke animatedly for some time and then he turned to me with a look of anguish. "This man is telling me about his wife", he said. "He says she was eaten by a tiger in the jungle last year!"

Mali

Eyeless in Mali

Melanie McGrath

Before her America travels and the publication of her acclaimed book, *Motel Nirvana*, Melanie McGrath spent some months touring West Africa. She met up with her boyfriend just before crossing into Mali. Their stay in Bamako, the capital, was dominated by the friendship they formed with a Malian student who introduced them to the popular culture of his country and its shadowy street politics. See also Melanie's pieces on Burkina Faso (p.101) and the USA (p.596).

Bamako begins where the desert ends, just at the place where warted stumps of baobab trees give way to a scatter of adobe huts, sheeny in the sun. These are the suburbs. From here the brown minarets of mud mosques at the capital's centre are as distantly grandiose as the World Trade towers might be to Coney Islanders. There is water in this dust, which is why the huts are here. Women with babies lassoed to their chests stroll along the side of the road forming caravans, each with an enamel bowl balanced on her head. Wherever the pump is, it is not visible to us. There are fewer swollen bellies here than in the savannah villages to the east and north, but the life is a country life all the same, which is to say that the men sit cross-legged in the dust and wait for the rainy season, when it comes, if it comes. No one bothers to protect themselves from the tornadoes of flies.

When I first arrived in West Africa it was the fly-blacked faces of country children with their runny eyes which most disturbed me. I took the triumph of insects to be a metaphor for despair. At some point between the Biafran war and the 1990s images of big-bellied infants had become so much a slogan that I could no longer see them and be horrified. So, it was the sucking mosquitoes, the blackflies and bluebottles and sandflies bloated with blood and sweat that spoke to me most eloquently of the interminable heat, and the impermanence of resistance. I realise now that patience and stoicism play a greater part in African life than they do where I grew up, but I did not see that then. When I look at photographs of myself from that time, I realise how beaten I was. There is a kind of tension on my face, which makes me look both quizzical and anxious, as if I had spotted something strange beyond the eye of the camera. Very often I am squinting, merely, I suppose against the heat haze and reddened dust. But always, always my arms are in a furious blur, whirring round and round in a hopeless, avenging war against the army of insect life.

At the bus station we take a taxi to the *Grand Hotel*. Since leaving Ouahigouya in northern Burkina Faso, I've lost about a stone in weight. Behind the leathern tan there I am, bloodless and weak. I imagine that my mother would have told me I had aged. Paul is more or less unrecognisable; rope thin and with a flame red scab across his face where the midday sun reflecting off the River Niger caught the tender skin and branded it. It was not until he had paddled to the far river bank that he felt the burn. As if that were not enough we are both scraping at a rash of blisters where desert sand has eaten into the skin of our limbs and buttocks. We are agreed that it is time for some luxury, for sanity's sake, and at any price. It is early afternoon. The temperature is in the late 40s and the air heavy with greasy Harmattan dust, which colours the town rosy rust and gives camouflage to the pink painted balustrades strung along the boulevards. Some Muslims hold that the Harmattan winds are God's way of reminding the faithful to keep fast over Ramadan. Whatever their cause they bring the Sahara a little closer each year. In the dust grow date palms, the first greenery we have seen in weeks. They give the city of Bamako a kind of ramshackle elegance, not unlike the more tawdry parts of the French Riviera.

It is Ramadan, so no one has eaten or drunk since sunrise and the streets are empty of pedestrians. Yet every time the taxi slows a gaggle of children appear from some alleyway or door and rush towards the vehicle shouting "*Il faut me cadeauteur!*" or simply "*Donne-moi!*" You hardly hear them before they are upon you. Neither of us dares wind a window down lest we are sucked from the car by a thousand marauding infant hands. The driver turns on his air-conditioning system, and the air begins to broil nicely. We swing off the main Avenue de Fleuve by the Cathedral onto the rue Gourand which leads down past bakeries and motorcycle repair shops towards the central market. All at once a crowd appears from our left and we find ourselves in the midst of some kind of ceremony or demonstration along with much of the rest of the city's traffic. The driver switches off his engine and we wait. The air-conditioning carries on autonomously, converting the car into first sauna then steam bath as the condensation of our breath evaporates from the vinyl cladding of the seats. I am painfully aware that when I walk out of the car and into the lobby of the most expensive hotel in Mali I shall be sporting a large soaking stain on my buttocks.

We can see militia now, managing the protest, if that is what it is, and moving people along. Some kind of bottleneck must have formed, because people are pressing against the cars in the middle of the road and all of a sudden there are bodies squashed against the windows of the taxi, blocking out the light. The car in front begins to sound its horn in time to a drumbeat up ahead. Our taxi driver joins in, then winds down his window and gesticulates enthusiastically in the air with his fist. It could be Naples in the rush hour, but it isn't. The taxi driver thinks these are students demanding that some soldiers responsible for firing on an earlier demonstration be brought to justice. The civil servants are out too, on strike in support of the students. The government hasn't paid them for a couple of months and they are running out of food and patience. "So you support them?" asks Paul. The driver shrugs in reply "I just don't want my car to get damaged. You know, it's all I've got."

The night at the *Grand Hotel* breaks a cherry or two; our first hot water (as opposed to the tepid, peppery stuff we've lived with for two months); an ancient copy of *Time* magazine, the only English read in weeks. Never mind that we already know the stories. Better in fact, because it removes the need to concentrate. Paul orders a club sandwich, and what arrives is a tower of sweet bread curled about the edges and teased with intimations of processed cheese, the whole sweating rather grimly in the air-conditioning. No ham, of course. A bite or two on and we realise it was the "club" rather than the "'sand-wich" which provided the initial appeal, being redolent of "luncheon clubs" and "country clubs": all those kinds of clubs we shake off contemptuously at home but are secretly drawn to abroad as symbols of mindless, guilt-free indulgence.

I suppose we should have seen from the beginning that Issa was an opportunist. He wore his aspirations on his sleeve. There was no pretence to it. What Issa dreamed of was to be rich and Western, maybe even white. Most young Africans, who have grown up in independent states and never travelled beyond, cannot conceive of the strength of the racism so rife in the developed world, but Issa, I know, had his suspicions. We should have seen from the clothes he wore, which spoke of his aspirations, the hopes he nurtured through his acquaintance with us, and other travellers before us. Where those around him paraded in magnificently embroidered tunics, Issa wore white polo shirts; where others were prone to dramatic displays of friendship, anger or joy, Issa was reserved and cool. What Issa wanted, I see now, was to be like us. And if I am honest, all we asked was that he enable us, somehow, to fit in. We looked to him to give us a part to play and put an end to the outsider's unease. Issa saw this, I think, and it explained his exquisite patience with our pitifully stumbling French, the way he oiled our conversation with helpful little turns of phrase and eased us gently into menu Bambara. In this respect he was a go-between, passing messages from the world he knew and despised to the world of his fantasies and in seeking to reconcile the two had perhaps himself become lost in the interstices.

Nonetheless, we thought him breathtakingly romantic; educated, self-assured, a student radical fighting for a multi-party democracy in a country where the people, had we stopped to consider it, were in truth disenfranchised less by politics itself than by poverty. Still, he made us feel privileged to be in on all the inside stories. He took us to the places where marches were held, he told us of arrests and beatings, he led us into whispering alleyways full of discontented youth. It was a true alliance of students and workers, he said, who had pressed Moussa Traore into promising a free vote in parliament which would herald the beginning of multi-party democracy in Mali.

For fifteen years Traore had stood before the crowds and cursed the International Banks, the Western loan sharks, the great conspiracy of wealth, while at the same time embezzling from the shrunken coffers of his own country dollars sufficient to build new towns, or end the water crisis. Malians were beginning to grow bored of the same old tales of World Bank chicanery and CIA scum and soon there remained no one else to blame except Traore and his entourage because, aside from a few development agencies and a scattering of Christian missionaries, no one else took the slightest interest in Mali. Almost imperceptibly, over a period of months, the rich diplomats, landowners and bureaucrats stopped attending cocktail parties at the Presidential palace and shed their friends in government and the military.

Issa pointed all this out to us, but we just didn't absorb its implications. Looking back, I can see that his political world was so alien we resisted intimacy with it. We were willing to take on only the most superficial kind of integration – a cult handshake, the correct way to tie a turban, which bakery to patronise. It is the convention in our world that there is only one effective political act – the act of voting. Between times we are content to become talkers, whingers, mere observers of a political scene which carries on, secure in its mandate, entirely without us. In Mali, by contrast, there are very many political acts – demonstrations, strikes, protests, even criticism is an act of great political significance because the government knows it has no mandate and can have no mandate while it fixes the vote and a part of its people starve. So instead it watches. The people and the government circle round each other watching, until one or other strikes. It's a game of reflexes.

We moved from the *Grand Hotel* to the *Pension Djoliba*, where Issa was staying. Our room was painted navy blue and had no windows. A fan flickered on and off with the electricity supply, then died. It was a kind of eyeless prison. I got sicker and we moved out, to a tiny shabby little room with a sunken bed and a window looking out over leafy boulevards. Our days passed on the balcony, watching the rose-coloured sun dive beneath the slate rooftops and corrugated iron shacks of Bagadaji district. Issa sang us songs, which we taped and whose rudiments we picked up by demanding repeats, and more repeats after the first. Issa spoke a dazzling array of languages; Bambara and Wolof, Fula, Malinke and a little More, the language of the Mossi people from the South. Most of these are unrelated; the African equivalent of speaking Russian, Magyar, Welsh, English, Portuguese and modern Greek. And Issa knew the songs of each, from fast-paced Wolof dance tunes to spiky, edgy Malinke ballads.

Now and then we would venture out to eat, taking Issa along as a kind of guest-cum-guide. He wove for us a path through the *Grand Marché* so that people would let us by without insisting on a Polaroid or some other "*cadeau*". I wished we had more to give, but a gift for one meant a gift for all, and to single people out would have been seen as an act of gross discourtesy. We would spend hours in the market, absorbing the smells of dried fish and pineapple, and poking about among the food stalls, challenging each other to identify hairy manioc from sorghum, pounded yams from millet flour. The women would compete for our attention and we would amuse them in turn by admiring their woven hair, or the whorl of African fabric some knotted round their heads whose tip would reach nearly a metre into the sky. As payment for our intrusions we would buy mangoes or tiny red bananas to distribute among the children around our feet, and so the show would continue.

After the market Issa would take us to a restaurant, warning us on the way about who to avoid, what to hide, which conversations never to begin. Bamako is an expensive place, and I remember that Issa would make a habit of choosing the most expensive dish on the menu, usually steak or lamb brochettes. Afterwards we resented this, although at the time it seemed a small price to pay for his company. Looking back, one can hardly blame him. Burkina Faso and Mali produce the most delicious beef and lamb I have ever eaten; but livestock is so prized that people taste it, if at all, only at the most important of religious festivals, living in the meantime on rice and yams and millet cous-cous. There are few green vegetables. A ubiquitous sauce made from palm oil and chilli renders the grain palatable. Richer families may throw a guinea fowl or scrawny chicken into the sauce pot, feathers and all. Nothing is ever wasted here. Animals convert into calories, old tyres into shoes and buckets, rusted piping into musical instruments.

When I became too ill to get out of bed, Paul rang the British consul, who evidently found our situation ludicrously mundane. Naturally we should expect to be sick, travelling through the Sahel in the heat of the dry season, in any season. He congratulated Paul that he, too, had not succumbed and urged us to be grateful for that, at least. "It's not a good time to be here, anyway, it's unstable," he said, without expanding. "Try the American Embassy", he added and hung up. This was good advice, at least. Dr Joel K Reismann proved embarrassingly welcoming. In truth, I think that embassy life was so cut off from the everyday actuality of West Africa – diplomats lived in a sweep of breezeblock houses with special shops to provide homesick American palates with a supply of potato chips and salsa sauce, air conditioning of a strength to defeat the African heat, sealed windows to block out the Harmattan dust – that no one ever succumbed to the endless round of malaria, hookworms, river blindness and bilharzia that blighted the lives of thousands of Malians. So the doctor spent his days alone and welcomed any opportunity to talk. He sent me away to produce a stool sample.

I never found out what it was that had made me ill because when I went back to the Embassy the next day, the place was deserted and padlocked up, for reasons that were obscure to me at the time, but are now quite clear. It is sometimes difficult to believe that anyone could have missed the signs of disquiet during those days in Bamako, but miss them we did and it was quite by accident that we were saved from the consequences of our own short-sightedness. But I am fast-forwarding and I want to tell you what happened exactly and how we came to know about it.

There is a single plane that leaves Bamako for Burkina Faso. Otherwise it is a twenty-four to thirty-hour drive along pitted dust roads in a *taxi-brousse* to the border. Sometimes, in the wet season, there is no passable route at all. Since I was too ill to contemplate such a journey, and the heat and dust had become unbearable, Paul and I decided to fly out on the next plane. As it turned out ours was the last plane to leave the country before the troubles began. But it was not the heat and dust which forced our hand in the end. Nor did we leave because of demonstrations and Issa's insistence that there would be trouble, or even because of what the British consul had, in his disengaged way, hinted at. As for the increasing presence of soldiers on the streets, we didn't notice them.

No, we left to save what remained of our respect for each other. A month in the Sahel had hardened us. Where we had been open we were self-enclosed, where we had delighted in conversational intimacies we were now dry and taciturn. I suppose we were little more than wary interlopers each on the territory of the other, with Issa the only connection between us. Later I saw that he had sensed this tension and capitalised on it, playing the role of conduit between us. This may not have been a conscious act on his part, but there is no doubt that he benefitted from it. It was to him we turned for our laughter, in him we confided our impressions, to him we confessed our ignorance. He was our temporary saviour because he saved us from the baldness of our relationship. It was not that Paul and I had ceased to care for one another's company altogether, but I think that whatever feeling remained between us was merely the memory of warmth. The heat of the desert had simply sucked out the rest.

Issa helped us pack and we rode together in a taxi to the airport. He was withdrawn and a little sullen, understandable in retrospect. Our minds were already too much in another country to take much notice. We exchanged kisses, embraces, addresses. Issa promised to come and stay. We wished him luck with his student agitations. You'll get there in the end, we said, because you deserve it. I recall that we gave him a present, but I can't remember what it was. We were in the air when we realised that Issa had stolen the most valuable piece of equipment we had – the professional tape recorder on which we had recorded our diary over the past months and our conversations on the balcony of the *Djoliba* hotel. Most of the tapes went too. So much for the kisses, the exchanges of confidence, the promises of friendship; even his songs were lost to us. And yet, how could we have expected otherwise? He had paid us, after all, with his company. For a short few days he had made us feel that we fitted in. What we had chosen not to see was entirely our own responsibility. If we felt betrayed, it was merely because we had not wished to understand that poverty puts a value on everything.

We found out about the coup two days later, in the marketplace at Bobo-Dioulasso in southern Burkina Faso. I was bargaining for a length of cloth and a scarf with a picture of Moussa Traore emblazoned across it. I remember that the cloth was printed with purple shells and that I wanted it a good deal because it reminded me of the sea. That always puts you in a weak position, wanting something badly. The owner of the cloth knew this too and was intransigent about the price. Eventually she gestured to the scarf and said she'd throw it in for free. She said that it wasn't worth so much now that Traore had been toppled. Paul and I looked back at her in astonishment.

Under a shade by the hotel swimming pool that afternoon we learned the details from the World Service. The army had put down a student protest with tear gas and rubber bullets. This brought others out until there were mass demonstrations on the streets of Bamako. Moussa Traore responded by ordering in more troops who were armed this time with heavy artillery. In the furore Younnussi Toure used his influence with parts of the army to stage a coup closing the airport and all borders. No foreigners were allowed in or out and there were curfews night and day. At least forty people died in the protest, mostly students. We do not know to this day whether Issa was among them.

read on . . .

Lieve Joris (trans Sam Garrett), *Mali Blues: Travelling to an African Beat* (Aus/UK/US: Lonely Planet Journeys, 1998). Belgian author Lieve Joris has a unique ability to move towards the heart of a new culture using, as a bridge, her deepening friendships with the people she meets. In *Mali Blues*, an account of a trip that takes her through Senegal, Mauritania and into Mali, she falls in with an immensely popular, though poor, musician, Boubacar "Kar Kar" Traore. Through him, she learns to look with Malian eyes at the tragedy and consolations of an impoverished village life, on the outskirts of Bamako and the disappointments of living on the brink of global musical success. There are moments when you question her right to publish the confidences they share – revelations about the death of loved ones, for instance, seem painfully private – but Joris is no prurient journalist. Every observation she makes seems to shore up a new respect for the close friends, characters and customs that surround her. And in the background to it all, there's the music.

Bettina Selby, *Frail Dreams of Timbuktu* (UK: John Murray, 1991). Selby's lively account of her bike ride across the banks of the Niger River from Niamey to Bamako. A wealth of descriptive detail, amply reinforced by colour photographs, make this a riveting read.

Mauritania

On the road with Fati Matou

Lucy Ridout

Lucy Ridout has spent much of the last fifteen years travelling and working in Asia and is the co-author of the Rough Guides to Thailand and Bali. In 1998 she went to Africa for the first time, to help her partner research his new book, *Sahara Overland*. Together they spent the best part of four months driving through the desert regions of Tunisia, Libya, Morocco and Mauritania. Most of the trip was done in their own four-wheel-drive car, but in Mauritania they went on a tour with a Dutch friend and two local guides, Jean and Fati Matou.

My heart sank when a European face appeared in the doorway of our hut and announced: "*Bonjour, je suis Jean et voici Fati Matou, mon aide et aussi mon épouse.*" Jean was to be our guide through the Mauritanian desert for the next ten days; a grey-haired Frenchman in his early fifties, he'd spent 34 years in the army and his final assignment had been a four-year posting in Atar, the remote town in the Sahara desert where we'd just pitched up.

It was in Atar that Jean had met his future wife, the lively young Fati Matou, now nineteen, who was to accompany us on our travels. The age gap was the thing that got me: the clichéd partnering of older expat male with young local female. I have spent a lot of time in Thailand in the last ten years, where my job as a guidebook writer has taken me to the resorts frequented by thousands of expat men who hire local "wives" by the week. This was the last thing I'd expected – or wanted – to see replicated in the Muslim nation of Mauritania.

Mauritania is in north West Africa, situated south of Morocco and west of Algeria, and three-quarters of the country lies in the Sahara desert. Thirty years ago, the population of Mauritania was almost entirely nomadic. Most families – including that of Fati Matou – lived in large camel-hair tents in the Sahara, relocating every few months to find fresh grazing grounds for their camels and goats. But in the early 1970s a severe drought decimated the livestock population and so, deprived of their traditional wealth, large numbers of people began to migrate to the coast. The young seaside capital of Nouakchott mushroomed dramatically, attracting ring after ring of temporary shanty-style dwellings, and continues to be the best place in the country to find work. When not leading tours, Jean and Fati Matou are based there too; Fati Matou's parents live in Atar. But not everyone gave up their desert roots. The nomadic life is far from extinct in Mauritania and it was our encounters with traditional desert-dwelling families that made the trip so memorable. Our tour with Jean and Fati Matou focused on the Adrar region of northwest Mauritania, a spectacular desert plateau bisected by huge sandy canyons that is still home to hundreds of itinerant Mauritanians who make their living from camel-herding. We travelled through the Adrar for ten days and rarely drove for more than three hours without passing a group of nomad tents. If we stopped to ask directions or exchange greetings, we were unfailingly asked into the tents for tea. It often turned out that Fati Matou had relatives in common with the nomads we met, but traditional Moorish hospitality is extended to any stranger, regardless of blood-ties – a custom that's essential in the desert where food, water, shelter and news are scarce, and the taking of tea is a ceremonial ritual.

The tea itself is Chinese green tea, boiled up in a tiny enamel pot with huge chunks of sugar and stewed for about ten minutes. The host then pours it repeatedly back and forth between tiny shot glasses, until each is lined with foam which stays in the glasses while the tea pot is reheated. Finally, each foamy glass is filled with piping hot tea and handed round. You knock the tea back in a couple of gulps – it's very strong and very sweet and said to be addictive – return the glasses, and the whole stewing, foaming and pouring ritual is then repeated. This happens three times and takes at least half an hour; to leave after only one or two glasses is rude and only done if you consciously want to offend your host. We of course did not, and enjoyed the drawn-out ceremonials for the chance it gave us to look around the inside of the nomads' communal tent-homes (*raima*), to ask them lots of questions (through Fati Matou) and to play with the children.

A typical *raima* houses a family of six; it's about five metres square and two-and-a-half metres high in the centre, with an open-sided front entrance which can be lowered at night or during sand-storms. The floor is covered in matting woven by the women from strips of rag and dried grass; bedrolls are tucked away in the corners and everyone sits on camel-leather cushions during the day. The women seem to spend most of their time in and around the tents, milking camels and goats, preparing meals, looking after the children and keeping house. We rarely saw their menfolk who during daylight were usually off with the rest of the camels or goats.

One morning, we spent an hour watching an entire nomad family pass our camp en route to new grazing grounds. The proces-sion began with about fifty camels high-stepping proudly in line under the watchful eyes of a couple of men. Then came the goats, shepherded along by two boys, followed on foot by the other mem-bers of the household, some of them leading camels and donkeys piled up with the family tents and the rest of their belongings. The rear was brought up by mothers with very young children, sitting on *howdah*-style chair-saddles and wrapped in indigo veils. As with most prejudices, my misgivings about Jean and Fati Matou quickly proved to be ill-founded, and their double-act became a pleasure to watch. Cheeky and forthright, Fati Matou turned out to be the perfect foil for Jean's pompous loquacity. He is the kind of man who likes to feel superior, and we quickly wearied of his unrelenting denigration of the Mauritanians. "See this road? Built by the Mauritanians. Pah!", and later, "They have no idea how to grow tomatoes, just look at this . . ." And so on. But Fati Matou took it all with good humour, jousting when she could be bothered, ignoring his jibes when she couldn't.

As we got to know her better, I started to understand a little of what she gets out of the relationship. Her husband is an active, energetic and educated man who positively discourages his wife from confining herself to the home and their two young children. He has taught her French from scratch, and she now speaks the language flawlessly and vivaciously; he likes to cook and is used to doing domestic chores himself; and he loves to take her with him when he goes searching for Neolithic stone tools or rock climbing. He has money too, not a huge amount, but enough to hire a live-in Senegalese girl to take full-time care of their little boys at home in Nouakchott, where they also employ a housekeeper.

For someone who grew up having to compete with ten siblings for the attentions and wages of her overworked mother, all this must make a nice change for Fati Matou. By all accounts it was quite a typical upbringing in the desert town of Atar. Her mother, an Arabic Moor, had had ten husbands before Fati Matou's father came along; divorce is very common in Mauritania, and very easy – for men. Apparently all the man needs to do is announce that he's had enough. For women it is "not so easy", but "not impossible". Fati Matou has three older sisters by three different fathers and is herself the oldest child of her mother's current husband, an extremely convivial black Moor whose darker African looks she has inherited. He is obviously extremely fond of his eldest daughter whose mum he has been married to for about eighteen years.

As in any country where health-care is poor and child mortality all too common, Mauritanian women feel obliged to keep on producing children. In the same month that the eighteen-year-old Fati Matou gave birth to her second child (laid out on a wooden table in Atar's hospital, her placenta chucked unceremoniously out of the front door), her own mother gave birth to her eleventh. Though Fati Matou and Jean definitely don't want that many children themselves, they too are painfully aware of how hard it is to keep a small child alive in Mauritania. Their third child, a little girl, got sick while staying with her grandparents in Atar and died within the fortnight, before Fati Matou and Jean even knew she was ailing. And their youngest boy almost went the same way – if his parents hadn't got back to Atar in time to diagnose severe dehydration he would have died overnight.

Who knows whether their children would have got sick at the couple's home in Nouakchott, where there's more money, more attention and, presumably, more medical knowledge and equipment.

Certainly Fati Matou's sons enjoy a more privileged upbringing than her own tiny brother and sisters. Fati Matou's father works as caretaker for a girls' school and the family live in two concrete buildings in the corner of the school yard. They use the school toilets, an open-roofed row of sixteen holes in the ground partitioned by waist-high walls, and bathe from buckets of water in the yard after dark. During the daytime Fati Matou's mother sets up a sweet stall beside the school gates and there's often a little family knot sitting on the street there waiting for customers and friends to pass by.

When we visited the Atar home, the Nouakchott toddlers stood out like sore thumbs with their smart leather shoes, fashionable romper suits and battery-powered robot toy. Fati Matou also looked out of place as she sat like a queen visiting her poor relations, with the Senegalese nanny in constant attendance; here she seemed quite different from the sprightly expedition assistant in the desert. Despite her new status, Fati Matou is fiercely protective of her family. That afternoon her mother had got into a dispute with the woman next door over the family's water supply. The neighbour became so incensed that she stormed round to abuse Fati Matou's mild-mannered mum, leaving her in tears. Fati Matou immediately flew round to the neighbour's, returned the abuse, threw a stone at her and turned off the mains tap to spite her, whereupon the neighbour summoned a policeman but it didn't take Fati Matou long to get rid of him.

Mauritanian women are known and admired for their forth-rightness. We were frequently surprised by the cheeky friendliness of the young women we encountered. They didn't seem to be cowed by the more restrictive Islamic precepts and were not at all retiring – they took a particularly keen interest in the two European men I was with! In Atar we were constantly followed by gaggles of laughing female students and when we stopped outside the school gates for a few minutes we were screeched at and prodded as if we were pop stars. The desert women were even more frank: at one nomad family's encampment, the young Dutch guy who was travelling with us was bowled over to be asked, after merely fifteen minutes' acquaintance, if he would like to marry Zing, their gorgeously plump, smooth-skinned eighteen-year old daughter. The proposal was accompanied by plenty of bawdy chuckling, but whether or not a straight answer was expected, none of the family was shy about the asking.

Perhaps because the women are so unabashed about their sexiness, I got no hassle at all from Mauritanian men, not even the kind of furtive, loaded looks I had experienced in Islamic Morocco and Tunisia. Though Mauritanian women are obliged, under possible threat of arrest, to wear a veil at all times in public, these are far removed from the cloak-like chador worn by women in Iran or even the robes of Moroccan women. Made of almost transparent loose-weave muslin, they are worn over Western-style skirts and dresses, draped around the head and body in a way that accentuates rather than masks the women's curves and graceful movements, rather like Indian saris. In Atar, eye-catching veils are the norm: lime green and orange were the most popular colours while we were there, with muted shades definitely out. Nomad women wear the traditional indigo veils which stain their skin a deep blue.

Mauritanians have traditionally admired large, well-padded women and they even have a special word – *smina* – to describe a desirably fat-bottomed female. This used to mean that young girls were forcibly fed a daily bowl of sugared camels' milk and ground dates to fatten them up for the marriage market. Fati Matou underwent this ordeal when she was about thirteen but protested so much that she was eventually reprieved. The milk and date mixture is sweet and nourishing and very good for new mothers and anyone else in need of building up, but it can cause health problems if consumed in excess. Because of his army training, Jean sometimes acts as an informal medical adviser to his neighbours in Nouakchott and he has seen several women patients whose complaints – of foot pains, backaches, breathing problems and sores – would all, he says, disappear if they halved their weight. Needless to say, Fati Matou, her sisters and her mother are now all slim in a fashionably Western way.

Travelling in the desert is tiring and sometimes nerve-wracking, and by the end of our ten days with Jean and Fati Matou everyone was exhausted, tourists and tour leaders alike. There'd been a particularly wearying experience towards the end when we got marooned in the sand dunes with a dangerously low supply of water. Again and again the car got stuck in the sand, and again and again the five of us burrowed and shovelled our way out of it; on one occasion we spent the four hottest hours of the day clearing the sand from under the car. It took us two-and-a-half days to cross this forty-kilometre stretch of low-lying dunes and by the time we reached the well on the other side I was furious at Jean's irresponsible behaviour. He had assured us that he knew the way, that it would take half a day, that he'd done it before, and that the route we'd wanted to take instead was inferior – all of which turned out to be untrue. And yet, even as we vented our annoyance to each other at the end of the tour, we all agreed that it had been an exceptionally satisfying trip. For all his faults, Jean is a very knowledgeable guide and we learnt things about Mauritania that only an expat (albeit a jaded one) could have told us. But for me, Fati Matou was the key to the whole experience. Spending a week and a half with an eloquent woman from such a remote and under-explored culture was a real privilege.

read on . . .

Lieve Joris (trans Sam Garrett), *Mali Blues: Travelling to an African Beat* (Aus/UK/US: Lonely Planet Journeys, 1998). Belgian author Lieve Joris expands the boundaries of travel writing by the apparently simple method of stepping into the lives of the people she meets. In *Mali Blues*, an account of a trip that takes her through Senegal, Mauritania and into Mali, she casts aside her plans to travel to the south of Mauritania after meeting Sass, a sociologist who was born in a nomadic tent and went on to study in Paris, cutting loose from family on the way. While joining him on his field research to the east of the country she discovers the poignant yearning he feels for the nomadic and Islamic way of life he long ago rejected.

Mexico

Reality

Jean McNeil

Jean McNeil is author of the *Rough Guide to Costa Rica*, and wrote on Costa Rica and Nicaragua for the *Rough Guide to Central America*. In 1995/96 she spent time in Mexico as a "tourist", hoping to take a break from work as a journalist and travel writer. Her journey took her to Chiapas, Mexico's southernmost state and scene of a long series of uprisings by the indigenous population, seeking justice in the face of five centuries of cultural and economic oppression. On New Year's Day 1994, the indigenous EZLN (Zapatista) rebels took over several Chiapas towns demanding basic human rights. The brutal response of the state, including the bombing of civilians, catapulted the region into front-page news. There followed peace negotiations between Zapatistas and the government but by September 1996 these had broken down over the question of indigenous rights, and at the time of writing (1999) the situation remains as volatile as ever. Foreigners and Mexicans from other parts of the country have flocked to Chiapas to show support for the Zapatistas and their enigmatic leader, the philosopher, poet and soldier Subcomandante Marcos. "Reality" is the story of Jean's encounter with four such travellers and of her time as a peace observer during the height of the post-insurrection tensions between the EZLN and the Mexican government. Jean McNeil's first novel, *Hunting Down Home*, is published in the UK, Canada and the USA.

November

The houses of the city are the colour of dried cranberries. At noon the sky is hot and close, the light glares like an animal and even with my sunglasses on, my eyes are forced shut. Strange angles of sunshine stalk the streets, which all end in empty plazas. Over them banners flutter in the green, white and red of the Mexican flag. Children follow me, whining "*Cómprame, Señora, cómprame*". What they mean is "Buy from me" but the phrase actually means "Buy me". I have six belts and two change purses and my shoes have been shined twice by shrewd boys who try to sell me overpriced newspapers.

I set out for the House of the Jaguar, once the home of Scandinavian anthropologists, experts on the Lacandón Maya. The house is like a fortress, with thick orange adobe walls studded with purple bougainvillea. I wander in and out of rooms stocked with the anthropologists' acquisitions: arrows, bows, textiles and sleek black-and-white photographs of the Lacandón, who stand white-smocked and splay-toed on moss-covered logs.

I meet them as we have coffee together in the old dining room. G— has brown eyes, thin lips, the brittle bone structure of the upper classes. Underneath her overlay of intelligence and warmth is, I think, something rather dark and disappointed. She and her boyfriend J— are both in their early fifties. J has a slack face; skin folds sag underneath his eyes and his jowls hang.

We meet for drinks and for breakfast for a couple of days. They ask if I want to come with them to *La Realidad* (Reality), one of the Zapatista "communities in resistance" in the *Selva Lacandona*, the Lacandón jungle that occupies much of the southeast quarter of Chiapas. Only eight months ago the area had been bombed by the Mexican army.

"Why are you going?"

"It's our holiday." J shrugs, then adds, "We want to."

I say I can't. I haven't come to Mexico to work as a journalist or a guidebook writer – although these are jobs I have done before in Latin America. I don't have press credentials and tourists are officially not allowed into the conflict zone. In fact, foreigners are deported for that kind of thing. Or sent to jail, and everyone knows you want to avoid Mexican jails. Besides, I get the feeling G and J are well-meaning but wealthy voyeurs, wanting to witness a struggle very far from their double-car garage lives in Guadalajara.

But that night in my pension room I hear a voice I haven't heard in a long time and which is probably left over from the days when I found myself in gun-toting mining towns in the middle of the Amazon. The voice needles me: "You got so close and you didn't do anything. You had a ticket to a really interesting experience, and instead you jumped on the bus to the nearest beach or ruin, with all the other tourists."

The next day I meet the couple they are travelling with, who carry EZLN badges and who have an entree into the village. The man is a musician with lanky grey hair and moustache. He wears a leather jacket and T-shirts with chancy political slogans: "*¡Para la Paz en Chiapas! ¡Que Fueran los Soldados!*" His girlfriend is also his manager. She seems bored and only perks up when she talks about how it will be once we are in the war zone. We all agree to meet for breakfast the next day, then to leave at about ten for the six-hour drive into the mountains.

J and the musician manage to solve most of Mexico's pressing social problems between San Cristóbal and Comitán, like members of a government-in-exile (if they were in charge, they'd sort it out). After Comitán we find a hot lowland road meandering through tended fields. Palms and leafy trees grow among bananas, cacao and *milpa* (maize). Suddenly there's a barrier and a man in a taupe suit resembling the safari gear worn by tourists leaps out at us. The Mexicans smile winningly at the official. "Beautiful day," they say.

"Where are you from?"

"*Mexicanos.*"

"*Pasaportes, por favor.*"

He signals to me to get out of the car. The Mexicans pile out wearily; the musician's girlfriend lights a cigarette. The official and I go into a hut where he sits on a thin iron bed. A kettle stands beside the bed on a flimsy card table.

Suddenly he points something at me – a small silver box. It's a camera, one step up from a disposable. "Wait a minute," I shield my face with my arms. "You can't do that. It's against the International Charter of Human Rights." I don't really know what I am talking about. Maybe it's the Geneva Convention on Human Rights. "*Señorita,*" the man says wearily, lowering his camera slightly. "You have no rights. You're a foreigner in a foreign country. You're entering a *zona de conflicto*. Don't you know that?"

"But why do you want to take my picture?"

"We have to keep a record of all the foreigners who enter this area. In case anything happens. How else are we going to identify you and notify your embassy?"

At this moment J enters the dark hut.

"What's going on?" he says, genially.

"I have to take the *Señorita*'s photograph," the taupe-suited man says.

"I don't want to have my photograph taken," I protest to J.

"Why don't we have a group picture then? Why don't you take all our pictures?" He turns, bright-eyed, to the official. "Come on, you should take the photographs of Mexicans too," his face pretends outrage. "What is this, favouritism for foreigners?" J takes me by the arm and leads us outside.

"No . . ." The immigration man follows.

J calls to G. "Come on, we're going to have a group picture."

The *migración* man gives me a pained look. I shrug. "Look." He raises his camera. By this time J and G have their arms around me and the other Mexican couple grin behind us. "A nice holiday snapshot," J says. "A nice group of Mexicans."

The *migración* man snaps the photograph, grimacing. "OK, now I really do need the *Señorita* alone." By now I feel a bizarre sympathy for this man who is trying to intimidate me, so I tell the others it's OK and pose for my photograph. A click from the silver box, me scowling into the sun. He lets us go.

Abrupt mountains stagger into the distance, each collapsing into valley bowls where zinc-roofed communities collect like residue cooked by the flat heat of micro climates. We drive slowly through the villages, narrowly missing children chasing small squealing pigs, grey and rough-shaped, that look like newly hatched Stegosauruses. We climb and descend as the afternoon disappears and is replaced by a blue twilight. On some passes we can see far into Guatemala, only a few kilometres to the south – mountains upon mountains, scattered among them the conical thrusts of volcanoes. We take turns looking through binoculars. I pick up the loop of circling osprey eagles.

Then night falls and two dark mirrors are draped over each side of the mountains. For the next three hours our headlights cut a path through the night. We descend the last kilometres to the village slowly. The road is heavily rutted, the car can't make it except a few feet at a time. Below us the village is dark, except for what looks like flitting amber fireflies.

We are met by a group of the fireflies, who turn out to be flashlights. From the darkness behind them shiny faces emerge.

"*Pasaportes, por favor*," one says, just like the immigration official.

"Excuse me, *Señor*. Are you going to keep my passport?"

He is a man in his forties, perhaps. I think I see a smile playing around his lips.

"Could I perhaps leave a photocopy with you?"

"Relax," J says and turns to the man, whom I will come to know as Ramón, the village *jefe*. "She's just had a photo session with the *migra*."

The *jefe* shines his flashlight in my face, checking me against my passport photo. He hands me back my passport. He turns to J and smiles. "So the *Señorita* doesn't cry."

I wake into a small grass field circled by a dozen shacks constructed from bamboo with roofs of corrugated iron. Later we sit down under a tree to wait out the tremendous heat of midday. The musician rolls a cigarette, looks around pensively. He tells me J is a *vívero*, a man who lives off rich women. Although I'm not sure; if you take away the accent, *vívero* means a man who keeps a plant nursery. But there is nothing about J to suggest a gardener.

J also turns out to be a venture capitalist, and a novelist. I start to read the novel which he has brought with him in manuscript form. It's about a left-wing middle-aged man who has failed in business and who goes to the jungle to help the oppressed.

In the afternoon G and I sit on a log, talking to some of the kids. An eight-year-old girl stands in front of us, her nose running, wearing a tattered yellow dress, a baby balanced on her hip.

"You're good with the children," I tell G.

"I used to have a daughter," G says it as if it has no connection to the compliment. She picks at the longer stems of grass between her legs.

"*¿Que pasó?* What happened?"

"She was playing in our driveway and went out into the street. Hit and run." She turns her face toward the mountains and stares at them hard, as if they were something other than mountains. "I still don't know who did it. She was eight years old. It's a long time ago now."

There's not much going on in La Realidad, so G and J, the musician and his girlfriend, get ready to leave the next day. They have dispensed their medicines and talked two days' worth of politics with the *jefe* of the village, who looks exhausted by the interchange. Beads of sweat dot the foreheads of J and G as they put on their sunglasses, standing by the car.

"Are you sure you want to stay?"

"No."

They both shrug. "Oh well."

I watch the car struggle up the first few kilometres of the road. With the going of G and J there will be no way out for at least a couple of weeks.

December

I have been given a role by CONAI, the organisation that mediates between the indigenous people and the state. I am to be an observer. I ask Maria, who is in charge – there seem to be many women, most of them thin, chic, hard-smoking, in the upper ranks of the organisation – what I am expected to do. She shrugs. "Just be here." From her posture, both impatient and bored, it's obvious she doesn't think this a challenge.

I am the only observer in La Realidad. I hear an Italian girl is staying in San José and a woman from Mexico City is in Guadelupe Tepeyac. We are all young women, under twenty; when I finally meet them I will see that we look alike, whether we are from Germany or England or Spain. We wear Indian trousers and elaborate sandals invented by surfers. Nothing stays dry; our shirts are marled and buttered by the humidity; our books, my moisturiser, cover-up stick and writing paper all smell of mould. We have lank hair. Our eyes are dull from weeks of eating only eggs as protein. The indigenous women remain spectacularly shiny, wear colourful quetzal-shaped barrettes in their hair and dresses of magenta and lime. They must think us ugly.

Tonight two photojournalists showed up in an ancient Cherokee soldered together by caked mud. One is Chilean, in his late twenties, a prematurely balding man with more wrinkles than he ought to have and the distracted air of an adventurer. The other the village has already nicknamed *el rubio* – he has bright red hair and freckles and is from Argentina.

We all sit in the village *comedor*, a table with two wooden benches underneath a blue tarpaulin, two dripping candles for light. We are served eggs, beans, tortillas and warm Fanta. The photojournalists tell stories of a year ago when they were deported for being at Ocosingo. Tomorrow they will go to San Quintin, see if they can hook up with someone who will take them deeper into the Lacandón. At nine o'clock we are the only ones awake. Most people in La Realidad are in bed an hour after the sun goes down and rise at 4.30.

I go and swing in my hammock. In the hut next door are the *jefe* and his men sitting around a kerosene lantern. They are planning a defence. Even though they have no weapons; it is not that kind of defence.

We are surrounded by mountains and the mountains are full of the army: tanks, helicopters, bomber-fighters, snipers. The tension is a result of the meeting places, outdoor shelters called *aguascalientes*, that the people of La Realidad are building for themselves. The state asserts they will be used for political meetings. Three months ago they bombed an *aguascaliente* in Guadelupe Tepeyac, the neighbouring village; a dozen people were killed.

The run-up to Christmas brings foreign journalists smelling violence. They hang out, sweating under the eaves of the school where I sometimes string my hammock, waiting for a revolutionary to pop out of the jungle.

"Where are the *comandantes*?" They sound like the kind of people who wait at the stage doors of theatres hoping to get an autograph from a star. The villagers point into a sky filled with leaping mountains. "*Allí están.*" The journalists look at me. Their eyes say: "Are they making fun of me?" I shake my head. They really are out there in the mountains.

From his jungle laptop and Internet connection, the revolutionary commander has issued a Christmas statement. "We are going to stop fighting," he says. They are tired of fighting this nation which has chosen to forget itself and its people. They are going to listen, talk, even though they will never forget. Their missives are printed as open letters to the country in the national newspaper. The leaders say, "We call this a war, a war against forgetting."

The women stay at the river washing clothes most of the day and talking. The men are out in the fields, tending maize. Today a boy shattered this rhythm by racing through the village on the back of a horse. He could barely stay on as he galloped back and forth to the men's shouts of encouragement. The women, knee-deep in the river, surrounded by laundry, look up like startled birds. The horse and horseman disappear up the hill in a cloud of fine red dust. When I ask Ramón he says he's a courier.

The silent noise builds. The wind has a tinny air. Voices sound metallic, our echoes sharpened. The plants shout at us. I don't know what to do with this feeling that something will happen; it is heavy, slows things down into a stunning lassitude. I have no idea what is going on in the outside world, what decisions they are making. I wish I knew some games, had a deck of cards, Scrabble. Some nights I think I can hear the mountains' corrugated breathing.

The days drag on. Helicopter patrols come twice a day now with the regularity of scheduled flights: once at 10am, once at three. There are also tanks, armoured jeeps, planes, helicopters. In these cloudy forgotten mountains the sight of jet fighters is like the appearance of rare and ferocious birds visiting from another planet. We are waiting, waiting for something to happen. Time slows down, stops dead, goes into reverse. Waiting, expecting, hoping – in Spanish this is all one verb: *esperar*.

Suddenly, a few days before Christmas, the silence lifts. At noon the sky is full of mechanical locusts. They fly so low we can see all the detail of their undercarriages, the individual rivets in their hulls. Our ears split with the scream of their engines. We can see the soldiers, their young surprised faces, sitting on the gunnywhales of the helicopters. For some reason in all the rushing about I think: "*La lucha, la guerra*". The struggle, the war. In Spanish they are both feminine words. I would have thought they'd be masculine.

Something is stroking me. I turn and find a young boy leaning against my leg. I know everyone in the village by now but I can't place this boy. I realise he is touching me for luck. The helicopter sounds come back, encircling us from all directions. The boy disappears.

They are going to bomb the shelter, the whole area. Everyone is running for the cover of the rainforest, terrified, calling for help.

As it turns out, they were just trying to scare us. The army went away before lunchtime to wherever they spend their afternoons. That night I spend looking at the trees; I can't really sleep. Coati rummage at my feet. Other sounds shear the night – birds, howler monkeys. I look up at the trees, towering above me, illuminated by the moon. The revolutionary commander is a poet, a good one. He has something to say about trees: it is part of their mission, he writes, to be guardians of the night.

January

Christmas and New Year come and the crisis is past. The government and the revolutionaries are going to get together. The two sides will talk in the National Indigenous Forum, scheduled for the second week in January. It is time to go.

I didn't get to know anyone very well in the village. Everyone remains exquisitely polite, but shy. I am an exotic stork, something admired but altogether too outrageously different to really enter into their lives. I imagine many anthropologists are stuck with this problem. However, after living among the dehydrated babies, the malnourished children, the village women who tell me their sisters living closer to town have been raped by soldiers, I see something of the current reality behind (or in front of?) the books and the headlines and what I learned in distant snowbound university classrooms from lectures about the colonisation, of Maya priests burned at the stake and their body fat used as face cream by the wives of the conquistadors, of a process of genetic dilution which included the systematic rape of indigenous women. The current face of this reality is less hysterically brutal, more about lack of protein, lack of opportunity, and the harassment of unarmed people by a highly armed army.

The only way out is the Red Cross convoy that will ferry thirteen *subcomandantes* to San Cristóbal. They are expected to arrive at one in the afternoon. By two the village is nervous. Then, one second the road is empty only to be filled suddenly with masked faces. Because of the dip in the road they seem to rise up from the ground. Balaclavas appear first, then the magenta and lime green dresses of the women, who wear scarves tied across the lower half of their faces. They all come on foot, silent, marching in step, holding hands like schoolchildren. The Red Cross drivers start their motors. The afternoon is hot and still. Everyone is poised to go.

We stop only twice, once for a marimba reception in a village along the way, where there is much kissing of babies and hasty speeches, then for a piss break. We all share cigarettes, even those of us who don't normally smoke. One of the better-known *subcomandantes* comes up to me. In photos he always wears the same clothes, a shirt of chocolate brown and a red scarf slung around his neck. He is small and lithe and walks with the springbok step of an athlete. On his wrist is an enormous gold watch. It looks like a Rolex, but how would a jungle revolutionary get a Rolex?

"What are you doing here?"

"I'm an observer."

He points to his eye. "A very good position. What have you observed?" Before I can answer the convoy leader shouts and we have to return to our vehicles.

We approach the invisible frontier that divides the "conflict zone" from the rest of Mexico. If we are stopped at the migration post where the official photographed me a few weeks before, I will be deported. The little man in his taupe suit emerges and waves to the driver of the lead vehicle. He opens the gate, the one that signals the border between the real and the imaginary Mexico. We pass through at sixty miles an hour.

In San Cristóbal the sun has slipped behind the mountains. I get a handshake from two of the officials. I go to Normitas with some of the conference people and wolf down a stringy steak. We eat *rosca*, the Epiphany bread. It is sweet and doughy. Inside are little plastic figures of Jesus. Whoever finds them has to make a crib for him; this will be celebrated on Candelaria, February second. My teeth hit something tough and I extract a tough tear-stained Jesus. Everyone cheers. In the restaurant they still haven't taken down the Christmas decorations. A tree winks in the corner, its little coloured lights flashing off and on.

We say quick goodbyes in the deserted cobblestoned streets. Then, suddenly alone, I take a walk on the high elevated sidewalks. The town shocks me with its payphones, restaurants that serve meat. In a few hours we have climbed nearly 3000m. The air is thin and flutters in my lungs; several times that night I wake panicked, certain I have stopped breathing.

Two days later in Mexico City I will read that the revolutionary commander has come out of the jungle, doing the same trip we did in an hour less. He travels alone, he cannot risk having anyone with him. He wears his one pair of tattered boots, he has not slept for three days.

Maybe it's the photographer's flash but he looks a little startled. His face has the deflated face of a man who has lost too much weight too quickly. He looks hungry.

read on . . .

★ **Sybille Bedford,** *A Visit to Don Otavio* (1953; UK: Eland Books, 1982). An enjoyable, intriguing and utterly sophisticated romp of a travel memoir from one of Europe's classiest writers. In the last gracious moments of post-war travel, before the backpackers barged onto the scene, Bedford leaves New York on the Sunshine Special bound for Mexico City and the sub-tropical Mexican south. With female friend E, a wry and slighty boozy American travel commentator, she survives an appalling journey, and begins a series of sojourns in small-town hotels. The eponymous visit is a chance encounter. A male cousin of E's joins them and persuades them to pay a call on a nearby don of his acquaintance. Don Otavio, "the kindest of hosts", offers them the run of a lakeside hacienda with seventeen servants in attendance. Halcyon days follow. Full of frank, witty and often profound reflections (especially on the futility and exhilaration of travel), Bedford's first published work and only travel book is a rare travel feast.

Harriett Doerr, *Consider This, Señora* (US: Harvest, 1994). This novel by the author of the award-winning Stones to Ibarra (1984; o/p) follows the progress of four American expats in a tiny Mexican village as they buy and sell plots of land, build houses, gain acceptance from the local inhabitants and develop their lives in unexpected directions. Doerr, who only started writing in her sixties, has an easy, eloquent style with a sympathetic eye for human frailties. She also has a genuine love and knowledge of Mexico.

Katie Hickman, *A Trip to the Light Fantastic, Travels with a Mexican Circus* (UK: Flamingo, o/p). Enchanting, funny and uplifting account of a year spent travelling (and performing) with a touring Mexican circus troupe.

★ **Mary Morris,** *Nothing to Declare: Memoirs of a Woman Travelling Alone* (1988; UK: Picador 1999/US: St Martin's Press, 1999). Weary of life in New York, novelist Mary Morris packs up her bags and goes to live in the small dusty town of San Miguel de Allende, north of Mexico City. Uncertain of her purpose, beyond escape, and knowing little of the language and culture of her new home she embarks on a long, sometimes painful, journey of self-discovery. Her travels take her from her little rented house in San Miguel, where she soon learns to treasure a close relationship with her impoverished neighbour, Lupe, down through southern Mexico and into the lush mountains and jungles of Central America. As with her second travel book *Wall to Wall*, Morris manages effortlessly to weave her own personal story with fine description and astute observations of the places and people she encounters.

Mongolia

Dancing in the village of delight

Louisa Waugh

 After working with young homeless people in London for five years, Louisa Waugh decided to move to Mongolia and explore a country which had long held a special fascination for her. She planned on living there for six months, but stayed for two years working as a writer and journalist in the capital Ulaanbaatar, followed by a further year in Tsengel, a remote village in the western Altai mountains. Louisa has recently moved to Scotland where she plans to finish the book she is writing about her time in Tsengel, which in Mongolian means "village of delight".

"Gansukh," I said, beaming helplessly, "I'm completely drunk." Smiling, Gansukh tutted and reprimanded me affectionately, her own eyes glinting from the numerous bowls of local vodka we'd knocked back to toast the bride and groom.

Gansukh and I had been working together for several months, teaching English at the small Tsengel village school, in the remote far west of Mongolia. When the school year finished she and her husband, Sansar-Huu, had invited me to spend the summer with them, in the Altai mountains beyond Tsengel, where nomads celebrate their weddings with raucous laughter, heartbreaking song and home-distilled vodka. This time with my nomadic friends was supposed to be the culmination of my six-month stay in the village, but I didn't

405

want to leave at the end of summer: there was too much to experience, learn and write about life in the mountains.

I'd already spent two years learning Mongolian and working as a journalist and editor in the dilapidated Mongolian capital, Ulaanbaatar, where, after a bloodless revolution, democracy had been secured in 1990. Following 75 years of rigorously enforced socialism and Russian domination, the market economy was now being pursued with an almighty vengeance. I was both fascinated and appalled by the political and economic implications of the reforms: the homeless children, the young entrepreneurs with their mobile phones and recently acquired American accents, and the dislocated older people, who told me they longed to return to a collective past they understood and felt part of. I wondered how these upheavals were affecting life in the countryside, where three-quarters of a million nomads are still living in their felt *ger* tents, herding their livestock across the arid steppe. I decided to find out by spending several months in the countryside, collecting anecdotes for a book about life in rural Mongolia after democracy.

Most of my friends in Ulaanbaatar thought I'd last about a week in the countryside, where there's still only very erratic electricity, and no night life. But, almost in spite of myself, I'd made my mind up, although I didn't have a clue where to go. It was a Kazak friend of a friend who first told me about Tsengel. Late one night, as we sat drinking beer in a dark, dank bar pulsating with Mongolian rock music, he described an isolated village, more than 80km from the nearest town, which was home not only to Mongolian herders, but also Shamanic Tuvan and Muslim Kazak nomads from the neighbouring central Asian republics. Tsengel, he explained, is built on the banks of the wide, treacherous Hovd river and has a small clinic and a school where children from nomadic settlements in the surrounding mountains board twelve to a dormitory. Their parents pay the fees in meat and wood.

Intrigued, I wrote to the village governor, Abbai, and offered to teach English classes at the school in return for accommodation and food. Ten days later I received a brief telex, saying the school was drawing up a schedule for me and asking that I come as soon as I could. I had a sleepless night, took a very deep breath and bought a one-way ticket to the airport nearest Tsengel, which was almost 2000km from Ulaanbaatar. "It's OK," I told my sceptical friends "I'll be back in three or four months. That's plenty of time to research my book." It was almost a year before they saw me again.

Within days of arriving in the village in mid-February, the naivety of my self-imposed timetable made me laugh out loud. Tsengel had no electricity or running water. I had never chopped wood, fetched water from a river or well, lit a fire, or cooked on a wood-burning stove in my life. I would have to learn to fend for myself, before I could even begin to unravel these resilient people and the traditions that bound them to their unlit wooden cabins, defiantly carved amid these barren, windswept mountains.

At first I was housed alone at the clinic, in a spooky, dark, freezing ward with faded Cyrillic UN posters on the chilly walls and a continual audience of schoolchildren banging on my window. After ten days I begged Abbai to move me and was offered a *ger*, one of the circus top-shaped felt tents which provide shelter for Mongolia's nomads. My *ger* was situated in one of the Tuvan teachers' *hashas* (fenced yards) and thus began my life with Gansukh, her husband Sansar-Huu and their two young children. They became my greatest friends. We shared the outside trench toilet, did our washing, sawed logs and fetched water together and spent our evenings relaxing in their candle-lit cabin, sharing stories and songs. Gansukh had taught herself a little English, but, in the absence of any other Anglophiles, my Mongolian was finally flourishing.

International Women's Day was celebrated just a few weeks after my arrival. Gansukh and I were invited "for tea" to the house of our neighbour Handaa, and found ourselves at a riotous, all-day party. The men had been sent out for the day and the house taken over by Handaa and her friends, their children, mothers and grandmothers. Every woman had brought a platter of meat and a bottle of vodka. We ate and drank, toasted each other for Women's Day, recited poetry, sang, laughed and hugged each other. By ten o'clock that evening I was waltzing round the room with a 55-year-old mother of eight and wondering why it had taken me so long to move west.

During the spring many of the village men travelled to the mountains to tend to their families' livestock, while the women remained in the village with the children. This was a particularly brutal spring for Tsengel, as dust and snow storms battered the village and weakened the herds after a long, freezing winter. Thousands of animals died. While Sansar-Huu was away, digging calves and lambs out of snow drifts, Gansukh and her friends, Tuya and Amraa, patiently taught me how to chop wood, light and keep my wood-burning stove going and cook dried meat. I also learnt to brew Mongolian milk tea dosed with salt and to gut fish freshly hooked from the Hovd River.

After acquiring a babysitter and a red lipstick, the four of us would storm off to the village disco. Held in a crumbling, generator-powered theatre and with an amazing, tilted dance floor that was almost a hillside, I have many fond memories of ancient, distorted dance records and practising my Mongolian waltz! At first the village men were too intimidated to ask me to dance (although the women waltzed happily with me and each other), but people were gradually becoming used to me living in their small, intimate community. Nomads who lived in settlements outside Tsengel would still gape open-mouthed at me as they rode through the village, but locals now visited my *ger* for tea, updated me on local gossip and shyly asked about life in England: whether we kept camels and sheep, how many children people had and what kind of food we ate. After so long away, I gradually realised my own perceptions of England were receding – I began to recall a perpetually warm country, where it never snowed and everyone lived as part of a nuclear family and next door to a cosy, oak-beamed village pub.

At the end of April, it was my thirtieth birthday. People greeted me all day, calling to me from their yards and doorways and presenting me with numerous bags of glistening boiled sweets and armfuls of plastic flowers. Two hundred people turned up to my party at the disco and I was finally cajoled into mounting the narrow, dark stage and crooning the Beatles. Gansukh, Tuya, Amraa and new friends from the school and disco cooked me a glorious, garlicky midnight feast and we sang and danced in my *ger* till we keeled over.

It was just after my birthday that I tasted the only true fear I ever felt in Tsengel. At the end of spring a mass of young herders were conscripted into military service for a year and poured into the village from their mountain settlements. Bored with waiting for trucks to transport them to the provincial capital, they drank vodka all day, brawled in the streets and broke into *hashas* at night. My cosy *ger* with its latticed wooden walls suddenly felt flimsy and vulnerable, as I dozed without sleeping properly and was warned by my friends to barricade my door. After the weekend disco, which for once Gansukh and I decided not to attend, four of the conscripts tried to break in to my *ger*. Sansar-Huu was away and I sat upright in my narrow bed, too rigid and intimidated to light a candle, or even scream for help. But anger finally triumphed over fear, as I rose to my feet, brandished my axe and swore venemously into the darkness. One man lingered at my door, pleading with me to let him in, until, feigning more confidence than I felt, I told him I was going back to sleep and he could visit for tea the next afternoon. I never saw or heard from him again.

By the beginning of May, people were waiting for rain to drench the parched steppe. But the elements threw down yet more snow and dust and the grasslands remained resolutely white and yellow. Vegetables had long run out and, like all the villagers, I was living on rice, dried meat and home-made bread. Gansukh and I slowly eked out my Ulaanbaatar-bought provisions. There was hardly anything to buy in the few kiosks in Tsengel. People usually bartered, exchanging sheep and goat skins for shoes, flour for salt, vodka for beef. When Sansar-Huu returned from the mountains for a few days, we shared fresh milk and yoghurt. But yields were low. This had been the harshest spring for a decade.

I'd gradually realised that Gansukh and Sansar-Huu had an unusually equal marriage. Gansukh taught at the school while Sansar-Huu, when he wasn't assisting his parents, did the housework and looked after their two children. Cosseted by tradition, most of the men I met in Tsengel did no housework, no cooking, cleaning or washing, and the women always rose first, to rekindle the cold stove. When I visited herders in their isolated settlements, halfway up mountains and accessible only by camel or horse, the women often looked exhausted, their dry faces prematurely aged by constant child rearing and the daily struggle to scrape a living from the unyielding terrain.

It wasn't until the beginning of June that the rains finally lashed down. My *ger* obligingly leaked, the felt walls were sodden, the canvas roof saturated. I had to live in the epicentre for several days, constantly mopping up streams that coursed through my home and ruined sacks of flour. But it was worth it, to see smiles unwrapping on people's faces and the steppe and valleys surrounding us erupt into green, moist pasture for the emaciated cows and camels to gorge themselves on at last.

Around this time Gansukh and Sansar-Huu suggested I spend the summer in the mountains west of Tsengel with them and Sansar-Huu's parents. Summer is the only kindness this climate bestows on the herders; people live on milk, cream and cheese, literally fattening themselves up for the lean winter ahead. When we moved to our summer camp at the end of June, the weather was glorious and I was looking forward to a long, warm rest, milking the odd yak or goat and learning to curdle cheese. But my blissful ignorance about the pace of summer nomadic life was shattered on impact.

We worked fifteen hours a day. Rising at dawn we milked the goats and yaks twice a day and the horses every two hours, fetched water, collected dung for fuel, sheared sheep with scissors, curdled thick cheeses, churned cream and butter and distilled our own vodka. I was totally wrecked by the end of the first week. While the men rode off on lengthy hunting trips, I helped to herd the families' 350 goats and sheep with Sansar-Huu's little sister and was immersed in the extended household led by his statuesque mother, Dere-Huu. But it wasn't all about work. After we'd completed the evening milking and rounded up the animals for the night, we would all curl up together on the grass *ger* floor and sip hot, frothing yak's milk. We bathed together in the freezing river and rode over the mountains to drink tea with Amraa and Tuya in their "nearby" valleys. There were resplendent weddings when the nomads' *gers* resounded with applause as well-fed guests, elegantly attired in their calf-length embroidered tunics and brilliant silk sashes, chorused yet another ode to love, the mountains, horses or everyone's mothers. Parties lasted till dawn, although people couldn't afford to lie in for the morning – there was too much to do. After a particularly memorable celebration (which involved the women whipping the men), we mounted our patient horses as the sunrise washed over us, and blearily cantered across the wild flower-drenched valley to our own settlement, where we spent the morning tethering and milking sixty frisky goats.

Gansukh and Dere-Huu escorted me on a visit to the formidable female shaman, Enkhtuya. This powerful young woman came from a lineage of female shamans stretching back nine generations. She had a smooth face, but the bearing of a much older, more tired woman. "I am," she told me quietly "the link between people and the spirits. I speak with animals and the mountains and I offer people the wisdom I receive from the spirits." I was a little afraid of Enkhtuya – and I believed every word she said.

By the end of summer I knew how to milk goats, yaks, cows and horses. I could tell by looking at a piece of dung if it would burn or just smother the flames. I could ferment my own milk, saddle my own horse and herd sheep. I also knew how to beat and roll sheep's wool into sheets of fresh felt for the *ger* walls. Dere-Huu, Gansukh and their family had taught me well. They had shared their lives with me that summer, teased and encouraged me, offered to find me a husband with a huge herd of his own, and taken me on a four-day, breakneck horse-riding trip to the most beautiful places I have ever seen.

I looked around me and knew with a quiet certainty that I wanted to stay in Tsengel until winter – until the river froze two metres thick and drivers and horsemen used the marble ice as a flat road across the valley. I wanted to witness a full cycle of the seasons and the work they dictated; to help slice hay for winter fodder with a crude hand-held scythe; to wake up to the burnished autumn colours Mongolians call "the short golden season"; to visit the sacred mountain where the legendary Ibex sheep roamed; and to go to Tuya's wedding. I sat down with Gansukh outside our *ger* and bluntly told her I longed to stay. I could train her to take over my classes when I left, I brokered, but I would have to move to a wooden house, it would be too cold for a *ger*. Would she help me to stay, talk to the school director and Abbai, the governor? Gansukh stared at me intently, frowning, and then laughed out loud. "Yes, yes! If you help me I can be an English teacher after you leave, then we don't have to wait for another foreigner to come . . . and I know Abbai has a house in his *hasha*. I will talk to him, but also to the school director because you'll need coal in winter and we can talk to Tuya and Amraa, they'll help and . . . Sansar-Huu, come here . . ."

I sat back against the warm felt walls and basked in the brilliant afternoon sunshine, because now time was on my side.

read on . . .

★ **Lynn Ferrin,** "Across the Steppes on a Horse with No Name" in *Travelers' Tales: A Woman's World,* **Marybeth Bond (ed) (US: Travelers' Tales Inc., 1995).**
Ferrin joins a group of fourteen American riders, plus assorted guides, cooks and a doctor, to spend a week crossing the steppes of Inner Mongolia on horseback. They gallop over vast bleak landscapes, spend a night in an oasis on the edge of the Gobi desert and marvel at the resilience of the people and the extraordinary depth of the star-filled sky. A most memorable package tour.

Morocco

Fear and shopping in Chefchaouen

Sue Bennett

Sue Bennett, an English lecturer, had been living for three months with her children, aged twenty-two, twenty and seven, in southern Spain when a German friend, Sina, suggested a weekend trip to the picturesque hill town of Chefchaouen in northern Morocco. With her previous travels limited to brief trips within Europe, she discovered that she was quite unprepared for the impact of entering Morocco, with its confusing mix of modern-day hustle and strong Islamic tradition. After a dramatic night-time border crossing and a hair-raising taxi ride from the port of Algeciras into the Rif mountains, Sue, her youngest son Charlie and Sina and her daughter, meet up with the enigmatic Clara and finally achieve the goal of the trip – they go shopping.

The trip to Morocco was arranged one morning in October, over the ritual "after school run" cup of coffee with Sina. The scorching heat of the summer had mellowed, Levante winds sandblasted our skins and torrential tropical storms now poured through the thatched roof of our cottage. The tourists had gone back to their own worlds and southernmost Andalucia had become extraordinarily monotonous.

Sina had lived on the Costa de la Luz for seven years and although fluent in German, Spanish and English she was finding work hard to come by. She intended to make enough money to live on for the next year by selling Moroccan pottery and jewellery at the forthcoming Hamburg Christmas Fair, and a trip to Morocco was necessary to buy stock. We were to stay with an old friend of hers called Clara, who was living in the small Berber hill town of Chefchaouen, high in the Rif mountains of northern Morocco.

Morocco had fascinated us since the start of the summer when we had first stood high above Algeciras on the Sierra del Cabrito and gazed across the narrow straits of the Mediterranean, the intriguing mystery of North Africa within our sight, almost within swimming distance. The purple Rif mountains towered above a parched, shallow coastline. Beyond, awesome in their alien magnificence, the mist-shrouded peaks of the Atlas mountains seemed to stretch for infinity, justifying the ancients' belief that they were pillars holding up the sky at the edge of their Mediterranean world.

The plan for the trip was simple. The next day I would meet my seven-year-old son Charlie from school at 2pm and then collect Sina and her daughter Coco, also aged seven. It would take about one-and-a-half hours to drive to Algeciras, followed by a ninety-minute ferry crossing. If all went according to plan we should have arrived in Ceuta at about 7.30pm, in daylight. Wrong. We finally arrived in Ceuta at 9.30pm, having watched the sun turn through an amazing range of orange and pink hues and sink in blazing glory over Tarifa and the Atlantic before we had even left the Port of Algeciras.

The ferry was nearly empty except for five or six elderly Moroccan men, loaded down with battered cardboard suitcases, carrier bags and boxes of electrical appliances. The delay had been due to a fault with the doors. Up on the deck, at the stern of the ship, we could see some of the crew trying to mend a rusty and problematic bolt. It was at that moment that we realised which doors they had a problem with. The big ones! The ones that stop water from flooding onto the car deck. I spent the first half of the journey fearing for our lives. Then we arrived. Fear? I had never experienced the full feeling in all my life until I arrived in Morocco.

Ceuta was fine. Ceuta (known to the Moroccans as Sebta) was a Spanish enclave and the eighteenth-century architecture resembled the streets and houses that had grown familiar to us in Cadiz. We took a taxi from the ferry port to the frontier. For obvious security reasons the driver dropped us some way from the first border crossing and, with some trepidation, we climbed out of the safe, warm car into the pitch-black African night.

The crossing was lit by stark bulbs that cast a cold green light over the wooden huts, housing the Spanish border guards. We walked towards this scene along a dark and littered road, with a sheer, rock cliff bordering one side and a long drop into a deep-black, velvet sea on the other. The heavily armed guards casually glanced at our passports and we passed through into no-man's land. From here the road was still unlit, but in the distance we could see the brash lights of Morocco. In the shadow of the rocky cliff three Moroccan boys were being searched, their bodies spread-eagled, movement prohibited by automatic weapons. By now I was having severe doubts as to the prudence of our weekend trip.

The Moroccan border was even more heavily armed, and the passport procedure slow and tedious. However, we were finally allowed to enter Morocco and walked into hell. Ahead, lit by a single arc light, stood a scattering of buildings, surrounded by a seething mass of cars and people; nothing was visible beyond except the Cimmerian night. As we approached, a cacophony of Arabic hit our eardrums. Our adrenaline was pumping as we were swallowed up into an alien world.

A tall young man, dressed from head to toe in fake designer sportswear, broke away from the crowd. He was insistent that he would find us a taxi. As he hustled us towards a battered old Mercedes, what seemed like hundreds of touts tried to pull us towards other taxis. Being the only foreign foot passengers on the last ferry of the night we were clearly a prime target. As Sina pushed the children into the back of the waiting car and jumped in behind them, I struggled with our rucksacks into the front passenger seat, men tugging at the door as I was pulling it shut.

Now the haggling began. We were trapped in a taxi that was now surrounded by a crowd of men, clamouring for our custom, and the taxi driver and his tout were doubling the price for the two-and-a-half-hour journey to Chefchaouen. Finally, we compromised and agreed an extortionate rate to Tetouan, the first Moroccan town. It was 60km short of our destination, but at least we'd be well on our way. By this time Coco had started to cry and Sina and I were on the verge of hysteria. Charlie was made of tougher stuff and appeared to be in his element when, finally, the taxi driver paid off his tout and we set off.

We travelled fast and furiously across a moonlit landscape, arid and featureless. Nearing Tetouan, our driver was chatting away to us in Spanish when suddenly he had a change of heart and offered to take us to Chefchaouen for the original price. Obviously he was dabbling in a little double-dealing with his tout. We agreed. The outskirts of Tetouan resembled anywhere in southern Spain, though dirtier and more decayed – and of course the graffiti was in Arabic. Driving through the more picturesque town centre we could see brightly lit cafés lining the streets, each crammed full of men dressed in traditional cotton *djellabas*. Many a head was adorned with a fez. Ahmed (we were now on first name terms with our driver) suddenly turned off the main thoroughfare and we disappeared into a maze of dark little back streets. Panic returned. I kept my voice low, so as not to scare the children. "*¿Donde estamos? ¿Donde estamos?*" We had turned off a major road clearly signposted for Chefchaouen, and were now travelling in the opposite direction. Ahmed stopped the car. Tall, unlit, silent buildings leaned over the empty, narrow, cobbled street. Ahmed uttered something that included the word passport. Sina was positive that he wanted us to hand over our passports. "No," I responded assertively, bordering on the aggressive.

For the second time that night, we compromised and in a moment of heroic madness I insisted on getting out of the car and going wherever it was that he wanted to take our documents. I followed him down an unlit alleyway, dragging my heart along in my sandals. In front of an ancient wooden door, he waited for me and knocked. God knows what I was expecting, but it certainly wasn't two apparently friendly policemen sitting behind a desk. Relief swept over me as they laughed companionably with Ahmed who was clearly telling them about his nervous charges. "*Lo siento*," I apologised for my ignorance and stupidity. In Morocco, in order to leave one area for another, taxi drivers are obliged to have documentation with details of their passengers logged with the local police. Whether this was for our protection, I never discovered. During the next 60km of our journey we were stopped five times by police and army roadblocks on dark and desolate stretches of mountain road – that document was demanded every time.

Their method thrilled Charlie, who was an avid *Men in Black* fan. First the dusty headlights would pick out a group of uniformed men standing by a jeep at the side of the road. As they flagged us down with their guns Ahmed would screech to a halt in a flurry of sand and rock – 90mph to nothing in three seconds. Next they poked a gun through the open window of the car and asked questions. Once they had discovered that we had the correct paperwork they were really friendly.

Ahmed's driving was something else. We had all slunk low in our seats as he squealed around hairpin bends, carving our way at breakneck speeds through the steep Rif mountains. After about an hour Ahmed slowed down slightly and started to fiddle about with his sock. Through the open windows of the car the pungent smells of the mountains wafted in on the warm night air, but even more pungent aromas were emanating from whatever Ahmed was doing in his lap with one hand. The son of a donkey was now rolling a joint. Not content with scaring us half to death he now wanted to get us busted. I started nagging him but he explained that there would be no more roadblocks now, only bandits. Great.

The hashish was brilliant. I wouldn't have normally accepted a joint from a strange taxi driver in the middle of the North African mountains. But Charlie and Coco were fast asleep, cradled in Sina's arms, and the more Ahmed smoked the faster he drove. My logic was that the more I smoked the less he would. Also at my first refusal he reacted as if I had insulted the whole of the Berber nation, particularly his father who had grown the potent substance on his farm just outside Ketama, the centre of the hashish-growing region. He was eager that we go with him now to visit his family. No. No. No.

Finally we reached Chefchaouen, and Ahmed stopped in a large tree-lined square outside a big hotel. Once again the car was quickly surrounded. There was absolutely no way we could get out; even Ahmed was panicking as he handed out *dirhams* through a narrow gap at the top of the window. Then, as if by magic everyone stepped back. A tall man in a suit demanded to know if the taxi contained two women and their children; as he herded us to safety he explained that Sina's friend Clara had asked him to look out for us and we could wait in his hotel until she came for us.

The children were now wide awake and starving so I fed them biscuits while we waited. Clara was a total shock. Everything about her seemed exaggerated, from the voluminous black woollen cloak enveloping her body to the large hooked nose which poked out from under the hood beneath bloodshot eyes, ringed black against a milk white face. Charlie's hand gripped mine tightly as she tweaked his ear and babbled Spanish into his face, but she was friendly and led us out into the night once again.

We had been deposited in the comparatively new part of Chefchaouen, where cars could move around with ease. Clara led us into the old walled quarters of the town, the *medina*, where no cars could pass. The roads, designed for people and donkeys, wound steeply up the sides of a mountain. A maze of narrow alleyways soon brought us to a huge square, flanked by numerous cafés where groups of men drank mint tea under the shelter of tarpaulins. Behind, a ruined castle shrouded by trees and dwarfed by a huge mosque dominated one side of the square. It had been a long time since anything but biscuits had passed our lips and I looked longingly at the cafés, but Clara was hassling us to hurry up. Also I realised that we were the only women to be seen in the square.

We were to stay in the hotel where Clara lived. We left the quiet bustle of the square and headed into the intricate maze of alleyways and passages of the *medina*. We turned and went down some worn narrow steps and entered a darkened passage, at the end of which stood a heavy wooden door, iron-studded, medieval in appearance and quite possibly in age. Clara banged on the door and a small shutter was opened through which we were inspected, obviously approved and finally, thankfully, admitted. Across a tiled entrance lobby we were led into a huge, galleried courtyard around the sides of which, through ornate pillared arches, we could see low wooden couches covered in brightly coloured carpets. We climbed a spiral staircase in the corner of the courtyard to the gallery above. Charlie and Coco were excited, leaning over the wrought-iron railings, gazing down on the courtyard and up to a midnight-blue, star-scattered sky, while we were introduced to our bedroom.

We slept like the dead, missing the dawn *muezzin*, but as the call to prayer is sung five times a day we were not too worried. It was shafts of hot sunlight that woke us and by ten o'clock we were sitting on the terrace of the "foreigners' café", drinking delicious coffee and eating *tostada*. We were in a prime position at one end of the huge main square, Plaza Uta el-Hammam, which we had crossed the night before. The souks were setting up for business and there was traditional Arabic music being played from every café and shop. Charlie and I were fascinated by every sight and sound, his eyes like saucers as he stared with blatant curiosity at everyone and everything.

Sina was keen to start shopping, I was keen to chill out and just drink in these surroundings. The exertions of the previous day had taken their toll and I needed to relax. A group of English people had joined us on the terrace and Charlie and I were devouring them. After three months of speaking only Spanish or pidgin English we couldn't get enough. Our new friends were frequent visitors to Chefchaouen. Because it was little-touched by mass tourism, they preferred it to Amsterdam. Since they were all surreptitiously rolling joints under the table our conversation led naturally to the region's main commercial product, hashish or *kif*. Although it is illegal to sell or to consume the drug in Morocco, discreet possession is tolerated. Every shopkeeper seemed to have a little screw of newspaper containing kif and a long-necked pipe on his counter or more often in his mouth. Perhaps this explains the incredible sense of relaxation and peace that pervaded the town.

As midday approached the main square filled up with the people of Chefchaouen going about their daily business: old women dressed entirely in black, bent-double carrying backbreaking bundles of kindling; men driving donkeys, similarly burdened; boys dressed in Western sports designer gear waiting for a chance to pester us with offers of top-quality hash, or a visit to an uncle's carpet shop.

Clara finally made an appearance, sporting a fresh *djellaba* and heavily kohled eyes. She had come to give us a guided tour of old Chefchaouen. We headed off up a steep cobbled street. All the buildings were a blinding white except for the lower half of the walls which were painted a vivid blue – apparently intended to keep flies out of the houses. Again I was struck by the physical similarities with rural Andalucia. However, time had stood still in this remote hilltown, the medieval Muslims and Jews who fled the Spanish Inquisition in Andalucia to Chefchaouen having left their indelible mark.

We climbed for nearly an hour, through the intricate maze of white-washed buildings which clung for dear life to the lower slopes of the twin-peaked Jbel Chaouen. We bought fresh bread, olives and some ewe's cheese and sat at the base of an ancient water pump to eat, then continued on our way. The children were hot and fractious but finally, turning a corner, there were no more houses, just a rickety gate and steep stone steps leading to a terraced garden café. Here we quenched our thirst with glasses of sweet mint tea, stuffed with fresh mint leaves.

The view from our mountain terrace, perched on the edge of a dramatic gorge, was spectacular. On the far side, the sheer rock face of the second peak of Jbel Chaouen rose incandescent in brilliant sunshine. Breathing in the pure air and drinking my tea I felt totally at peace.

The next item on our itinerary had to be shopping. We had already checked out many of the shops on our way up the mountain but comparing prices and quality, which varied greatly, was a mammoth task and took the whole afternoon. We saw treasure houses brimming with the most fantastic traditional crafts. Brightly coloured Berber carpets, huge brass plates, small silver tea pots, exquisite Berber necklaces, earrings and bracelets – more like shackles than pieces of jewellery – stacks and stacks of Moroccan pottery, strikingly simple with stunning colours and designs and astonishingly cheap. There is a good choice of crafted wood in Chefchaouen and, of course, leather to die for. It is a shopper's paradise. I wanted everything, particularly a beautiful shuttered window frame, intricately carved and decorated in rich blues, terracotta and gold. The time for buying was the next day.

Shopping in Chefchaouen was a unique and lengthy experience requiring the patience of a saint. The first rule I learnt was that you do not ask to look at anything unless you intend to buy it. There are a few tourist shops that will allow you to browse but on the whole Moroccans do not understand the concept of window-shopping. I wandered into a carpet shop dreaming of the day that I could come back to Morocco with some money, and the next moment the shop-keeper was laying carpets out and rapidly quoting prices; they were incredibly cheap, but he obviously expected me to haggle and ultimately to buy. It took an hour for us to escape, with Clara promising to go back and purchase one of the rugs another time. She was not very pleased with me. Our next experience of shopping was everything I had imagined.

The Bazar Berber, in the rue Abi Hassan, was an Aladdin's cave. We had inspected its wares the day before and the quality was good and so were the prices. When we arrived and started to talk quantity we were made to feel like princesses, the immense cavernous rooms our domain. The shop was in fact a typical courtyard house, similar to our hotel but on a much larger scale, consisting of five floors, all of which we were invited to explore at our leisure while the children were fussed over and given gifts of stuffed camels made of leather.

Sina concentrated on the more commercial ground floor, choosing from a plethora of baby *tajine* pots, suitable for serving salt, pepper and spices, ashtrays, brass-framed mirrors, soapstone dishes, wooden boxes, embroidered bags – the list is endless – while I wandered about upstairs. Every corner and area of floor was piled with things. Every wall and gallery railing hung with rugs and leather goods. The higher I went the dustier everything became and the more intriguing. I found piles of rough terracotta cooking pots, blackened where they had been fired for days in pits of ashes, ancient leather now stiff and dry, racks and racks of traditional Berber clothes, brightly coloured silks, braided and embroidered and decorated with tiny mirrors and beads.

After an hour or two of browsing the owner of all of this treasure insisted that I accompany him to the very top floor. A precarious climb led to a roof terrace where I was served endless glasses of mint tea and we chatted about the beauty of Chefchaouen and, of course, the wonders of his shop. It *was* wonderful, so far removed from my normal reality.

Totally exhausted by shopping we eventually dropped our booty off at the hotel and found a restaurant that did not resemble a smoking den and spent the afternoon eating. We started off with a communal dish of Moroccan salad, a bed of lettuce piled high with chopped tomatoes, cucumber, sweetcorn, peppers, masses of olives, all doused in olive oil and lemon juice. For our main course we chose the traditional staple, *tajine* and couscous. Tajine is a slow-cooked stew often with a mix of meats and lots of vegetables flavoured with herbs and spices served on a bed of couscous. *Harrisa*, a condiment made from hot chillies, garlic and olive oil was served in little dishes so that we could add our own heat to the meal. Last came irresistible pastries. Described as "gazelle's horns" and "coiled serpents", these were stuffed with almond paste and sprinkled with icing sugar and cinnamon – truly divine.

Sadly the next morning we had to leave our medieval time warp and return to twentieth-century Spain. Clara needed to go to

Tetouan, and offered to give us a lift to Ceuta. The drive in her ancient camper van, decked out with voluminous drapes, joss-stick holders and candles, felt more like flying. Charlie and I clung on for dear life, as once again I found myself fearing for our lives as we sped through the fantastic gorges and ravines of the Rif mountains. As we neared Tetouan Clara slowed down for a donkey laden with bundles, on top of which sat a fat man. Behind trudged a woman swathed in heavy woven cloth, her face hidden by the traditional *hijab*. Thirty kilometres later we returned to the Western world. Southernmost Andalucía suddenly seemed extraordinarily modern.

Running through Fes

Margaret Hubbard

Margaret Hubbard, who works as an English teacher in Scotland, set off to Morocco for a month's holiday. Although she had long been interested in Islamic culture and had already travelled in the Middle East, this was her first trip alone to a Muslim country. Margeret is an avid Marathon-runner and tends to keep in training regardless of where her travels take her.

I knew that there were likely to be difficulties in travelling as a woman alone around Morocco. I'd been warned by numerous sources about hustling and harassment and I was already well aware of the constraints imposed upon women travellers within Islamic cultures. But above and beyond this I knew I'd be fascinated by the country. I had picked up a smattering of Arabic and the impetus to study Islamic religion and culture during trips to Damascus and Amman (both times with a male companion). Also I already had enough experience of travelling alone to know that I could live well with myself should I meet up with no one else. So, a little apprehensive but very much more determined and excited, I arrived at Tangier, took the first train out to Casablanca and found a room for the night. It was not until I emerged the next morning into the bright daylight of Casablanca that I experienced my first reaction to Morocco.

Nothing could have prepared me for it. Almost instantly I was assailed by a barrage of "*Voulez-vous coucher avec moi . . . Avez-vous jamais fait l'amour au Maroc . . . Venez avec moi madame . . . Viens m'selle*". Whatever I had to say was ignored at will and wherever I went I felt constantly scrutinised by men. Fighting down the panic I headed for the bus station where, after a lot of frantic rushing to and fro (I couldn't decipher the Arabic signs), I climbed onto a bus for Marrakesh.

It wasn't that the harassment was less, in fact it was almost as constant as in Tangier. But wandering through the Djemaa el Fna (the main square and centre of all life in Marrakesh) amongst the snake-charmers, kebab-sellers, blanket-weavers, water-sellers, monkey-trainers, merchants of everything from false teeth to handwoven rugs, I became ensnared to such an extent that my response to the men who approached me was no longer one of fear but rather a feeling of irrelevance.

Marrakesh proved to me that I was right to come to Morocco. There was too much to be learned to shut out contact with people and I heard myself utter, as if it were the most normal reply in the world, "*Non, monsieur, je ne veux pas coucher avec vous, mais pouvez-vous me dire pourquoi ils vendent les dents fausses* [false teeth]/*combien d'années il faut pour faire des tapis à main/pourquoi les singes* [monkeys]". That first night I returned to my room at 2am more alive than I had felt for months.

I'd also stumbled upon a possible strategy for pre-empting, perhaps even preventing, harassment. Moroccan hustlers know a lot about tourists and have reason to expect one of two reactions from them – fear, or a sort of resigned acceptance. What they don't expect is for you to move quickly through the opening gambits and launch into a serious conversation about Moroccan life. Using a mixture of French and Arabic, I developed the persona of a "serious woman" and from

Marrakesh to Figuig discussed the politics of the Maghreb, maternity rights, housing costs, or the Koran, with almost anyone who wanted my attention.

It became exhausting, but any attempt at more desultory chat was treated as an open invitation and seemed to make any harassment more determined. That isn't to say that it's impossible to have a more relaxed relationship with Moroccan men. I made good friends on two occasions with Arab men and I'm still corresponding with one of them. But I think this was made easier by my defining the terms of our friendship fairly early on in the conversation. As a general rule whenever I arranged to meet up with someone I didn't know very well, I chose well-lit public places. I was also careful about my clothes – I found it really did help to look as inconspicuous as possible and almost always wore loose-fitting blouses, longish skirts and occasionally also a headscarf.

After exploring Marrakesh for five days I took a bus out over the Atlas mountain range to Zagora. The journey took twelve hours and the bus was hot and cramped but, wedged between a group of Moroccan mothers, jostling their babies on my lap and sharing whatever food and drink was going round, I felt reassured, more a participant than an outsider.

This was also one of the few occasions that I'd had any sort of meaningful contact with Moroccan women. For the most part women tend to have a low profile in public, moving in very separate spheres to the tourists. There are some women's cafés but they're well hidden and not for foreigners. For me, the most likely meeting place was the *hammam*, or steambath, which I habitually sought out in each stopping place.

Apart from the undoubted pleasures of plentiful hot water, *hammams* became a place of refuge for me. It was a relief to be surrounded by women and to be an object of curiosity without any element of threat. Any ideas about Western status I might have had were lost in the face of explaining in French, Arabic and sign language to an old Moroccan woman with 24 grandchildren the sexual practices and methods of contraception used in the West. "Is it true that women are opened up by machine?" is a question that worries me still.

I arrived in Zagora on the last night of the festival of the King's birthday. It was pure chance. The town was packed with Moroccans who had travelled in from nearby oases, but I met only one other tourist – a German man. We were both of us swept along, as insignificant as any other single people in the crowd, dancing and singing in time to the echoing North African sounds. At the main event of the night, the crowd was divided by a long rope with women on one side and men on the other, with only the German and I standing side by side. I felt overwhelmed with a feeling of excitement and wellbeing, simply because I was there.

From Zagora I headed for Figuig and the desert, stopping overnight en route at Tinerhir. It's possible that I chose a bad hotel for that stop but it was about the worst night that I spent in the entire trip. The men in and around the hotel jeered, even spat at me when I politely refused to accompany them, and throughout the night I had men banging on the door and shutters of my room. For twelve hours I stood guard, tense, afraid, and stifled by the locked in heat of that dismal hotel room. I escaped on the first bus out.

Further south I met up with a Danish man in a Landrover and travelled on with him to spend four days in the desert. It was a simple, businesslike arrangement: he wanted someone to look after the van while he slept and I wanted someone to look out for me while I slept. I can find no terms that will sufficiently describe the effect that the desert had on me. It was awesome and inspiring and it silenced both of us. On the rare occasions that we spoke we did so in whispers.

I also found that the more recent preoccupations that I had about my life, work and relationships had entirely slipped from my mind, yet strangely I could recall with absolute clarity images from over ten years ago. I remain convinced that the desert, in its simplicity, its expansiveness and its power changed me in some way.

At Figuig I parted company with the Dane and made my way in various stages to Fes. I tended to find myself becoming dissatisfied after travelling for a while with a male companion. Not because I didn't enjoy the company, which was more often than not a luxury for me, but I used to feel cheated that I was no longer at the forefront and that any contact with Moroccans would have to be made through him. This is often the case in Islamic countries where any approaches or offers of hospitality are proffered man-to-man, with the woman treated more or less as an appendage. I was prepared to go on alone however uncomfortable it might become as long as I was being treated as a person in my own right.

In Fes I discovered yet another, perhaps even more effective, strategy for changing my status with Moroccan men. I am a runner, and compete regularly in marathons and I'm used to keeping up with my training in almost any conditions. Up until Fes I'd held back, uncertain of how I'd be greeted if I dashed out of the hotel in only a track-suit bottom and T-shirt. My usual outfit, a long skirt and blouse, was hardly suitable for the exercise I had in mind.

After seriously considering confining myself to laps around the hotel bedroom, I recovered my sanity and sense of adventure, changed my clothes and set off. The harassment and the hustling all melted away. I found that Moroccans have such a high regard for sport that the very men who had hustled me in the morning looked on with a respectful interest, offering encouragement and advice as I hurtled by in the cool of the evening. Furthermore I became known as "the runner" and was left more or less in peace for the rest of my stay. After this I made it a rule to train in all the villages and towns I stayed in on the way back to Tangier. Now when I run I conjure up the image of pacing out of Chaouen towards the shrine on the hillside, keeping time with the chants of the *muezzin* at dawn.

Returning to Tangier I felt as far removed as it is possible to feel from the apprehensive new arrival of the month before. I felt less intimidated by and more stoical about my status as an outsider and I had long since come to accept the fact that I was a source of income to many people whose options for earning a living are sorely limited.

Walking out of the bus station I was surrounded by a group of hustlers. I listened in silence and then said, in the fairly decent Arabic that I had picked up, that I had been in the Sahara and had not got lost so I didn't think I needed a guide in Tangier; furthermore, that I had talked to some Tuareg in Zagora who told me that it is a lie that Moroccans buy their women with camels; please would they excuse me, I had arrangements. I spent the next few days wandering freely around the town, totally immersed in plotting how soon I could return.

read on . . .

Esther Freud, *Hideous Kinky* (UK: Penguin, 1993/US: W. W. Norton & Co., 1999).
Freud's wonderful debut novel, written from the perspective of a five-year-old, drew heavily from her own childhood experiences of traipsing around Morocco with her naive and idealistic hippy mother and slightly older and more streetwise sister. Romanticised in the way that childhood memories often are, and shot through with colour, humour and a wonderful

array of characterisations and anecdotes, the book succeeds utterly in capturing the zeitgeist of Morocco travel in the 1960s. In doing so Freud touches on the perennial and often bitter struggle between children and parents about whose needs prevail. It's her talent that she manages all this with such affection and humour.

Fatima Mernissi, *The Harem Within: Tales of a Moroccan Girlhood* **(1994; UK: Bantam, 1997/US: Perseus, 1995).** The feminist author of *Beyond the Veil* (1975; UK: Al Saqi Books, 1985/US: Indiana University Press, 1987), a ground-breaking work on women and Islam, has written a riveting memoir of her childhood in the confines of the family harem. Her account moves between life behind the monumental gates of her father's house in Fes and visits to her grandfather's farm – the country harem – where, unlike the women in the city, nine co-wives enjoy the freedom to ride horses, climb trees, go fishing and swim in the river. These spirited characters, among them Tamou, the warrior who appeared out of nowhere, "dagger dangling from her hip", and won Mernissi's grandfather's heart, may leave the most lasting impression but this is a book filled with memorable women. Each has her own way of transcending domestic boredom, be it moments snatched dancing to illicit love songs on the radio, long nights of story-telling or simply escaping into dreams. Each too has her own answers to the young Mernissi's persistent questioning about segregation, the meaning of the word "harem" and why it is women and not men who are locked away behind high walls. Enhanced by the author's scholarly footnotes these questions provide valuable insights into the nature of Islam and its impact on the everyday lives of Moroccan women.

Elizabeth Warnock Fernea, *A Street in Marrakech* **(1975; US: Waveland Press, 1988).** In 1971 Elizabeth Warnock Fernea, an American academic in Middle Eastern Studies, moved to Marrakech for a year with her anthropologist husband and three children, aged eleven, ten and eight. Her frank, detailed and illuminating account of their stay in the *medina*, should touch a chord with all parents hoping to embark on a cross-cultural family adventure. The uphill task of overcoming the suspicion and hostility of their neighbours pales against the daily grind of explaining and justifying their travel plans and local customs to their perplexed and sceptical children. And some moments are hard to justify indeed, such as when her ten-year-old son returns from school repeatedly bruised, or her daughter confides that she is too fearful of punishment to risk moving or speaking in class. The social anthropology can sometimes seem a digression from a gripping, if fairly raw, family story.

Edith Wharton, *In Morocco* **(1920; US: o/p).** Wharton dedicated her book to General Lyautey, Resident General of the Protectorate, whose modernising efforts she greatly admired. By no means a classic, it is nonetheless worth reading for glimpses of harem life in the early part of the twentieth century.

Nepal

Living Goddess

Isabella Tree

Isabella Tree began travelling as a child with her parents and younger sister, first to Kashmir and then, in the 1970s, to Ladakh when they were among the first tourists to enter the country after the opening of its borders. She went back to the Himalayas after leaving school, catching the tail-end of the hippy era and shacking up in a flat in Freak Street, Kathmandu. Fourteen years later, as a fully fledged travel-writer, Isabella returned to look for the Living Goddess, a haunting inspiration from her teenage days in Kathmandu. In 1997 she won the Travelex Travel Writers' Award for Best National Sunday Newspaper Feature.

Isabella Tree is the author of the celebrated travel book *Islands in the Clouds*, an extract of which appears in the Papua New Guinea chapter (p.471).

I slipped up in something as Laxmi hurried me through the backstreets and in my agitated state of mind I fancied it was blood. It was dusk and difficult to tell. It was probably nothing more than the usual back-street puddle – a confluence of sewage and urine (human, dog, cow, buffalo, goat), slops from a washing-bucket, the remains of yesterday's rain. But the smell of blood was still in the air, and there were flash-backs of blood-spurts when I closed my eyes at night.

A week earlier I had seen Kathmandu as I never could have imagined her. From something of a Cinderella in my eyes – kind-hearted, pure, a princess in rags – she'd shown herself to be a bloody, axe-wielding maniac. The metamorphosis had me reeling and by the way I could almost feel the blood-stains travelling up my trousers, smell the blood still lingering in the air, I knew I wasn't quite back to normal.

We had arrived during Dasain, the biggest festival in the Nepali calendar, when Durga, the avenging goddess, triumphs over the forces of evil. It's a festival that celebrates the end of the monsoon and the beginning of the rice harvest. It's a time, specifically, for families – the Nepali equivalent of Christmas. Medieval, hand-powered ferris wheels and huge bamboo swings, or "*pings*", are set up. Everyone gambles – it's the one time of the year it's legal to do so – and even children are allowed to put down bets on board games in the street.

At the start of the holiday Kathmandu is at a standstill. For eight days her streets, normally choking with traffic, are silent. Even the ring-road, a log-jam at the best of times, has a chance to relax. It seemed we couldn't have chosen a better moment to arrive. The rains had rinsed a window in the pollution – you could even see the mountains, icing-sugar peaks, above the haze. And we'd driven into town from the airport in fifteen minutes flat – like the old days.

But this peacefulness was misleading. Kathmandu was not closing up shop, putting its feet up, but getting ready for the kill. While Hindus sharpened their knives, Buddhists, in implicit collusion, prayed for those who were to be given to Durga: for the goats assembling in their hundreds in Tundikhel park; for the geese and ducks massing down Kantipath, for every buffalo tethered to a stake, for every chicken in every backyard.

At midnight on the eighth day of Dasain, on the black night of Kala Ratri, the drums had sounded at the shrine of Mul Chok in the ancient heart of Kathmandu, and 108 buffaloes and 108 goats had their throats slit. These represented demons that threatened the city. They were just the first of thousands to go. Early the following day standing beside Laxmi, my guide, on the visitors' balcony over Kot Square, I had watched another 108 beasts and 108 goats decapitated with a single slice of the kukhuri.

That day (called simply the "ninth", or Navami), in every household there were the twitchings and kickings of a sacrifice. In the temples, people slithered up to the priest holding their offerings, their bare

feet leaving skidmarks on the tiles. In the streets, motorbikes and rick-
shaws were sprayed from the jugular of – remarkably – a still-bleating
goat. The wheels of cars were bloodied, too, and the bonnets of buses.
And at the airport each Royal Nepal Airlines aircraft got its due:
another head lopped off, another rolling-eyed, lolling-tongued loosen-
ing of life. Kathmandu was being purged.

It was a frenzied day and one that left flutterings of anguish in
the solar plexus. It seemed the opposite of why I had come, the
antithesis of the quest that had returned me to Nepal. I had come back
to look for a goddess, but not the Gorgon who had met met me on
arrival. I was looking for the Living Goddess, for a real, breathing,
beautiful child, the girl I had once glimpsed at a window, fourteen
years ago, the Royal "Kumari" – emblem of Kathmandu.

I had first seen the Kumari when I was eighteen, in my "gap
year", when Kathmandu was still a hippy mecca. Flower-power was
well on the wane but up here, somehow, they strung it out for just a
bit longer. This was where the weirdest and wonderfullest of the
bona-fide flower children had washed up – not quite in the bloom of
their youth by the time I got to them, their beatific faces etched
with crows' feet and smile-lines, their skin sagging off the bones; but
still using phrases like "peace, man", "good for the *kharma*", "pass
the *chilum*".

"Human driftwood" was how the proprietor of Yin Yang Hostel
liked to describe them. The rest of Kathmandu called them "freaks". I
thought they were wonderful. Even the posters pasted up by the
embassies around town begging for word from someone's son or
daughter – some long-haired layabout too lazy or selfish or off their
face to stay in touch – failed to tarnish the romance of it for me.

I shacked up with friends in a two-room flat above Peace Air
Travel in Freak Street, sold my Walkman for a pair of shoes that
looked like Cornish pasties and some tie-dye shirts that ran, grew my
hair, smoked pot, ate hash cookies, drank *bhang lassi*, and lolled about
all day trying to empty my mind of everything I could think of. There
was a lot of talk about "cosmic enlightenment", "reaching *nirvana*",
"the third eye". I think I knew even then that it wasn't working, that
all this dreamy self-analysis was coming up with nothing, that the
Nepalese were beginning to resent us spiritual cuckoos getting it
wrong – and for not spending enough money while we were at it.

Shortly before the rest of my life picked me up by the Tibetan *yaket* and threw me onto a plane bound for university, I stopped by the Kumari Bahal, residence of the Living Goddess, barely a stone's throw from our flat, on the other side of Durbar Square. So absorbed had I been contemplating my own navel, I'd hardly given the sights of Kathmandu a second glance. I made a hurried last-minute effort and, raising a condescending eyebrow to a group of French tourists, stepped between two snarling lions and into the courtyard of the Royal Kumari.

It was quiet and other-worldly in that courtyard, even with the tour group murmuring among themselves. A patch of sunlight fell on a small tree. Carved wooden balconies and windows, intricate as lace, looked in on all sides. Serpents and fishes and monkeys, peacocks and lotuses, gods and goddesses twined about each other, binding Buddhist and Hindu as one in a gesture of co-devotion.

Hundreds of years ago, so the legend goes, the King of Kathmandu used to play dice with the goddess Taleju, the protective spirit of the Kathmandu Valley. One day the King made an improper advance, and the goddess was so angered that she threatened to withdraw her protection But the King begged her to stay and at last she relented. But so as to put herself beyond temptation's reach, she agreed to return only in the body of a pre-pubescent girl.

We waited while an attendant counted and pocketed his *baksheesh*. Then, like some paid-up Romeo, he called up to a window framed in gold-leaf on the third storey. "Eh, *Devi*!" – "Hey, Goddess!" Moments later there was a flicker of movement behind the shutters and the goddess appeared. She could only have been four or five years old but she was made up like a woman on a good night out. Her eyes were black with kohl like the eyes of Shiva, her lips were red, her clothes were red, her hair piled up under the famous peacock crown, and she was dripping in jewels. In the centre of her forehead was a third eye.

She looked down on us mere mortals for a few, dutiful moments before turning back to her devotions. But in that brief glance I read a mystery that had been missing from all the Om-ing and ah-ing that had been going on in Freak Street. I'd been searching for my inner child in a haze in some rat-ridden hole when she was personified right here for all to see, in a palace, one minute's walk away across the square. That look – a petulant, bored, sulky look – seemed designed to put me in my place. It warned me not to go away thinking I had understood anything about the real Kathmandu.

Fourteen years later the freaks had all gone, evaporated into respectability or the after-life. Of all the wacky vegan restaurants I'd frequented there was only one left and that had been tarred with the designer brush: black chairs and white formica tables and a canned version of Simon and Garfunkel's *I'd Rather Be A Sparrow* . . . playing in the background. It was empty. Our flat was now a sweat-shop making trousers with turn-ups and T-shirts that read:

NO one rupee
NO rickshaw
NO hashish
NO change money
NO problem!

Kathmandu had quadrupled in size. The population of Nepal had rocketed from 10 to 25 million with hordes of people descending on the capital to look for work. The demons of the West had caught up with Kathmandu: unemployment, deforestation, drug-addiction, crime, industrial pollution, river pollution, depletion of the water-tables, the cult of the car. Where there had been the jangle of bicycle bells, there was now the thrum of engines, exhaust fumes and the horns of thousands of irritated drivers.

The area around Durbar Square, though, was an oasis of quiet. It had been sealed off with bollards – Covent Gardenified – to prevent motorists gridlocking its narrow streets and to give the medieval buildings some relief from the invading miasma. And here, in the eye of the storm, in her secret chamber on the third floor of the Kumari Bahal, the child-goddess still perched on her throne, keeper of the soul of Kathmandu.

Of course, she wasn't the same child I had seen all those years ago. As soon as the Kumari bleeds – be it a scratch or a graze or, in the end, menstruation – the goddess abandons her and, insubstantial for a while, hangs around in the ether until she can possess another, unsullied, vessel. There had been two child incarnations (including this one) since I'd last been here. And this Kumari was as inaccessible as ever. Only her priestly entourage and her caretaker, I was told, or Nepali supplicants seeking her blessing, could be given an audience.

But more than ever, I was intrigued to know more about her. She had possessed much of my imagination for all these years and there were still so many questions I had unanswered. What was it like to be taken away from home at the age of two, to be isolated, worshipped and adored, to have such power, to hear the pleas of childless women and the yearnings of grown men, to perform rituals day after day, to hold a city in the palm of your hands, to look down on gawping tourists like me, to have the King of Nepal kneel at your feet; to feel the inspiration within you; to be a goddess?

Aware of my obsession, Laxmi had managed to arrange an interview with the Kumari who had reigned before this one. The girl we were about to meet, he told me, was now fifteen. Like all the Royal Kumaris before her, she would have undergone rigorous testing before she was chosen. She would have been born into the elite Buddhist *Sakya* caste of silver- and gold-smiths, and her parents would have put her name forward to a special committee, consisting of five Buddhist priests, a Brahmin priest and the royal astrologer. They would have checked her horoscope for propitious signs and finally received her, along with several other candidates – all between the ages of two and four – in a room in the Royal Palace, the Hanuman Dhoka, for a physical examination.

There, she would have been subjected to an ancient process of elimination. The committee would have scrutinised her for 32 physical perfections, the most obvious being that she was in perfect health, had black hair and eyes and no blemishes or bad body smells. The other aspects they were looking for were disconcertingly Lolita-esque. The Kumari must have thighs like those of a deer, for example, a neck like a conch-shell, a tongue that is small and sensitive and moist, a voice as clear and soft as a duck's, eyelashes like those of a cow; sexual organs that are small and well-recessed, feet and hands that are soft and firm. Strangely, for a child, she should also have forty teeth, cheeks like a lion, chest like a lion, and body like a banyan tree.

But it was the last test that had me unnerved. It would have been carried out a few weeks after the physical examination as final proof that the goddess had possessed this one particular child. On the black night of Kala Ratri, the eighth day of Dasain, the little Kumari-elect would have been led to the inner courtyard of Mul Chok where the goats and buffaloes had spilt their blood. Inside, the 108 buffalo heads would have been laid out in rows, butter-wick candles flickering between their horns. In the shadows lurked men with faces of demons. The child would have walked clockwise round the courtyard, in complete composure, then entered the shrine of Bhagmati, the terrible eight-armed goddess now splattered with gore. Finally, having betrayed not a flicker of fear, the priests would have led her to an upper story in the palace to worship her as the deity.

It was not just the thought of those executions last week that had me dragging my feet in the dark. It was the realisation that the Living Goddess was not the lovely creature she had seemed. Or rather, that I'd assumed her to be. To my Western eyes, despite the lipstick and the eye-black and the look of sultry disdain, I'd imagined this little girl as a symbol of charity and innocence – a female Christ-child perhaps.

Now I learnt that the Kumari goddess, and the demon-slayer I'd run into over Dasain, were one and the same. That the Kumari is Taleju in one aspect – the dice-playing temptress – but she is also Durga, the Mother Goddess, fierce as a tigress protecting her cubs. Those carvings on the balconies of the Kumari Bahal were not some benign guardian angel – they were images of Durga. The buffaloes and goats that got the chop in Mul Chok were demons that threatened the city. In her guise as Durga, the living goddess has them torn apart so she could bathe all her temples in conciliatory jets of their blood.

That the Kumari is a child is almost an irrelevance. It's her virginity – her eroticism, even – that give her her power: the unambiguous, awesome power of a woman untamed by man. This is why she dresses in reds – the *rajas* colours of married women: the blood red, scarlet, purple, pink, and not the *sattvik* whites and yellows of purity. This is why the people who seek her blessing are those with menstrual problems, or who are haemorrhaging or coughing blood. They come to seek help not from a goddess who is untainted by blood, but from one who revels in it.

I was no longer sure who, or what, would be waiting for us at the end of these alleyways, what the Kumari would be like, even three years after the goddess had left her. With all the traumas of severed heads and demons, the orphaned isolation, kingly indulgence and priestly repression, the prospect was daunting. Not to mention what had happened to her since that moment of her own, natural bloodshed: the immediate de-thronement; her return, jewel-less, crown-less, make-upless, to a family she no longer knew, to the horrors of insignificance.

Laxmi stopped at a door in a tiny odiferous courtyard down a dead-end street. I could feel a pulse choking under my ribs. He called up to a third-floor window. There was a rustle behind the shutters – oddly reminiscent it seemed – and a chink of light threw a blade into the darkness. In the split second before her father unlocked the door, the face of the ex-Royal Kumari passed above us like a moon between clouds. She was breathtakingly beautiful, unmistakable though I'd never seen this one before.

She was not in the room we were shown into and for a moment I wondered if I'd imagined her. But there were signs of her presence: a glass cabinet full of dolls and toys donated by tourists, a photograph of the little Kumari in full regalia – a beautiful, mournful child, and beneath it, as if by way of explanation, a sticker that read in English, "Smile on face, cry in heart".

We sat, Laxmi and I, on low chairs at a formica coffee-table, the inquisitors, while her father, beaming from ear to ear, ordered us tea. In came a disappointingly pasty woman in a sari – her mother.

After an interminable ten minutes of chat, and with no warning, the ex-Royal Kumari slipped into the room and took up her place on a sofa at the far end. She was wearing a purple *kurta* pinned at the neck with a tiny brooch, and a black knitted waistcoat. But it was an effort to notice these things. Her shyness and her beauty were intoxicating. She averted her eyes from us most of the time, gazing instead at the fingers twisting in her lap. But occasionally, when she heard Laxmi translating my questions, she would flash us a glance and a smile of such brilliance it made one want to weep.

Scarcely had she entered, however, than her two elder sisters stormed the place like pantomime dames. They were pretty-ish but big and fat and pushy. They were thrilled to find an audience for their English and intercepted my questions with lightning reflexes. They told me about the selection process, how they used to visit the Kumari, how they would bow and call her "God-sister", how she would play with her dolls, and occasionally the caretaker's children, how she was made up and dressed every day, of the queues of people waiting to see her. But all the while my blood boiled with frustration as I tried again and again to fire words past their defences.

Eventually, after half an hour, they upped and left. I thought the ex-Kumari would feel free to talk. But I was wrong. The ugly sisters had been playing a part that had evolved out of necessity. The more I tried to coax my subject to speak, the less she seemed able to do so. My questions were like chains that threatened to choke her. She would utter a word, a single, tiny, trilling sound that Laxmi and I strained to catch; then her parents would expand it into an answer. It was as if they were needed to magnify her thoughts, as if they were the channel between ether and the earth.

Yes – the Kumari suggested, in this roundabout way – she had wanted to play outside, to run and skip with other children, but she was a goddess so naturally she couldn't. Of course she wasn't frightened by all the blood on Kala Ratri. Yes, she had felt different as the Kumari.

She was the Devi then – the goddess.

The answers came back like rays of light through water. They were illuminating in a way, but they were difficult to pin to anything. I was hoping for pearls of wisdom, for a confession, for transports of religious fervour, for some of the defiance I had seen in the reigning Kumari. But her response left me empty-handed and disorientated.

Her answers about present life were a little more direct. But then this was straightforward. The hardest thing, she indicated, was negotiating the people and traffic in the streets. Until then she had only walked the length of her chamber. On the few occasions she had showed herself outside the Kumari Bahal, like on the festival of Indrajatra, she had been carried in a chariot. Life as a mortal was, literally, about finding one's feet.

She was at school now and having a hard time of it. As a goddess she was omniscient so, although she received schooling from her caretaker, it hadn't prepared her for ninth grade. She felt distant from the rest of her class. The principal still addressed "*namaste*" to her first, in deference to her past. She felt happier at home now, though she had felt angry and awkward at first.

And what of the future? Would she ever like to marry, have children? She smiled, a bashful yet sorrowful smile. Her parents didn't bother to expand. The likelihood of finding a man brave enough to marry her were remote. Most Nepalese men believe this would be the kiss of death, they would die horribly on the wedding-night if they married an ex-Kumari. Even men who were educated, worldly and less prone to superstition would be reluctant to take on a woman who might demand to be treated like a goddess, who wasn't used to doing the shopping.

The interview ended, an anti-climax. Most of the questions I had written down in my notebook had been crossed off unanswered. Yet the meeting had been mysteriously, circuitously, inspiring. She radiated sanctity this lovely, lonely creature and I had been moved in a way that made mockery of my journalistic interrogations. The emptiness at her core – that absent distraction, that serene, ethereal gaze – were how I imagined a person to look at the moment of death. An empty, beautiful shell. It had been been pointless – I saw that now – to ask about her time as a goddess. But I came away, at least, with an idea of what it was for her to be one no longer.

Outside, the world was a sordid place. A couple of crack-heads tried to beg money off us. Dogs fucked on a rubbish dump. Someone was crapping in the gutter. And back on the fume-filled thoroughfare the traffic jerked and blared though it was almost eight o'clock. A low-pressure smog had descended on the city. Somewhere beyond the cacophany, in the quiet of Durbar Square, it was comforting to remember that other little girl perched on her throne ready for battle. A few spots of rain began to fall as we headed for a rickshaw, and thunder rolled around the foothills in a long, protesting growl.

A sociable climber

Dawn John

Dawn John was more familiar with boardrooms than backpacks when she left her job and family in Britain to trek alone in Nepal. John, however, is no stranger to adventure: at 21, the former teacher gave birth to twin sons in a mission hospital in Ghana. Since then, she has gone on to have a successful career in the charity sector, and is currently director-general of the British Wheelchair Sports Foundation.

Two weeks before Christmas, I decided enough was enough, and resigned as a director of one of Britain's largest charities. Each of my three sons' response was: "What an opportunity at your age to rethink your life."

Early next morning, the phone began ringing: "How are you?" (the consensus being that I'd taken leave of my senses). Bouquets of flowers arrived, three job offers were floated, and numerous friends and colleagues inquired about what I would do next. Feeling too foolish to say I didn't know, I replied that I was going trekking in Nepal.

At 47, overweight and more familiar with a boardroom than the great outdoors, this news was met with stunned silence and then offers of company. No, I replied firmly, I was definitely going alone.

Out came the travel sections of the newspaper. I phoned, booked a flight to Kathmandu, and had my doctor pump me full of antibodies. I bought the necessary guidebooks and began looking forward to my departure in early January. All that remained was getting the right gear.

It was huge fun to breeze into outfitter shops in a designer suit and high heels, and announce to condescending young salesmen that I needed the gear for hiking in the Himalayas. I also found that the first rule of buying backpacking kit is to spend, spend, spend. My hiking boots remain the most expensive footwear I have ever bought, and initially the most uncomfortable. I practised wearing them around the house, tripping up and down stairs, much to everyone's amusement. A jacket with zip-in fleece lining came next, followed by special gloves, socks, a ridiculous hat with ear-flaps and a sleeping bag suitable for temperatures down to -20°C. In this fetching green-and-yellow combination, I looked like a huge wriggly caterpillar. Oh well, the indignity couldn't get any greater than the assistant shouting across the pharmacy shop, "This woman wants worm tablets. Are these OK?"

The first time I put on my shiny new backpack I fell over backwards. I looked in horror at the complexity of adjustable straps and clip-on extras. But eventually I mastered which strap adjusts what, and could change the weight from shoulders to bum quickly and efficiently, which impressed me enormously. I learned how to wear my two-pack – a large backpack on my back and my day bag on my front. It's quite comfortable once you accept that you look ridiculous anyway.

It was strange to leave my husband at Heathrow for the company of my fellow travellers: all young, relaxed and hippyish. What, I wondered, was I doing here? My backpack shone like a new penny amid their well-worn exhibits. In Qatar, I changed planes for the final leg and met Sarah, a young woman off to advise tourists at a remote luxury wildlife camp – despite the fact she had never set foot outside Europe before. She was shocked that someone her mother's age should be exploring alone. I was equally shocked that she should be offering advice.

As we flew further into the Himalayas, the Annapurna mountains were suddenly all around us. Each mountain was identified by George, an aid worker based in Nepal. At Customs, he rushed up to offer a lift to my guesthouse. I swung my back-pack over one shoulder, my day-pack over the other, and threw them into his waiting Land Rover. I soon found that the amazing thing about travelling alone is that people talk to you, offer help and advice. What was to make this journey special was the amazing people I met – all with stories to tell and aspirations to share.

Staying at the *Kathmandu Guest House*, I wondered why more hotels weren't like this. With rooms ranging from $2 to $60, a mix of people, a quiet garden, fax, international telephone, films showing: it's a great meeting place for a real mix of people. Gathered around a large brazier on cold nights, everyone meets to drink beer, eat, exchange stories and information.

The streets of Kathmandu are crammed with people during the day, but deserted at night, with restaurants and bars closing by 10pm. It seemed that marvels awaited around every corner of this congested city, and even when lost in the poorest area, one is greeted by smiles and greetings of *namaste*. During my first week in town, I met Lisa, an articulate Canadian lawyer who worked for Amnesty International. Though about sixty and suffering from Nepal tummy, she showed enviable commitment to her work. We visited a number of temples together, fending off gentle but persistent offers for guide services.

Lisa was one of many solo women I met during my first days. There was also Lucy, an American who had broken her journey home following three years in Greenland doing development work. She found the noise and bustle of Kathmandu too much. We walked the streets searching for Buddhist retreats, but all were closed for holidays in January and February. Here we met Janet, a young English teacher who was following a spiritual path while working locally. I shared a boozy dinner at a Mexican restaurant with Margaret. An attractive, intelligent woman in her fifties living in Kathmandu, she did nothing all day and had somehow lost her way. When asked what she felt she would be good at, she replied, "Inspiring other women". She gave me directions for one of my best treks.

One of my favourite companions was Sally, a 45-year-old Aussie woman. She had no formal qualifications and had spent her life visiting different countries, working where possible. She was smartly dressed in a silk shirt and slacks, but owned nothing and wanted nothing. She made little of the fact that she had just been mugged and knifed in Delhi. Carrying no money, she was "damned" if she would give the guy her torch. Unfortunately, she hadn't seen his knife.

Before I left Kathmandu, George wanted me to have a typical Nepalese meal. We started at my guesthouse with a beer, chased that with a pint of draught lager at a pub frequented by famous climbers, and continued through back streets to a local restaurant where we were the only non-Nepalese – and I was the only woman. Nepalese men danced, sang, played music and drank together. We were served a delicious *dal*, constantly refilled from an antique pot. We had an enjoyable evening and it was only when we got up to leave that I realised that I couldn't feel my face – it was numb. This was my first introduction to *raksi*, and I certainly treated the local firewater with more respect after that.

After the pleasures of Kathmandu, it was time to start hiking. I took a short flight to the mountain town of Pokhara and dumped my gear in a pre-booked hotel, full of partying Indians who did their best to ignore me. I walked about a mile up the road to the lakeside, where I sat in the sun enjoying a late lunch of cold beer, chilli chicken and fried rice. At the next table was an apparition – a beautiful six-foot-tall Viking with long red hair, dressed in a lime-green sari and hiking boots. Henrietta was a Danish artist, working mainly with photo images. She and I talked, found a guide, and agreed to leave the next morning for a two-day hike. First, though, we set out on a short walk to check if she was going to kill me. She was obviously very fit and I needed to show I could manage to hobble along at a credible pace.

But I passed muster, and we later enjoyed dinner together around the fire and met a young Dutch flight attendant also trekking alone. She was off the following morning with two Nepalese men she had met in Durbar Square in Kathmandu, a notorious pick-up spot. I worried about her until we re-met by chance and had dinner together in Kathmandu two weeks later.

The next morning, I set off with Henrietta and our guide, Amit, who had brought a porter to carry our small shared bag. We began walking at 10am, first crossing bamboo poles suspended over a fast-running river, then climbing at a steady rate. As I struggled, elderly locals strode past, disappearing in the distance. Henrietta sang as she marched, anything from lullabies to *Rule Britannia*, depending upon her mood. The ever-changing view was mystical and each change of direction brought a new vista. The haze and clouds added to the ethereal atmosphere. At 5pm, we stopped and dressed in all the clothes we possessed to watched the sun go down over Machhapuchhre and the Annapurnas. This was a moment to share with your closest, and the one time I regretted travelling alone.

In complete darkness, we scrambled down to our lodgings – a modest family home that Amit had led us to earlier – surprised that what had appeared a clear path in daylight was not so at night. By foul-smelling candlelight, Grandma had prepared *dal* and we shared *raksi* from a dirty plastic container with an old rag stuffed in the neck. Ambrosia! We clambered up a few rickety steps to our sleeping bags, with the front of the room open to the elements. It was -15°C and the family dog was eaten by a cougar during the night, but we slept like logs.

Waking at 5am, we almost missed the sun rising over distant hills. The fairytale scenery prompted constant daydreams as we walked up and down dales, meeting villagers everywhere. We stopped to have tea with three isolated women and their children. They knew no English and I spoke no Nepalese, but we shared jokes as they tried to give me an egg to take home. Using hand gestures, I explained it would break if I tried to carry it home. The older woman, who looked 65 but was probably younger than me, took off one of her two family bracelets to give to me. She owned very little and wanted me to have a gift. I was really touched. If I had been carrying anything to give in return, I would have loved to have accepted. So we laughed some more and left reluctantly. A row across the lake, a few miles' walk and we were back on the road to Pokhara.

On the eight-hour bus journey back to Kathmandu, I met a very handsome Ghurka who gave me insights into the Nepalese way of life, explaining all about a funeral procession we passed. When he left the bus on the outskirts of Kathmandu, I had a much better understanding of life in Nepal. When I had to leave the bus, I had no idea how to get my large backpack down off the roof. In desperation, I asked two fierce-looking young Afghani men if they could help. Piercing blue eyes stared into mine. "Pleasure", one said, and hauled himself onto the roof to throw down my bag. I was off once again with my pack looking for a taxi to my guesthouse.

I re-met many fellow travellers still in Kathmandu, plus British-born Jackie, who was with her Aunt Ada. They rushed like dynamos to collect visas for an upcoming trip to India and shop for Jackie and her Nepalese husband's lodge, *Forest Hideaway*, near Bardia, in a remote national park seventeen hours west of Kathmandu, along the India border.

In the spirit of adventure, I suddenly decided to join them for the long journey. Leaving at dawn, we drove all day and into the night, past ox carts and through dense jungle. We finally reached a remote clearing: no electricity, water, telephone or transport, only a spacious compound with a restaurant, bar and mud-thatched rooms. It was wonderful. After a warm welcome and cold beer, I unrolled my sleeping bag, drew the cords tightly, ignored the rats rustling in the thatched roof and went to sleep.

The next morning, I went tiger-hunting with two guides, each about 5ft tall and armed with a stick. As we walked through dense elephant grass, it occurred to me that if a tiger or elephant were 10ft away, we wouldn't see it in time to steer out of harm's way. I clambered over branches and forded a number of deep river flows. We watched two different types of crocodile and identified which were vegetarians, as this might prove useful.

A couple of nights later, real danger loomed: the area was attacked by rogue elephants. Through the thickness of my sleeping bag, I heard the crashing, chanting and banging of drums. I lay there wondering whether to go out, but decided there was little I could actually do to be helpful, so I rolled over and went back to sleep. The next morning over breakfast, I took a ribbing about my no-show and how I managed to ignore the danger of being trampled.

Soon it was time to return to Kathmandu. Sad goodbyes were said, and I rode the first thirty miles over rough road in an ancient army jeep. Schoolchildren along the route came out to wave to me, and at first I waved back enthusiastically until I began to feel rather foolish. We arrived at the bus stop, and I decided to ask for the loo. I was directed through tin shacks to a moveable tin shed perched on short wooden stilts in the middle of a paddy. The site was fifteen inches deep in human waste, but I needed a loo and this was it. I then walked up and down the wet fields for ten minutes afterward to clean my boots. No more rice for me. I didn't eat or drink again until I reached Kathmandu, as I was not ready for a repeat performance.

The bus eventually turned up with two VIP seats reserved for me: an unpadded bench at the front of the bus. It must be admitted that the Nepalese are not good travellers. At each turn, there was the sound of deep retching. I was grateful for my front seat. We stopped regularly for refuelling and snacks, and I saw many buses turned upside down in the bushes.

We eventually reached Kathmandu, no worse for wear. By now I had more friends here than in my hometown. Walking through the streets, I met friends, shared meals and ran into a couple that I had even met in Bardia. Rupert, Irene and I found that we had friends in common in West Africa – small world.

But soon it was time to go home to my own world. I arrived at Heathrow late at night, wearing my hiking gear and carrying my well-travelled pack, and was met by my distinguished grey-haired husband carrying a bouquet of roses. I am not an intrepid traveller. I enjoy the easy life of nice hotels, rental cars and taxis, but they weren't an option in Nepal. Not only did I not miss them, but I enjoyed pitting my wits against transportation or accommodation problems. If you are fairly careful, it is great fun travelling alone. You can make all your own decisions, visit where you want to and stay as long as you like. There is a whole world of experiences and friends you haven't yet met. Would I do it again? Try to stop me.

read on . . .

Arlene Blum (preface), Maurice Herzog, *Annapurna: A Woman's Place* (1978; US: Sierra Club Books, 1998). Twenty years ago, Arlene Blum and twelve other women set out for Annapurna in the Nepal Himalayas, to make the first ascent of the world's tenth-highest mountain by an American and by a woman. It was a huge achievement, which hardly needs the abundant woolly metaphors (mountains left to climb, difficult goals to strive towards, and so on) to make it well worth republishing.

★ **Monica Connell,** *Against a Peacock Sky* (UK/US: o/p). Beautiful, impressionistic rendering of life among the *matawaali* (alcohol-drinking) Chhetris of Jumla District, capturing the subtleties of village life in Nepal.

Katharine Bjork Guneratne, *In the Circle of the Dance: Notes of an Outsider in Nepal* (US: Cornell University Press, 1999). Guneratne accompanies her anthropologist husband to rural Nepal and tries hard to integrate herself into village life. Her participation in a traditional women's circle dance seems to symbolise her eventual acceptance. Her frank, conscientious and insightful account of setting up home in the village and tackling the many and various communication problems should be riveting reading for anyone considering a lengthy stay in the country.

Rajendra S Khadka (ed), *Travelers' Tales: Nepal* (US: Travelers' Tales Inc., 1997). Another excellent anthology of extracts and original compositions distilled from over five decades of travel to Nepal. Notable entries include Monica Connell, Jan Morris and Barbara Scot.

Dervla Murphy, *The Waiting Land: A Spell in Nepal* (1967; UK: Flamingo, 1998/US: Overlook Press, 1990). Having spent six months working with Tibetan refugees in Dharamsala at the end of her epic bicycle journey from Ireland to India, Murphy turns her attention to their plight in Nepal. Though captivated by the "friendly gaiety and inconsequential craziness" of Kathmandu, she chooses to spend most of her time organising work, shelter and other necessities of life for some 500 refugees in the less colourful but equally appealing town of Pokhara. Here, much to the horror of the Nepalese community who "suspect the integrity – or even the sanity – of a European who fails to maintain European standards", she lives simply, sleeping on the floor of her tiny room and washing herself and her clothes in the river. But this is a book as much about Tibetans in exile as about Nepal. Writing with her usual blend of honesty, insight and, above all, respect for diverse cultural traditions, Murphy is particularly forthright when dwelling on the day-to-day difficulties inherent in trying to support a disenfranchised people without depriving them of their spirit of integrity and independence.

Durga Pokhrela and Anthony Willet, *A Shadow over Shangri-La: A Woman's Quest for Freedom* (US: Brassways, 1996). Brutally interrogated and imprisoned for eight months following her participation in the struggle against the ruling Panchayat regime, high-caste lawyer and activist Durga Pokhrel spent her time in prison petitioning for others less privileged than herself. On her release she fled Nepal, attended Harvard and married a British development specialist, co-author of this memoir. Pokhrela's accounts of her prison experiences make harrowing reading yet her tone of unflagging optimism and determination to survive carry you through. An inspiring tale, which lapses into a rather formal style from time to time but keeps its integrity of spirit.

Barbara J Scot, *The Violet Shyness of their Eyes: Notes from Nepal* (US: Calyx Books, 1993). Motivated by the desire to so some good for the world's second-poorest nation, Scot takes a voluntary job teaching English in a Nepalese village. Before long she is questioning the premises of voluntary work, the value of English within rural villages and reconsidering who benefits whom. While never skirting the hardships and injustices she encounters, Scot's growing respect for the Nepalese way of life is palpably expressed. Her eye for evocative detail, from children shivering at village taps to the stale-sweet smell of an overcrowded bus, combine with a mass of everyday anecdote to create a sympathetic and vivid travel memoir.

New Zealand

Champagne at Welcome Flat

Gail Andrews

Gail Andrews is a Canadian writer living in Toronto. After graduating from university, she and her closest friend since childhood, Marketa Havlik, set off for a year touring and working in New Zealand and Australia. This is just one of many stories from that year. Gail is currently working on a screenplay which she wrote in New Zealand.

A candle flickers beside us, casting light over the pool. Steam rising from the water clogs our eyes and noses. We open the champagne. Exploding like a gun in the night, the cork slams into a nearby bush. A sweet reward for a long trek. I pour the champagne into two semi-fragile plastic glasses and set them down on their stubby plastic stems.

We are neck-deep in a bubbling hot spring, nestled against the bottom of New Zealand's largest glacier. A candle jammed into the neck of a bottle, a glowing indigo Timex watch and two well-used towels lie at the edge of the pool. The watch says it is midnight soon. Two German boys come down from the trail and strip naked except for their glasses, sliding their thin tanned bodies into the opposite end of the spring. In the sky we can barely see the black craggy silhouettes of the mountains. A bright moon hides behind one of the peaks. On the ground it is dark, except for a comforting circle of light thrown by the candle. Four rounded reflections from the Germans' spectacles shine across the pool, causing me to giggle.

All the others are asleep – a hut full of hikers who care little for New Year's Eve. All they really want is some rest. They will be rising at five and six am to climb again. Most will go back the way they came, over the Fox Glacier and back down the other side. Since the watches are not co-ordinated, there is some confusion as to when it turns midnight. We drink the champagne anyway. One minute past twelve is no different from 11:59, 12:02. And it isn't. The same still calm hangs in the air before as after, the glacier in its millennia shrugging off another human year with complete indifference. We splash around a little more, then call it a night. The quiet here is catching.

This hot spring is a favourite with mountain climbers, who soak in its soothing mineral waters after a gruelling climb from the other side of the glacier. They even call this area the Welcome Flat. We cheated, driving ourselves around the mountain and trekking in on the Copland Trail. The hot springs are our destination, rather than a bonus prize. Not to mention that, this early in the New Zealand springtime, the rocky, icy climb over the glacier is more than slightly beyond our level of expertise. Even the hike had taken us all day. We arrived shortly after dinner, not long before some of the weary climbers were drifting off to sleep. Our backpacks were both crammed with food. As North American as we are, we could not fathom New Year's Eve without champagne. Besides the bottle of bubbly, we had also hauled a large number of chocolates, cheese and milk powder. *Fettuccine Alfredo* was on the menu for dinner.

Two months of trekking through this country had brought us to an understanding: we are soft-core hikers, willing to brave anything as long as the food tastes good. We learned this lesson the hard way, after an arduous three-day hike on Stewart's Island for which we were notoriously unprepared. We brought a loaf of bread, some cheese and several pears for three days. It was only through the kindness of fellow travellers that we managed not to starve or get ill. Warding off hypothermia with cups of warm tea from the billies of strangers was lesson enough. Our trip to Stewart's Island had given us respect for the power of this country and an understanding of the capacity of our bodies to explore it. We trekked all over New Zealand, from southern tip to northern extremity, well aware that we should not be able to do what we were doing and accomplishing our goals time and time again.

Today, we had reason to be proud. Mud slides had recently destroyed the banks of several rivers, washing out the track and all signs of the proper direction. We left this morning from the coast and trekked for eight hours, over the longest, roughest stretch of the Copland Trail. It was as if the hot springs were not letting us get off that easy, making us work like the others for a chance to soak in its warmth. We were terrified and brave enough to try our first river ford on the last night of the year. Up to our knees in muddy run-off, convinced we were at the limits of extreme trekking. Many times we were forced to climb up raw piles of dirt, bare rocks and boulders which had been uncovered by the slide. We did not know the way. Only at last, when we saw others returning, could we be sure that we were on the right track. We could have been anywhere.

Where we finally came to rest was at the top of the Copland valley, in which nestled the Welcome Flat hut. With padded mats for sleeping and gas-powered stoves which roared when lit in the centre of the hut, it was heaven: two floors of warm, dry space. On 1 January, we wake to an almost empty cabin. The hikers are off and the sun sits well risen in the sky. It is probably 8:30 in the morning. We make porridge for breakfast, with brown sugar and travel mugs full of instant coffee. Our one concession to being on a hike is the instant coffee, a dreaded substance which reminds us that we are far from town. We dress, roll our sleeping bags up off the floor mats and stuff our gear back into our packs. Leaving our heavy knapsacks at the door of the hut, we stroll out onto the porch. Someone has killed a possum, probably for the screeching noise it was making during the few precious hours of climber's rest. We walk up toward the spring, leaving the bloodied grey body lying in front of the hut.

During the day, the warm water repels us. The hot spring bubbling in its yellow mud is not so refreshing in the heat of New Zealand's fast-approaching spring and summer months. A taut swing bridge lures us away from murky steam. From the middle of the bridge, we see farther up the valley where a long, wild rush of spring water streams away from the shiny white glacier. Jagged mountains look down on all sides. Blue skies sparkle above their peaks. Along the valley floor a long clear river runs with the most intense clarity.

Pebbles shine from the bottom, each stone visible from the surface. The cold run-off is clear and inviting. Walking along an old path through already thigh-high grasses at the edge of the stream, we notice the mud slide has not affected this part of the valley. Mountain walls and river beds lie undisturbed.

We walk as far as the path will let us. My legs are glad for the long stretch, grateful for flat land after the arduous trek the day before. Walking freely and chatting infrequently, we are good travellers, comfortable enough in silence to admire what transpires around us. We have been friends for ten years. What brought us to New Zealand was different in motive, but the experience we share is the same. Sweat beads at my hairline and I stop to tie my sweatshirt around my waist. How beautiful the stream looks, flowing brightly to my left. After several kilometres, I am too hot for comfort. The water seems clean enough to drink, but when we stop and rest, I regretfully drink the warmish liquid from our thermos. I know the crystal-clear waters in this country are not always fit for drinking, even though they seem it. A reasonable chance of getting sick is still a chance I am not willing to take. Sliding my day pack from around my waist, I sit down on the edge of river bank and strip my feet of socks and boots. Cold pierces my toes when I dangle them in the stream. Removing her fleecy green jacket from her waist, Marketa wipes sweat from the back of her neck. We are both ridiculously hot. We have to go swimming.

We strip naked in the wide-open privacy of the valley. The cold is excruciatingly good. We splash like infants in a pool in the park at home. I plunge my pale white body into the stream, paddle fiercely in an attempt to cool off and warm up at the same time. A few seconds feels like several minutes. No wonder; I am swimming in freshly melted ice. The glacier chuckles in the distance. Our clothes lie like trophies in the grass and I fish my camera out of one of the pockets. We take pictures to prove to ourselves, and to everyone else, how truly stupid we are. Then we climb out of the stream. Clothes off, into the water, out of the water, get a picture, get back into our clothes, shiver all the way back to the cabin, have lunch.

They say you spend the rest of your year the way you spend New Year's Day, a fact I have been keenly aware of, each hour of every January first since I was a kid. There was the year I became so hung over, I was sick all day. There were years I lay guiltily on the couch in flannel pyjamas watching bad television. There was the year I went cross-country skiing with my father in fresh powdery snow, crossing acres of fabulous green cedars and laughing together as he fell time and time again. And then, there is still this year to come.

read on . . .

Janet Frame, *The Complete Autobiography* **(UK: The Women's Press, 1999/US: George Braziller, 1991).** Though widely acclaimed for her novels, short stories and poetry, Janet Frame is probably best known for the wonderfully rich and complex autobiography which inspired Jane Campion's award-winning film, *Angel at My Table*. The first two of three volumes tell of her childhood and adolescence in New Zealand, growing up in the 1920s and 1930s in a poor but intensely literate family, through to her isolation as a student and a series of spells in mental hospital where she was diagnosed with schizophrenia. In the third part Frame sets sail for Europe, gains success as a writer and, seven years later, returns to her much-loved homeland where she is astonished to be the centre of attention, "as famous, rich, a woman of the world, sane, insane, inevitably different from the shy unknown who had departed". This is a beautifully written, moving, funny and disarmingly honest account of emerging from the magic of childhood into the dark realms of supposed madness and the salvation found from writing fiction.

Norway

Cod and cloudberries

Kirrily Johns

On completing university in Australia, Kirrily Johns decided to embark on an adventurous tour of Europe, which took her through London, France, Spain, Turkey and Russia. An old college friend of hers, Clare, introduced her to Melinda, a fellow Australian, also on a gap year, and Therese, a Norwegian who was just about to return home for the end of the summer vacation and the start of the new academic year. Before their money ran out and the inevitable employment in London ensued, Kirrily travelled with her new friends to the far north of Norway, in search of Therese's summer retreat and the midnight sun.

"Come to Norway," Therese enthused. "We can all stay in my family's cabin in Hamaroy. My grandmother will be happy to see us and we'll have so much fun." I imagined the four of us, Therese, Clare, Melinda and I whiling away a lazy summer in a cabin on an island well above the Arctic Circle, lying on the grassy roof and staring at a light night sky. Therese had already coloured in a few details from her childhood summers, but even without these happy reminiscences it was an offer too enticing to refuse.

Various plans were arranged, discarded and changed, but eventually we agreed that Clare would join me in Barcelona, where I was stuttering to the end of a Spanish course, and that, together, we'd travel north picking up Melinda en route. Therese would go on ahead to prepare the cabin and meet us all at the ferry port of Hamaroy. It turned out to be a mammoth trip: a hundred hours on trains through seven countries, all without a shower and very little sleep.

Cheerful and optimistic, Clare and I sped from Barcelona to Paris on the night-train, although it had transpired that our reserved seats did not exist. Clare wilted visibly on the journey, reacting badly, it seemed, to something she'd eaten just before catching the train, but we arrived more or less intact at the Gare du Nord, where the Eurostar trains to Paris hurtle in from London Waterloo. Melinda had assured us she would be on one of them, and indeed she did finally stride down the platform, backpack swinging and a grin on her face. We had time only for a hello and a hug before we had to whisk her away to buy a ticket to Brussels. The carriage, once we found it, was to be shared with a Saudi family of six, who consumed an astonishing number of litre bottles of Coke a day. "It's not cheap," the father complained.

We had planned to spend a night in the Belgian capital, but were distracted by the sight of a train heading for our next destination, Copenhagen. We paid for reserved seats and leapt on. Unfortunately, a very large troupe of boy scouts had decided to make the same journey. As they did not have reservations, three hundred straggly boys, wilting under backpacks, sleeping bags and saucepans, parked themselves in the corridor outside our compartment, destroying our plans for a safe snooze. There were sniggers, smiles and cheeky waves; some even wore Viking hats. The boys collapsed into a noisy squashed heap for the night, while we took comfort in Belgian chocolates.

By the time we arrived in Copenhagen, the whiff from our carriage was overpowering, but we rejoiced in a brisk stretch around the streets, filling our stomachs with a picnic before returning to the station. After enduring nights of heads vibrating against glass and hourly disturbances, we decided to treat ourselves to a sleeping compartment, so that when we next awoke it was to a green fuzz outside the window, the pine forests of Norway. We greeted our close green horizon with an excited shriek. By the time the train was heading from Oslo to Trondheim, three hundred miles to the north, its passengers had turned into tall hikers dressed in knickerbockers and knee-length red socks, who carried long walking sticks. We had a day to kill at Trondheim, so we went to find a café and took advantage of endless free refills of warm coffee. Afterwards we struggled with the

Norwegian menu, attempting to learn some words, thrilling to the prospect of hot food.

Back on the platform the crisp summer air had begun to work its way into our tired bones and we had to dance frenziedly to keep warm. Other passengers conspicuously consulted their tickets and made hand signals – which we later discovered meant "They are crazy". Once again underway, we snuggled into our sleeping bags and gossiped of dreams and the past, trying not to disturb too much of the carriage with our bursts of laughter. Drifting in and out of sleep and tunnels I saw a hazy vision of every shade of green, and vast fjords of blue glitter flashed by. Bathed in a low light, rugged peaks, forests and expanses of water emerged into my line of sight. It was summer and I was surprised to see so much snow on the mountains.

Reaching Bodo in the north, the only thing that separated us from Therese was a fjord and a ferry that didn't leave until evening. A good-looking boy at the tourist information office courteously rang Therese's grandmother to tell her that we would be catching the late ferry. She lived not far from the holiday cabin, where Therese had already been staying for a week. The ferry was not due to depart for some hours, so in bored anticipation we plodded a circuit around the town looking at closed shops and sheltering from the drizzle in cafés and the information bureau.

At last the ferry arrived at Hamaroy and pulled alongside a drooping timber dock dotted with red wooden sheds. Therese was waiting for us. She swung her arms wildly and shouted "*Elg!*" It was the one Norwegian word she had managed to teach us in our time together in London. It meant moose. "*Elg!*" we enthusiastically responded, ignoring the surprised looks of the dockers. We jumped off the boat, hugged and blurted out the highlights of our epic travels while Therese ushered us towards the car she had borrowed.

Hamaroy is a watery area of lakes, fjords and beaches. Our cabin had red timber walls and, as promised, a tufty green grass roof. We stepped inside, thankful to get out of the chill, moist air, and gazed admiringly at the wooden floors and walls brightened by cosy rugs and coloured furniture: a blue table, red couch, traditional wooden sten-cilled chest and lots of gorgeous clutter. Within moments we made ourselves at home, and settled into delightful chatter, staying up until five or six o'clock in the morning. The talk took in all kinds of trivialities and profundities: food, men, what we wanted from life. The pattern was set, and over the next few days we teased confessions out of each other, made brownies, knitted socks (in Therese's case), and talked on and on while the fire crackled in the grate, going to bed in the small hours and not waking till afternoon.

The light would dwindle to pale at about 11 o'clock in the evening and return refreshed one hour later at midnight. "I feel revived when I come up here," Therese said. The same charm had begun to work on us.

We knew Therese in London as a wild city girl, happy in a miniskirt, snakeskin and heels, but here she seemed equally content to sit knitting by the fire. Intelligent, confident, easily bored and impulsive, her interests ranged across a huge spectrum from opera to rock to fishing. She and her parents live in Oslo, coming north to Hamaroy every summer to visit her grandma and replenish stores of energy for the rest of the year. One day we found ourselves dancing on the grass roof, to the sound of Roberta Flack emanating from the chimney, against a 360-degree backdrop of mountains and water. All dreams seemed possible.

Therese was intent on sharing her pride in her homeland, and in the afternoons took us exploring. She had an explanation or story for every site we visited, knowledge gleaned from a lifetime of summers. She pointed out a hole in the ground where the locals smoked salmon, and a haunted house which was the scene of a stolen first kiss. She led and we followed, our considerate translator and guide in this land of strange light. We decided to look for cloudberries, small round pale yellow berries that have a subtle strawberry flavour and are a local delicacy. Like real Norwegians out for a hike, we took chocolate in case of being trapped in a snowstorm, although it was the middle of summer and snow was highly unlikely. We set off through wild flowers and rocky ground towards the beach. Patches of earth were concealed by soft moss and shrubs, which bounced under our feet.

No-one will tell you where the wild cloudberry bushes grow, nor how many berries are stored in their fridge. The ones we found we stored in our stomachs, and we quenched our thirst with water tasting of earth from a stream that flowed down from the mountains. A walk alongside the beach provided a range of sensory experiences, not least the ooze and squelch of grey mud between our toes. We listened to sheep bells clanging and looked for shells. The wind blew through the scrub and across the rough sand. At midnight the sun was visible on the horizon as a streak of weak light. We puffed our way back to the car.

On another occasion Therese bustled us aboard a sailing ship which was heading up the fjord: the *Anna Rodge*, built in 1886. She had gleaming decks and bright white sails. Mid-fjord the engine was cut, and the crew went to work, sliding up masts, yanking on ropes and unfurling the sails, which then spluttered into life. Then, in complete silence, we sailed on amongst the craggy rocks and mountains. On board we were approached by a woman who wanted to know how we liked Norway, and asked to be photographed with us. Later, Therese informed us that she was a well-known Norwegian actress, here to participate in a festival to celebrate the work of a distinguished author called Hamsun. When the ship docked at Tranoy, a tiny settlement of coloured wooden houses, we went to visit an exhibition of work inspired by Hamsun that was being held as part of the festival. An artist, Arne Moen, a middle-aged man in checked shirt and a beard, with a knife tucked into his belt, was curating his own pieces. He chuckled and basked in our art history student admiration, then, after chatting about his work, made us all delicious heart-shaped waffles.

Therese had organised the trip in her usual enthusiastic and spontaneous style, and had not mentioned that the boat would drop us back at the far side of the island. She had assumed there would be a bus. Not speaking the language or knowing our way around, we followed her every whim, but it emerged that hitchhiking was our only option for getting home. So we waited by the road and all four of us stuck out our thumbs. For part of the way we were given a lift by a genteel elderly couple, but then we had to walk for some time, thumbs out and singing, before a sports car whizzed past, stopped, and reversed back. Inside were two large and spotty young men, and a back seat full of food and sex videos. As our alternatives were limited, we squashed in. The music was turned up, the car accelerated, and in no time we were dropped at our door. The next day they returned: "Is there a party?" they asked.

"No," we replied. It emerged that Therese had mentioned the possibility in Norwegian, as a parting "thank you" when we clambered out of the car. They had clearly washed the car and ironed their shirts in honour of the non-existent event. They sat and stared at the floor while we ate dinner. Then they left.

Therese's grandmother was a friendly presence who hovered in the background throughout our stay, dropping off gifts of food or sending them via Therese. She was shy of us foreigners, who spoke none of her language and had to mime all the time, and preferred to leave us to our antics. Occasionally, though, we would pass her on the gravel path from the cabin, and we'd all break into smiles and waves, racking our brains for some gesture to show our appreciation of the copious quantities of bread and cakes she supplied us with. The fresh bread was offered with a variety of toppings, including mayonnaise, salami, caviar and *Brunost*, a sweet caramelised cheese.

In honour of the Hamsun festival, a bonfire and an outdoor tango concert were arranged on the rocks by the lighthouse. We arrived late to what was a substantial gathering, where the tango dancing was well underway. Therese's cousins gave us wreaths made of wild flowers, which by old custom were worn at midsummer (intended to represent purity, but now a dying tradition). All eyes followed the dancing, and many joined in, including us with our own sketchily improvised version. People said kindly, "You dance the tango so well", but none of us came even close to the standards of the slick and accomplished couples manoeuvring around us. In the cold night air, the thoughts of hot Argentine passions made us shiver. Later, we warmed our hands and faces by the bonfire and looked out over the sparkling fjord, above which jutted the blue and pink Lofoten mountains. The light grew more rosy and the mountains became dark silhouettes as dawn approached and the fire died.

We were to catch fish the next day for Therese's grandmother's kitchen, so in the family boat and navy boiler suits we rowed down the fjord towards the sea. At first the water was rough but then it adopted a calm and mystical silver blue. There were no other boats; ours was surrounded by the dazzling beauty of the land and seascape. We threw the lines into the water and held on. Suddenly and unexpectedly my line was yanked hard by the weight of a hooked fish. I started to haul it in and discovered that it was a sizeable cod. Therese taught us how to hold the fish and pull out the hook without it squirming too much. We learnt to gut a sharp cut of the belly, a hand in the slimy goo, rip and sever the head. For dinner that night we had an exquisite cod with sour cream. On another night, we had whale. All thoughts of political correctness went to the wind while

Grandmother cooked a cream stew of delicately sliced whale flesh, which had a distinct flavour and tender texture. It was quite an experience.

Therese taught us more than how to gut fish and how to appreciate whale flesh: she shared numerous insights on Norwegian art, literature and culture, and showed us a landscape almost too wild to describe. Like most Norwegians she understands the beauty of her country. She respects its heritage and feels safe in its wildernesses. At a local supermarket I met an Australian woman who had hitchhiked to Skutvick fifteen years earlier, where she had met and married a local man, and lived ever since. "It's the Norwegians," she told me, when we tried to pin down the charm of the place, "they have a special knowledge. They just think on a much deeper plane than anyone else."

read on . . .

Janet Garton, *Contemporary Norwegian Women's Writing* **(UK: Norvik Press, 1995/US: Dufour Editions, 1995).** An excellent collection of essays, short stories and extracts of plays, from the beginnings of Norway's "New Wave Feminism" in the 1970s to the more fantastical literature of the last decade.

Mary Wollstonecraft, *Letters Written during a Short Residence in Sweden, Norway and Denmark* **(1795; UK: Penguin, 1987/US: University of Nebraska, 1976).** For reasons never made entirely clear, Wollstonecraft, author of *A Vindication of the Rights of Women* and mother of Mary Shelley, travelled Scandinavia for several months in 1795. Her letters home represent a real historical curiosity, though her trenchant comments on the state of Norwegian society often get sidelined by her intense melancholia.

Pakistan

Hotel Holiday

Kathleen Jamie

Kathleen Jamie is best known as one of Scotland's most accomplished poets. At age nineteen she won the prestigious Eric Gregory Award and has since published four volumes of poetry, each to critical acclaim. She grew up in Midlothian and now lives on the north coast of Fife with her two young children. In the intervening years she has travelled widely, including two long solo visits to Pakistan, which formed the material for her travel book *The Golden Peak* (see p.469). Setting the scene of the incident in Karachi that she describes below, she writes: "I was making my way home, slowly, after a long trip to China and northern Pakistan. Thin and tired, I took a night-flight from Islamabad to Karachi. I had a ticket from Karachi to London. Karachi was hotter than hell. All I had to do was put up for a couple of days, and argue my way onto a flight home. The flights were always overbooked. The hotel I chose at random was clean, and on a relatively quiet side-street. I didn't need any more hassle."

The room had no view: one window looked onto the corridor, the other into a nasty concrete well formed by buildings packed together. I didn't like it, so looked at the fan. And what if the fan came away from the ceiling, came chopping down to the bed where I lay? What if a fire broke out? Where to jump? Three floors down a pit. You're tired. I told myself. Time to go home.

There were fissures in the green-washed plaster, a line of ants travelled up and down a crack beside the door. I watched them, waiting for the ants to bear away time, moment by moment, until the long day was over. I watched the ants until the air was hot and I was bored enough to go out into the corridor.

Behind the open doors of the other rented rooms, men in vests and baggy trousers were rising. From the corner of my eye I saw how they scratched their bellies, carefully brushed their moustaches. I kept my head down, didn't want the men to catch me looking. The walls at each end of the corridor were built of open-work breeze-blocks. If you looked through the gaps of this rough screen you could peer out at the city: flat roofs and TV aerials, buildings half built or half torn down, a mash of wires, wheeling birds. Below, Suzuki-rickshaws turned the corners from alleys into streets, the first traffic horns crowed at the rising sun as the city went to work.

There was a time when work meant a few fishing boats being pulled down the sand to the languid sea. Where was the sea? The desert I'd flown over last night? Out there in the grey-pink haze. The eyes of the preening men followed me back down the corridor; or perhaps I had just imagined it. I locked the door, adjusted the curtain, lay on the bed and waited for the ants to do their work. What's wrong? I asked, and answered myself, *just really tired*, unsettled by the changes, the midnight flight, the hours at the airport waiting for time to pass until I could move safely into town like a peasant at dawn.

So the city was going to work. Me, I could take another shower and, in the privacy of my room, lie under the turning fan. It was still getting hotter and the drains were foul. Before it was too hot I would go for some food, a wander in the bazaar. Now, in the city, my clothes shamed me. Rich girl, Western girl, can't you keep your clothes clean, can't you buy more? No. I had no more money. The fan wobbled on its stem. What if it *did* sheer off? Metal fatigue. I lay on the bed, covered my eyes with my arm.

★ ★ ★ ★

Someone was knocking. It seemed unlikely, a mistake, so I did nothing at first, but he knocked again. I rose from the bed, draped a *dupatta* over my *shalwar kameez*, and twitched the curtain. A man not much older than myself, perhaps thirty, was standing back, waiting. He was dressed in the Western manner, a white tennis shirt and jeans. Jeans, in this heat. He knocked again, and again stood back waiting for me to answer, as I would. After all, I was brought up to look at people if they spoke to me, to answer their knocking, and not be rude.

"I am manager," he said, "*Hotel Holiday*. I am come to check room."

This was laughable.

"I am sleeping. The room's fine."

"I am checking."

"I am sleeping."

"Okay, sleep. I will check room. Sleep, please."

He came in, checking the room. He was manager, he could go where he liked. He began to move around the room. Checking, elaborately. He flicked the electricity switches with thin fingers. The bare bulb glared on, off, and the fan stopped, wobbled briefly, then resumed speed and its dull thudding. He assessed the door, ignoring the string of ants. As he crossed the room I stood between the two single beds, one untouched, one with a rumpled sheet. He shouldn't be here, but now the room was full of him. He pressed his hand to the window, three storeys up the tight dirty pit. He looked at the floor, at my rucksack and book, at the little table with a water-flask and my scatter of objects. He looked at my dirty clothes steeping in a wash-pail beneath a rim of grey scum.

Soon he would look at me. He tilted back his head to check the ceiling.

"It's still there," I said, "the ceiling."

"Sleep, please."

"No."

Now he dropped his gaze to me. With a long arm, he indicated the rumpled bed. In a sense, his own bed. Mr Manager.

"Is okay."

So ludicrous I wanted to smile. To smile while he was showing me the bed would have been a wrong thing to do.

"Now you have checked, everything is in order, please leave."

A thin face, black moustache; tall, thin legs in his jeans.

"You are lone?"

"Please leave now."

"You, what country are? Student are?"

That Urdu phrasing, carried into English.

"How long you are Pakistan, how many days?"

He was edging toward the door. If I took a small step forward, he took one back. It was alright. But now he stopped, right between me and the exit. That was silly, I told myself. He was still asking his questions: husband, family, country. You are? You are country? Father? Husband?

Childrens? Brothers? No childrens?

Soon he'll be gone, I thought, I will shut the door, bolt it. Then I will wait until the ants bear away the moments. No, I'll go and ask the fat uncle at the desk downstairs to tell me what the manager looks like.

I bet he doesn't look like this manager, the one moving slowly toward the threshold, his clean white shirt, jeans. It occured to me he may have chosen this outfit specially. It occured to me that he didn't realise he was blocking my exit. It was not a deliberate manoeuvre.

At the last moment, he turned to face me, one hand on each side of the door frame.

"You want fucking?"

"What?"

"You want fucking?"

"Just get out."

★ ★ ★ ★

I don't feel safe, don't feel safe, don't feel safe in the Hotel Holiday. Round my head like the madly cheerful theme-tune of a TV gameshow. I put on the works: *dupatta*, shoulder bag securely over my head, the vast grubby-white shawl with little flecks of mirror sewn on, to reflect the world back on itself should it look at me. *I don't feel safe in the Hotel Holiday*. I could take my things and walk out. It would be simple if my passport wasn't locked in a drawer behind the fat uncle's desk. He sat under a picture of Mecca and a board of keys. As I handed over mine, my keys, my room, I asked about the manager. The description matched.

"You want to see manager?" asked the fat uncle.

"Thank you, I don't."

★ ★ ★ ★

The hotel's entrance was on an alley between two thoroughfares of Saddar Bazaar. In the bright sunlight outside, a young man was stripping down a motorcycle. It was not the manager. A café on the corner, open to the street, served noisy men with tea and *paratha* as the fans turned over their heads and a family of kittens mewed about their ankles. I looked from under my shawl. The manager was not there. At the tourist office they recommended the YMCA, but I was a woman, they wouldn't take me.

They said there was a YWCA on Jinnah Road. I walked out of Saddar Bazaar to Jinnah Road through a quiet street, where low modern buildings hid behind purple scented shrubs. A tonga clip-clopped by, a taxi. I tried to walk slowly, to breathe the flowers' scent and still my mind.

Though the huge mirror-flecked *chador* covered my hair, shoulders, breasts, though I wore *shalwar kameez*, I was walking on the street. A man was coming towards me. He was in Western clothes: tight white trousers and a red shirt. I, wearing Eastern, walked toward him, trying not to look at him as the space between us narrowed. As we passed, predictably enough, he grabbed my breast, then began to run. I turned and yelled, called him a cowardly little bastard as he minced away in his tight white trousers. *But I am playing by the rules. I stayed in my room. When I come out, I am covered*, like a naughty squawking parrot who has learned to screech obscenities. Run, yes run, you cowardly bastard.

For a long time my breast felt the painful grasp of his hand, as amputees are said to feel a ghostly limb. I didn't wonder whether, for an equally long time, at some other place in this hot noisy city, that man was holding the swell of my body in his hand; and if so, whether the sensation was cherished or abhored.

Perhaps Jinnah Road would be a street of scented shrubs, the YWCA a low quiet building. Maybe there would other single girls there, young women from Europe, from Pakistan. It would be a laugh. We could sit in the shade of trees and drink tea, friends for the day.

The scented street led me back into a busy bazaar with stalls of watches and shopping trolleys, fryers of samosas, an ice-cream parlour. I walked too quickly, dabbing sweat from my face with the shawl. Once, I had a conversation with the keeper of a silk shop He said: "*it is because of pornography*". Through the shawls, behind the door of the hotel room they see the same woman, the *Anglaise* with short hair and no husband, the same as in the pictures circulated among friends. Imagine! She is here! In your hotel, on your very street. Remember, he did ask as if it were a service: you want fucking?

Jinnah Road was fast and dirty with fumes, bad diesel, twostroke.

Painted trucks tinkled and blared. The noise and heat of buses, Suzukis, horses, motorbikes twined together up into the hazy sky. The only way to cross was by a footbridge where hawkers sat offering services: you want fortune telling? dentistry? jewellery? My bag was by my side, and I touched it now and again, checking. The airline ticket was in there, the very little money I had left; certainly not enough for a good hotel. But no passport. I had no fear of being robbed, but touched it like an amulet to ward off the poverty which reached out to me, gently. A girl with a stud in each nostril waited until I was standing over her then hissed, and swiftly, woman to woman, lifted her shawl to show her dry breast, and the weak baby on her lap. I snarled at her, then was ashamed.

A laughable sign in the grounds of the YWCA read "Peace Zone". The lower half of the notice was obscured by black dirt from the thundering traffic. A path crossed a sorry garden to an eroded stone building which at first seemed deserted; I looked into several featureless rooms before discovering three people, all Pakistani, who stood looking at a heavy typewriter on a desk. Even within the stone rooms the traffic noise was unbearable. They said it was 100 rupees a night. They said, if I would wait over there, Mrs Jones would be summonsed. Mrs Jones would show me a room and explain the Rules and Regulations.

I never met Mrs Jones. I turned heel and left before she had a chance to arrive, back onto the Jinnah Road. Christian Association. Rules and Regulations. I'd be home soon enough. For now I'd rather pay 70 rupees, put up with Mr Manager, make up the rules and regulations as we went along.

★ ★ ★ ★

The next day I lay on the bed in my room of the *Hotel Holiday*. Only the fat uncle was at the desk downstairs, no sign of the manager. I had eaten and slept. The ants had borne away a whole day toward the leaving of the plane. There was a knock at the door. I thought about ignoring it, but it would be rude, like walking away before Mrs Jones arrived. We have rude, they are shame. It is rude to ignore the knock. It is shame to open the door to a man. The knock came again.

I lifted a little pair of sharp scissors which fitted neatly into my closed hand. The blade rested against the ball of my thumb. The manager was again in Western clothes, clean and fresh, but he looked down at his feet as I opened the door.

"Yesterday . . ." he began, then stopped.

"Yes?"

"What I say. Very wrong. Very wrong words."

Silence. Thrown. A voice in my head said "disarmed". It was more important than ever to conceal my scissors. Dis-arm.

"Very wrong, what I said. I sorry. You are angry."

"I was angry. You mustn't think that . . ."

But if I was going to presume to tell him what to think, then I was too late. He had done his thinking. At home, with his family, at the table-tennis club, all round town, wherever he went. As had I. Both of us with the sensation of the encounter pressed on our minds. Funny how we both came back.

"I sorry. Please. I go now."

When I left the hotel for the late evening flight, he wasn't there, only the fat uncle who presented a bill for three days. I had budgeted for two, it was that close.

"No, you are 24 hours more!"

"No! I am two days only. Two nights!"

"But now is other night. 70 rupees more."

"I do not have 70 rupees more."

I sat bad-temperedly on a small sofa beneath a Chinese picture of a kitten, my rucksack beside me. The fat uncle sat beneath his calendar with a picture of the Kabba'h. We glared at each other.

"I will telephone the manger!" he said and reached for the green phone.

I relaxed. "Please do."

The fat uncle spoke, casting me glances. I looked about the reception room. The few postcards on the wall, an exhortation from the Koran. I could picture the manager in his jeans and tee-shirt, his black moustache pressed into a mouthpiece in some other place; at home, at a café. I was causing trouble, but it would be alright. Me and the manager. At length the fat uncle hung up and looked sourly across the desk.

"Mr Manager say is okay. Is okay. Two days only. 140 rupees."

As he spoke he unlocked the drawer, took out my passport and slapped it on the desk.

"Now you are go."

I picked up the passport, and went.

"But madam, who drives the motorcycle?"

Nicki McCormick

Nicki McCormick puts a new spin on travelling overland: in 1996, a chance comment by a fellow traveller in India prompted her to buy an ageing Enfield Bullet motorcycle, which she decided to drive all the way home to London, through Pakistan, Iran and Turkey. This is the story of her travels in Pakistan with her bike, "Betty". Since returning, she has led tours to Iran, contributed to various magazines and to *The Adventure Motorbiking Handbook* (Compass Star) and is currently finishing a travel book of her journey, "*But Madam, Who Drives the Motorcycle?*".

Half a day's drive west of nowhere, three rusty oil drums by the roadside revealed themselves to be a petrol station. As fuel was being filtered through a scrap of cloth, the inevitable crowd gathered. Faces pressed closer and the questions began:

"You lady? You man?"

"Lady."

"LADY?! Alone? No husband?"

"Uh huh."

"But madam," my interrogators demanded, "Who drives the motorcycle?" This was rural Pakistan, where unaccompanied young women on motorcycles are so far removed from people's concept of "female" as to be impossible. Even in India, where odd foreigners are commonplace, I'd been an oddity. Now with Betty, the Enfield Bullet I'd bought in Delhi and ridden round India, I was making my way slowly back to Europe. We were proving to be quite an arresting combination.

A wild-looking man sporting a shock of spiky black hair and a grubby *shalwar kameez* rushed from the back of the crowd. Something about "Bazaar! Bazaar!" – he seemed to be insisting on a lift up the hill to the Fort Munro village. The crowd all agreed the situation was urgent, so despite my reservations about taking strange men on the back I motioned him to clamber aboard.

Fort Munro, once a British hill station and army garrison, was a ghost town of deserted, dilapidated luxury villas, silent and faintly eerie. No sign of a shop, let alone a bazaar, but my passenger gee-ed me on like some deranged horseman until I spied the government-owned resthouse. A modern but tasteful concrete edifice, it was perched on a small knoll among fruit trees and cultivated slopes, its rose gardens incongruous against a backdrop of mountainous desolation. Disentangling himself from my luggage, my companion informed the English-speaking manager that we were checking in together.

"Excuse me? Is it correct, madam, that you are travelling with this gentleman?" queried the manager politely.

"What! It most certainly is not. He wanted a lift up here, and I agreed as there is no other transport."

After profuse negotiations and a final check that was I absolutely sure of my decision, my disappointed admirer was led off to be driven back down to the village, his hopes dashed.

That little excitement finished with, I asked the price of a room. At 500 rupees (£10) it was way outside my meagre budget, so I said I'd camp instead. The manager, Salim, suddenly became animated. "No, madam, you can't possibly camp! It's far too dangerous!" I silently agreed with him – the tribesmen engaged in rifle practice in the rose gardens were making me edgy – and was relieved to see the price tumble as I halfheartedly insisted I'd be fine in my tent. The only guest, I spent the evening on the veranda listening to tales of the days of the Raj.

"At the top of the hill," crooned Salim, "is a tiny British cemetery, and there is buried Maud Evelyn. She was the only daughter of Sir Oldham, the last Viceroy of Multan, the wife of Captain Ferrar, Indian Army Punjab Commission. She died here on October 13, 1906, aged only 26. Her husband was so heartbroken that he stayed by her grave for 35 years until his death. He begged to be buried with her, but his body was shipped back to England against his wishes so they were finally parted."

Charming and well-educated, the stout, middle-aged manager was the perfect host, until he casually slipped into the conversation, "So, do you need your own room tonight, or would you prefer to share mine?" I acted suitably horrified and haughty, demanded my own room and barricaded the door, just in case. But Salim seemed to have already forgotten the incident.

At dawn I paid a visit to Maud Evelyn. Two thousand metres above the world, against a backdrop of bare jagged mountains, lie five lonely British graves from the turn of the century. Two were for the young babies of army wives: how was it to give birth to and bury a child in such isolation? Remote even now, this hilltop was once even more inaccessible, yet it was a haven from the heat and dust of the plains. What was life like for the young women who followed their husbands to such places? Despite the image we have of pampered memsahibs of the Raj, I suspect many of them must have been pretty tough women.

Long sharp shadows on the hills shortened and softened; faint murmurs of activity rose from the waking village in the valley far below. Betty's engine shattered the morning stillness as I bade farewell to Maud Evelyn and her compatriots and headed, with more than a hint of trepidation, for the distantly visible pass that would lead to Baluchistan.

The road into the province of Baluchistan is known locally, with some justification, as "Robber Road". But no bandits were to be found, only friendly restaurateurs who insisted I devour extra chapattis (for strength) and a family in a jeep who flagged me down for photos.

They explained, with eloquent throat-slitting gestures, that I was 30km down the wrong road, a road I would be wiser not to take. The desert scenery ahead was tantalising, but I took their advice and retraced my route to the main highway.

Climbing northeast into the mountains that form the foothills of Afghanistan, storm clouds threatened, dusk was approaching and the road dwindled to a muddy track. I felt alarmingly insignificant and alone, and wasn't quite sure how far the next town was. Suddenly I found myself pinned under the bike in a pool of slippery ooze. A group of camel drivers, looking every inch the ferocious tribesmen I'd been warned about, ambled round a corner. Masking my fear with a forced grin and a nervously friendly wave, I appealed for help. They realised I was female and rushed to my aid as I righted the bike. "Very strong. Very brave," they gestured, but, concerned for my safety, commanded a passing motorcyclist, who was obviously terrified of them, to stay with me till the next town.

I reached Ziarat, another hill resort and former capital of Baluchistan, at nightfall. "Come and meet my family," insisted a man I asked directions of. I followed him through metal gates into a high-walled courtyard. Inside were sixty-odd women in their Friday holiday finery. I was flabbergasted. So were they, and the whole crowd froze as this mud-encrusted foreigner was led into their midst. Then long-forgotten English lessons were summoned forth and questions came flying from every direction. "Where are you from? Where is your husband? How did you come here?"

I had questions of my own. What is this gathering? Why are there no men around? I had walked into a women-only extended-family "picnic". Like a visiting celebrity, women and girls fought to shake my hand, others looking shyly on from the back. Meanwhile, someone had arranged for me to camp for free in a nearby hotel grounds. All too soon the family had to leave, and a matriarch tried to press a leaving present of cash into my hands. I accepted instead her phone number in Quetta and promised to come for dinner in a few days.

The manager of the hotel clucked sympathetically at the state of the bike, boasted approvingly of my adventures to everyone within earshot, arranged for several buckets of hot water and the use of a bathroom, then rustled me up the best biryani on earth. On the house. And that was the end of another good day in Pakistan. In fact, most of them were good days. And the ones that weren't were more to do with bikes and bureaucracy than being a woman alone.

As in many countries low-level lechery is frustratingly pervasive, but the strict separation of Pakistani men and women in fact makes life easier for the female traveller. Constant "romantic" offers can be more irritating than unnerving. It's usually more a case of, as in Salim's case, "well, we've heard what these Westerners are like – you never know if you don't ask . . ." Because the penalties for touching a woman are so severe (in many areas it is considered justifiable to kill a man for merely looking at one's sister), men will look, men will proposition, men might occasionally attempt the odd furtive grope if crowds permit, but never once did I feel physically threatened. In response to the endless enquiries, I used to reply that no, I was not single, I was married to my motorcycle. "It needs just as much attention as a husband, but if it gets too troublesome, I can sell it! And you had better beware, sir, my motorcycle it is very jealous!"

Humour seemed to defuse most awkward situations, whereas reacting angrily merely provoked laughter and more teasing, especially among young men. Almost everyone I met was intensely proud of their country and eager for travellers to think the best of it. I learned to act shocked and disappointed if someone so friendly, in such a hospitable country, dared think shameful thoughts, or to declaring myself the "daughter" or "sister" of any potential suitor. By putting the man concerned into a "protector" role, all the hassles were stopped before they started. A friend had suggested carrying photos of my family – the sight of a fierce-looking father, even on paper, works wonders in cooling the libido of even the most ardent of admirers! Paradoxically, the further away you are from Western media sources and touristy areas, the safer you are likely to be, and the unavailability of alcohol (apart from my own cravings) is also a blessing – sober suitors are much easier to deter than drunk ones.

Being alone, I was thrust into the role of "honorary man", a welcome alternative to being invisible in the shadow of a male companion. Yet women, even fearless, slightly crazy intrepid explorers, are there to be looked after. Time and again rooms were found in full hotels, passers-by stopped to assist with puncture repairs and mechanics would give the bike extra attention because they didn't want to feel responsible for me breaking down later. And, as a woman, I was welcomed into the intimate world of the family.

In Quetta, the last Pakistani city before the desert crossing into Iran, I spent an evening with the Luni family, they of the picnic. An uncle, accompanied by a bevy of excited children, collected me from my hotel. After formal greetings to the father of the house, I was whisked away into the women's world, jealously guarded as their "catch". Away from the men, the women were bawdy and relaxed, teasing me mercilessly for my ineptitude with babies and marvelling that I could be unmarried at the advanced age of 26 (one woman of my age was shortly to become a mother-in-law). Female members of the extended family, escorted from their homes by their sons, filtered in all evening and the room became a jumble of lounging bodies, clambering children and banter.

Though many women in Pakistan rarely have contact outside the family circle after marriage, that family is often vast and its female members form a woman's social circle and support network. Men are superfluous, was Aunty Parvin's opinion, merely there to provide children and financial support. She qualified this by saying how lucky the Luni women were to have such good husbands. None of the (regretfully few) women I met in Pakistan expressed the slightest urge to mix in the "men's world". "We have our life, they have theirs, we are all happy," declared Aunty Parvin.

As we tearfully hugged goodbye and I re-entered the men's world of motorbikes and mechanics, the greatest wish they had for me was to return one day a married woman with children. I was content to return to the comfortable familiarity of life on the road, but it came as a shock to realise that they were more likely to pity than envy my freedom to roam the world.

read on . . .

Kathleen Jamie, *The Golden Peak: Travels in Northern Pakistan* (UK: Virago, 1994). With Benazir Bhutto still in power and the Gulf war threatening, poet Jamie takes a bus across the China border to the provincial town of Gilgit in northern Pakistan where she spends three seasons staying both in an old colonial hotel, the *Golden Peak* of the title, and with a local Shia Muslim family. In her account of this stay, written with a lucid honesty, and effortlessly beautiful prose style, she introduces us to the people, paradoxes and aspirations of a segregated Shia Muslim and small-town way of life. Her everyday observations are made with an uncompromising sympathy that takes you deeper beneath the surface of her friendships and encounters. Some moments are hard to forget, such as her account of witnessing the ritualised grief of the yearly Muharram procession, when the entire male polulation of Gilgit walk the streets beating themselves bloody: "Two boys broke from the crowd and ran to a roadside stone, ostensibly to sharpen their blades, but they took a long time over it, like schoolboys excused to go to the toilet." Jamie's only travel book must rank as an unsung modern masterpiece of the genre.

Emily Eden, *Up the Country: Letters from India* (1838; UK: Virago, 1984). A fascinating collection of letters recording the author's experiences as "first lady" to her unmarried brother, George, who, in 1835, was appointed governor-general of India. She describes in vivid detail their two-and-a-half year tour up the country, to Lahore, now within Pakistan.

Christina Lamb, *Waiting for Allah: Benazir Bhutto and Pakistan* (UK: Penguin, 1991). Gripping journalistic account, which would benefit from some serious updating, of Benazir Bhutto's accession to power in December 1988. It follows the action up to her dramatic departure less than two years later, but could hardly predict the even deeper mire of corruption into which she would eventually sink.

Dervla Murphy, *Full Tilt: Dunkirk to Delhi by Bicycle* (1965; UK: Flamingo, 1995/US: Overlook Press, 1987). Despite her regrets at leaving Afghanistan, on this first of her epic bicycle journeys Murphy soon falls in love with Pakistan. Here the familiar discomforts of food deprivation and aching muscles are joined by heatstroke, biting sandflies and a terrifying ride in a tiny plane, "scraping through the Himalayas", but nothing puts this intrepid Irishwoman off her stride. At one stage, negotiating a series of glaciers in an impending thunderstorm and faced with a river to cross without a bridge, she and her equally resilient bicycle, Roz, finally plunge into the icy water with the help of a cow whose neck provides a comforting armhold, thus avoiding the "awkward situation" of becoming unbalanced in a raging torrent of melted snow. Accounts of such gruelling endeavours are mingled with mainly sympathetic human encounters, and musings on the relationship of Man and Nature always a favourite theme.

Dervla Murphy, *Where the Indus is Young: A Winter in Baltistan* (1977; UK: Flamingo, 1995). Murphy returns to Pakistan several years after her first trip with her daughter Rachel, nearly six and already initiated into the rigours of travelling with her mother in Southern India. Their destination is Baltistan, also known as "Little Tibet", an area of 10,000 square miles between China and Kashmir. On arrival in this intimidating landscape, "whose scale, colour and texture combine to create an impression of the most savage and total desolation", a pony is eventually purchased and the pair set off to trek through five valleys, including the perilous Indus Gorge. Luckily Rachel is accurately described as a "natural stoic" (given to doing arithmetic in times of stress) and together they cover miles of rocky, often icy terrain, staying mainly in very basic resthouses along the way. As usual it is Murphy's passion for truly remote places and respect, if not always affection, for communities untouched by the "polluted mainstream of our horrible consumer society" that shine through.

Papua New Guinea

Islands in the clouds

Isabella Tree

Isabella Tree first went to Papua New Guinea in 1986 on a two-week stopover on her way to Australia. An English friend who had taught at the capital, Port Moresby, in the early 1970s, insisted that she get in touch with a remarkable ex-student of hers, a Highlander called Akunai. Akunai had grown up in a tribal village reminiscent of a stone age civilisation – the wheel had yet to be discovered, metal and glass were unheard of and there were no beasts of burden. His father, who was converted by one of the first missionaries to make tribal contact, sent him to missionary school, where his aptitude for study led to a place at an elite school in the capital and then university. This educational quantum leap continued via postgraduate studies in Sydney and several years of travel within Europe, America and Japan until he settled in Moresby as a local businessman and politician.

Isabella meets Akunai: "He had a kind, intelligent face and eyes that twinkled with amusement . . . not the kind of refinement I had bargained for." He takes her on a trip to his village and soon they make plans to explore the country together by jeep and helicopter, flying between Highland villages and gold-mining frontier towns and across the border that bisects the Papua New Guinean section of the island from the Indonesian province of Irian Jaya.

Islands in the Clouds, Isabella's acclaimed account of this journey, was shortlisted for the Thomas Cook Travel Book Award in 1997 (see review on p.478). In the extract below Isabella, Akunai and Busybee, a fellow Eastern

471

Highlander who, armed with a *busnaip* or bushknife, acts as their bodyguard against the bandits or hostile tribes that line the route, travel by truck through the northwestern province of Enga to the goldmining township of Porgera. They find themselves caught up in a sing-sing (a protest dance) on the way.

As we left the joys of Kaiap Lodge to face the uncertainty of the journey ahead, the mood in the truck fell as flat as our spare tyre. There were more abandoned vehicles along the road as we continued west beyond Wabag: great piles of junk rusting beneath the casuarinas. Only one village had taken advantage of the scrap metal to reinforce its traditional defence walls with a patchwork of car doors, heavy truck parts and tyres. Busybee was unusually quiet in the back, his explosive comments reduced to a contemptuous "tut".

A few miles down the road we began to climb again, carefully navigating the bends in anticipation of a tanker coming the other way. Eventually we reached a plateau of blue, grassy plains. Flocks of swallows wheeled high overhead, and dozens of kites were swooping down into the band of insects above the *kunai*. This was the Laiagam Valley, at 7200 feet the highest in the Highlands.

The people we passed along the road became increasingly tribal in appearance. The women were often bare-breasted; the men carried axes and had decorations of some sort in their hair – a sprig of fern or grass, some flowers or a feather. Some wore hats made from the fur of a silky cuscus or bead necklaces of shells or bone. Many of the men had painted their faces with yellow clay or charcoal. Even the women wore face-paint, at liberty – unlike women in the east – to indulge in self-decoration. We passed some children completely smothered in leaves. Dressed for the ultimate game of hide and seek, they vanished laughing and squealing into the undergrowth like mischievous elves.

Akunai had once complained to me about the loudness of Europeans. But the Engans seemed to revel in noise, jumping up and down, shouting, and running after our truck with whoops and yells. It was Akunai and Busybee who were now singled out as objects of curiosity. An Eastern Highlander was even rarer in these parts than a white person, and ran considerably greater risk of getting an arrow in his chest. Busybee wound his window up despite the warmth of the sun.

By now the gardens had changed dramatically. In the Goroka or Hagen valleys, *kaukau*, taros and yams would be planted in round mounds only four foot across; here, there were domes of earth half the height of a man and the length of a car. They rose up, bare and majestic like gigantic egg cartons, the tiny shoots of new plants occasionally pricking through the surface. Where the crops were riper, the mounds were green and overgrown with creepers bearing the little mauve trumpets of the sweet-potato flower. Between the mounds, the earth was packed hard to repel rain, but inside – and this was the secret to their size – festered a rich organic compost of vegetable matter and manure. Up here, where frosts were frequent, the *kaukau* mounds were designed like giant incubators, fostering the plants in a cocoon of warmth and sustaining them with nutrients.

Busybee and Akunai were clearly daunted by these gargantuan gardens. "Small is beautiful," said Akunai. "We don't build monstrosities like this in the east."

"*Ol i bikpela tumas*," agreed Busybee, "*ol i maunten*" (which, translated roughly, means "all are big, too much, all are mountain").

And like Jack and the Beanstalk, we were about to meet our Giant round the very next bend.

Despite the frequency of villages, over the last mile or so the road had become deserted. I had assumed that this was a mark of remoteness. The countryside around us had once again closed in and the road was climbing beneath the limestone pinnacles. It seemed likely that the villagers were out hunting in the montane forest or working in their gardens. So it was startling to find them massed in our path, a human blockade, as we turned another bend. Shrill whistles sounded as we drew up to the crowd, like a thousand traffic conductors out of control. The noise had a galvanising effect, whipping the whistle-blowers into near frenzy.

The crowd swarmed around our truck as we pulled to a halt; they were shouting, shaking their spears and beating on the sides of the vehicle, their faces fired with excitement. Some of them had red rings around their eyes and yellow spots on their cheeks. They were protesting about the existence of the new road and were using a traditional *sing-sing* to assert their power. Two tankers and another truck were marooned in front of us, their drivers locked inside their cabs for safety.

From a short distance away came the thud of *kundu* drums, slowly building in volume until a band of dancers came into sight. This was what the crowd had been waiting for, and attention thankfully

473

switched back in their direction. Drawn on by the thought of photographs I got out of the truck and sank into the crowd, followed hesitantly by Akunai.

The dancers were fierce and warlike, blowing whistles and sweeping up in a phalanx suggestive of an armed assault. Puffs of dust rose from the road as they stamped their feet in unison, raising their knees high to get the full effect of the march, and kicking up their long sackcloth aprons before them. Their buttocks were covered with great bushes of tanget and their calves bound with bark and grass bandanas. On their foreheads and around their necks they wore the distinctive crescent-shaped discs of the kina shell. Their faces were painted black. Bushy tufts of cassowary feathers tossed about on their heads, increasing their height by an impressive foot and a half. The crowd parted reverently before them, intoxicated by the rhythm of the whistles and the drums, and then fell back as the dancers pulled rank and faced them, thirty strong, like some nightmarish platoon trooping its colour.

I was causing a stir in my corner of the crowd and as many faces were turned towards me as they were to the parade ground. But I was too preoccupied with my camera to notice an irate warrior approaching and shaking his axe. Eventually someone pushed me towards him and the man let rip with words of violent abuse.

I tried to apologise and shook my head uncomprehendingly, but he gesticulated all the more and began prodding me towards the periphery of the crowd. Two of his henchmen came up and muscled me down the side of a bank. Akunai was nowhere in sight and the truck, with Busybee sitting on top of it, was more than forty crowded yards away. I was being jostled and beginning to despair when one of the onlookers threatened, "You give him *planti mani*. Him manager *bilong sing-sing*. Him *bikpela* man. He say you pay for snap-snap – *kisim poto.*"

It seemed miraculous to be offered an escape and I gave him all I had in my pockets. He snatched the twelve kina without complaint and I was left to fight my way back to the truck, bruised and tearful with shock.

Busybee seemed as relieved to see me as I was to reach him, although from his vantage point on the roof of the truck he had perfected an air of disdain and detachment. The *busnaip* lay unsheathed against his leg. Only when Akunai came battling towards us did he feel his job was over. He slid down to the ground and into the back seat.

We took advantage of the first break in the crowds to speed off down the road.

As the sound of the *sing-sing* was left behind, our relief was overwhelming.

"We nearly became the next headlines for the *Post Courier*," laughed Akunai: "'Three People Hacked to Death by Wild Tribe in Enga!'."

"Did you see that guy with the axe and all that body paint?"

"You should have seen the blokes I was stuck with over the other side," said Akunai.

The tension of the moment was diffused. On reflection, however, the incident took on a different perspective. We had been precisely what the warriors had been protesting about – outsiders using the road. And we had walked into the proceedings with the arrogance of uninvited guests. It was scarcely surprising that the local *big man* had demanded reparation, particularly from a Westerner – a representative of the people responsible for the road in the first place. To my mind, as well no doubt to his, he had reasserted his authority by reminding me of my status – an unwanted foreigner in someone else's land. The feeling of being an intruder began to haunt me.

The road wound steadily upwards. There were no more villages and we could rest assured that there would be no more *sing-sings*. Up here there was only forest, deep dark tracts of it filling the gorges and swathing the pinnacles. Busybee and Akunai had never seen forest like this: gigantic and dense, dripping with moss and epiphytes, alive with the presence of birds skimming the treetops. This was virgin territory, so high and impenetrable that it had never been cleared for gardens or firewood. It had even repelled the more recent interests of logging and settlement. The forest existed in its manifold glory as it had done for tens of thousands of years. It almost certainly contained species and subspecies as yet unknown: plants, butterflies and insects with no name; botanical mechanisms and biological dependencies never before imagined; trees larger than those on record; a whole world yet to be scientifically investigated.

The road dissected the forest like a ribbon-tailed snake. Money sang out from the scrunch of quality gravel, from the evenness of its surface, from the generous lay-bys designed for passing tankers and lorries, from the gradient and angle of its bends and from the way the road followed the contours of the mountains it traversed. This was a feat of modern engineering and superhuman endeavour. It led us on beguiled.

When we finally caught sight of Porgera, with its shanty towns and airstrip, it was from one of the road's superior lay-bys. The cliff face dropped away on our left-hand side, falling 2500 feet to the valley floor. The morning air had dried the limestone on the road. From halfway down the mountain we could see great puffs of powder agitated by dumper trucks on the move. Everything in the valley – trees, houses, vehicles – was veiled in dust like an over-exposed photograph. After miles of travelling through rainforest it seemed we had stumbled on the flip side of Shangri-la – an oasis of tin and dust, of machinery and Nissen huts.

Akunai surrendered the driving seat to me. This is not Papua New Guinea, he seemed to be saying, this comes from your world – it's not up to me to see us through.

But the view from our lay-by was just the beginning. As we descended into the valley, past the busy construction work of the new runway designed for jet aircraft, through a checkpoint, past stalls of dusty bananas and black-market petrol, it became clear we were nowhere near the mine itself. This was the "unofficial" face of Porgera. This was where dependants of the mine workers set up their camps, where the traders and merchants sold their wares at vastly inflated prices – fourteen kina for a chicken, noted Busybee, appalled, compared to ten kina in Wabag and six in Goroka. Villagers had built huts in clusters along the roadside. Akunai noticed from the variations in design that they belonged to different tribes. On the slopes of the mountain new *kaukau* gardens were being dug.

We drove on for another mile before we reached the mine site proper. A network of roads and prefab buildings with corporate logos identified the township of Porgera. The original airstrip, a hard runway for Hercules transport planes, took pride of place in the heart of the town, its perimeter fence isolating one half from the other. The mining compound itself, heavily fortified with guards, dogs and three sets of tall barbed-wire fences, dominated a position to the north-west of the settlement. The roads were busy with people: some walking purposefully in boiler suits and hard hats; others, bemused and in traditional dress, watching from the roadside. There was a sense of urgency about the place which, combined with an awesome display of high technology and heavy security, gave a James Bond feel to it all. The human ants scurrying about this surreal world seemed as dispensable as thousands of extras.

A crowd had gathered in the compound of a large, official looking building, and as we approached a fight broke out and spilled onto the road around our truck. There were shouts from all sides and fists flying from a tangle of assailants. A man was stabbed in the arm and, quick as a flash, the skirmish was over, satisfied for the moment by the drawing of blood. No one waited around for the police to arrive. A landslide had obliterated the police station at Porgera and, temporarily, offenders were being locked up in empty steel cargo containers.

We had passed almost unnoticed in the fracas, but anonymity was beginning to weigh more heavily upon us than our prominence an hour or so before at the *sing-sing* on the road.

"This is no good," said Akunai. "Too many different tribes in one place. This place is trouble."

We drove around aimlessly, increasingly depressed by the acres of chicken wire. To the north of the town was a large gully, with a yellow river of sludge from the mine flowing along its bed, and a dismal settlement of bush houses and corrugated iron clinging to its sides.

"This is group from Eastern Highlands," said Akunai, registering familiar faces. But he didn't want to stop.

We headed on up through the town towards the mine site, although without permits or identity cards there was no strategy in this. There were "Danger", "No Unauthorised Personnel Beyond This Point" and "Keep Out" signs posted on the fence; and women walking past went barefoot in the dust with *bilums* on their backs. Two dusty pigs wandered on the wrong side of the fence.

A tanker appeared from nowhere and dust obliterated our vision. As the chalk settled, we found ourselves opposite a padlocked entrance presided over by sentries in a patrol box. Just then a couple of company jeeps drove up, and in a flash of impatience I put my foot on the accelerator and tacked onto their convoy. Akunai had been right: this *was* more my world than his, and I was more prepared to take risks. If we were challenged he wouldn't have felt able to bluff his way out, or even pull rank. I, on the other hand, could rely on some affinity with management, even though I had no place here, simply because we were all white in a black country. It was an advantage that Akunai, despite his missionary upbringing, his European friends and his Australian education, did not have. We passed through the gates without question, and I even managed a gracious wave of thanks to the sentry as he closed the gates behind us.

read on . . .

Isabella Tree, *Islands in the Clouds: Travels in the Highlands of New Guinea* (Aus/UK/US: Lonely Planet Journeys, 1996). Tree describes her journey with Highlander companion Akunai in clear, uncluttered prose, disclosing acute observations, reflections and wonderful dialogue (much of it written in pidgin), while maintaining the respect and integrity of her friendship. Nothing is exaggerated. Readers learn how children had to run through the jungle territory of hostile tribes on their way to school, hoping to avoid an arrow through the neck; and what it feels like to slash a path through a field of wild orchids, or join Vietnam veteran pilots in death-defying flights across the treacherous interior mountain ranges, or dig delicious maggots out of a rotting sago palm. Tree's intelligent fascination with all aspects of New Guinean Highland life and her concern for the future of its land and people are reflected in this beautifully composed and salutary book.

Peru

The mild bunch on the Inca Trail

Kate Robbins

Kate Robbins is a freelance travel journalist currently living in Amsterdam. She has been fascinated by travel for as long as she can remember, fuelled at a young age by the adventures of the children's book character, Paddington Bear, who came from "deepest darkest Peru". She has visited a great number of countries, studied for several years in the USA and contributed features to many UK and US publications. Kate finally made it to Peru in 1998 when, together with seven assorted travellers and two guides, she walked the Inca Trail to Machu Picchu.

As we reached the top of Warmiwanusca Pass, known disconcertingly as "Dead Woman's Pass", Julio told us to join hands in a circle. "OK everybody, on the count of *uno*, *dos*, *tres*, shout *ariba*, *ariba*, *ariba*," he ordered. At 4198m above sea level we barely had enough puff left to breathe but somehow the eight of us managed quite a rousing group "*ariba*" which echoed down the Inca Trail and got lost in the cloud forest below.

The trail to the lost city of the Incas, Machu Picchu, takes you through river valley and cloud forest, past Inca ruins and snow-capped mountains. It is the most popular and arguably the most stunning hike in Peru and as I soon found out you don't have to be a rufty-tufty, leather-skinned mountain man or woman to accomplish it.

I'd booked the trek with the well-respected Peruvian Andean Treks who are based in Cuzco, which was where I joined a group of seven other adventure-seekers to walk the Inca Trail. We were a mixed bunch with a wide range of backgrounds, interests, personalities and ages.

"Sshh!" said 68-year-old Bob as he pointed up to the branch of a moss-covered cedar tree. "It's a scarlet-bellied mountain taniger."

"Is it edible?" asked 21-year-old Corrie who for every five minutes of the past hour had been asking Julio, our guide, when it was time for lunch. But we did have one collective interest, the desire to see Machu Picchu and one shared fear, the walk that would lead us there. We began the trail at Kilometre 77 in the village of Chilca and followed the Urubamba River that winds its way from the tropical Amazon Basin to the white pinnacles of the Andes. Julio and Ivan, our guides, set the pace. They never rushed us, just encouraged us and provided lots of opportunity to rest en route as they gave information on the flora, fauna and folklore of the Andes. "Look here," Julio instructed us, pointing at a red-flowered cactus. "This very old medicine used by the Quechuas [indigenous people] to calm fever."

However, at the end of the first morning it was a remedy for aching feet and fatigue that was needed. And by the time we'd climbed through a eucalyptus grove to the first minor ruin of Llactapata, where we shared our lunchtime feast of cold chicken, fresh bread and bananas with curious local children, I was beginning to wish that I'd gone on a few preparatory hikes before coming away. Or at least strolled to the corner shop. And I wasn't the only one who was suffering.

"God, I'm gagging for a ciggie," said eleven-stone Barbara. "But I swore I wouldn't have one." Barbara, a self-confessed choco-holic couch potato from Perth, had booked her trip to Peru on a whim after splitting up with her long-term boyfriend. "I did it because he said I was boring," she told me. "You should have seen his stupid face when I told him that I was going to walk the Inca Trail in Peru, which reminds me . . .". Barbara foraged around in her daypack for five minutes before bringing out a "Happy Snapper" instamatic camera. "Take my picture will you, mate? I want proof of every bloody step I take on this mountain otherwise no one will believe I did it." I took a picture of her lying on her back in the sun shoving a Snickers bar in her mouth.

The first evening we pitched our tents at 2750m on a flat, grassy plain near the village of Huayllabamba. As soon as the sun dipped behind the summit of Mountain Veronica and the temperature dropped to freezing I wrapped myself up in the soft alpaca-wool blanket that I'd haggled for in Cuzco market and stayed in my tent sipping hot chocolate. But some members of our group were hardier than I. Greg, who was studying tropical medicine in Lima, was determined to have a shower whatever the climate and had carried a contraption called a sun shower on his back all day. The sun had heated the water (brought from Cuzco) inside a plastic container as he'd walked along, which had given the rest of us hours of amusement. "You won't be laughing when I'm the only clean one left at the end of these five days," he finally snapped at Barbara, sick of all her wisecracks. That evening we all gathered on the mountainside to watch Greg disappear behind a bush with his sun shower. "Let's nick his towel," suggested Barbara who was fast becoming the self-appointed camp comic. It had seemed like a jolly jape but for hours afterwards Greg had shivered uncontrollably, unable to get warm after standing naked on the mountainside searching for his towel, which he unaccountably found hanging from a nearby tree. "Better warm and dirty than clean and cold" soon became our group's motto. The sun shower was never seen again.

On the second day Julio gave us coca leaves to chew because we were about to negotiate our way to 4198m above sea level, the highest point on the trek. Although cocaine is derived from the coca plant, in its pure form coca tea is drunk and coca leaves chewed by the Quechua people to alleviate the symptoms of altitude sickness. "This is more like it," said Barbara whose withdrawal from nicotine was taking its toll. "With any luck now I'll fly up this sodding mountain." Without ceremony she stuffed a bundle of leaves in her mouth and set off with a determined look in her eye. As we climbed further up into the cloud forest a soft, icy mist began to fill the air and I donned my red plastic poncho, woolly hat and gloves for extra warmth. Today it was the creamy breasted canistero that caught Bob's eye as it darted between the wild orchids and purple lupins. Much to his amazement, Corrie, whose stomach was full of an ample porridge breakfast, took a keen interest in his ornithological observations. "Really, Bob? And is the canistero a migratory bird?" I heard her ask, trying to make up for yesterday.

We lunched in the middle of an egg-shaped Inca ruin that was originally used by the Incas as an emergency shelter and food store. When we reached the second pass of the day the clouds were thick and the mountains had vanished behind them. By the time we reached the campsite it was teeming with rain and morale was low.

"We need to make an offering to the gods to change the weather," said Julio solemnly. I looked anxiously at my companions. Which one of us would it be? Surely not me, I was too thin! We all looked at Barbara. "Piss off," she muttered, her sense of humour dampened by the rain. In the meantime Julio had taken a bundle of coca leaves from his pocket and held them up to the sky. "I'll place these beneath a stone. The gods will see them and recognise our gift. But first we have to blow the clouds away."

I looked at Greg. Thank god there was a doctor among us because Julio was losing it. "Are you sure you haven't had a little too much of that coca yourself, Julio?" I asked. I felt a bit stupid standing on a mountain ridge in the rain watching a forty-year-old man trying to blow away the clouds. But at that moment the thought of pitching the tents in the rain was so unattractive that after a couple of minutes every one of us had joined in and was blowing with great concentration. Anything was worth a try.

That evening the stars came out to play and the clouds hung low beneath the snow line. Camping above the clouds – what a strange and mysterious place to sleep, spoiled only by the fact that my tent was pitched on a slope and the rustling of chocolate-bar wrappers coming from Corrie's tent kept me awake with envy for hours. I awoke bad-tempered with a rumbling stomach and in a heap at the bottom of my tent, but was cheered when I discovered that the gods had looked kindly upon our offering. The clouds had lifted to give us clear views of the mountains. We left our mud bath of a campsite early that morning, hoping that the sun would continue to shine throughout the afternoon and that our wet clothes and equipment would have a chance to dry out.

Again the trail took us through cloud forest, thick with giant leaves known to the locals as elephant's ears and used as umbrellas during rainstorms. Luckily we didn't need them today and as we descended down the carefully engineered Inca steps the temperature rose and our Peruvian llama wool hats were replaced with less ethnic baseball

Kirrily Johns (right) and friends in Norway

Carolyn Steele and Ben in Canada

Barbara Lynch in Spain

Louisa Waugh in Mongolia

Kate Robbins on the Inca Trail, Peru

Margaret Jailler's daughter, Fayida, in Shetland

Carina Marong in The Gambia

PETER KYLE

Anita Roddick in Albania

Joy V. Harris's nieces in Paris

JOHN MILES

Dawn Hurley in Yemen

caps. We stopped walking at one o'clock and, like a well-drilled army corps, pitched our tents, rolled out our bedding and went on emergency standby to blow the clouds away.

It was day three now and our whole existence had begun to revolve around food. Dinner, in particular, was an event that we all dribbled at the thought of and where we all showed our true colours. There was none of the usual politeness associated with dining with strangers. We quarrelled over the last drop of vegetable soup, compared our portions of pasta and fought unashamedly over tiny morsels of chocolate cake. Julio dubbed us the "Great Greedy Gringos".

On our final day we each found a new source of energy. This could have been due to the sunshine, the hearty porridge we'd enjoyed at breakfast, the anticipation of reaching the Lost City or the fact that Julio had let slip that they sold pizza at a café in a nearby village. But there was definitely a new spring in our steps as we climbed up through the last of the cliff-hanging cloud forest to Intipunku, the gate of the sun. Sadly, when we reached the Inca gate the clouds had again rolled in and it was impossible to see Machu Picchu so we sat in a row and waited. After only half an hour the city slowly began to emerge from behind the veil of mist and drizzle. Another fifteen minutes and the Lost City was completely revealed. In celebration Barbara lit her first cigarette for five days. "That is just fan-bloody-tastic," she said. "Yeah," we all agreed, nodding, not really sure whether she was talking about Machu Picchu or the sudden inhalation of nicotine. Either way the past four days' walk had been worth it for that first glimpse of the Lost City alone. It took the Incas over a century to build Machu Pichu and the ruins were lost for four hundred years, quietly nestling on the foothills of Machu Picchu mountain, until the American historian Hiram Bingham came across them by accident in 1911. The site has since been gradually restored and cleared of foliage until a stone jigsaw revealed a maze of temples, pathways, houses, ceremonial baths, meeting halls and other curiosities. My favourite had to be the romantically named Intihuatana (hitching post of the sun), an enormous carved rock pillar used not for telling the time but for telling the time of year.

Our final campsite was on the banks of the river, below Machu Picchu. I was relieved to discover that the ground was flat and that just along the road were the hot springs of Aguas Calientes. Although I was a bit dubious about the colour of the water (a yellowish green) Julio assured me that this was due to the high content of natural minerals. "Is good for you, trust me," he said unconvincingly as he fished out a large dead beetle. But after four days of not washing I plunged in. "Wouldn't it be great to have a beer now?" I mused. A small serious boy who had been sitting quietly nearby suddenly leapt to his feet and sprinted off but within minutes he was back. "Beer, *cerveza*, beer, *cerveza*," he shouted excitedly, passing us bottles of ice-cold local beer.

We soaked away our aches and pains, swigging our beer merrily, smug in the glory of completing the trail and secure in the knowledge that we could get the tourist train back to Cuzco the next day.

read on . . .

Dervla Murphy, *Eight Feet in the Andes: Travels with a Mule from Ecuador to Cuzco* (UK: Century, 1985/US: Viking, 1986). After Coorg and Baltistan, Murphy's third trip with her daughter Rachel, now aged nine, takes them across the Andes, accompanied by Juana, a much-pampered mule. Together they walk and ride, depending on the state of Juana's feet, across rocky mountain ridges and through long green valleys, camping on bumpy ground along the way with only basic provisions. Luckily Rachel is as resilient as her mother who, on observing "much ice on tent and gear" records that, "Poor Rachel looked rather wan: she was obviously hungry and cold, yet uttered not a word of complaint". The next stage of their journey is told in Rachel's own wonderfully graphic words (including spelling), ending with evident relief at finding a hotel and somewhere with food. Murphy displays her usual awe and admiration of untamed landscapes but, compared with other journeys, dwells little and with less sympathy than usual on the people encountered.

Poland

Rubble and life

Laura Pachkowski

 Canadian Laura Pachkowski moved to Britain in 1989 where she first studied film and later took a Master's degree in creative writing. Uninspired by her television job and after a series of personal disasters, in the autumn of 1997 she decided to follow her Polish and Ukrainian roots and take a train journey to Central and Eastern Europe. She describes herself as a hopelessly impractical traveller but sometimes cannot resist the urge just to get up and go. Currently she lives in Bristol where she works for a charity that rehabilitates Cambodian landmine amputees. She has also recently had a short story published, entitled *This Land is Our Land*.

After my flat in North London burnt down, I spent a month sorting through the rubble, dealing with the loss-adjusters, the builders and the latent anger of my landlord and neighbours, who didn't want me to stay in the apartment building - as though the freak electrical fire were in some way my fault. I felt lucky to be alive but limped fed-up through the aftermath of the fire. The recent bust-up of a long-term relationship didn't make things any better. With the appearance of all these sudden endings in my life, I was overwhelmed with a desire to get away from England.

It was a good time to pack in a paper-pushing job in the television industry. Friends suggested I travel to Koh Sumai in Thailand or to a Greek island; anywhere near water, they said, to "heal" myself.

485

Instead I booked a cheap flight to Prague as a starting point from which to explore eastern Central Europe. I had Poland on my mind.

Like so many North Americans, I had grown up among many bowdlerized family myths and half-truths about great-great immigrant ancestors from deepest, darkest Eastern Europe. Yet with all the borders of the region shifting over time, I could never work out where exactly they had come from. Whether my ancestors were Marchland Poles (on my father's side) or Ruthenians (on my mother's) mattered less these days than the fact that they had got out. Besides, my family ethos had always been firmly forward-looking. Success, material possessions and hard work (even if you hated it) were where it was at. The fact that my great-grandparents had the first TV/car/sausage grinder in their rural Canadian community was supposed to fill me with immense pride. Ironically, this particular great-granddaughter, not having had home contents insurance, was now homeless and owned nothing.

My plan was to tour Central Europe by train, visit the Eastern Polish borderlands and then travel on to Western Ukraine, to the Carpathian Mountain basin where my forebears, earlier this century, were serfs and forest workers on the outskirts of L'viv. It was an ambitious itinerary given my state of mind and I knew that my inability to speak any foreign language was going to be a problem, but I was also looking forward to the challenge.

I heard my first warnings about Poland in a café in Prague where I met Tanya, a well-dressed woman who worked as an office manager for a firm of solicitors.

"Ah, but my boss is a pig! Western women don't realise what freedoms – OK, they're still not there – but they don't realise what basic freedoms they have . . ." she told me over a single glass of wine, ". . . but going to Poland on your own? I wouldn't do it. No way."

"Is your boss Polish?" I asked.

"No, French Canadian."

Tanya further regaled me in rapid-fire broken English with stories about the Polish mafia, of desperate groping men, of women being drugged, raped and robbed. She spoke of these things as a great nuisance rather than as life-threatening events. She was amazed that I was travelling alone. What little she told me of her own life, she conveyed in dismissive tones. I began to suspect she wasn't Czech. Sure enough, when pressed she admitted she was Latvian. She finished her drink with a flourish, wished me luck and went home to her unemployed husband.

It had been a relief to speak to Tanya; I had not met many friendly Czechs and had little patience with the other Westerners in the café, mostly young American women on the Bohemian trail, trying to look the part with dyed hair, notepads and determined expressions. I watched as they entered in dribs and drabs and occupied half-tables. They gazed longingly at the Czech bartender, Sergei, a handsome Slav so innocently oblivious to their attentions that he became all the more attractive for it. There were furious scribblings and endless cigarettes in the expat café that evening but I, as a lone female traveller, had come here to get drunk in safety.

Several glasses of wine later, I found myself walking to a nearby tram stop, along a deserted stretch of Art Deco blocks in the Holsovice district. Mozart's *Requiem* heard from a nearby church gave way to rapidly approaching footsteps from behind. I picked up my pace and moved to the centre of the road but the footsteps followed. I was suddenly grabbed from behind by a man who rasped "Ciao" in my ear. I froze, never having been so blatantly seized by a stranger before. I could feel his whiskered face against mine and could smell booze on his breath. I finally remembered to scream and ran to the tram stop only a few yards around the corner. Thankfully, his bravery deserted him and he fled.

I had let my guard down. Maybe I was pushing my luck travelling alone in this part of the world. I went back to my private room, crawled under the hand-embroidered duvet and tried, unsuccessfully, to forget about the encounter.

The next day I queued patiently with sombre-looking African and Asian nationals for a visa at the Polish Consulate. I had carried an awkward surname throughout my life, one that tied tongues and sometimes had negative connotations. Surely here, I hoped, it would carry some clout, but the staff at the Consulate were not impressed. After a two-hour wait, I was charged the equivalent of forty pounds and summarily stamped and approved by po-faced civil servants who were more concerned with anticipating lunch. On the sliding scale of acceptability my money and I were rated highly. My new international friends were not so lucky.

The train journey into Poland was slow and clunky with random, pneumatic halts along the way. Inside my carriage, a paunchy Russian trio with smelly feet were en route to Kiev. Outside, the horizon was punctured with television towers and baroque steeples. The forests and smoke-stacks of the Czech Republic gave way to the cultivated fields and smoke-stacks of Poland. I could barely contain my excitement and bounded in and out of my train compartment, up and over the indifferent Russians.

I alighted at Kraków's Główny Station to the piped music of Steeleye Span. On the streets outside I was assaulted by rampant advertising: Adidas, Versace, Playboy, Fruit and Vegetables. Identical streetside stalls sold identical consumer goods. Bananas and soft porn, cabbages and hard porn. Streams of provocatively dressed young people laughed and swerved their way through the kiosks of this trash Mecca. I had known that Poland embarked on radical economic reforms in the late 1980s but hadn't expected the more vulgar excesses of capitalism to be taken so seriously.

The Tourist Office sent me to a private rented room in a communist-style, concrete, high-rise estate out in the distant suburbs, which I imagined jazzing up to make it look like something out of a Kieslowski film. The reality was not at all art house and I had to hold my nose against the smell of garbage and urine as I rang the bell.

My host, Helena, was a large woman in a flamboyant floral blouse. She didn't speak English but communicated the basics through mime. I squeezed myself and rucksack into the cubbyhole room, fell upon the fold-away bed and was greeted from all angles by photographs of Pope John Paul, a quiet reminder perhaps that smoking, drinking and sexual thoughts were not welcome here. I grimly remembered the lack of privacy in Roman Catholic spaces from my own childhood. Helena finally closed the door and left me in peace, only to barge back in a few minutes later.

"*Studenicky? Studenicky?*" she demanded.

Wanting some privacy, I half nodded. She frowned and walked out.

A few minutes later she came back again. "*Muzeum? Muzeum?*" she asked, obviously still perplexed. I smiled as if to say yes.

This time she had returned with boiled sausages, custard buns and black tea (*herbata*). She seemed slightly more appeased now that I was eating. I was touched by her kindness but worried by the wariness in her smiling face. In the room next door I could hear the unmistakable canned laughter of a Polish version of *Let's Make a Deal* on her television.

Later I took the tram into town. It was October and Kraków's Old City was flooded with hundreds of excited and excitable Polish schoolchildren. As we marched single file through the beautiful, narrow, baroque streets, I found myself the butt of incomprehensible jokes. It became apparent that I had not inherited any Polish genes, for all around me fair, fine-featured Romanesque Slavs in trendy clothes put my darker, eastern Slavic features and bargain-basement dress sense into sharp relief. I pulled my fake fur coat closed around me. The buttons were missing.

My self-consciousness worsened. In fin-de-siècle-style cafés and milk bars I sat next to packs of teenagers, families and couples about-to-become families. I tried to feel tougher and made a big show of reading my guidebook as if to say I AM A TOURIST NOT A PROSTITUTE! The only other unchaperoned women visible were gypsy girls, some as young as seven or eight, eating *borscht* in restaurants, and their mothers, who lurked and hustled outside for cash. I admired the young girls' independence and indifference, but wondered how long it would be before they had this beaten out of them by the well-documented and worsening violence and racism facing the Romany community in Eastern Europe.

Back on the streets my simple Polish "*Prosze*" (please) and "*Dziekuje*" (thank you) were not understood. People barged in front of me to get on trams. My calls weren't getting through to England. I got lost. Museums were inexplicably shut and churches were open for Prayer Only. Without monuments to look at, I began to drift aimlessly with no purpose. In a coffee bar, I poured salt into my coffee instead of sugar. The woman serving me, as well as the customers, found this insanely funny. I tried to make a dignified exit and she followed me out the door on the pretext of sweeping the doorway and laughed again.

It started to rain. I wished for practical clothing; a Goretex jacket perhaps, though I owned no such thing. I felt vulnerable and craved familiarity so settled for a nearby McDonald's, where I was greeted on entering by the sound of Gregorian chanting. When the rain had stopped, I wandered out of the Old City into a poorer quarter with darker, more run-down blocks, where I found a bench to sit on, but I felt uneasy there. It was as though some vital life force had drained out of me, down through my money belt and my feet into the paving stones where it lay trodden underfoot and forgotten.

It wasn't long before a young gypsy girl approached me. I braced myself for chicanery but she surprised me by stroking my fake fur coat in frank admiration. Her eyes lit up when she saw my red velvet hand-bag. I felt a little guilty at my own mistrust and without thinking emptied my bag of its contents and gave them to her. She grabbed them with a smile and ran off. I was feeling a little better. It was dark by then and I made my way back through dimly lit streets balancing map, money and bananas. To make matters worse my trousers were falling down. I was losing weight.

At Helena's, I scrutinised the map a little more closely. I had been in Kazimierz, the old Jewish ghetto. The eerie discomfort I experienced seemed to grow and become part of something bigger, something uglier. That night I dreamt of occupation and relocation, and of the man in England who loved me but not quite enough to love me exclusively. My insomnia was back. I opened the window and lit a cigarette. I racked my brain for some answers as to where my life was going. Within seconds Helena broke into my room in her night-gown and slippers. At first I was concerned that I had woken her, that she was worried about burglars and intruders, but her expression was unmistakable: "What's the matter with you?" Something silent passed between us and all gestures of congeniality ended; we became ene-mies. My madness and rude manners now confirmed, I had become an interloper in her home. "What's the matter with you?" I sheepishly went to bed.

The next morning I took a local bus to Oswiesicim, the town with the grim legacy of hosting Auschwitz-Birkenau. Polish boys cackled and teased me in German from the back of the bus, but I did-n't care. I was getting used to the attention by now. The sun was shining and the rolling foothills of Silesia were glowing with autum-nal colours so I gazed out of the window and lost myself in the scenery.

I have read a lot about the Holocaust and maybe not untypically for a lapsed Catholic have a strong interest in Jewish culture. Mostly I wanted to visit the camp because I was haunted by vague memories of ignorant, and perhaps unthinking, family anti-Semitism. My grand-mother laughingly called me a "dirty Jew" every time I tried to sell her back the sweets she had given me as a child. Even worse, I was disturbed by rumours that Ukrainians (my mother's ancestry) had acted as Nazi henchmen by pushing Jews into the gas chambers. I sup-pose I harboured the dubious touristic intention of seeing for myself. The bus dropped me outside the camp where the Nazis exterminated Jews, gypsies, Poles, homosexuals, Communists and anyone else con-veniently categorised as non-Aryan. In the parking lot, bored and slightly desperate taxi drivers touted for business. I purchased a coffee from a hot-dog stand and the attendant counted out my change in German. It started to rain so I paid the equivalent of seven pounds for an umbrella.

Inside KL Auschwitz I, the smaller of the camps, one could see the Poles' desire to preserve and explain the memory of the Holocaust by repairing and repainting some of the grimmer barracks, and setting up sanitised exhibitions. I marched in and out of the red brick prison blocks with the ubiquitous Polish school groups. The children's faces were gloomy with horror and maybe boredom too. According to the guidebook, places of special interest were the Gas Chamber, the Wall of Death (collective gallows), the Commandant's House and the Cinema, but I was especially moved by the collections of prisoners' confiscated possessions: an entire roomful of spectacles, another of hairbrushes, another of prosthetic limbs – the left-behind paraphernalia of human lives.

The exhibition hailing the Polish resistance made me feel more hopeful, but I learned too about the Sonderkommando and Kapos, Jews and others, who upheld and carried out the orders of the SS. It was strange to take small comfort in the fact that if any of my ancestors had been unlucky enough to get a job in the Sonderkommando, they would have eventually been sent out by their successors in the same manner as their victims – through the chimney.

I took the special express bus to the larger camp, KL Auschwitz II – Birkenau, and the heavens really opened. While the few other tourists there contented themselves with surveying the scene from the dry confines of the watchtower, I made a special effort to walk through the mud. I must have made quite a sight – a lone woman combing the concentration camp in a downpour. I felt I wanted to see everything, take it all in, look for clues, as if there were any rationale for such destruction. I remembered the fire in my home.

Finally I took the long, straight walk from the site of the unloading ramp, where "selections" were made, to the remains of the crematoria which the fleeing Nazis had dynamited as the Russian troops moved in. More rubble. A memorial. I was struck by the silence of the place and the apparently reassuring forest surrounding the camp. On my photographs, developed back in England, strange white blobs appeared on the negatives above this spot. Never a believer in the supernatural, I only half joke that they are an eerie exposure of the ghosts of Central Europe. Outside the camp one of the bored Polish cab drivers, whose relatives lived in Chicago, tried to strike up a conversation, tried to drum up some business with me, but I felt like exploding. It was all so humdrum and workaday.

On the train back into Kraków I remembered how an English friend told me not to visit Auschwitz alone, that it would screw me up. But I felt strangely calm and humbled. Perhaps the morbid pilgrimage did function as a sort of healing for all my losses. At Auschwitz, I confronted something infinitely greater than any of the petty vagaries of my own life. At Kraków station I took the escalator up to street level where I was "arrested" and fined by a drunken representative of Polish State Rail for lighting a cigarette in what looked like the street, but was still, it seemed, actually within the confines of the station. It was a little scam but it worked. He asked if I were German but upon seeing the Polish name in my passport demanded that I immediately hand over a hundred *zlotys*. My name carried no weight with him either. Maybe it was worse that I carried a coveted Canadian passport. Too tired to argue, I handed over two days' worth of my budget. Telling him to spend the money on something worthwhile I strode away.

Anger liberated me: after this incident my trip turned around. I travelled to the mountain resort of Zakopane and calmed down a lot. Perhaps I became a little more travel-wise. Perhaps I needed those first two weeks of travelling to divorce myself from all the depressing emotions I had brought with me on the journey. I did consider taking a bus to L'viv, where I had wanted to trace my ancestry, but on seeing it was named the Chernobyl Express decided against it. Maybe another time, I reflected, when I felt stronger . . . In many ways it was a relief to leave Poland but as I wound my way south towards Hungary, I realised that I was much more confident than I had ever felt before. I had found my feet, so to speak, and even began to utter phrases of the local languages with ease. My fears about my future faded into the background and I even began to meet people and have a good time. I will not forget Poland in a hurry, or what I brought away from it.

read on . . .

Janina Bauman, *Winter in the Morning* (UK: Virago, 1991) and *A Dream of Belonging* (UK: o/p). Bauman and her family survived the Warsaw ghetto, eventually leaving the country following the anti-Semitic backlash of 1968. *Winter* is a delicate and moving account of life and death in the ghetto. Less momentous, but also historically important, the second volume of her autobiography, *Belonging*, tells of life in the Communist Party and disillusionment in the early post-war years.

⭐ **Slavenka Drakulic,** *How We Survived Communism and Even Laughed* (UK: Vintage, 1993/US: Harperperennial Library, 1993). Croatian journalist and novelist Drakulic set out to convey the realities of life under communism in Eastern Europe by focusing on the mundane, and mainly domestic, details of everyday living. Her witty and often poignant tales of overcrowded apartments, the frantic search for cosmetics, the stockpiles of plastic bags, and hoarded food and medicine, the frisson of guilt and gratified ambition she feels on buying her first second-hand fur coat in New York, or her sense of being stifled by the old rhetoric when interviewed by an American academic feminist; add up to an exposé of Eastern European politics far more astute and accessible than any theoretical treatise. Her collected essays, *Café Europa: Life after Communism* (UK: Abacus, 1996/US: Penguin, 1999) continues with the same deceptively light tone of enquiry, this time delving into notions of Europe from within the Eastern European imagination.

Isabel Fonseca, *Bury Me Standing: The Gypsies and their Journey* (UK: Chatto & Windus, 1995/US: Vintage, 1996). After Albania, Slovakia, Bulgaria and Romania, the author's quest to understand the history and daily lives of gypsies takes her briefly to Poland where Warsaw's Central Station received the first wave of families migrating west after the revolutions of1989. Five days spent "loitering" in stations and visiting refugee camps where many gypsies are housed add up to a grim picture of an unwanted people, shunned by the Poles but equally divided by country of origin among themselves.

⭐ **Eva Hoffman,** *Lost in Translation: A Life in a New Language* (UK: Penguin, 1989/US: Penguin, 1990). Standing at the railings of a Canada-bound passenger ship, watching her beloved Poland slip away from her, the teenage Eva Hoffman experiences her first severe attack of nostalgia or tęsknota – "a word that adds to nostalgia the tonalities of sadness and longing". In the first section of her immensely moving and thoughtful memoir, which she titles, "Paradise" in contrast with her subsequent "Exile"in Vancouver, Hoffman describes the vibrant, irrepressible cultural life of post-war Kraków, where her Jewish parents instill in her the imperative to clutch hold of and enjoy each moment. She does, but her bright and cluttered memories only add to the pain she feels on finding herself lost in the bland suburbs of early-1960s Canada. Hoffman's more conventional travel narrative, ***Exit into History: A Journey through the New Eastern Europe*** (UK/US: Penguin, 1994), is a somewhat academic and journalistic enquiry into the post-communist landscape of Eastern Europe in the early 1990s. Inevitably her account is now dated but the sections on Poland stand out for their combination of shrewd political insight and human warmth. In ***Shtetl: The Life and Death of a Small Town and the World of Polish Jews*** (UK: Secker & Warburg/US: Mariner Books, 1998) she once more returns to her dual Polish and Jewish roots, this time to probe the deep ambivalence that coloured relations between Poles and Jews on the eve of World War II and throw new light on the motives which influenced Christian villagers' decisions to rescue or betray their Jewish neighbours when the Nazis invaded. A sober, heartrending book of immense integrity.

Russia

Back to Moscow

Caroline Walton

Caroline Walton, a writer living in London, first visited Moscow as part of a tour group in the late 1970s. It was the beginning of a twenty-year involvement with the country that led her to study Russian language, history and politics and, after the break-up of the Soviet Union, return to live and work, as one of very few foreigners, in Samara, an obscure provincial town. During that time she researched and wrote two books, *Little Tenement on the Volga*, about her experiences in this small conservative and militarily sensitive backwater, and *Russia through a Shotglass*, the century's political upheavals and purges as seen through the eyes of a Russian tramp.

Her latest trip back to Moscow was inspired by a more personal piece of research. She was asked by a family in England to visit the Russian capital for them and trace the history of an elderly Russian relative who had been forced to emigrate from Soviet Central Asia after her husband and father had been arrested as "capitalists".

Tuesday October 7, 1997: Will the city be wracked by mafia violence and nationalist hatred? Will commercial ugliness scar the landscape? I am returning to Russia after a four-year absence, and although in Britain I take press reports with a very large pinch of salt, I am a little apprehensive that I might find Moscow transformed into just another Western-type city, swallowed up by the global economy.

I have been commissioned to write the life story of a ninety-year-old lady who now lives in London. In 1932 this remarkable woman left her home in Soviet Central Asia, put on a veil and walked into Afghanistan with her four-year-old son. After an epic journey, which involved being smuggled into Palestine in a fishing boat, she joined her husband in London in 1936. I am going to Moscow to stay with her niece, Panina, to find out what happened to those members of the family who remained behind.

Sheremetevo airport: There is a long queue at passport control. Peroxide blonde, gum-chewing girls scrutinise each passport with inexorable slowness. Looking at their heavily made-up faces I feel a surge of irrational joy. At least some things haven't changed.

Outside the airport a drab autumn landscape greets me, unmarred by Coca-Cola signs. I am relieved to find that Russia still soothes my Western eyes.

Panina brings me home to her flat in the southeast of the city. Although it is late in the evening kiosks are open outside the metro station, and we drop into a store to stock up on cheese and sour cream. "This beats the Holloway Road for convenience shopping," I think.

Indeed, Panina tells me that Moscow is now a perfectly feasible city to live in, providing you have enough money. Shops and markets are crammed with food and clothing, you don't have to go to McDonald's if you want a quick cup of tea and a snack, and the metro runs like a dream. The provinces are another story. Compared to the rest of the country Muscovites are privileged: new money floods into the capital and some finds its way to the city's inhabitants (but by no means to all of them). Beyond the capital most people's survival depends on barter and the food they can grow.

* * * *

Wednesday morning: I rush out to greet the onion domes of St Basil's in Red Square, and am amazed to find the cathedral open to visitors. Panina has lived in Moscow for fifty years and she has never known it to be open. We buy our tickets - foreigners pay more, which I think is only fair – and wander through twisting corridors and little chapels. Icons are guarded by young and old women, who sit warming their legs by electric heaters.

"I am a retired construction engineer," says one elderly attendant, "with a higher education. They pay me mere *kopecks* to guard the icons but my pension comes to nothing so I have to work. I got a lot more under communism . . . and they call this democracy!"

The famous GUM department store is horrible, full of Christian Dior. I might as well be on Bond Street. We hurry through and Panina takes me to her synagogue on a side street. This serene old building revives my spirits; they rise still higher as we wander home through alleyways and courtyards – the hidden, beguiling heart of Moscow.

★ ★ ★ ★

Thursday: I wait at the metro for Panina's daughter, Shura. On the square in front of me a market is in full swing: as busy and bustling as any back home in London. A *babushka* war breaks out: three old ladies are standing by a wall peddling packs of cigarettes; when another approaches with the same intention they crowd around her, shouting and shoving her so hard that she gives up and totters away. I look at their hard, angry faces – reflections of their unimaginably hard lives. Yet these are only their public faces; to some young person each will be a kind aunt, a beloved granny.

Shura arrives and as we walk she tells me about her life: "My friends and I – university-educated women – live by picking up crumbs from the table of the nouveaux riches. They want cultured public relations managers to give their businesses a good image; they want their children to be literate so they employ us as tutors. But they are bloodsuckers all the same."

We wander down back streets and slip into a tiny church where a service is being held. Tall thin women bow before icons and cross themselves many times; one bends to kiss a priest's hand. With their heads bound in scarves, they look as though they have just stepped out of icons themselves. I watch them with the feeling that there is a thick glass wall between us. 'What was Lenin thinking of?', I wonder. 'In this country faith is everything.'

To my great joy, Shura takes me to a flat where the poet Anna Akhmatova used to stay when she visited Moscow. It will soon be opened as a museum but is not quite ready. The custodians are kind to me, as a foreigner, and show me into Akhmatova's former bedroom. Reverently I stand in the austere cell, stroking her bedcover, lightly touching her typewriter and smiling at the little fish and crab carved into the wooden frame of her door.

Meanwhile the custodians have laid out tea and cakes. We sit down to discuss Pushkin and Shakespeare and the trials of Akhmatova's life. 'This is why I keep coming back,' I think, 'this overwhelming hospitality, the chance conversations that last for hours, and the way this country awakens my sense of the past.'

★ ★ ★ ★

Sunday: Panina takes me to Peredelkino, a writers' colony just outside Moscow. She has two friends who live here, in a green-painted wooden *dacha*, its three rooms crammed with old furniture and paintings. Despite being rather tipsy, our host takes us in a tour of the settlement. We begin with the house of writers, then Boris Pasternak's *dacha*. We visit his grave in the local cemetery, next to stones of people who died in Chechnya and at Chernobyl.

Ivan the Terrible's chief executioner lived here, by the local church. I imagine Ivan's secret police riding out from this spot, with dogs' heads and broomsticks on their saddles, to sweep the land clean of the Tsar's enemies. My head swims with this vision of ancient and cruel Russia.

On the road back to the *dacha* I get a glimpse of modern and cruel Russia. Pretty little *dachas* like my host's are being burnt down and huge brick mansions erected behind high security fences. A holy spring has been encased in metal, and now resembles a urinal. A plaque beside it commemorates "Bogdan and Ludmila, killed in 1995".

"New Russians," remarks our host. "Mafia. They are taking over Peredelkino. Some of them are threatening our neighbours. They persuaded the local authorities to cut off their electricity and telephone. I expect they will turn their attention to us next."

"Doesn't it make you angry?" I ask, as a bull-necked man in a Toyota jeep sweeps past us and swings in through gates in a high concrete wall. Behind it lies a *dacha* that used to belong to Valentina Tereshkova, the first woman in space.

"It's just part of the historical process. You had it 300 years ago, with your robber barons, merchant adventurers, pirates and slave-traders. Yes, the new Russians are vicious and vulgar, but they'll send their children to Moscow University, Oxford and Harvard. The next generation will be more cultivated."

As Panina and I get up to leave our host, who has been swigging vodka all evening, staggers to his feet. "Dear ladies," he slurs, "allow me to escort you to the station."

Panina takes his arm, keeping him upright, while I lead the way with a torch. 'This is typical,' I think, 'the women still do everything here, while letting the men think they are in charge.'

On the little electric train a young peasant with a pink, potato-like face sits opposite, beaming at us and trying to butt into our conversation. Finally Panina turns to him: "We have just been eating the most delicious herring."

"I can tell you have," he replies, "by your smell."

Potato-man proceeds to tell a "joke" about a Jew and the KGB. I look away in disgust. Panina laughs. Later I question her.

"It's okay," she explains. "I don't feel conscious of anti-Semitism here but I like to test the water with people. If I had told that young man I was a Jew he would have said 'Oh, but my boss is Jewish and he's a great fellow; so are my Jewish friends.' "

"I go to Israel for a few weeks each year to visit family, but my home is here. I don't want to emigrate. I like living in a big, cosmopolitan city. Moscow is not Russia. Once you get used to living here you don't want to go anywhere else."

★ ★ ★ ★

Monday: Eating out in Moscow used to be a problem: you were faced with a choice between grim canteens — usually without the luxury of chairs — or a five-course banquet with mandatory champagne and vodka in a disco setting of mirror balls and East European pop music. Today Shura takes me to a pleasant restaurant for lunch; it is modestly priced, all items on the menu are available, and there is no obtrusive music. I am thirsty and ask the waiter for a cup of tea.

"But you haven't finished your soup!" he cries, in brave defiance of service culture.

I want to kiss him for that.

★ ★ ★ ★

Friday, Sheremetevo: I have filled in my customs declaration incorrectly and have to redo it (in triplicate) before they will let me through. As I struggle with the forms a beggar woman sticks her hand under my nose.

"You have not picked the right moment," Panina tells her softly as I begin to panic that I will miss my flight.

Finally I am allowed through. I kiss Panina goodbye and stumble off into a shining glass labyrinth of perfume and whisky bottles. There seems to be no information or indication of how to find one's departure gate. Flustered, I buttonhole a member of ground staff and ask her in Russian for help. She shrugs and walks off without a word.

'This airport just about sums up the new Russia,' I think, as I find my gate with the help of some Japanese businessmen.

But as I board my plane, I relax, relieved that the Russia I love lives on, squeezed between capitalist excess and the Soviet behemoth that refuses to die.

read on . . .

Caroline Walton, *Little Tenement on the Volga* **(available via the author c/o Women Travel).** Walton describes her experiences as one of the first Westerners to set up home in Samara, a small conservative town and militarily sensitive backwater. Her latest book *Ivan Petrov: Russia Through a Shotglass* (US: Garrett County Press, 1999) is a biographical account of a Russian tramp who survives the Stalin and Khrushchev years before seeking refuge in England.

Louise Bryant, *Six Red Months in Russia* **(UK/US: o/p).** Bryant's pacey and humane first-hand account of the revolution in Russia has been somewhat lost in the shadows of the more celebrated journalism of her Communist lover, John Reed. Her dynamic, mercurial writing, including interviews with Lenin and Trotsky, deserves better.

Christina Dodwell, *Beyond Siberia* **(UK: Sceptre, 1993/US: o/p).** After travelling in Africa, Papua Guinea, Turkey and China, often on horseback, one of Britain's hardiest women explorers turns her attention to the remote peninsula of Kamchatka, Russia's Far East and "a land of permafrost and volcanoes . . . of bears, sables, caviar and gold". She tells of travelling with a song and dance troupe entertaining the scattered communities of reindeer herdsmen, of driving runaway dog sleds, tracking bears and skiing across frozen sand dunes down to the sea. Dodwell's passion for charting new territory, her warm-hearted curiosity about people, not to mention the obscure nature of her destination, make for a rewarding read.

Martha Gellhorn, "One Look at Mother Russia", from her collected travel writings, *Travels With Myself and Another* (1978; UK: Eland Books, 1983/US: o/p). In the late 1970s, when travel throughout the Soviet Union was entirely governed by the whim of the state agency, Intourist, Gellhorn broke her self-imposed boycott of Russia to visit an elderly author whom she admired. Her almost seismic impatience with the bad manners and prohibitions she encounters during her week veers sometimes into slapstick, such as when she can't find any decent food and gatecrashes a US Embassy party to gobble the canapes. An enjoyable cringe that somehow also manages a serious look at the iniquities of the totalitarian regime.

Mary Morris, *Wall to Wall: A Woman's Travels from Beijing to Berlin* **(UK: o/p/US: Doubleday, 1991).** Morris has a gift for combining insightful travelogue with an intensely personal account of her own history and ongoing quest for self-discovery, In *Wall to Wall*, she is driven by her grandmother's stories of the Russian Cossacks and pogroms of her ancestry to make an epic journey from China, through the Soviet Union and on to Berlin. The journey takes place in 1986, when the second wall is still a formidable physical and political barrier and the ripples of glasnost and perestroika have only just begun to spread. Two momentous events magnify her growing sense of unease about her journey, the Chernobyl nuclear disaster and the revelation that she is in the first stage of pregnancy. Morris manages to write as eloquently about the doubts and tedium of travel – the thousands of miles whizzing past a grimy train window, the anonymous hotel rooms – as about her impressions of place.

Irina Ratushinskaya, *Grey is the Colour of Hope* **(UK: Hodder & Stoughton, 1989/US: o/p).** In 1983, 28-year-old dissident poet Irina Ratushinskaya was sentenced to seven years of hard labour and five years of internal exile. This memoir follows the four years that she spent as part of a tiny group of female political prisoners, isolated from the mass of ordinary "criminals" due to their dangerous influence. A humbling portrayal of six women locked in a dignified, caring and utterly courageous stand against appalling oppression.

Larissa Vasilieva, *Kremlin Wives* **(UK: Weidenfeld & Nicolson, 1994/US: Arcade, 1994).** A fascinating glimpse at some KGB files on the women who paced the Kremlin, from the imprisoned wives of Molotov and Kalinin, to the free-loving Alexandra Kollontai and the media-sophisticate, Raisa Gorbachev. Unfortunately Vasilieva's research is thrown together with a mass of jumbled speculation and unattributed detail that takes away most of its edge.

Scotland

Northern rocks

Margaret Jailler

Margaret Jailler went camping in Shetland with her daughter Fayida, then aged four. Having visited the Orkney isles and Barra in the Outer Hebrides, she was intrigued by Shetland's particular Norse culture and also by its paradoxical mix of physical isolation and cosmopolitan people. In fog and fine weather the pair explored the islands by bus and on foot, dragging their accommodation on wheels behind them. They currently live in South London where Margaret runs an organic vegetable home-delivery service. A graduate in film-making from the Royal College of Art, she also works occasionally as a lighting-camerawoman in the field of art and experimental documentary films.

At the gateway between the North Sea and the North Atlantic, the cluster of islands which make up Shetland are almost as close to Norway as they are to mainland Britain and, level with the southern tip of Greenland, not that far from the Arctic Circle. However, due to its strategic position in some of the world's richest fishing grounds and, more recently, the construction of Europe's largest oil terminal at Sullem Voe, its people are neither insular nor backward-looking. After poring over travel books, I imagined Lerwick, the capital and only town of any size, to be like some Wild West frontier town where Russian trawler crews, Norwegian whalers and men from the oil rigs gambled and whored and stocked up with dry goods before returning to the inhospitable wastes of the North Sea.

We descended into Sumburgh two days before Shetland was enveloped in a warm mist that prevented either landing or take-off for another week. Shetlanders are used to being cut off by fog, but I felt as though we'd stumbled into Brigadoon. We headed for Lerwick, an elegant Victorian town where, even in summer, the wind whistles down Commercial Street fit to take your coat off. Though we did not bump into a single drunken Russian, Lerwick did feel like a frontier town. Built on a promontory in the Sound of Bressay, its seafront is dominated by docks and a harbour. While the main shopping street comprises mostly small family businesses, there are two enormous supermarkets on the outskirts of town and a place that sells nothing but bottled butane. During our stay in Shetland we often hitched rides into Lerwick with people on their way to stock up at one or other of these three places.

Fayida and I spent two days in Lerwick buying provisions, visiting the charity shops and luxuriating at the well-appointed Clickimin leisure complex, which, along with Shetland's well-constructed network of roads, is evidence of the prosperity that North Sea oil has brought to the islands. We also visited the tourist office on Market Cross and planned a loose itinerary. The basis of this was that we would begin at the most northerly point and work our way south, back to the airport at Sumburgh, visiting Lerwick every few days for more supplies and tourist information. My only other resolutions were to avoid organised coach trips and to try not to neglect Fayida's interests.

Those first two days were rough. The bag containing all our camping equipment was painfully heavy, even to drag, and Fayida complained constantly that she didn't want to be in Shetland. She missed her friends, her toys and the TV, and she didn't want to walk. Our return flight was not for another two weeks; I struggled with futile thoughts of how the whole trip was a terrible mistake. The turning point came on the third day when we were leaving Lerwick for Unst, the most northerly isle. On our way to the Viking bus station the bag on wheels was cutting off the blood supply to my fingers and I could bear the endless complaints no longer. We stopped in the road and, as I flexed my painful fingers, I described to her a hell worthy of Dante into which we would surely descend unless we tried to view things more constructively. I think that what swung it for Fayida in the end was the packet of fruit pastilles I produced rather than anything I'd said. For the next two weeks I made sure that I was never without them.

A relay of post buses and vehicle ferries transported us from the mainland, via the island of Yell to Unst. By mid-afternoon we had reached the village of Haroldswick, which boasts the most northerly post office in Britain.

As far as I could see through the fog, Haroldswick was flat and deserted. A pale sun and the sound of lapping waves were the surest means of orientation. I found it eerie and, glad that Fayida was not similarly affected, turned my gloomy thoughts to practical matters. This would be our first pitch off a campsite; my first criterion was a water supply and my second was nearness to people. After clearing it with people in the only shop I pitched nearby, next to a standpipe in the grounds of an unoccupied house.

We were sitting in the mouth of the tent, brewing up soup, when a wiry, dark-haired man in his late thirties approached. He was a little the worse for drink which, combined with the thick Shetland dialect he spoke, meant that I had to ask him to rephrase much of what he said. Finally, after some good-humoured effort on both sides, I understood that we had camped outside his deceased uncle's house and that, although he didn't mind, he felt he should warn us that, on this, the first anniversary of his uncle's death, his father might be upset about it. He said that if his father approached us we should say that he, Frank, had given us permission. I was later to realise that this warning was more a pretext for an introduction, since in fact his uncle had only rented the house from a distant laird.

Fayida and I spent the next two hours wandering about this scattered community, veiled in fog. I tried with little success to get some sense of the geography while Fayida responded with measured curiosity to the squat ponies that trotted along with us behind their fences. No sooner had we returned to the tent than Frank visited again, this time with the gift of a jar of instant coffee. In the course of the next hour he told us of his past army career, his broken marriage and the long and unsociable shifts he had just been working in his maintenance job at the nearby Saxa Vord RAF base. He explained that it had been several weeks since he'd had anyone to talk to and now he couldn't stop. Then he invited us for tea at the house which he had built for himself and his wife and which he had named "Lonabrak", the Norse word for the sound of a wave retreating over shingle. I was charmed that there should even exist such a word and, since I too had been lacking adult company, we accompanied him to his house. His was a sad story and I could imagine how difficult the gloomy Shetland winters would be for anyone of a brooding nature.

Frank's house was cluttered with the belongings of his deceased uncle and the momentoes of his own army career. In the absence of the family he'd planned he seemed compelled to offer his protection to Fayida and me in the form of countless small gifts. I refused most of them on the grounds of needing to travel light. Among those I accepted were a finely illustrated book of birds which had belonged to his uncle (and to which I referred daily for the rest of our holiday), an old calendar with a photograph of the 1961 class of Haroldswick primary school, all dressed in home-made Viking costumes, and some items of army issue survival kit, including sachets of dried food and some matches which would apparently light under water. Fayida remained glued throughout to the 36-inch colour TV which was tuned to a satellite cartoon station. Increasingly conscious of the risk I was taking in visiting this man, and worn out by his pressing generosity and the effort of trying to follow his conversation, I finally decided it was time to leave. I believe there is such a thing as a woman's touch and this house lacked it, almost wantonly. Once outside the claustrophobic squalor, we ambled circuitously back to the tent.

Fayida slept deeply that night while I lay wondering whether we would be disturbed by another visit from Frank or some of the men spilling out of a nearby RAF disco, or worse, the ghost of Frank's uncle. This was to be the first of several occasions on which I was grateful for the over-riding influence of tiredness on my imagination.

Early the next day we relocated to the youth hostel in Uyeasound in the south of Unst. Here we teamed up with two young men, an Italian student of architecture and a English teacher, to walk through the Hermaness bird sanctuary, along the most northerly coastline. The fog, which made this expedition quite risky, lifted enough for us to see thousands of screaming gannets wheeling around stacks and arches white with guano, and sheep perched in impossible places. From a distance the rhythmic babble of these colonies sounded through the fog, like the sinister throb of some enormous engine to which we drew inescapably nearer. On reaching the cliffs the sound was almost deafening. Beyond the gannet colonies, on the wave-dashed rocks of Muckle Flugga, we saw Britain's most northerly light-house, designed by Robert Louis Stevenson's father and said to be the location for the writing of *Treasure Island*.

All my concerns that Fayida and I might not be able to keep pace with our companions were unfounded. On the few occasions when it did happen they lingered discreetly, taking photographs or sipping water, but for the most part Fayida showed astonishing stamina for a four-year-old. She delighted in the springiness of the peat under-foot and the way the boggy water filtered through her sandals. We shared out the fruit pastilles and kept a tally of the puffin carcasses left by skuas. At last Fayida seemed contented. Late in the afternoon the four of us hitched back to the youth hostel without difficulty. It had been a refreshingly uncomplicated day.

That evening we pottered on the beach in front of the youth hostel and met a startlingly self-possessed girl of about the same age as Fayida. She informed us that this was her beach and, accompanied by her second-in-command, an ancient lurcher called Max, she took us on a tour of inspection of her "prisoners". These were a dozen or so large, ink-blue, beached jellyfish, in the centre of each of which she'd placed a small rock "to stop them escaping". At length she turned her attention to Fayida and asked, in a strong accent, "Is he a boy?" Fayida's father is from Zaire and her hair is a mass of tight curls. I don't expect this girl had never seen anyone quite like her before.

After another brief trip into Lerwick, we travelled east to Walls for the agricultural show. By now I was feeling more confident about the travelling and we frequently hitched when there was no bus service. The ease with which we secured lifts was like plucking fruit from a tree; despite the unforgiving landscape, our experience of Shetland was that it was both bountiful and providential in its care of us.

The Walls agricultural show offered more evidence of the pleni-tude that this seemingly inhospitable island can yield up through hard work and ingenuity. Besides the livestock categories, which captivated Fayida, there were those which are traditionally women's. These included home produce, knitting and spinning, and flower arranging. My favourite was the wild flower category and I was deeply impressed by the knowledge of generic names which nearly everyone in the tent seemed to share.

I found the appreciation of nature to be one of the rare and refreshing qualities common to all Shetland people. They are conscious of sharing use of the land with the wildlife, for which they have a rich vocabulary of folk names. At one point I had a conversation with a man in his early twenties about the subtle colourings of the rabbits you see when walking the cliffs at dusk and the way quizzical seals swim alongside you. This man was not a naturalist though, and his observations, merely those of a country person, wouldn't have sounded strange coming from the lips of a Thomas Hardy character.

The Walls show ended with entertainment in the village hall. A line-dancing sketch had us joining in the laughter without understanding a word of the dialect. There were fiddle virtuosos performed by the very young through to the very old, and a reading of Christine de Luca's poetry, written in dialect and read by her old schoolteacher, which brought back images from my own rural childhood and with them the regret that Fayida will never experience such freedom as long as we remain in the city.

Our holiday was half over and by now I'd come to terms with the idea that in two weeks we wouldn't see most of Shetland. By this time I'd also seen enough to know that we couldn't leave without visiting the wild and wuthering coastline at Eshaness and staying in Johnny Notions' cottage. This historical property, like many others throughout Shetland, has been opened up by the regional tourist board as a "camping bod". As cheap as a campsite, and with roughly the same facilities, these old buildings provide welcome shelter from the elements and a glimpse of the fisherman–crofter's habitat.

Each time we arrived in a truly remote place, as we said goodbye to the last person we would see for a day or two – usually the bus driver – he or she would invariably want assurance that I'd come prepared with enough food. There would be an unstated note of apology (about the lack of amenities) in this enquiry and my affirmative reply was always met with a mix of relief and respect, presumably because the ease of shopping in London had not eroded my capacity for forward planning. I was always touched by these enquiries, which were perhaps made more readily because of "the bairn".

Eshaness was probably the remotest place we visited but was far from being god-forsaken. The god of all things animal and elemental ruled here, and a vengeful god he was. Flotsam and jetsam – traces of frail humanity spat out by the raging sea onto towering cliff-tops – were everywhere to be seen. Among plastic fish crates and lobster pots, crops of fluorescent pink and orange buoys nestled in eye-stinging contrast with the intense green of grassy hollows. In a day spent walking a significant stretch of the coastline, we saw hundreds of skittish rabbits and colonies of indolent seals, but not one human being. The scattered evidence of people's past attempts to work the land – small stone enclosures in which sheep now cropped the over-grown cabbages – served as a reminder that nature only lends the rights. We sheltered behind one of these constructions to eat our lunch and found in it a litter of tiny kittens waiting snugly for their mother. Fayida and I sang loudly in this wilderness, keeping always back from the edge because of the strong winds, the squally showers, not to mention the downward slope to the precipice. If anything happened to us the bus driver, who I'd asked to collect us after two days, would be the first and only person on the island to notice us missing.

Johnny "Notions" Williamson was an eighteenth-century weaver. He became a local hero when, without medical training, he devised a smallpox inoculation that averted an epidemic. The door to his one-room cottage is only five-feet high and the ceiling less than seven, though Johnny himself was perhaps no shorter than his contemporaries.

I was a little unnerved by the isolation of the cottage. We had one neighbour and he, as far as I could tell, lived alone in a caravan and spent his time banger-racing on the empty roads in an old Cortina. He'd spotted us at a distance earlier that day and now, as the light faded and we prepared for sleep, I tried not to imagine his face peering in at the window. In some ways I was glad not to have electricity; there were no curtains so lights inside would have made me feel even more vulnerable. By an effort of will I superimposed the face of my own fear with the enquiring and steadfast features I imagined Johnny Notions to have had. Fayida slept immediately while I was obliged first to tiptoe to the outhouse, the hairs prickling on the back of my neck. On returning I placed a bottle on its side behind the unlocked door so that at least we might waken to receive our guest.

On our last visit to Lerwick we took a boat trip round the islands of Noss and Bressay. From our vantage point below the cliffs we saw, smelled and ducked large colonies of gannets. We also saw seals and dolphins at close range. The deep waters were teeming with fish and each time our guide cast his fishing line, which had six hooks on it, he'd reel it straight back in with as many thrashing mackerel attached.

We said our last goodbye to the capital and spent the remaining few days ambling south. The southern landscape is gentler, with many fine white beaches and fewer cliffs. We spent most of our time beach-combing and building fires from driftwood. Fayida was contented but I had left my heart in the north and felt ready to leave.

read on . . .

Mairi Hedderwick, *Eye on the Hebrides: An Illustrated Journey* (UK: Canongate, 1998). An illustrated travel memoir by the much-loved Scottish illustrator and author of children's books. Hedderwick's knowledge of and rapt interest in the islands of the Hebrides, where she spent her childhood holidays and returned as a young adult, are rendered in appealing, if occasionally over-sentimentalised, watercolours and sketches. The text is evocative enough of landscape but can lapse into somewhat cute observations of people.

Bettina Selby, *The Fragile Islands: A Journey Through the Outer Hebrides* (1989; UK: Ulverscroft, 1994). Robust cyclist and traveller Bettina Selby spent a long summer exploring these "thinly covered scraps of rock", accompanied by an equally hardy bicycle and a small tent. Her keen interest in both people and wildlife is accompanied by a deepening concern for the future of a region whose wasteland is expanding as its faltering economy drives much of the younger population overseas. A well-observed account by a writer not afraid to air her views.

South Africa

Bussing them in

Sarah Johnstone

Taking a bus tour of Soweto may be the safest way to visit, but London-based freelance writer Sarah Johnstone found there's a hidden price to be paid for cultural voyeurism: enduring your fellow passengers. Johnstone has written for the *Independent on Sunday*, *The Times* and *The Face*. See also her piece on Libya (p.357).

"Well at least they're doing something," the man from Australia nodded in the direction of our hosts. "Not like the Abo who sits there and takes." Now, if that's the sort of dumb-headed remark you'd never expect to hear in the middle of a bar in the heartland of the new South Africa, try visiting Soweto on a package tour.

I don't normally go around recommending package tours, but after I'd spent some time in Johannesburg's affluent white suburbs, I had to escape, and this tour seemed like the safest way to see Soweto, even if it did make me as guilty of cultural voyeurism as everyone else on the bus.

"Tell me, was there any time you did not feel 100 percent safe?" asked George, the tour guide, as the humid morning's trip came to a close. Well, now that you mention it, George, there was the old man yelling in Zulu at our parked minibus. Then, there was a heart-stopping moment when you stepped away for a moment and left us staring into the face of a menacing-looking bloke. Sure, bus tours

510

might be the safest way to visit, but I still couldn't put out of my mind those countless stories of hold-ups that dominate whites' dinner-table conversation throughout this troubled land.

Since 1994, when Nelson Mandela walked out of political mythology and into the Parliament building in Cape Town, it's been possible to visit South Africa without risking the sort of dubious looks usually reserved for elderly German exiles in Paraguay. But a journey to Johannesburg and its environs, including Soweto, is full of other perils. At the time I visited, in 1997, the police told me that fourteen people were murdered on an average day, seventeen were raped and 100 were mugged. Another 24 had their car hijacked at gunpoint while just popping down the shops for a pint of milk or something.

No longer able to rely on repressive policing to shield them them from fellow citizens poorer than themselves, and suddenly finding those fellow citizens armed with AK-47 rifles, white Johannesburgers have been left feeling very nervous in this post-apartheid era. Very nervous indeed. Not that blacks aren't targets of crime as well, but some are so paranoid you almost have to hold a pistol against their heads to persuade them just to drive downtown. Although tours to Soweto began operating about ten years ago – well before the downfall of apartheid – many white South Africans have never set foot in a township.

However, fuelled by a mix of political fervour, curiosity and fear, I decided there was nothing for it but to throw in my lot with a local guide and a bunch of other pasty-faced Westerners. In less than an hour I started regretting it, as the stupid questions flew. "Do children from Soweto go to school?" "Can you take me to a witch-doctor?". Never mind the risk of being shot, the scariest thing about visiting Soweto has to be your fellow passengers.

"We know that there were a lot of lies talked about Soweto in the past," asserted George after picking us up in Johannesburg and driving us 13km to the bustling taxi stand at the township's entrance. "We want people to see the truth about Soweto. We know there were a lot of people in other countries who were against apartheid."

But the bunch of us who marched in baggy shorts and other bits of shapeless attire past the colourful market stalls and the long queues for minivan taxis hardly look like the crusading types. A German woman seemed to have trouble hiding her distaste as we picked across the mud and dirt into a very makeshift café. The suburban Yanks among us looked uncomprehending as they surveyed the chaos.

All the same, it's perfectly understandable why Soweto should prove such a drawcard for Mr and Mrs average tourist. The name became synonymous in the 1970s and 1980s with the riots and uprisings against the National Party regime. Its poverty came to represent the inequities of apartheid. Plus visiting Soweto is a great way to impress your friends back home with how intrepid you are, virtually without having to leave your seat.

My first glimpse of this vast sprawl of townships revealed it to be not quite what I'd expected. Although there are pockets of squalid-looking tin-shacks, Soweto also has all the features the modern urban dweller has come to take for granted – brick houses, schools, libraries, sports grounds, a university and a well-established mafia.

Apart from the townships' two-dozen millionaires, there are a few local, self-styled "gangstas" who are also thought to have broken the six-figure barrier through one scam or another. Rumour has it that the Mr Bigs of South Africa's infamous car-jacking syndicates are white. At every turn, as we wound our way through the red dusty streets, there was someone polishing his BMW, shining up his Mercedes. There was even a guy with mobile phone in hand, taking a break from washing his silver BMW, only a few feet from a group of squatter-camp inhabitants collecting water from an open pipe.

Any visit to Soweto soon involves its most-famous local boy made good, the former president. George showed us the Orlando football stadium, where Mandela staged his homecoming rally after his release from prison in 1990. He told us tales of the gifts lavished on him by rich locals. He showed us rainbow murals where the face of the township's "main man" radiates down, next to another of the most enduring icons of the anti-apartheid movement, the pietà-like image of murdered schoolboy Hector Peterson being carried from the carnage of the Soweto riots.

The monument to Hector Peterson, a few miles away, is probably as close as the township gets to a tourist attraction. As we stopped at the memorial where the thirteen-year-old was gunned down by police in June 1976, George spent some time and care explaining how the trouble began. Inspired by the Black Consciousness movement of the 1970s, students decided they wanted to be taught in English rather than Afrikaans, the language of the oppressor. They stayed away from school. They demonstrated. Things swiftly got out of hand. "If you have any questions, feel free to ask," George coaxed us. Umm. . . Given the chance to ask something sensible, we suddenly fell silent.

Next, we piled back into the bus to look at some houses. Gazing at people's homes is something you spend a disproportionate amount of time doing in Soweto, leading some commentators to remark that all of the buildings are alike. That's not true, though. Some of the government-built versions come with the deadly "luxury" of asbestos roofs, while other tall, skinny edifices reserved for lone widows are fairytale reminders that you're almost in another world. Looking at the squat cinder-block structures and the corrugated iron annexes, it's weird to think that Sowetans had to organise rent boycotts to get the government to deliver on its promise to allow them to own these homes.

Winnie Mandela's house was a barrow of bricks. Her abode high on a hill in Diepkloof extension – nicknamed Diepkloof expensive – is a mansion by township standards, and notorious for being the place where Stompie Mketsi was killed in an incident involving the ANC youth football league, and Winnie's reputation began its downhill slide. The house has the added distinction of representing probably the only collaboration between Jane Fonda and Libya's Colonel Muhammed Gaddafi. George told us that both contributed to funds to build the house after the Mandelas' earlier home was firebombed.

Winnie's decision to remain there, while her former husband departed for the leafy streets of one of Johannesburg's ritziest neighbourhoods, has earned her the fierce loyalty of the locals. "We feel the ANC has betrayed Mrs Mandela," George said forcefully. "Aha," we nodded, but once again fell into a sheepish silence as we piled back into the bus. After, we drove down the only street in the world with two Nobel Prize-winning residents (at least nominally, as both Nelson Mandela and Archbishop Desmond Tutu now spend their time elsewhere) and gaped at the makeshift dry-cleaners' shop in a painted caravan, the green flags fluttering above the witch-doctors' homes, and waved back at the children who waved at the bus.

Nothing we saw, though, seemed to spark quite so much interest as the simple "Welcome To Soweto" sign. We'd already been travelling some time when we happened upon it, and it provoked a scramble to get off the bus. A cheerful British father and his son started taking pictures of each other standing in front of the sign. Others posed in front of the shield and nine spears representing Soweto's tribes.

Five minutes later, when we called in on some of George's relatives in Orlando, the same father distinguished himself by pushing the rest of us aside as he raced to videotape the family living room, with its faded orange-and-brown decor and tattered football posters. By the time we stopped for a drink at *Wandi's Place*, things were getting distinctly weird. We filed past a giant can of Castle lager into the dimly lit *shebeen*, or pub, and George went over to chat with the guides from the other tour groups which had also stopped here. The place was full of loud, half-pissed bores boasting about the last time they were on safari or when they climbed the Matterhorn. I wedged myself into a corner to escape them and overheard some gob-smacking comments. As we emerged, the British man with the camcorder was looking particularly pleased with his new T-shirt, proclaiming "I was in *Wandi's Place*, Soweto".

"Feel free to ask anything," George coaxed us one final time, as we hopped back in the bus and continued on our merry way. Suddenly, a man in the back started saying something. George looked expectant. "Yeah, say, can you turn the air-conditioning up?" the man drawled. By now, I was beginning to think it wouldn't be such a bad thing if our sorry bunch of gormless voyeurs were hijacked after all, as we took a last turn in a neighbourhood where one of the township's millionaires had been trying to sell his house. He couldn't find a buyer, though, on account of its street number: 666. "If you were to buy that house you would be the first white person living in Soweto," George suggested.

That would take a lot of courage. A lot of courage, indeed. Maybe if you had that much sang-froid, you wouldn't even bat an eyelid at these busloads of damn fool tourists driving round and round in circles, just checking out your 'hood.

Jazz in the city

Jo Hutton

Jo Hutton is a London-based musician and single mother who went to Johannesburg to visit friends and to trace Stephen Phiri, a Sowetan musician she has admired ever since finding one of his records at a jumble sale, aged fifteen. Though she failed to find Phiri, she and her sons, Jake and Liam, discovered the pleasure of breaking through racial barriers in the jazz clubs of Rockey Street. Jo teaches music in schools and colleges, and gives workshops on music technology and recording to women's groups and people in prison.

"I'm sorry, Madam, but you won't be able to travel with that ticket." My heart sank. I looked at my kids, waiting patiently in the queue, and back at the official behind the airline desk. I couldn't believe it. Two years of saving for this trip, all my careful checking and re-checking suitcases and travel documents, and I had overlooked the simple fact that my passport stated my maiden name and my ticket had been issued in my married name. I had no document to prove the connection, only the living proof of my two sons beside me. I pointed this out to the official, who sent me to the customer-service desk. My heart was racing as we ran to the other end of the airport. Agonising minutes passed as I listened to a stream of phone calls attempting to verify my identity. Finally, I was permitted to sign an indemnity form, and before long, we were back on course to Johannesburg. As the plane took off, my son Liam screamed, "Ra, wicked!", loud enough to make everyone laugh. I pressed the recline button and began to relax for the first time in six months.

Our six-week trip was a well-deserved holiday for my sons Jake, nine, and Liam, six. We would visit with a close friend who lives in Johannesburg and I would learn more about South African music. As a saxophone and flute player, I have long nurtured an infatuation with

515

the simple but haunting sounds of South African jazz, and I was looking for one man in particular: a certain saxophonist named Stephen Phiri from Soweto, who played on an old record I had found at the age of fifteen at a jumble sale, and which has had a profound influence on my life ever since.

Our friends live on Rockey Street in Johannesburg – a sort of Portobello Road, with snobby shops at one end, grungy drug-deal warrens at the other, and funky street stalls and clubs in between. It's home to a large student population and has always been known for its racial mix, even during the apartheid years. That was true of our house too. We were staying with a young couple, teachers in a local school, and their two kids; my close friend Amanda who works crazy hours as a hairdresser for TV and video; a young Sowetan man who now plays rugby professionally for Johannesburg, and his girlfriend.

Like other houses on our street, our windows were fortified with fierce-looking iron bars, but this didn't seem to make much of a difference to the easy-going way everyone lived. The security gate was always open, and there were always people coming and going. Everything seemed surprisingly relaxed. It wasn't at all how I had imagined life to be in this notoriously violent city.

Wandering around Rockey Street confirmed the impression. The street was buzzing with colourful stalls – luscious fruit and veg stands attended by gorgeous women in traditional robes and wraps. Shop fronts, walls and signs boasted bright African colours. Unlike London, everyone seemed to walk so "easy", whether they were women balancing baskets on their heads or men with a backwards lean and casual swing. We were the only white people around, but Jake and Liam seemed unfazed by this new culture.

Still, appearances can deceive. The first day, we decided to walk home through the back streets. As we ambled along, I realised that the surrounding neighbourhood and atmosphere was suddenly very different. The houses were squalid and I could sense resentment and anger in the looks we attracted. Just as I was wondering if we should turn around and go back, a car-load of men pulled up, jumped out and started shouting angrily at me while pointing to Jake and Liam. I was terrified until a passer-by translated for us: "This is dangerous place for you. Walk fast and hold hands with your children. You want them kidnap?" These angry, frightening men were just concerned for my safety. We walked on quickly, and, as suddenly as before, we were back in a friendly street.

After that first day, I never again felt threatened or intimidated walking with my boys in the streets. Perhaps this was because we didn't look like we had much money or because the Rockey Street community welcomes those who want to be part of it. In London, we live in a racially mixed part of town, and we had discussed the possibility of encountering racism in South Africa before we left home. Yet, once we arrived, the boys seemed determined not to deal with any kind of racism, and I realised that it was from them that I would best learn how to overcome my own anxieties. As my friend Amanda said, "It's people who look frightened and aloof who have problems. If you give off a friendly vibe, you won't have any trouble".

We took her advice to heart, and the boys made many friends on Rockey Street. I followed them into places where I would never have dared go on my own. Jake, bursting with enthusiasm and confidence, would march into a bar, straight up to the pool tables, put his money on the table and wait his turn for a game – much to the amazement of the clientele. He simply didn't notice any tension created by our presence. If he did, he was much more skilled than I was at ignoring it. Almost always, he succeeded in breaking through it, and we made many friends through him.

Music was another way of finding common ground. In Johannesburg, music is everywhere. One morning, I woke up to melodic whooping and screeching. It was the sound of dustmen coming down the road, performing a traditional South African song, where one person shouts something and then they all harmonise for the chorus. It sounded wonderfully rich and warm, perfectly in time and tune. I wish our dustmen did that at home.

Rockey Street was a haven for live jazz, with a club located every hundred yards or so. My friends knew many of the club owners, so it wasn't long before I was invited to sit in on the flute on a couple of numbers. I played with one band where the keyboard player was blind, the saxophonist had a limp, and the leader, Simba Morre, had a huge scar on his face. They were old guys from Soweto, who played the sweetest, most soulful jazz I have ever heard. Another band we met was made up of traditional Zulu musicians, who played a deeply resonating instrument I'd never heard before: a horn from the impala antelope. Everywhere I went, I asked about Stephen Phiri, but no luck.

We were now getting into the rhythm of life in Johannesburg. The boys had started going to school with the other kids in the house, leaving me free to meet up with musicians and do some playing and recording. After a month, though, I agreed to fulfil my promise to the kids of going on safari. We booked three days on the Pilanesberg Game Reserve, a long bus journey away. As we set off on our "safari", everyone was laughing at the lengths to which this city-slicker was willing to go to keep marauding insects away – sprays, creams, burners. Our tent would be positively glowing with chemicals. Unfortunately, we didn't take the side-effects into consideration, as Jake later developed an allergic reaction to the sprays, and his neck swelled hugely.

When we arrived, we realised we were the only people with a tent, as the site was mainly occupied by luxury-caravan owners. This was our first encounter with Afrikaaners – square-jawed, well-fed, with values rooted firmly in the past. Our little tent and my single-mum status made us something of a novelty, and we were soon taken under the wing of the campsite managers, Big Laz and Mighty Elicen. Big Laz was well over six foot, drove a big truck and had a deep voice with a big smile. Mighty Elicen was very small with a soft voice and gentle manner. At breakfast, due to diminishing funds, I ordered just coffee and one breakfast for Jake and Liam to share. Mighty Elicen was offended: "What's this? One breakfast for three? Growing boys must eat." I was very embarrassed. "Sorry, I don't have much money," I said. For the rest of our stay, Mighty Elicen discreetly brought us three huge breakfasts for the price of one.

While we were there, we went on safaris and the kids played in the pool. One day, a group of African schoolchildren arrived, and dived in. Every single white Afrikaans person in that pool jumped out, grabbed their stuff and ran for cover. The schoolkids and the boys carried on swimming. I couldn't help but think this was a good image of the current situation: the Afrikaans on the run, as the Africans get on with life.

At the end of our short trip, Big Laz drove us to the bus station, and we returned to Johannesburg with only a little bit of time left before our scheduled return. I have to admit, I was feeling tired and looking forward to home. Travelling on your own with children is very rewarding and creates endless opportunities for meeting people. But it's also exhausting being away from your normal support system. I had failed in my search for Stephen Phiri, but had found all the friends and music I had hoped for – music that speaks the language of change to anyone who wants to listen.

read on . . .

Margaret McCord, *The Calling of Katie Makanya: A Memoir of South Africa* **(UK/US: John Wiley, 1998).** A unique record of the life of Katie Makanya, a black South African woman, born in 1873, who lived through colonisation, the Boer War and the establishment of apartheid. Well educated but also a very fine singer, Makanya went to England with an award-winning choir which performed for luminaries including Queen Victoria, returning to South Africa to start a family and dedicate herself to helping her people. Concealing her education, she worked for a time as a servant until she eventually found a long-term job as assistant to the American doctor Jack McCord, whose daughter recorded and reported this story. Using hours of taped interviews with this remarkable eighty-year-old woman, Margaret McCord creates a wonderfully vivid and detailed portrait of an "ordinary yet extraordinary" life, experienced at a time in South Africa's history when the black population seldom, if ever, had a voice.

Sindiwe Magoma, *To My Children's Children* **(UK: The Women's Press, 1991/US: Interlink Publishing Group, 1998).** A fascinating autobiography, initially started so that her family would never forget their roots, in which Magoma traces her life from the rural Transkei to the townships of Cape Town, and from political innocence to wisdom born of bitter experience.

Emma Mashinini, *Strikes Have Followed Me All My Life* **(UK: The Women's Press, 1995/US: o/p).** Moving account of this diminuitive but unstoppable trade unionist, who defied both injustice in the labour market and the deep sexism of her colleagues during her tireless struggles from the 1950s to the 1980s.

Dervla Murphy, *South from the Limpopo: Travels through South Africa* **(UK: Flamingo, 1998/US: Overlook Press, 1999).** This is the story of three long bike-rides made in 1993 and 1994, before and after the elections which marked the dawning of a new South Africa. As in most of Murphy's travel accounts, she uses a diary format to chronicle her journeys around the country, meeting all kinds of people from slum-dwellers to businessmen, frankly recording her views as she attempts to unveil the development of a newly liberated but still complex and multi-layered society. Despite being in her early sixties, her stamina appears more or less undented by either the distance covered – literally thousands of miles – or the basic sleeping quarters she almost seems to prefer. She is also as undaunted as ever in the face of hostility, for instance when her overtures are frequently ignored or, more dramatically, when strip-searched in a police cell. This book, along with her many previous volumes still in print, further consolidates Murphy's position as one of the most quirky, entertaining and intrepid women travellers writing today.

Gillian Slovo, *Every Secret Thing: My Family, My Country* (UK: Little, Brown & Co., 1997). Slovo's intensely moving memoir recounts what it was like growing up as one of the three daughters of Ruth First and Jo Slovo, prominent white activists dedicated to campaigning for the liberation of South Africa against apartheid. But this is much more than her own story. Beginning with the day in 1982 when Ruth was killed by a parcel bomb delivered to her office, Slovo manages to combine a deeply personal and revealing tribute to her parents with an often harrowing picture of the fear and insecurity of a difficult childhood. Added to this volatile brew are rare insights into the last phases of the South African struggle up to and beyond the release of Nelson Mandela. It is partly the detail, as in her mother's feet, poking out of the bomb wreckage "clad in the t-bar, tan high-heeled shoes that had been her favourites" or her father's secret notebooks which he threw away as soon as they were filled in his "cramped, curling almost childish hand" that makes this such a compelling book. It is also finely written with an impressive honesty that never strays into self-pity. Slovo has published some good novels, including thrillers, but this is by far the most gripping.

Spain

The foreigner and the shepherd

Barbara Lynch

Barbara Lynch worked in Britain as a professional fundraiser, hating every minute of it, until she reached forty. She then decided to study photography, and at the end of the course went for a short holiday in Andalucía. Following a small advertisement – "Learn Spanish in Spain. Small mountain village. Courses and accommodation" – she found herself in the near-deserted village of Ferreirola in the Alpujarras, a mountainous area south of Granada. She stayed on, bought the house she had formerly rented and partitioned off a part to lease out to holiday guests. Then she met Juan, a passing shepherd, and her life shifted onto an entirely new path.

Barbara has now lived for five happy years in her remote village, the last three of them with Juan and his flock. She earns a living by offering holiday accommodation and photography courses to other escapists.

The ferocious July sun had already begun to sink behind the peaks of the Sierra Nevada as we began the switchback ascent into the high mountains. I had no map, only an aerial photograph of my destination, which was a small language school run by a Danish/Italian couple in the remote mountain village of Ferreirola. I peered at it closely, whenever the light or lurchings of the car allowed. My "taxi driver", a local man who had offered to help out when I had asked for directions at a bar in Orgiva, knew Ferreirola well but was unconvinced that the language school I was looking for existed. "*Nada, nada*," he would repeat, with a good-humoured shake of the head. There's nothing there. In the picture you could just about make out a few lightly toned shapes of roofs amid a seemingly arid landscape, bleached featureless by blinding sunshine. I had to agree that it didn't look promising.

Forty minutes later we swung off the main road and drove downhill straight into the sunset. The landscape was irradiated; every tree, every rock seemed to bounce back a new tone of light. The car stopped to allow a flock of sheep to cross. If I were a real photographer, I thought, I'd get out and take a picture. But I was too tired, so I sat there while the sheep swarmed past and the image impressed itself in my memory.

A helpful old woman, dressed in black, dismissed all the doubts that had piled up on my journey by waving me towards a blue door set in a wall. Nodding and pointing she ushered me through. Behind was a small patio garden that led onto the terrace of the Sierra y Mar language school. Inger, its Danish co-owner, was waiting to greet me.

Within a day or so I had slipped into a dream-like routine. Spanish lessons on the terrace in the morning were followed by a walk to the small bar for several beers, and then lunch and a siesta. I lived in a tiny stone *casita* with a single bed, table, chair, and a pole on which to hang my clothes. A branch grew out of the whitewashed wall, with several leaves which I dampened daily. I could lie in bed and watch the moon over the mountains, visible even during the day, and that month I saw for the first time my own shadow created by moonlight. Nature seemed overpowering. I was drugged by the summer sun, horrified by the constant invasion of insects and deafened by the relentless screaming of the cicadas. Each day grew hotter and hotter until by the end of July, even the short walk to the spring just outside the village was an effort.

The village was a small one, but even so it had suffered a massive depopulation over the last few decades. When I arrived there were barely more than thirty people and most of those were over sixty. The Alpujarras has so little employment nowadays that the young migrate to the cities to work, notably Granada, and return only for holidays, sporting their new cars and city clothes. The old men are left to tend their almond and olive trees alone and to produce huge quantities of fruit and vegetables – enough for the extended families that they once had around them. Their wives congregate in the square at two o'clock for the daily bread van and gossip. While they wait, Sebastian the village sage and drunk, quotes chunks of *Don Quixote* at them and tells dirty jokes that set them all twittering like plump blackbirds in slippers.

Over the years they have seen many foreigners come and go at the language school, and they are quite tolerant towards them. Inger came initially for flamenco lessons and found herself entranced by both the village and Guiseppe, or "Sep", her Italian partner who had been living here. We became good friends and spent hours talking and making chutney and jam from windfalls. "Too much fruit in paradise," I faxed a friend at home. "Send recipe for chutney."

One day Inger and Sep took me to see a house that was for sale. We were curious to see what it was like inside and I had already begun to do what a lot of tourists do, dream that a wonderful interlude could be prolonged, perhaps for ever. The house was huge. There were galleried spaces, low doorways, and wooden beams. The entire roof had been made into a terrace that looked out at the mountain range separating the village from the rest of the world. We admired the views and talked to the elderly Swedish woman who was showing us around. Even though I had just sold a flat in Glasgow and therefore had some money, I did not think of buying the house. Not then. A month later however I found myself returning with a lease for six months, negotiated by Inger, and the vague idea of a sabbatical from the life in Britain to which I had no particular desire to return.

On the day that my furniture arrived, so did my landlady. I'd been living in one room with a borrowed bed and spending hours sitting on the balcony. My letters home were ecstatic, if weird, and I'd been moon-gazing again. A dog had adopted me and I had a lizard living in one of the skylights. And still I had no idea what I was doing in this little village where nothing really happened. Piecing together the landlady's strange English it became clear that she wanted me to move out, immediately.

She had at last found a buyer, someone local, and had decided to accept about half of the price she had originally been asking. The removal men had just finished carrying my boxes of books upstairs and I was horrified at the prospect of having to find somewhere else to live and store all my belongings again. So I said that I would buy the house from her if she gave it to me for the same price. It came to every penny I had in the world. Later, when I tried to work out how it had all happened, an English woman called Angela said, "You don't choose Ferreirola, it chooses you." Angela had bought a piece of land with three friends, intending to build a holiday house on it, and when that fell through she lived on it herself, in a teepee. She knew what she was talking about.

My house might not have been as open to the elements as Angela's, but that first winter I thought that I would freeze to death. The huge rooms, pleasantly cool in summer, turned into ice boxes when autumn came and I had to go out to get warm during the day. I spent hours on the roof reading the complete works of Jane Austen, an odd choice perhaps but extremely soothing. Periodically I made forays into the surrounding countryside, scrumped apples and nuts, and exchanged a few words with the old men working ancient terraced plots of land created by the Moors. On Fridays I scrounged a lift to a larger village and carried my supplies home from market in a rucksack. Sometimes I went for days without speaking to anyone at all. At night I huddled round a wood-burning stove given to me by my Spanish teacher, and watched old Westerns on the television. I found it strange that both the Mexicans and the cowboys spoke Spanish.

There were nights when I would begin rearranging the furniture at three in the morning. You're not right in the head, I told myself. You need more human contact. The old people in the village were courteous to me but no more, except for Piedad, my neighbour. Shamelessly she plied me with questions whenever we met and peered into my shopping bag every time I returned from Pitres. "How old is your mother?"' she asked twice a week, and, "How much did you pay for your house?" Most days my answers seemed to disappear into some kind of vacuum, so in search of slightly more lucid company I started going to the bar.

The local wine is deadly – like sherry and just as alcoholic, it goes down more easily after the first glass. I spent a number of nights translating English pop songs for the barman before stumbling home to sleep for twelve hours. After a while I was on nodding terms with a few more people, but I still felt dislocated, cut adrift from the human race. It appeared I was trying to forget something – the work ethic, my previous life, God knows. Luckily I suffer from terrible hangovers so it became clear after a time that no matter what kind of expatriot I might be, I was not going to turn into an alcoholic.

I was offered a temporary job teaching English, which forced me to go out of the village more and meet people. There were other foreigners hidden away, painting or making a slim living selling tofu or herbal remedies to visitors and other "blondes" as the Spaniards called us. Some were women on their own or with children. All seemed very brown and confident as they bought their vegetables in the market. I needed to make a living too and hit on the idea of renting rooms to visitors, so I registered the house with an agency. At first I moved out when it was let and stayed in a friend's summer house, but then, with help from my sister and brother-in-law, rebuilt part of the house to divide it back into the two living units it had once been. I became a landlady. The people in the village nodded approvingly and directed lost visitors to my door. They even learned my name.

One morning I was sitting with a book on the balcony and heard a horse pass by. I glanced down and saw a wild-looking young man sitting on it, smoking a cigarette.

"*Hola*," he said, "So" ("*Whoa*") and the horse stopped. We had a sort of conversation in my broken Spanish and his almost indecipherable Andaluz accent, and then he went off down the path. The next morning he was there again. Same white horse, cigarette and gappy grin. He had a particularly nice grin, but what I really fell for was his dog.

"What's your dog called?" I asked.

"Juan," he said, "the same as me. You can have him if you like."

Juan passed morning and evening for a couple of months. I could hear him singing as he came up the path and found myself drawn to the balcony. He would ask me to go out to the Sierras with him and the sheep, but I was too scared to go. People had told me stories about shepherds, how wild they were and how they got into fights and burned the countryside over land disputes. They were only slightly less popular than the gypsies, whom nobody trusted.

On a spring evening I came across the sheep charging along a narrow track in a cloud of dust. They wore heavy copper bells around their necks and the noise was incredible. I stopped, not sure how to get past, and Juan appeared, beating a path through their woolly backs with his stick. "You've got a lot of sheep," I said inanely.

"Yes," he replied, "three hundred. When are you going to come out for a drink with me?"

I heard somebody say, "Not tomorrow, the next day."

"The day after tomorrow? Good, I'll pick you up." And off he went singing and whistling to the dog.

The day after tomorrow arrived and so did Juan, on a motor-bike. I was relieved it wasn't the horse, though I'd not been on a motorbike for twenty years. I eyed it sceptically.

"I'm not sure I know how to do this."

"It's easy," he said. "Just lift up your leg and get on."

So off we went to the mountains to drink dreadful red wine in his village and be stared at by men in the bar.

For the next few months people stared at me constantly. Word soon got around that Juan had "captured" a foreigner, and they were fas-cinated to see what sort of woman would take on this hairy ruffian. "You'll have to shave off your beard now, son," old women said to him in the street and he smiled proudly. "Could be," he would reply. To me the women gave monster-sized vegetables and tips on how to cook them. There was general approval of our unlikely match, but being a public fig-ure was a bit of a strain after so many months of seclusion. The first time I helped Juan bring the sheep back to their pen in his village, for exam-ple, it seemed the entire population stood in their doorways to watch.

"Are there usually so many people here in the evenings?" I asked, blushing and embarrassed by the attention.

"No," he said matter-of-factly. "They've come to look at you. And the sheep, of course."

That was three years ago, and people are used to me now. "Is she English?" asked one old man of Juan recently, for all the world as if I were a new kind of vegetable he had persuaded to grow here. I still go out sometimes with "the girls", as Juan calls the sheep. As I write this, it is lambing time and some days I have to bring the newborns home by car so that Juan does not have to carry them. This morning we went to buy two splendid white goats, mother and daughter, who were shoved complaining into my very small hatchback for the jour-ney back. I am getting quite good at negotiating mountain tracks with protesting passengers on board.

"What's the matter with you, Juan?" asked his friend Manolo, the goatherd, last spring. "Why isn't she pregnant yet?"

"We're still practising," replied Juan, causing Manolo to whoop with delight and rush off to tell his brother.

Sunday morning

It's 11am and I'm sitting in bed eating burnt toast and reading Hemingway's *Death in the Afternoon*. Having already missed the cool part of the day I've decided to stay put until evening. Suddenly I hear footsteps in the *tinao* outside where the balcony hangs over the street, then a frantic hammering on the front door and shouts of "¡Juan! Juan!"

"*No esta* ("He's not here")," I shout back.

"¿No esta?" bellows the voice, incredulous and belligerent. I'm clearly conversing here with someone of formidable lung-power

"No," I holler back, "He's up in the Sierras."

Juan is staying up in the summer pastures with the sheep. Every few days he returns, bandit-style, for more supplies and a few home comforts. Lately he's been coming home more often, complaining that he can't get a decent night's sleep in his little stone house due to the mice gnawing at the beams that support the roof. Odd that this has never particularly bothered him before.

By now I've realised that the man outside the bedroom window is the very one that Juan has been trying to get hold of to buy his lambs and not some enraged assassin. "Wait," I shout, thinking of the nice Scottish couple who are eating breakfast in the rental part of my house, "I'm coming." I can hear more shouting as I hurl on my dressing gown and head for the door.

Enrique the lamb-buyer is a gypsy, somewhere between thirty and forty, short and slightly plump, but definitely majestic. He has oiled black hair and a dapper moustache. He's wearing black flamenco trousers, a little too long, Cuban heels, and a very white shirt of some synthetic material that drapes beautifully around his hairy chest. Unfortunately (and I am a sucker for these) he is not sporting either a silver belt buckle or flat hat, but he does have a splendid shiny black walking stick which he twirls as he speaks to me.

He has only slightly lowered his voice at my appearance in the street. I'm in a long white dressing gown and slippers, and my hair's down. I probably look like a white witch or an ageing princess depending on your view. Enrique takes no notice of my appearance although the dreary, bespectacled son or nephew who is lurking in the shadows boggles slightly.

These days I'm quite used to conversing with strange men in my dressing gown and I don't bother apologising any more for my dishevelled state. Once I complained to Juan that these men who turn up at all hours and bellow in the street for him were so rude. "They're not rude," he said patiently, "they're gypsies."

The lamb-buyer shoots questions at me like the Grand Inquisitor and I dutifully tell him when Juan will be back and yes, he does want to sell the lambs. When he hears that they are a three-hour climb away he decides to return on the following Tuesday: those Cuban heels would never make it and the stick's ornamental. I attempt unsuccessfully to get his phone number, and he snorts incredulously when I explain that we haven't got a mobile phone yet. I hear myself apologising weakly and get annoyed. I think the imbalance of our outfits is beginning to get to me. I wish I had a wife with a long plait to iron my shirts.

Attempting to redress the balance I tell him sternly not to come too late on Tuesday or Juan will have gone. "Right," he says. "Early." I realise that I have let myself in for a repeat performance at dawn.

Sighing, I go back into the house. As I'm closing the door I notice a neighbour in the fig tree just outside, only his face and basket visible. I think of the Cheshire Cat. "Picking figs?" I ask, having by now mastered the Andalucían art of stating the obvious. "Are they ripe?"

"Some," he answers, "but they're difficult to reach."

"Right," I reply, realising that I'm wittering and that this kind of nonsense can leave you seriously doubting your intellect. So I shut the door and head back to bed.

Flamenco fever

Nikki Crane

Nikki Crane is a former dancer who now works for an arts development agency in the east of England, helping to promote dance to the public. In her spare time she teaches others her passion – flamenco dancing, a craze that's been gathering momentum in Europe over the last decade. To inject some authenticity into her steps, she travels regularly to the south of Spain, using specialist holiday firms who offer high-calibre tuition in a package of performances, *juergas* (parties) and outings, often scheduled to coincide with major Andalucían festivals.

Joining the queue at Stansted Airport, I glanced nervously around to see if I could spot Sian, my companion for the trip. Sian is fairly new to flamenco package holidays. Normally she's to be found charging around the Somerset countryside in walking boots and waterproofs, with her dog, Millie, padding alongside. But like myself and everyone else queuing up at that particular check-in desk, she had an addiction to indulge and needed to get to Andalucía for her fix.

I whiled away the time examining my fellow passengers. The outfits seemed more extreme than on previous trips I had taken, but the basics were familiar: the telltale rose in the hair, the brightly coloured shawl thrown self-consciously over the Marks and Spencer raincoat, and the unmistakable haughty look. There was a mix of ages – from thirty-somethings to a fairly large number of women in their fifties – and even a scattering of men. Sadly, any hope of sharing the flight with a bunch of virile matadors was dashed by the reality of receding hairlines, paunches hanging over waistbands, crumpled jackets and sagging shoulders.

We must have seemed a strange, if not hopeless, set of candidates for a flamenco troupe, yet there was no doubting the passion we all felt for the dance. For some it was the fiery, sensual opera *Carmen* that had first sparked the flame; for others, the eroticism of international flamenco star Joaquin Cortes; or happy memories of Benidorm from holidays past; or perhaps just a romantic attraction to the gypsy life. Whatever, we knew that a dance class at a local fitness centre or a demonstration in a church hall would never be enough. We had to come to Spain and try for the "authentic" experience. Also, it's amazing how the sight of lush bougainvillaea and the feel of Mediterranean heat on the skin can improve one's dance technique.

Our comfortable hotel was on a pretty street lined with citrus and overhung by wrought-iron balconies. We checked in and, feeling like members of a school party, crowded into the "dorms" for excited late-night chatter. Sian and I opted to share a room, so as to give each other full moral support. The next morning saw a frenzy of changing and exchanging outfits, of more theatricality than usual with the make-up. Dressing up and acting the drama queen were not only perfectly acceptable but even seemed an essential initiation into the group.

Down at breakfast the pecking order and social pattern for the week was being set. Who was in the top stream for tuition? Loud voices established the ranking. "Are you in Group A?" "Do you know where to go?" Others kept their counsel, quietly terrified of exposure. Would they be able to keep up with the rest of the class? A particularly bossy woman emerged to take charge of the rabble. I had seen this kind of flamenco zealot too many times before, carefully dressed in matching attire, twitching with a sense of urgency and the need to organise jolly get-togethers. Naturally, she was fully versed in all the arrangements for the week, down to the finest detail. Sian and I sank into the background.

After a briefing from the holiday company we trooped off, convoy-style, to our classes, at which point Sian and I separated. All around, bags were overflowing with flamenco paraphernalia: high heels with metal tips (a glorified hobnailed boot for use when the passions rise), castanets and all the usual colour and frills and spangles.

Of course, a different picture awaited us at the dance studio. Enter Concha, our tutor for the week. A gravel-voiced Garbo figure, fifty-ish, feisty, cigarette in hand, she possessed a formidably disdainful stare. No frills or flowers for her, just a plain black practice skirt and a T-shirt, with no embellishment: pared-down, no need to make a statement. And then the movement began. Concha exuded all the colour and vibrancy you could ever hope to see in a dancer; sexuality oozed from every gesture. There was coolness and heat, as if to say, "I will chew you up and spit you out – keep your distance."

On examining the gaudy array in front of her, Concha's response was a mixture of wry amusement and raised eyebrows – "What are they doing here? Are they serious?" – before she got down to business, attacking the raw material in her charge with evident relish. I shuffled nervously to the back, immensely relieved that I had finally opted for a low-key black outfit. I was convinced, as the guitarist began to play, that there was about to be an outbreak of a very English emotion: embarrassment. These fears were confirmed as I witnessed the agonising contrast between the depth and earthiness of Concha's movements and our own self-conscious, overstated posing. Worst of all, it was being captured on video, for us to squirm over at leisure.

The archetypal handsome, swarthy-skinned and black-eyed guitarist caused more than a slight tremor in the class. He seemed oblivious to our awkward attempts at flirting, pouting, glowering, and instead threw himself moodily into his music.

To compound matters, in strolled the daughter, Desiree, all slim lithe body, full mouth and glistening mane of black hair, which, as she danced, tumbled loose from its pins as if on cue. Again, that irresistible nonchalance, with a hint of petulance waiting in the wings. As if by the flick of a switch, the guitarist's sullen demeanour vanished. He was now on full voltage, the *bulerias* rhythm whipping through the strings and sound ricocheting from wall to wall.

We had no chance of having the same effect on him but I comforted myself with the knowledge that flamenco, maybe more than any other dance, celebrates the voluptuous figure, positively embraces the ample bosom and the rounded hips. What you really need for a true initiation are a keen sense of rhythm, earthy sexuality, and a modicum of the right temperament. Perhaps these in themselves were a tall order for a group of middle-aged British women. As for Lycra, in which most of the class was at least partly clad, why give yourself a hard time? A piece of old gingham curtain made into a skirt, and a baggy top, will perform just as well. Just be sure that there is enough fabric to swirl up and engulf you when the dance reaches its climax.

After class, shopping was the order of the day. Each of us hoped to find that special frock to wear at one of the evening gatherings and dance in to maximum effect – that is, if one could squeeze into one's chosen chic little number after continual consumption of *patatas fritas* and tapas of *tortilla*, *boquerones* (marinaded anchovies) and fried fish. Hopping from bar to bar and consuming small platefuls of whatever local delicacy catches the eye is all part of the Spanish experience and it's just too easy to forget that you'll be spending the rest of the week in front of a mirror, scrutinising every contour.

Sian and I met up again, and were just about to make our getaway to the shops when a determined hand tugged at my T-shirt, and the morning's familiar loud voice boomed, "We're all meeting up at one o'clock to go over what we've just learned." I politely declined – it was hot, after all, and would soon be time for a siesta – but my excuse was waved aside. "I've already arranged it, everyone's going to be there," she insisted.

We made our exit, but only after I'd promised to attend one of her informal rehearsals in the morning. We almost ran from the hotel, hurrying down roads without even bothering to consult a map until we came across a small alley. At the end, in an old bullring, was a market. A range of stalls overflowed with garish flower decorations for hair and costume, and heaps of fusty polka-dot flamenco dresses. Whether they would fit or not and how I would transport them were of little importance. I managed to convince myself that these were the genuine gypsy articles and, in a blind rush of shopaholic adrenaline, purchased a job lot, plus a brand new suitcase to carry them back in. Predictably, when I got home, I sold almost all of it, horrified at what appeared, in the cold light of an ordinary English day, to be about as authentic as an airport souvenir doll, and twice as tacky. Some, though, had a decided retro charm – straight out of the 1960s and subjected to the full flower power treatment.

Back at class some participants were finding the going tough, especially the few who were past retirement age. Blistered feet were par for the course, but there were also wounded egos and the odd dispute about the air conditioning. The "professional" elements in the class were not keen to expose warm muscles to a possible chill, but others were gasping for air in the stifling heat. Of course, no flamenco class would be complete without a few frayed tempers and this was the perfect opportunity to vent all those pent-up emotions and throw open the lock of English reserve. For once, we could flail our arms in the air, exercise our face muscles with anguished expressions, stamp our feet petulantly, and unleash our passions without fear of reproach.

Or so we thought, until a group of frighteningly talented young Spaniards arrived early at the studio for their lesson one day, and creased up with laughter on witnessing the curious circus before them.

Going through this humiliation was an essential ingredient of our encounter with Spain; through it we felt we had drawn closer to the passionate heart of another culture. And going home took some readjustment. Back on English turf I sensed a sudden loss of vitality and purpose, yet there also remained with me a little smugness, a slight hint of superiority, and just a faint echo of stamping feet.

read on . . .

Karen Connelly, *One Room in A Castle: Letters from Spain, France and Greece* **(UK: Black Swan, 1995; US: o/p).** Following the success of her award-winning memoir of a year spent in rural Thailand, Connelly moves to Southern Europe where she plucks impressions from the edges of provincial life in France, Spain and Greece. Skilful and astute beyond her years – she was in her twenties when she penned most of this work – she mixes autobiography, fiction and poetry to frame her impressions of her travels. Her slightly oblique observations of gypsy life on the streets of Guernica in the Basque Country live up to the startling promise of her earlier work.

Lucia Graves, *A Woman Unknown: Voices from a Spanish Life* **(UK: Virago, 1999).** Daughter of the poet Robert Graves and his wife Beryl, Lucia Graves grew up on the island of Majorca. After graduating from Oxford University she married a Spanish jazz musician and returned to Spain where, until the break-up of her marriage twenty years later, she raised a family and worked as a songwriter and translator in Barcelona. Descriptions of her idyllic early childhood, her gradual awareness of the impact of Franco's dictatorship, and a long period of immersion in her husband's Catalan culture, are interwoven with vivid portraits of some of the ordinary Spanish women who played a central role in her life. An absorbing if at times melancholy memoir, especially revealing about the dilemmas of feeling caught between cultures.

Elisabeth Luard, *Family Life: Birth, Death and the Whole Damn Thing* **(1996; UK: Corgi Books, 1998/US: o/p).** In the first two-thirds of this book, award-winning food-writer Luard enthusiastically recounts the family life she helped to create. In jaunty prose, peppered with child-rearing tips and recipes, she covers her marriage at nineteen to debonair 1960s writer, Nicholas Luard: early motherhood (with an achingly brief mention of the loss of two of her babies through rhesus blood problems): their move with their four young children to a cork forest in the south of Spain and the joy and resourcefulness with which they all adapted to Andalucían country living. Then, with the scene set, she discloses the heart of the book. In 1991 her confident, bright and beloved eldest daughter, Francesca, tests positive for HIV and, shortly before Christmas 1994, dies. The closing movement of this book focuses on the family's response to Francesca's illness and the tragedy of her loss. One chapter is written by Francesca herself, an all too brief and unspeakably moving account of an intelligent, generous young woman contending with the diagnosis of a stigmatising illness and the onset of death. The eloquence, honesty and utter humanity of her words leave an indelible impression.

★ **Rose Macaulay,** *Fabled Shore* (1949; UK/US: o/p). Few books have had greater impact on the way people travel than the first and only travel book by celebrated English author Macaulay. Her description of her automobile tour from Port Bou to Cape Vincent along the coast of Spain in the immediate post-war period opened the floodgates of mass tourism to the costas. The "little *playa* of Torremolinos" was never to be the same again.

Sweden

Island fantasies

Dea Birkett

Distinguished broadcaster, journalist and travel writer Dea Birkett has long held a fascination for barely inhabited islands. Nearly a decade ago she travelled over four thousand miles aboard a chemical tanker to reach Pitcairn Island in the South Pacific where she lived for several months, semi-marooned with the island's 38 residents. Her controversial and critically acclaimed travel memoir, *A Serpent in Paradise*, was the first to throw light on that utterly insular community. Her book recounts her tenuous and ultimately unsuccessful attempt at integrating herself amongst her island neighbours and the disturbing realities of becoming isolated as an outsider with no other means of forming friendships or escaping. In contrast, the tiny island of Runo, in the Stockholm Archipelago, where she recently holidayed with her boyfriend and their toddler daughter, offered the illusion of blissful isolation. Dea also discovered that it brought out, strange proprietorial fantasies and, for the two-week duration, a fiercely guarded privacy.

Dea Birkett's first travel book, *Jella: From Lagos to Liverpool, A Woman at Sea in a Man's World*, won the Somerset Maugham Award in 1993. She also recently co-edited *Amazonian: The Penguin Book of Women's New Travel Writing*, and has lived and travelled with an Italian circus.

When we dream of Paradise, it is an island. It is tear-shaped and sea-lapped. It is lonely, remote and utterly free from the anxieties and expectations of modern life. And because it is a tiny island, it is conquerable, it is yours.

I have dabbled in this dream. I have woken with the blistery sun, bathed naked in the calm waters beneath my timber home, and dined on fish cooked over an open fire.

My island was called Runo, just 400 metres square, one of over 24,000 islands (nobody knows exactly how many) in the Stockholm Archipelago, some no bigger than a beached whale. In the winter, the brackish Baltic Sea freezes, and the only way to reach Runo is a treacherous walk over the ice. But in the summer, a tiny boat-taxi took us – myself, my boyfriend and our toddler daughter – from Stavnas on the mainland.

The boat-taxi's skipper seemed to have swaggered from the pages of a Jack London novel. Dour and taciturn, Jepsen (pronounced Yepsan) did not deign to talk to us, but tugged on his droopy moustache. Pulling up before a half-built wooden pier, Jepsen twitched his hand towards a small grey sea-bound hillock with a timber chalet teetering on top. "Runo," he said, in a husky drawl, making it resound like the name of a warmongering Viking god.

We clambered over the rocks. There was jungle of ferns and bushes, blanketed with lichen. Wild mushrooms flourished in the spongy mess rotting the tall pine trees. There was no soil, just huge boulders, the sort a child stands on top of to declare themselves King. On Runo, we were the royal family. The smell of the pine cones crunching underfoot was intoxicating.

Runo may have been 400 metres square, but it was tough terrain. Behind our chalet, which my daughter christened the Magic House, rose our very own moutain, at least fifty metres high. But the loose shingle and smooth rocks made it – to my inflated island-induced imagination – a dangerous and challenging climb. Only a few footsteps from the safety of our chalet, there was Adventure.

Our neighbours were goats. But what elsewhere might have seemed a domesticated farmyard pet were wild and threatening on Runo. They became untamed beasts lurking in the undergrowth, with massive spiked horns. Once, one chased me, surely with the intention of goring me, and I had to run over the rocks to escape certain injury.

Fears fester on an island. And I became, therefore, astonishingly brave. I pictured myself not as a mere holidaymaker, but as explorer and warrior. I could conquer hostile territory and subdue wild beasts. I could release energies which lay buried in my safe urban existence and unearth the primitive in my soul.

Even buying a pint of milk was turned into a mental and physical challenge. The nearest store was on Runmaro, a neighbouring island with two hundred inhabitants, and the only way to reach it was to take the small wooden boat tied to our pier. The inlets between the islands had to be carefully navigated; in some places, the water was so shallow that rocks lurked only inches under the surface. We needed to arm ourselves with charts, lifejackets, oars in case the tiny outboard engine faltered, and untold courage, before setting out for the shop.

Other islands were in sight, dotted about us like ships in the rippling sea. Occasionally, and especially at night, you could hear the inhabitants talk, although all in a language I couldn't understand. Echoing along the inlets and bouncing off the boulders, their voices sounded like the Norse gods conversing with the wind and the stars. Once, on a becalmed evening, the sound was so clear that when I heard someone sneeze several islands away I exclaimed, without thinking, "Bless you". The mouth of the fish breaking water to catch flies sounded like an orgy of kissing.

The Scandinavian summer gave early mornings and long nights, buzzing with midges. Our watches were packed away, and we rose, ate and slept when we wanted, and seldom dressed. One night, with the sun still struggling to warm the rocks at 10 o'clock, a mist appeared, rolling over the water and obscuring everything, even the shore below our house. We were truly cut off from the rest of the world.

The chance of losing all contact with other humans was both attractive and terrifying. It turns all island dwellers into hoarders. I threw away nothing, and became over-vigilant in my housekeeping. Was there going to be enough fresh water? What if we ran out of wood to cook on over the open fire? I panicked when I opened the kitchen cupboard and found only two loaves of bread, and saw that our eggs were down to a mere dozen. What if the mist didn't lift? What if the engine on our boat failed and we would not be able to reach Runmaro for weeks?

There was a serpent even in our patch-sized Garden of Eden. Island living didn't unleash talents and traits that the city had smothered. It brought out the woman in me and the man in my man. In our Swedish Family Robinson, he skippered the boat, he caught the fish, he gathered and chopped the wood for the fire. I cleaned and cooked and looked after our daughter like a cavewoman. But even worse, I enjoyed doing these things.

I didn't much like the person I was becoming. Rather than an unencumbered free spirit, I quickly turned proprietorial. Runo's size and seclusion fed the fantasy that we actually owned the island, a piece of Paradise. This was my mountain behind the house, my slippery rocks, my waterfront.

Soon, visitors were unwelcome. They were only objects of interest from afar. Who was that paddling up our creek? Where were they going? If a craft approached, I would run down to the shore and glower out to sea, warding them off with my eyes.

We waited on the pier with our bags for Jepsen to take us back to work, to worries and to continental land. Next week, another family would move into the Magic House, clamber over our rocks and climb our mountain. Our departure had the pain of surrendering. I put on my watch and turned home.

Jazz in the snow

Kate Westbrook

The jazz singer Kate Westbrook has travelled all over the world. She began her career as singer/instrumentalist with the Mike Westbrook Brass Band, a group of versatile musicians who played anywhere from concert halls to city parks. She subsequently married Mike and has since earned her living performing and touring. For two decades she has gone back to Sweden every other year or so, in all seasons and in all musical guises.

Very early on in the life of the Westbrook Brass Band, before they had a manager, I wrote to the *Kulturhuset* arts centre in Stockholm suggesting that we might play there. The director of music, Johan

Etzler, sent back a charming letter, inviting us to come. Over the decades Johan has become a close friend, and Sweden one of my favourite countries. The Swedes, though apparently so reserved, really respond to our music and I have the warmest feelings for the people and the countryside.

My most recent visit was to perform with a southern Swedish Big Band, the Tolvan Band, playing a piece that Mike and I had created using themes and arias from the work of Gioacchino Rossini. I had toured with Tolvan before. They are excellent musicians and great people to work with (even if they do chew gum a lot, only removing it to eat or to put their instruments in their mouths). On this occasion the band was joined by soloists from other parts of the country – a cellist, a bass player, an accordionist, a percussionist, as well as Mike and myself from England.

I was the only woman in the band. Not unusual in a country like Britain, but slightly surprising in Sweden, where I have come to expect more enlightened attitudes. Nevertheless, I was never made to feel uncomfortable as the sole female. It may well have been an advantage that I only speak a few words of Swedish and so have no idea what people are saying to each other. Usually when travelling I at least make an attempt at the native tongue – I speak French and Italian fairly well, and sing in several languages (including a Swedish dialect song) – but I've barely made any progress in Swedish since my first trip. It's all too easy to become lazy when everyone, even in the most remote corners of the country, speaks English so well.

On this trip with Tolvan we had a rehearsal period in Lund, at the southwestern tip of the country, before setting off on tour around Scandinavia in a fine big bus. It was autumn, my favourite season in Sweden. The silver birches had turned, along with all the other deciduous trees, and harebells lingered in the scrubby heath and flat grey rocks. Farms dotted the landscape, many of them painted a marvellous deep terracotta red, reminiscent of parts of New England. I've been told that the red paint was originally used for the boat bottoms of fishing fleets, and was taken up as a cheap protective cover for wood-frame buildings, proofing them against the severities of the climate. A white line painted around the doors of barns points up the entrance in the dark, and the window frames of the houses are usually painted white too.

In the windows, above the ubiquitous gingham and lace cotton curtains, hang coloured hearts made from wood, or small glass ornaments, or dried flowers in bunches. The Swedish love arranging domestic trivia like this, and really go to town at Christmas, when small children wear crowns of evergreen studded with lighted candles. Travelling round Sweden at Christmas time I have seen moose in a snowy landscape, and skiers hiking across the flat countryside on short skis. I have seen people pushing sledges bearing children, or wood, or groceries. On reaching a downward slope the "driver" steps onto the long runners at the back and rides down. When the ground is level again the tall handle at the rear of the sledge serves to steady the person pushing, rather like an elegant wooden zimmer frame.

Once, we were travelling in the coldest part of the winter with a small band, in an English minibus. This is the equivalent of going to the North Pole in a cotton frock. The inside of the windows towards the rear of the vehicle were caked with ice, and our skimpy tyres skated about on the surface of the road. At one point we were driving along a straight stretch beside a frozen lake when suddenly the bus performed a graceful pair of revolutions in the face of an oncoming truck, and landed in snowbound reeds at the lakeside. Within seconds an ambulance arrived out of nowhere, made sure that no one was hurt and disappeared again into the white empty landscape. Eventually we were helped by passing motorists to push the bus back onto the road and, miraculously, made the gig that night.

In such severe weather it's always good to have what's known as a "suede shoe gig", where the performance space and sleeping quarters are under the same roof or have inter-connecting doors so you don't have to mess up your suede shoes by going out in the street. A few years ago our trio (Mike and I and saxophonist Chris Biscoe) went to play in Härnösand on the east coast – not as far north as the Arctic Circle but north enough. Again it was winter, with the temperature at minus 24°C and falling. We were booked into a hotel only a short walk from the club, but during these few steps the moisture in our noses froze, tickling uncomfortably, and every breath hurt. The water in the inlet was iced over, leaving tankers and boats stranded like beached whales. Upstream a factory emitted a vile smell, made sharper still by the intense cold. There was a large illuminated print-out of the temperature and time over the other side of the bay, and I spent much of the night staring out of the window in fascination as the recorded temperature dropped, and numbered minutes and seconds ticked by. The only other lights in view were the appallingly clear stars.

With these long, dark winters, the suicide rate is high. During interminable journeys on the road, and in spite of myself, I frequently found my thoughts turning to death. There's a skeleton in the city museum in Stockholm, dating from two thousand years ago or more: a small person, buried in the foetal position. Oddly enough, I found this a very comforting image. Having summoned that creature to my mind's eye I could return to my book or get into conversation again.

After the long winter come the welcome signs of spring and the big thaw. Great icicles fall from the eaves of buildings, creating a real hazard in town for pedestrians. Everywhere there is deep slush, and the streams, rivers and lakes are full. Water is never very far away in Sweden.

Swimming in the summer is a bracing experience, with no Gulf Stream to take the cold edge off the sea. Inland lakes aren't much better, but the sun can feel wonderfully warm, shining late at night and coming back after only a few hours. The Härnösand promoter told us that she hates the summer. It is so short that she feels under tremendous pressure to get a tan, to have barbecues, and to relish the fact that it never quite gets dark. And the weather is not all the people of Härnösand have to be concerned about. The concert promoter also told us of the terrible effect the Chernobyl disaster has had on the region, which received one of the highest doses of radioactive fall-out outside Kiev. Local people are still bitter. They're no longer able to supplement their tables by gathering berries, fungi, and roots, and won't be able to again for many years.

On the autumn trip with Tolvan we were booked to play towns and cities in the south of the country before heading on to Gothenburg, a town which I find reassuringly familiar. Over the years I have been to the same hotel, the same clubs in Gothenburg and, on the whole, they change very little. I was outraged on this occasion when "our" Chinese restaurant, where the waitress used to expect to see us every year or so, had been transformed into an anonymous Japanese place. Although Gothenburg has a jazz club, the *Nefertiti*, for some reason we have never played there. We have, however, played in the rather grand theatre, the university, and in the art gallery flanked by sculpture and fine paintings. For several seasons we did concerts in a shambolic private museum/club owned by Sven, a dear friend. Touring as we do, we make friends along the way and intense bonds spring up, kept alive with occasional letters and postcards and rare visits. Sven was ancient and tall, immensely cultured and gracious, living with the cancer that made him as pale as Swedish porcelain and with his hair dyed brick red. He has since died and the venue has closed down.

From Gothenburg we travelled north to Stockholm. This time, instead of icing up, the bus overheated badly. We watched videos in the sweltering atmosphere until we could stand it no longer. In a rain-soaked industrial wasteland, we unloaded our gear and waited while relief buses were summoned, both inadequate. The original bus was fixed at last; the journey took eleven hours in all and we turned up at the club, tired, damp and late for the soundcheck.

Stockholm's *Fasching Club* has been host to all the great American and European jazz musicians. The room is long and narrow with a balcony round one end, and the management are forever trying to make the space work, in spite of its awkward skinny shape. They've tried putting the band below the balcony so that those above look down on the tops of the musicians' heads. They've put the stage on one side of the room, flanked by two blocks of audience. It was like this the night I sang there with Tolvan, meaning, in effect, that I spent the evening turning from one side to the other, or else looking straight into the eyeballs of the sound engineer who had his desk against the wall opposite the bandstand.

Almost all our Stockholm friends turned up for the concert. Poor Frippe, with his clean-shaven upper lip and chin, and wispy beard below, and emphatic be-bop talk that keeps him just this side of madness, clutching an alto saxophone and forever waiting to "sit in". Lovely deaf Gunilla, who spends all night driving taxis after the *Fasching* closes, was there, fragrant and in peach silk. One of her delights is to feed *surströmming* to the many jazz musicians she knows. Considered a great delicacy by the Swedes, *surströmming* is rotten her-ring and, as one musician so elegantly put it, "makes a bad fart smell like a breath of fresh air".

These days the *Fasching* can only afford to put on jazz a couple of nights a week, though one of my favourite Swedish singers, Monika Zetterlund, can still be heard there at regular intervals. She has performed with the best Swedish and American jazz instrumentalists. At the Memorial Concert for the assassinated prime minister, Olaf Palme – a champion of the arts who had many close friends among the artists and intellectuals of his country – she sang a politicised Swedish version of *As Time Goes By*, lamenting the country's loss to an audience mute with shock.

Apart from the *Fasching Club*, Stockholm has a number of small jazz clubs, and a Radio Station concert hall where we once played a lunchtime concert. With the Radio Band, and various other groups, we have performed at the handsome concert hall in the *Kulturhuset*, an arts complex in a modern shopping mall, overlooking a fine example of 1950s' fountain design. Despite the drug addicts who inhabit the underground pedestrian area outside, I feel quite safe walking round here on my own. Indeed Stockholm is a lovely capital in which to wander. A great sweep of water reaches right into the heart of the city, where the public and commercial buildings are situated, bringing with it a glorious light and all the attendant bustle of a port. The old town is quaint and well-heeled, while the newer parts are spacious and clean, if a little soulless. There's a delightful sculpture down at the water's edge, of a person, apparently below ground, raising the lid of a manhole cover and poking his nose out into the air. He has been there, fooling passers-by, for at least twenty years.

The Museum of Modern Art, jutting out on one of Stockholm's many promontories, is one of my favourite haunts. The collection is good, and they occasionally host concerts in the main gallery. It's a splendid thing to listen to music with a backdrop of Matisse's massive collage of "Apollo". You can get a good cup of coffee in the café, too, along with those strange bright green cakes that appear in every Swedish eatery.

With Tolvan we went to Västerås, stopping off several times to eat in motorway cafés. The menu never varies at these places, and the choice, though limited, is good. There's *Pytt i panna*, hash with an egg on top, very tasty nursery-type food. Or *Köttbullar*, which are meatballs served with Lingon berries (cranberries). I like the large flat wheels of crispbread that hang on specially designed wooden spikes, that never seem to go stale and that go with absolutely anything. The Swedes boast that country people eat bread made from the bark of trees but I've never come across it.

On reaching Västerås, we drove into an industrial estate, totally deserted and cloaked in darkness with warehouses towering between vast areas for loading and unloading. In the centre of this concrete park stood a small single-storey building, entirely on its own. Inside this odd venue there turned out to be a restaurant with a stage at one end, a manager who loves the music, and, later in the evening, a packed house and a terrific reception. It was all very Swedish.

At the end of a tour we often move on with the band to Finland. Though in the aftermath of two ferry disasters it will never feel the same again. I used to love taking the overnight boat from Stockholm to Turku or Helsinki, especially in the depths of winter with the sea frozen over, the small islands of the archipelago standing out dark against the glistening whiteness, and a great roaring noise of ice being riven by the prow of the ship. After the *smörgåsbord*, we would go up to the main lounge where there was invariably a singer with electric keyboard and rhythm box churning out ABBA songs (even the most sophisticated Swedes are proud as punch of ABBA). Then we would take a last look out on deck before turning in. Stepping back inside from the darkness to the light, it was always startling to be confronted by the sight of lots of gypsies. Many of the travelling people have family in Sweden and come from right across Russia and Finland to take these boats, bedding down for the night on the elaborately patterned carpet in all their finery. The women wear massive crinoline skirts, layer upon layer, each shot with gold or silver on vibrant colours. Small girls in elaborate dresses are festooned with ribbons and cloth flowers, while the men and boys wear tight-fitting waistcoats and flamboyant shirts. It was like stepping from the cold north air into a painting by Delacroix or Matisse.

read on . . .

Agneta Pleijel, *The Dog Star* (UK: Peter Owen, 1992/US: Dufour, 1993). Powerful, emotive tale of a young girl's approach to puberty, by one of Sweden's leading writers.

Mary Wollstonecraft, *Letters Written during a Short Residence in Sweden, Norway and Denmark* (1795; UK: Penguin, 1987). For reasons never made entirely clear, Wollstonecraft, author of *A Vindication of the Rights of Women* and mother of Mary

Shelley, travelled across Scandinavia for several months in 1795. Her letters home represent a real historical curiosity, though her trenchant comments often get side-lined by her intense melancholia.

See "Read on . . . journeys and other places" (p.653) for reviews of *Amazonian, Serpent in Paradise and Jella*.

Syria

The Gates of Damascus

Lieve Joris

Belgian-born Lieve Joris is one of Europe's foremost travel writers. Two of her six books, *The Gates of Damascus* and *Mali Blues*, are currently published in English – translated with exceptional fluency by Sam Garrett – as part of Lonely Planet's acclaimed Journeys series. In *The Gates of Damascus*, extracted below, Lieve returns to the Middle East to stay with her friend Hala, a spirited, warm and ironic Damascene. The two had met at a conference in Baghdad when they were both in their mid-twenties. In the eighteen years since, while Lieve had been travelling as a writer and journalist around Europe, other parts of the Middle East and Africa, Hala's life had become constrained as a result of the arrest, torture and political imprisonment of her left-wing husband. Left to look after their only daughter, Asma, with only her precarious income as an academic, and under the continual threat of surveillance by the mukhabarat, President Assad's secret police, Hala is forced to seek security within the often stifling confines of her family.

In the extract below Hala takes Lieve to visit her husband's family home in Damascus. Hala and Asma stand out from their in-laws, who descend from a poorly educated family of woodcutters, and expect women to adhere strictly to customs of purdah.

Our taxi driver almost runs over a woman. It frightens me, but Hala just laughs. "Wait, you haven't seen anything yet!" Large signs bearing edifying messages have been posted in the city centre: "If you see someone commit a traffic violation, give him an angry look. These are the words of our leader, Hafez al Assad". But according to Hala, it's his own soldiers who cause the most accidents. Like the president, many of them come from the mountains in the north; they're not city people. A soldier here once ran over a two-year-old boy. It was the talk of the town, but none of the newspapers dared to write about it.

My amazement at everything I see amuses Hala. Only now does she realise that she's become used to the strangest things. "You have to meet Ahmed's family," she says. "My family's nothing by comparison! Before I met him I didn't even know such households existed in Damascus."

"What's so different about them?"

"I can't explain it, you'd have to see them to believe it."

As we're walking through the old town one afternoon, Hala stops in front of a door with a little copper hand on it. She uses it to knock on the door. We hear excited female voices and then someone asking: "Who's there?"

Ahmed's mother opens the door. The women, who had fled in all directions like frightened birds, reappear laughing. They are Ahmed's sisters, sisters-in-law and their children. While we sit in the whitewashed courtyards new faces keep appearing at innumerable doors in the upper galleries. After a while I lose count completely.

"How many people actually live here?" I whisper to Hala.

"I wouldn't know, it's a surprise to me every time I come by." One of Ahmed's sisters is visiting from Amman; she's brought her mother-in-law with her, and a little niece Hala has never seen before.

The men are nowhere to be seen: they work during the day in the lumberyard owned by Ahmed's father; or they're asleep, for some of them work at night. The women look at me inquisitively. One of them breast-feeds her baby; giggling, she asks whether women do that in my country as well.

Do I have a husband? And children? These are questions I'd rather avoid; the answers are so disappointing. If I tell them I'm married, they'll wonder why my husband allows me to travel alone. That there are women who choose not to have children is something they can't understand at all. But Ahmed's mother looks at me so expectantly that I say to Hala: "Tell her my husband and I are unable to have children."

Her look is full of compassion. "Is it because of her or her husband?" she wants to know. I regret my lie immediately.

Why did Hala take me to the *souq?* Ahmed's sisters sputter; she should have shown me the modern shopping streets of Damascus! But Hala says they wouldn't know their way around there themselves, because the men do all the shopping in this household. When the women do go out, Ahmed's mother always chaperones.

We drink coffee and Asma disappears into the house with her cousins. Everything here is in constant motion: children are taken out of bed, others are put in, and Hala and I quickly become part of the ever-changing decor – no one seems to mind that we're speaking a different language.

Time doesn't exist in this family, Hala says; they never look at the clock. They live according to a rhythm barely influenced by the outside world. How often they've invited her to a lunch that wasn't served until six in the evening! The girls are raised very differently from Asma: they only go to school until they turn twelve and they can barely read or write, but they know many more female secrets than Asma – nothing is kept from them.

Sometimes a group of women leave the house to visit relatives. These outings are a real exodus: when one of Ahmed's sisters-in-law visits her family, she not only takes her children, but also her mother-in-law and a couple of Ahmed's sisters. If dinner is served late, they can't go home – they don't travel after dark – so they have to spend the night.

When she met Ahmed at the university, Hala thought he was alone in Damascus. He had a Jordanian accent and didn't talk about his family – she assumed that they had stayed behind in Amman. In fact, he never talked about himself at all. Politics, that was his subject, and when Hala suggested spending a weekend with friends he just kept talking politics and never even tried to touch her.

One afternoon during a second weekend she simply pulled him into the woods. He was clumsy – she could tell he had never been with a woman before. That evening he began discussing politics again, wiping the sweat from his forehead with a handkerchief and glancing at her in confusion.

Her father was disappointed that she wanted to marry Ahmed. A family of woodcutters, what would they have to talk about! She was still young, she had all the time in the world – what was her hurry?

"Yes, what was the hurry?"

"I wanted respect," she says. "I couldn't go on living an independent life, I had to think of my reputation. People here don't know the
difference between freedom and prostitution."

"Were you in love with him?"

"No, not really." She laughs. "It wasn't very romantic. I thought
I could live with him, that's all."

Another knock on the door causes the women in the courtyard
to flee in all directions, but they breathe easier when they hear the
voice of Rashid, Ahmed's younger brother. He's a slim young man
with his hair slicked back – he looks like Ahmed. We were just getting
ready to leave, but that's out of the question now. Rashid invites us to
come into the house and sends one of his little nephews out to buy
local ice cream with pistachio nuts.

Hala says no one ever sits in the parlour, but Rashid is bent on
showing it to me. Heavy Damascene furniture, cabinets inlaid with
mother-of-pearl and high-backed chairs – objects that require a lot of
space, but here they're all crammed together. A clock with a picture of
the Ka'aba shrine in Mecca is ticking away on the wall.

In the living room a tinted photograph of Ahmed hangs in a
gilded frame above the TV. At home Hala has a small black-and-white
print of the same photo; I'd recognised it as Ahmed immediately.
When I was last in Damascus, he had offered to stay with a friend. I
liked him for that, for not feeling threatened by Hala's friendship with
this stranger she had met in Baghdad.

In these surroundings I suddenly see him in another light. He's
not an exceptionally handsome man, but his eyes radiate masculine
pride and self-confidence. Rashid has the same look. It has to do with
the natural authority he holds over the women in this house, the outside world he represents to them. It confuses me to think of Ahmed's
pride in connection with such things – it doesn't fit the image I had of
him until now.

Hala had told me that Rashid raises pigeons. "He sits up on the
roof with his friends for hours," she said. "You have no idea of the
kinds of things they do up there." "Feed the pigeons," I ventured, but
she said there was more to it. She was so secretive about it that I
became curious. Rashid laughs shyly when I ask to see his pigeons.
The roof is men's territory: women never go up there; they're not

even allowed to hang up the laundry on the upper floors when there are no men in the house. But you can't refuse a foreign woman a request like that.

We climb the stairs to the top floor, a group of children in our wake. As soon as we step onto the narrow wooden ladder leading to the rooftop terrace, feathers begin swirling down around us. The light on the terrace is blinding, and we stand there blinking at the sea of roofs, domes and minarets spread out before us. Rashid disappears into one of the pigeon coops and proudly shows me a couple of new female pigeons. "They're very expensive," Hala says, "you wouldn't believe what he'll pay for one of those birds."

Rashid releases about thirty males. They fly in tight formation above our heads, in ever-widening circles. "The neighbours have pigeons too," Hala says. "When they let them go at the same time they sometimes get caught in each other's flight." That's the sport, as it turns out, the neighbours waylay each other's pigeons.

Hala was right: this has nothing to do with the pigeon racing I remember from my youth, with the old men who met in cafés smelling of tobacco and flat beer. This sport belongs to the closed ranks of the old Arab city. The *kashash al-hamarn* (pigeon racers) usually don't have a good reputation: people say they're mama's boys who can't make it out on the street, but who play the hero up on the roof; they say they take drugs and can't be counted on to keep their word.

"But what do they do with each other's pigeons?"

"That depends," Hala says. "A while ago, Rashid caught a beautiful pigeon that belonged to one of the neighbours. He wrung its neck and left it on their doorstep. Now it's war. Sometimes the arguments become so heated that they actually start fighting. Every once in a while you hear that someone in the old city has been stabbed over a pigeon."

The birds continue to circle, but there's no sign of the neighbours. I think of Ahmed. How was he able to reconcile his revolutionary ideas with these family practices? Hala is leaning over the balustrade; she signals to me to come over. Far below us is the street, and the doors with their hand-shaped knockers.

"I'd get tired of this real fast," I say.

"But not Rashid and his friends !" Hala whispers. "Maybe one of them has a pair of binoculars so they can look into the neighbours' houses. Who knows, maybe a woman throws them a secretive glance; maybe they can watch her dress." She laughs at my amazement. "A closed society looks for windows facing out. That's why the men of this house keep their women on such a short leash: they know the dangers that are out there. Rashid doesn't even let his friends know his wife's name. If he wants coffee or food up here on the roof, he whistles down and she puts a tray on the stairs. When one of his friends is leaving, Rashid bends over the railing and yells: '*Yallah!*' Then all the women rush into the house."

Hala was here once when a group of Rashid's friends came by. "All the women had to go inside, but I peeked through the kitchen window. I saw about eight men go up the stairs, their heads wrapped in black-and-white chequered shawls. One of them stood out: he walked differently and his face was completely hidden by the shawl." She gives me a conspiratorial look. "You'll never guess; it was a woman!" Later on she noticed that the men hadn't gone up to the roof, but were leaning over the railing of the third floor: they took turns going into the little room where the woman must have been.

"Do the women here know that these things go on?"

"I think so. Rashid's wife complains about it sometimes. Every once in a while he sends her off to her family for a few days, and when she comes back she can tell that someone has been sleeping in her bed, even wearing her clothes."

"And she puts up with that!"

"She doesn't know any better. She's better off than she was before! Her father wouldn't even let her watch TV, and when he comes to visit she just sits in a corner, quiet as a mouse. Rashid's mother chose her for her strict upbringing."

It makes me think of Abdelgawad, the family patriarch depicted by the Egyptian writer Naguib Mahfouz in his *Trilogy*: he spends every evening in a brothel, but beats his wife when she dares to go to the mosque on her own.

"What if his wife had an affair, what would Rashid do then?"

"Kill her," Hala says without hesitation, "don't doubt it for a moment." Not so long ago, one of Ahmed's married sisters had such an argument with her husband that he left her alone in their home for days on end. Ahmed's father was worried: what would happen if she was hanging up the laundry and a man whistled at her? And what if someone saw that happen and told everyone about it? Then, he wailed, he would have to cut her throat to preserve his honour.

Rashid holds a new female pigeon in the air and makes cooing sounds to lure the males back to their coop. They react immediately. In one fluid motion they land on the roof and meekly let themselves be locked up. Rashid laughs. "Did you see that?" He lets us go down the narrow ladder first, to where the ice cream awaits.

"You should marry a man like Rashid and have a bunch of children," Hala says on our way home later that afternoon. "After ten years of that, you could definitely write a book about Syria."

The very idea! "You don't think I'd have enough energy after ten years to even put one word on paper?"

"Why not?"

I can't believe she's serious. During the last few days she herself has kept trying to work out some research data for the university. She never gets far: Asma, Tete, Shirin, they all seem to be standing in line to pull her away from her writing table. The long sheets of paper on which she writes are always getting lost in the shuffle between Asma's drawings and soccer coupons. She thinks I'm extremely disciplined, even though I do nothing but keep up my diary. "Tell me the truth: you don't really believe that, do you?"

Hala laughs mysteriously: "I only got to know this country's problems once I was married. You could always try it, couldn't you?"

read on . . .

Lieve Joris, trans by Sam Garrett, *The Gates Of Damascus* **(Aus/UK/US: Lonely Planet Journeys, 1996).** With palpable sympathy, perceptiveness and deft prose Lieve Joris describes the year she spent sharing a tiny flat in Damascus with her ex-communist friend Hala and Asma, Hala's eleven-year-old daughter. Hala, whose identity you hope is well disguised, becomes Joris's mediator and guide into the domestic, cultural and political heart of contemporary Syrian and Arab society. The intelligence, wit and warmth of this educated Syrian woman, which shines out from every page, are shown to be her most powerful tools in coping with the constant threats of surveillance by the secret police, the intrusions of her demanding family and her fury at the injustice and waste of her husband's long political imprisonment. But Hala has her blind spots too. Her belief in global Zionist conspiracies is chilling to encounter and this, together with the claustrophobia of the lifestyle she clings to, becomes a source of tension between the friends. Through her intimate portrait of Hala, flaws and all, Joris traces the corrosive effects of fear of imprisonment or the social necessity of toeing the line as a good Arab woman and prisoner's wife. With her combination of frank open-mindedness, wide-ranging research and a gift for entering into others' lives, Joris has produced one of the most powerful and important evocations of a modern Arab society.

Gertrude Bell, *The Desert and the Sown* **(UK: Virago, 1985).** Bell was an indomitable society woman who indulged her passion for travel, becoming a respected historian, archeologist and linguist. She befriended T.E. Lawrence during their time at the Arab Bureau in World War I and ended up founding Baghdad's National Museum. This book describes her 1905 journey from Jerusalem to Alexandretta but is better on the people she meets than the places she visits.

Agatha Christie, *Come, Tell Me How You Live* **(UK, HarperCollins, 1999).** In the 1930s Christie accompanied her husband, Sir Max Mallowan, on many of his excavations in northeastern Syria. This entertaining and brief memoir captures her impressions of the landscape and people during the country's mandate era, but says nothing of the history being so assiduously dug up by her spouse.

Freya Stark, *Letters from Syria* **(UK: o/p).** A series of letters written in the late 1920s, most interesting in their open depiction of the hospitality of the locals to the ruling French, particularly in the Hauran which had recently seen a prolonged revolt. See also Malise Ruthven's *Freya Stark in the Levant* **(UK: Garnet, 1994),** a selection of the estimated fifty thousand photographs Stark took in the Middle East in the early part of this century.

Tanzania

The school that we built

Zoe Murphy

Zoe Murphy spent two months as a volunteer builder for HELP (Humanitarian Education and Long-Term Projects), an organisation started by students at Edinburgh University in 1990. After raising the necessary funds to construct a much-needed primary school in Tabora in central Tanzania, Zoe and a group of nine fellow students flew to the country to begin work on the site. It was her first trip overseas, although she has since travelled to India and the Caribbean.

My first impressions of Tanzania were gleaned from the back window of a road-worn Morris Minor. Driving from the airport at Dar Es Salaam to the local YMCA, where we would spend the night, I saw endless factory facades, dirt roads and roadside stalls selling mountains of oranges. In open-front shops, enormous cuts of meat swung from great hooks, swarming with flies in the midday heat. Barefoot women weaved their way slowly along the side of the road, babies slung across their backs so they could support the weight of the parcels on their heads. Men sat idly in the shade of the stalls playing games with old bottle tops. At the traffic lights, we were approached by young boys selling car aerials, mouse traps and penny chews. It all seemed a magpie's nest of Western mass culture, yet profoundly alien at the same time.

Strolling out in a small group for a bite that first evening, we were approached by a friendly young man offering to change money.

Since it was a national holiday and we hadn't been able to buy Tanzanian shillings, Steve, one of the volunteers, offered up $100 for exchange and I went in for $20. I watched the trader count out a wad of shillings and nodded at his friendly advice to beware of the "many cheating people in this country". He placed the money in an envelope, and asked Susan to hold up a note up to the light so as to confirm the watermark. It must have been at this point that he swapped our envelope for one stuffed with shredded newspaper. An old trick, we later learned. Frustrated and feeling foolish, we retreated back to the security of the YWCA, each making a mental note that we would trust to our common sense in the future.

The next day, we boarded the train for the 26-hour journey to Tabora. The second-class compartment was a six-person sleeper. Fortunately the large window allowed in just enough breeze to waft away the smell of urine that emanated from the small sink below it. The time passed and we played cards, read, sang, dozed and chatted as we wandered up and down the corridor. People smiled when I greeted them in Swahili, though I wasn't able to get much further than "*mzuri*" (very well, thanks). English-speaking Mr Meenor, the conductor, told us that the engines were actually quite powerful but because the tracks are so old and narrow, any speed over 30mph risked derailing the whole train. Rusting metal corpses of over-adventurous trains lay testament to this, strewn at regular intervals along the side of the tracks.

I lay on my middle bunk, level with the window, and let my eyes drift over the vast landscape, taking in the passing villages constructed from mud and sticks, with their herds of cattle and kids running and waving alongside the tracks. Exhilaration ran through me. Here I was, finally in Tanzania. I still found it impossible, though, to imagine the life that would be waiting for me at the end of the journey. I wanted the familiar train ride to go on forever, and yet was impatient for it to end. With the other students, I laughed at the prospect of our group – including students of geography, theology and astro-physics – mixing cement and getting our spades out. At least we were in this together. It was a comforting thought.

When the train first creaked to a halt, it was night-time. Flame torches revealed vendors offering a banquet of food: boiled eggs, roasted nuts, grilled chicken and beef, papaya. Women and children calling out in Swahili approached train windows holding aloft baskets of samosas and branches of bananas. People took their fill and then dropped coins into expectant hands. It was the ultimate drive-thru experience. At 4.30am, the train finally pulled into Tabora, where our local sponsor, Ruth Mnyampi, and a few others were awaiting our arrival. They greeted us with tremendous enthusiasm, plying us with questions about our journey and general welfare before ushering us through the pitch darkness into the back of a van. We were to stay in the house of Habib Albhai, a widely respected local man, while he stayed with his brother.

Arriving at the house, we found there had been a power cut. So it was by the light of gas lamps that we found our string and tape, hung up our mosquito nets, and bedded down in the empty house, full of curiosity about all that awaited us in the morning.

Our first day was spent meeting the six principal members of Tabora's Education Council, which involved speeches of thanks from the community for our commitment to the project and the financial assistance we had provided. Each of us had paid £175 towards the construction costs as well as raising the money for our flights and any extras. Liaisons with Ruth had given us a general idea of the price of cement, equipment, the architect's fees and a couple of workmen to help us along. We were happy to do all the labouring ouselves but, as none of us had any experience, we needed people working alongside and showing us what to do. A classroom for some thirty children was no easy undertaking – a fact that had not escaped some of the Education Council members. They seemed somewhat bemused that the majority of us were white women who had come from Britain to do what they saw as a man's job. Yet, this didn't lessen in any way their expressions of gratitude.

Work began almost immediately. We walked the thirty minutes from the house through the town to the school site and stood surveying a plot of land the size of a football pitch, overgrown with grass and old maize stalks. The enormity of the task we had agreed to take on suddenly hit me. With three spades, two hoes and three scythes between us, we began trying to clear a site large enough for a classroom, toilets, office and water tank. It took days of back-breaking labour.

Every morning we began at six, when it was still pitch-black and cold, and would return exhausted by the work and the heat at the end of the day. I was scratched and bruised, and had deep calluses on my hands from threshing and digging in the narrow foundation trenches. My shoulders and back ached from stooping to pull out the roots of plants. More often than not, we were dehydrated because we couldn't boil and treat the water fast enough. My flimsy straw hat did little to ward off the brain-melting rays of the sun. The first weeks were incredibly frustrating as there were very few visible signs of the labour we were putting in. The architect was incompetent and we wasted a lot of time in futile discussion about plans – a lot of pomp and bureaucracy, but little action.

In a small town, where most of the youngsters have never seen a white person before, we were enjoying star status. We gathered a daily audience at the site. From the distant safety of their doorways, or hidden from view, came cries of "*Mzungu, Mzungu*" (white person). As they got braver, they got closer. They were particularly curious about our hair and skin and would stand giggling and staring from a safe distance until one day Tim, six foot and skinny with a mop of red curly hair, ran after them shouting in Swahili, "I like to eat small children".

After a while, they threw caution to the wind and crept silently towards us, took our tools and started digging with spades that were bigger than they were. One little girl, about eight years old, stood there every day holding a baby in her arms, much too useful for household work to be permitted to attend school. She used to stand and watch me in silence. On my last day she ran up to me and grabbed my hand. She said something in Swahili, of which I only caught a few words, then handed me a small cloth doll of uneven stitching and a wide red smile.

We amazed ourselves at how quickly we got used to living without electricity and washing with a bucket of cold water, perfect for water fights in the dark. It took me slightly longer to relinquish my toilet roll in exchange for the beaker of water next to the squat toilet, but when you've got to go, you've got to go, as we each discovered in turn. There were certain things we missed. Family and friends for a start. We all looked forward to Ruth's postal delivery service every day at the site. With no access to phone or fax, our only method of reaching anyone was by mail, and even that was unreliable.

Fantasising about Western food became a favourite pastime, as our diet was extremely bland and repetitive. Steve and Tim were always hungry and would lie in the sun talking about burgers, steaks and big juicy chickens. We had £3 per day out of our main budget to feed the entire group, so we ate rice, vegetables and bread. Ruth and her mother gave us a few tips but generally we were left to fend for ourselves. Yet, any feelings of despondency that we had were far outweighed by the knowledge that we were doing something worthwhile. We also took pleasure in mixing with a new community and way of life, working alongside locals who gave their time and energy to help us, and supping "Safari" beer in the bar with them at sunset.

Ruth and a young teacher-in-training, George Roberti, became our greatest friends and constant companions. They were often on site with us, checking progress and adding a little linguistic clarity when necessary to ease communication with the architect and workmen. We also had a great deal of fun together, often heading out to traditional dance evenings where men and women contorted and shook their bodies in staggering fashions. The women, who wore cloth and padding wrapped around their buttocks in order to accentuate their movements, were mesmerising to watch and surprisingly sexual. Their powerful depiction of femaleness allowed me see more clearly the beauty of our bodies.

One evening George took me and two other volunteers, Tim and Steve, to the local cinema, Diamond Talkies, to see Jackie Chan in *Police Story 3*. The cinema was an old school hall, high-ceilinged and echoey. Wooden chairs had been pushed together to accommodate as large a crowd as possible, leaving us literally rubbing shoulders in the hot, dank atmosphere. The film was run from a shaky projector that was out of sync with the sound. From the level of the shouts and laughter and scraping of chairs, this did not detract from anybody's enjoyment of the film. Mr George, our building mentor, who had shown us how to make and lay bricks, was there, as was Museven, one of the local guys who had been coming down to the site to help out. On the way in, Museven had bought me two bubble gums and a boiled sweet. It was hard to tell whether or not this amounted to a "date".

In the final weeks of the project, construction proceeded at an incredible pace. We couldn't mix cement fast enough. As soon as the bricks had dried, they were added to the now sturdy-looking walls. Yet in the penultimate week of the project, both Susan and I fell ill with amoebic dysentery, contracted from impure water. It hit us from nowhere, and brought on fever, relentless vomiting and diarrhoea. We cut sorry figures, yo-yoing to the bathroom 24 hours a day. Sometimes we would turn to each other, saying, "Looking good, Susan", "You too, Zoe", and laugh weakly before stumbling to the toilet once again. I'd be lying if I said I never once thought of giving up the project, especially during those dark days of illness, but there seemed to be no real grounds for self-pity. Everybody had had their fair share of ill health. Keith had once spent an afternoon on a rehydration drip.

Overall, my trip to Africa affected me in many ways I didn't anticipate. I experienced new extremes of emotion, fatigue and exhilaration. I was touched by the people I worked for, who had so little yet gave their time, energy and friendship so generously. I was proud to give something back. Also, as a young woman travelling overseas for the first time, the journey was an awakening to a new sense of self. Finding myself in a context so different from anything I knew, I was able to gain a wider perspective on my home life, relationships and future. I also became aware of myself as a white Western woman, whose skin colour was respected, feared and hated. I was struck by the extent to which economics dictate life options and attitudes.

There were many difficult times, but also many occasions for laughter and fun. Yet, most importantly, on the field overgrown with grass and maize stalks there now stands a school, echoing with alphabet chanting and nursery rhymes.

read on . . .

Dervla Murphy, *The Ukimwi Road: From Kenya to Zimbabwe* **(UK: Flamingo, 1994/US: Penguin, 1996).** Once again Murphy takes to the road with her bicycle, but what is planned as a carefree journey across sub-Saharan Africa turns into a harrowing introduction to the continent's problems. AIDS looms largest, having reached epidemic proportions in most of the countries visited, including Tanzania where, soon after crossing the Ugandan border, Murphy meets a nurse whose every patient is infected. Her usual enthusiasm for rough living in remote places is thus tempered by reflections about the state of a country burdened also by lack of resources and the aftermath of Nyerere's "agrarian socialist" revolution. One of the most outspoken, and therefore controversial, books by an amazingly resilient traveller, still seeking adventure in her sixties.

Thailand

Monkey brain

Rebecca Hardie

Buddhist meditation courses in Thailand intrigue many travellers, including Rebecca Hardie, who found that chasing Nirvana is hard work indeed. London-based Rebecca is a seasoned traveller, who has recently returned from an extended trip from Cairo to Cape Town. See also her account of backpacking in India with her mum (p.257).

In the whole of the Chiang Mai night-market, there are no white clothes. I need white garments to cover me, to hide the parts of me that monks are not allowed to see. There are trinkets and gaudy faux-designer clothes, glinting artefacts and swathes of subtle Thai silks: nothing suited to my impending status as a Buddhist novice. But my search eventually leads me to a fabric shop, where I am able to get my hands on two lengths of plain white cotton – one to serve as a sarong, one as a shawl to wrap around and over my shoulders. I have shunned the seduction of the material goods around me for the austere garb of a nun. I am ready for the long journey to Nirvana.

The next afternoon, I leave the urban landscape of Chiang Mai for the breezy countryside of Northern Thailand. After a short journey, I arrive at the temple where I am to stay, Ram Poeng – a rash of gold against a green forest. Intense curlicues of colour rush upwards into pinnacled roof-beams, towering fingers of ceremonial light flashing towards the heavens. Odd that such a materially disdainful religion as Buddhism should be so showy, so immaculately gilded and cloisonné.

Passing through the gates, I am met by a young monk, Tanat, who is in charge of initiating Western visitors. He shows me to the female accommodation and asks me to put on my white attire and wait until I am called for my commencement ceremony. He leaves me to settle in, to take stock of my surroundings.

Here, I am a world away from the comforts of Chiang Mai. My room has a mud floor and the bathroom is ensuite: outside, roof open to the arching blue of the sky, hemmed in by palm-frond walls. There is a bucket of water, a hole in the ground. This, then, is my solitary confinement. I wrap myself in white, swaddle my Western self in the adopted spirituality of the East. I am excited, and I am fearful.

Tanat's American wife – who is being primed for teacher-training – takes me through the Vipassana handbook, the prostration ritual and the breathing and walking meditation movements that I must master before my ceremony with the abbot of the monastery. She teaches me how to sit cross-legged. She teaches me the chant of Universal Loving Kindness: the means with which to begin each session. I am keen to get it right. I have no idea what a jerky or mis-placed movement, what an insincere expression of loving kindness, might mean in this new grand scheme of things.

The ceremony is full of flowers and candle flames, heady incense, impenetrable Thai words and glitzy photos of past teachers. The abbot sits before me and I repeat after him as I swear the eight precepts of the Buddhist moral code. I am confident about my will to abstain from "any kind of erotic behaviour" and "intoxicating sub-stances", but I'll be relieved if I manage to refrain from "dancing, singing, music, going to show wearing garlands and beautifying with perfume and cosmetics". By the time I have handed over my eleven white lotus flowers, eleven orange candles and eleven incense sticks for the ceremonial blessing, my feet are so asleep it is all I can do to stum-ble out into the receding day. At seven o'clock I go to bed, my stom-ach growling furiously in the silence of the early evening.

The temple bell rings at four in the morning, then at six for breakfast and ten-thirty for lunch. There is to be no eating after this time, I am taught that morning. Tanat sets down the rules and regu-lations, and they sound easy enough. No sleeping during the day; no phone calls or letters; no visitors; no writing; no reading; no leaving the temple gates without permission; no immersion heaters for cups of tea. Talking itself is not recommended, but "cheerful, simple, unharmful, friendly talk is fine". The most important rule, Tanat stresses, is to not talk about your meditation practice with anyone, not to compare notes, not to quantify your experiences or your progress. Each person here is an island, with their own tides and temperaments; one shape must not and should not try to fit itself to the geography of another.

We go over the meditation movements again. The nut of the idea of Vipassana, Tanat tells me, is that by encouraging the mind to settle on the simplest, most unthinking events of life, a mindfulness of the wider plains of existence will result. Breathing – in, out, in, out – is the focus of sitting meditation. Stepping – left foot thus, right foot thus – is the focus of walking meditation. By paring down our perception of the atoms of our worlds, we can perhaps build awareness and understanding of the more complex blocks of experience. Mindfulness, Tanat teaches, is the opposite of clumsiness. It is the ability to see clearly, to transcend the ordinary obstacles that can clutter our lives.

I am given the task of five hours of sitting and walking meditation, in quarter of an hour stints, to complete in the next 24 hours. I am eager to begin. To see the clutter disperse, to feel the sureness of my own feet, to occupy my own space. And what could be more tempting for someone who is sometimes accused of being alarmingly cerebral, than the opportunity to sit right inside one's head for hours at a time?

But it simply didn't happen like that. That very first day ended in tears. Alone in my room, sitting crippled from my cross-legged yogic leanings, I swivel my eyes back right into my head, right onto the very act of breathing, the substance of the in-breath, the release of the out. The axes of life themselves. Quarter of an hour, fifteen measly minutes, and I can't keep at it for a second. Thoughts form behind my back and flick up and inwards to my brain, but no sooner do I spot them, no sooner am I lurching towards them with my hands out to strangle the very life out of them, than they stop.

Thoughts, it seem, exist only in retrospect. And they have slippery tails that curl away in a trice. As soon as I notice that I am thinking, that thinking changes, and I watch it change, and however hard I try to delineate to myself what is going on, it goes on regardless, and I become stuck in a kind of limbo between my thoughts and my attempts to watch those thoughts.

Walking meditation is no better, because there is the sheer distraction of physical movement to taunt me. And the noise of the outside, temple world. The bell and the children and the sounds of chanting, the birds and the rumble of distant cars, the frisson of cool trees. Yet it is breaking the rules to ponder how jam-packed-crammed-bursting-full our heads are, every nanosecond of every second of every minute of every day. I am quickly, and grudgingly, dispirited.

This continues over the next couple of days, and I am prescribed increasingly longer sessions of sitting and walking meditation to complete in 24 hours. There are slices of time when things appear to be getting better; some pass more quickly than others, some induce a kind of sleep-state where I am aware of very little at all. And those are the good ones; ones unhampered by the newly unleashed frenzy of my mental circuits. Or by hunger, by pain, by tiredness, by a lurking sense of anxiety, by missing people, by wanting a long cold luminous lager, by wanting to scream at the useless, pointless, stupid self-inflictedness of it all.

I want to write in my diary, or an outlet of any kind. I am not permitted to catch any reflections of me – not in mirrors, nor in the faces of friends, not in words or books. In none of the old familiar places. There is just me, myself and I to hinge myself to, and I am an uncontrollably chattering monkey brain.

But Tanat did say that novices are prone to violent mood swings. Mood avalanches, volcanoes, tempests and forest fires, more like. The days are now no more than strings of hours hooked together by meal-times – the food is filthy – by the torture of meditation, by going to bed, and by lessons from Tanat.

I learn that Vipassana "is not an escape from the trials and tribulations of everyday life, nor an asylum for disgruntled misfits." Nor, silly me, is it "a rest cure, a holiday or an opportunity for socialising". I learn that, as a woman, I cannot go to the first floor of the library lest I come across a monk meditating on his own on the ground floor below. Should such an impure thing come to pass, I will have offended his precepts and so have to undergo rigorous penance procedures. I delight, mindfully, in imagining what that might mean. I also learn that anyone caught masturbating has to sit out their punishment in a chalk square that is drawn carefully around them.

I begin to eye Tanat warily, to wonder where religion crosses the line into cult, where leadership bleeds into the charisma that can blind the willing, and why on earth I should be doing this at all. The five hindrances – craving senses, anger, sloth or torpor, worry or restlessness and doubt – would, if checked by mindful awareness, become confidence, energy, mindfulness, concentration and wisdom. To counter hunger, pain, thought, drowsiness or any other distraction whilst meditating, all one has to do is to observe that distraction gently, and banish it by calling it repeatedly by its name.

In my room, or walking up and down the path outside, the serene incantation of "hunger, hunger, hunger" simply does not seem to do the trick. "Fucking pissed-off, fucking pissed-off, fucking pissed-off" doesn't either. And I am bored. Bored with my failure, bored with my frustration, bored with the very speed of my brain, bored with going to bed at seven and getting up at four, bored with eating lousy food, bored with not talking to anyone except to say, "Mmmm, delicious greens we're having this morning, eh?" Bored with my seeming inability to keep my mind, my oh-so-finely tuned mind, on the job at hand. But mostly, alone in my bed again, I am bolshy-adolescent-bored with the morass of limits that suddenly seems to be me.

I very nearly give up. Very nearly jack it all in for the familiar chaos of the real world of pizza and mattresses, sleep and gossip and getting pissed. But slowly, imperceptibly, my most-secret mindful eye relaxes. I begin to listen and watch for longer periods at a time; I stop panicking just a little. I discover that ice-cream isn't food, really, but a liquid that can be imbibed even after ten-thirty in the morning. I allow myself a bit of chat with the other Westerners – two Dutch girls, pasty and worn in their now-grubby whites; an emaciated Swede due to marry a Thai woman; a cheerful South American woman addicted to mental retreats – and give myself a break from the puritanical drive to do the isolation-thing right.

I start to look around me and appreciate where I am staying. I join in on Sunday lunch, when the parishioners of the temple come and bring food and alms, and the entire community sits down cross-legged and shares news and laughter. I watch the miniature monks fashioning toys out of debris, trying all the while to mindfully stifle their childish shrieks. I discover that the nuns cook secret, and better, food for the local cats and dogs.

I start to trust Tanat and his lessons. I glean glimpses of the distance from oneself and the material world that could possibly result in a finer, more balanced way of seeing. I begin to feel my heartbeat – its sound and the inevitable movement of blood around my body – and the necessary force of my breathing. I begin to regain control.

By the end of the week and my closing ceremony, I am emerging from a gloomy chasm of self-obsession. And in repeating the abbot's words, I can feel myself preparing once more to face the real, obstacle-strewn world. I think of the lagers and cigarettes ahead, and I am certainly not sad to be leaving. But then again, I muse, casually eyeing my monkey-brain thoughts, maybe I wouldn't mind coming back sometime and doing it all again.

A familiar charm

Madeleine Cary

Until 1990 Madeleine Cary juggled her life as a single parent with a career as a media producer. That year her son Ky, aged sixteen, was killed in a tragic accident. After some time trying to recuperate and heal with family and friends she decided it was time to seek life-affirming experiences again. With a backpack, a few savings and no clear itinerary in mind, she flew to Bangkok, marking the beginning of ten months' low-budget trip through Southeast Asia. She currently lives on the south coast of England where she writes short fiction for radio and various publications and is currently completing her first novel. See also her piece on Malaysia (p.370).

I awoke on my first morning in Bangkok to the quickening rhythm of bells from the neighbouring Buddhist temple. At five in the morning there were no travellers or tourists to be seen; only the local Thai community, the saffron-robed young monks, the crisply uniformed schoolchildren, the street vendors and peddlars going about their business. The overnight rainfall had left a fresh damp air that was being injected with the dawn aromas of incense and smoking woks. Petrol fumes and the chaotic blasts of horns and revving engines announced the frenetic city life starting up just streets away.

Fourteen years earlier I had awoken in this same city about to embark on a 1970s drop-out adventure. I thought of where life had taken me since then and how, having just turned forty, I was now embarking on a year's lone travel in Southeast Asia. A deep personal tragedy had brought me to a watershed. I gazed at the activity on Bangkok's bustling streets and promised myself to use this year to find confidence, purpose and peace again.

Why I chose Thailand as the place to start owes much to my distant memories of the place. I was acutely aware of how tourism and the backpacker trail had brought about a major transformation. Others had warned me that I would not recognise the place. However, something enduring and comforting about the Thai culture and people had lured me back. It was at least a relatively familiar place to begin and I refused to believe that the entire country had been over-run with foreign businessmen, lager louts and hippies looking for cheap thrills.

Millions of visitors pass through Bangkok every year and yet I was still startled by their sheer numbers when I arrived in the city. I felt conspicuous with my squeaky-clean rucksack and my general demeanour which vacillated between naive excitement and a novice's paranoia. The majority of younger travellers had a uniform appearance of tie-dyed baggies and beaded hair. This was no surprise but I was taken aback by their "cooler than thou" attitude. In areas developed to cater to the needs of the backpacker, like Khao San Road, the local people have adopted all the fashions and manners of their Western counterparts. I stayed for two nights in this area and found few people approachable. During the day I explored the city; when I entered the old Thai suburbs, enjoying a spicy soup at a street market, or taking tea at an old shack by the river, I began to remember the familiar charm of Thai life.

As soon as my jet lag lifted, I took a train heading south from Bangkok, intent on finding my own way through the southern peninsula, trying, like many a lone wanderer, to plot a route away from the tourist and hippie trail. My first port of call was to be Hua Hin, a town on the eastern coast which the guidebook described as a "delightful seaside resort the Thais are keeping for themselves". When I arrived I drove through the quiet back streets in a rickshaw and was delivered to an old-style guesthouse where two young Thai women received me warmly, offering me a cheap, clean room. I settled in and felt at peace for the first time since leaving England. Until, that is, I set out to investigate the place at dusk and found that, beyond the old town, bars, neon lights and discos flooded the street and everywhere I looked, lithe young Thais, both male and female, were accompanied by large, well-heeled Western men. I was angry at first at the ill-researched guidebook and then felt amused by the irony of the situation. In trying to escape the backpackers, I had ended up in a beach resort where prostitution was veiled behind the guise of holiday romance.

Later that evening I sat on the guesthouse balcony with the two young Thai women and discovered they were both from rural farming communities and had come to the place to seek a fortune. One had a young baby and the three of them shared room and board in the lodgings in exchange for looking after guests. Their real earnings came from foreign "boyfriends" and much of their money was sent home to their village families. They clearly saw themselves as following a path which meant freedom from poverty, but it left a disturbing impression of the nature of Western exploitation.

For the next few weeks I travelled on public transport from one small town to another, trying to avoid the coastal "resorts". Thai bus and train travel was cheap, regular and reasonably comfortable. I rarely met other Westerners on these trips as most of them used the network of air-con tourist buses which shipped them en masse from one popular resort to another. Obviously, buses packed with wealthy Westerners make good targets for bandits and pickpockets and it was no surprise that tales of unfortunate incidents usually involved this expensive and exclusive means of transport.

I enjoyed the rhythm of those first few weeks of travel. Every day I would make a journey by bus or train alongside amiable Thais and enjoy the fantastic views unfolding through the windows: rice paddies, rubber plantations, jungles, rolling hills and sharp, jagged mountains. I watched the pattern of daily life in remote farming settlements, villages or small towns. Everywhere, Buddhist temples adorned the environment. I never felt harassed but frequently felt I was being looked after. It was hard to feel lonely when a toothless old lady would offer me some rice cake or a helpful bus driver would go off his route to deliver me to suitable accommodation. Often I would leave the bus and have a host of concerned, smiling Thai passengers waving to me. After finding a cheap place to stay, I would wander out to watch the magical transformation on the Thai streets as dusk fell. Night life is almost as bustling as day life in Thailand. Street food stalls appear and serve up delicious steaming concoctions within minutes. House shutters are open revealing tableaux of the family life within. Markets are a sensory delight, their cornucopia of exotic produce and domestic goods displayed together in incongruous partnerships; pigs' heads hang next to haberdashery; mounds of tobacco are flanked by dried fish; flowers and strings of sausages sway together from overhead rafters.

Although I had learnt the power of contact through just a smile and a few gesticulations, I was aware that my inability to speak their language was becoming a problem for me. Thai is tonal and very difficult to grasp and I had failed to pick up more than a rudimentary collection of words. I started to feel inadequate; was I so conditioned by Western verbosity that I was incapable of relinquishing the need to verbalise and intellectualise for a while? Then an incident occurred which acted as a catalyst.

I had crossed the peninsula to the western coast and was coming into the province of Phang-Nga, which was reputed to have unique geographical features: huge limestone rocks rose up from the sea in remarkable formations, some of which housed ancient caves with prehistoric drawings. Interested in exploring the area, I arranged to go on my first organised tour, a cut-price expedition that promised a guided boat trip to the rocks and caves and, later, a visit to a floating village built on rafts. On the morning of departure, however, it turned out I was the only low-budget traveller in town and so I had to take the tour alone. For some reason, the English-speaking tour guide failed to appear. Thus I was chauffeured round the magnificent sights by a taciturn old Thai boatman who chewed on his cigarette and gazed out to sea the whole time. I felt a childish disappointment and sat in a sulk as we sailed around the weird and beautiful seascape. I had been secretly hoping that I would meet other travellers on the tour, or, at least, have a tour guide to converse with in English. I realised then that my capacity to take joy from the experience was being hampered by my inability to share my impressions and sensations verbally. I surrendered to my Western conditioning and decided to go on the backpacker trail.

It was not difficult. I was close to the area where the impact of tourism is mushrooming at an incredible rate out from over-developed Phuket to the surrounding islands and coastal resorts. On a boat crossing to the island of Ko Lanta, I was approached by several young Thai touts. Already English was the common language again. Each tout brandished photo albums of their resort, usually the same Polaroid visions of grinning guests, palm-lined beaches, grass huts and sunsets as the next. I took pot luck with a place named "Paradise" and was herded into a pick-up truck with several other travellers when the boat docked. And so I finally got to experience the pleasures and pains of mingling with other backpackers. I indulged in verbal diarrhoea for days, incessantly articulating everything that had happened on my travels so far. I was not alone. Others would arrive, dump the rucksack, order a coconut shake and be off on a three-hour monologue before they even asked where you were from. The rapid turnover rate meant that different people arrived every day – I probably met at least fifteen different nationalities in the space of five days. Eventually, however, it all started to feel repetitious. Travellers' tales were becoming predictable; ideas and impressions were hackneyed; attitudes were often surprisingly reactionary. One evening a Swiss hippie waxed lyrical, claiming that the song *Message in a Bottle* said it all about the state of the world. When he started quoting Phil Collins lyrics, I went to my hut to pack. It was time to return to my previous lone travelling routine.

I headed back to the mainland and travelled down to Satun, the mainly Muslim Thai province that borders Malaysia. In the evenings the Thai national anthem was pumped out over the streets on loudspeakers just to remind these traditionally rebellious people of their Thai citizenship. I relished the varied and fascinating Thai culture with renewed enthusiasm and intended to get the best out of my last two weeks before my visa expired. In an effort to get to the nearby island of Ko Tarutao, a national park of reputed stunning beauty, I stumbled across a bizarre place that gave my sojourn in Thailand its final fling. Boat trips to Ko Tarutao were over for the season but there was a small vessel heading out to Ko Bulon, an island which was not even mentioned in the guidebook. I thought I had finally found an untarnished gem, an authentic, unspoilt Thai island.

Ko Bulon was a complete surprise. The island consisted of a small Thai community in transition from living off the fishing and farming trade to developing the place for low-budget tourism. It was all in embryonic form when I arrived yet already there were several Westerners encamped, almost permanently, in self-made beach huts and tree houses. Mostly they were exiles from Europe and North America who, for love of the country, or addiction to its drugs or lifestyle, had worked out the best way to reside longterm in Thailand. Ko Bulon was close to the island of Langkawi in Malaysia which meant the two-month Thai visa could be easily renewed in a 24-hour trip across the border.

In a sense, Ko Bulon was a microcosm of modern Thailand. Local people seeking a livelihood and security were prepared to cash in on the Westerners who sought an escape into a free and sensual lifestyle. It was a strange synthesis and helped me understand more clearly how the onslaught of tourism had occurred in the country at large. What was different about Ko Bulon was the fact that the foreigners at least made some attempt to adapt to the Thai community. Many knew fluent Thai and some even lived and worked with the Thai families. I was staying in an area owned by the patriarch Bang Lee and his huge extended family. One of his daughters-in-law ran the local store, a bamboo-stilted platform with shelves of produce and hardware. She had befriended a Thai-speaking Icelandic woman who helped her with the store and the children. I got the feeling it was necessary to be vetted and passed by these two strong women before you could be accepted into the community. I was lucky enough to be invited to dine in the storeowner's living quarters on my first evening and she liked the way I amused and entertained her children. I was offered a tent to sleep in on the beach. Later, when the crushing heat made it too hot for a tent even overnight, I was given floor space in someone's treehouse.

Bang Lee had already built a few basic beach shacks and a spartan restaurant for the occasional travellers who, like myself, found the place almost by accident. He was planning a major conversion to cope with a future influx of backpackers and tourists and was already chopping down the beautiful trees which lined the beach so that there would be timber for bulding. Ironically, it was the Westerners who lived in the community who took greatest offence at this development. They bombarded Bang Lee with eco-conscious arguments but he, naturally, was irrevocably caught up in visions of future fortune and power.

Not all the Westerners saw Bang Lee's plans as a threat, however. One, an enterprising American who, despite mastering the Thai language and donning a sarong, still hung onto his cultural roots, was planning his own free market profit-making scheme. He had bought an old Thai fishing vessel and converted it into a "tour boat" to provide island cruises. Keeping investment risk to a minimum, he had "converted" the boat by installing a curtain around a hole in the floor for a toilet and nailing a canopy of tarpaulin onto the top of the captain's cabin as the sleeping quarters. The maiden voyage was due to take place while I was there. It was only when I saw the motley collection of backpackers the American had roped in for the tour that my curiosity got the better of me. Some New Age West Coast Americans, an Australian environmentalist, a French academic and two Swiss secretaries made up the passenger list. Meanwhile, the American's partner and Captain, Mr Chang, had recruited two young island boys and a local boatman for his crew. The combination of these characters convinced me that, if nothing else, the boat tour would provide a psychologist's dream of group dynamics. I talked myself into a free trip in exchange for help as a deckhand.

As expected, the journey offered more excitement in the shifting dynamics between the people involved than in the experience of touring the tropical islands. My role as "social director" was quickly established as I acted as a buffer between the increasingly annoyed guests and the churlish American who had overestimated his skills in handling people. They felt they had been overcharged for the experience of living in cramped and primitive conditions for five days at sea. He felt they were expecting too much. Before long there was rivalry and conflict on board. The environmentalist was upset by the Thai crew's behaviour as they threw beer bottles and cigarette butts into the sea. He would sit crosslegged chanting to the ocean for forgiveness. The Europeans fell out with the American; the women joined forces against the men. In time, however, after a few outbursts of temper, moods settled and group bonding occurred. Relationships shifted, a New Age couple decided to split up and a romance blossomed between the boatman and a Swiss secretary. In only five days we had undergone an intense experience which left most of us more in touch with ourselves and our companions. I had discovered a role that would be given to me many times in the forthcoming months: playing "agony aunt" to all and sundry. I had also learnt how to cook Thai food in a dangerous and noisy engine room, how to swim against the tide, how to remove sea urchin spines from a foot. Ultimately, we all seized the moment and took delight in the beautiful island locations we visited. We befriended monkeys, snorkelled in coral reefs, bathed in crystal waterfalls and all took turns at night fishing hauls. We visited communities of nomadic sea gypsies and learnt Thai songs from Mr Chang, whose only English consisted of "I love you" and Elvis Presley lyrics. Finally, on our last night at sea, we held a wild singing and drumming party, raving on deck under a full moon as the old boat creaked over the Andaman sea.

I was so reluctant to leave Thailand that I overstayed my visa time by two days, incurring a small fine at the border. It was hard to believe that only two months earlier I had started out from Bangkok in a defensive shell. As I passed a shop window, a young woman with a glowing tan and confident gaze stared back at me. I was stunned when I realised I was looking in a mirror.

read on . . .

▣ **Karen Connelly,** *Touch the Dragon: A Year in Thailand* (1992; UK: Black Swan, 1996/US: Turnstone Press, 1995).** A startlingly perceptive, funny and stylish debut travel book by a young Canadian woman adjusting to family life in northern Thailand. Connelly, then seventeen, arrived in Denchai in the late 1980s on a Rotary Scholarship. In her lyrical account of a year spent living above a liquor store in a small farming and merchant community, attending to the endless rules and customs of her hosts and grappling with a phonetic language that everyone speaks but her, she reveals her background as a precociously accomplished poet. Connelly entered literary history in 1993, when this book made her the youngest ever winner of the Governor General's Award, Canada's top prize for non-fiction.

Cleo Odzer, *Patpong Sisters: An American Woman's View of the Bangkok Sex World* **(US: Arcade, 1997).** An American anthropologist's funny and touching account of her life with the prostitutes and bar girls of Bangkok's notorious red-light district. The story strays onto somewhat dodgy ethical ground when she begins an affair with a pimp (thus joining the sex tourists she so roundly criticises) but Odzer nonetheless manages to deliver an enlightening and thought-provoking portrayal of life in the Thai sex industry.

Louise Williams, *Wives, Mistresses & Matriarchs* **(1998; UK: Phoenix, 1999).** Williams' exploration of the lives of women in contemporary Asia contains three chapters on Thailand. The first is based on an interview with one of the country's most powerful businesswomen, the second with a factory worker and the third with a young woman forced into prostitution. These are only brief life stories but Williams has a sympathetic ear and her subjects provide interesting, if sometimes harrowing, insights into the concerns and experiences of women in Thailand today.

Tibet

Monastery baby

Wendy Teasdill

Wendy Teasdill, an experienced Tibet traveller, is the author of **Walking to the Mountain** (Asia 2000), about a lone trek that she made to Mount Kailash in western Tibet almost a decade ago. She currently lives in Somerset, England, with her husband and three daughters, where she teaches yoga and writes articles on travel, children and yoga. She has recently completed a pregnancy yoga book (Gaia Books) and is working on a new book on Tibet.

"*Das Baby ist ganz nass* ("That baby is completely wet")," confided one elderly German woman to another.

I attempted a philosophical reply: "*So ist das Leben* ("Such is life")". It would have been more honest, of course, to have retorted: "*Ihre Kleide sind wasserpruf und warm und sie ist ganz fröhlich*" ("Her clothes are waterproof and warm, and she is quite happy")." I might also have added the German translation of "And you might give me a hand with the push-chair through the mud, rather than criticising in that self-righteous manner."

We were going around the Tibetan monastery of Labrang in the pouring rain. We being myself, my husband and our fourteen-month-old baby, Iona. Not to mention the zygote of our next baby, nestled secretly in my womb – but I wasn't acknowledging her yet. We were going around with a party of Germans because they happened to be there that day and we knew the guide, who had suggested we come along. It was an unfortunate configuration. Some of the group seemed to think that we hadn't paid for the tour, and so were shutting doors in our faces at every turn. We (who had paid – in China, the system's the system), and who had done the tour on several past visits to Tibet, were becoming increasingly put out by their high-handed manner.

Iona was the only one who was happy. We entered the chanting hall. "Oh dear," whispered a rather anxious woman in front of us, "Won't the baby be scared?" The lights were dim: 35-watt bulbs sprouting from spindly wires were outshone by the richer glow of lamplight, and the shadows sank deep and long over the skeletons and protector deities painted on the walls. To their surprise, however, Iona let out a gleeful whoop.

The monks were her friends. At the sight of her, they grinned indulgently and waved. *Malas* (strings of prayer-beads) were proffered. Many of them knew her already, as we had been here for several weeks, and Iona was a familiar sight around the monastic town. Labrang is one of the six famous monasteries of Tibet belonging to the Gelugpa (reformed) order headed by the Dalai Lama. Though there is Chinese influence in the golden curly roofs of the temples, the monks' quarters are entirely Tibetan: low, flat-roofed dwellings made of earth, stone and wood, they fan out across the wide valley, covering several square kilometres.

On sunny days, we would go down and watch the monks debating in the orchards by the road; on duller days, we would take butter tea with them in their rooms. Iona found butter tea a very pleasant substitute for breast-milk from time to time. We had seen the monks' photo albums and Iona had cut her teeth on many of their beads. And every day, rain or shine, we would circumambulate the monastery at least once – a circuit of two miles or so. Iona was just learning to walk. I let her out of the pushchair and she toddled off into the monks' open arms, shrieking with joy.

I had already taken her to Buddhist retreats in India, such as Dharamsala and Ladakh, where she loved to listen to the rising and falling sounds of the prayer rituals. And I had been pregnant with her on a previous trip to Tibet. So bell-ringing, chanting and, most of all, the deep sonorous swell of "Om mani padme hum" had all the familiarity of wombsounds to her. She even looked like the monks. I had celebrated her first birthday in Ladakh by taking her to a lama, who gave her a blessing, a Tibetan name, and cut the first lock of her hair. Then I took her home and shaved her head. In many parts of Asia, children have their hair shaved when they reach their first birthday. It makes sense to me: the shaving of the baby-hair is the end of baby-hood and the hair grows thick and strong afterwards.

Now, months later, Iona's hair was growing in a smooth pelt of bristles, just like the monks' own hair, albeit blonde. She was also wearing a Tibetan coat of maroon homespun wool, which a friend in Ladakh had given her for her birthday. Despite her little purple wellington boots, she looked more like them than us. Om mani padme hum: "Glory to the jewel in the heart of the lotus" – so goes a rough translation of the eternal Tibetan mantra. We prized Iona away from the monks, returned their *malas*, and the tour continued. Torches were produced, and feeble lights shone on the demons and tortures of various hell-realms.

I lingered behind the others at a dusty altar, regarding the soft glow of the proffered lamps. I held my hands to the glow, and then brought its blessing up to my heart, throat and head in appreciation of body, speech and mind. Then, acting on intuition, I brought my hands down toward my lower abdomen. At this moment a monk glided from the shadows, and offered me holy water from a black kettle. I received it in the palm of my hand, and it was from this moment that the new baby was acknowledged. Silently I gave great thanks, and moved on.

Another day, we climbed up a steep and narrow clay path, out of sight of the main monastery, to Labrang's nunnery. We were going to deliver a message and a gift to one of the nuns from one of the female foreign followers of Tibetan Buddhism. The nunnery was established over a hundred years ago, but the abbot of Labrang insisted it remain out of sight and unfunded. The tradition continues to this day: the nunnery is still invisible and impoverished. It is common practice for nuns to be treated as very much inferior to monks. If you ask a Tibetan nun why she is a nun, she will inevitably reply: "So I can be reborn a man in the next life." And why? Because the teachings of Tibetan Buddhism are passed down from male teacher to male pupil by word of mouth. Women can only receive high teachings from women, and the only way around it is to go to Taiwan, where the

Mahayana female chain has survived intact – an option open to foreign followers of Tibetan Buddhism but not, ironically, to Tibetan nuns.

As well as having limited access to the teachings, nuns are often required to return to their families at harvest time to do the heavy work. In many respects, they are the true torch-bearers of the mystic spirit of Tibetan Buddhism, whose dictates require humility and forbearance, whatever the circumstances.

We asked for the nun we wished to see by name, and a bunch of children led us up to her. I had Iona on my back this time, and one little boy in particular delighted in reaching up to hold her hand. His head was shaved, all but for one rope which dangled sturdily from his crown; his clothes were tattered and black, and his hands were blacker. Iona crowed in delight and the boy revealed a gleaming white row of teeth. The "nunnery", when we finally came to it, was a very humble affair: a simple earthen room set into the hillside, containing a bed, a stove, a kitschy calendar adorned with kittens, and little else.

The nun seemed a little vague, and when we handed her the parcel, she turned it over with a disinterested air, before serving us with tea and scabby, stunted apples. A dozen other nuns appeared from similar dwellings on the hillside, smiling and taking it in turns to gently hold Iona back from the fire. They insisted that I take their photograph, all of them, with Iona. I have the photo on the wall now: they are all grinning like Cheshire cats and Iona looks to be in her element.

Many Tibetans told us Iona was certainly a reincarnated Tibetan. Of course, I am romantically inclined to believe this, and there were many instances of "proof". There was the time, for example, when, without having seen anyone else do this before her, Iona went up to a particular rock, and began to bang her forehead against it in veneration, in the way that Tibetans do, laughing the while. As the rock turned out to be particularly sacred, the Tibetan monks tended to treat her like a goddess after that. But Iona just laughed. To her, there was nothing occult or weird about the monks chanting, the murals, the darkness, the rain, the travelling, the rock: it just was what she was used to.

We spent a happy month or so in Labrang before renting a jeep and going down through the mountains on a three-day trip to the Chinese city of Chengdu. From there, we took a plane to the Tibetan capital of Lhasa. This was a new way of travelling for me: before I had met my husband, I had always travelled in China by public transport, and in Tibet by hitch-hiking or on foot. I had also always travelled alone. So had he, come to that. We had been introduced by mutual friends, and Iona was the consequence of our meeting. Though both of us have found our wings a little snipped by parenthood, we've gained more than we've lost: apart from the sheer joy that she gives us, Iona has opened up channels of communication undreamed of even by the solitary foot-traveller. Suddenly we were no longer oddities to be pitied and helped, but regular human beings.

Tibetans and Chinese could relate to us in a way they could not before. At one point, stuck in a traffic jam because of a mud-slide, I took Iona out for a walk. Iona lost her shoe in the mud. I retrieved it. A village woman beckoned us to where she was squatting on a hillock above the road and, with a can of water, and a ladle, helped me wash the shoe. No words were spoken, but we might have spent our whole lives working side by side, looking after mud-spattered little ones. We communicated in the universal language of motherhood.

Tibetan women were fascinated by our equipment: they examined at great length our baby buggy, which cruised like a four-wheel drive over the roughest terrain, and the sling with which I strapped Iona to my back for mountain-walking. They were always voted "*Yagadoo!*" ("Good") with a smiling thumbs-up. These items would, of course, be impractical for them. For example, Tibetan mothers adopt the Chinese split-trousers method instead of nappies. This involves a lot of mopping up, but is useful when the children are a little older and play outside. But I wouldn't fancy putting a baby with split trousers in either a sling or a pushchair.

For my part, I was intrigued with how they managed the small babies. Nomads pack rags with dried sheep's dung, which acts as an organic Pampers by absorbing the moisture. Most interesting, however, is the method used by Tibetan nomad mothers on pilgrimage. They wear thick homespun coats that come to the floor and are belted at the waist to form a bulging pouch. Often I saw a woman pop a hand into her pouch and scoop out an entirely naked baby, which she would then hold to the side of the path with a soft "shush"-ing noise. The baby – sometimes just a few days old – would then oblige by excreting neatly. Whether due to the impact of the cold or an extremely intuitive bond between mother and baby, I couldn't say - but it works.

Once we reached Lhasa, we again rented a jeep and went up to the nunnery and hot springs of Terdrum. High up in the mountains, Iona and I both became listless with altitude sickness. Neither of us had much appetite for the vegetables and rice I cooked over our mountain stove, yet we couldn't sleep either. Because I was feeling so woozy it took me 24 hours to figure out what was wrong – the jump to Lhasa hadn't seemed to affect us, but the long and gradual incline to Terdrum had finished us off. We had gone too far, too fast.

Altitude sickness is a funny expression. I didn't feel sick, just vague and floaty. It was only when I discovered I could scarcely climb the hill to the nunnery that I realised there was something wrong. As for Iona – instead of dashing around with her usual zest, she became a listless heap in my arms. In retrospect I wonder why I didn't worry more but, of course, the affect of altitude sickness is to cancel out worry.

On the second night a Westerner of forgotten nationality appeared in our room. He was anxious to impress us with his knowledge of Buddhism and reeled off a long list of all the lamas he had met, the holy places he had visited and the practices he had performed. He was leaving the following day. When I asked if he had any space in his jeep for us, as the baby had altitude sickness, he seemed to positively recoil. Then he mumbled a few words about the jeep being full already and disappeared. The monastery tour group seemed saints by comparison – at least they had acted out of concern for the baby.

Still, our altitude sickness wasn't too bad: our lips hadn't turned blue and we were still functioning in a low-key sort of way. We ate and did much less than usual and drank considerably more. Though we couldn't circumambulate the holy mountain, we lay quietly in the hot thermal waters and chatted with the Tibetan women pilgrims who gathered around us. As the full moon rose they began knocking back bottles of fermented barley wine, becoming fiercely drunk in the process. Fortunately we were in bed – though not asleep – by the time they decided to have a midnight dip, and were copiously sick into the water.

The bathing areas were sectioned off by stone walls, but there was an open washing area by the side of the stream that was a boon for nappy-washing. I had been washing terry nappies (not to mention the rest of the clothes) by hand for six months, and took great pleasure in the way they sparkled when I hung them out to dry. Here I draped them over the bushes and marvelled at their brilliance against the azure blue of the sky. Pampers and washing machines have nothing on the pioneer satisfaction of washing nappies with a bar of Chinese washing soap and a bit of elbow grease.

We returned to Lhasa on a pilgrim bus. As soon as we had descended a thousand feet, Iona and I recovered our vitality. Iona sat at the back of the bus, holding hands with a rather gaunt, hollow-eyed Tibetan boy a couple of years older than she. I wondered if he was ill but knew there was no way I could separate them. They sat there, grinning away, brother and sister born worlds apart, destined for different futures, united in a few hours of companionship. Tibetan Buddhism teaches that to live with awareness in the moment is the greatest wisdom. To an adult, with responsibilities and cares, it is very difficult. To Iona and her friend, it was child's play.

read on . . .

Alexandra David-Neel, *My Journey to Lhasa* (originally subtitled: *The Personal Story of the Only White Woman Who Succeeded in Entering the Forbidden City*) **(1927; UK: Virago, o/p/US: Beacon Press, 1993).** In her fifty-fifth year, French explorer and inveterate traveller David-Neel disguised herself as a mendicant nun, with her plaits inked and lengthened with yak's hair and charcoal smeared on her face, and set out across the Sino-Tibetan frontier. Accompanied by Yongden, the young priest who later became her adopted son, she trekked for four and a half months through blizzards and ice to enter the fiercely isolated and xenophobic capital where she lived undetected in the shadow of the Potala Palace for a further two months. Small wonder her writings, which include details from her rigorous researches into Tibetan Buddhism, became an instant and enduring classic.

Justine Hardy, *The Ochre Border: A Journey Through the Tibetan Frontierlands* **(UK: Constable & Co., 1995/US: o/p).** Hardy's first travel book tells of her journey with four women and a male photographer through the Spiti Valley, a remote region of Tibet, protected from the Chinese invasion and, in 1992, only just opened up to outsiders. As with the recent *Scoop-Wallah* (see p.274), she seems in her element writing about people, namely her motley bunch of companions, their guides and the various Tibetans they meet along the way. An entertaining, if somewhat superficial, read, as much about the dynamics of group travel as about the hidden wonders of Tibet.

Isabel Hilton, *The Search for the Panchen Lama* **(UK: Viking, 1999).** In 1995 when the exiled Dalai Lama selected a new Panchen Lama, the boy he chose was arrested and has become one of the world's youngest political prisoners while the Chinese government has enthroned its own representative. In her trademark detailed and unflinching style, Isabel Hilton details the whole sorry story of the search for the new lama.

Pamela Logan, *Among Warriors: A Woman Martial Artist in Tibet* **(US: Vintage Departures, 1998).** Logan, a third-degree karate black belt, crosses Tibet in her attempt to enter the forbidden mountainous region of Kham, home of the Khampa horsemen renowned for their guerrilla resistance against the occupying Chinese army. Her strength, stamina and self-discipline hold her in good stead as she cycles through high snowy passes, treks along precipitous tracks, and battles with the elements with only a few pilgrim encounters and cups of yak butter to sustain her.

Charlotte Painter, *Conjuring Tibet* **(US: Mercury House, 1996).** Painter presents us with a view of Tibet as seen through the eyes of an American writer-narrator who travels illegally into the country and seeks out a famed ***khandro*** (holy woman). In a series of notebook entries a picture is "conjured" of an ancient culture transformed and desecrated by Chinese oppression and state-backed vandalism. A passionate and astute documentary novel, which uses moments of fantasy writing and deeply personal musings to evoke even more effectively the catastrophe of the Chinese annexation.

Jetsun Pema, *Tibet: My Story* **(US: Element Books, 1998).** Jetsun Pema was a young girl when a group of elderly lamas arrived at her home to examine her brother on his knowledge of the sacred texts from a previous incarnation. They were sufficiently satisfied by his answers to install him as the new Dalai Lama. A privileged, though inevitably, reverential, view of the "eternal Tibet" before the Chinese invasion.

Trinidad & Tobago

"Dominique's a mas maker, not a lady!"

Dominique De-Light

Dominique De-Light, a carnival artist, photographer and freelance writer, is co-author of the *Rough Guide to Trinidad and Tobago*. She first travelled to Trinidad in 1996 in the hopes of finding work as a "mas maker", or costume artist, in the run-up to the February carnival. She had already worked, for a brief spell after leaving university, as a volunteer for the Notting Hill Carnival in London. In Trinidad she managed to arrange a job with the Callaloo company, the island's most prestigious carnival band, who were producing costumes by the internationally acclaimed designer Peter Minshall.

In November, whilst sleet and rain dominated the British skies, I started work with warmth in my bones and sun in my heart. Each morning I caught a "maxi-taxi" from Port of Spain to Chaguaramas, a thirty-minute journey past small fishing villages, rocky coastlines and coconut-littered beaches to arrive at the Callaloo mas camp. The "factory", as it was known, was an old US Army machine shop that had been transformed into a cavernous, light and airy space full of old costumes, tools and stocks of cane, fibreglass, wood and material. An air-conditioned sewing room stacked with bales of material competed with a small air-conditioned office for the coolest area to work in. The rest was a gigantic oven masquerading as a production area and a store room. In the corners cardboard boxes piled to the ceiling kept dust out of old costumes and hid the building's main occupants, the thousands of vicious mosquitoes that were to persecute me daily. There was a well-equipped workshop, dubbed "the engine room", where Murphy, the master mas maker, worked magic with wood. A makeshift kitchen had been set up at the rear where Joan, the cook, toiled for hours over huge cauldrons of cow heel soup or chicken foot stew. The sweet smell of food filled the factory and the delicious dishes soon filled the stomachs of the hardworking, ravenous crew.

The Callaloo company called itself a family; it was certainly close-knit and required dedicated loyalty from its workers. It held a prestigious reputation in Trinidad and this along with its cliquey workforce was enough to intimidate any foreign newcomer. At first I was watched closely. As a young, white, English woman entering a traditionally black, male, Trini bastion, I had a lot to prove. Women in the camp usually did sewing or decorative tasks; I, on the other hand, wanted to enter the realm of the "engine room", using power tools and constructing costume frames. A source of entertainment for many was seeing me use a "cutlass" (machete). Murphy pointed out the historical irony of "a British lady" using a tool traditionally used by the slaves on the plantations. However as the men laughed, a female colleague shouted out, "Why are you surprised? Dominique's a mas maker, not a lady!"

Gaining respect was not only a battle with the men, but the women too. I challenged the traditional sexual division of labour within the camp. To some who prided themselves on their feminine wiles, I was a threat; my desire to work in the "male jobs" was obviously a cunning ploy to steal their men. I felt hurt by the cool reception I received initially from the women of the camp. I had hoped, in my naivety, that the macho environment would have encouraged female solidarity. I found it hard working so intensively with so little support. In London I was used to a large social network and understanding friends. Here I was utterly alone, surrounded by men who believed silence signalled strength, and women who viewed me as a threat to be ignored or belittled. I was determined not to let these lows get to me. I loved the work, the banter, the physical challenge. I was in a constant state of extreme emotion, but at least I knew I was living; making the most out of life, not settling for an easy, mundane existence.

Initially I worked from drawings, trying to recreate the shapes, colours and textures of the designer Minshall's vaguely sketched head-pieces. During the prototype stage experiments were suggested by management but they were also open to new concepts, as long as the ideas proved effective, cheap and quick to produce. Most of the techniques I had to learn afresh as many of the ideas I brought with me from Notting Hill were either too expensive, too inaccessible or considered too poor quality for Callaloo.

Regal outfits were created from recycled materials, the result of long experimental processes and production stages. Crushed bottletops became glittering pendants, dried leaves backed with nylon net became headpiece decorations, palm leaves were woven into hats and belts. None could be identified once painted, gilded and placed in position. I watched closely as colleagues painlessly bent chicken wire into the shape of birds, or gilded palm leaves to make them resemble old worn gold – a little bend here and a crease there, and a piece of coloured transparent plastic became a wonderful ruby with a convincing glow.

Each night I rattled home to my rented room in the Port of Spain, my hands a piece of collage in their own right. Varnish, glitter and paint held together hands cut from wire bending, blistered from the glue gun and sprinkled with an unhealthy dose of fibreglass splinters. Luckily I have no desire to be a hand model.

In many ways the work was an ideal job, flexible, creative and collective. Chatting to my colleagues I slowly got to know them as we exchanged ideas, life stories and jokes. This congenial atmosphere had its price – the hours were long, at least ten hours a day and they increased the closer we got to carnival.

Once the production process started, the creative element of the work disappeared. At three weeks, with three thousand costumes to produce, time and organisation became essential. We were creating artistic theatrical costumes, but at the end of the day it became a production line like any other. Costumes were broken down into units and unit cost, and the factory was reorganised to ensure full production potential. Everything boiled down to numbers. Five thousand of this, two hundred of that, people working on a component with no idea which costume it was for. Long discussions took place at each stage of production, to try and create the quickest way out of the boredom. Knowledgeable crew members suggested labour-saving ideas to management, using artistic terminology relating to aesthetics, knowing full well that the same idea would be dismissed if "it's only to ease the workload". Even at this late stage, artistic sensibilities took priority over speed.

My sanity depended on my team workers. Horrors occurred if I was placed with slow, disorganised individuals. My day suddenly became wonderful if I discovered a person with initiative, common sense, and a desire to work fast and with attention to detail. Soon I searched out the same people, knowing we worked well together, and close friendships were made. Hundreds of yards of fabric had to be hand-painted with cut-out sponges. Five of us worked running up and down twenty-foot tables, sponges in one hand, heavy, wooden paint trays in the other. We became a human painting machine, working in perfect harmony – wetting, scrunching, sponging and splashing and turning ordinary brown cotton into ornate fabric.

I was working with the core crew. Praise was unheard of in this team of young, hard-working men, I had no idea how I was doing. The team leader criticised me constantly, which unknown to him would reduce me to tears on my tea break as I sat alone under the mango tree. After weeks of self doubt I challenged him. His explanation was he had to test me; he knew British people and they always sacrificed quality for speed, it was his responsibility that I did not do the same. Being used to a culture where time is money and speed is of the essence, I struggled with this new positive revelation that quality and artistry was more important than finishing the product. I found it refreshing to work with people of such high standards, though as the deadline grew nearer I noticed a few others who seem a little less concerned with attention to detail.

As the weeks progressed, the working hours increased. Each day I felt I could not cope with less sleep but each night I worked an hour more and slept an hour less. Twenty four hours a day, seven days a week were spent working in the carnival camp. We had no time for an outside life, the factory was our world. The beach was across the road, but I swam there only once, too often caught up in my work to even take a stroll to the water's edge. A sense of camaraderie developed, based on our dedication to carnival. Cut off from friends and family, with a final deadline that had to be met, little food and even less sleep, people were at their most raw – with only their commitment and love for the art form keeping them going. Working under similar conditions every year meant that friendships were close but also suffocatingly claustrophobic as everyone knew everyone else's private business. Uncertain of the work politics and social etiquette, I gingerly stepped around the minefield of who was involved with whom, who could be trusted and who was two-faced. I survived but not before a few explosions blew up in my face.

For the final weeks before carnival few people got more than three hours rest a night. Sleep generally meant finding a hole somewhere in the factory amongst material scraps, under tables, or even a workbench covered in sawdust and glue. I learnt to sleep with soca music blasting in my ears as the radio was never turned down – to ensure those who were still working stayed awake. Hard physical work, lifting gallons of paint, running and jumping off and on tables in a climate of eighty percent humidity and temperatures between 29 and 36°C, ensured I would collapse deep asleep despite the noise and blood-hungry mosquitoes. Dreams were perturbed, full of the repetitive actions of production. Counting thousands of plastic spoons used in necklaces, cutting endless leaf shapes out of chicken wire for headpieces, knotting yards of strips of gold lamé to create ornate tassels. I thanked God for small mercies – at least I wasn't doing Sam's job: drilling holes in 10,000 bottle tops with a drill bit that could only take six pieces at a time. He was there hunched over the drill for a week, with a placid smile and patient expression. Unshakeable from his task, he was determined to finish. His first son was born whilst he worked, but Sam would let nothing interrupt his mission.

As dawn rose, my colleagues so lively throughout the night, drinking vast quantities of rum whilst they worked, would fade into space cadets. Like zombies they walked aimlessly, sporting "darkers" (sunglasses) as the harsh light of day became too much for their battered senses. They would crash out on the nearest available table; cigarette butts still hanging from their mouths and hands clasped around empty glasses or an unfinished beer.

The last week of work and all I could wish for was for it to be over. I had become obsessed with the fantasy of sleep, a soothing bath and a soft bed. Carnival at this stage no longer mattered to me. Yet the intense build-up had wound me up like a spring. I was determined to enjoy the festival, I felt I deserved it. For weeks the carnival camp had been my life. No carnival fetes for carnival workers, for us the outside world didn't exist. Jouvert, a street party starting at 2am and ending at dawn, signals the start of the carnival. Suddenly in the camp, Todd the manager, climbed on the table and shouted across the hubbub, "Jouvert has started, carnival is here". People downed tools, jumped in a van, headed downtown and started to party though they'd had no sleep for three days. It was total madness. Exhausted and covered head to toe in paint and mud – traditional Jouvert garb – pumping soca tunes inspired energy to rise from deep within me. I was surrounded by thousands of people packed together, jumping up behind a sound truck on the streets of Port of Spain. Adrenaline pumped through my body. Dazed but ecstatic, I started to dance like I've never danced before. Surrounded by darkness, jostling between eerily painted mud-covered faces, I was swept along by the crowds and the rhythmic beating of the percussion band. Hours later as dawn rose, recognisable faces emerged from the mud creatures surrounding me. We wearily climbed back onto the truck to go for a quick "seabath" – to rid us of our body paint – before going back to work.

On Carnival Monday, the rest of Trinidad was out on the streets partying away. In the camp new costumes were still being started. Major individual pieces began to be assembled at midnight with only eight hours to go. Suddenly from nowhere huge thirty-foot structures of aluminum and fibreglass appeared. I was amazed at the speed and skill of my co-workers despite their sleep-deprived and alcohol-induced state. Shane, the wizard welder wielded his sparking machine with an attention to detail one would have thought impossible if you'd seen him a few hours before. Meanwhile I tried to cope with a brain soft as jelly and the body co-ordination skills of the newly awakened Frankenstein.

It was these huge costumes that I had been waiting for, eagerly anticipating spending hours on careful detail, learning the skills and scientific knowledge to ensure the costume is properly balanced and will not collapse under the weight of decoration. Yet when I finally have the chance to watch and learn I start to slump with exhaustion. A wad of gold sheet plastic is pushed into my hands and I am asked to make two hundred shaped stars for the Queen costume. After weeks of monotonous work, the moment finally comes to contribute to the most ornate costume of all, but with no sleep for 42 hours I sadly admit defeat and fall asleep on plastic bags full of material scraps. People grab glue guns, material and sequins, and a huge effort by the crew ensures the magnificent King and Queen costumes are completed. I, meanwhile, sleep soundly in the corner. A few hours later I wake to see elegant thirty-foot net wings bedecked with glitter and gold leaves. A twenty-foot circular backpack has appeared, studded with stars and fake gold roses, with sparkling trailing trains of shining satin spotted with light-catching decorations. The King and Queen costumes are finally completed; it is midday on Carnival Tuesday and time to meet up with the band on the road before we miss the whole event.

In true carnival tradition, things do not go smoothly. The crew is nearly electrocuted as the huge aluminum costume frames clash with the electricity wires on the route to town. I am too exhausted to be of any help. No time for dark humour or recriminations, though, as we speed towards the meeting point. As dusk approaches on Carnival Tuesday I am finally on the road with the band. The masqueraders surround me, bedecked in costumes I have only before seen as limp forms waiting to be decorated. Now they have life, as the participants swirl their cloaks in time to the music, their fluid, shimmering bodies ensuring that every piece of gold and glitter painstakingly placed by the mas maker catches the light – reflected and refracted, it blinds me with its intensity. People carelessly dance, letting loose all inhibition, heedless of the time and effort taken to create their outfits. Music, movement and an essential vitality are what it's all about now. The masqueraders have been dancing all day around the streets of Port of Spain. Loud soca music, hot tropical sun and plenty of free-flowing rum have the blood pounding, the head spinning and the body jumping. The highlight of the day has arrived – crossing the main judging point at the Queen's Park Savannah. Filmed for local television, participants suddenly become self-conscious, then the energy that is the spirit of carnival fills them all. They become one with their costume, playing it to its utmost, making it move, dance, float and jump; giving the best performances of their lives.

"A funny old place"

Polly Thomas

Born and raised in West London, Polly Thomas first travelled to the Caribbean aged seventeen, spending three months in Jamaica with a friend who was visiting her father. Since then, she has presented a programme about the island for Radio Four, in between freelance research and writing commissions. In September 1997, she travelled to Trinidad and Tobago for the first time, and spent two months staying with friends before returning to Trinidad the following January, when she stayed for four months to research and write the Rough Guide to the islands. Her first commission for Rough Guides was as co-author of the Jamaica book.

As my departure date drew closer, an overdose of preconceptions brought on mixed feelings about going to Trinidad and Tobago. Seduced by stories of home, spun by London-based Trinis, and a longstanding passion for roti and my local Notting Hill carnival, I had wanted to visit since my teens, but was unsure how the islands would compare to the Caribbean I'd already got to know, love and – occasionally – hate during years of researching and holidaying in Jamaica. I knew that T&T, with its oil rigs and gas reserves, its burgeoning manufacturing and export industries and its strong dollar meant a far more stable economy. I also presumed that without the four hundred years of slavery that the black Jamaican psyche has had to contend with, Trinbago society would be less belligerent, free to approach life without militancy in the face of a newer servitude to the tourist dollar.

Once I actually arrived in Tobago – the smaller isle of the twin T&T republic – my first impressions left me feeling about as comfortable and at home as they did naive and unenlightened. From the plane window, the inevitable sandy beaches had seemed all present and correct, and as usual, a draught of sweet, balmy air had caressed my parched, air-conditioned skin the moment the plane doors opened. The hooting, gesticulating drivers and the airport hustlers – "Hey

Miss Lady, you need a rental car/hotel/guide?" – were all unmistakably Caribbean, but on some aspects I was completely thrown. Though I could process the thickest of Jamaican drawls without too much effort, I found myself struggling to understand the unfamiliar, singsong intonation of Tobago. Despite my credentials as an independent, confident woman traveller, my so-called familiarity with the region and my months of preparation, I realised this "expert researcher" was somewhat at sea and my ignorance left me reeling. In Jamaica, I at least knew how to avoid being treated like the average tourist, decked out in pastel colours, with cleavage and antennae out for an exotic holiday romance; or else wandering around with red eyes, crumpled shorts and a bedraggled T-shirt emblazoned with "Ganja University". Well-pressed skirts and blouses, walking purposefully but not hurriedly, a tactfully employed sense of Caribbean etiquette ("good mornings" and "good afternoons" are all-important) and trusting my instincts (if I thought a man had a sexual interest, he usually did) had previously ensured that I was taken seriously and avoided most potentially sticky situations. Here, though, I didn't know how to even *start* interpreting the signals which might indicate what category people were placing me in – I wasn't even sure if the categories were the same. To cap it all off, it seemed even more vital to make a good impression in an island so small that my one friend there had warned me that my arrival – "the female travel writer" – was already a topic of gossip.

To get to know the islands in any depth, I'd need to see them through an insider's eyes, and with this in mind, I'd arranged to base myself at the home of Nick, an old school friend and his emigrant family. Bearing cold Carib beers, we set off from the airport along the island's sole pothole-free main road, accompanied by jeeps and swish saloons. I saw vast groves of tall and graceful palms. Glints of turquoise sea swung into view, and the showers of brilliant bougainvillaea, hibiscus and ixora in the gardens of wooden homes on stilts combined to complete the Robinson Crusoe fantasy painted in Tobago's brochures. Below the palms, though, the grass was brown, the earth caked and arid, and the hillsides that bordered the highway charred by bush fires. I'd arrived in the middle of the slow and traditionally wet season, and had expected the usual over-abundant lushness of tropical greenery, but the annual "Petit Carem" – a month-long break in the rains – had left the land as parched I'd been told it looked in the summer. Restaurants and guesthouses had put up their shutters until the winter hordes returned, the faceless concrete hotels around the airport all boasted "VACANCIES" and the patrons of rum shops slunk in darkened interiors, hiding out from the blistering efficiency of a sun that felt hotter than anything Jamaica could come up with. To my uninitiated eyes, Tobago looked almost soporific, a lacklustre resort gripped by over-dependence on a dwindling foreign presence.

Arriving at Nick's family home, we settled in for a discussion on the ins and outs of Tobago. I told them of the warning a Trini friend had given before I left: "It's a funny old place. It's friendly, and it's beautiful, but you'll never get below the surface", she had laughed, and Nick agreed, painting a picture of an impossibly close-knit, even clannish society in which most people were distantly related, everyone knew each other if only by face and even the disinterested were up-to-date with intimate details of each other's lives. Pointing out the bright blue bottles strung up in a neighbour's garden to ward off *maljo* (the evil eye), he told me that T&T's African-derived Orisha and Spiritual Baptist faiths are far stronger in Tobago than in Trinidad, and that a deeply mysterious spiritualism underpinned Tobago society. He described the collective slant of Tobago living, best displayed at harvest festivals where most of the island congregate in a remote village for a day and a night of visiting, gossiping, dancing, eating and consumption of illegally brewed babash rum. None of this bore any relation to the jaded resort towns, the fenced-off all-inclusives and the urbane hustler mentality that I'd come to expect, suggesting instead a society that had more important things to think about. Keen to find out the reality for myself, I persuaded Nick to take me out for a late swim and my first lesson in Tobago's ways.

Climbing aboard Nick's dirt bike, we headed for a favourite swimming spot on the Caribbean coast. Strong waves and decidedly green water hinted at my first surprise − rather than the mirror-calm bath water I'd anticipated, this was cool and turbulent, invigorating to say the least. But you could body-surf and somersault in the waves, and I was immediately taken under the wing of a group of diaphanously-clad middle-aged ladies who instructed me in the importance of the medicinal afternoon "sea bath" they were taking. This was also new to me − in Jamaica, local people and tourists rarely share the same beaches let alone a decent conversation. Already, it seemed that the endlessly frustrating tourist/local dichotomy that had seemed inevitable elsewhere in the region was inapplicable in Tobago, and I wasn't missing the manicured golden sand, the beach chairs and the frothy drinks one bit.

Via Nick's knowledge of the island and his countless introductions, I received a crash course in Tobago, my list of hotels to check out, restaurants to sample and beauty spots to find dwindling fast as I became immersed in an enthralling pond of paradoxes, small, incredibly complex but almost always good-humoured. Through Nick's girlfriend Andrea, who worked in the island's busiest bar, I found the female companionship that I had always missed while travelling alone; in the Caribbean, single tourists are often rightly viewed as a threat by local women who've seen one too many crass holiday "romances" whereby the women get "exotic" fornication, and the men might gain some dollars and the chance of a ticket out of it all. I found none of this resentment in the women I met in Tobago; if they liked me, they preferred to treat me as just another sister, to advise me on which men to avoid and which could be trusted, to act as my guardians if they thought anybody was getting too fresh and, more usually, to chat and share the burdens of everyday life "in the tropics" as they wryly sighed, more than conscious that being surrounded by blue sky and beaches does not equal paradise.

Once the young "gigolos" realised that their valuable time and best lyrics were wasted on me, they too allowed me into the fold, sharing jokes, offering games of pool or launching into extended philosophical arguments. I had found that I was often treated with some scepticism when I drove around on my own – the very traditional Tobagonian psyche couldn't cope with an unchaperoned young woman – and asking a local man to accompany me put older people at ease as well as simplifying long hunts for lesser-known waterfalls and providing invaluable insight into local customs. At the end of a week where one man had spent every day on the road with me, I was paid the ultimate compliment when he turned to me with a wicked grin and announced: "Polly, the more I get to know you, the less I want to fuck you." That I had become more than just a walking opportunity for a flirt meant a lot. The longer I remained on the scene, the more I became a part of it and the more I was accepted as simply me. I found this support incredibly strengthening.

My working mission, twinned with Nick's introductions, had allowed me a sort of dual status – part tourist, part semi-local – and nowhere was this more obvious than in the succession of bars and clubs that every Tobagonian under thirty gravitates to after dark. Stopping off in Canaan or Carnbee to pick up my female escorts, I'd join the regulars on a tour of western Tobago's bars, a nightly routine that would inevitably end up at the *Golden Star* – part nightclub, part soap opera, where the dramas of the day would be publicly ironed out to the comments of the crowd. The highlight of the week was Sunday School, not an opportunity for Bible class but a weekly open-air fete held between the confines of an indoor bar/disco and the clapped-out concrete roof of a seldom-used beach facility at Buccoo Bay. Schooled by the masters, I would arrive at about 11pm and spend an hour happily people-watching on the terrace as we delighted in who had turned up with whom and which of the beach bums (their term not mine – Tobago hasn't yet reached the Rent-a-Dread/Rastitute heights of Jamaica) was indulging in a particularly scandalous method of seducing the women. I was able to dance to my heart's content without being grabbed by an eighteen-year-old (they start young), and, being English, I was always warmed by the countless offers of a rum, a beer or a plate of food from one of the coolers that local people, avoiding the bar prices, brought with them.

Trinbago hospitality was endless, and during my six months on the islands I was invited to countless "limes", semi-organised social gatherings that revolve around food or drink. These ranged from a drunken "Rum and Curry Duck Lime" where I nearly learned to play the local speciality card game, All Fours, to a fishermen's fete, where I found myself in the dark, in the sea, drinking white rum with a seawater chaser from the bottle.

Towards the end of my second trip, I was joined by my best friend and her three-year-old, who came from England for a holiday. After blissful relaxation in Tobago and a cramped stint in my rented Port of Spain apartment, we headed for Trinidad's rugged northeast coast and the lime that taught me what T&T was really all about. Our destination was the sole hotel and focal point of tiny fishing village Grande Riviere, a remote and appealing collection of weather-beaten homes sitting pretty between thick tropical forest and a staggeringly beautiful horseshoe beach. I'd felt a special bond with the village and the people since I'd stayed there with co-author Dominique during my first trip. This time, we had again planned to stay only a couple of nights, but after a hike through the bush to a waterfall on our second day, we were loathe to return to the heat and the hassle of Port of Spain. "You can't go," chorused Chance and Nigel. "We're cooking iguana tonight and we're having a party." The day before, a middle-aged Canadian couple who were the hotel's only other guests had helped some local boys remove an iguana from one of their forest traps, and there was to be a lime in its honour; wild meat is one of T&T's most sought-after delicacies, iguana being known as particularly "sweet".

After a meal at the hotel (it seemed the safest bet) we walked down the empty main street to a tiny bar whose owners had been persuaded to open up for the occasion. On the verandah outside, Grande Riviere's youth contingent and the Canadians were gathered, listening to Nigel and Anthony argue over seasoning ingredients and appropriate cooking time for lizard meat. The bar owner offered us her bedroom so that my friend's child could sleep, and after much fussing the iguana was served up in a rich sauce that did little to mask its decidedly green and very scaly skin. The Canadians turned pale. Soft-shelled and dirty yellow, the eggs were judged to be the best part, and were sucked dry with much smacking of lips as we divided our time between trying not to retch and holding our sides at the avoidance tactics of the Canadians, who'd spent the majority of the day confidently boasting of their plans to "eat lizard" but were a little less jaunty when it came to the crunch. Once the iguana was nothing but skin and bones, we headed for the main bar to dance with varying degrees of finesse and a lot of humour to innumerable versions of a Jamaican rhythm track called *Joyride* which was the current village favourite.

As I attempted to settle the bar tab the next morning, I asked Nigel if sharing their iguana and their lime with visitors was usual. Though I hated to admit it, such an event would have been unlikely in most of Jamaica's jaded and cynical resorts, where spare time is not usually spent entertaining tourists for the sheer joy of it. "Only if we like them," he replied, and in his simple acceptance and genuine friendship, I realised that without concerning itself with the task in the least, T&T had ensured that our relationship was only just beginning.

read on . . .

Amryl Johnson, *Sequins for a Ragged Hem* (UK/US: Virago, 1988/1989). Intense and personal portrayal of Trinidad, Tobago and other Caribbean islands by a woman born in Trinidad but living in Britain: "the 'ragged hem' of the title refers to the rape of slavery and all this had done to my people. 'Sequins' are the colour and sparkle they have woven into the state of being in exile." A poet, Johnson writes with a powerful, and angry, eloquence about revisiting the ghosts of her past against the backdrop of a region still haunted by the legacies of colonialism. There are also some marvellously funny moments, like the crab race on Tobago when, amid howls of laughter from the audience, the eventual winner is accused of having dragged a dead crustacean across the finishing line. A must for anyone seeking an "inside outsider's" view of life in the Caribbean.

Lucretia Stewart, *The Weather Prophet: A Caribbean Journey* (UK: Vintage, 1996/US: o/p). Stewart's restless journey begins and ends in Trinidad where she lands with no plan, other than to island-hop through the Caribbean as the fancy takes her. Typically, on her second day she meets Gina, a feisty single mother who offers to rent her a room and quickly fills her in on the nature of Caribbean men in general, "more hot than sweet", and the nuances of Trinidadian culture. Based on several visits to the Caribbean, this book offers a host of thoughtful insights into the "real world" beyond the resorts. In places it is also very entertaining.

USA

Las Vegas, in denial

Melanie McGrath

Following the success of *Motel Nirvana*, about her journey through the New Age heartlands of the Southwestern desert states (reviewed on p.620), Melanie McGrath returned to the US and checked into downtown Las Vegas, America's "desert Disneyland" and "purpose-built escape from its puritanical traditions". For three months (twenty-six and a half times the average stay) she casino-hopped, and chatted to bar girls, mobster attorneys and gaming agents while delving behind the myths and corporate propoganda that pass for history in America's glitziest town.

Melanie McGrath is currently completing a novel about London, where she has lived for many years. An avid virtual traveller, she chronicled the rites of passage of the digital generation in her 1998 book *Hard, Soft and Wet* (see p.621), and uses the Internet as a workplace. Actual travels have been just as varied. See accounts of her journeys to Mali (p.378) and Burkino Faso (p.101), also included in this book.

Debbie settled herself into the hot tub.

"Some day I'm gonna meet a Mr Right," she said, tying up her hair. She had the Blonde, Browned and Boobed look you see everywhere in Las Vegas, the look of expensively reprocessed flesh. A high-quality human luncheonmeat look.

A dove landed on the date palm beside us. I looked up and saw a series of green and orange flares snaking across the night sky.

"What d'you think that is?"

"Oh just some old missile tracing," Debbie said. "It'll be in the paper tomorrow." She turned the subject. "Did you see the La Hoya fight?"

I hadn't, though I knew there had been a lot of money riding on it. Debbie had served drinks at the fight. She'd met a number of nice gentlemen and given them her phone number. Evidently, she was hopeful and I thought it would be mean to remind her that we were in Vegas, the city of a thousand private escorts, topless bars and nice gentlemen with wives and kids back home.

"I don't think they should let older women be cocktail waitresses," said Debbie, contemplating her future, "Cellulite is so offputting."

I said I thought that was one way – a very Las Vegas way – of looking at it and we fell silent. A rush of traffic took over. The air was thick, as though carrying rain.

"I'll be a greeter by the time I start falling apart," said Debbie. Her orthodontic work made a clicking sound. "It's more dignified, though I'll be married by then, of course."

Las Vegas is full of half-lit Debbies. Seven thousand people move into the city every month, drawn by the sheeny lights and the non-stop dollar bills. But few ever get what they came for. Las Vegas is a temporary mirage, a city built to deliver the average dreams of the average visitor on their average 2.8-day stay.

★ ★ ★ ★

It was a hot September night and I was stuck in a line of taxis heading out towards the airport. Eight hundred flights take off and touch down at McCarran airport every day, ranking it among the ten busiest airports in the world.

Last year there were 30 million visitors. Next year there will be more. I'd been living in Vegas eleven weeks – twenty-six and a half times the average stay – researching a novel, and my mind had grown used to blanking out the vast electronic billboards, the lines of topless bars and advertisements for cheap eats and loose slots. On that September night, I drove into the neon cloudshine with a feeling of disquiet. Everyone knows Vegas is a made-up world, a desert

Disneyland, but I had been trying over the weeks to build up a picture of the town beneath the smile and what I had found was troubling me.

If there is a single truth about Las Vegas, it is that nowhere on earth so efficiently evades it. In a city whose $5.7bn-a-year gambling business it is to serve up pleasure, reality doesn't sit so well as fantasy. Vegas is a city in denial of the facts. A city where the birds are scared from the trees by ultrasonic bleepers to stop them pooping on passers-by, where prostitution is illegal but there are seventy pages of Yellow Pages ads for private entertainers, where to water a single golf course costs $12m a year. Reality is Las Vegas's Mrs Rochester, its shameful hidden secret, stashed away and going quietly bonkers unregarded.

As I drove by the Little White Chapel a couple in an Oldsmobile were getting married at the 24-hour drive-thru window, one of the 100,000 weddings registered in Vegas every year. The week before an article had appeared in the local paper announcing that from now on the marriage register would be available on the Internet, apparently as a convenient resource for hung-over newly-weds desperately seeking the name of the person they'd married the night before.

Vegas is set to collide with the facts before too long. Mrs Rochester is knocking at the door. Currently the fastest-growing city in America, Las Vegas, Nevada is only just beginning to wake up to its problems. The smog is now as bad as in LA. The suburbs grow virtually uncontrolled in a town not used to planning. Sewage and water systems are struggling to keep up. Las Vegas's schools are turning out illiterates and there is a serious street-gang problem.

You cannot drive more than a couple of hundred yards without witnessing some traffic accident, the joint product of overcrowded roads and endemic alcohol abuse. And if that were not enough, Vegas is the compulsive gambling and suicide capital of America.

"You know what they call Las Vegas?" a taxi driver once asked me. "No."

"Lost Wages." Lost Wages. It was a joke I would hear a hundred times.

As I was driving, a radio newsflash announced that the El Nino storm was heading for Lost Wages, bringing four inches of rain to a city whose average yearly rainfall is only four inches. The air smelled electrical but chain gangs of tourists were still tramping up and down the Strip in their regulation T-shirts and shorts and I wondered if they knew what was coming to them.

My car, a perky jalopy from Rent-a-Wreck, pooped past *Carl's Jnr* burger bar where a man had been shot dead a day or so before. Tonight the place was full, all evidence of the murder carefully obliterated. Guns are two-a-penny in town.

Only the previous evening, an employee of an off-Strip gun range had offered me an uzi for $300, saying he could pack it so that customs would never know. He said it was light and woman-friendly, handy for self-protection.

The cult of individualism that stocks gun ranges encourages Las Vegas to avoid its problems. A population accustomed to being subsidised by the gaming and rooming taxes imposed on out-of-towners, to paying no state income, inheritance or capital gains tax is suspicious of collective needs. When the question of failing schools was raised a while ago, Vegas residents suggested that casinos fork out for improvements.

I drove on south, past the Corinthian plinths, the pyramid, the Ferris wheels, the third-size Statue of Liberty which make up the Strip's phenomenal skyline. A group of men in suits – most likely conventioneers from one of the city's 3000 annual conventions – tumbled out of the Riviera Hotel and into a mini-bus, headed perhaps for one of the string of legal roadside brothels across the Clark County line in Lincoln and Nye.

"One day this will be a great archaeological enigma," prophesies Myram Borders, head of the Las Vegas News Bureau. "An Egyptian pyramid next to an Arthurian castle next to a Roman villa next to a volcano next to a pirate ship."

By the end of 1998, there will be more: the 1.3bn Bellagio, inspired by the Lake Como resort; the $750m Paris with its replica Arc de Triomphe and River Seine; the $1.5bn Project Paradise, the $2bn Venetian. In the hunt for profit Vegas has created an expectation it must now fulfil. Its visitors demand reinvention, so after five years of marketing itself as a family destination, Vegas is growing up. Family Entertainment Vegas is dead. Long live Adult Resort Las Vegas.

As happens after every good succession, there will be a spring cleaning of the facts and Vegas's past will be hastily rewritten to suit its most recent incarnation. For now, though, the official version goes something like this: In 1942 mobster Bugsy Siegel motors in to a one-cactus town of twenty thousand lost souls with a dream and the dirty money to make it happen. Four years later the *Fabulous Flamingo Hotel* opens on the two-lane highway to Los Angeles and the Las Vegas Strip is born. But Bugsy doesn't live to enjoy the fruits of his success. A shower of bullets blasts his face and drowns his life away.

By the mid-Fifties, the Strip is smoking. Sinatra is frontlining at the *Sahara*, Dean Martin is drunk in the *Dunes* and Sammy Davis Jnr is playing to an all-white crowd on weekend furloe from the Southern Californian suburbs. The movie stars are moving in and before you know it, Las Vegas, Nevada has become the world's most famous little town, a desert oasis watered by a silver stream of money.

East Coast banks won't touch the place. It takes a loose alliance of Mormon bankers and mid-west mobsters to bankroll the city's swish new resort hotels and carpet-joint casinos and Vegas becomes a financial frontier where racketeering, tax evasion and money launder-ing are accepted modus operandi. Millions are skimmed off the gam-ing Drop and despatched to the Chicago and Cincinnati Outfits and every so often someone's bones turn up in a shallow grave out in the sage, but still, everyone knows everyone; and everyone knows that no-one who sticks to the rules gets hurt.

By the Seventies the silver stream of money flowing through Mob 'n' Mormon town has burst its banks and the East Coast financiers and Wall-St listed corporations are beginning to change their minds about the world's most famous little town. A tidal wave of Hiltons and Sheratons washes that silver stream sparkly clean and brings in its wake more investment capital than the Outfit could have mustered in a century. With the help of the FBI, the Mob is gradually squeezed out.

Out go the dingy gambling dens, the late-night lock-ins, the mom-and-pop casinos and up go the megaresort hotels. By the late eighties the world's most famous little town has grown up into a big fat city, a bursting sprawl of smog and shopping plazas and gated sub-urbs and backed-up freeways all decked out in the venal, unearthly beauty of the Las Vegas Strip.

It's hard to piece together the unwanted details, the inconvenient facts, the bits in between. Early on in my stay, I rang Robert McCracken, a well-known local historian and we fixed up a time to meet. The following day his daughter called to say her father had become suddenly indisposed.

"I'm here for a few weeks yet," I offered.

The daughter coughed.

"I think my father is likely to be too busy," she said.

"For twelve weeks?"

"Yes," she said. "For twelve weeks."

What kind of town is it, I asked myself, where the local historian won't talk?

Vegas has rewritten its past, cutting out the inconsistencies, the uncomfortable clots of fact. The librarian at the University told me that "researchers have only really just got interested in the city's history," and there are few books. What I did find out is that the official line – from Frontier Vegas and Bugsy Vegas through Rat Pack Vegas and Mob Vegas to Corporate Vegas doesn't allow for the diverting complexities of the place. For example: it wasn't so much the Mob 'n' Mormons who built Las Vegas as the Jews. Bugsy Siegel and his boss, the Mob financier Meyer Lansky, were Jewish. Casino moguls Sheldon Adelson and Steve Wynn are Jewish too. The town boomed not because gambling was legal but because the railroad ran right through it. And far from being the centre of licence it likes to think itself, Vegas was racially segregated right into the mid-Seventies. (Twenty years before Bugsy Siegel booked Lena Horne to perform at the *Flamingo* but made her sleep elsewhere and instructed the chambermaid to burn her bedlinen.)

The trouble with the schematic history is not so much that it isn't true, but that no-one really cares either way. So long as the narrative fits the present's purposes, which is to say so long as the past boosts the present's profits, there are few in Vegas who will bother to question it. History has in large part been privatised. Almost every historical "attraction" in and around Vegas – from the Liberace Museum and the Bonnie Springs Frontier Town to the Ethel M Chocolate Botanical Garden – is a company enterprise, designed more to push product than to present the past.

In the northwest of the city lie the remains of a crude stone fort built by Mormon settlers in 1855. A tiny, stain-rimmed plaque marks the spot and on all the occasions I drove past it, I never once saw anyone there. The News Bureau's official list of attractions includes:

World of Coca-Cola, the Favourite Brands International Marshmallow Factory and Ocean Spray's Cranberry World West. Mormon Fort doesn't get a look in.

Still, the official history does have some claim to the truth for Vegas is, as it suggests, a city periodically colonised by competing interests with the single aim of making money, a boondock serving impulses greater than itself, a libertine and libertarian space where the ordinary rules of exchange and social relations do not apply, a brilliant and gaudy gutter built to catch a silver stream.

In this respect, Corporate Las Vegas isn't much different from Mob Las Vegas. Back in the eighties, an investigation into corruption in Atlantic City, New Jersey, where gaming is more highly regulated than in Vegas, "found everything, just everything", according to the Vegas columnist, John L Smith.

Money laundering, corporate tax evasion, embezzlement, insider-trading and illegal stock manipulation. "It's hard to pin down," Smith told me, "because the corporations control access to their information and employees so tightly. Back in the Mob days the mobsters would either talk to you or not." I couldn't draw him further. He would only say: "Hey, Las Vegas is a company town!"

The Mob swells its profits by expanding its reach, but listed companies are always under pressure to increase their shareholder dividends from existing operations, and casino stocks are both notoriously overvalued and volatile.

"They've gotten greedy," observed John Smith, meaning that every part of a hotel-casino operation is now expected to turn a profit. In the Mob days, a casino would only report its overall results. Free lounge acts and big-fee stars were often just loss leaders designed to bring in the gamblers. That's all gone.

Virtually nothing's for free in Vegas any more. Room rates are rising, show tickets can hit $100 a head and the famous buffets aren't as cheap as they used to be. Even the fat-fee stars who used to give Vegas its glitter have gone, replaced by long-running shows carefully managed to appeal to Germans and Jamaicans and Japanese.

I went along to one of these new-style shows at the Riviera. They put me next to a couple from Dundee. A photographer came and snapped a pic ($10). We ordered our watery drinks and smiled weakly at one another. A troupe of topless dancers burst from backstage and displayed their breast implants. Mr Dundee shifted in his seat and began to look uncomfortable. There was a juggler, followed by another bout of breasts. A cavalcade of motor bikers performed some death-defying stunts. There were more breasts. A magician made a woman disappear. Some breasts appeared, this time with nipple fixings. The music throughout was canned, as by now was Mr Dundee. We shuffled out without making eye contact. Bye bye Sinatra, so long Streisand, howdy *Starlight Express*.

In Vegas, every big flea has a flea on its back to bite it, and if the corporations play games with fact, so swindlers in turn cheat them. Around $70m a year is lost through cheating – by switching in loaded dice, marking the backs of cards, past-post betting, false shuffling, counterfeiting chips and slot tokens, paying off dealers and gaffing slot machines. A competent gang can fix a slot machine in six seconds, less if security is in on the scam, switching the reels to a jackpot or using optical wands to daze the machine's scanner into releasing the contents of its coin hopper. One cheat, Tommy Glenn Carmichael, allegedly ripped off $34m before getting caught. Mike Cassell, an agent at the Nevada Gaming Control Board told me: "We arrested a guy who'd cheated $8m out of video poker machines. He was someone's grandpa kind of thing. He did it for the buzz, to beat the machines." Many casinos see cheating by outsiders as a cost of business. "If you make a slot machine sensitive enough to distinguish between genuine quarters and fakes, it's also sensitive enough to go off at the smallest thing and that slows up play," said Mike.

The casinos are only really paranoid about insider cheats. One medium-sized casino ran an incentive scheme: the dealer with the highest table won first dibs at the shift rota, which may not sound much, but when your income is dependent on tips, it's a significant incentive. You don't make much on graveyard. So the story goes, one of this casino's blackjack dealers had a sick wife, and he badly needed to be able to take the early shift so he could pick his kids up from school. He knew that if he asked for special dispensation, he'd be shown the door. So this dealer began removing the tens from his card decks in order to lower the punters' odds at winning and so increase his table earnings.

After a very short while he was discovered and dismissed, but not before word had got round that the casino had employed a crooked dealer. Overnight, its custom vanished and within days, it was bankrupt.

The morning after my disillusioned drive along the Strip, El Nino finally broke, blowing rain in sheets. For the next day and night runoff roared through the storm drain next to my room and made it impossible to sleep. On the second morning, a blue scar appeared in the sky, followed by a shadowy sun. I ventured out and took a stroll. Down by the palm tree there was Debbie, sitting alone in the hot tub with the floodwater lapping at her ears and her eyes immersed in Cosmopolitan.

"If you've got a weakness, Vegas will find it," John Smith said.

Debbie's weakness was for persistent fantasy. Mine was for gloom. There is something about Vegas that kills your spirit as it pleasures your senses, a sort of undeadness. Looking back, I can see it begins with a loss of sensibility, a numbness brought on by the overwhelming blare of lights and the feeling of disorientation which comes from living in a city where midnight is a reiteration of midday. There's a belting unquietness to Las Vegas. As a matter of survival anyone who stays must learn to tolerate its profligacy, the gobbling light, the pouring water, the alpine wastes of food, the routine degeneracy of booze and greed and tits 'n' ass. There is simply too much to be angry about to be able to continue being angry.

If there is a lonelier place on earth then I have yet to find it. At night, with the lights pinking out the darkness, Vegas is the sparkliest, the swirliest and the smiliest. I'd often spend my nights quite happily hopping casinos, enjoying an expansive terrain of anonymous gambles and unnoticed exits. It was the kind of freedom that, as a woman, is unavailable to me elsewhere. But Vegas is a vampire. The dawn arrives and the city shrinks and then it hits you.

You are utterly alone. Not alone among the stars and not alone among friends. Just plain solitary. It's then you notice the flashes of female body parts on the discarded pages of the freesheet escort mags which struggle along in the breeze like wounded birds, the boozers slumped in bus stops, the pickups parked outside the porn stores. It's then you remember that the waitress in your local diner won't smile at you because she assumes you'll have left town tomorrow.

You start to feel sorry for yourself, embarrassed by your nighttime confidence. You remember how little anyone cares. You're mawkish in your solitude and your mind plays back to the Debbies with their dreams of glittery jobs and Misters Right and you realise that Vegas lonely is whole other kind of lonely. You wonder how its manifest illusions ever took a hold.

For a while, I could gamble away my blues but I am not a true gambler and blackjack doesn't take me out of myself for long. Perhaps I'm too familiar with the tricks casinos play to keep gamblers at the tables. A mathematician called Jess Marcum (who had helped develop the neutron bomb), worked out that a craps player staking $200 a game for 25 minutes has a 1.15 to 1 chance of winning $1000 before he loses $1000, whereas the same player staking $1 a game for 2 months reduces his chances to 1 in 2 trillion.

Casinos are miniature laboratories of behavioural science, where daylight and clocks are banished to give the impression that time has infinite elasticity, where the carpets, the lights and sounds are all designed to draw you in. Slot machines at the ends of rows are brightly coloured – predominantly red – to attract attention, and tend to pay out frequent small sums in imitation of the patterns of positive reinforcement American researcher Skinner discovered to increase motivation in rats. The centre machines are pastel-coloured for those slot-hogs whose eyes have tired of red. Most slots have one-arm bandit handles to increase the player's feeling of having a role in the outcome, though the position of the reels is actually determined by a computerised random number generator set inside the machine.

It's unwise to underestimate the power of such psychological tricks. During one October weekend in 1991, the Chicago neurologist Alan Hirsch sprayed a pheromonal scent called Odorant 1 into the slot casinos at the Las Vegas Hilton and increased the house Drop by 45 percent.

The only reality Las Vegas has not yet learned how to cheat is the persistent presence of mortality. But even then it has a go. Up in the northwest of the city lies the sunset-pink pall of Sun City, an "age-restricted community", where Southern California's over-55s play golf and save themselves the discomforting memento mori which might come from having to engage in a world full of folk any younger than themselves. I drove up there one day and got shown around. We strolled from golf course to hot tub to pool. Every so often a trophy wife jogged past, making an uncomfortable, almost vulgar show of youth.

My companion said that whatever you might think about age-restricted communities they were "a clean way to bolster the economy".

Perhaps it's not surprising with so many retirees moving to Vegas that it is more profitable to be an undertaker in Nevada than in any other part of the USA. I learned this at the Association of Funeral Directors, a group of 6000 undertakers gathered in Vegas for their annual convention. It was, coincidentally, the anniversary of my father's death and only a week or so after I had personally received a death threat, from Oscar Goodman, a Vegas attorney who represents many of the mobster-types in town, and played himself in Scorsese's movie of the Seventies mobster period, *Casino*. We were at a fund-raiser for a school and I'd crossed him over something. He leaned in to me and whispered: "There's a four-foot hole waiting out in the desert for you." It was a joke of sorts, but all the same, what with that and my dad's death, my mind was rather tied up in mortality.

Though you had to walk through a Star Trek exhibition, a casi-no and a coffee shop to get to it, I found the display of coffins, hearses and all the vast paraphernalia of death at the convention vaguely comforting. Here, it seemed to me there was at least a glimpse of reality, albeit rather stark.

As luck would have it, the American poet and undertaker Thomas Lynch was at the convention. I'd read and enjoyed his book of memoirs, *The Undertaking*, and I was curious to know what he thought of Vegas.

"It's a place where people have turned pleasure into sickness," he remarked.

"Don't you find it soulless?" I asked.

"No," he said. "Everywhere has a soul."

★ ★ ★ ★

I was beginning to think that death might actually be the key to understanding the real Las Vegas. The official history touches on Las Vegas's long-time proximity to the Nevada atomic weapons test site, but focuses on the city's attempts to make light of its dark-hearted neighbour. During the Fifties, when mushroom clouds were regular fixtures over the Las Vegas horizon, the Chamber of Commerce sponsored a Miss Atomic beauty pageant, there was an atomic hairdo (a version of the beehive) and the casinos served Atomic cocktails.

Tourists would be bussed out to vantage points to watch the mushroom clouds. Never mind that the downwind population living to the northeast of Las Vegas began to suffer birth defects, that somewhere between 10,000 and 75,000 children developed thyroid cancer. Vegas celebrated. The NTS brought good jobs and better money and most likely Vegas didn't feel it had a choice.

Unable to shake my new idea, I went up to the Nevada Test Site, sixty-five miles north of Vegas. It was at the NTS (which, along with the Nellis Airforce Range, occupies an uninhabited area of five thousand square miles of the Nevada Desert) between 1951 and 1992 that 928 atmospheric and underground atomic and thermonuclear devices were tested, twenty-four of them jointly with the UK.

LaTomya took me through security ("Warning: unauthorised personnel present, no classified discussion") and we drove out to Frenchman Flat, where many of the early atmospheric tests were conducted. It was an eerie grey colour. The sagebrush and creosote bushes seemed dead to me, but LaTomya said that was just the way the desert looked. Actually, it wasn't the way the rest of the desert, brightened by El Nino's rains, looked at all, but I didn't care to argue.

Scattered about were the twisted remains of materials experiments and Doom Towns, where mannequins dressed as Fifties (nuclear) families were placed in Fifties homes and blown to shards. We passed by animal pens, where living pigs and sheep were blasted into clouds of blood. "Remnants, where they exist, are kept frozen here on Site," said LaTomya.

We drove a hundred and fifty miles that morning, passing huge falls in the earth carved out by bombs and huddles of experimental huts and bunkers and razor-wired areas marked: "Hazardous, do not enter." As far as the eye could see, the road was layered where the quakes from bombs had folded it. We passed a sign reading: "Stop for convoys with blue flashing lights."

"Who needs to be told to stop for an A-bomb convoy?" I asked.

"You'd be surprised," said LaTomya. "People overtake. You can even get a parking ticket here. The sheriff comes round." As if that anchored the place and somehow made it normal.

We passed by the grey stump of a mountain melted by the unexpected venting of a bomb three times the size of the one dumped on Hiroshima.

"You can't go into Smoky without radiation suits and special clearance," said LaTomya, pointing to the nub of rock.

"I think I'll pass," I said.

Some parts of the NTS have been closed off permanently. Plutonium Valley, for example, is a no-go, and if Congress approves, by 2010 Yucca Mountain in the southwest corner could follow it, becoming a permanent repository for 80,000 metric tonnes of high-level nuclear waste – a sort of plutonium cemetery.

I couldn't resist asking about Area 51, where the US Airforce supposedly keeps the remains of UFOs and aliens.

"There is no Area 51," said LaTomya. "But the area you mean is up by Groom Lake." I suggested we drive over and take a peek.

"We can't do that," she said. "We'd get into trouble."

We drove instead to Sedan Crater, an alluvial cone 1280 ft wide and 320 ft deep, part of a 1962 test to investigate the possibility of using A-bombs to widen the Panama canal. The blast shifted twelve million tons of soil, but it was months before it was considered safe for scientists in radiation suits to venture into the crater, so they gave up on the idea of widening the canal.

Thirty-five years later nothing grows in Sedan. A hot wind fell over the lip. There were piles of tyres at the crater's base.

"They must be using it as a dump," volunteered LaTomya.

I do not pretend to be objective. Sedan Crater is the nearest place to hell I have ever been.

We sat in the Fifties canteen in Mercury, the Test Site town, and ate school dinner food. At the height of the Cold War one thousand people lived here, but it's a ghost town now, the perfectly preserved bowling alley and movie theatre used as stores.

I spread out my official map of the NTS and retraced our day's journey with my finger. The map was quite obviously partial.

"This isn't a true representation is it?"

LaTomya looked uncomfortable.

"No," she said.

★ ★ ★ ★

That night I found Debbie in the hot tub again. I said: "Aren't you scared about that missile we saw the other day?"

"Oh no," she said. "Things like that don't bother me."

Perhaps it isn't so surprising that Vegas thrives on a denial of the facts, when the gates to hell are only sixty-five miles up the road.

I came grudgingly to admire Las Vegas. It is America's only purpose-built escape from its puritanical traditions. And in a culture where the rich are often confused with the morally righteous, Vegas's lack of hypocrisy is remarkable. Money will buy you just about everything in Vegas except virtue.

Often I was tempted to be offended by the city's amorality, but with hindsight I realise that Vegas doesn't make us what we are. We are, in varying degrees, what Vegas knows us to be: greedy, libidinous, celebratory, scared, infantile, orgiastic, experimental, conforming and conservative.

★ ★ ★ ★

Towards the end of my trip, my mother came to visit. We drove down Tropicana Avenue and hit the Strip at the New York-New York hotel. It was night and the lights shook like aspens. We drove past the pink porte cochre of *Caesar's Palace*. We watched the fake volcano going off.

"Isn't this just marvellous," my mum said, giggling with pleasure.

We ate double-decker icecreams among the cords of brilliant neon and below us, invisible to the eye, flowed the thick water of the silver stream. Thomas Lynch, the poet undertaker, told me his aunt always used to say that life is wonderful if you can resist temptation and wonderful if you can't. That night we watched the smudge of traffic and we felt our best selves. Mum didn't notice the vacant lots, the dust of building sites, the drunks slumped at the bus-stops. She saw what Vegas wanted her to see. "It's so enormous and tacky and beautiful," she said.

And she was right. It was.

"Yaow baby! Turn that up!"

Diane Brady

Diane Brady is a Canadian writer for **Business Week**. Prior to her recent move to New York she was based for four years in Hong Kong from where, as travel and aviation correspondent for **The Asian Wall Street Journal**, she travelled as far afield as Beijing, Bali, Delhi and Taipei. This is the second time she has lived in New York. In the late 1980s she was a student at Colombia University where she studied journalism and began to live out her suburban fantasies about life in the big city.

While growing up in a leafy Ontario suburb, my most enduring fantasy was to join a street gang and live in New York. Our neighbours were born-again Christians with teenaged children, which meant a steady supply of comic books featuring drug addicts and hippies who later found God. My friend Jamie and I, after rifling through his sisters' collection, agreed that the best parts came *before* the characters named Jesus as their personal saviour – when they got to roam around in hip-huggers, leather and long hair. The city's seedy image was bolstered in my mind by a steady diet of the 1970s sitcom *Welcome Back Kotter* and occasional peeks at *Saturday Night Live*. Ah, to be a slimmer ten-year-old me in Brooklyn, with my biker jacket, tight jeans and cool friends like John Travolta. It would be another decade before I actually saw the Big Apple. On every camping trip to Maine, my father would veer off the New York State Thruway mere miles before it hit the city. The first time I managed to drive that route myself – while heading to a New Haven debating tournament in university – I finally made it all the way.

As we rumbled past the boarded-up buildings and graffiti-lined streets of the South Bronx, I thought I'd landed in heaven. Every car seemed to pulse with rap music. Every corner seemed a collage of fascinating faces. The buildings looked like works of art with curly-haired heroes and stylised names spray-painted on the outside. The street scenes were better than any theatre downtown, with arguments and bragging broadcast to anyone passing by. I took out my camera. A huge woman in orange leggings laughed and waved. I loved New York.

Was this the city I'd dreamed about? Perhaps not, but it was still pretty good. There were more rich people than I had imagined: high-heeled women walking tiny clothed dogs and apartment dwellers who hired uniformed men to hail them taxis or open their front door. Even the toddlers looked more sophisticated than me. Who knew Ralph Lauren made such tiny clothes?

Who cared? I relished the grit – signs that said "Don't Even Think of Parking Here", steam belching from sewers, the loud-mouth antics of Ed Koch, and black men who called me "sister". Times Square was the place to lose money in a shell game. Central Park was where people played saxophone into the night. Whadda place! After finishing university in Toronto, I signed up at the city's Columbia University for graduate school.

It was the 1980s, when New York was still an armpit in the eyes of the nation. I briefly dated a man named Larry the Fixture King whose hobby was buying discarded doorknobs from Dominican land-lords to sell to yuppies. Then I moved on to Marty, a wealthy entre-preneur with a SoHo loft who collected Fiesta tableware and dreamed of starting the American Museum of Ice Cream. He also insisted he was not married and barely 35. I suspect he lied but I ended up dump-ing him because he seemed too rich. I was young and preferred hang-ing out at *Tom's Diner* or grubby bars with my Jewish pal Chris. Then there was the rest of New York. One of my favourites was the man who collected cans outside my apartment. New York's five-cent return policy, combined with the fact that most storekeepers made it difficult to return your own cans, had created a minor cottage indus-try. Thomas was one of a small army of men ferreting through the garbage to compile huge bags of cans that they would then cart to a supermarket until some disgruntled manager agreed to count their wares. He was meticulous in combing the landscape, politely asking students if they'd finished their drinks as they lounged in Riverside Park and arranging times to pick up donated empties. It was Thomas who introduced me to "We Can" – a non-profit redemption centre aimed at sparing collectors the humiliation of waiting around stores. "Best city on earth," he told me while sipping a can of cola one spring day. "Why would I leave?"

Good question. Some of us had to leave for jobs and visa reasons. Canadian writers were about as popular as Mexican dishwashers in the eyes of immigration officers at that point. With a hint of sadness, I went home.

In early 1999, I moved back to find a find a fresher and much hyped Manhattan. Mayor Rudolph Giuliani, a discipline-minded autocrat who first won my attention with his wife's brief appearance in *The People vs Larry Flint*, had long led a campaign to clean up the undesirable elements. The subway cars were stripped clean of colourful graffiti. Times Square had become more of a spot for toddlers to buy Tweetie-Bird toys than for stupid college kids to get ripped off in shell games. Every street corner seemed to boast a Starbucks or pedestrian barriers to help cars move more easily. Thanks to full employment or the advent of recycling bins, can collectors seemed in short supply. Was it just me, I thought while staring at a massive poster hawking mutual funds for sale, or had the city lost something?

Beneath the renovated brownstones of Harlem and fresh-scrubbed department stores, though, the city's heart was still pumping strong. Where else would people endure long lines outside a library to see a collection of maps? Walking into the Museum of Modern Art, I listened as a duo earnestly debated the evolution of Jackson Pollock's paint splatterings. "This is perhaps his most evocative piece," said one man with a gray goatie and checkered slacks standing beside a huge mural of drippings. "It's so emotional," his younger friend agreed. "Yet such control!"

Over at the Metropolitan Museum of Art, a homeless man was yelling "Only payfive cents; it's free!" outside. Saks Fifth Avenue was still staffed with coiffed sales girls who smirked "Can I help you?" the minute you touched a tester lipstick. Try it on and they would add "So how many would you like?" before loudly complaining that it's tough to make a living with people like me wasting their time. Even *Sylvia's*, my favourite Harlem restaurant, seemed refreshingly familiar with its sweet-potato pie and homestyle service. "Hello again," chirped the chubby waitress. Did she remember me or, more likely, did I have a dime-a-dozen face? And did it matter when, within minutes, she'd be telling me to eat up because dessert is on the way?

Some parts of New York simply can't fall victim to the fastidious fingers of Giuliani and gang. Central Park is still a magnet for men wearing tiny silk shorts while roller-blading in February. A new form of primal scream has emerged on the city's 5800 subway cars. Officials called it *scratchiti*, where vandals use keys, coins or razor blades to scratch names on the pristine metal doors. Even efforts to stomp out jaywalking have inspired protests among pedestrians and police alike.

St John the Divine, on the Upper West Side, remains mildly grungy with its Keith Haring memorials, poet corners and other hallmarks of a hip urban church. It was also host to the most inspiring funeral I've seen – a joyous tribute to Muppets founder Jim Henson, complete with Big Bird and a big brass band. We had slipped into the reception afterwards by striking up a silly conversation with actress Daryl Hannah and her sister – "So, um, did you know him too?" – while sticking close as they made their way past the crowd. Composer Paul Williams had winked at my sister, one of the few adults who stood at eye level with him. Ah, New York!

Although the city might now boast the world's highest number of pretentious nightclubs, where men in cheap jackets decide who gets beyond the velvet rope, it also allows extreme access to people and places. In Los Angeles, stars can hide behind big fences or fancy cars. In New York, they're out buying bagels or yelling at cabbies with the rest of us. And New Yorkers tend to leave them alone. Director Steven Spielberg looked like another middle-aged baseball fan as he and his wife wandered around the Jackson Pollock show, keeping their debate about his work barely audible. Rod Stewart was picking his teeth when I saw him at Central Park South. During one elevator ride at *Essex House* hotel, I turned to a coiffed slender man and said, "You're David Bowie." There was a pause. "Yes," he said icily as he walked out of the elevator. "Of course it's David Bowie!", snapped the bellboy. Jesus, where was I from?

Like a lot of people in New York, of course, I was from out of town. In fact, the more eccentric residents are rarely born in the city; they grow up slightly weird in Idaho, but find their spiritual home in New York. That much had not changed: the purple-haired guitarist from Minneapolis, the Japanese art student who roller-blades to school, the fledgling actress from Buffalo and the former wannabe gang chick from Burlington. A growing band of Wall Street types may have joined the mix but that army just ebbs and flows with the times.

The rich may also be richer but they still live around the corner from the poor. Thanks to prolonged good times, stockbrokers now spend thousands to cram into studio apartments while veteran New Yorkers pay a fraction to dance about in their rent-controlled lofts. Even those in penthouses hear the horns of the city. Rap artists live in the same buildings as bankers; the rich roam through Central Park with the bums. And they both fight for space on the lawn whenever a free concert comes up.

And maybe my dreams had changed a bit with New York. When looking for cheap apartments in the city (ha!), we tripped across a fifth-floor walk-up I absolutely loved. It had an excellent rooftop for those raucous raves and a cute little alcove in the tiny kitchen. "It's very, uh, artistic", muttered the broker, a greasy little man in a leather jacket. Then I noticed the stained tub that stood eight inches deep, the bunk bed in the living room, and the huge pipe pointing into our window, not to mention a complete lack of security on the shabby roof. And that five-storey uphill climb! Even the ten-year-old rebel in me wanted a bit more luxury. Besides, this armpit had a $1600 monthly price tag. Three bedrooms in a decent if dull neighbourhood may cost three or four times as much, and both will contain some woman reading a romance novel who flatly informs you that she's the broker and will need and extra fifteen percent to book the deal.

Restaurateurs have discovered that diners will actually pay $25 for a dish of pasta and order fine wine to accompany their eight-ounce burgers. But Chinese takeaways still adhere to some unspoken rule that a family of five can gorge on chicken balls and rice for less than the price of a starter in a midtown restaurant. Hotdogs still cost $1 each or even less if the vendor is about to wheel away his cart. Bagels now come in more than a dozen different flavours but few fans stray beyond sesame and poppy seed. *Roy Rogers* fast food hasn't abandoned its fixins' bar.

And New Yorkers haven't abandoned their air of jaded incredulity. "Can't say I've seen that," shrugged our apartment handyman when confronted with a toilet bowl that had mysteriously split in half. "How am I? Don't get me started" remains a greeting of choice, followed by "You paid what?". Every once in a while, when salsa music drifts quietly from across an apartment courtyard, an enthusiastic voice might even shout "Yaow baby! Turn that up!"

A trip to the "last frontier"

Lorna Menzie

Lorna Menzie works as an advertising copywriter in London. Inspired by a magazine article about "the greatest dog race on earth", she flew to Alaska with the aim of witnessing the race for herself. This was the first time she had travelled alone.

"Alaska. Where men are men and women win the Iditarod." So read the headline of a Sunday supplement article about the gruelling sled dog race that takes places every year in Alaska. Launching off from the state capital, Anchorage, the competitors travel on six-foot long sleds pulled by up to twenty husky dogs for over a thousand miles through the earth's most inhospitable territory. It's the ultimate test of Alaskan machismo; it was therefore somewhat galling when a petite woman called Libby Riddles swiped the first prize from under the men's noses in 1985. Since then a woman called Susan Butcher has won on three occasions.

Reading about the Iditarod and Libby Riddles' cunning win I became hooked. I decided to write off to The Race Organisers, Nome, Alaska, and see what happened. To my surprise I received an unbelievably enthusiastic letter back from a dog racer, or musher, called Matt, describing the excitement of racing and insisting I had to come and see it for myself.

I had no other contacts, but with three weeks' holiday ahead I felt I could do something a bit more adventurous than drink *glühwein* in the Alps. With the incredulous laughter of my friends still ringing in my ears, I boarded the plane to Anchorage. The month was February, not a time of year recommended by the American Tourist Board.

If Anchorage hadn't been a strategic refuelling spot on the way to the Far East, I doubt whether the plane would have bothered to even set down. Glancing at the cabinload of Japanese businessmen, I got the distinct feeling I would be disembarking alone. I settled down in my seat to see what I could learn from the few guidebooks I'd managed to find.

After a few pages I began to sweat. Layers of thermal underwear didn't help (I was convinced I'd be walking off the plane in a blizzard), but more uncomfortable were the statistics. Long dark nights, cabin fever, alcoholism and lawlessness provide conditions for the highest incidence of rape and murder per head in the United States. Alaska is nearly half the size of Europe; I reasoned that it couldn't be homicidally dark everywhere and, with a population of only 460,000, I might not bump into too many people.

We eventually touched down in Anchorage in brilliant sunshine at a warm 0°C. The town was definitely low on charm. The airport bus meandered past standard issue shopping malls and empty office blocks, testimony to the oil, gold and mineral rushes that have come and gone. Having found out the high cost of hotel accommodation, the only pre-planning I'd done was to reserve a youth hostel bed. The uninspired grid system of First, Second and Third Avenue and A, B, C Streets meant that at least the bus knew where to drop me off.

I arrived at lunchtime, when the hostel was as eerily empty as the malls we had passed, but by early evening the place began to fill up with the long-stay residents. Many of them were sitting out the winter here, waiting for the lucrative summer season when they could get jobs in the tourist trade or the canneries. By mid-evening things were definitely looking up. Mavis "all my exes live in Texas", myself and five others from the hostel went on a spot of bar-hopping to *The Buckaroo Bar*, *Fly-by-Night* and *Chilkook Charlies*.

Yes, this is ten-gallon hat "good ol' boy" country. The atmosphere wasn't over-friendly, but then again neither was it at all threatening. It was great fun and a good way to get to know the people I'd be living with for a while.

It was quite a night, especially for Bonnie, my Mormon roommate who was on orange juice only. It wasn't until after quite a few drinks in several bars that I realised Bonnie was missing. We'd driven about twenty miles and I was beginning to get worried as she was good fun but fairly unworldly. Some of us retraced our steps, only to return in the small hours, still Bonnie-less. To my amazement, there she was waiting outside the locked hostel. She'd fallen asleep under the table in *The Buckaroo Bar* and a friend of the barman had given her a ride into town. I realised that although it doesn't hurt to be a little circumspect, you shouldn't judge everybody by a few statistics you might read. I discovered, too, that travelling alone you get to do things and be with people that normally you might choose to avoid. It didn't have to change my personality, but I did have to dump some of my preconceptions.

Two days later, I was beginning to wonder what the hell I was going to do in Anchorage for a week before the race started. Then, over the telly and a jumbo bag of corn chips, up came the offer of a ride north.

Having left at home my boyfriend and travelling companion of seven years, it was weird to be with a couple without being part of one. Doug was from California and his partner, Kumi, was Japanese. We agreed we'd share the petrol and visit some of his friends along the way.

The ride north was spectacular. Frozen lakes and towering rock-faces gave way to snow-drenched forests. First thing in the morning, the ice froze into delicate lace patterns hanging from the trees. It was a magical, totally silent landscape. Occasionally the stillness would be broken by the sight of caribou deer or an eagle overhead. The scarcity of civilization and the sheer scale of Alaska makes it staggeringly remote and beautiful. So far I hadn't seen a husky dog team, but I'd experienced more than I could ever have imagined. The trip was already worth it.

Reaching the outpost of Circle, fifty miles from the Arctic, took two days. Still not an igloo or polar bear in sight – just plenty of sunshine and, thirty miles down the road, Circle's answer to a health farm.

It was during the Klondike gold rush that Circle first appeared on the map. Conditions for the gold prospectors were appallingly harsh, so when natural hot springs were discovered nearby they were well-used. Bearing in mind that the mighty Yukon River at Circle is frozen solid at that time of year, you could see why the springs are still popular. The gold rush brought thousands to this desolate spot, where brothels and gambling dens soon sprang up to relieve the miners of their hard-earned cash. Nowadays all that is left is the *Hot Springs Hotel*.

I took myself off for long sessions in the outdoor pool. The natural heat of the water at 59°C served the dual purpose of keeping me very happy and heating the greenhouse, from which you can enjoy fresh tomatoes even when the outside temperature hits minus 31°. Floating on my back, and looking up at the cloudless blue sky with huge overhanging icicles just visible through the steam, I felt extremely content. As nobody visits the hotel mid-week, we had the undivided attention of the backwoodsmen running the place. Bobble hats glued firmly on, both indoors and out, they were very gentle hosts and revelled in telling tales of harsh Alaskan life to us wet-behind-the-ears townies.

My return to Anchorage was a huge anti-climax. Not having checked the dates Matt had given me a month earlier, I'd missed the pre-race meeting. This is where details of the thousand-mile route are given and the rookies, or novice racers, receive tips from the old timers. Basically, it's a big get-together and sounded fun. The hostel seemed stark and boring and no place to nurse my abject disappointment.

As the going had suddenly got tough, I headed straight for a shopping mall. I'd seen in an advert that Libby Riddles, the first woman to win the race, was going to be signing at a bookstore. Libby Riddles was surprisingly interested in my quest and kindly fixed me up with the vital transport to a couple of race checkpoints. She was charming, and so affable that it made the thought that she'd trounced the competition even sweeter. Lasting two weeks, the going is physically and mentally exhausting. Libby had made a calculated but extremely risky final push, mushing through a blizzard in temperatures approaching 15°C below, to win the title with a two-and-a-half-hour lead.

Not having done my homework, I hadn't taken in that being in a wilderness you wouldn't be able to watch the race beyond the first few checkpoints; and that transport was needed, even to those. When they say wilderness in Alaska, they really mean it, so I was particularly grateful for Libby's help.

At 8.30am downtown Anchorage was packed out with spectators, stewards, helpers and wagons unloading hundreds of feverish huskies onto the slush. The atmosphere was electric. While the dogs were barking and slavering to be off, the mushers were in a frenzy, packing and repacking their sleds, since every extra pound carried can cause trouble later on. Each team has up to twenty dogs and separating and sorting them into their harnesses was quite a feat. At the start of the race the mushers, one to each sled, were allowed some help, but once they'd passed the first two checkpoints they were completely on their own. Among the many potential hazards are frostbite, blizzards, losing the trail and – possibly worse than anything – encountering moose which, despite their dopey appearance, won't hesitate to savage a dog.

Libby had fixed me a ride to the checkpoints with an old friend and race enthusiast called John Kelly, who'd spent his working life on Arctic ice stations in the American navy. His ambition, which he'd eventually achieved at the age of sixty-two, had been to walk the Iditarod trail alone. As the last team disappeared through the woods, we repaired to the Chinese restaurant to swap stories.

The next morning I woke with the nagging feeling of "Now what?" The fanfare of the race was gone and I was at a serious loose end. After only one morning of pacing the hostel, the answer came in the form of a Swede called Lars. Another passionate racing enthusiast, he thoughtfully suggested that I could go south with him, to Homer on the beautiful Kenai Peninsula, and stay with the friends he'd made the previous year. At the same time we could follow the racers' progress on TV and in the papers. That very afternoon we took off for Homer on a scheduled flight.

Putting up a stranger at a moment's notice didn't seem to bother Liz, Edwin and Michael at all. They were all escapees from the softer mainland states of Washington and Oregon, enjoying the less pressured lifestyle of mending fishing nets in winter and working as lifeguards at Homer's indoor pool to pay the bills. They had also started up and were voluntarily running Homer's answer to marriage guidance counselling.

Unemployment, alcoholism and depression brought on by the short daylight hours combine to bring trouble to the lives of the townspeople. The Native Indian population has the difficult task of trying to survive in modern Alaska while maintaining their traditions. There are also three Russian villages in the area which have staunchly resisted the outside world. The original inhabitants came to the Kenai Peninsula long ago, having been expelled by the Tsar for their extremist views. These people still adhere to the doctrine that if you disobey your husband, he has a right to beat you. If your disobedience continues, the same task falls to the local priest. Seeing the freedoms enjoyed by other women, some of the sect had become a little disaffected and had sought help. It was part of my hosts' task to put the women in safe houses while the couples found a less violent solution to their marital troubles.

Not only did I have great admiration for these new friends, but they were brilliant company as well. By day I took myself on long walks, for which they lent me snow-shoes so that I could explore the vast wood behind the house. I found them very unwieldy and preferred to stick to the well-beaten tracks which afforded a wonderful view of the mountains without any danger of running out of road to walk on.

Walking the ten miles into Homer, I gave up counting the number of people who stopped to offer me a ride. People thought it rather odd that I was walking all the way for enjoyment. I suppose you get used to anywhere if you live there long enough, but trudging along, taking in the white peaks and glaciers surrounding Kachemak Bay, was quite something to me.

In the evenings after work we all hung out together. I cooked Liz, Edwin and Michael a full-works roast dinner one night – they amazed me by going totally crazy over the roast potatoes. It was nice to share something so ordinary from our culture that they thought was positively exotic.

On my last night the three of them asked me to take part in a quasi-Indian ritual, something they did partly in reaction to the overwhelming number of devout Christian sects in the vicinity. After dark we climbed through the deep snow at the back of the house until we reached a mound, a good half-mile from any neighbours. They stood me on the mound of snow, which was decorated at four corners with moose bones and a crow's wing, and we stared up at the night sky, thick with stars. Then, shaking their home-made moose-hide rattle, they slowly began to encircle me, chanting good wishes for my journey home to England.

read on . . .

Melanie McGrath, *Motel Nirvana: Dreaming of the New Age in the American Desert* **(UK: Flamingo, 1996/US: Pica Books: 1997).** In her compelling debut travelogue, McGrath takes a sharp and sardonic look at the New Age communities of

Southwestern America. A committed insomniac, and a questing but critical outsider, she immerses herself in the auras, chakras, past lives and mystical gadgetry that clutter the small towns at the desert fringes, and mulls over the results in motel rooms, empty diners and on endless stretches of tarmac. The accumulative effects are peculiarly dispiriting, echoing the emptiness of the brilliantly evoked desert landscape. Her final, explosively personal chapter, called "Prozac Dreaming", contains one of the most lucid arguments yet against the ready use of anti-depressants, feel-good therapies and New Age charlatanism as any means of achieving some degree of spiritual depth. "What is Nirvana, in the end," she asks rhetorically "but a painless, pointless sleep?" In her second book, *Hard, Soft and Wet: The Digital Generation Comes of Age* (UK: Flamingo, 1998), McGrath explores the future of online culture. Helped in her first tottering steps by her Californian friend Nancy, who works at the forefront of software marketing, McGrath soon launches herself into virtual relationships and transglobal adventures. Already seriously dated in feel and content, it endures as an excellent chronicle of the first online generation.

Maya Angelou, *I Know Why the Caged Bird Sings* (1979; UK: Virago, 1984/US: Bantam, 1993). First and arguably the richest of a five-volume autobiography by one of America's most renowned and multi-talented black women writers. Angelou leads us from her difficult early childhood in the 1930s, growing up with her formidable grandmother in Stamps, Arkansas, through to her move to her mother's home in San Francisco where, aged sixteen, she gives birth to a son. Subsequent volumes trace her experiences as a single mother, waitress, singer, actress, dancer, black activist, editor and writer in California, New York, Europe and Africa. Maya Angelou is an utterly stirring and hugely popular storyteller.

Simone de Beauvoir, *America Day by Day* (1954; UK: Victor Gollancz, 1998/US: University of California Press, 1999). Written in 1947 and now published in English for the first time, this captivating diary is as astonishing for its freshness as it is impressive for the range and depth of de Beauvoir's insights on this her first ever journey to the USA. Armed with a few introductions, some lecture dates and the avid curiosity of the French intellectual, she spends three giddy weeks in New York before setting off across the country by train, car and Greyhound bus. Impressions of places, people and attitudes are recorded in marvellous detail: the Hudson River, smelling of "salt and spices"; the drunk couple in a Chicago dive, dancing "with a joyous abandon that verges on madness and ecstasy"; the contempt of American women for the servility of their French counterparts, although "the tension with which they twist around on their pedestal conceals a similar weakness". Throughout her journey, meeting mainly artists, musicians, college students and fellow intellectuals, de Beauvoir questions everything, from the position of blacks and the nature of jazz, to American obsessions with wealth, fame and individual freedom. Startlingly relevant today, this exhilarating view of post-war America by one of the century's most influential feminist writers is a definite classic.

Josie Dew, *Travels in a Strange State: Cycling Across the USA* (UK: Warner 1995/US: Bulfinch, 1996). This somewhat naive, yet spirited travelogue by one of Britain's youngest cycling scribes traces her erratic eight-month journey from California to Nova Scotia via Hawaii, pedalling nearly all the way. An entertaining read, packed with wacky observations and bizarre encounters as Dew weaves her path along the coast, through cities, up mountains, and even braves the freeway (keeping to the hard shoulder) where astonished motorists stop to offer beer, advice and the odd prayer.

Joan Didion, *The White Album* (1979, UK: Flamingo, 1993/US: Noonday Press, 1990). The second of Didion's classic essay collections documenting states of the American psyche over three decades – the 1960s, 1970s and 1980s – focuses mainly on California, where her razor-sharp eye is applied to some of the characters and events that helped shape that middle era. In her distinctive style – part introspective, part detached - she writes of hanging out with the Doors and Janis Joplin, visiting the Black Panthers in prison, watching Nancy Reagan picking flowers before a film crew, the early days of the Women's Movement, brushes with the Hollywood movie industry, each time revealing an amazing facility for capturing the essence of what is being observed. A writer, both journalist and novelist, who easily endures the test of time.

Didion's latest collection, ***Sentimental Journeys* (UK: Flamingo, 1993/US:** published as ***After Henry*, Noonday Press, 1992),** uses a series of encounters, events and news stories, from the 1988 campaign trail to the famous "jogger murder" in Central Park, to dissect the culture of America's major cities – Washington, Los Angeles and New York. Incisive and beautifully written, as is her earlier portrait of a city, ***Miami*** (1987; UK: Flamingo, 1994/US: Vintage, 1998), which fiercely analyses the political background and complexities of a place which no longer shares the prevailing culture or language of the rest of the country.

Carrie Fisher, *Postcards from the Edge* (UK: Picador, 1987/US: o/p). Fisher starred as Princess Leia, the goody-two-shoes heroine of the original ***Star Wars*** trilogy, and later – faced with the mother from hell, the pressures of teenage stardom and the unstoppable force of the Hollywood Movie Machine – caved in to drugs before cleaning up her act, rebuilding her relationship with Mom and writing the book (also made into a film). Diary extracts combine with narrative and memory flashbacks to create this often funny, embarrassingly honest memoir.

Melissa Holbrook Pierson, *The Perfect Vehicle: What is it about Motorcycles?* (UK: Granta, 1997/US: W W Norton & Co., 1998). Pierson, a New York poet and intellectual, has crafted an engaging and profound treatise on "motolust"; an affliction she's been happily stricken by for over a decade. "Riding on a motorcycle can make you feel joyous, powerful, peaceful, frightened, vulnerable, and back out to happy again, perhaps in the same ten miles," she writes. Her debut memoir is persuasive stuff, as much for the great ungreased as for hardened aficionados of the road-swallowing machines. And she's good on the roadside aspects of real life too, like heartbreaks and the ever-present fear of accidents.

Irma Kurtz, *The Great American Bus Ride* (UK: Fourth Estate, 1994/US Simon & Schuster, 1993). After thirty years living as an American expatriate in London, Irma Kurtz sets off to explore the length and breadth of her own "baffling country" by Greyhound bus. Starting in New York, in three months and ten days she weaves her way across a vast array of landscapes but it is the people she meets and observes in the close confines of some 65 buses who fuel this vivid and highly entertaining portrait of America. Protected by, yet wholly at ease with, the anonymity of middle age, Kurtz revels in the freedom to watch and record the bizarre selection of characters who enlighten (and occasionally burden) her journey.

Mary Morris, *Angels and Aliens: A Journey West* (US: Picador, 1999). In this latest memoir Morris takes to the road as a single parent, exploring the world of sun-seekers, spiritual believers and cults that thrive in southern California. As always, she combines her observations of the people and places she visits with a very personal struggle to come to terms with her own inner conflicts, in this case an unsatisfactory relationship with her daughter's father.

Julia Scully, *Outside Passage: A Memoir of an Alaskan Childhood* **(UK: Souvenir Press, 1999/US: Random House, 1998).** Evocative yet oddly detached memoir of an impoverished childhood, growing up as a teenager among sailors, gold-miners and Eskimos in the barren reaches of the Alaskan frontier. The main theme of the book is survival as Julia, her mother and sister struggle through the war years overshadowed by the unspoken memory of the father's suicide several years before. A bleak yet compelling account of hard times, intensely lived.

Uzbekistan

Mosques, ministries, and the "Stairway to Heaven"

Liz Williams

As part of her work for a British educational consultancy, Liz Williams provides advice on English language courses to agencies in some of the former Soviet Republics, including Kazakstan where she lived for a while in 1996 (see p.340). She visited neighbouring Uzbekistan for the first time in June 1997 when she was sent on a week-long trade mission to recruit students for English language schools. Here she found a more strictly Islamic society, with traditional attitudes to women and the family.

My first impressions of Tashkent were filtered through a haze of pain, after having contracted food poisoning at London's Heathrow Airport. Travelling through the dark streets in the early hours of morning I immediately experienced déjà vu: Tashkent is one of those identikit Soviet cities, very similar to its more northerly neighbour Almaty. Although the name might conjure up visions of a glamorous vanished past, there is very little left of its former glories. The old city was flattened by an earthquake in 1968, and teams of labourers, shipped in from throughout the USSR, rebuilt it in record time along typical Soviet lines. Wide streets are arranged in a grid pattern, opening onto squares bordered by bland, monumental public buildings.

The next day, I stepped rather weakly out into a bath of heat. I'd arrived in June and the temperature was already up in the nineties. I was in Uzbekistan for only a week, as part of a trade mission to recruit students for English language schools. That first day, however, was a Sunday, so we were bussed around the city to see the sights.

Uzbeks are famed for the closeness of their family life, the strictness with which they raise their children, and their devoutness. Kazaks and Uighurs, their ethnic neighbours, speak of them with approval. Signs of a resurgent Islam are increasingly apparent: the *madrasas*, religious schools for young men, are reopening and their peaceful courtyards are once more filling with students. The first place we visited was the Abdul Khanim Madrasa. Quiet precincts hid a little grove of mulberry trees and the workshops of local craftsmen. Later on, less exquisite but more practical items could be bought in the Chorsu Bazaar. The intention behind the bazaar was obviously to reproduce one of the heavenly azure domes of Samarkand's famous buildings, although the result looked more like a UFO had landed. Inside was a chaotic melange of goods – everything from engine parts to cinnamon. Vendors in monochrome Uzbek hats squatted along the perimeter, selling dried fish and small wizened apples, and a pall of throat-catching smoke from the *shashlik* (mutton kebab) stands hung over everything. Other sights included the imposing Earthquake Memorial, where a Soviet Hero stood with hand outflung, protecting his wife and child from the uneasy forces of nature. Locally, however, he's become known as Alimony Man, since his wife appears to be · assaulting him from behind. We were also taken into one of Tashkent's most surprising attractions: the Metro. Marble-floored, so clean you could eat your kebab off it, and bedecked with cascades of chandeliers, the Metro was impressive – but I was unable to record its wonders photographically because it's a restricted area (a relic perhaps of Cold War paranoia, but I like to think that it's in case envious Westerners might seek to reproduce its unique delights elsewhere, in New York, say, or on London's Northern Line).

By Monday I had recovered from my malaise and embarked on an exhausting round of visits and interviews. First was the Ministry of Education, a decaying office block in what passes for Tashkent's downtown. My colleague Donald and I sat through a less than exhilarating hour while the Minister reeled off statistic after statistic: "We have had a very productive year." I bet. Uzbekistan's finances are in the same dire state as most of the other ex-Soviet satellites, and it is host to an eclectic range of environmental disasters, foremost among them the poisoned salt-flats where the Aral Sea used to be. There's not a lot of spare cash to spend on anything else.

The Uzbeks are more traditional, and more sexist, than their northern neighbours, the Kazaks. At one of the universities, Donald was courted while my questions passed unanswered. At the end of the session, we were all given a huge ceramic plate, but I'm afraid I did not feel that this was adequate compensation. Revenge came later in the afternoon, when we visited a local women's networking group. Here, I was feted and Donald was ignored. The Uzbekistanis should perhaps be more circumspect: some surprising people end up here. At an Ambassadorial reception later that evening (held in the garden and less grand than it sounds) I met an unassuming blonde woman in a dress with daisies on it; only later did we find out that she was Britain's first female astronaut, Helen Sharman.

Prudently, we avoided eating in the hotels (one German guest had asked for a breakdown of his bill and discovered that he had been charged per slice of tomato) and headed instead to one of the numerous *shashlik* cafés and *chaikhanas* which were dotted all over the city. There were some excellent teahouses, including the *Arpapoya*, situated among willows by the canal. This sold not only the inevitable *shashlik*, but quail-on-a-stick, good *plov* (mutton pilau) with pine nuts and almonds, and green Chinese tea. We got invited to a "home restaurant" in one of the back-street areas. God alone knows where it was, but the food, served by a Ukrainian girl with trendy emerald fingernails, was excellent. The following night we had a significantly less impressive dinner at one of the flashier hotels, consisting of the same ingredients, for twenty dollars more.

On Thursday, once the visits were over, we got our day out: a visit to Samarkand. The road there ought to be wreathed in glamour and legend; instead it winds through interminable acres of grey-green cotton fields until you reach the low hills surrounding the city. It looks startlingly like parts of Wales. We began with an extremely dull visit to British American Tobacco, a hangar-like factory on the outskirts. I find that I have largely blanked this event from my memory: you shouldn't have to face the relentless thrust of capitalism in old Samarkand, but then, the city was always a trading place, and I found the contrast between the modern outskirts and its ancient heart rewarding.

Our whistlestop afternoon tour began with the Registan, one of the old Silk Road marketplaces. An enormous courtyard was flanked by three famous *madrasas*: the Sher Dor, the Tilla Kari and the Ulug Bek. They were crowned with immense blue domes and their facades were covered in intricate calligraphy and forbidden images, apparently a legacy of Zoroastrianism. The principles of that ancient religion are based on fire and light, and signs of these remained in the colours of the Registan: blue as a summer sky, golden as the sun. Lions and deer pranced across the portals of the Sher Dor. Within the Tilla Kari, or "gilded" *madrasa*, the mosque it contained was covered with ornate and dazzling gold. I've seldom been silenced by marvels, but the Registan rendered me speechless.

Behind the Sher Dor and the market, where I purchased a collapsible Uzbek hat from an astounded old woman, lay the Bibi Khanum mosque. It was reputedly built by Tamurlane's Chinese wife as a gift, which she then somewhat undermined by indulging in a flirtation with its architect. Tamurlane was not amused and repaid the architect's treachery with execution. Despite earthquake damage and neglect, and its shaky beginnings, the proportions were still stunning. Just along from the market was the Shah-i-Zinda mausoleum, an eerily beautiful street of tombs containing the remains of Tamurlane's female relatives. We climbed the "Stairway to Heaven" which led up to the tombs, making sure that we counted the steps: if you lost track, you lost your chance of entering paradise, not a risk I was prepared to take. The tombs, all of which date from the fourteenth and fifteenth centuries, were the colours of water – aquamarine, cobalt and turquoise. It was a strange place; the dead seemed very close and the silence hung over it like a veil.

Herded back into the coach, we drove post-haste to the Ulug Bek Observatory, which was the workplace of Tamurlane's astronomer grandson. Unlike the rest of his savage family he was a peaceful, enlightened man, but unfortunately his progressive scientific enquiries were not universally appreciated: he was beheaded by his devout son in 1449. The observatory was torn down, but has now been rebuilt and houses a charming museum with panoramic views across

Samarkand. When we visited, a little group of people were performing an energetic and flamboyant dance outside. I still don't know why!

By this time, various members of the party were surreptitiously glancing at their watches and walking rather quickly around the sights. It later transpired that they had arranged to meet friends for a dance of their own, in the local belly-dancing restaurant back in Tashkent. They commented on this as being a lewd and salacious performance, unsuitable for another woman's eyes. Casually I mentioned that I used to do Egyptian dancing myself. There was a short astounded silence, and the conversation was hastily changed. Ah, British businessmen, innocents abroad . . .

Despite the rush we managed to see Tamurlane's mausoleum, the Guir Amir. The warrior lay beneath an immense slab of jade, so dark that it appeared almost black. The mausoleum was decorated with invocations to Allah, but there were uneasy hints of an older, shamanistic worship, like a horse's tail flung from a pole, looking anachronistic among the sophisticated designs of Islam. Apparently, however, it designated a Muslim saint, Tamurlane's tutor. It is said that Tamurlane's spirit was not content to be consigned to his tomb, and wailed every night for a year. Only the release of the prisoners whom this terrifying leader had captured allowed his ghost to rest in what might pass for peace.

Exhausted by sightseeing, we slumped on the bus and were rattled back to Tashkent, stopping off at a *chaikhana* en route for a quick bowl of *plov* and a beer, and thereby enraging the dance-bound members of the party. We did not, alas, make it back in time for their planned evening's indulgence. The next day, after a last walk in the shady park opposite the hotel, where Marx once stood and now Tamurlane's statue arrogantly rides, we were escorted to the airport and the journey home.

Venezuela

By dugout to the Yanomami

Linda Ballou

Linda Ballou travelled to Venezuela with her husband, Mike, and their friend, Rick. They flew to Puerto Ayacucho, a river port and border post on the upper Orinoco from where, supported by a small crew, they set off to explore some of the tropical waterways that run through the Amazonas. Though her companions were male, she felt that her approach to the journey and interactions with the people she encountered "emanated from a distinctly different woman's perspective". This was especially true of her meeting with Bettina, a member of the Yanomami tribe. Among numerous jobs to support her adventures and travels, Linda Ballou has worked as a snake catcher in India, a magic-wand seller with a circus, a newspaper reporter, a librarian and a charter boat cook. Her interest in aboriginal tribal peoples began thirty years ago when she came to know the Irulas of South India. She currently lives in Florida.

The cross-cultural connections and fervent friendships offered by travel rank way up high as motivations for my personal wanderlust. They can occur in the most unlikely places.

I met Bettina when we stopped at Coromototeri on the banks of the Rio Casiquiare in search of a Yanomami guide. Her nostrils and cheeks were pierced with slender sticks, her gourd-shaped breasts were crisscrossed with strands of blue and white beads, and the pregnant bulge of her belly was covered by a length of red cloth wound around

629

her middle. I admired how she stood there on the rock landing so erect and proud. And I liked the way her dark eyes expressed amusement as much as surprise at the unexpected visit of three gringos and two Venezuelan boatmen.

Her husband Enrique, the village chief, was away hunting, Bettina explained. (Taboos prohibit the use of their Yanomami names but Spanish names, bestowed on them by missionaries are readily substituted.) They could not provide us with a guide she told us, in her careful mission Spanish, because her brother had been killed by a member of the tribe we were seeking. By the Yanomami code of retaliation and revenge, members of her village were now at war with them and refused to go to their territory.

Not much different from the so-called civilised world, I mused, but her words gave me pause. I began to wonder just what I thought I was doing probing Venezuela's remote Amazonas in search of one of the last bands of unacculturated tribal folk left on earth. All my lofty sentiments about learning better ways to live on the planet from stone age hunter gatherers began to seem facile. Maybe these people living in isolation in their rainforest fastness just wanted to be left alone. Maybe I was just looking for justification for another adventure.

But I kept my misgivings to myself and let the momentum of the expedition carry me on. Fortified with cassava bread, which had the texture and flavour of thick cardboard, we followed the southwesterly flow of the river.

At San Carlos on the Rio Negro, we exchanged our sixteen-foot aluminum boat for a 32-foot-long dugout with a canopy roof. And at their village at the mouth of the Rio Pasimoni, we added two Curipaco Indians to the crew. Cacimiro and Antonio knew the idiosyncrasies of the backwaters we'd be travelling. Cacimiro even spoke a little Yanomami. The dugout (known locally as a bongo) was a slender craft better suited to manoeuvre the narrow shallows of our route. It also suited my romantic notions of tropical river travel a whole lot better than the tacky little outboard we'd been crammed into for the last four days.

Cacimiro kept vigil at the bow using his heart-shaped paddle to guide the bongo around obstacles, while ritually scooping river water into the manioc gruel that he swilled throughout the day. He'd brought along an ancient shotgun held together with wire. His sharp ears were attuned to the calls of the wild and occasionally he'd signal Antonio to pull over to the bank. Quickly and silently he'd disappear into the jungle, fire a single shot, and return bearing a blue-faced crested bird the size of a chicken. It would go into the stew pot at the end of the day.

We made camps on the riverbanks, hanging our hammocks and mosquito nets beneath tarps suspended from trees. One night Cacimiro led us to an abandoned Indian fish camp where a couple of low thatch tent-like huts had been built on a flat granite outcrop next to some racks for drying fish. Although we had to share these quarters with the insects and lizards already in residence, we stayed cosy and dry despite a downpour lasting much of the night.

In the morning I basked on the warm rocks, my belly full from a breakfast of grilled piranha, and daydreamed about living there. I imagined weaving baskets and gathering jungle fruit, paddling a small dugout up hidden creeks, wearing orchids in my hair and visiting Bettina to see her new baby. I didn't want to leave, but the others were calling me.

Our route followed branches of rivers that turned into streams and then into creeks. We no longer saw pairs of macaws flying overhead nor heard the chatter of flocks of green parrots. But brilliant blue butterflies, their colour and proportions as exaggerated as cartoons, fluttered slowly across our bow. Escorted by pale river dolphins, we reached the Rio Baria. Even on the best of our maps it appeared only as a vague squiggle losing itself in uncharted tributaries probably extending into Brazil. Somewhere in that tangle lived the Yanomami tribe we were seeking.

The Baria had so many twists and turns that at times we seemed to be going in circles. Clusters of palm trees formed little islands around which there was barely enough water to pass, and the low-lying banks began closing in on us. Branches of trees on the river's edge drooped under the weight of orchids and bromeliads. Though the air had become dank and oppressive, there was a compelling primeval beauty about the place.

The mosquitoes and jejenes, a particularly noxious type of biting gnat, were thick and ravenous. Even our tightly woven mosquito netting was no deterrent to their hunger for our bodies. Their bites caused me to toss and turn so much that one night I dislodged the clothing stashed at the foot of my hammock. In the morning I found my underwear and socks on the ground, chewed into confetti by leaf-cutter ants who were beating a single file retreat waving white flags snipped neatly from my sports bra.

Antonio nosed the dugout slowly through the coffee-coloured water, guided by hand signals from Cacimiro on the bow. The previous months of torrential rains had left a legacy of collapsed banks, broken branches and fallen trees to obstruct our passage. At one point three trees crisscrossed the river, forming a tangled fence blocking our course. It looked impenetrable to me. But Cacimiro began chopping at one of the tree trunks with his machete. Its dense tropical hardwood rang like a gong when he struck it, but the chips flew. Meanwhile, Nilo hung monkey-like from the branches of one tree to hack at the limbs of another. With all of us pitching in we were eventually able to clear enough of the jumbled mass so that we could push and pull and squeeze the bongo through.

We continued to hack our way through logjams until we finally reached an impasse. Even Cacimiro had to admit that it would take more than machetes to cut through the trunks of dozens of thick trees blocking our way. The uncontacted Yanomami tribe would remain hidden from our curious eyes. Though I never admitted it to the others, I was secretly pleased.

I was also pleased to return to Coromototeri. We stayed there for two days while Jose and Nilo took the bongo back to San Carlos. Bettina once again met us at the landing, this time with her husband, the chief. "Leenda!" she shrieked when she saw me, and we beamed at each other like long-lost friends.

Her tribe now became the beneficiary of the trade goods we had expected to bring to their enemies. We gave them knives, fish hooks, our remaining machetes, and bolts of red cloth. In return they offered us a hut to sleep in and freedom to wander the village and enter the huts of the chief's extended family.

Bettina hustled me off with a conspiratorial grin, as though we'd planned this get-together and had lots to catch up on. In her window-less hut I stumbled into the hot coals of a hearth on the floor before my eyes adjusted to the dark. She and the other women howled at my clumsiness as I danced around on one foot. After I settled down Bettina worked patiently to pare down the quills of two chartreuse parrot feathers to fit the small holes of my pierced ears. Only then, apparently, was I fit for public display.

Decked out in my new green feathers, I let Bettina take me "shopping". My currency was the beads and safety pins I had brought along as personal trade goods. Safety pins might seem like an odd item, given that the Yanomami, even the mission influenced groups, wear little clothing. But it turns out they are troubled by an insect that lays its eggs under their skin. The safety pin provides a better tool than sharpened bamboo for digging these out, plus it can be kept handily clipped to their necklaces of beads. My pins and beads were both desirable items, and I did a brisk trade in baskets, agouti-tooth knives and bamboo arrow-point quivers. One man came back after the completion of a trade and, looking embarrassed, indicated that he wanted his quiver back. Wondering if this was what was meant by Indian giving, I handed it over. He pulled off the snakeskin cover, extracted a slimy wad of tobacco leaves from among the arrow-points, popped it under his lower lip, and bashfully returned the case to me.

Bettina stood quietly to the side during all these transactions, but I noticed that she seemed unable to take her eyes off the red rain hat in which I'd carried my beads and pins. Shoving the rest of them into my pockets, I held the hat out to her. She came closer, removed the monkey fur headband she wore and placed it on my head, then took the hat I offered and pulled it over her neatly cropped hair. We smiled into each other's eyes, needing nothing so crude as language to communicate our mutual feelings. Though our cultures were at opposite ends of the spectrum, we were not so very different. We looked for affection; we liked a good bargain.

Later we sat on the rocks beside the river and watched the small freshwater dolphin play. Bettina stroked the blonde hair on my arms, and then placed my hand on her protruding stomach. "*Shori*," she said, "*shori tute*." There was one word of Yanomami I knew well. Before leaving Florida I had acquired a new cat and named her Shori, the Yanomami word for friend.

During the night I was awakened by the shaman's chanting, which went on for hours. At first it sounded alarmingly contentious, and a small shiver of fear went through me. The Yanomami, after all, are known for suddenly turning upon their guests with murderous rage. But once I got used to his occasional thunderous outbursts, the rhythmic resonance of the shaman's voice became spellbinding. I began to listen closely to see if I could make out anything of what he – or the spirits he'd summoned – were saying. Thanks to the pages of Yanomami vocabulary that Rick had compiled, I had memorised a number of their words. For a long time I understood nothing. Eventually I began to pick out the odd word here or there. But finally I heard a pattern. "*Napu . . . hapo . . . parawa . . . tote hiwa . . . tote hiwa.*" The shaman repeated a phrase using those words like a refrain.

"He's saying," I leaned out of my hammock and whispered into the pitch-black hut with utter certainty, "'The river has brought the strangers; it is good, it is good.'"

read on . . .

Lisa St Aubin de Terán, *The Hacienda: My Venezuelan Years* (UK: Virago, 1997/US: Little Brown, 1999). This remarkable, eloquent book tells how the author, at seventeen, marries a Venezuelan aristocrat and moves from South London to her husband's hacienda in a remote part of the Andes. There, she struggles to learn how to become la Doña, running the estate and fighting illness, poverty, ignorance, the weather and extreme loneliness, while her wayward and increasingly violent husband descends semi-publicly into madness. Astounding both for the toughness of its protagonists and the delicacy with which the story is told, the narrative covers the seven years that de Terán spends on the lush but often unforgiving hacienda, which she says have had a massively formative effect on her career as a writer. Disarming honesty is matched by the tactful respect (eventually) accorded her by the tenants and workers on the estate, who depend on her for their survival and with many of whom she forms an enduring bond.

Yemen

Behind Yemen's veil

Dawn Hurley

Dawn Hurley is a Canadian based in London. She travelled and lived in Yemen for seven months while working for a British independent film company headed by her partner, John Miles. She has worked extensively in scriptwriting and has had a short story published in *Quality Women's Fiction* magazine. This account was written before December 1998, when three British nationals and an Australian were murdered by terrorists in the Yemeni desert. The country is no stranger to violence, having traditionally been ruled by tribal law and ripped apart by a succession of civil wars, yet until recently travel was considered relatively safe.

I felt like a pack horse. Sweat dripped down my back as I lugged our gear up the winding dirt path of Jabal Sabir, a ten-thousand-foot-high mountain in the heart of Yemen. My partner John was already off photographing the terraced mountainsides; in those remote highlands *qat* and coffee plants provided a lush backdrop to the clusters of fortress-like villages that perched precariously on the mountain-tops.

We were researching the best location to make a documentary film on this ancient kingdom, and wanted to find a community which revealed some of the fascinating aspects of daily traditional life. We had journeyed to Yemen before kidnappings had become a commonplace risk for some travellers: the Yemen that we experienced included guns and tribalism, but virtually no aggression towards Westerners. Few tourists travelled in the places that we did – we headed for isolated spots and wanted to feel the true heartbeat of a country that had remained, to outsiders, shrouded in mystery for centuries.

We had been living for a while with a family of Yemenis in Sana'a, the mud-walled capital, which is also one of the oldest cities in the world. The family thought we might find what we were looking for in the highlands, so we hired a four-wheel-drive and set off to explore. With the midday sun pulsating above me, I wished I had on a loose pair of shorts and a T-shirt, but out of respect for Islam, the country's dominant religion, I had opted to cover my arms and legs. Usually I wore a headscarf too, which resulted in fewer lascivious looks from men, and silent approval from local women. In Yemen, being female didn't just mean changing my dress code, it also altered my "girl power" quotient from high to almost non-existent. Yemeni men did not view me as John's equal, more as an attractive appendage. For some strange reason, John did not seem to mind this at all.

I had always to walk a little behind the men, and not initiate too many conversations. It appeared that a lot of Yemenis see Western women as characters from the American soap *Dynasty*, ie bed-hopping bitches. I guess we did look quite brazen compared to women who walked the streets swathed head to toe in black *sharshafs*, almost all aspects of their identity hidden to the world. Some even covered their eyes, so that they could only see out through a layer of black gauze.

While John snapped away unencumbered, I slogged on upwards, silently wishing I were a man so I could wear one of their long cool white *thobes*, sling a *djambia* dagger (which resembled a long curved phallic symbol) around my waist, and basically get a little R-E-S-P-E-C-T. But I didn't feel miserable for long.

Up the path strode a group of local women, chatting away in Arabic and balancing on top of their heads loads which looked as though they weighed more than I did. I was surprised to see the women's faces uncovered, and their colourful headscarves and dresses bloomed around them like desert flowers. They walked lightly, not seeming to feel the burden of their bundles – or their womanhood.

"*Salaam wa alaikum!*" they chorused.

"*Wa alaikum salaam!*" I replied.

As one of the women put down her bundle and inspected my blonde ponytail, I bandied about some of the stilted Arabic that I had picked up in Sana'a. The woman, who turned out to be called Jamila, faced me, her eyes shining in symphony with the gold jewellery draped around her neck. She wiped her hand across her brow, indicating the heat, then tapped me on the head. I thought she might be angry with me for not covering my hair; after all, we were in the mountains, and I guessed that the dress code might be more strict than in the city, but I was off the mark. Chatting excitedly, the women began to buzz around me while one of the younger girls reached into her bag. She uncoiled a long red and white hand-painted scarf and held it up. The other women nodded. Brown work-worn hands then gracefully wrapped the material around my head in the traditional style. Jamila pulled out a flower that she had used to decorate her own head-dress and tucked it behind my ear.

"*Kwayis*," she said. She approved of my new look.

At this point John sauntered up to discover what the commotion was all about.

"*Zowge?*" she asked.

"Yes," I replied.

Even though John and I only lived together in London, we decided to travel as a married couple. For an unmarried man and woman to travel together in Yemen would definitely have been a *faux pas*. Most of the Yemeni girls I'd talked to never consorted with men other than those of their immediate family, and often never even saw their husbands until their wedding day. Furthermore, there were more men to be seen holding hands on the streets of Sana'a than in all the clubs in Soho.

The group of women proceeded to grill John about my lack of gold jewellery; all of them dripped delicate filigreed gold from their ears, necks, wrists and fingers. I guessed that the silver wedding band bought in a Cairo market for two pounds fifty looked a little shoddy by comparison. John's cheeks reddened and I started to get indignant, caught up in the collective sentiment. "Yeah, where's my gold?" I thought. "I'm worth it, aren't I?" These women definitely thought so, because one unclipped a large chunky necklace and draped it around my neck.

"*Shokran*," I thanked her, knowing, unfortunately, that this was just a loan.

I could just understand enough of what was being said to know that the women were going on to the next village to attend a wedding. They tugged at our sleeves as a sign of invitation. John took the backpack and we followed the women on up the mountain.

In the village we approached a towering stone house, its façade stuccoed in a white, lace-like pattern. *Takrim* windows, typical of Yemeni architecture, glinted in the colours of a peacock feather. John was whisked away by a man wearing a *djambia* and *thobe* just like the ones I'd been hankering after earlier. Now, however, I was very pleased with my headdress. Men and women do not mix at Yemeni wedding celebrations: I had attended several weddings in Sana'a, so I knew that John would spend his afternoon with the men chewing *qat*, smoking water pipes filled with fragrant Yemeni tobacco, and possibly taking part in a traditional *djambia* dance, in which the men form a large circle to symbolise tribal unity. Accompanied by two drums, the leader begins the steps, which are simple at first and then become more intricate as the music quickens. The dancers hold their daggers aloft, whirling them skilfully between themselves and the other men. One by one they drop out until only the best dancer and the leader are left, locked in a graceful combat. As a Western woman, I had in the past been privileged to be admitted to join the men. No man, however, was ever permitted to join the women's wedding party. What I was about to experience, no man would witness.

In the foyer of the house, kept cool by the mud walls, the women adjusted their dresses and headscarves, and I could hear a carnival of voices from down the hall. The hostess, Aisha, came out to welcome us. She was wearing a long dress in the style of the women of Jabil Sabre, heavily embroidered at the bodice with richly coloured threads. She greeted everyone, including me, by clasping hands, then passing over one of hers to be kissed, and taking mine back to return the gesture. Our hands travelled back and forth several times, which showed that I was warmly welcome.

Aisha led us into the *mafraj*, the main room of the house, which was painted white with high ceilings. Hordes of children played boisterously, or suckled at the breasts of women sat two or three deep around the edges of the room. The mothers propped themselves up on cushions specially designed for sitting on the *mafraj* floor. To add to the chaos of children, friends tried to sell each other wares like stockings and soap mittens by throwing them backward and forward across the room like jugglers. Before we had a chance to join the party a young girl approached, carrying a clay pot attached to a chain. She poured a fragrant smoke of incense over our bodies; skirts were lifted slightly so that smoke could rise underneath, sealing in the warmth of the scent.

We found a place on the crowded floor, sitting with the "grandmothers", who oozed the authority of those who have lived long and carry the wisdom of the world in the folds on their faces. They smiled at me and offered me *qat*, their cheeks already bulging with the mildly narcotic leaf. I'd chewed it many times before and had become quite fond of the whole leaf-chewing ritual. Although acrid at first, the juice from the leaves soon becomes unnoticeable as your senses are heightened to a point of extreme wakefulness. It's almost like drinking ten cups of strong coffee, but without the accompanying nausea and stomach rot. I accepted the offer and started to fill my cheeks. The women who had invited me along emptied items for sale from their bundles, and bundles of *qat* flew overhead as the women exchanged gestures of welcome and friendship.

My limited command of the language made conversation predictable: husbands, children, Yemen. My company seemed shocked to discover that John and I had been "married" for three years but still had no children. When I reassured them that we wanted at least five to form a little tribe of our own they appeared much relieved. I was glad that my nose didn't start to grow and give the game away.

In between conversations the older women puffed languorously on the wooden mouthpieces of the *madah'ah*. In the centre of the room, our hostess had placed four large silver trays, each laden with four of these water pipes, all of different heights. Their long hoses were swathed in velvet and coiled around the bases like a nest of colourful snakes. It was a privilege to possess the fragrant smoke, so when a pipe was passed to me I felt honoured to accept it. The soft smoke complemented the taste of the *qat*, and any harshness was smoothed away by drinking from the jugs of water flavoured with cardamom which were placed around the room.

A drum and a high-pitched guttural cry intruded into the tranquillity of my smoke-filled haze. The cry came from a group of approaching women, and those in the room joined in – a sure sign that the bride would soon appear! Then she was there, parting bodies to either side of the room as Moses parted the waters of the Red Sea. Two young girls clad in white gowns rustled towards the bride's throne, carrying tall white unlit candles. Like pageboys, they stood on either side of the chair. Regal, yet shy, the bride walked through the sea of faces to take her place at the head of the room. A shaky hand reaching out for a tissue betrayed her nervousness. Her hands and fore-arms were painted in black *naqshe*, a body decoration similar to henna which, according to tradition, was painted on the bride's hands and feet just before the wedding ceremony. Each pattern is like a distinc-tive signature, whose elaborate design might also ward off the evil eye.

I wondered if the paint and ritual might also help her deal with wedding night jitters, when she would lie for the first time on her spe-cially prepared bed. Her new husband would spill her virgin blood on a specially prepared sheet, which the following morning he would show to her parents and then enjoy a hearty (and specially prepared) breakfast. She can have been no more than sixteen.

The drums continued to beat, and extra percussion was added by fingertips tapping on the bases of metal bowls. The steady rhythm har-monised beautifully with Arabic song. Clapping and chatter accompa-nied the lead singer, while a group of guests moved into a cleared space to dance. They stood side by side, holding hands at right angles to the chest, raising their hips and moving forward to the beat of the music. Every movement exuded a controlled sensuality. As the dance speeded up enthusiastic onlookers let out their throaty cry, gyrating their tongues to produce waves of sound. Unfortunately, I didn't remain an onlooker for long. Jamila pulled me up to dance, so I rose despite knowing that I was about to make a spectacular fool of myself. I did *try*, but rhythm is not my strong point. The other guests didn't seem to mind my Western wiggle and clapped and cheered through-out the song. As I sat down, perspiring, I was offered more *qat* and *madah'ah*. I felt girl power seeping back into my bones.

The sun was beginning to sink low. Suddenly Aisha called me from the proceedings, so I said "*Masalamah*" to bid my new friends goodbye and was led down a hallway to a small wooden door. Behind it was a quiet room with another five women in it, and I was taken over to an ancient woman sitting on a bed. She pulled me towards her for inspection, commanding respect with a gleam in her eyes. I sensed that this was the family matriarch. She politely asked me several basic questions, and I thanked her for allowing me into the family home to share in the wedding celebrations. Then she gestured to one of her daughters, who disappeared into an adjoining room and reappeared holding a Jabil Sabre dress with the elaborate embroidered front, its folds spilling over her arms. I was taken aback when the smooth fabric washed over my head-dress and down my body. The dress was for me.

Rejoining John outside the house, I entwined hands with him and it felt to me that we descended the mountain on equal footing. The *qat* had made us quiet and contemplative, but the energy of the wedding surged between us in a male-female synapse. Images of the day flashed across my mind, searing themselves into my mental photo album. Even though I have not seen the women of Jabil Sabre since that day, I can still flip through these pages in my memory; I can conjure up the day, smell the incense, hear the song, and feel the warmth of the women's companionship.

It was difficult for me to leave without feeling a little choked. I took heart from the women's strength of character and from the way that they had welcomed me into their fold. As John and I wove our way back down the mountain path I felt freshly buoyant, free of that morning's despondency. I wore my new dress proudly and with pleasure, knowing that I had glimpsed behind the veil that concealed the community of Yemeni women from the view of the outside world.

Zimbabwe

A term at Eaglesjail

Tatum Anderson

At 22, Tatum Anderson's teaching experience was limited to tutoring individual pupils at home in London, when she accepted a job at a private school in Harare, teaching physics to about 100 teenagers barely younger than herself. She is currently a magazine writer in London and the author of "A sista and a mzungu" (see p.365), about her travels in Malawi after the end of term in Zimbabwe.

The headmaster's jaw dropped when I met him at the airport. So did mine. I'd flown thousands of miles to teach in Zimbabwe to be met by a white man. He was not expecting a black woman to be teaching physics O- and A-level.

A friend had recommended I try teaching in Zimbabwe, and after writing to countless organisations and schools, I was offered a post to replace a physics teacher who was taking a term's sabbatical. I knew when I was offered the post I wouldn't be working in a bush school. But I wasn't prepared for the weird ex-colonial timewarp of the Zimbabwean private-school system with its uniforms, school songs and hockey matches straight out of an Enid Blyton novel. I had no idea what I'd let myself in for. As we drove through Eaglesvale's school gates, the headmaster said to me, laughing: "The kids call it Eagles*jail*."

Set on a huge plot of land, it was all encompassing, with an almost pristine maze of school buildings including many that looked like pre-fabs. There were extensive games lawns, separate girls' and boys' hostels and a dining hall in the middle. The school's philosophy seemed to be that everything is done, or not done, on threat of punishment.

Many of the seventy or so teachers and school staff lived with their families in houses on the property. A few of the younger teachers like myself were assigned a room in the boarder's hostels. In exchange for looking after the boarders, I was given free room and board. I was shown my sparsely furnished room in the girls' hostel and introduced to Tuni, or matron. She was a fierce-looking old lady with a harsh Afrikaans accent but a rather kindly nature, who lived by herself in rooms at the bottom of the hostel building.

I was already a little shaky when I first met my form class, twenty sixth-formers, just after seven in the morning. A bell that sounded like a World War II black-out siren had blasted me out of bed at 5.45, and I had woken up with a multitude of mosquito wounds on the bits of my face that I'd missed when I had smeared on repellent the night before.

Exhausted after a sleepless night of worrying, I found it impossible to focus properly on the register. Gradually the bursts of laughter grew into an uproar as I mispronounced one after another Shona and Afrikaans surname. I had only ever taught children one at a time; my teaching experience was limited to tutoring science and maths GCSE and A-level in the comfort of my own home in London. The prospect of being responsible for such a large amount of children in a foreign country had not really dawned on me.

Suddenly I had classrooms full of pupils, a pile of lesson plans and letters of introduction from the previous physics teacher. I was swamped and absolutely petrified. The other teachers told me not to smile on my first week, because that was a sign of weakness. My face did not crack for at least two, and in return I got monosyllabic, unenthusiastic responses. The upper sixth form seemed faintly amused because, at the age of 22, I looked only slightly older than they did.

I taught about 100 children – a seventh of the school. There were six classes in all, with students who ranged in age from fourteen to nineteen. The children were a mixture of races, coming from Zimbabwe, South Africa and Zambia. Some were day-scholars, some were boarders. Gradually, the indistinguishable mass of names and faces had transformed into personalities. George, who was more interested in rugby than school; Twanda, who told me horror stories about going on safari; Farai, who apparently was a troublemaker in every other class but was very attentive once we talked about Manchester, where he had family; the hockey-playing girls, who always got full marks; Adrian, who seemed to be obsessed with clubbing despite being very obviously underage; Ritu, who was much better at physics than I was at her age.

I got to know the diligent ones, as well as the ones who couldn't wait to leave school because they knew they could inherit their parents' farms with no qualifications. There were also ones who were dumped in the girls' hostels, even though their parents lived in Harare, and never had visitors at the weekends to take them out. After a few weeks of playing with magnets, electrical wires and slinky springs, the ice was broken.

My day did not stop with teaching or looking after the boarders. Although protesting that the last time I played hockey was at the age of eleven, I was appointed co-hockey coach, in addition to being the only physics teacher. The first lesson was a nightmare. The other coach, who had been a member of the Zimbabwean Olympic team in her youth, hadn't turned up. I had no idea of the rules and had to oversee forty pubescent girls in the under-sixteens hockey game. The game turned into chaos as rules were broken and arguments erupted, fuelled by the girls who had already swapped best friends three times that day and were feeling hard-done-by. Internal politics were destroying the team, but I did my best during the term as mediator, asthma-inhaler-holder and agony aunt. Despite that, we were regularly thrashed at hockey matches all over Zimbabwe.

With sport in the afternoon, I had almost a full school day, which lasted from 7am until 1pm each day, and was busy planning lessons, setting up experiments and marking books in the free periods. The whole surreal experience was made manageable by Martin, one of the other teachers, who had an escape route in the shape of a car and provided plentiful supplies of Marmite at breakfast. Then, I discovered a PC with computer games in the apparatus room and with

Dan, an English gap-year teacher, we would go and shoot aliens instead. We would visit Emmanuel, who taught in the junior school and had an apartment attached to the hostel where we could gather and cook food, watch television and escape from the hostel world.

Other than that, life outside Eaglesvale was a mixture of shopping, cinemas, bars and clubbing. Mpume, one of the other teachers, took me clubbing by ET, an emergency taxi. ETs were battered old cars, appallingly unroadworthy, into which would be crammed an average of eight people, half of whom would sit in the boot. Once Martin left his car in a garage to be fixed after an accident. He was told for weeks that it wasn't ready, then one day he saw it being used as an ET around Harare.

I tried not to take ETs very much, although the school was some way out of Harare. I would beg lifts from friends' parents, or hop on the school buses going into town. Every so often, we would jump in the car and leave Eaglesvale for the weekend. Once, we borrowed an old jeep and watched wild zebra and giraffe at a farm owned by one of the teachers' friends. That night we were woken by a rabid wildcat which chased us around the house. We would eat fresh papaya and mangoes for breakfast from the garden and, once, took a breakfast picnic to a game park where we ate, surrounded by kudu and impala. Another time, we went up to Dombashawa, a huge dome-shaped rock just outside Harare, to watch the sunset.

With weekends like those, Monday mornings were even more hideous than in London. The school routines, however, were becoming more familiar and, despite my moans, I discovered that I enjoyed teaching. The pupils had passed the stage of being polite to prevent punishment, and were now courteous because they wanted to be. I got the general impression that my pupils' hatred for physics was decreasing during the term. I certainly got funny looks when we ran up and down the stairs to measure energy changes or were caught playing with huge springs.

At night, I would generally be found marking books, often by a paraffin lamp during the frequent power cuts, or pacifying girls whose bedtime coincided with the start of *Beverly Hills 90210* on the television. Being one of the few people in the hostel with a torch, I was often to be seen herding the girls to the dining room, which had a separate generator where I would have to test the little ones on their spellings, read them bedtime stories and then later make sure their mosquito nets were tucked in around their beds.

One of my responsibilities as a teacher living in the hostel was to escort pupils to church on a Sunday. I would take children, black and white, to a church whose Christian denomination formed the basis for the apartheid regime in Southern Africa. The ironies of life in Zimbabwe constantly bowled me over.

Sharon, a white fourteen-year-old, had sat at the back of my physics class and looked uninterested. She had visited me in my room in the hostel to ask for help the night before a test and listened with distaste to the reggae music on my Walkman. After a while she seemed to thaw out and would throw herself instead into answering as many questions in class as possible, whether right or wrong. One day she asked me, "Ma'am are you black or coloured?" She decided without waiting for an answer that I was coloured. I had no idea at that stage what she meant.

Shortly afterward, I was given a government form asking the ethnic origin of my students, with categories that included "Black", "White", "Coloured" and "Asian". Until then, I had not realised that coloured or mixed race was considered a race in itself, one of the by-products of southern Africa's apartheid regime. In one coloured household, the comments about "The Africans" and the sorry state of Zimbabwe made me realise how ingrained this separate indentity had become, despite having been so artificially defined and imposed.

The teachers, who had their own houses, all employed maids and manservants who waited on them hand and foot. Even at the school, the cleaning staff were barked at both by teachers and pupils. I found it impossible to be called Ma'am by a technician who was old enough to be my grandfather, or let someone do my cleaning and laundry when they already had enough chores to do. I got to know Douglas, who was a sort of odd-job man. I would be working in the classroom when he came to clean up and gradually we got talking. He was trying to teach himself English A-level at home because, in the district where he lived, it was just too dangerous to go out to evening classes. By the end of term, I had taught him how to use a computer to write up his essays and he had taught me some Shona in return. He put his foot down when I offered to show him how to play computer games.

The war that had paved the way for Zimbabwe's independence in 1981 was still vivid in the memories of the older generation, and I was surprised by how little social mixing went on, even fifteen years later. The children were bothered to a lesser extent. There were more best-friend combinations of Shonas and Afrikaaners at Eaglesvale than I would ever see on my travels around Zimbabwe. The older children, however, were much more likely to stick to their ethnic groups than the primary school children.

By the end of the term, I was tired. I had written, adjudicated and marked 100 exam papers and lost count of the number of reports I had written. Fourteen weeks with only two days' break at half-term had almost finished me off. It was tough, but I learned a lot about crisis management, crowd control, and how to deal with completely alien situations. I also glimpsed the quiet social protocols that you only see when you are an outsider, and can take a step back from what everyone assumes to be the norm.

Three years on, I'm still in touch with many friends that I made in Zimbabwe. Soon after I left, I was offered more work at the school, and even contemplated going back for another term. On my travels around the country and further afield I often bumped into my pupils and we'd greet each other like old friends. But a small taster of the world outside an urban private school in southern Africa had whetted my appetite, and I wanted more. I never went back to teach at Eaglesvale.

read on . . .

Doris Lessing, *African Laughter: Four Visits to Zimbabwe* (UK: Flamingo, 1993/US: Harperperennial, 1993). As an outspoken opponent against the former white minority government, Doris Lessing was banned from her homeland for 25 years, so it is with understandably intense feeling that she finally returns in 1982, two years after Zimbabwe's independence. This and three subsequent visits, in 1988, 1989 and 1992, form the basis of this richly evocative, penetrating and highly personal portrait of a country beset with problems as it struggles to emerge from its colonial history. As Lessing travels far and wide, simultaneously revisiting her past and commenting on the new Zimbabwe, every facet of life is examined: the attitudes of white farmers, including the brother with whom she "never got on" but shared a "mysterious understanding"; the devastated wildlife; the increasing corruption of the Mugabe government; the threat of AIDS; the failure of the "new townships"; and the positive impact that small projects, like a "meagre little school where remarkable people teach", can have in the countryside. A largely pessimistic account but passionately told by one of this century's most assured, provocative and inspiring British women novelists.

further reading

Read on . . . anthologies

The following list represents a selection of our favourite collections of women's contemporary (with the exception of Dea Birkett and Jane Robinson's excellent compendiums of Victorian ladies abroad) travel writing. We consider some of the stories contained (Kate Pullinger, Sara Wheeler, Lesley Downer, Clare Boylan, and many more) to rank with the best examples of short travelogues. Enjoy the browse.

★ **Dea Birkett and Sara Wheeler (ed)**, *Amazonian: The Penguin Book of Women's New Travel Writing* (UK: Penguin, 1998). A wonderfully rich and eclectic mix by established travel writers, novelists and an actress. Although limited to only eleven contributors, each one is given full reign to experiment with and extend the genre, and does so with stunning effect. See particularly virtuoso pieces by Sara Wheeler (on Bangladesh); Kate Pullinger (on England and Canada) and Lesley Downer (on Ghana). The last is also featured in this book.

★ **Dea Birkett**, *Spinsters Abroad: Victorian Lady Explorers* (UK: Gollanz, 1993/US: o/p). A concise and well-researched look at the button-booted spinsters who launched themselves across the further reaches of the Empire, by the distinguished British writer and broadcaster. In unravelling the motives and perspectives of these women, amid a rich store of impressions and historical detail, Birkett allows us to judge for ourselves if these are the role models we wish to follow abroad.

★ **Marybeth Bond (ed)**, *A Woman's World* (UK/US: Travelers' Tales Inc., 1995). Following the success of their early collections of travel writing relating to specific countries, the excellent Travelers' Tales series branched out into this anthology covering the "inner and outer panoramas of women's journeys". Extracts (from writers such as Eva

Hoffman, Tracy Johnston and Robyn Davidson) are mixed in with a range of new travel pieces to provide an inspiring spectrum of women's contemporary experiences. Although understandably biased towards the Americas (nearly a third of the journeys are within US and Mexico), there are sufficient wild and far flung travel adventures to satisfy the most exacting wanderlust.

★ **Sarah Champion (ed)**, *Fortune Hotel: Twisted Travel Stories* (UK: Hamish Hamilton, 1999). Like *Wild Ways* below, this collection is mainly fiction but striking in the authenticity of the travel predicaments it covers. Electrifying tales abound, by new and established literary stars – Esther Freud's and Emily Perkins' stories of how love can peter out on long, slow days abroad are definite highlights. It's a shame, however, that they're almost swamped by the bizarre design. Contents and headings are presented as motorway signs glimpsed in reverse, a trendy idea but we all know what happens when you read in cars.

★ **Margo Daly and Jill Dawson (ed)**, *Wild Ways: New Stories about Women on the Road* (UK: Sceptre, 1998). A collection of travel-inspired short stories that offer such a strong sense of place that they nudge the boundaries between travelogue and fiction. Louise Doughty's backpacker on the trail round Guatemala; and Emily Perkins' teenager who knowingly surveys her mother's

Canadian travels from the back seat of the car, are just two of the brilliant protagonists and scenarios that spice this book.

★ **Katherine Govier (ed)**, *Without a Guide: Contemporary Women's Travel Adventures* (UK: Rivers Oran Press, 1994/US: Hungry Mind Press, 1994). Seventeen major, and international, literary figures, from Alice Walker and Annie Proulx to Hanan al-Shaykh and Margaret Atwood (whose piece on the Ecuadorean Galapagos Islands is featured in this book) present their own particular travel moments. Sadly overlooked in the UK, this anthology contains some extraordinary pieces of travel writing, such as the Irish poet and author Clare Boylan's poignant and knowing account of trying to re-establish a relationship with her mother by whisking her around the sights of London. A gem that demands relaunching.

★ **Elaine Lee (ed)**, *Go Girl! The Black Woman's Book of Travel and Adventure* (US: The Eighth Mountain Press, 1997). A strong sense of roots and identity permeates this first ever volume of travel stories by contemporary black women. Contributors include well-known writers like Alice Walker, Maya Angelou, Audre Lorde and Colleen J McElroy as well as less known names, such as Rosalind Cummings-Yeates, Joy V. Harris and Constance García-Barrio whose accounts are featured in *Women Travel*. United in spirit but also richly varied in the range of voices, destinations and experiences featured, this is another great American book which deserves distribution in the UK.

★ **Lucy McCauley (ed)**, *Women in the Wild: True Stories of Adventure and Connection* (US/UK: Travelers' Tales Inc., 1998). More women's stories from the Travelers' Tales series, this time focusing on forays into the natural world, from high adventure – rafting a river in Borneo, diving in the jungle and hang gliding over Big Sur – to more meditative journeys where women consciously explore the wildness of their own natures. Robyn Davidson, Annie Dillard and Louise Erdrich are just three of the impressive cast of writers who make this such an inspiring read.

★ **Mary Morris with Larry O'Connor (ed)**, *The Virago Book of Women Travellers* (UK: Virago Press, 1994/US: published as Maiden Voyages, Vintage, 1993). A selection of women's travel writing ("the best and the bravest"), covering three hundred years. Idiosyncratic, as any anthology of such scope is bound to be, Morris's selection nonetheless provides a wonderful progression of women's travel writing from the first airings of "inner journeys" in work such as Ella Maillart's, to the radar alertness of Joan Didion's city scans.

★ **Jane Robinson**, *Wayward Women: A Guide to Women Travellers* (UK/US: Oxford University Press, 1991). Very readable annotated bibliography covering sixteen centuries of women's travel writing – from the Abbess Etheria who journeyed to the Holy Land in the fourth century, to such modern adventuresses as Dervla Murphy and Naomi James. Robinson's second compilation, *Unsuitable for Ladies: An Anthology of Women Travellers* (UK/US: Oxford University Press, 1995), serves as a companion volume, arranged geographically and featuring extracts from some two hundred of the writers listed before.

★ **Lisa St Aubin de Terán (ed)**, *The Virago Book of Wanderlust and Dreams* (UK: Virago, 1999). Highly entertaining and unusual compilation of writings about longings, dedicated to "women who have had the courage to say 'yes' to life, whether that means daring to go, or daring to stay". Among the diverse collection of writers who let fly their imaginations are Zora Neale Hurston, Angela Carter, Karen Blixen, Janet Frame, Dorothy Parker and Shena Mackay.

Read on . . . journeys and other places

The following section collects together travel narratives that relate to either longer journeys or destinations not covered in the country chapters.

Diane Ackerman, *The Rarest of the Rare: Vanishing Animals, Timeless Worlds* (UK/US: Vintage, 1997). Poet and naturalist Diane Ackerman unites botany, zoology and travel into a truly significant literary achievement. Her powers of observation and reflection are so vivid, and the knowledge at her disposal so formidable, that your imaginary landscapes cannot help but be transformed by reading this book. Whether writing about the precarious clifftop existence of the short-tailed albatross in Japan, or the golden lion tamarin in the jungle of Brazil, she draws the reader into her passionate concern not just about the endangered creatures and habitats that she visits (often at some personal risk), but also for those rare people who are custodians of their little remaining safety. A magical book.

Julia Blackburn, *The Emperor's Last Island* (UK/US: Vintage, 1991/1993). Celebrated novelist and biographer Julia Blackburn delves through the minutiae of Napoleon's last, stifled years on St Helena, a barren and windswept island in the middle of the South Atlantic. Although her book succeeds more as an essay on the corrosive tedium of imprisonment than as a piece of historical research or travel literature (she does sail there herself, in a brief and fairly uneventful rounding-off of her research), her description of the island's changing landscape lingers on. A deft, beautifully crafted and quirky account of how an Eden of fruit trees became a forbidding rock and how one of the world's most powerful tyrants ended up on a see-saw with a courtier.

☒ **Dea Birkett**, *Jella: From Lagos to Liverpool: A Woman At Sea in a Man's World* (1992; UK/US: o/p). In her prizewinning debut travel book, Birkett recounts how she signed up as a crew member on a working cargo vessel sailing back from Nigeria to Liverpool. The only woman on board, nicknamed Jella – meaning small boy – by the West African crew, she describes the strategies she resorted to as a means of fitting in; learning to steer the ship; ignoring the strained atmosphere at porn video showings; and effacing herself in massive boiler suits. More riveting than any docusoap and illuminated by Birkett's scalpel-like observations and analysis, this is a compelling memoir. It's also a fascinating insider's guide to longitude, latitude and the traffic of the seas.

In her second book, *Serpent in Paradise* (UK: Picador, 1997/US: Doubleday, 1998), Birkett pursues her fascination with the Bounty Mutineers whose descendants still live on Pitcairn Island, the speck of volcanic rock in the South Pacific where Fletcher Christian set their ship aflame. After two years of persistent correspondence, she persuades the fiercely private Pitcairnese to let her live among them, and then boards a chemical tanker for the 4000-mile journey south. Birkett's tale of learning island lore and contending with the peculiarities of Pitcairn culture and the simmering antagonisms of minute-town life is entirely gripping, as well as intelligently and succinctly composed. There's a controversy, however, at the heart of this book that the author explicitly stirs. It concerns the ethics of exposing, through publication, the lives that ordinary people wish to guard from public scrutiny. A tough, and divisive debate, and one which Birkett has opened with consummate literary skill.

Annie Caulfield, *Kingdom of the Filmstars: Journey into Jordan* **(Aus/UK/US: Lonely Planet Journeys, 1997)**. Drawn to Jordan by her love affair with Rathwan, a Bedouin tour guide, Caulfield offers a special insight into the odd corners of Jordanian society. Nomads, refugees, artists and policemen form a rich cast as she explores the capital, Amman, and journeys into the rural and desert heartlands, including a riotous stay "on the women's side of the tent" in Rathwan's family home. An informative and witty account that's refreshingly upfront about the complexities of negotiating a relationship across two very different cultures.

Kuki Gallmann, *I Dreamed of Africa* **(UK/US: Penguin, 1992/1995)**. Gallmann's emotionally charged memoir swiftly transfers from her native Italy to Africa where, in 1972, she, her beloved husband, Paulo, and their three children settle down to a new life on the vast ranch they establish in the highlands of Kenya. Details of this privileged existence, the wholeheartedness with which she embraces the spirit of her surroundings, her passion for wildlife – all are memorably captured. However, it is the tragedies that punctuate this story and the extraordinary resilience with which she confronts her unbearable losses that make it such a haunting read.

⭐ **Colleen J McElroy**, *A Long Way from St Louis* **(US: Coffeehouse Press, 1997)**. African-American poet McElroy has written a truly unique account of her experiences of world travel, from childhood memories on the road as an "army brat" to motorcycling across the Australian desert some fifty years later. These, plus trips to Peru, Japan, the former Yugoslavia and a host of other countries, are all lyrically evoked in a series of vignettes in which the writer's personal thoughts on family, love, race and her passion for dancing are skilfully interwoven with more general observations about places visited and people encountered along the way. Poetic, humorous and bursting with spirit, this is one of the most engaging collections of travel memoirs around.

⭐ **Jan Morris**, *Destinations: Essays from Rolling Stone* **(UK: Oxford Paperbacks, 1992/US: Oxford University Press, 1982)**. These seemingly effortless essays capture the essence of places as diverse as Washington after Watergate, Delhi under Mrs Gandhi, Panama on the eve of the US treaty debate, and Cairo at the time of the Israeli–Egyptian peace talks. "Manhattan", in which Morris reconstructs New York as it greeted returning GIs in 1945, is widely thought of as the single best article ever written on the city.

⭐ **Mary Morris**, *Wall to Wall: A Woman's Travels from Beijing to Berlin* **(UK: Flamingo, o/p/US: Doubleday, 1991)**. Morris has a gift for combining insightful travelogue with an intensely personal account of her own history and ongoing quest for self-discovery. In *Wall to Wall*, she is driven by her grandmother's stories of the Russian Cossacks and pogroms of her ancestry to make an epic journey from China, through the Soviet Union and on to Berlin. The journey takes place in 1986, when the second wall is still a formidable physical and political barrier and the ripples of glasnost and perestroika have only just begun to spread. Two momentous events magnify her growing sense of unease about her journey – the Chernobyl nuclear disaster and the revelation that she is in the first stage of pregnancy. Morris manages to write as eloquently about the doubts and tedium of travel – the thousands of miles whizzing past a grimy train window, the anonymous hotel rooms – as about her impressions of place.

Anne Mustoe, *A Bike Ride: 12,000 miles Around the World* (UK: Virgin, 1992/US: o/p). A former headmistress in her mid-fifties sets off on a whim to cycle around the world. Told with humour and an often disarming modesty, this straightforward account of her epic journey across Europe, India, the Far East and the United States shows just how far an indomitable spirit can take you.

Pamela Petro, *Travels in an Old Tongue: Touring the World Speaking Welsh* (UK: Flamingo, 1998). Zany account of the American author's quest for Welsh-speaking communities around the globe, motivated, quite simply, by her passion for everything Welsh. From Norway to Argentina via Japan, she visits fourteen countries in five months, zealously pursuing every contact – from Eleri who despairs about the difficulties of maintaining a Welsh-speaking house in Singapore, to the elusive Effie Wiltens, "a Dutch woman who went to Wales on holiday and never got over it".
Recounted with enthusiasm, wit and a sure gift for observation, Petro's whistlestop tour covers not only places and people but also the nuances of Welsh language and culture. An original, funny, deceptively informative book that appeals to travellers and linguists alike.

Melissa Holbrook Pierson, *The Perfect Vehicle: What is it about Motorcycles* (UK: Granta, 1997/US: W.W. Norton & Co., 1998). Pierson, a New York poet and intellectual, has crafted an engaging and profound treatise on "motolust", an affliction she's been happily stricken with for over a decade. "Riding on a motorcycle can make you feel joyous, powerful, peaceful, frightened, vulnerable, and back out to happy again, perhaps in the same ten miles", she writes. Her debut memoir is persuasive stuff, as much for the great un-greased as for hardened aficionados of the road-swallowing machines. And she's good on the roadside aspects of real-life too, like heartbreaks and the ever-present fear of accidents.

Lisa St Aubin de Terán, *Off the Rails: Memoirs of a Train Addict* (UK: Sceptre, 1990). From childhood, when at the staggering age of eight she discovered trains as an entertaining means of truancy from school, this wonderfully eccentric author developed a love of railways which "hovers now somewhere between the improbable and the insane". Here she traces some of her numerous journeys, from accompanying her mother on the luxurious Moscow to London Occident Express, rattling from Buenos Aires deep into Patagonia, to crossing Italy and France and, finally, riding the El in Chicago. An escapist's dream.

Sara Wheeler, *Travels in a Thin Country* (UK: Abacus, 1995/US: Modern Library, 1999). A pacey, informed account of a six-month solo journey zig-zagging the entire length of Chile by one of Britain's most renowned new travel writers. Wheeler manages to pack in an extraordinary diversity of experiences, from camping in Patagonia to hitching a lift on a supply boat around Cape Horn, and relays it all with verve and scholarly flair.

Travel she wrote

Women Travel's 25 essential contemporary travel books

For the following selection we've allowed ourselves only one title per author (although their other recommended books are included in the country and journey chapters) and have tried to represent the rich pickings of travelogues, memoirs, autobiography and essay collections either grouped under the label "travel" or which convey such a strong sense of place that they might easily be. Most of the titles were published recently, the majority within the last four years, with the odd post-war classic, such as Sybille Bedford's, slipped in. (Each of the titles below, listed alphabetically by author, is reviewed at more length within the book.)

Sybille Bedford
A Visit to Don Otavio
(1953; UK: Eland Books, 1982)
Witty and sophisticated romp through 1950s Mexico by one of Europe's classiest writers. (p.404)

Annie Caulfield
The Winners' Enclosure
(UK: Simon & Schuster, 1999)
Comedy scriptwriter unearths the Australian history of her Irish great-uncle, who became a famous jockey. Funny and deceptively informative. (p.58)

Dea Birkett
Jella: A Woman at Sea in a Man's World
(1992; UK/US: op)
British travel writer joins the merchant navy for the voyage from Lagos to Liverpool. (p.653)

Karen Connelly
Touch the Dragon: A Year in Thailand
(1992; UK: Black Swan, 1996/US: Turnstone Press, 1995)
Lyrical account of a year spent in rural Thailand by seventeen-year-old, prize-winning Canadian. (p.572)

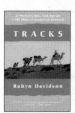

Robyn Davidson
Tracks
(1980; UK: Picador,
1998/US: Vintage, 1995)
A lone camel trek across
the Western Australian
Desert and an instant
classic of epic and
introspective adventuring.
(p.58)

Miranda France
Bad Times in Buenos Aires
(UK: Weidenfeld & Nicolson,
1998/US: Ecco Press, 1999)
Twenty-something British
"stringer" contends with
Argentinian angst, self-
absorption and pursuit of
supermodel looks. (p.36)

Joan Didion
The White Album
(1979; UK: Flamingo, 1993/
US: Noonday Press, 1990)
Incisive reflections on
the American psyche in
the late 1960s and early
1970s from one of the
country's sharpest social
commentators.
(pp.158 & 622)

Martha Gellhorn
Travels with Myself and
Another
(1978; UK: Eland Books
1983/US: o/p)
Celebrated war
correspondent's candid
accounts of the journeys
she most loathed. China
and Russia feature notably.
(pp.149 & 500)

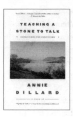

Annie Dillard
Teaching a Stone to Talk:
Expeditions and
Encounters
(1982; US: Harper Perennial,
1992)
Ecuadorian jungle treks,
Arctic musings and total
eclipses, evoked with clear
virtuosity. (p.180)

Eva Hoffman
Lost in Translation: A Life
in a New Language
(UK: Minerva, 1991/US:
Penguin, 1990)
Hoffman emigrates from
her beloved Poland to
Canada in the late 1950s,
losing the nuances of
language and identity in
the process. (p.493)

Slavenka Drakulic
How We Survived
Communism and Even
Laughed
(UK: Vintage, 1993/US:
Harper Perennial,1993)
Witty and poignant tales
of life under Communism
in Eastern Europe. (p.493)

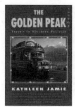

Kathleen Jamie
The Golden Peak: Travels
in Northern Pakistan
(UK: Virago, 1994)
Scottish poet settles into
the routines of a
segregated Shia muslim
town in Northern
Pakistan. A sympathetic
account of startling clarity.
(p.469)

Lieve Joris
The Gates Of Damascus
(Aus/UK/US: Lonely Planet
Journeys, 1996)
Tells of a year shared with
a Syrian sociologist whose
husband has been
imprisoned under Assad.
Offers remarkable insights
into a modern Arab
society. (p.552)

Jan Morris
**Destinations: Essays from
Rolling Stone**
(UK: Oxford Paperbacks,
1992/US: OUP, 1982)
Seemingly effortless essays
on places as diverse as
Washington after
Watergate and Delhi under
Mrs Gandhi. (p.654)

Doris Lessing
**African Laughter : Four
Visits to Zimbabwe**
(UK: Flamingo, 1993/US:
Harper Perennial, 1993)
Banned from her
homeland for 25 years,
internationally renowned
author returns to her
homeland and launches a
passionate critique. (p.647)

Mary Morris
**Nothing to Declare:
Memoirs of a Woman
Travelling Alone**
(1988; UK: Picador 1999/
US: St Martin's Press, 1999)
American novelist packs
her bags and goes to live in
a small dusty town north
of Mexico City. (p.404)

Fatima Mernissi
**The Harem Within: Tales of
a Moroccan Girlhood**
(1994; UK: Bantam
1997/US: Perseus, 1995)
A riveting memoir that
shifts between the author's
restricted girlhood in her
father's home in Fes, and
the relative freedoms of her
grandfather's farm. (p.426)

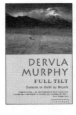

Dervla Murphy
**Full Tilt: Dunkirk to Delhi
by Bicycle**
(1965; UK: Flamingo 1995/
US: Overlook Press, 1987)
Murphy pedals from her
native Ireland, through a
frozen Europe and onto
the overland route to
India. (pp.9, 298 & 470)

Melanie McGrath
**Motel Nirvana: Dreaming
of the New Age in the
American Desert**
(UK: Flamingo, 1996/US:
Pica Books, 1997)
Incisive browse around the
New Age communities of
the Southwestern desert
states. (p.620)

**Melissa Holbrook
Pierson**
**The Perfect Vehicle: What
is it about Motorcycles?**
(UK: Granta, 1997/US: W.W.
Norton & Co., 1998)
Diva poetess and
motorbike fanatic explains
the thrills and spills of
biking in the US. (p.622)

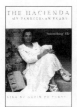

Lisa St Aubin de Terán
The Hacienda: My
Venezuelan Years
(UK: Virago, 1997/US: Little
Brown, 1999)
At 17, de Terán married a
Venezuelan aristocrat and
moved to his hacienda in
the Andes, only to discover
that it was downhill from
there on. (p.634)

Sara Wheeler
Terra Incognita: Travels in
Antarctica
(UK: Vintage, 1997/US:
Random House Modern
Library, 1998)
Everything you ever
wanted to know about the
vast frozen wilderness of
Antarctica. (p.24)

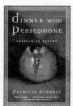

Patricia Storace
Dinner with Persephone
(UK: Granta, 1997/US:
Random House, 1996)
American poet and fluent
philhellene spends a year
among friends in Athens
mulling over modern and
classical icons and political
conundrums. (p.243)

Jan Wong
Red China Blues: My Long
March from Mao to Now
(UK: Bantam, 1997/US:
Anchor Doubleday, 1997)
A fascinating account of
daily life in Cultural
Revolutionary China.
(p.148)

Isabella Tree
Islands in the Clouds:
Travels in the Highlands of
New Guinea
(Aus/UK/US: Lonely Planet
Journeys, 1996)
Tree and a Highlander
friend travel through the
tribal areas and gold-
mining towns of PNG
and Irian Jaya. (p.478)

Stay in touch with us!

ROUGH*NEWS* is Rough Guides' free newsletter.
In four issues a year we give you news, travel
issues, music reviews, readers' letters and the
latest dispatches from authors on the road.

ROUGH GUIDES: Travel

Amsterdam
Andalucia
Australia

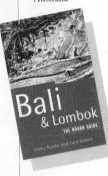

Austria
Bali & Lombok
Barcelona
Belgium &
  Luxembourg
Belize
Berlin
Brazil
Britain
Brittany &
  Normandy
Bulgaria
California
Canada
Central America
Chile
China
Corfu & the
  Ionian Islands
Corsica
Costa Rica
Crete
Cuba
Cyprus
Czech & Slovak
  Republics

Dodecanese
Dominican
  Republic
Egypt
England
Europe
Florida
France
French Hotels &
  Restaurants 1999
Germany
Goa
Greece
Greek Islands
Guatemala
Hawaii
Holland
Hong Kong
  & Macau
Hungary
India
Indonesia
Ireland
Israel & the
  Palestinian
  Territories
Italy
Jamaica
Japan
Jordan

Kenya
Laos
London
London
  Restaurants
Los Angeles
Malaysia,
  Singapore &
  Brunei
Mallorca &
  Menorca
Maya World
Mexico
Morocco
Moscow
Nepal
New England
New York
New Zealand
Norway
Pacific Northwest
Paris
Peru
Poland
Portugal
Prague
Provence & the
  Côte d'Azur
The Pyrenees
Romania

St Petersburg
San Francisco
Sardinia
Scandinavia
Scotland
Scottish Highlands
  & Islands
Sicily
Singapore

South Africa
Southern India
Southwest USA
Spain
Sweden
Syria
Thailand
Trinidad & Tobago
Tunisia
Turkey
Tuscany & Umbria
USA
Venice
Vienna
Vietnam
Wales
Washington DC
West Africa
Zimbabwe &
  Botswana

AVAILABLE AT ALL GOOD BOOKSHOPS

ROUGH GUIDES: Mini Guides, Travel Specials and Phrasebooks

MINI GUIDES

Antigua
Bangkok
Barbados
Big Island of
  Hawaii
Boston
Brussels
Budapest

Seattle
Sydney
Tokyo
Toronto

Dublin
Edinburgh
Florence
Honolulu
Jerusalem
Lisbon
London
  Restaurants
Madrid
Maui
Melbourne
New Orleans
St Lucia

TRAVEL SPECIALS

First-Time Asia
First-Time Europe
More Women Travel

PHRASEBOOKS

Czech
Dutch

Egyptian Arabic
European
French
German
Greek
Hindi & Urdu
Hungarian
Indonesian
Italian
Japanese

Mandarin
  Chinese
Mexican Spanish
Polish
Portuguese
Russian
Spanish
Swahili
Thai
Turkish
Vietnamese

AVAILABLE AT ALL GOOD BOOKSHOPS

ROUGH GUIDES:
Reference and Music CDs

REFERENCE
Classical Music
Classical:
  100 Essential CDs
Drum'n'bass
House Music
Jazz
Music USA

Opera
Opera:
  100 Essential CDs
Reggae
Reggae:
  100 Essential CDs
Rock
Rock:
  100 Essential CDs
Techno
World Music
World Music:
  100 Essential CDs
English Football
European Football

Internet
Millennium

ROUGH GUIDE MUSIC CDs
Music of the
  Andes
Australian
  Aboriginal
Brazilian Music
Cajun & Zydeco

Classic Jazz
Music of
  Colombia
Cuban Music
Eastern Europe

Music of Egypt
English Roots
  Music
Flamenco
India & Pakistan
Irish Music
Music of Japan
Kenya & Tanzania
Native American
North African
Music of Portugal

Reggae
Salsa
Scottish Music
South African
  Music
Music of Spain
Tango
Tex-Mex
West African
  Music
World Music
World Music Vol 2
Music of
  Zimbabwe

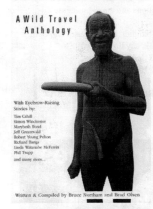

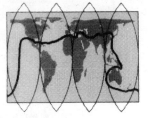